COASTAL NAVIGATION
FOR THE
SMALL BOAT SAILOR

BY JEFF MARKELL

TAB BOOKS Inc.
BLUE RIDGE SUMMIT, PA. 17214

FIRST EDITION

FIRST PRINTING

Library of Congress Cataloging in Publication Data

Markell, Jeff.
Coastal navigation for the small boat sailor.

Includes index.
1. Navigation. 2. Boats and boating. I. Title.
VK555.M37 1984 623.89 83-24119
ISBN 0-8306-1628-4 (pbk.)

Front and back cover photographs by Carol A. Stickles.

Contents

Acknowledgments

SEVERAL INDIVIDUALS AND ORGANIZATIONS HAVE been extremely helpful in the preparation of this book. I should like to thank the U.S. Coast Guard, specifically Keith Tasker and Ted J. Kosloski. They supplied photographs of the various aids to navigation shown in Chapter 3.

Many thanks to the U.S. Weather Bureau, National Oceanic and Atmospheric Administration, and Mrs. J. C. David; she culled their files for the excellent photographs of the various types of cloud formations found in Chapter 8 on Weather.

Thanks also to Bob Sellby, president of Davis Instruments Corp., and Henry Davidson, president of Recmar Marine Corporation. Recmar Marine supplied the charting instruments (parallel rules, dividers, course protractor, and drafting triangle) used to work out the charting examples given in Chapter 5. Davis Instruments provided the pelorus, the hand-bearing compass, the range finder, and the hand-held speedometer used in Chapter 5 to describe dead reckoning and piloting. Davis also supplied the hand-held wind-speed indicator shown in Chapter 8. Presidents Sellby and Davidson were a most friendly and helpful pair of presidents.

And finally, particular thanks are due to Ms. Lynn Stewart. It was she who edited descriptions in the manuscript that failed adequately to describe, and explanations that failed adequately to explain, as well as innumerable elementary errors in spelling and punctuation.

Introduction

MAYDAY - MAYDAY - MAYDAY; THIS IS THE boat *FAIRWIND*, Whisky Yankee Alfa three six eight two calling Coast Guard - MAYDAY - MAYDAY - MAYDAY.

The Coast Guard responds. Conversation between the two reveals *FAIRWIND* to be a 26-foot inboard/outboard. It has a white hull, white superstructure, and blue decks. There are four people aboard and seven lifejackets.

The boat left port about an hour and a half ago to go fishing. She suddenly started taking on water rapidly. Water is coming in faster than the bilge pump can pump it out. There is nothing they can do about plugging the leak because they cannot see where the water is coming from. The weather is clear with a lively breeze and a choppy sea running.

The Coast Guard is ready and able to go to their assistance, but they can do nothing. The skipper of *FAIRWIND* cannot give them the one small piece of information they need to help him because *he does not know where he is!*

If the Coast Guard can keep the skipper of the *FAIRWIND* on the air long enough to get directional bearings on his radio transmissions, they might be able to fix his position. If so, they might get to him in time, and then again they might not. Crucial time has been wasted.

This scenario might seem absurd; unfortunately it is not. All too often small boat operators get in trouble and then discover they do not know their position accurately enough to direct an assisting vessel to their location.

Fortunately, emergency situations are comparatively rare. Nevertheless, there are many other reasons for a prudent boatman to want to keep track of his position at sea. By following the shortest *safe* course between two places, considerable fuel can be saved, and today fuel is not inexpensive (or had you noticed!).

Rocks, shoals, and other dangers can be avoided by keeping track of where *you* are and where *they* are located. Bending the propeller on a rock or punching a hole in the hull is likely to ruin your entire day. Reasonably accurate timing of departures and arrivals certainly make boating a more enjoyable pastime. It can also help to avoid a good deal of worry, and at times discomfort and inconvenience as well.

By following the simple procedures given in this book, you will be able to locate the position of your boat at any time with reasonable accuracy. With this information, you can then pick the shortest and safest route to your destination. You will also know just about what your arrival time will be.

Chapter 1

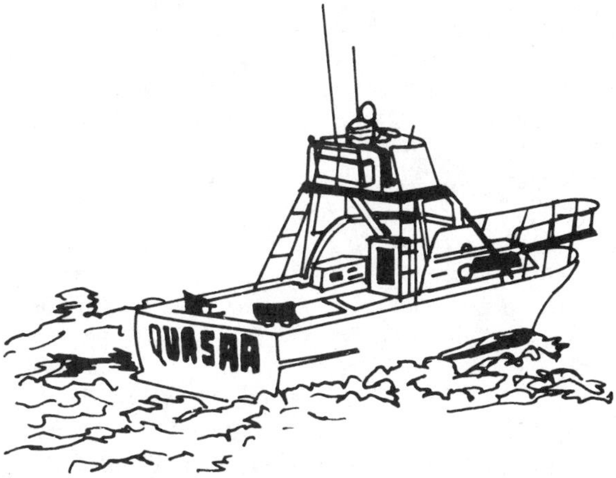
QUASAR

The Earth and Navigation

TO THE AVERAGE PERSON WHO HAS A SMALL boat and perhaps goes fishing on the weekends or just likes to sail around for the fun of it, the term *navigation* might have a rather awesome ring. Many people feel that navigation is an extremely difficult and complicated skill that requires a great deal of time and effort to learn. While it is entirely true that some aspects of navigation are complicated, it is also true that every time you have gone somewhere in your boat and returned, you have navigated!

The word navigation is derived from two Latin words: *navis* meaning ship, and *agere* meaning to direct. Thus navigation is the process of directing the movement of a vessel from one place to another. Isn't that exactly what you have done? Certainly there is also an implied meaning to the word navigation that the vessel is directed safely.

The entire subject of navigation has been divided into four basic sections: piloting, dead reckoning, celestial navigation, and the most recently developed area, electronic navigation. Of the four divisions, the casual small boat operator is primarily concerned with the first two—piloting and dead reckoning. Depending on boat size and equipment aboard, electronic navigation could also be of some importance.

PILOTING

While historical authorities differ somewhat, there is good reason to believe that people have been navigating vessels of various types on many bodies of water for somewhere between 6000 and 8000 years. Piloting was certainly the very first form of navigation. Its elementary form was the use of visible landmarks to help the earliest sailors keep track of their position at sea.

As far back as Homer's *Odessey*, we have an example of written *Sailing Directions* for voyaging through the Mediterranean Sea, giving complete and accurate descriptions of islands, landmarks, harbors, wind and weather conditions, and sailing times. Homer's descriptions are so complete that much of Ulysses track was reconstructed and even resailed as a demonstration by a British yachtsman in the 1960s.

The same use of visual signs that was basic then is still basic today. Happily by now we are a great deal further down the road in terms of providing the mariner with detailed and accurate information as to what he is seeing. National Ocean Survey (NOS) provides extremely accurate charts of our coasts and harbors. They show many natural features such as the shape of the coastline, location of conspicuous hills, and general appearance of the land such as wooded areas, or grassy, sandy, or rocky sections.

They also show many prominent man-made structures such as chimneys, towers, tanks, bridges, large buildings, and other features that are visible from at sea. In addition, they locate very accurately the various man-made aids to navigation specifically constructed and maintained for this purpose. These include lights buoys, daybeacons, foghorns, lighthouses, bells, whistles, gongs, and radio signals for direction finding. These are explained in Chapter 3.

On many small boats where navigational instruments as well as space to store them are very limited, the mariner will be heavily dependent on sight and sound to find charted landmarks to guide him. On somewhat larger boats, an electronic depth sounder or a radio direction finder might be available to supplement the sensory information, but sight and sound will remain basic. Vessels large enough to be equipped with radar, loran, consol, decca, or other sophisticated electronic navigational equipment are beyond the scope of the small-boat weekend sailor to whom this work is directed.

Essentially, piloting is the part of navigation that enables the sailor to locate his position and where he is heading by recognizing and using charted objects. Some of these will be natural landmarks, some will be man-made constructions, and some are objects specifically constructed only for the purpose of guiding the mariner.

DEAD RECKONING

Dead reckoning is used when you are starting from a known geographical location, at a specific time, to project the position of a boat forward mathematically in space and time. To do this, geographic directions, time periods, speeds, and distances are used. The origin of the term *dead reckoning* is believed to lie in an old sailing ship term *deduced reckoning.* This term was normally written in the ships log as "ded. reckoning."

When using this method, the course and speed of the boat are both projected purely mathematically. No allowance whatsoever is made for any type of off-course movement regardless of whether movement is caused by wind, current, sloppy steering, or anything else. Granted—wind, cur-

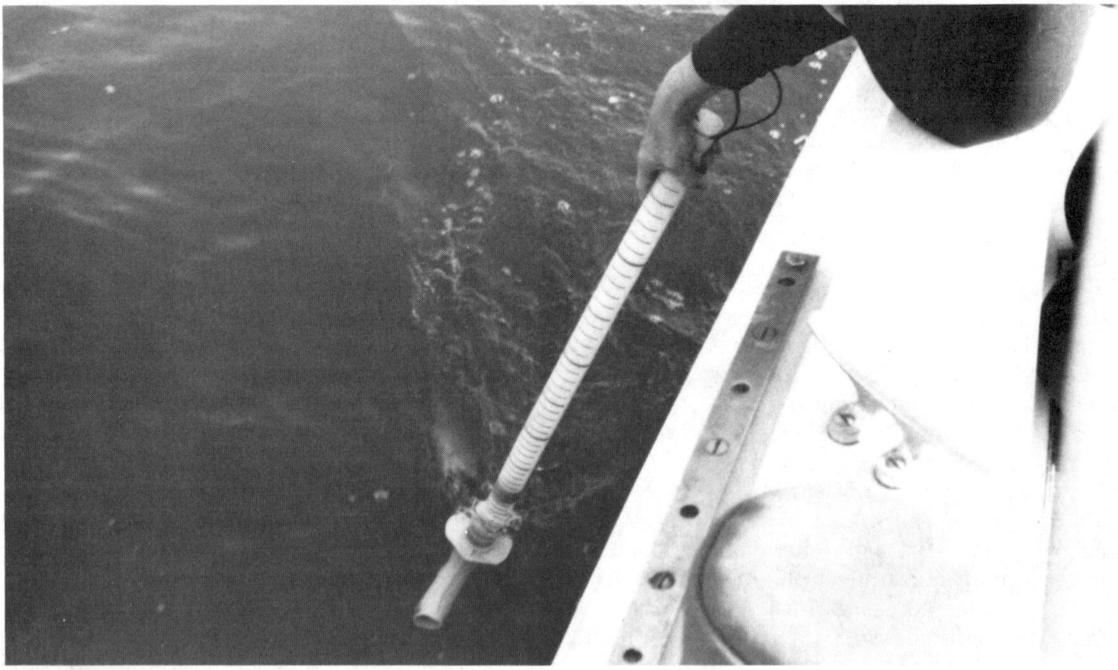

Fig. 1-1. Hand-held knotmeter.

rent, and steering errors normally will put you somewhat off course. When correctly worked out, however, a dead reckoning or DR position is fairly near your actual position and gives you a starting point to which corrections can be made to show the actual position.

Dead reckoning courses are determined by finding the direction of a line on a chart connecting one position with another. Speed is speed through the water, as shown by knotmeter readings, or it can be found by the use of a speed table based on engine revolutions as indicated on a tachometer. Many small boats do not have a knotmeter; and if you have an outboard, you will not have a tachometer either. No problem. Speed can be found with adequate accuracy by using one of several inexpensive hand-held speedometers that are available (Fig. 1-1).

As explained in Chapter 5, dead reckoning (DR) courses and projected positions at various times are laid out in advance of sailing. Once under way, they are periodically corrected to show actual positions that reflect the effects of wind, currents, and steering errors. This is accomplished by means of observations and bearings on landmarks and aids to navigation. Such observations are part of routine coastal piloting procedures.

Dead reckoning is used to plan an intended trip. Before starting a cruise, the sailor determines the direction in which the vessel will head. Distance from starting point to final objective is found by measurement on the chart. With the distance known, the running time can be computed using the time, speed, and distance formula shown in Chapter 5, by simply deciding on a speed. Alternately using the same formula, speed can be found by specifying an arrival time and working back from that time.

CELESTIAL NAVIGATION

Celestial navigation leaves many people in complete awe. Without reference to anything on earth except the horizon, the location of a vessel is found by means of observations of celestial bodies such as the sun, moon, stars, or planets. An accurate timepiece, a current Nautical Almanac, a reliable instrument called a sextant, for measuring angles, and one of several mathematical "sight reduction tables" are necessary. With these for tools the position of a ship as of a particular time can be found to within a mile by a good navigator under decent conditions.

The small boat sailor making coastal runs is seldom out of sight of land; and when he is, it is for only short periods of time. When running along the coast, position is determined by the use of charted objects either ashore or afloat close to the coast. Celestial sights are unnecessary. In addition, positions based on charted landmarks are vastly more accurate than those obtained by using celestial bodies.

The same sextant that is used to take celestial sights has uses in coastwise navigation as well. Until recent years, the sextant was by definition an extremely expensive and delicate instrument, and certainly unsuitable to risk carrying on a small boat. More recently, comparatively inexpensive plastic sextants have become available. These are by no means as accurate as a high-grade marine sextant. For the angle measurements needed in coastal work, however, they are accurate enough. These uses are also discussed in Chapter 5.

ELECTRONIC NAVIGATION

A variety of electronic systems are currently available for determining the position of a vessel by means of radio signals. Transmissions from various sources are received and analyzed by shipboard equipment, and result in positions that can be accurate to within a few feet! These systems are not suitable for small boats and they are not at all necessary.

Many small boats operating close to the coast have no electronics at all aboard, except perhaps for a transistor radio tuned to a local ball game. A knotmeter is a worthwhile device for a modest investment. A depthsounder is another useful and affordable device for the small boat, as is a portable radio direction finder. The use of these instruments is discussed in Chapter 5.

The ship-to-shore radio telephone is an electronic safety device and communication instrument; it is not a navigational instrument. Some people might think calling the Coast Guard, asking them to take bearings on your radio, and then tell you where you are qualifies as navigation. This is *not* an acceptable thing to do unless you are in deep trouble and lives are in danger.

Responsibilities of the Navigator

Regardless of the methods used, the job of the navigator is to give the answers to these questions:

- ☐ What is the present position of my boat?
- ☐ What is the direction from here to the desired objective?
- ☐ When will we get there?

Of these three questions the first is by far the most important. The navigator must start with a known position at a known time. Without these two elements as a beginning, there is no way for him to have the faintest notion as to either where he is going or when he will get there.

Further, in order to explain how to pinpoint the present position of a boat, let me first define the navigational meaning of the term *position*. In this application, the word means a point on the planet that is precisely identified by a system of geographic coordinates that form an imaginary grid over the surface of the earth.

The point being identified will be stated as lying on a particular parallel of *latitude* specified in degrees, minutes, and tenths of minutes of angle. At the same time, that point also lies on a meridian of *longitude*, also identified in degrees, minutes and tenths of minutes of angle. Latitude lines run east and west; longitude lines run north and south. Our

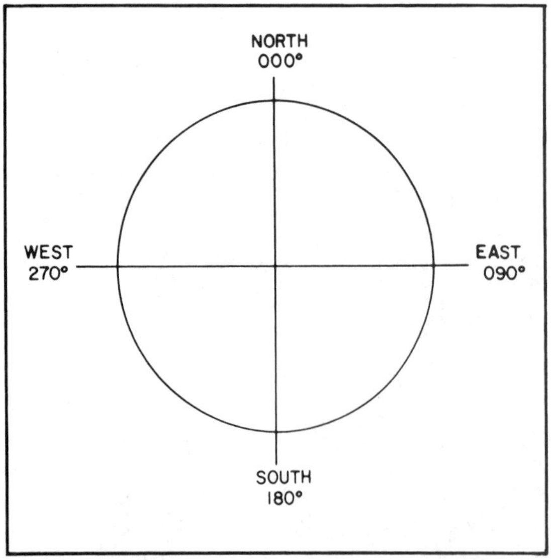
NORTH
000°
WEST
270°
EAST
090°
SOUTH
180°

Fig. 1-2. Directions measured in degrees from north (000 degrees) to east (090 degrees) to south (180 degrees) to west (270 degrees).

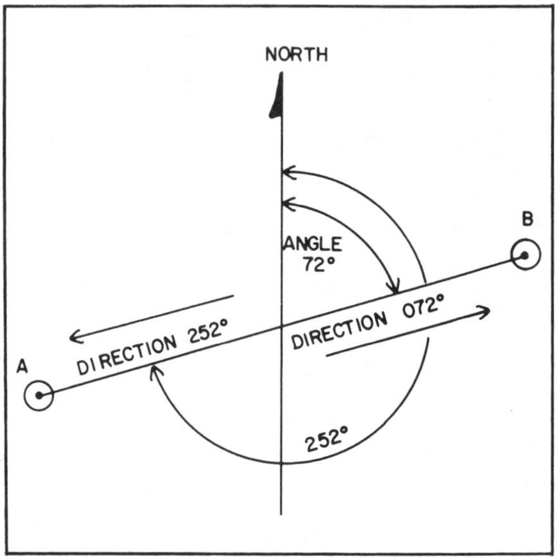
NORTH
B
ANGLE
72°
DIRECTION 252°
DIRECTION 072°
A
252°

Fig. 1-3. Measuring directions clockwise from north (000 degrees).

position is at the point where the two intersect. The source of these angular measurements is further explained later.

Once we know our position we need to know the *direction* from there to wherever we are going. Direction is also expressed in degrees of angle. This time the angular measurements start with north as the reference (Fig. 1-2) and go around a full circle of 360° clockwise, from there through east to south to west and back to north. Note that navigational direction angles are always expressed in three-digit numbers. North is not 0°; it is 000°. Due east, which is 90° away from north, is given as 090°. Of course, from 100° on up to 360° they are all three-digit numbers anyway.

To find the direction of travel necessary to get from place A to place B (Fig. 1-3), draw a line on a map (in our case a chart) from one to the other. Then measure the difference in angle between this direction and north. The angle happens to be 72°, but the direction of travel is 072° (three-digit number, remember?). To find the direction of travel from B to A, measure the angle clockwise all the way from the north to the line pointing to A. This turns out to be 252°. Yes, as you might have heard, there are different kinds of north. That is covered in Chapter 4.

The question as to when we expect to reach

our destination depends on two factors: how far is it from the starting point, and how fast are we traveling. Distances on the water are measured in nautical miles and tenths of miles. Note at once that the *nautical mile* is different from the mile as measured on land. A mile on land (called a *statute mile*) is 5280 feet. The nautical mile is considerably longer, measuring 6076.1 feet. While it might seem absurd to use the same word—mile—to refer to one distance on land and another at sea, that is the case.

How fast the boat travels toward its destination is measured in *knots*. A knot is a nautical mile per hour. The word refers strictly to a measurement of speed. You will often hear it used incorrectly to refer to distance as, "We have gone 5 knots in the last half hour" meaning that we have moved 5 nautical miles. Actually, to travel 5 nautical miles in half an hour the boat speed would be 10 knots.

POSITIONS, DIRECTIONS, AND DISTANCES

The basis of navigation is finding positions, directions, and distances. The first step in learning how to do this is to understand the system that is used to locate places accurately on the surface of the planet by means of latitude and longitude.

The earth is not perfectly round; it is a bit fat in the belly. The diameter through the poles is just under 6865 nautical miles. Around the equator, it is just under 6888 nautical miles—a monumental difference of about 23 nautical miles. For practical purposes it can be considered round. It rotates around an axis running through it from the *north geographic pole* to the *south geographic pole* (Fig. 1-4). The fact that I am referring now to geographic poles must be emphasized. Later, when I discuss the compass, I will discuss *magnetic poles* that are not located on the earth's axis of rotation.

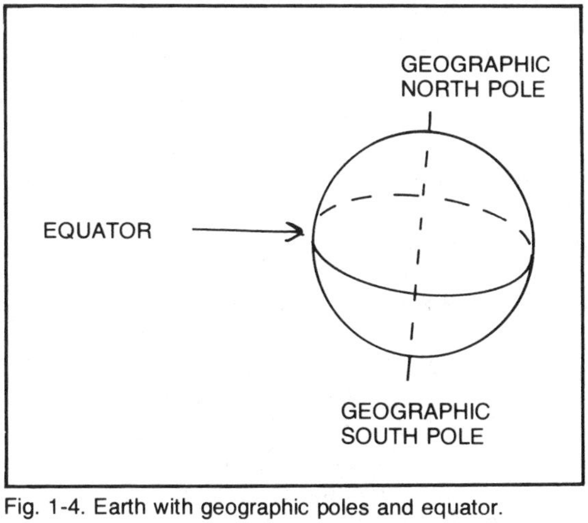
GEOGRAPHIC
NORTH POLE
EQUATOR
GEOGRAPHIC
SOUTH POLE

Fig. 1-4. Earth with geographic poles and equator.

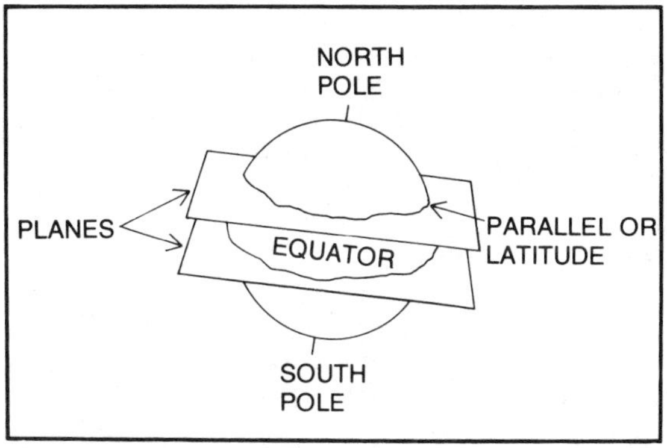
NORTH
POLE
PLANES
EQUATOR
PARALLEL OR
LATITUDE
SOUTH
POLE

Fig. 1-5. Planes creating parallels of latitude.

LATITUDE

Halfway between the poles, along a line around the planet equidistant from both, is the line called the *equator*. Being equidistant from both poles, the equator divides the earth into two halves, or *hemispheres*. Moving north and south away from the equator, a series of planes (Fig. 1-5) parallel to that of the equator locate the *parallels of latitude*. The latitude of a particular position on the surface of the earth is given as the angle of its plane as if measured from the center of the earth (Fig. 1-6).

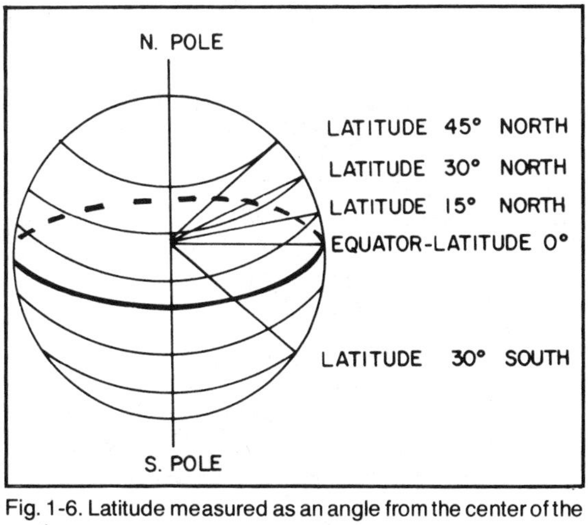
N. POLE
LATITUDE 45° NORTH
LATITUDE 30° NORTH
LATITUDE 15° NORTH
EQUATOR-LATITUDE 0°
LATITUDE 30° SOUTH
S. POLE

Fig. 1-6. Latitude measured as an angle from the center of the earth.

If the angle was measured toward the North Pole, the latitude is noted as latitude north (Lat. N). If measured toward the south, the designation is latitude south (Lat. S). Thus a latitude given as 30° has no meaning until you know whether it is north or south.

The latitude of any position is given in degrees, minutes, and tenths of minutes of angle. For example, a position is at latitude forty-one degrees, sixteen and four tenths minutes north. That is written; Lat. 41° 16.4° N. The procedure for actually finding such a latitude on a chart is explained in Chapter 2.

Because the numbering of latitude starts with 0° at the equator (there is no angle between the equator and itself), the numbers end at 90° north and 90° south, because 90° is the angle between the equator and either pole. The use of the word parallels in relation to latitudes emphasizes the fact that they are concentric circles parallel to the equator and each other that grow progressively smaller as they move toward the poles.

LONGITUDE

Longitude is the other series of lines around the planet that is used to pinpoint a position. As mentioned above, these lines run north and south. They cross all parallels of latitude at right angles, and pass through both poles (Fig. 1-7). Because they all pass through both poles, they differ from the

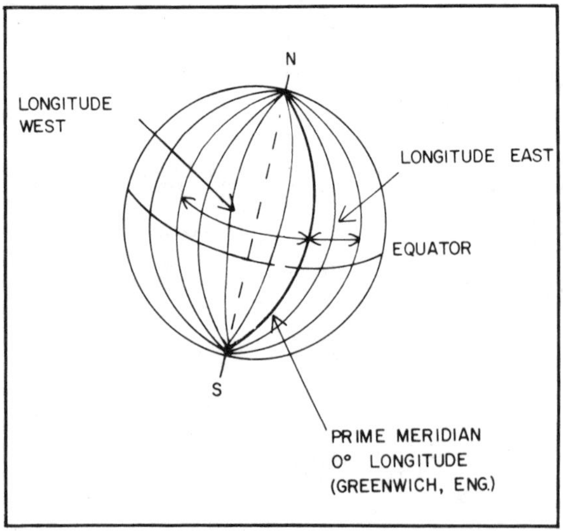
N
LONGITUDE WEST
LONGITUDE EAST
EQUATOR
S
PRIME MERIDIAN
0° LONGITUDE
(GREENWICH, ENG.)

Fig. 1-7. Longitude—prime meridian and meridians east and west.

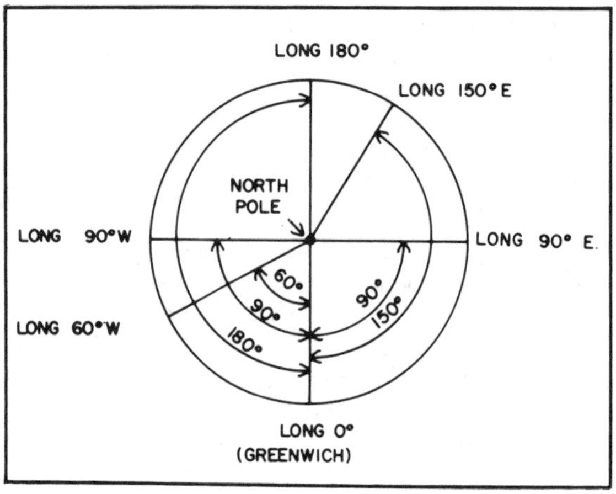
LONG 180°
LONG 150° E
NORTH POLE
LONG 90°W
LONG 90° E
LONG 60°W
60°
90°
180°
90°
150°
LONG 0°
(GREENWICH)

Fig. 1-8. Longitude measured from 0 degrees to 180 degrees and W—viewed from the North Pole.

latitude circles in that they are all the same size.

These circles are called *meridians* and are also numbered in degrees of angle. The numbering system starts at the *Prime Meridian*, which is longitude 0°. Because it passes through the original site of the Royal Observatory at Greenwich, England, is sometimes referred to simply as Greenwich.

Longitude is measured both east and west from 0° to 180° (Fig. 1-8). All longitudes between 0° and 180° must be labeled east (Long. E) or west (Long. W) just as latitudes must be labeled north or south—and for the same reason. Without such labels the numbers would mean nothing. Longitude, like latitude, is described in degrees, minutes, and tenths of minutes of angle. The longitude of one-hundred twenty-three degrees, thirteen and six tenths west is written: Long. 123° 13.6′ W.

Now that we have two sets of reference lines around the planet—latitude and longitude—any point on its surface can be precisely described as being at a specific latitude (north or south) while being at the same time at a specific longitude (east or west). By means of the two coordinates, we have placed it exactly. As a matter of custom, latitude is always given first when defining a position. A position then could be written: Lat. 33° 21.2′ N, Long. 118° 19.1′ W. When transferred to a nautical chart, this position lies a short distance north of Avalon Bay, Santa Catalina Island off the coast of Southern California. The procedure for finding such a position is explained in Chapter 5.

DISTANCE

In distance, one degree of latitude is always 60 nautical miles. This makes 1 minute of latitude conveniently 1 nautical mile. Incidentally, this explains the peculiar length of the nautical mile: 6076.1 feet. Multiply 360° (a full circle) by 60 minutes per degree. The total is 21,600 minutes. At 1 mile per minute, this gives the circumference of the earth at the equator as 21,600 nautical miles. But that is wrong; in school they told you the earth is 25,000 miles in circumference. Right? Look again. That 21,600 was *nautical* miles. Multiply that again by the conversion factor to statue miles—which is 1.1516. Now we get 24,875 statue miles. Will you settle for that? The fact that 1 minute of latitude equals 1 nautical mile provides us with a simple and convenient way to measure distances on the chart (as you can also see in Chapter 5).

NAVIGATIONAL TERMS AND ABBREVIATIONS

A good many of the terms used in navigational discussion are completely new and unfamiliar to the beginner. Worse yet, a number of familiar words take on completely different meanings in connection with navigation than they have in ordinary conversation. When there is a standard abbreviation in use for a particular word, it is given as well.

bearing (B)—The direction of a place or object when looking toward it from another place. Bearings are given in degrees of angle from 000° to 360°. Bearings may be True (TB), Magnetic (MB), or Compass (CB), depending on the source of the north reference line. A bearing may also be Relative (RB) if the bow of the boat is used as the reference.

course (C)—Direction toward which a boat is to be steered. It may be given as True (TC), Magnetic (MC), or Compass (CC). The direction to be steered will be in degrees from 000° to 360°.

course over the ground (COG)—The actual course of travel (Fig. 1-9) of the boat over the earth. This will always be a very wobbly line because of the combined effects of wind, current, seas, and steering errors.

course made good (CMG)—A direct line connecting the point of departure with the point of arrival. This is the net result of all the irregularities in the course over the ground. It too will be marked in degrees from 000° to 360°.

deviation (D)—The difference between the compass reading and the magnetic direction. It is caused by magnetic effects on the boat. It differs from boat to boat and changes with different headings on the same boat.

danger bearing (DB)—Bearing on a fixed object that marks on one side or the other the limit of safe waters. The chart shows which side is safe.

dead reckoning (DR)—Computed course or

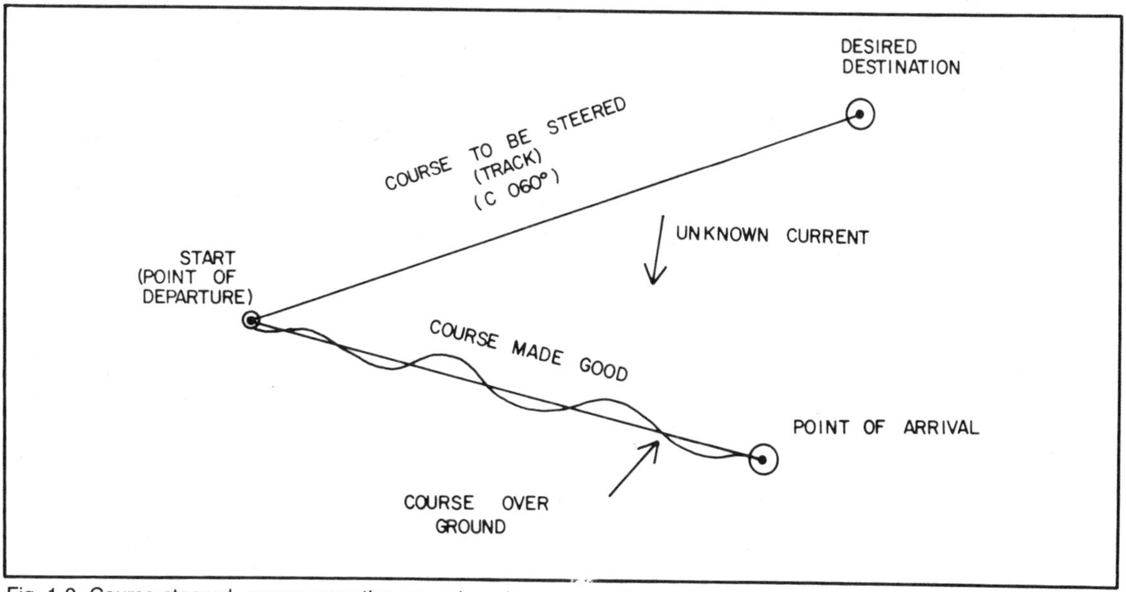
DESIRED
DESTINATION
COURSE TO BE STEERED
(TRACK)
(C 060°)
UNKNOWN CURRENT
START
(POINT OF
DEPARTURE)
COURSE MADE GOOD
POINT OF ARRIVAL
COURSE OVER
GROUND

Fig. 1-9. Course steered, course over the ground, and course made good.

position of boat without regard for wind, current, or steering errors.

Defense Mapping Agency Hydrographic Center (DMAHC)—Source for charts of foreign waters, *Sailing Directions* for foreign waters, sight reduction tables for celestial navigation, and various other navigation publications and information.

estimated position (EP)—DR position of the boat corrected by imcomplete data on wind, current, or other effects. More probable position than the DR, but not as accurate as a fix.

estimated time of arrival (ETA)—The time you hope you will get there!

fix—Position of boat at a specific time established with a high degree of accuracy by any of several methods. See Chapter 5.

high water (HW)—High tide. Given in feet above chart datum or in time on the 24-hour clock.

heading (Hdg. or SH)—The direction toward which a boat is pointing at any given instant. The heading is constantly changing due to the effects of wind and sea on the boat as well as the steering efforts of the helmsman as he attempts to keep the boat pointed toward the desired destination.

knot (K or kn or kt)—Measure of speed. One knot equals 1 nautical mile per hour.

latitude (L or Lat)—Angular distance north or south of the equator.

line of position (LOP)—A line somewhere along which the boat is or was at a particular time.

low water (LW)—Low tide. Given in feet above or below chart datum or in time on the 24-hour clock.

magnetic north (M)—Direction the compass will point if undisturbed by any local magnetic effects or materials.

mean high water (MHW)—Average of all high tides in feet above charted datum.

mean higher high water (MHHW)—Average of the higher of the high tides when there are normally two tides of unequal height. This situation, called diurnal inequality, is commonly found on the West Coast of the United States. (See Chapter 6.)

mean lower low water (MLLW)—Average of the lower of two unequal low tides. Also found on the west coast of the United States.

mile (mi)—The standard unit of measurement of distance on the water. At sea, the international nautical mile equals 6076.1 feet. On land, on the Great Lakes, on the Intracoastal Waterways, and on the navigable river systems such as the Mississippi River or the McCellan-Kerr Arkansas River System, the statute mile of 5280 feet is used. The meaning of "mile" depends on the waters being sailed.

National Ocean Survey (NOS)—Agency that produces charts of United States waters, tide tables, current tables, *Coast Pilots*, pilot charts, and other publications useful to the navigator.

speed over the ground (SOG)—Actual speed of travel over the earth. Often quite different from speed through the water due to the effects of wind, current, and steering.

time (T)—Times of departure, arrival, bearings, course changes, fixes, or other significant events are properly noted in four digits according to the 24-hour clock.

track (TR)—Actual path of the boat. The same as COG.

variation (V)—The difference between magnetic north and true north. It changes considerably in different locations and can be easterly or westerly. The variation for the area in which you are sailing will be found on the chart.

Chapter 2

QUASAR

Nautical Charts and Coast Pilots

AT SEA, THE NAUTICAL CHART TAKES THE PLACE of the familiar road map used ashore. The information the chart provides is of far greater importance to the boatman than anything the road map can provide to the motorist. To the motorist ashore, the road map is very helpful. To the boatman at sea the chart is an absolute necessity.

WHAT THE CHART TELLS YOU

The first thing the chart shows is the shapes of the areas of land and water and the contour of the coastline. That contour is shown to scale and with a very high degree of accuracy. This makes possible very precise distance measurements.

Along with its contour, the nature of the coastline is shown as well. The specialized symbols used on charts to show coastline and land features visible from sea are given in the Appendix excerpts from *Chart No. 1* parts A, B, and C. Part A gives the conventional symbols for indicating whether the coast is flat or rises in cliffs. Also indicated is the kind of material that forms the shore: sand, rock, gravel, or coral. Part B lists descriptive abbreviations that will be found printed on the chart. These identify various coastal features: rivers, mountains, rocks, swamps, islands, and many others. Part C illustrates symbols used to show vertical land contours, and some types of ground cover such as grassy, bushy, or wooded areas. Prominant inland features, such as hills or mountains, are also accurately located. Heights above sea level for prominant hills or mountains are often given as well.

In addition to all readily visible natural features, the chart shows all prominant man-made constructions. These include bridges, tanks, spires, distinctive buildings, railroads, highways, airports, and many others. Some of these items, while not fully visible from sea, are still potentially useful to the coastal navigator. For example, an airport might be invisible from sea, but the aircraft landing and taking off from it most certainly are visible. Positioning an airport by virtue of its air traffic can be very useful to the boatman as an aid in locating his position.

A railroad track might also be invisible from sea. Nevertheless, the sound of a train whistle at night or in a fog can be just the additional piece of information needed to confirm an estimated position. A major highway is seldom a good visual landmark from a couple miles to seaward, but the lights from traffic on that highway can be a very useful guide at night.

Such readily visible constructions as bridges,

spires, radio transmitter towers, tanks, and various distinctive buildings are very accurately located by the charting agencies before they are added to navigational charts. They can be used for line of position bearings with the same confidence one can have in the specially maintained aids to navigation such as lighthouses, ranges, buoys, and beacons. Any type of fixed landmark ashore is far more reliable than the most elaborate floating aids to navigation. Storms, strong currents, or various types of damage can dislocate or inactivate floating aids. They will not move a tank, a chimney, or a bridge.

For a number of years, I was involved in supplying the Coast & Geodetic Survey—now the National Ocean Survey—with information for updating and maintaining 28 charts covering Puerto Rico and the Virgin Islands. The accuracy required and the thoroughness with which information was verified, were indeed impressive. As an example, if a channel had been dredged, they didn't want my soundings or anyone else's. They wanted the official report from the dredging company as verified by the Corps of Engineers.

The exact location of a radio station transmitting tower is specified on the station license. Before the station can go on the air, the FCC verifies that the tower is located precisely where the station license says it is to be. NOS then uses the station license location as the authority for its charted position. Nothing less authoritative will do.

The navigational chart not only provides a tremendous amount of information, but that information is checked and cross checked for accuracy before it is allowed to appear on a chart. Charts are continually being updated as information comes in to NOS from various sources. An old chart could be seriously in error. Keep your charts up to date; then believe those charts not your hunches.

In addition to the various natural and man-made landmarks, charts show the exact locations, types, and distinguishing characteristics of the many man-made *aids to navigation*. These include lighthouses, ranges, beacons, and a variety of buoys (discussed in Chapter 3).

In addition to the information the chart gives regarding visible objects of various kinds, it also includes considerable data regarding things that are not visible or that are visible only part of the time. Depths of water are well charted as are numerous kinds of underwater obstructions and hazards such as shoals, bars, and rocks where a vessel could go around. Kelp beds in which a vessel could become entangled are marked, and so are areas of growing coral where a vessel could come to grief. Submerged wrecks, wrecks awash, and other isolated hazards such as submerged piles are noted.

In summary, nautical charts show all the information the charting agencies can develop that will both assist the mariner to keep track of his position, and help him avoid all known hazards.

CHART PROJECTIONS

Because the earth is essentially spherical, neither it nor any portion of it can accurately be represented on a flat surface, such as a chart, without some distortion. The smaller the area being shown the less the distortion will be. The larger the area the greater the distortion. To deal with the distortion that results from representing the three-dimensional earth on two-dimensional surfaces, various methods of "projecting" the sphere onto a plane have been devised. Each deals with distortion in different ways. Each different projection method in common use owes its popularity to the fact that it minimizes one or more kinds of distortion. Invariably, this is accompanied by some exaggeration of other types of distortion. Therefore, the projection method to be used for a given purpose will be selected on the basis of the type of distortion deemed most important to minimize.

In order to understand what is meant here, consider the fundamental problem involved in producing a projection. A sphere is termed geometrically "undevelopable" because it cannot be laid out flat without greatly altering any pattern placed on its surface. Other surfaces do exist that are "developable:" they can spread out flat without altering any designs or patterns drawn on them.

One such surface is a cylinder (Fig. 2-1) another is a cone (Fig. 2-2). Either one can be simply cut from top to bottom and laid out flat without distorting anything previously placed on its surface. If a portion of the surface of the earth is first projected onto either a cylinder or a cone, it can then be laid out flat to produce a chart without further distortion.

Although there are other projection methods in addition to cylindrical and conic, a full explanation of these methods is not necessary here. In

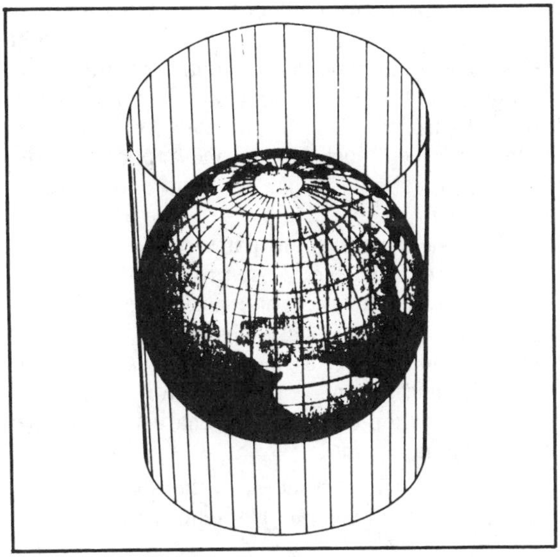

Fig. 2-1A. Cylindrical projection.

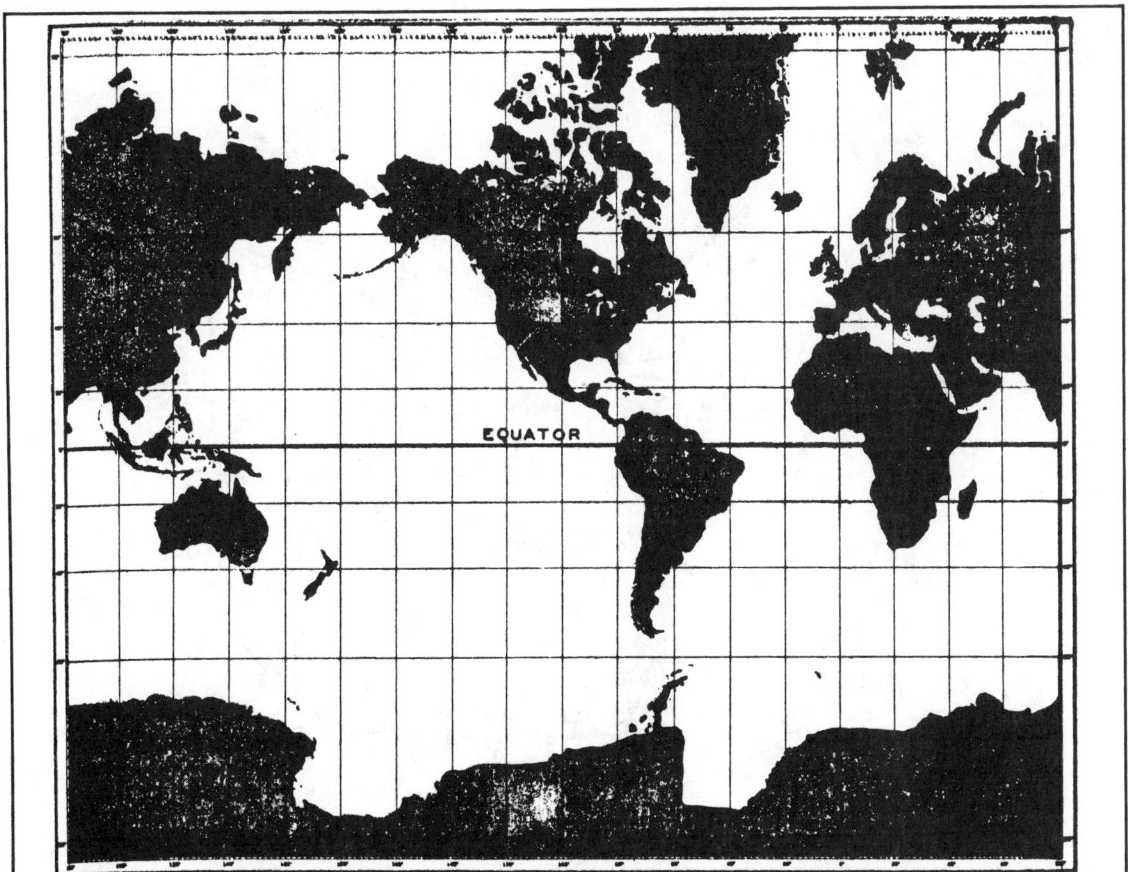
EQUATOR

Fig. 2-1B. World map in Mercator projection.

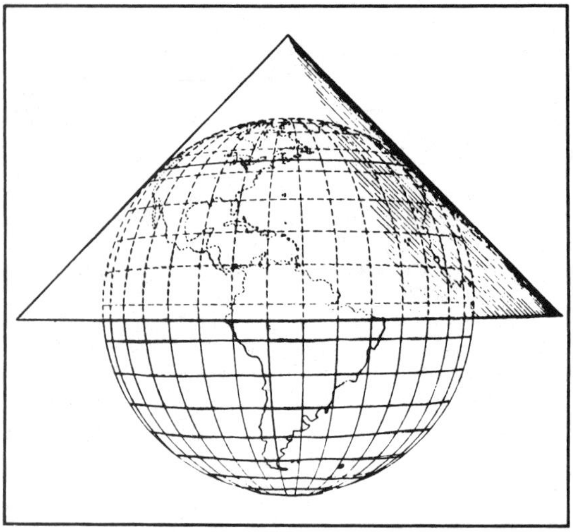

Fig. 2-2A. Conic projection.

coastwise navigation, no charts based on other projections will be needed. The other projection methods used in mapping are gnomonic (Fig. 2-3), orthographic (Fig. 2-4), and stereographic (Fig. 2-5). All three are used in various land mapping applications, and each has marine applications relating to celestial navigation. Those do not presently concern us.

At first glance, some parts of the earth—as shown in one or more of these projections—appear less distorted than the same areas seem in the projections used for coastal charts. Nevertheless, there is good reason for the methods used in compiling our charts. In a projection to be used for marine navigation the following characteristics are of primary importance:

☐ Correct presentation of the shape of geographical features such as land and water areas.

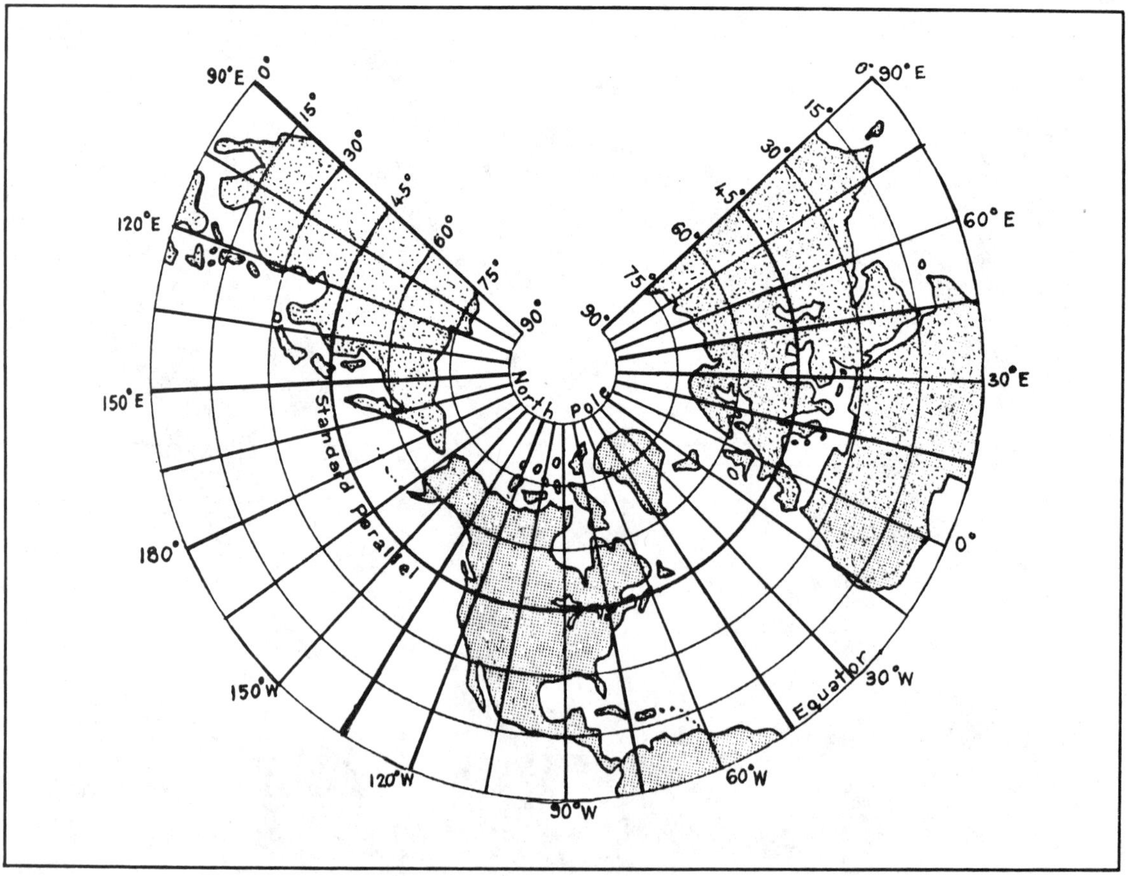
90°E
0°
15°
30°
45°
60°
75°
90°
120°E
150°E
180°
150°W
120°W
90°W
60°W
30°W
Equator
0°
30°E
60°E
North Pole
Standard Parallel

Fig. 2-2B. Conic map of Northern Hemisphere.

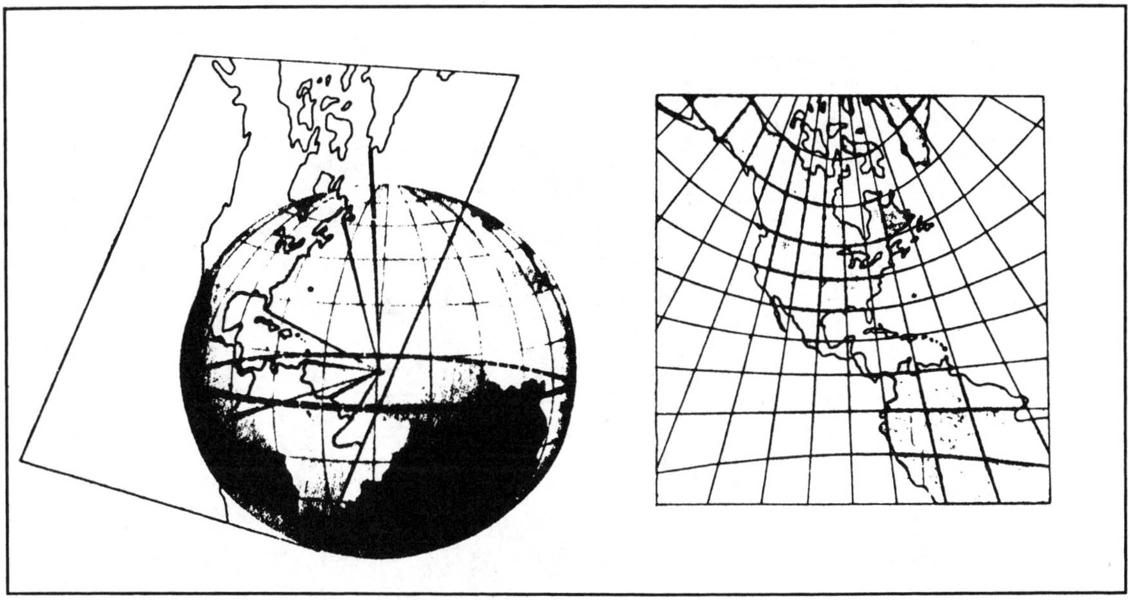

Fig. 2-3. Gnomonic projection.

□ Consistent scale and relative sizes of land and water areas.

□ Correct angular relationships of objects to each other and the planet to permit correct determination of directions.

Charts of the comparatively small areas required for coastwise navigation could provide these characteristics if based on *any* projection method. The agencies responsible for producing the charts, however, have settled on the Mercator projection (Fig. 2-1B), a cylindrical method, for United States coastal and harbor charts, and a very few of the Great Lakes charts. The great majority of Great Lake charts are based on polyconic projection, the remaining few are Lambert conformal (another conic method).

MERCATOR PROJECTION

Those readers who are happily agog over the wonders of contemporary technology have a sobering moment in store. A great majority of all of the nautical charts presently in use both in the United States and throughout the planet right now, in the twilight years of the 20th Century, are based on a projection method devised by Gerardus Mercator, whose world chart was first published in the year 1569! For the purpose of constructing *nautical charts*, his method has not been significantly improved upon since then!

As shown in Fig. 2-1, parallels of latitude and meridians of longitude are shown as horizontal and vertical straight lines. Right away there is a very obvious distortion. Instead of converging, the meridians are parallel. This immediately stretches objects out in an east-west dimension. To bring objects back to proper shape, at the cost of exaggerating their size, the spacing of the horizontal parallels of latitude increases as they move north and south away from the equator.

In a world chart, or a large area sailing chart of the Atlantic or Pacific Ocean this variation in spacing of latitude parallels is certainly obvious. In charts of relatively small areas, such as appear in the harbor and coastal series, it is not really noticeable.

The Mercator projection is considered *conformal*; this is an important characteristic in a nautical chart. This means that angles and angular relationships are correctly represented, and directions can be correctly measured with reference to any parallel, meridian, or compass rose. On a Mercator chart, a course line can be drawn between two points, its compass direction found, and it can then be sailed by simply following that direction all the way.

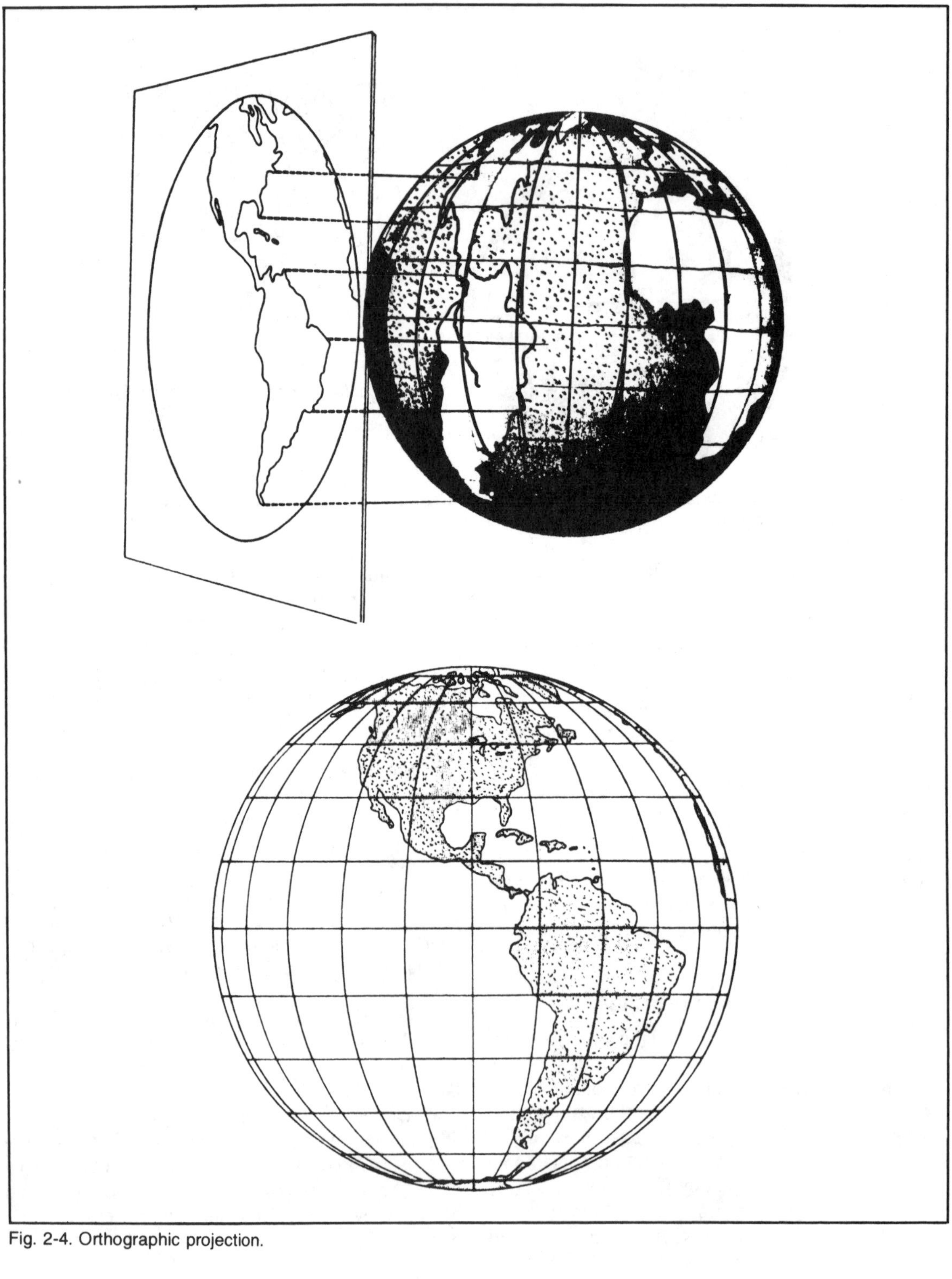

Fig. 2-4. Orthographic projection.

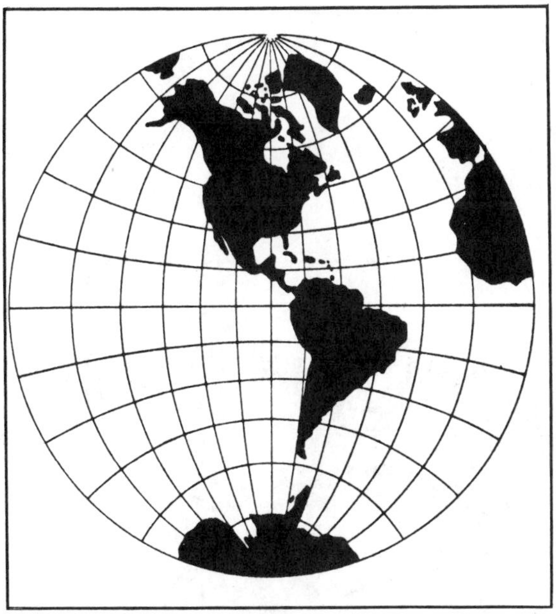

Fig. 2-5. Stereographic projection.

In order to preserve true shapes, an east-west distortion was compensated by a matching north-south distortion. Distances can be correctly measured in any direction on small area Mercator charts. This is fully explained in Chapter 5.

Because correct angular relationships are maintained on a Mercator chart, the angular relationship of our vessel to charted objects ashore or afloat can be found and plotted on the chart giving an accurate location or *fix* on the position of the boat at a specific time. It is then possible to tell how to get from the present position to the desired objective.

By comparison with a globe map of the world, a Mercator projection results in gigantic distortions at high latitudes. Greenland, Canada, and Alaska, as examples, become absurdly huge. Above latitude 50° north or south, deformations of land shapes over large areas become extremely pronounced. Latitude 70° north or south is about the limit of usefulness of the equatorial Mercator projection. Because most readers will be operating at latitudes laying between about 20° and 45° north, they will be well within the useful limits.

POLYCONIC PROJECTION

A majority of Great Lakes charts are based on the polyconic projection. Those who operate in that area will need to be acquainted with this method. It is based on developing the surface of the earth on a series of cones, using a different one for each parallel of latitude (Fig. 2-6). Due to the large number of cones used, this method preserves shapes and relative sizes considerably better than the Mercator. Distances are correct along any parallel and along the central meridian of a particular projection. Scale increases along other meridians as their longitude increasingly differs from that of the central meridian.

Parallels of latitude appear on a large area polyconic projection (Fig. 2-6B) as arcs of nonconcentric circles, and meridians show as curved lines converging toward the poles. All these curved lines are the reason polyconic projections are not as commonly used for marine navigation at the Mercator. Instead of using Mercator's handy rectangular grid, directions have to be measured on the polyconic chart from the meridian of a specific location. Particularly on small area charts, it works out in practice that use of the nearest compass rose is entirely satisfactory. On small area charts, the curvature of the parallels and the meridians is not objectionably noticeable.

LAMBERT CONFORMAL PROJECTION

The Lambert conformal projection is primarily used for aeronautical charts and for great circle nautical charts used in planning long ocean voyages such as a trans-Atlantic or trans-Pacific crossing. Because there are 14 small craft charts in the Great Lakes series derived from Lambert conformal projections, a brief description of this projection is included for the sake of completeness.

The Lambert is another conic projection; instead of postulating multiple cones, a single cone intersecting the surface of the earth at two parallels of latitude is used (Fig. 2-7). By altering the parallels to equalize the distortion along both meridians and parallels, this projection becomes conformal (angular relationships are shown correctly). This is a particularly desirable feature.

Another desirable feature is that a straight line on the Lambert chart very closely approximates a great circle, which is the shortest distance between two points on a sphere (Fig. 2-8). Radio signals follow great circle paths allowing them to be plotted directly on a Lambert chart. This feature has made Lambert charts popular for aeronautical navigation

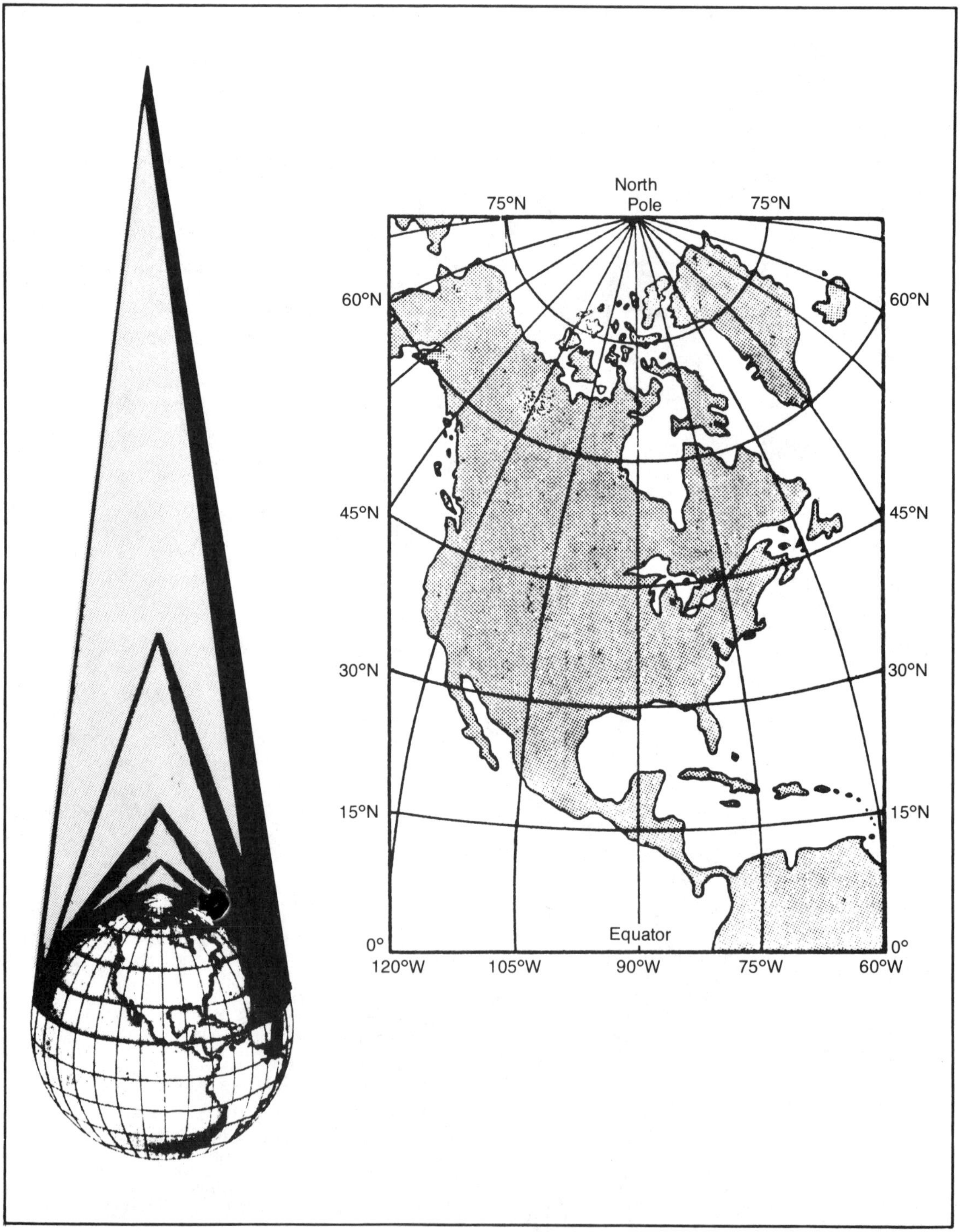
North
Pole
75°N
75°N
60°N
60°N
45°N
45°N
30°N
30°N
15°N
15°N
0°
0°
Equator
120°W
105°W
90°W
75°W
60°W

Fig. 2-6. Polyconic projection.

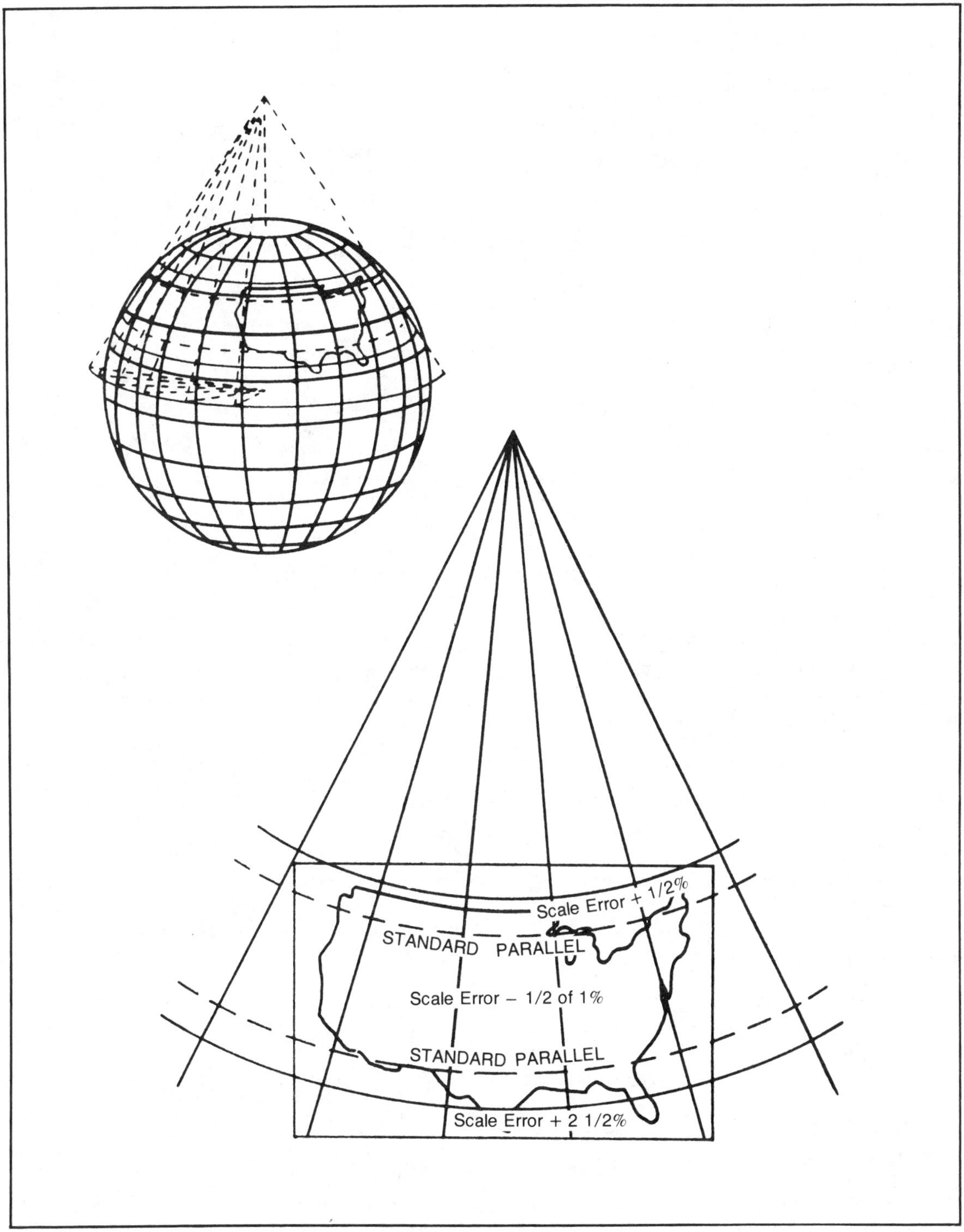
Scale Error + 1/2%
STANDARD PARALLEL
Scale Error – 1/2 of 1%
STANDARD PARALLEL
Scale Error + 2 1/2%

Fig. 2-7. Lambert conformal projection.

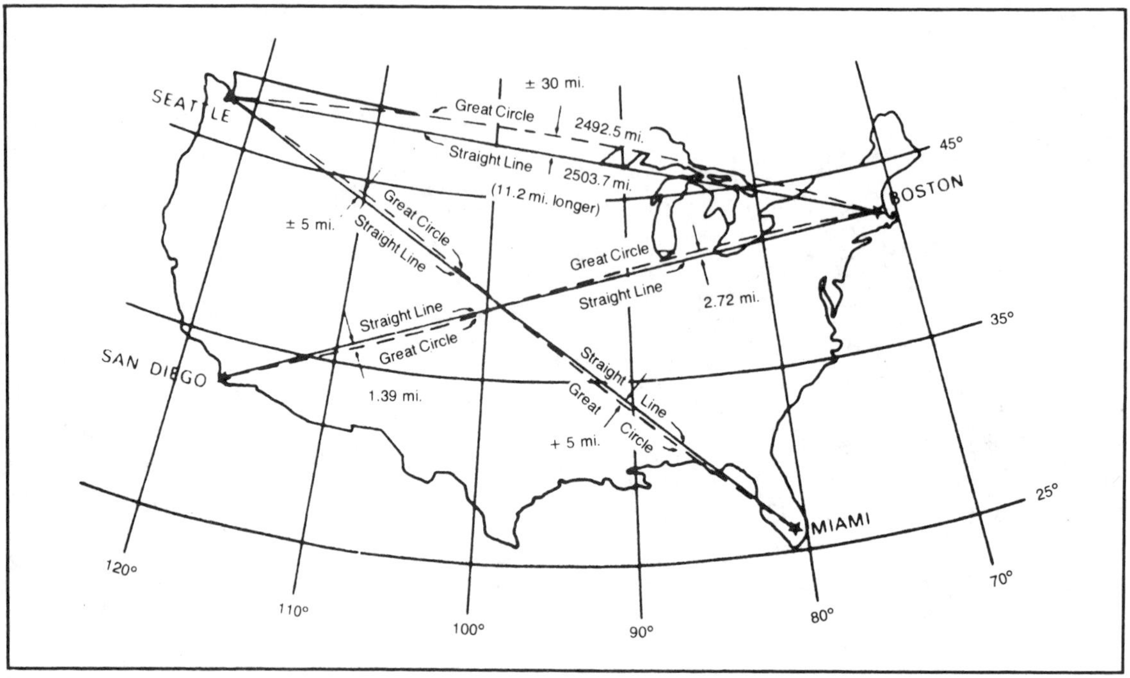
SEATTLE
± 30 mi.
Great Circle
2492.5 mi.
Straight Line
2503.7 mi.
(11.2 mi. longer)
45°
BOSTON
± 5 mi.
Great Circle
Straight Line
Great Circle
Straight Line
2.72 mi.
Straight Line
Great Circle
35°
SAN DIEGO
1.39 mi.
Straight Line
Great Circle
+ 5 mi.
Circle
Line
MIAMI
25°
120°
110°
100°
90°
80°
70°

Fig. 2-8. Great circles approximate straight lines on Lambert conformal projection.

because aircraft use radio aids extensively. In marine applications, except for long passage planning, the Lambert chart has not—and is not likely—to replace the Mercator.

CHART SOURCES

Charts of different areas and types are produced by different government agencies. Most boatmen operating in United States coastal waters will use charts issued by the National Ocean Survey, a part of the Department of Commerce. The charts from this agency cover the United States coastal waters, ports, harbors, and rivers as far upstream as there is tidal action. The NOS charts also include the Hawaiian Islands, Alaska, Puerto Rico, and the Virgin Islands. What was formerly the Lake Survey has been incorporated into NOS so that NOS also handles the charts for the Great Lakes and related lakes and canals.

Charts of all foreign waters are issued by the Defense Mapping Agency Hydrographic Center (DMAHC). Some of these charts are based on United States surveys, but many are based on surveys made by other nations. Some are virtually direct reprints of foreign charts.

Charts of major inland river systems such as the Mississippi, the Ohio, and the Arkansas are supplied by the Army Corps of Engineers.

WHERE TO OBTAIN CHARTS

Charts covering the reader's nearby waters are probably available at local marine equipment suppliers. All of the producing agencies have extensive networks of authorized distributors throughout the country. If, for some reason, local distributors are inadequate or nonexistent, contact the appropriate one of the following agencies:

National Ocean Survey, NOAA
Rockville, MD 20852

Defense Mapping Agency
Hydrographic Center
Washington, D.C. 20390

Army Corps of Engineers
Lower Mississippi Valley Division
Box 80
Vicksburg, MS 39180

Army Corps of Engineers
Omaha District
215 N 17th Street
Omaha, NE 68102

Each of these issuing agencies publishes catalogs showing the areas covered by each chart and the prices of each one. These catalogs are particularly helpful when you are planning a trip into unfamiliar waters. They contain the information as to what charts exist covering the intended route.

CHART TYPES AND SIZES

Conventional NOS charts vary considerably in sheet sizes. The smallest are about 22 × 29 inches while the largest are 36 × 54 inches. On small boats where customarily there is no large area where charts can be laid out, the 22-×-29-inch size is already large. A 36-×-54-inch chart would be impossibly gigantic! Fortunately, the small-boat in coastal operation will seldom have need for any of the charts issued in that size.

The NOS issues 5 series of charts. The first two, *Sailing* and *General Charts*, will seldom be used by the small-boat coastal navigator. Both are intended for offshore navigation. The largest area conventional charts for which the reader will have use will be *Coast Charts*. These are specifically intended for entering from sea, leaving ports, and close-in coastal navigation. Once port area has been entered, the *Harbor Charts* supply very complete details.

It is the *Harbor Charts* that will be most useful to the small-boat operator. They show complete soundings of the areas they cover, *all* aids to navigation, and all important landmarks. They make possible very accurate positions from bearings on a wide choice of objects.

In addition to the four series of conventional charts noted above, NOS also publishes—specifically for the convenience of the small-boat operator—a series of *Small Craft Charts*. In contrast with the conventional charts that are intended to be stored either flat or rolled, the *Small Craft* series come folded down. They are a far more convenient size for use on vessels where a chart table is nonexistent and storage space is very limited. These charts consist of several sheets printed front and back, accordian folded, and placed in a protective jacket.

The chart and its jacket contain, in addition to the usual navigational information, much other data useful to the small boatman. The locations of marinas, repair facilities, supply and service facilities, as well as local tidal, current, and weather information are given. *Small Craft Charts* are printed on somewhat lighter paper than conventional charts. They will not stand up to the amount of plotting, erasing, and replotting that a conventional chart will take, but they do have much valuable information not found on conventional charts.

Those operating on inland rivers will find one very great immediate difference between the NOS charts and those of the Corps of Engineers. The inland river charts give no depths of water. This results from the great seasonal changes in those depths. Although no depths are given a route line is usually shown. It follows the line of the greatest depths. The river charts are often issued in book form, with a book covering a considerable stretch of river. Distances are given in statute miles rather than nautical miles.

River chart books include a variety of miscellaneous information of interest to the boatman. There are tables of mileages between points along the river, information regarding bridges and locks, radio communications channels, locations of marinas and available services, and data on various types of recreation facilities. These include launching ramps, campgrounds, picnic grounds, and trailer parks.

READING THE CHART

On every chart, located at a place where it will not interfere with navigational information, is a title block. See Fig. 2-9. Here the correct name of the chart is given with the type of projection (in this case Mercator). Next comes the scale to which the chart is drawn (1:40,000 here). Then comes the unit of measurement for depths (feet in this instance) and the datum level used (Mean Low Water on this sample is noted). The chart name is descriptive of the area of the waters it covers. The projection is Mercator most of the time.

SCALES

Scales of charts vary with the different series and the geographical areas covered by individual

UNITED STATES – EAST COAST

DELAWARE – PENNSYLVANIA – NEW JERSEY

DELAWARE RIVER

WILMINGTON TO PHILADELPHIA

Mercator Projection
Scale 1:40,000 at Lat. 39°51′

SOUNDINGS IN FEET
AT MEAN LOW WATER

TIDAL INFORMATION

Place	Height referred to datum of soundings (MLW)			
	Mean High Water	Mean Tide Level	Mean Low Water	Extreme Low Water
	feet	feet	feet	feet
Wilmington, Del	5 3	2 9	0 0	−4 0
Chester, Pa	5 4	2 9	0 0	−4 0
Billingsport, N J	5 5	3 0	0 0	−4 5
Phila Pier 9N, Pa	5 8	3 1	0 0	−5 0

(463)

ABBREVIATIONS (For complete list of Symbols and Abbreviations, see C & G S Chart No 1)

Lights (Lights are white unless otherwise indicated)

F fixed	S-L short-long	OBSC obscured	Rot. rotating
Fl flashing	Occ. occulting	WHIS whistle	SEC sector
Qk quick	Alt alternating	DIA diaphone	m minutes
Gp group	I Qk interrupted quick	M nautical miles	sec seconds

Buoys

T B temporary buoy	N nun	B black	Or orange	W white
C can	S spar	R red	G green	Y yellow

Bottom characteristics

Cl clay	M mud	hrd hard	bk black	gy gray
Co coral	Rk rock	rky rocky	br brown	rd red
G gravel	S sand	sft soft	bu blue	wh white
Grs grass	Sh shells	stk sticky	gn green	yl yellow

21 Wreck, rock obstruction, or shoal swept clear to the depth indicated
(2) Rocks that cover and uncover, with heights in feet above datum of soundings

AERO aeronautical	R Bn radiobeacon	C G Coast Guard station
Bn daybeacon	R TR radio tower	D F S distance finding station

AUTH authorized Obstr obstruction P A position approximate E D existence doubtful

HEIGHTS

Heights in feet above Mean High Water

AUTHORITIES

Hydrography and topography by the Coast and Geodetic Survey
with additions and revisions from the Corps of Engineers

Fig. 2-9. Chart title block.

charts. The *Coast Chart* series ranges from 1:50,000 to 1:150,000. The *Harbor Chart* series goes from a scale of 1:5,000 to 1:40,000 (making them considerably larger in scale than the *Coast* series). The geographical area shown on *Harbor* Charts is smaller than that given on the *Coast* series, but the various features are drawn much larger.

Because the matter of "large scale" and "small scale" is occasionally confusing try looking at a couple of scales as fractions. An object drawn in the scale 1:50,000 is 1/50,000 of its actual size. Seen another way 1 inch on the chart represents 50,000 inches, or .685 miles. A scale of 1:150,000 shows features at 1/150,000 of actual size. The same 1 inch now equals 2.06 miles, and that is a much greater distance, meaning everything being shown must be *drawn much smaller*. It is therefore a *smaller* scale. The *Harbor Chart* scale of 1:5,000, by contrast, shows geographically much smaller areas, but drawn vastly *larger*. It gives all manner of detail impossible on the smaller chart scales; 1:5,000 is thus a very large scale.

DEPTHS AND DATUM LEVELS

The unit used for depth soundings on *Coast Charts* will usually be fathoms. *Harbor Charts* are sometimes in fathoms and sometimes in feet. The title block will tell which. The meaning of datum level used for those depth soundings calls for some explanation.

Tides and tide tables are covered in Chapter 6. In advance of that discussion, it will be news to few readers that all salt water coastal areas and waters well up the estuaries of many rivers are subject to daily tidal variations in depth. There might be two fairly equal tide changes per day, there might be two quite unequal changes each day, or there might be only one change in a day. Therefore the depth soundings given on charts must be adjusted to a low enough base level so that the mariner can safely expect to find at any specific location at any time *at least* the depth of water shown on the chart.

This has led to the use of various datum levels depending on the tidal variation pattern found in different charted areas. In some areas, the average of the daily low tides is used. This is called Mean Low Water (MLW). Where there is considerable difference between the two daily tides, Mean Lower Low Water (MLLW) is a safer datum level to use. At some places, there is enough difference between the low waters on different days of the month that it is safer to base charted depth soundings on the average of low water spring tides. These are the minimum low tides of the month. They are noted as Mean Low Water Springs (MLWS).

EDITIONS

The location of the title block and its information varies depending on available space. The chart number, its edition number, and edition date will be found in the lower left-hand corner (Fig. 2-10). The chart number is repeated in all four corners. If there has been a revised printing of a chart, the revision date will follow the edition date in the lower left corner. It is most important to use the latest available charts. Also keep them up to date by correcting them to include any information given in *Notices to Mariners* since the last revision.

NOTES

In the vicinity of the title block—and scattered about at various other places that are considered suitable—will be found various information notes. See Fig. 2-11. Because the charting agency felt that the information noted was important, the sailor is wise to study the chart carefully to be certain that he has seen all such notes. Then determine whether they apply to him and if so in what ways.

Water depths are shown (Fig. 2-12) by the

10th Ed., June 2/79

18765

LORAN-C OVERPRINTED

CAUTION

This chart has been corrected from the Notice to Mariners published weekly by the Defense Mapping Agency Hydrographic /Topographic Center and the Local Notice to Mariners issued periodically by each U.S. Coast Guard district to the print date shown in the lower left hand corner.

Fig. 2-10. Chart lower left corner sample with chart number, edition number, and data.

CAUTION

Improved channels shown by broken lines are subject to shoaling, particularly at the edges.

CAUTION

Temporary defects in aids to navigation are not indicated on this chart except where a buoy replaces a fixed aid. See Notices to Mariners.

CAUTION

Southeast Channel Entrance is subject to continual change.

1240

Caution

Extremely heavy tide rips and strong currents may be encountered in the vicinity of the islands shown on this chart.

9030

CAUTION

Vessels entering Long Beach Channel should pass eastward of lighted whistle buoy "LB," and vessels departing should pass westward.

5147

CAUTION

The shoreline is subject to continual change in this area.

887-SC

CAUTION

Mariners are warned to stay clear of the protective riprap surrounding navigational light structures shown thus:

NAVAL TRIAL COURSE

The line of buoys in the entrance to Penobscot Bay between Latitude 44°01′ and 44°08′ mark a Naval trial course. Vessels must keep clear of this course while trial tests are in progress.

1203

PLANES OF REFERENCE

Depths charted in Caloosahatchee River and St. Lucie River are referred to mean low water. Depths in the Caloosahatchee Canal are referred to a low water elevation which is 10 feet above mean sea level. Depths-in Lake Okeechobee and St. Lucie Canal are referred to a low water elevation which is 12½ feet above mean sea level.

1289

PRIVATE BUOYS

Private buoys are maintained in most of the bays, ponds and inlets on this chart.

259

DUMPING GROUNDS

Regulations and permission for dumping in the areas indicated may be obtained at the office of the District Engineer, Corps of Engineers, New York, N.Y.

INTRACOASTAL WATERWAY

Use chart 845-SC. The depths and channel markers are not shown hereon.

1247

ST. LUCIE INLET

The channel is subject to continual change. Entrance buoys and lights are not shown because they are frequently shifted in position.

Use chart 845-SC.

1247

VEGETATION

The land is generally heavily wooded. The woods decrease in density with the elevation, leaving the higher elevations bare.

8148

STORM WARNINGS

The U.S. Weather Bureau displays storm warnings on the following lightships:

Pollock Rip (41°36′-69°51′)
Nantucket Shoals (40°33′-69°28′)
Ambrose Channel (40°27′-73°49′)
Scotland (40°26′-73°55′)
Barnegat (39°46′-73°56′)
Five Fathom Bank (38°47′-74°35′)

For a complete list of storm warning stations, see large scale charts.

1108

STORM WARNINGS

The U.S. Weather Bureau displays storm warnings at the following approximate locations:

Custom House, Boston (42°21.5′-71°03.2′)
Boston C. G. Station (42°22.1′-71°03.1′)
Boston Lightship (42°20.4′-70°45.5′)
Deer Island Light Station (42°20.4′-70°57.3′)
*Old Colony Yacht Club (42°18.0′-71°02.7′)
*Hingham Yacht Club (42°15.7′-70°53.7′)
Pt Allerton C. G. Station (42°18.4′-70°54′)
*Winthop (42°22.1′-70°59.3′)
*Seasonal

246

Fig. 2-11. Miscellaneous standard chart notes.

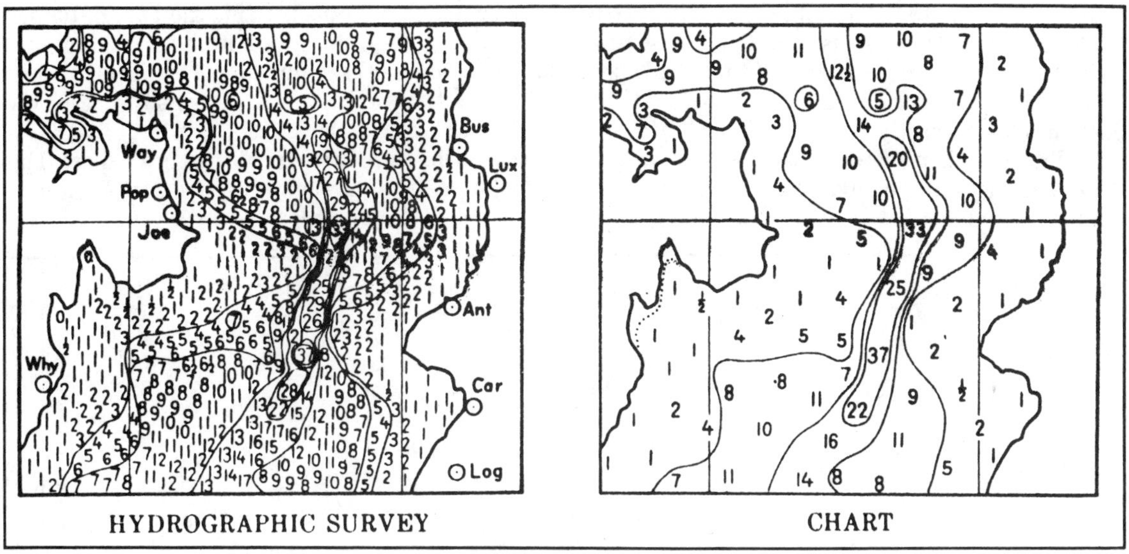
Bus
Lux
Way
Pop
Joe
Ant
Why
Car
Log
HYDROGRAPHIC SURVEY
CHART

Fig. 2-12. Comparison: survey boat sheet and chart.

many small numbers scattered over the water areas of the chart. Whether they refer to feet or fathoms is determined by looking at the tile block (Fig. 2-9). The depths charted are a very small number of the total soundings that the survey ship made when the area was last surveyed (Fig. 2-12). Only enough are charted to give the sailor a clear picture of the contour of the bottom. Where there are many and rapid changes in depths, the soundings given will be close together. Over areas where changes are gradual, the spacing is wider.

COMPASS ROSES

One of the most desirable features of the Mercator projection is that it's "conformal" angles and directions are correct. To make use of this fact, compass roses (Fig. 2-13) are placed at convenient locations on each chart. The outer circle of each rose shows true geographic directions in degrees: 0° = true north, 90° = due east, 180° = due south, and so on clockwise around the rest of the circle.

Inside of that is another circle of degrees tilted so as to show the directions the magnetic compass would read in that particular locality if it were uninfluenced by any magnetic effects on the boat. Variation, this local difference between geographic north and magnetic north, is fully covered in Chapter 4 dealing in detail with the compass. Merely note at this point that it is from the compass rose on the chart nearest to your position that the local variation is to be determined.

LATITUDE AND LONGITUDE SCALES

At the right and left margins of the chart will be found the latitude scales for the area covered. On the top and bottom borders are the longitude scales. Charts of the *Harbor* series will have borders of the type shown in Fig. 2-14; those on *Coast* series charts will be of the Fig. 2-15 type. With the aid of these border scales and a pair of dividers, the exact latitude of any point on the chart can easily be found.

To find latitude, simply place one leg of the dividers on the point in question and the other on the nearest marked parallel of latitude. Now move the open dividers to the scale on the border and read off the latitude by counting the difference between the marked parallel and the unknown point. Remember, north is toward the top of the chart. If the unknown point is above the marked parallel, you add (latitude increases as you go north, right?). If the unknown point is below the marked parallel, subtract the difference from the latitude marked.

With the latitude known, now repeat the process using the nearest marked meridian of longitude to determine the unknown longitude. Do not forget that in the United States all longitudes will be west because we are west of Greenwich. The east side of the chart is the right-hand side; west is to the left, and thus longitude is going to increase from right to left across the chart. With latitude and longitude known, a location on the surface of the earth has been exactly determined.

With the chart border scales shown in Fig. 2-14, latitude and longitude can be expressed in degrees, minutes, and seconds. This is the most precise notation method. Using the type of border given in Fig. 2-15, locations are given in degrees, minutes, and tenths of minutes. This is not as precise a notation method as the other, but we are now dealing with charts that cover much larger areas on which all features are drawn much smaller. The same degree of precision in measurements is neither possible nor necessary.

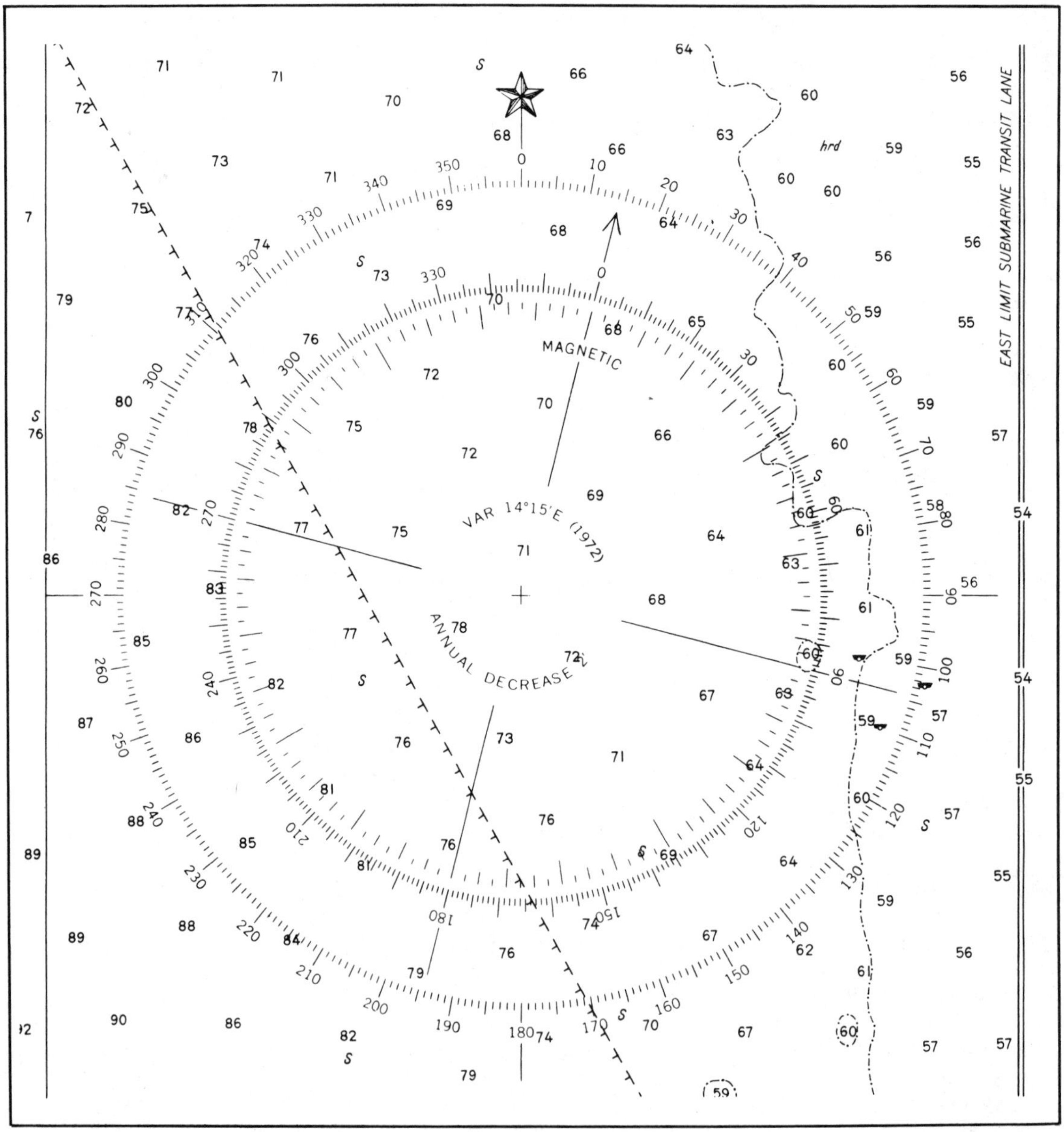

MAGNETIC
VAR 14°15'E (1972)
ANNUAL DECREASE
hrd
EAST LIMIT SUBMARINE TRANSIT LANE

Fig. 2-13. Typical chart compass rose.

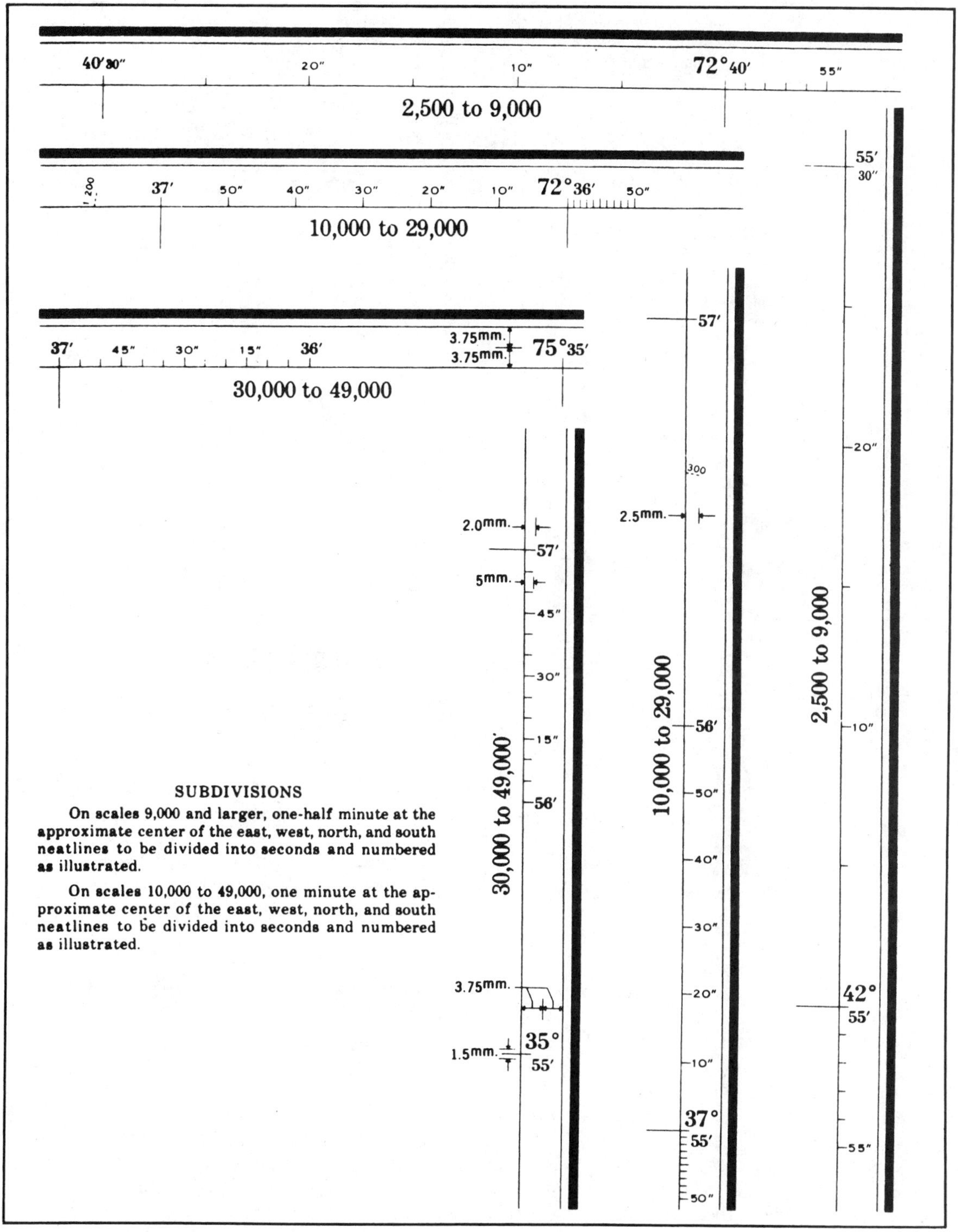
40′30″
20″
10″
72°40′
55″
2,500 to 9,000
55′
30″
1:200
37′
50″
40″
30″
20″
10″
72°36′
50″
10,000 to 29,000
37′
45″
30″
15″
36′
3.75mm.
3.75mm.
75°35′
30,000 to 49,000
57′
20″
2.0mm.
57′
5mm.
2.5mm.
45″
30″
15″
56′
10″
56′
50″
40″
30″
20″
10″
30,000 to 49,000
10,000 to 29,000
2,500 to 9,000
3.75mm.
1.5mm.
35°
55′
42°
55′
37°
55′
55″
50″

SUBDIVISIONS

On scales 9,000 and larger, one-half minute at the approximate center of the east, west, north, and south neatlines to be divided into seconds and numbered as illustrated.

On scales 10,000 to 49,000, one minute at the approximate center of the east, west, north, and south neatlines to be divided into seconds and numbered as illustrated.

Fig. 2-14. Typical borders for harbor series charts.

Scale	Interval Project. lines	Interval Project. figures	Interval Border subdiv.
50 000	5′	5′	1/10′
60 000	5′	5′	1/10′
80 000	10′	5′	1/10′
100 000	10′	5′	1/10′

Scale	Interval Project. lines	Interval Project. figures	Interval Border subdiv.
125 000	10′	5′	1/5′
200 000	20′	10′	1/5′
250 000	20′	10′	1/5′

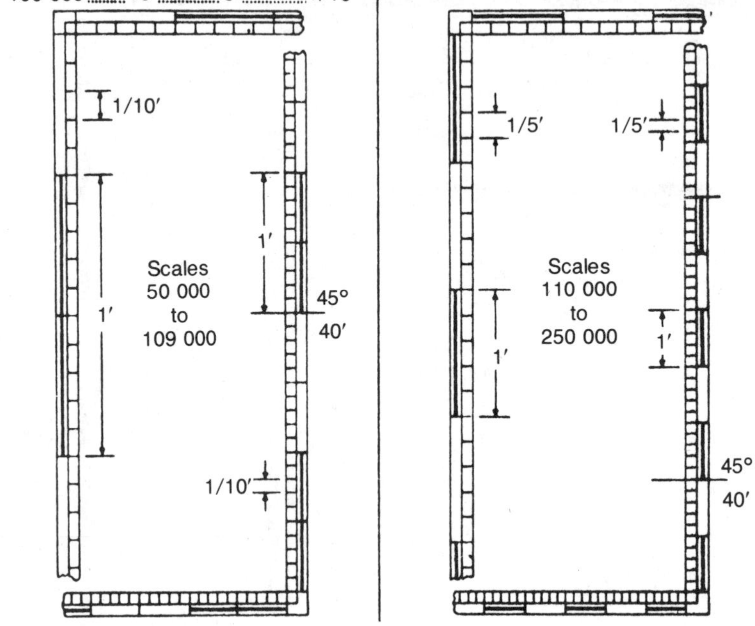
1/10′
1′
Scales
50 000
to
109 000
1′
45°
40′
1/10′
1/5′
1/5′
Scales
110 000
to
250 000
1′
1′
45°
40′

Fig. 2-15. Typical borders for coastal series charts.

DISTANCE

In Chapter 1, during the discussion of latitude, I mentioned that 1° of latitude on the surface of the earth is equal to 60 nautical miles, thus 1 inch of latitude equals 1 nautical mile. One of the virtues of the Mercator projection for nautical charts is that—in addition to being conformal, permitting correct course and bearing directions to be determined—distances can also be measured.

All charts of the *Harbor* series, and many of those in the *Coast* series, contain a scale of miles similar to that shown in Fig. 2-16. As the conversion to metric measurement progresses in the United States more scales giving meters and kilometers can be expected to appear.

On charts having borders of the type shown in Fig. 2-15, distances are easily measured using the border latitude scale on the chart sides because that scale is graduated in minutes of latitude and tenths. The number of minutes and tenths equals the number of nautical miles and tenths. If it is desirable to express the measured distance in some unit other than nautical miles, a short exercise with a handy pocket calculator will be needed to make the conversion.

SPEED

All *Harbor Charts* have a logarithmic speed scale (Fig. 2-16) with which speed over the ground can be found by simple graphic means using only a pair of dividers. Running time and distance run must be known. Directions for the use of this scale will be found printed directly under the scale itself. If the vessel has a tachometer a procedure for working out a table of speeds through the water, given in Chapter 5, can be used. Speed through the water and speed over the ground can be very different numbers.

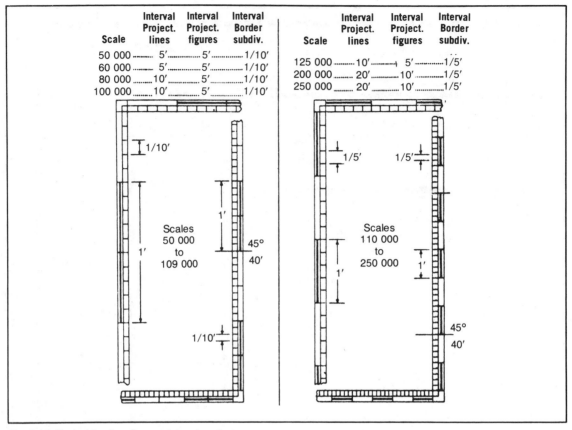

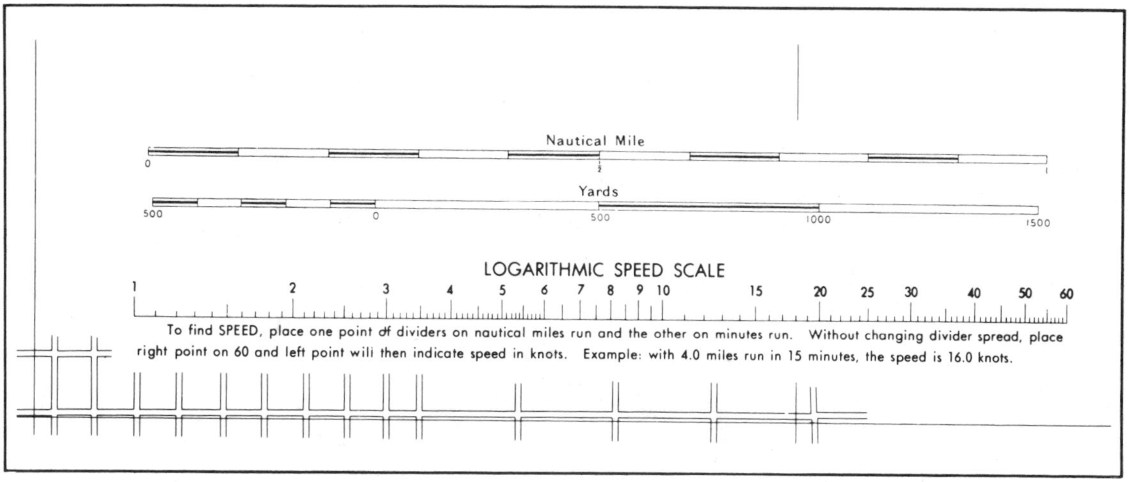
Nautical Mile
0
½
1
Yards
500
0
500
1000
1500
LOGARITHMIC SPEED SCALE
1 2 3 4 5 6 7 8 9 10 15 20 25 30 40 50 60
To find SPEED, place one point of dividers on nautical miles run and the other on minutes run. Without changing divider spread, place right point on 60 and left point will then indicate speed in knots. Example: with 4.0 miles run in 15 minutes, the speed is 16.0 knots.

Fig. 2-16. Scale of miles and speed scale from harbor chart.

STANDARD SYMBOLS AND ABBREVIATIONS

I strongly encourage you to obtain a copy of *Chart No. 1*. It is published in pamphlet form and it contains all of the various symbols and abbreviations used on United States charts. They are printed in the exact sizes and colors in which they appear on the charts. Not only does this provide an ideal way to become familiar with the more commonly encountered symbols, it also constitutes a handy and authoritative reference for the identification of any symbols or abbreviations encountered that might be either fairly rare or simply unfamiliar.

Chart No. 1 is divided into lettered sections running from A through U. Each section deals with a category of either symbols or abbreviations. Depending upon an individual's area of operation, and the charts covering that area, some sections of *Chart No. 1* will be far more useful than others. Some parts however, will be important to everybody.

In addition to Appendix excerpts from *Chart No. 1*, parts A and C, all sailors will be well advised to be particularly familiar with sections K, L, M, and O (also reproduced in the Appendix).

Section K deals with the many kinds of lights that are maintained as night aids to navigation. It also includes the abbreviations that will be found on the chart alongside the various symbols describing the color and characteristics generally encountered such as flashing, occulting, quick flashing, interrupted quick flashing, group occulting, and others that are explained in detail in Chapter 3 in the section on aids to navigation.

Section L deals with buoys and beacons. Some of these are floating aids to navigation, and others are fixed either in shallow water or ashore. The specific aids symbolized in this section are also covered in Chapter 3.

Many of the radio and radar aids shown in section M call for equipment well beyond what will be available to the average weekend sailor. For those who want them, ultracompact, self-contained, self-powered, multi-channel radio telephones operating on the marine band are available. I have had one of these for several years, and I have found it very satisfactory.

For those who are interested, some very compact self-powered combination portable radio/radio direction finders can be obtained. The use of these instruments are explained in Chapter 5 in connection with methods for locating positions.

All charts should be carefully studied to note the existence and determine the location of any of the various hazards and obstructions shown in section O. Some of these will be immediately familiar to a sailor accustomed to the charted territory. Nevertheless, it is not safe to assume merely because a person has been sailing a particular area for the last 10 years that he or she knows all the various dangers that exist there and exactly where they are. This is one of the most difficult categories of items for the charting agencies to keep up to date. A

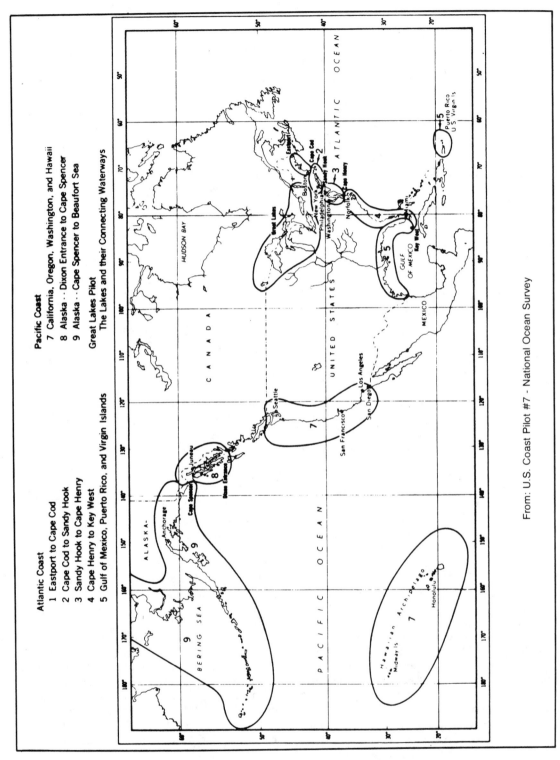

Atlantic Coast
1 Eastport to Cape Cod
2 Cape Cod to Sandy Hook
3 Sandy Hook to Cape Henry
4 Cape Henry to Key West
5 Gulf of Mexico, Puerto Rico, and Virgin Islands

Pacific Coast
7 California, Oregon, Washington, and Hawaii
8 Alaska - - Dixon Entrance to Cape Spencer
9 Alaska - - Cape Spencer to Beaufort Sea

Great Lakes Pilot
The Lakes and their Connecting Waterways

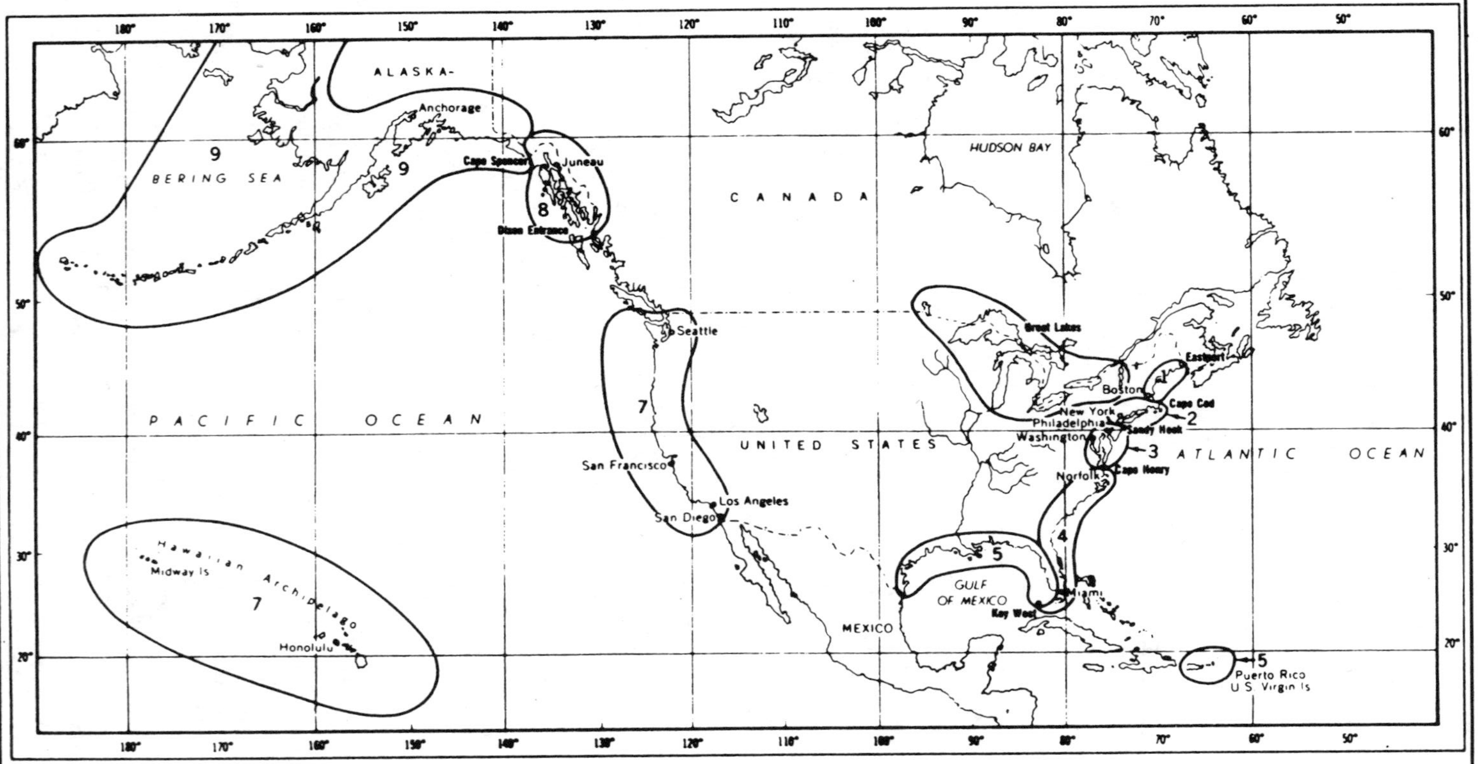
ALASKA
Anchorage
Cape Spencer
Juneau
Dixon Entrance
BERING SEA
CANADA
HUDSON BAY
Great Lakes
Eastport
Boston
Cape Cod
New York
Philadelphia
Sandy Hook
Washington
Cape Henry
Norfolk
Seattle
San Francisco
Los Angeles
San Diego
PACIFIC OCEAN
UNITED STATES
ATLANTIC OCEAN
GULF OF MEXICO
Key West
Miami
MEXICO
Puerto Rico
U.S. Virgin Is
Hawaiian Archipelago
Midway Is
Honolulu

From: U.S. Coast Pilot #7 - National Ocean Survey

Fig. 2-17. Map of Coast Pilot areas.

wreck awash might be fairly easy to see—easy, that is, until it rots away and becomes a sunken wreck. A sunken wreck becomes invisible and more dangerous because of that.

Similarly, the sea can break down a rock awash so that it becomes submerged, invisible, and twice as dangerous. Never trust the limits given for coral reefs. Coral is constantly growing. Move in the vicinity of coral with the utmost caution. When the sun is low—making your visibility below the surface of the water poor—do not move in the vicinity of coral at all!

COAST PILOTS

In addition to publishing and continually updating several hundred charts covering a couple million square miles of United States waters, your National Ocean Survey also publishes nine *Coast Pilot* books. These cover the same waters and provide a vast amount of information of vital concern to the navigator, but impossible to include on the charts. Each of the *Coast Pilots* contains detailed sailing directions for the area it covers keyed to each of the charts for that area.

Each chart number is called out in geographical sequence (north to south on the East Coast, south to north on the West Coast). The information provided for each chart differs depending on what is of primary importance in that area.

Although there are nine *Coast Pilots* published, most boatmen will find that one of them covers the waters in which he sails with a good bit to spare. You are unlikely to need more than one. The nine books (Fig. 2-17) are:

Atlantic Coast
Eastport to Cape Cod
Cape Cod to Sandy Hook
Sandy Hook to Cape Henry
Cape Henry to Key West
Gulf of Mexico, Puerto Rico & Virgin Islands

Pacific Coast
California, Oregon, Washington & Hawaii
Alaska - Dixon Entrance to Cape Spencer
Alaska - Cape Spencer to Beaufort Sea
Great Lakes Pilot

All *Coast Pilots* begin with fairly long chapters containing a general explanation of how the *Coast Pilot* states its information. Also given are which United States government agencies are involved in maritime activities. Then standard distress and radio communications procedures, sources of radio weather and storm warnings, and times and frequencies of time signal broadcasts are found. This is followed by general information regarding charts, aids to navigation, signals of certain specialized vessels, and general navigational restrictions.

Chapter 2 contains parts of the Federal Navigation Regulations that are of importance in the area covered by the particular *Coast Pilot.* These regulations deal with specifics relating to radio communications, boundaries of Inland Waters within the concerned area, anchorage regulations, and specific anchorage areas in different harbors. Then drawbridges and how to signal each one, various local marine traffic regulations, limits of designated restricted areas, and regulations relating to canals and locks are given.

Chapter 3 continues to fill in the local background dealing in a general way with the regional tidal conditions, currents, and kind of weather, and climatic conditions to be expected. Also included are recommended routes to be followed on passages between various major ports.

Following Chapter 3 are differing numbers of chapters in different *Coast Pilots* describing in detail every port and harbor as well as every significant object along the coast between ports. The remarks in these chapters refer the reader to the charts that show the features being discussed. Useful landmarks are pointed out. Distances in nautical miles between significant points are given. Local weather peculiarities are noted. Normal velocity and sets of currents are mentioned along with local peculiarities that might catch the mariner unawares.

Information regarding small craft facilities is given along with notes on availability of fuel, repairs, and supplies. Major aids to navigation are pointed out, and exact latitudes and longitudes for them are stated. Heights above water in feet for prominant lights are noted. Radio channels for communication with local harbormasters will be found along with local harbor regulations.

Any significant local hazards to the mariner are emphasized. By combining the very specific local guidance given in the *Coast Pilot* with the navigational information available on the chart the boatman is well prepared to make a coastal passage. He may be confident that he knows what hazards he might encounter, and where, as well as what to look for in the way of both aids to navigation and natural and man-made landmarks to help him keep track of his position and progress.

At the back of each *Coast Pilot* will be found a group of useful tables. Climatological tables are provided for various important ports in the region. These supply monthly data on temperature, precipitation, humidity, winds, and cloud cover. Meteorological tables for points scattered over the region give monthly averages on winds, wave heights, visibility, barometric pressure, and wind direction. Surface water temperatures and densities in the region are found in another table. There will also be tables of distances between important ports. Several helpful reference tables are also included for the determination of wind speed by sea condition and distance of visibility of objects at sea. Conversion tables are included for degrees to points, nautical miles to statute miles, and feet to meters. Plus, there is a table for estimating running time based on speed and distance.

While a *Coast Pilot* is by no means a ponderous volume, it measures about 8 × 10 × 1 inches thick. On smaller boats, a suitable stowage place may be difficult to provide. This should not be a problem. The time to read the *Coast Pilot* is not when you are already at sea, but beforehand when the preparations are being made.

Ahead of time, read over the *Coast Pilot* with the charts laid out for reference. Note on the chart objects indicated as likely to be helpful or hazardous, as the case may be, and put the *Pilot* away. It has served its purpose. Of course, if stowage space is available by all means keep the *Coast Pilot* aboard.

Chapter 3

QUASAR

Aids to Navigation

As a study of charts will show a number of hazards lurk in coastal waters. Any of these hazards can endanger, or at the very least embarrass, the unwary boatman. Seldom indeed does a natural landmark exist close enough to such a hazard to be usable as a warning marker. Consequently, an extensive system of man-made *aids to navigation* has been devised both to serve as warning of unseen dangers as well as markers to guide the mariner along safe channels.

The term aid to navigation refers to any object, device, or mechanism (fixed in position or floating, but certainly external to the vessel) that is specifically placed to assist the navigator either accurately to locate his position or safely to avoid a known hazard. These man-made aids to navigation fall into two general categories: fixed aids and floating aids. Fixed aids are objects located in known positions ashore (such as lighthouses, radio beacons, or ranges) or aids located in water shallow enough that they are fixed to the bottom (such as beacons or offshore light towers). Floating aids are buoys of many different kinds, plus a very few lightships. Most of the old lightships have now been replaced either with offshore light towers (so-called Texas Towers), or large unmanned navigational buoys.

FIXED AIDS

The largest, most powerful, and most important aids to navigation are the lighthouses. In some cases, they are located on the mainland. In other cases, they might be placed on offshore islands. In yet other instances, they might be built up as markers on particularly important or dangerous shoals. These aids are each entirely individual as regards to their physical size, structure, intensity of light, and the flashing pattern of the light (which is termed its light *phase characteristic*).

Lighthouses are positioned at points of major importance: prominant coastal headlands, entrances to major harbors, or on isolated danger points of which the mariner needs to be warned. The actual structures vary with the importance of each light as well as the particular requirements of the location such as the kind of ground on which it is to stand and the kind of wind and sea conditions to which it will be exposed (Figs. 3-1A through 3-1D). The average person conjuring up a mental picture of a lighthouse will probably think of the typical tapered, cylindrical masonry structure terminating in a large light on top. A good many, particularly the older ones, do conform to this stereotype. Other

Fig. 3-1A. A typical light station (courtesy United States Coast Guard).

structural shapes and construction methods are in use as well.

In any event, the purpose of the structure is to support a powerful light at some considerable height above sea level, and possibly a fog signal and a radio beacon as well. It might also contain living quarters for the operating personnel. In many cases, the fog signal, radio beacon, and living quarters are in an additional building or buildings close by. Both the height of the light and its intensity are determined by the distance at which it is intended to be visible.

Most of the old lightships that used to mark, offshore, the entrances to major harbors or serve as shoal warnings in heavily trafficked waters have been replaced with offshore light towers (Fig. 3-2). These are a good deal more uniform in size, shape, and design than the lighthouse. They normally consist of an 80-foot square deckhouse supported on four large steel corner legs. These stand on pilings driven 300 feet into the sea bottom. At one corner of the top deck, which serves as a landing platform for helicopters, is a combination light and antenna tower. It supports a light with a nominal range of 18 miles. The same tower contains the radio beacon antenna. These towers also operate powerful fog signals.

VISIBILITY OF LIGHTS

The distance at which a light will first be seen is dependent on which of two factors limits its visibility: its *nominal range* or its *geographic range*.

The nominal range is determined by the intensity of light. This distance is defined in the *Coast Guard Light Lists* as the maximum at which the light may be seen in clear weather. Clear weather, in turn, is defined by the Weather Bureau as an atmospheric condition such that visibility is 10 nautical miles.

Geographic range is limited (Fig. 3-3) by the curvature of the earth. Appendix Table A-1 gives distances to the horizon for various heights above sea level. If the height of the light in a lighthouse happened to be 100 feet above sea level, the curvature of the earth will intercept that light at a distance of 11.4 nautical miles regardless of its luminosity. Even if the light is bright enough to be seen for 30 nautical miles and the height is doubled to 200 feet, the earth will still intercept it at only 16.2 nautical miles.

Even in a very small boat, the sailor's eye is not going to be at sea level (at the very least it will be some few feet above). As an example, let's assume the eye of the sailor is 6 feet above sea level; the horizon will be 2.8 nautical miles from the sailor's position. That sailor's eye height of 6 feet has thus extended the geographic range of the 200-foot high light by 2.8 miles to a total of 19 nautical miles. Having caught sight of the light and if that sailor now sits down, reducing his height of eye

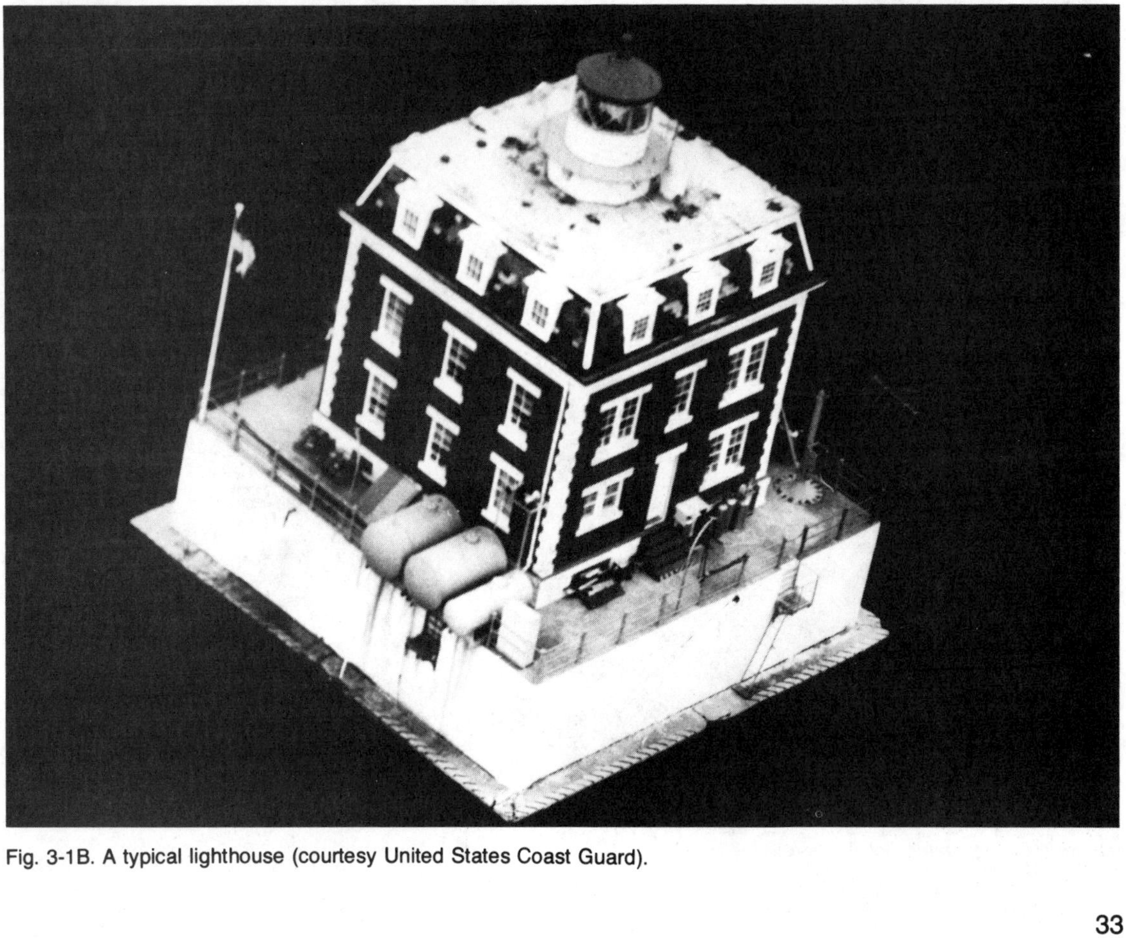

Fig. 3-1B. A typical lighthouse (courtesy United States Coast Guard).

Fig. 3-1C. The Cape Henry Light Station near Virginia Beach at the south side of the entrance to the Chesapeake Bay (courtesy United States Coast Guard).

Fig. 3-1D. The Brandywine Shoal Light Station, Delaware Bay (courtesy United States Coast Guard).

AMBROSE

Fig. 3-2. Off-shore light towers.

by 3 feet, he will at once also lose sight of the light because he had reduced his visual distance to the horizon by .8 of a mile.

Both lighthouses and offshore light towers have lights of such great luminosity that the factor limiting their visibility is invariable geographic range rather than nominal range except, naturally, for times when fog, haze, rain, or other weather or atmospheric conditions are interfering with visibility in general.

CHARACTERISTIC LIGHT PATTERNS

The lights mounted in aids to navigation are not simply lights turned on at night and off in the daytime. In order to distinguish them from each other, and from nearby lights serving other purposes on the shore, each is lighted according to a distinctive repetitive pattern of on and off cycles. This repeated pattern of on and off is termed the *light phase characteristic*. These light phase characteristics can be infinitely varied by altering the time durations of lights and darks. Thirteen basic patterns, shown in Fig. 3-4A, have been chosen for use with navigational aids.

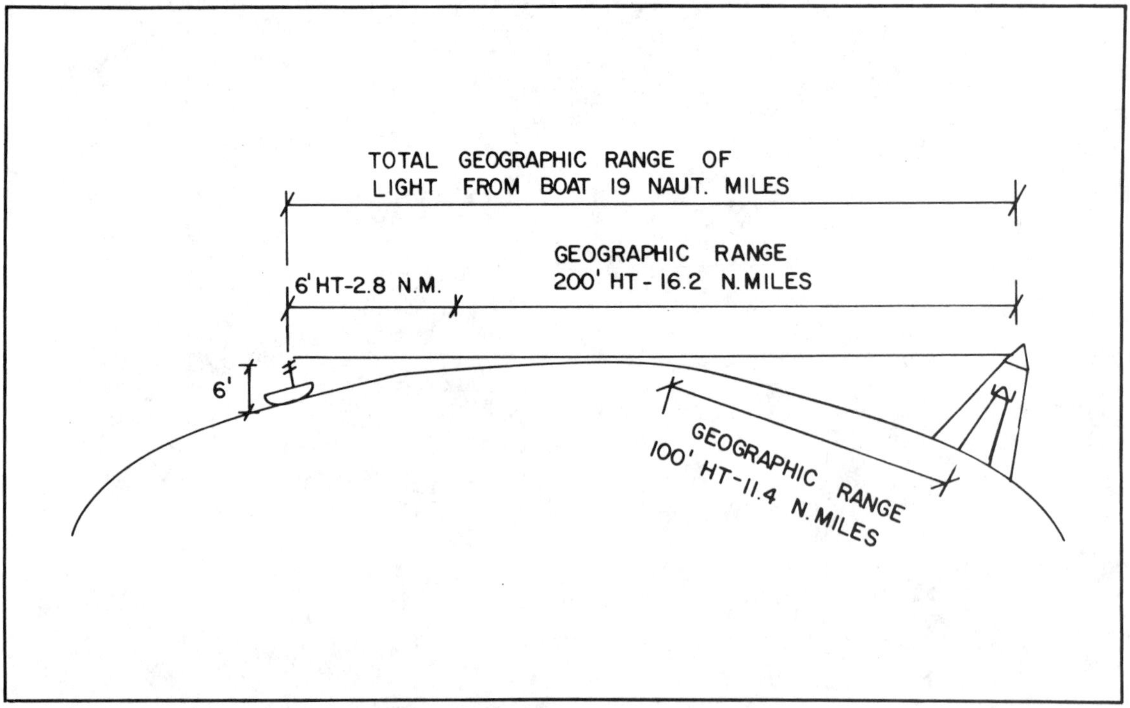
TOTAL GEOGRAPHIC RANGE OF
LIGHT FROM BOAT 19 NAUT. MILES
GEOGRAPHIC RANGE
200' HT - 16.2 N.MILES
6' HT-2.8 N.M.
6'
GEOGRAPHIC RANGE
100' HT-11.4 N.MILES

Fig. 3-3. Diagram of the geographic range of a lighthouse.

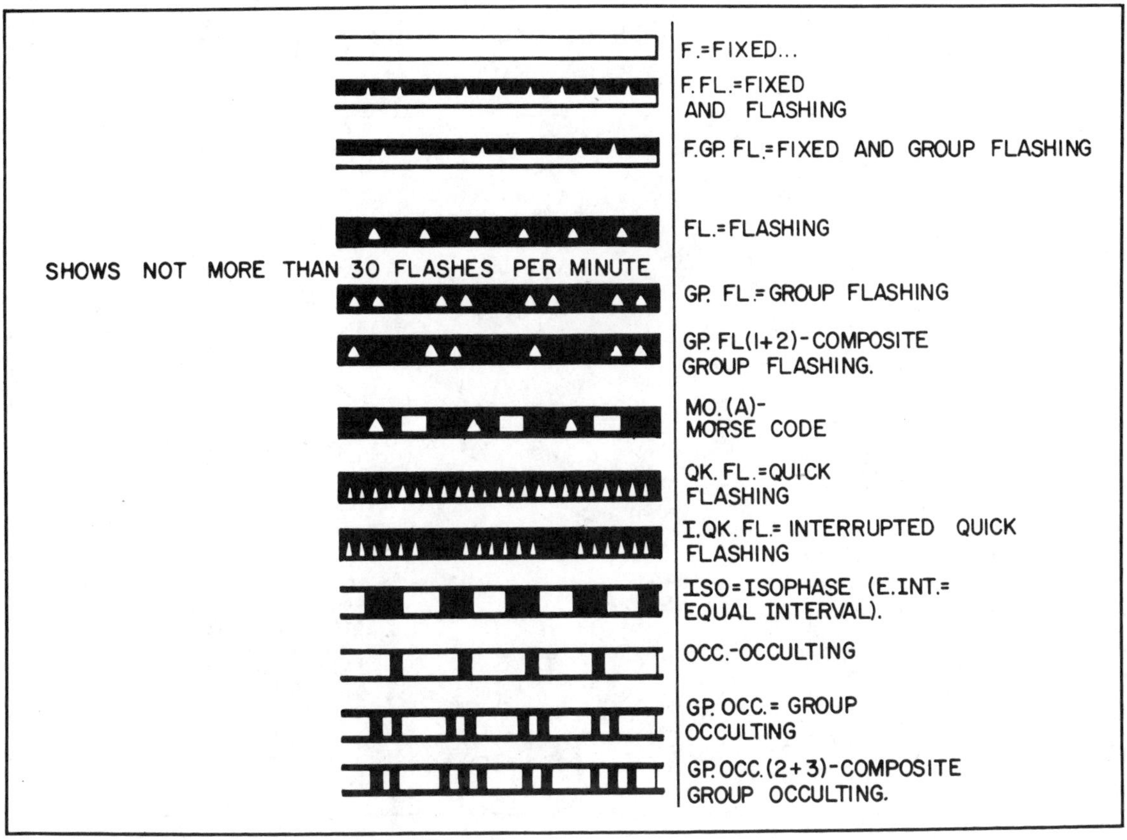

F.=FIXED...
F. FL.=FIXED AND FLASHING
F.GP. FL.=FIXED AND GROUP FLASHING
FL.=FLASHING
SHOWS NOT MORE THAN 30 FLASHES PER MINUTE
GP. FL.=GROUP FLASHING
GP. FL(1+2)-COMPOSITE GROUP FLASHING.
MO. (A)- MORSE CODE
QK. FL.=QUICK FLASHING
I.QK. FL.= INTERRUPTED QUICK FLASHING
ISO=ISOPHASE (E.INT.= EQUAL INTERVAL).
OCC.-OCCULTING
GP. OCC.= GROUP OCCULTING
GP. OCC. (2+3)-COMPOSITE GROUP OCCULTING.

Fig. 3-4A. Basic light phase characteristics (13 types).

Fixed (F). A light shining with a continuous, steady intensity. These are uncommon because there is nothing about a fixed light to help the mariner distinguish it as an aid to navigation rather than another ship or any of innumerable fixed lights ashore.

Fixed and Flashing (F.Fl.). This is a big improvement in making the light identifiable to the mariner because the higher intensity flashes repeating in a steady pattern immediately separates this light.

Flashing (F.Gp.Fl.). Here the distinctive repeating group of flashes will help further to distinguish the aid to navigation from any other erratic lights in the vicinty.

Flashing (Fi.). This is defined as a single flash of light recurring at regular intervals. This light is off more of the time than it is on, and it flashes on no more than 30 times each minute.

Group Flashing (Gp.FL.). A light that repeats at regular intervals flashes in groups of two or more. There might be three flashes, then a pause, and then the three flashes are repeated.

Composite Group Flashing (Gp.Fl. [2 + 3]). In this case, the groups of flashes are of different numbers and alternate between 2 and 3. The numbers 2 and 3 are examples only. They could be any other two numbers.

Morse Code (Mo. [any letter]). A light which by means of flashes of different duration spells out one or more letters in Morse Code. A short flash followed by a long one is "A," for example, or a long followed by 2 shorts is "D."

Quick Flashing (Qk.Fl.). Steadily flashing at regular intervals, off more of the time than it is on, but flashing at least 60 times each minute.

Interrupted Quick Flashing (I.Qk.Fl.). Regular repeated cycles of some number of seconds of quick flashing interrupted by dark intervals.

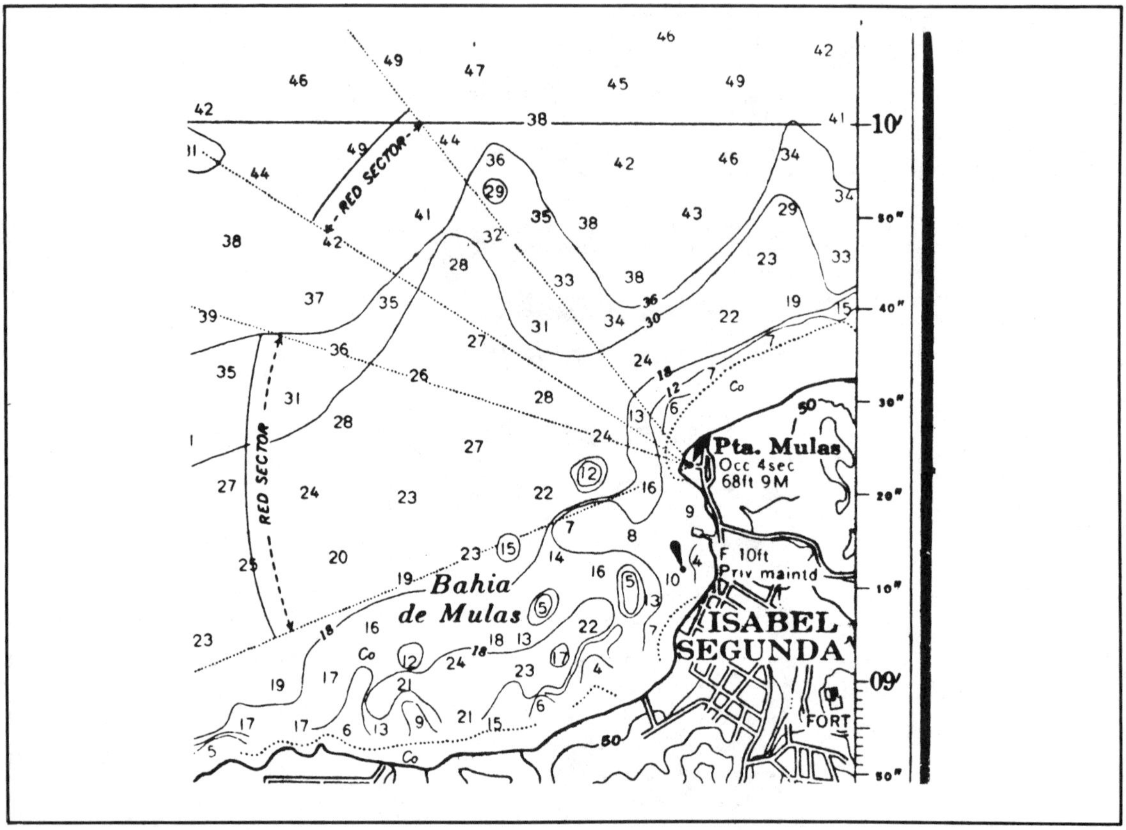
RED SECTOR
RED SECTOR
Pta. Mulas
Occ 4sec
68ft 9M
F 10ft
Priv maintd
Bahia
de Mulas
ISABEL
SEGUNDA
FORT
10'
09'
Fig. 3-4B. Chart section: sectored light.

Equal Interval (E.Int). Alternating intervals of light and dark of equal duration; perhaps 1 second on followed by 1 off, or 2 on and 2 off.

Occulting (Occ.). A light alternating regularly off and on, but on for longer intervals than it is off. This is the reverse of the flashing characteristic.

Group Occulting (Gp.Occ.). This is the reverse of Group Flashing. The light is on more of the time than it is off, and it drops off in groups of two or more "offs."

Composite Group Occulting (Gp.Occ. [3+4]. The reverse this time of Composite Group Flashing. This time it occults in groups of different numbers.

Many of the preceding light-phase characteristics will vary considerably as to the length of time required to complete one cycle. That cycling time is termed the "period" of the light. For example, a light designated on the chart as "Gp.Fl. 4 10 sec." specifies a light that flashes four times followed by a pause. That pause is timed so that the first flash of any cycle is 10 seconds after the first flash of the last cycle.

In view of the variations possible in both characteristics and periods of lights, it is easy to maintain sufficient difference between the lights visible from any particular position at sea to avoid confusion. The characteristic patterns and periods of lights described apply not only to lighthouses and offshore light towers, but also to all other lighted aids to navigation both fixed and floating.

SECTORED LIGHTS

Some lights are located in positions that cannot be safely approached from all the directions in which the light is visible (Fig. 3-4B). Some approaches lead across rocks, shoals, or other hazards. In such cases, the light will have a red sector that becomes visible to the sailor when any danger lies between him and the light. As long as a white light is seen, it may be approached directly. If a light is seen showing the correct light phase characteristic—except that it is colored red—make a course at 90° to the bearing of the light until it turns white so that the vessel is now in a position from which a safe approach can be made.

FOG SIGNALS

Any sound-producing device located at a charted position and operating during times of reduced visibility will qualify as a bona fide fog signal. After all various conditions other than fog can reduce visibility at sea to the point where the sailor can well use whatever audible help he can get to keep track of his position. On many occasions, rain, haze, or smog partially, or completely, obscure the various visible marks he normally uses as guides. At that point, any available sound signals that can be reliably identified are welcome indeed!

Major lighthouses and offshore towers are equipped with powerful mechanically operated fog signaling devices of any of several types.

Diaphones produce a two-toned horn signal. A horn blasts for some seconds, and then suddenly drops considerably in pitch continuing to blast for some additional time. It is a mournful sound indeed, but one that can be the most beautiful music in the world at times.

Diaphragm Horns produce a blast of steady pitch. Occasional duplex or triplex horns of different pitches produce a multiple pitch blast.

Reed Horns such as diaphragm horns produce a blast of steady pitch.

Sirens produce the familiar cyclical rising and falling tone repeated over and over again.

Whistles and **bells** are sufficiently familiar sounds that comment is unnecessary.

In general, lighthouses and offshore light towers are equipped with horns or diaphones. These will sound off with characteristic blast patterns of one to three blasts with length of blasts, durations of pauses, and durations of complete cycles varying, similarly to light patterns, in order to help the mariner identify from which station the sound is coming. The characteristic sound pattern of each lighthouse or other sound-producing aid is given in the *Light Lists* published by the Coast Guard. The small vessel coastal sailor is making short enough hops that his chances of becoming confused between major sound-producing aids is slight indeed. If you hear a horn at all, you'll probably know what it is!

At manned lighthouses and offshore towers where a continuous watch is kept on the operation of the aid, fog signals are started when visibility gets down to 5 miles. Stations not so manned might not sound off as promptly in conditions of reduced visibility. There is also always the horrid possibility of mechanical or electrical failures interfering with proper operation of these devices.

WARNINGS REGARDING FOG SIGNALS

Fog signals are dependent on the propagation of sound waves in air. Moisture content in the forms of humidity, rain, fog, snow, sleet, or other precipitation, particulate content (smog), and temperature variations or inversions can all affect the movements of sound in air. Unfortunately, it is just during times of reduced visibility, when one would most like to be able to rely on sounds, that atmospheric conditions tend to make those sounds most unreliable because:

☐ Fog tends to muffle sounds making both apparent distance and direction confusing.

☐ Due to atmospherics, a fog signal might seem louder further away than when close at hand.

☐ Very often fog signals cannot be heard above engine noise. Periodically shut off engines in order to listen when running in fog.

☐ You can be in a fog bank at a time when it is clear at the lighthouse so the fog signal is not in operation.

☐ Sound signals in fog must be regarded somewhat suspiciously. Act with extreme caution.

Many aids to navigation other than lighthouses and offshore towers are equipped with sound-producing devices. A major group of such aids are the sound-equipped buoys. These include bell buoys, gong buoys, whistle buoys, and horn buoys.

RADIO BEACONS

The radio direction finder can be used to determine lines of position based on many radio transmitting facilities, including the marine radio beacons maintained by the Coast Guard. These facilities, as well as how to use them, are discussed in detail in Chapter 5 in connection with Positioning.

The Coast Guard operated network of marine

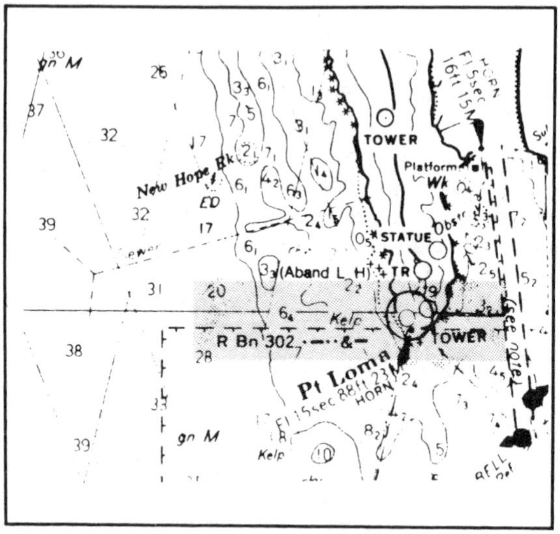
TOWER
Platform
New Hope Bk
STATUE
(Aband L H)
TR
Kelp
R Bn 302
TOWER
Pt Loma
HORN
Kelp
Fig. 3-5. Chart section: aid with radio beacon.

radio beacons broadcasts on low frequencies in the range between 285 and 325 kHz from lighthouses, offshore towers, the new large navigation buoys, and a number of carefully located minor stations along the coasts. These beacons appear on the standard navigation charts and appear in the *Light Lists* published by Coast Guard as well. The distances at which they can normally be heard varies from perhaps 10 miles for the minor marker beacons up to about 200 miles for a major beacon. The information given on the standard charts (Fig. 3-5) covering radio beacons includes the radio beacon symbol centered on the transmitter location, the broadcasting frequency of the beacon, and a pattern of dots and dashes indicating the characteristic signal broadcast by that station. The major radio beacons broadcast continuously 24-hours a day. Some minor ones operate in groups broadcasting on the same frequency, but in sequence. Each one is for a minute at a time followed by one of the others. Sequenced beacons are identified on the charts by a Roman numeral following the three-digit Arabic number that indicates the station broadcast frequency.

RANGES

In addition to the major fixed aids to navigation (the lighthouses and offshore light towers), a great many minor fixed aids are maintained as well. In many cases, these minor aids are of far greater importance to the small-boat operator than the major ones. One of the most useful types of minor aids is the range (Fig. 3-6). A range consists of two markers which, when sighted in line with each other, mark a safe channel.

Because range markers are fixed aids standing either on land or in fairly shallow water, the safe channel they mark begins at some distance forward of the front marker and may be of limited length as well. The mariner thus would certainly stand into danger by going too close to the front marker and could also possibly get into trouble by following the channel too far out. The chart of the area must be checked to determine the limits of the safe channel and to find additional aids to use as guides to keep you within those limits.

Ranges are among the very best aids to navigation available because they are firmly fixed in known locations and mark very clear lines of position. They thus provide the mariner with the means to pinpoint his whereabouts with extreme accuracy.

Although the term *range* generally applies only to pairs of structures built specifically as aids to navigation, any two known objects can be used as a range. For a couple of years, I kept a boat in a small harbor called Las Croabas on the East Coast of Puerto Rico. The entrance was via a narrow channel between two coral reefs, and it was totally unmarked. The channel could be safely entered by lining up a power pole on the shore with a small red shack halfway up the hill behind and using the two objects as a range.

A wide variety of shapes, sizes, and designs have been used in making range markers in the past. Many are still in use. The Coast Guard has now standardized on a vertically striped rectangular daymark (Fig. 3-7) with its longest dimension vertical. A considerable variety of colors can be used depending on what will stand out well from the surrounding background, but the basic pattern remains the same—consisting of three stripes. The two outside ones are the same color with the center one contrasting.

Because of their great value as accurate positioning aids, many ranges are lighted in order to make them useful at night as well as during daylight hours. Such lights may be white, red, or green, whichever is felt to stand out best from the surrounding objects and lights in the immediate vicinity.

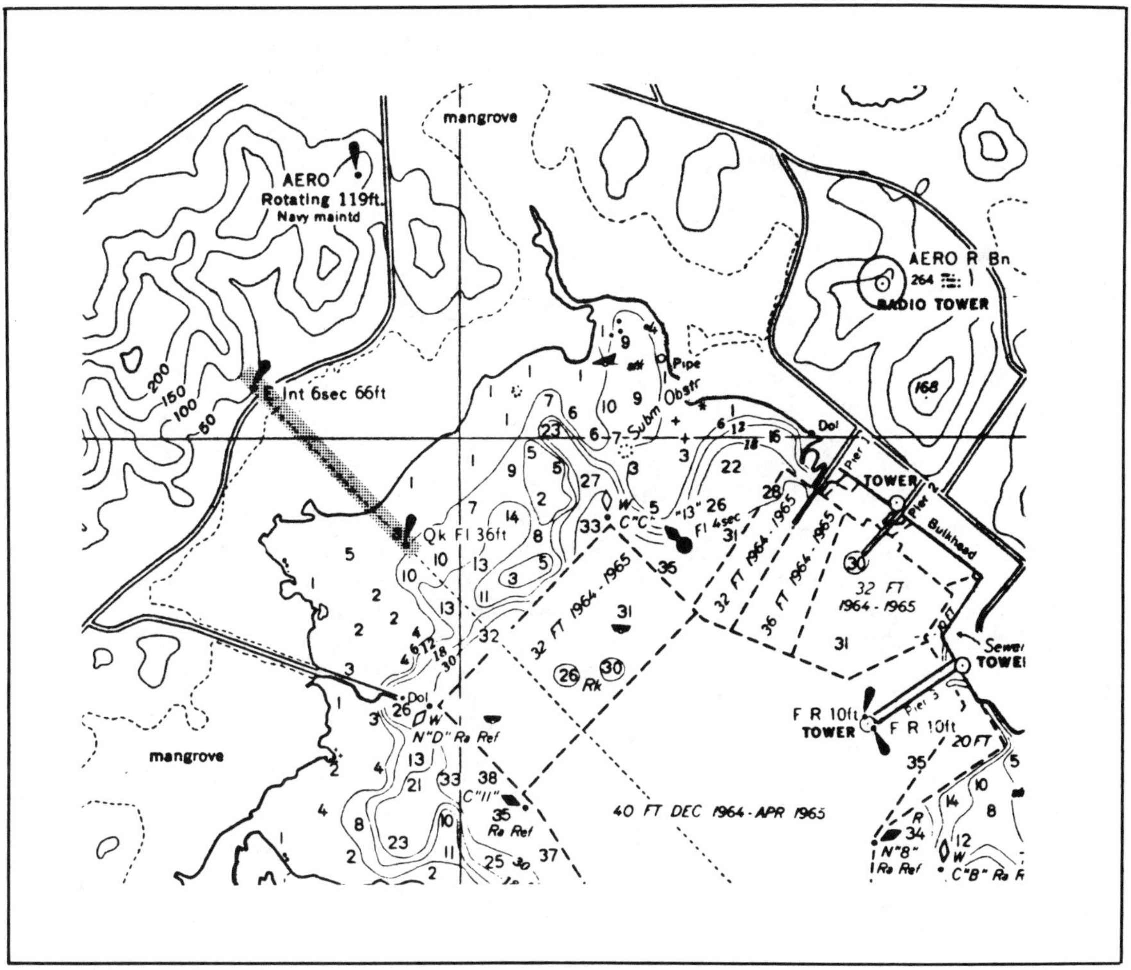
mangrove
AERO
Rotating 119ft.
Navy maintd
Int 6sec 66ft
Qk Fl 36ft
AERO R Bn
RADIO TOWER
Pipe
Subm Obstr
Dol
TOWER
Pier
Bulkhead
Fl 4sec
32 FT 1964-1965
36 FT 1964-1965
32 FT 1964-1965
Sewer
TOWER
F R 10ft
TOWER
F R 10ft
20 FT
N"D" Ra Ref
C"11"
Ra Ref
40 FT DEC 1964-APR 1965
N"8"
Ra Ref
C"B" Ra Ref
mangrove

Fig. 3-6. Charted range.

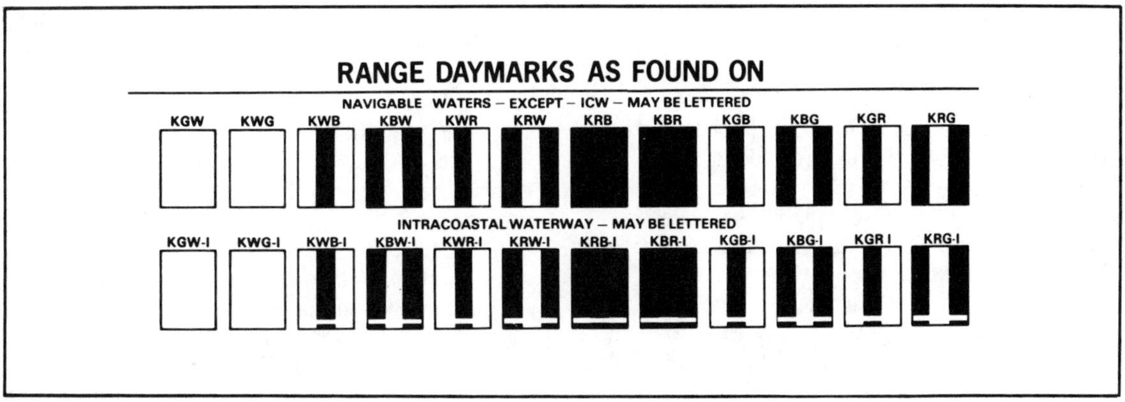
RANGE DAYMARKS AS FOUND ON
NAVIGABLE WATERS – EXCEPT – ICW – MAY BE LETTERED
KGW
KWG
KWB
KBW
KWR
KRW
KRB
KBR
KGB
KBG
KGR
KRG
INTRACOASTAL WATERWAY – MAY BE LETTERED
KGW-I
KWG-I
KWB-I
KBW-I
KWR-I
KRW-I
KRB-I
KBR-I
KGB-I
KBG-I
KGR I
KRG-I

Fig. 3-7. Present type United States Coast Guard range markers.

Front and rear lights will most often be the same color, but with different light-phase characteristics. In order to line them up as a range, both lights must be visible together; consequently the light-phase patterns will tend toward those that are on more than they are off—the occulting types. In some cases, a lens is used to intensify the light output along the center line of the range, decreasing on either side.

DAYBEACONS

Another very common fixed aid to navigation is termed a *daybeacon* or simply *beacon*. These too show up in a fairly bewildering variety of shapes and colors depending on whether they are part of the general system of Aids to Navigation on Navigable Waters (Fig. 3-8) part of Aids to Navigation on the Intracoastal Waterway (Fig. 3-9), part of Aids to Navigation on Western Rivers (Fig. 3-10), or perhaps belonging in the Uniform State Waterway Marking System (Fig. 3-11), or even a privately maintained beacon set up by a yacht club, a fishing club, or some commercial interest. One thing they all have in common is that they stand fixed in shallow water or on the shore close to the water's edge.

The beacons maintained by the Coast Guard along navigable waterways, including the Intracoastal Waterway, and those posted by the Corps of Engineers along the Western Rivers are of three shapes: square, diamond, and triangular. The colors and patterns painted on these simple shapes vary considerably depending on where they appear, as is apparent in Figs. 3-8, 3-9, and 3-10. The most commonly seen shapes are square and triangular. Square beacons mark the port (left) side of a channel and triangular beacons are to starboard (right).

The state systems use diamonds, circles, and simple rectangular signboards carrying a printed message.

Support structures for beacons vary with the conditions they will be required to withstand (Fig. 3-12). A single post is used wherever possible. In many cases, however, several posts or piles bound together to form a moderately elaborate structure are required in order to withstand the winds, wave action, icing, or other destructive forces to which a particular beacon will be exposed. Due to support problems, daybeacons are limited to use in shallow water locations. Due to their firmly fixed positioning, they constitute—for the navigator—extremely reliable aids when they are available. The Coast Guard likes them also because, although they periodically need repainting, they do not have to be hauled, and scraped before repainting and accurately relocated afterwards as must be done with buoys.

LIGHTED BEACONS

Lighted beacons, or minor lights, are fixed aids with the same general physical appearance as daybeacons, except that a light has been added. Where a lighted beacon marks the side of a channel, it will have the same light color and phase characteristics as would a buoy marking the same side of the channel. The intensity of a beacon light is about the same as that of a lighted buoy. Its visibility is often better because it is often placed higher above the water. Being fixed in position, it does not bob about with the movements of the water.

In some crucial locations, minor lights are also equipped with fog sound signals—either a horn, a bell, or a siren. Such signals can be remotely activated from a manned station in the vicinity, or in some instances they are operated continuously during those times of the year when fogs are likely (which might be for months at a time). The on and off switching of the light will be accomplished by the same type of light-sensitive control that is used on lighted buoys. Remote control by personnel from manned stations is unnecessary.

CHARTED LANDMARKS

While the great variety of charted landmarks are certainly not in the category of aids to navigation maintained specifically for the purpose of assisting the navigator to guide his vessel in safety, they most definitely help him accomplish this even so. While not constructed or maintained as such, they are obviously *charted* with intent that they be used as navigational aids.

For the small-boat operator, such objects can be particularly useful. He often sails in areas where there is too little commercial or general navigation to justify the Coast Guard maintaining a network of either fixed or floating aids of the normal types. As long as the navigator can accurately locate an object on the chart, he can then use it to determine where he is relative to it or to some hazard he must avoid. What that object is or how it got there matters not. It is well worthwhile for the small-boat operator to

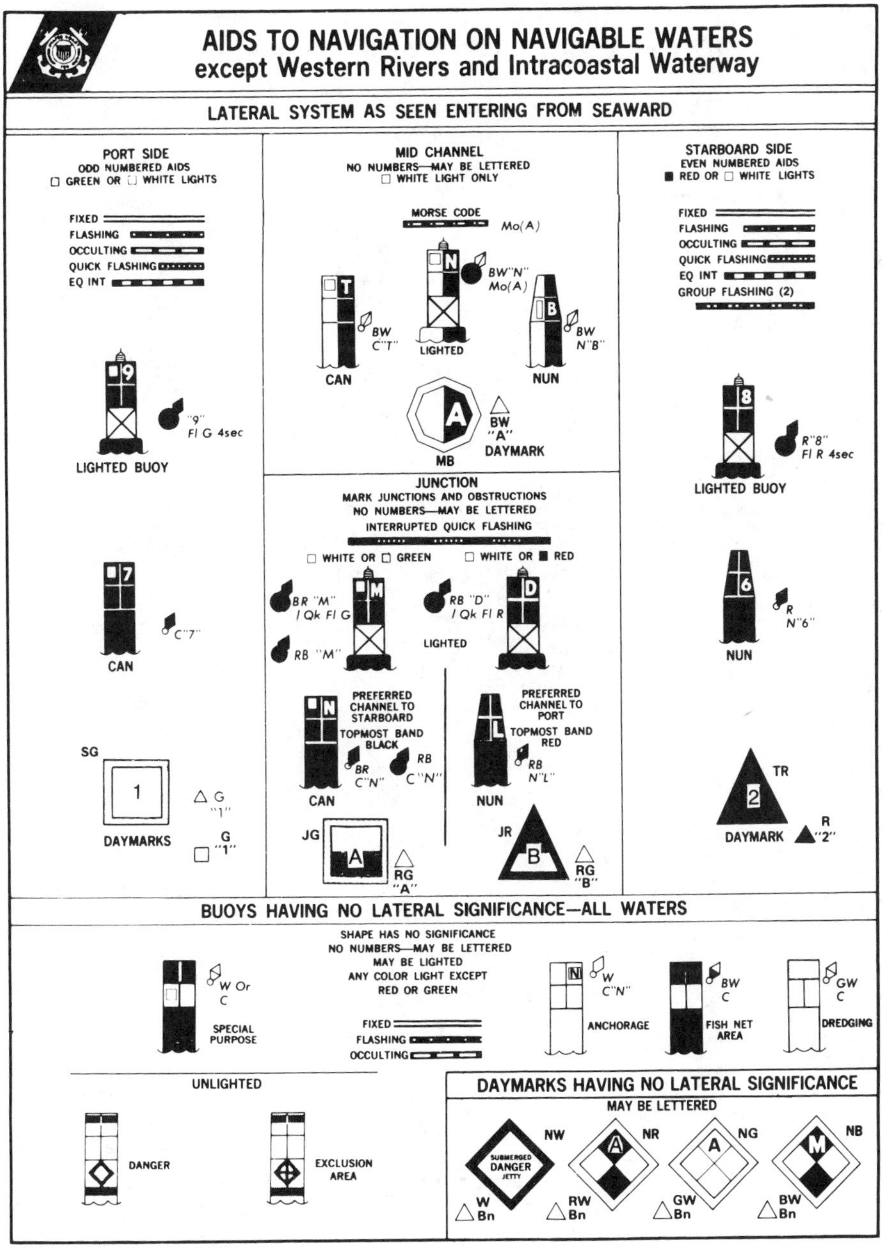
AIDS TO NAVIGATION ON NAVIGABLE WATERS
except Western Rivers and Intracoastal Waterway
LATERAL SYSTEM AS SEEN ENTERING FROM SEAWARD
PORT SIDE
ODD NUMBERED AIDS
GREEN OR WHITE LIGHTS
FIXED
FLASHING
OCCULTING
QUICK FLASHING
EQ INT
"9" Fl G 4sec
LIGHTED BUOY
C"7"
CAN
SG
G "1"
DAYMARKS
G "1"
MID CHANNEL
NO NUMBERS—MAY BE LETTERED
WHITE LIGHT ONLY
MORSE CODE
Mo(A)
BW"N" Mo(A)
BW C"T"
LIGHTED
BW N"B"
CAN
NUN
BW "A"
MB
DAYMARK
JUNCTION
MARK JUNCTIONS AND OBSTRUCTIONS
NO NUMBERS—MAY BE LETTERED
INTERRUPTED QUICK FLASHING
WHITE OR GREEN
WHITE OR RED
BR "M" I Qk Fl G
RB "D" I Qk Fl R
RB "M"
LIGHTED
PREFERRED CHANNEL TO STARBOARD
TOPMOST BAND BLACK
BR C"N"
RB C"N"
CAN
PREFERRED CHANNEL TO PORT
TOPMOST BAND RED
RB N"L"
NUN
JG
RG "A"
JR
RG "B"
STARBOARD SIDE
EVEN NUMBERED AIDS
RED OR WHITE LIGHTS
FIXED
FLASHING
OCCULTING
QUICK FLASHING
EQ INT
GROUP FLASHING (2)
R"8" Fl R 4sec
LIGHTED BUOY
R N"6"
NUN
TR
DAYMARK
R "2"
BUOYS HAVING NO LATERAL SIGNIFICANCE—ALL WATERS
SHAPE HAS NO SIGNIFICANCE
NO NUMBERS—MAY BE LETTERED
MAY BE LIGHTED
ANY COLOR LIGHT EXCEPT
RED OR GREEN
W Or C
SPECIAL PURPOSE
FIXED
FLASHING
OCCULTING
W C"N"
ANCHORAGE
BW C
FISH NET AREA
GW C
DREDGING
UNLIGHTED
DANGER
EXCLUSION AREA
DAYMARKS HAVING NO LATERAL SIGNIFICANCE
MAY BE LETTERED
SUBMERGED DANGER JETTY
NW
NR
NG
NB
W Bn
RW Bn
GW Bn
BW Bn

Fig. 3-8. Coast Guard sheet; Aids to navigation on Navigable Waters.

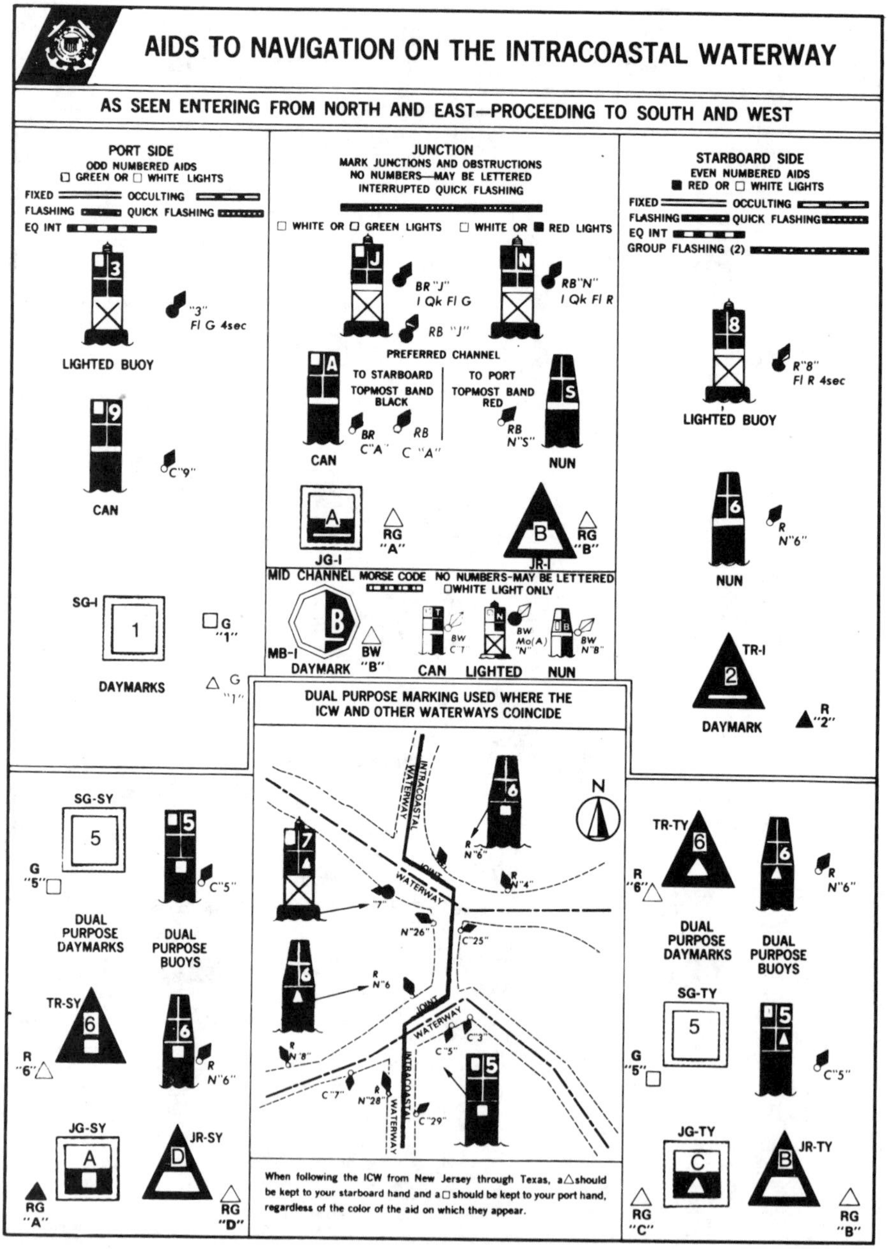
AIDS TO NAVIGATION ON THE INTRACOASTAL WATERWAY
AS SEEN ENTERING FROM NORTH AND EAST—PROCEEDING TO SOUTH AND WEST
PORT SIDE
ODD NUMBERED AIDS
GREEN OR WHITE LIGHTS
FIXED
OCCULTING
FLASHING
QUICK FLASHING
EQ INT
LIGHTED BUOY
CAN
DAYMARKS
JUNCTION
MARK JUNCTIONS AND OBSTRUCTIONS
NO NUMBERS—MAY BE LETTERED
INTERRUPTED QUICK FLASHING
WHITE OR GREEN LIGHTS
WHITE OR RED LIGHTS
PREFERRED CHANNEL
TO STARBOARD TOPMOST BAND BLACK
TO PORT TOPMOST BAND RED
CAN
NUN
MID CHANNEL
MORSE CODE
NO NUMBERS-MAY BE LETTERED
WHITE LIGHT ONLY
DAYMARK
CAN
LIGHTED
NUN
STARBOARD SIDE
EVEN NUMBERED AIDS
RED OR WHITE LIGHTS
GROUP FLASHING (2)
LIGHTED BUOY
NUN
DAYMARK
DUAL PURPOSE MARKING USED WHERE THE ICW AND OTHER WATERWAYS COINCIDE
INTRACOASTAL WATERWAY
JOINT WATERWAY
DUAL PURPOSE DAYMARKS
DUAL PURPOSE BUOYS
When following the ICW from New Jersey through Texas, a △ should be kept to your starboard hand and a □ should be kept to your port hand, regardless of the color of the aid on which they appear.

Fig. 3-9. Coast Guard sheet; Aids to Navigation on Intracoastal Waterway.

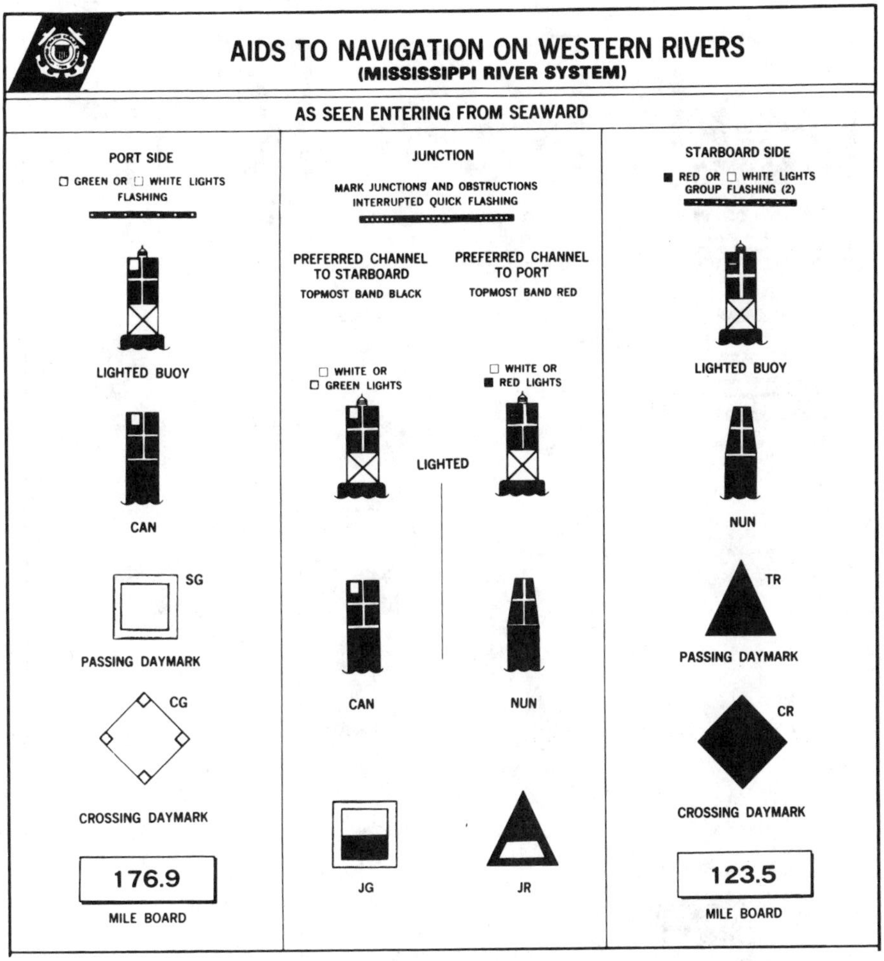

AIDS TO NAVIGATION ON WESTERN RIVERS
(MISSISSIPPI RIVER SYSTEM)
AS SEEN ENTERING FROM SEAWARD
PORT SIDE
GREEN OR WHITE LIGHTS FLASHING
LIGHTED BUOY
CAN
SG
PASSING DAYMARK
CG
CROSSING DAYMARK
176.9
MILE BOARD
JUNCTION
MARK JUNCTIONS AND OBSTRUCTIONS INTERRUPTED QUICK FLASHING
PREFERRED CHANNEL TO STARBOARD
TOPMOST BAND BLACK
PREFERRED CHANNEL TO PORT
TOPMOST BAND RED
WHITE OR GREEN LIGHTS
WHITE OR RED LIGHTS
LIGHTED
CAN
NUN
JG
JR
STARBOARD SIDE
RED OR WHITE LIGHTS GROUP FLASHING (2)
LIGHTED BUOY
NUN
TR
PASSING DAYMARK
CR
CROSSING DAYMARK
123.5
MILE BOARD

Fig. 3-10. Coast Guard Sheet; Aids to Navigation on Western Rivers. Effective in 1987, black can buoys will be painted green.

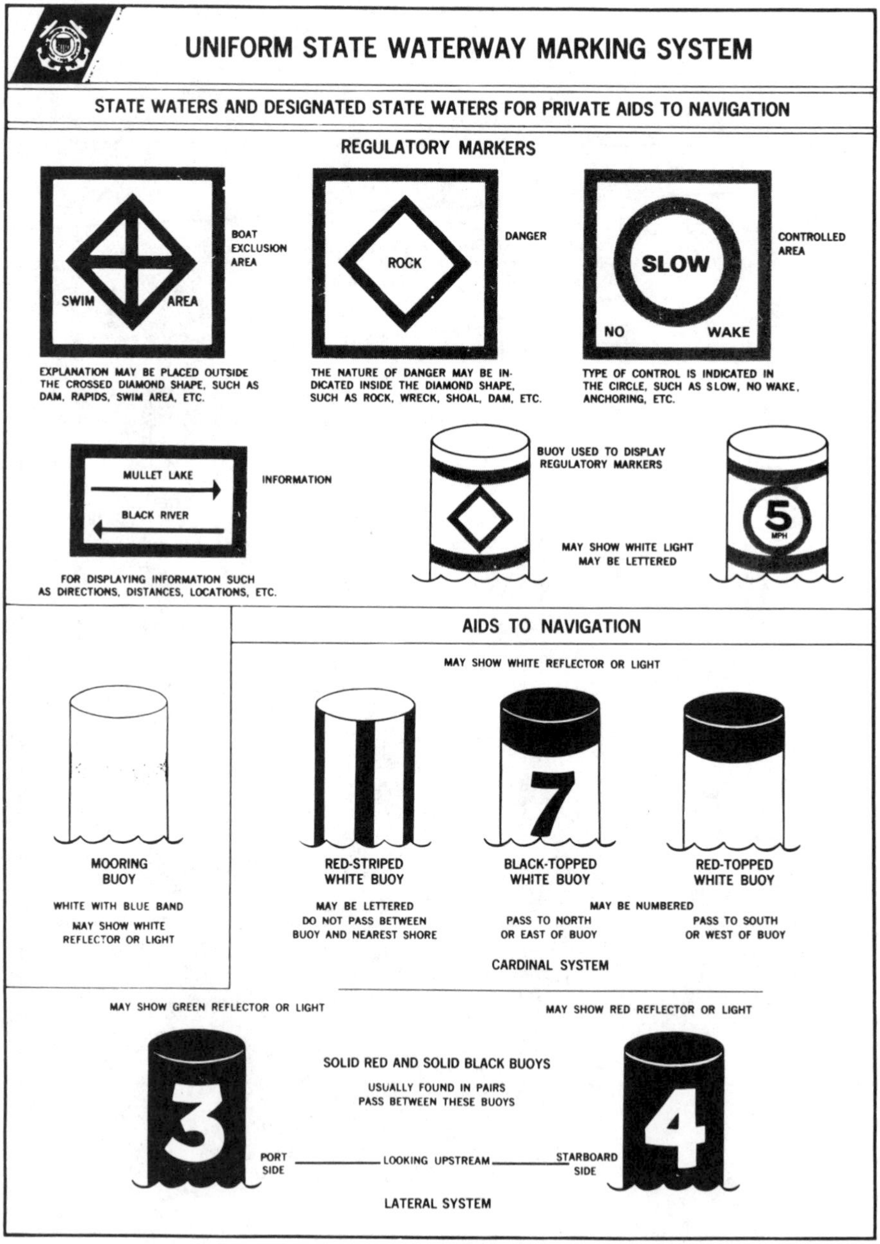
UNIFORM STATE WATERWAY MARKING SYSTEM
STATE WATERS AND DESIGNATED STATE WATERS FOR PRIVATE AIDS TO NAVIGATION
REGULATORY MARKERS
SWIM AREA
BOAT EXCLUSION AREA
ROCK
DANGER
SLOW
NO WAKE
CONTROLLED AREA
EXPLANATION MAY BE PLACED OUTSIDE THE CROSSED DIAMOND SHAPE, SUCH AS DAM, RAPIDS, SWIM AREA, ETC.
THE NATURE OF DANGER MAY BE INDICATED INSIDE THE DIAMOND SHAPE, SUCH AS ROCK, WRECK, SHOAL, DAM, ETC.
TYPE OF CONTROL IS INDICATED IN THE CIRCLE, SUCH AS SLOW, NO WAKE, ANCHORING, ETC.
MULLET LAKE
BLACK RIVER
INFORMATION
FOR DISPLAYING INFORMATION SUCH AS DIRECTIONS, DISTANCES, LOCATIONS, ETC.
BUOY USED TO DISPLAY REGULATORY MARKERS
MAY SHOW WHITE LIGHT
MAY BE LETTERED
5
MPH
AIDS TO NAVIGATION
MAY SHOW WHITE REFLECTOR OR LIGHT
7
MOORING BUOY
WHITE WITH BLUE BAND
MAY SHOW WHITE REFLECTOR OR LIGHT
RED-STRIPED WHITE BUOY
MAY BE LETTERED
DO NOT PASS BETWEEN BUOY AND NEAREST SHORE
BLACK-TOPPED WHITE BUOY
RED-TOPPED WHITE BUOY
MAY BE NUMBERED
PASS TO NORTH OR EAST OF BUOY
PASS TO SOUTH OR WEST OF BUOY
CARDINAL SYSTEM
MAY SHOW GREEN REFLECTOR OR LIGHT
MAY SHOW RED REFLECTOR OR LIGHT
SOLID RED AND SOLID BLACK BUOYS
USUALLY FOUND IN PAIRS
PASS BETWEEN THESE BUOYS
3
4
PORT SIDE
LOOKING UPSTREAM
STARBOARD SIDE
LATERAL SYSTEM

Fig. 3-11. Coast Guard sheet; Uniform State Waterway Marking System.

2

Fig. 3-12. Daybeacon (courtesy United States Coast Guard).

study carefully the charts of the areas where he customarily operates looking for just such landmarks to supplement the existing aids to navigation in the vicinity.

A commercial radio station broadcast antenna is a particularly good landmark. It is a tall, thin structure that is a good shape for sighting. It is located on the chart with extreme accuracy and provides an excellent base for a line of position. As a warning to air traffic, it has to be lighted at night. When you are used to its position, it serves as an excellent night aid. By no means unimportant is that with an RDF it can be used as a guide in a fog.

A tall utility or factory chimney is another good thin object to sight on. Also some tall chimneys are lighted and that makes them useful at night as well. In general, look for narrow objects rather than wide ones because they will yield more accurate lines of position. But use whatever is available to supplement the government aids. Always remember the regular government aids were planned to meet the needs of larger vessels making longer voyages than those of the weekend sailor who goes many places lacking such aids.

FLOATING AIDS

Lightships are essentially floating lighthouses that are anchored offshore either to mark hazards in heavily trafficked areas or to mark entrance channels to major ports. Hulls are uniformly painted red with the name of the station in large white letters on the side (Fig. 3-14A). Each lightship has a powerful light with a distinctive phase characteristic, a radiobeacon, and a fog signal. The nautical chart shows the light characteristic and nominal range of visibility, gives the frequency and distinctive signal of the radiobeacon, and notes the type of fog signal. Complete details are found in the *Light Lists*.

Lightships ride to a single bow anchor and so they will swing somewhat with wind and current. The position shown on the chart for a lightship is the point at which its anchor is placed. When observed, the ship itself will be some small distance down wind or down current (whichever happens to be stronger at the moment) from the point shown on the chart.

All lightships are self-propelled; they are capable of steaming under their own power to and from station for routine maintenance. When a lightship leaves its station, it is always replaced by another ship marked RELIEF. While the relief ship might look somewhat different from the normal one on a particular station, it will make all of the same light, sound, and radio signals as the one that is permanently anchored there.

Most lightships are being replaced by either

Fig. 3-13. Lighted beacon (courtesy United States Coast Guard).

COLUMBIA

Fig. 3-14A. Lightship (courtesy United States Coast Guard).

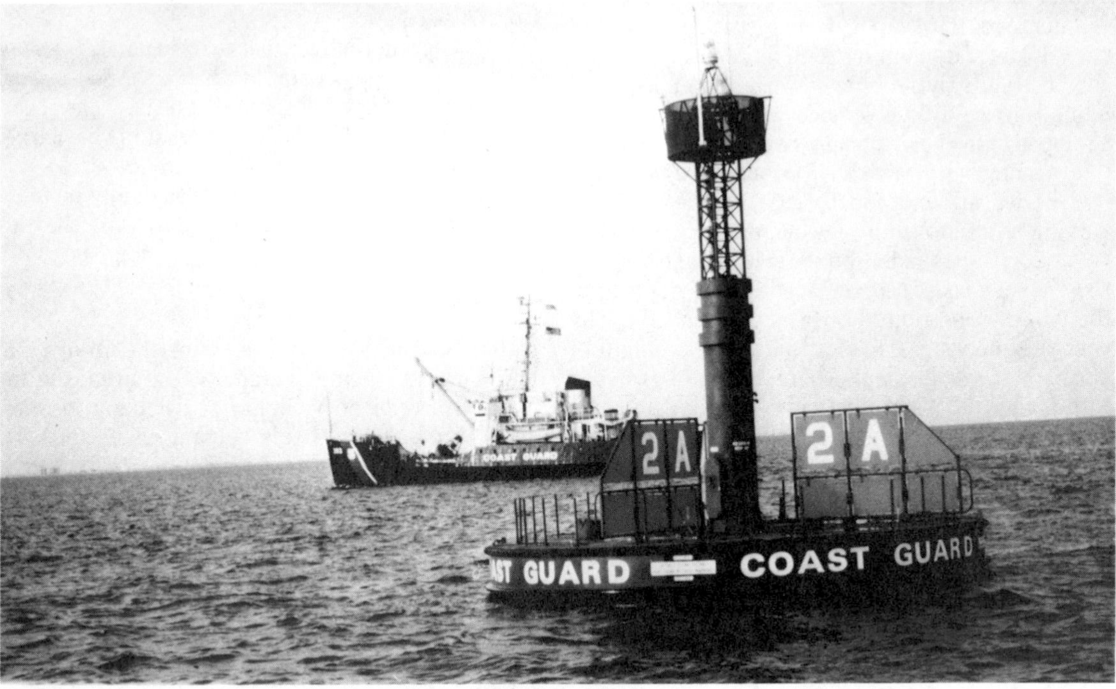
2A
2A
GUARD
COAST GUARD
COAST GUARD

Fig. 3-14B. Superbuoy (courtesy United States Coast Guard).

offshore light towers or large navigational buoys, sometimes jokingly referred to as super buoys. Where feasible, the offshore tower has the advantages of being fixed in position—not swinging with wind and sea—and its light is considerably higher—increasing its visibility.

The large navigational buoys (Fig. 3-14B) are equipped with a light, fog signals, radiobeacons and instruments for collecting weather and oceanographic data for transmission to shore stations. They can be placed in position for a small fraction of the cost of constructing an offshore tower. In addition, they do not require a crew because all functions are automatic. They have the disadvantages that the light is not placed nearly as high above the water as that of the offshore tower. And because they are floating aids rather than fixed, they are subject to the same types of damage and storm dislocation as any other floating aid.

Buoys

Buoys comprise a considerable group of floating objects. They vary widely in size and shape and share only the common characteristic that they are all anchored or moored at locations shown on the charts. By means of distinctive symbols, letters, and numbers the chart indicates shape, color, and type of light and sound signal (if there is any). Buoys are basically daytime aids. Those equipped with lights become valuable aids at night and those equipped with sound signals (bells, gongs, or whistles) become very valuable in fog as well as at night.

Buoys are moored to cast concrete blocks varying in weight from a few hundred pounds up to several tons, depending on the size of the buoy, and the type of sea and current conditions that occur at the mooring location. The buoy is attached to the concrete mooring, called a *sinker*, by a length of chain that will be somewhere between two and three times the water depth in length. With a chain that long, obviously the buoy is going to move with wind and current around the exact location shown on the chart. That location is actually the place where the mooring sinker is dropped.

While aboard a Coast Guard buoy tender while some buoys were being set, I was immensely impressed with the skill, care, and accuracy with which this is routinely done. To give an idea of what is involved, the sinker (weighing perhaps several tons), the buoy (which is not lightweight), and the connecting chain (another heavy load) all have to be picked up and swung over the side of the ship while the ship is being maneuvered into a position such that the boom holding all this heavy gear is precisely over the charted buoy location. At that exact moment, the whole business is dropped. When it is dropped, the ship has to be at a stop. This can be a neat trick when there is a fairly strong current or a lively breeze blowing—or both.

While the sinker is right on the charted buoy location, the buoy is, at best, somewhere nearby. It is certainly close enough for all practical purposes, but the point to remember is that it is not exactly in the position shown on the chart in the same way as a beacon or a lighthouse. Also note that it is rather like a boat at anchor in that it swings around its mooring. Consequently, it will be out of charted position in different directions and by different distances at different times.

A further caution regarding buoys is that, because they are chained to a mooring on the bottom, they can be moved a considerable distance out of position by storms, collision, or other accidents or even destroyed completely. Any time a boatman sees a buoy that appears to be out of position or missing, this should be reported at once to the Coast Guard.

Accepting the fact that buoys cannot be found in charted positions with the same accuracy that can be expected of fixed aids, note that they mark channels and hazards that cannot successfully be marked for the guidance of the sailor in any other way. In addition, while a buoy might occasionally be found quite far out of position, most of the time they are pretty darn close to where they are supposed to be.

Buoy Types

Depending on the importance of the item being marked, the volume of traffic in the area, the frequency of reduced visibility at the buoy location, and the types of vessels relying on it, the buoy picked to mark a particular position will be one of four general types. These are unlighted, lighted, sound buoy, or combination buoy.

The vast majority, somewhere around 80 percent of all buoys, are unlighted. They are of distinctive colors, shapes, and markings, but have neither lights nor sound signals. For the most part, they will appear in one of two shapes (Figs. 3-15A and 3-15B). One is called a *can* and the other is called a

Fig. 3-15A. Unlighted nun buoy on station in Lake Erie (courtesy United States Coast Guard).

nun. The above water parts of both are made up of steel plates to make them radar reflective. The can gives the appearance of a flat-topped cylinder while the nun appears as a cone with its point up.

Can buoys are painted black (green by 1987) and are used to mark the left-hand (port) side of the channel when returning from seaward. When they are used to mark a shoal or hazard, they are also to be kept to the left when passing. The identifying numbers will always be odd numbers.

Nun buoys are painted red and mark the right-hand side of the channel when returning from seaward. If you can remember the three Rs, *R*ed *R*ight *R*eturning, it might help to avoid some confusion. Nuns also will mark some type of hazard that should be passed on the right-hand (starboard) side. Nuns will be even-numbered.

When two channels meet or where there is an obstruction or shoal well out in the fairway, the junction buoy marking this can be either a can or a nun. In either case, it will be painted with alternating stripes of black or red. If the top stripe is black, the shape will be a can and the preferred course is to treat it as a cam and leave it to the left. When the top stripe is red, the shape will be a nun; therefore it is preferable to leave it to the right.

Midchannel buoys are painted with black and white vertical stripes. They are numbered and can be either can- or nun-shaped. The shape has no significance. They may be passed close at hand on either side.

Some other unlighted buoys that might be encountered (Fig. 3-8) and having no favored passing side are solid-yellow quarantine, green-topped dredging, and solid-white anchorage buoys. Shape has no importance and none of these will be numbered. Some of the buoys will be lettered.

Lighted buoys (Fig. 3-16) consist of a metal tank serving as a float above which a metal skeleton is built, which carries above it the light. Lighted buoys, while shaped differently, are painted and numbered in a manner similar to unlighted buoys. Black, odd-numbered buoys will be on the left side of the channel returning from sea while red, even-numbered buoys will be on the right (*R*ed *R*ight *R*eturning).

Black buoys will normally carry green lights, but on occasion white will be used to increase the distance of visibility. Red buoys have red lights but again exceptions are made to extend distance of visibility by changing to white. No colored lights other than red, green, and white are ever used on buoys. When you see anything other than those three colors, it is *not* a buoy.

Lighted buoys are powered by batteries placed in the float tank. These batteries will operate the light for many months between replacements. To extend battery life, most lights are equipped with photo-sensitive switches to shut them off during daylight hours.

Lighted buoys have varying light-phase characteristics, as do both lighthouses and fixed

13A

Fig. 3-15B. A standard black can buoy (courtesy United States Coast Guard).

B

Fig. 3-16A. A straight-sided lighted buoy (courtesy United States Coast Guard).

26
Fig. 3-16B. A lighted tapered buoy (courtesy United States Coast Guard).

aids equipped with lights. These characteristics all fall into the basic patterns previously described (Fig. 3-4), but in general very simple patterns are used for lighted buoys. Black and red (port and starboard) channel markers are most often either flashing, (Fl.), quick flashing (Qk.Fl.), occulting (Occ.), or equal interval (Eq.Int.). Midchannel buoys painted black and white will have a white light flashing a Morse code "A" (dot-dash). Junction or obstruction markers painted red and black will probably have an interrupted quick flashing characteristic as an attention getter.

Sound buoys, like lighted buoys, consist of a float tank surmounted by a metal skeleton structure holding the sound signaling device that can be one of several types.

Bells are hung inside the skeleton frame with four clappers hung externally around them. As a result of wave motion, different clappers hit the bell at irregular intervals to produce a single sporadic tone.

Gongs are similar to bells except that a gong buoy has four bells with one clapper each (instead of one bell with four clappers). As the result, a gong buoy produces four different tones at irregular intervals rather than the one tone produced by the bell buoy. In cases where both bells and gongs are used along the same channel, the gongs will be on black buoys on the port side while bells will be to starboard on red buoys.

Whistles are actuated by an air pump that operates due to the motion of the buoy in the sea. To operate well, these need rather more active sea movement than bells or gongs; they are more often found toward the seaward end of channels.

Horns are not common because they are electrically operated and therefore require more maintenance than the sea-activated bells, gongs, and whistles. Being electrically powered, they can be distinguished from other sound-producing buoys by the regularity of their signals.

Combination buoys (Figs. 3-17A and 3-17B) are equipped with both lights and sound signals. These buoys are used at locations considered important enough to be identifiable in daylight, at night, or in reduced visibility. The structure is like that of either a light-only or a sound-only buoy. It consists of a float tank above which a steel skeleton frame supports the radar reflector, the sound signaling device, and on top is placed the light.

28
Fig. 3-17A. A lighted radar reflector bell buoy (courtesy United States Coast Guard).

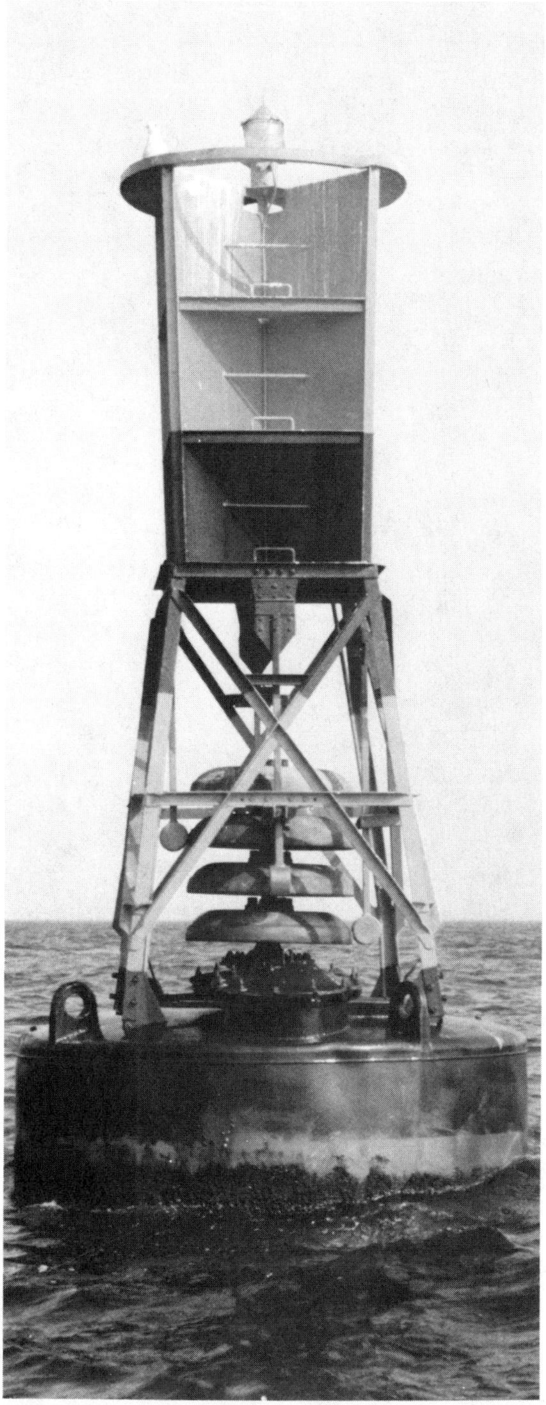

Fig. 3-17B. A lighted radar reflector gong buoy (courtesy United States Coast Guard).

The sound signals are the same types found on sound-only buoys: bells, gongs, whistles, or horns. Lights will have the same colors and light-phase characteristics as light-only buoys. This means that green lights are on black buoys with odd numbers marking the left-hand side of the channels. Red lights go on red buoys with even numbers marking the right-hand side of the channel.

LATERAL BUOYAGE SYSTEM

The United States system of using shapes, paint colors, numbers, and light colors to indicate the side on which a buoy should be passed is known as the *lateral system*. It is a very simple system, and it should be thoroughly understood by anyone operating a boat on any of the waters falling under federal jurisdiction. All buoys in those areas conform to this system.

The basic procedure is to start at the seaward end and work inward through bays and harbors or up rivers to the head of navigation, using black buoys with odd numbers to mark the left side of the navigable channel and red buoys with even numbers to mark the right. Unlighted, lighted, sound, and combination buoys are all distinguished by paint colors and numbers to signify which side of the channel they mark. Consequently, when proceeding from seaward, three successive buoys, all red and all even-numbered, could be of different types all marking the starboard side of the channel. Nun 6, unlighted, could be followed by Bell 8, followed by Red 10, flashing three seconds, followed by another nun. In addition to showing by symbols the locations of buoys, the chart also gives (Fig. 3-18) the numbers and enough additional information so that the mariner knows what shape and color to look for as well as whether to look for a light or listen for a sound.

Not all channels lead from seaward. Also some channels start out from seaward and, passing around behind an island at some point, begin returning *to* seaward. As a vessel passes up the East River between Manhattan and Brooklyn, it is returning from seaward. As it goes on into Long Island Sound, it will suddenly find itself returning *to* seaward the red buoys on the right changing to black and numbers becoming smaller rather than larger. Again your trusty chart will show this color and number reversal.

When running parallel along the Atlantic

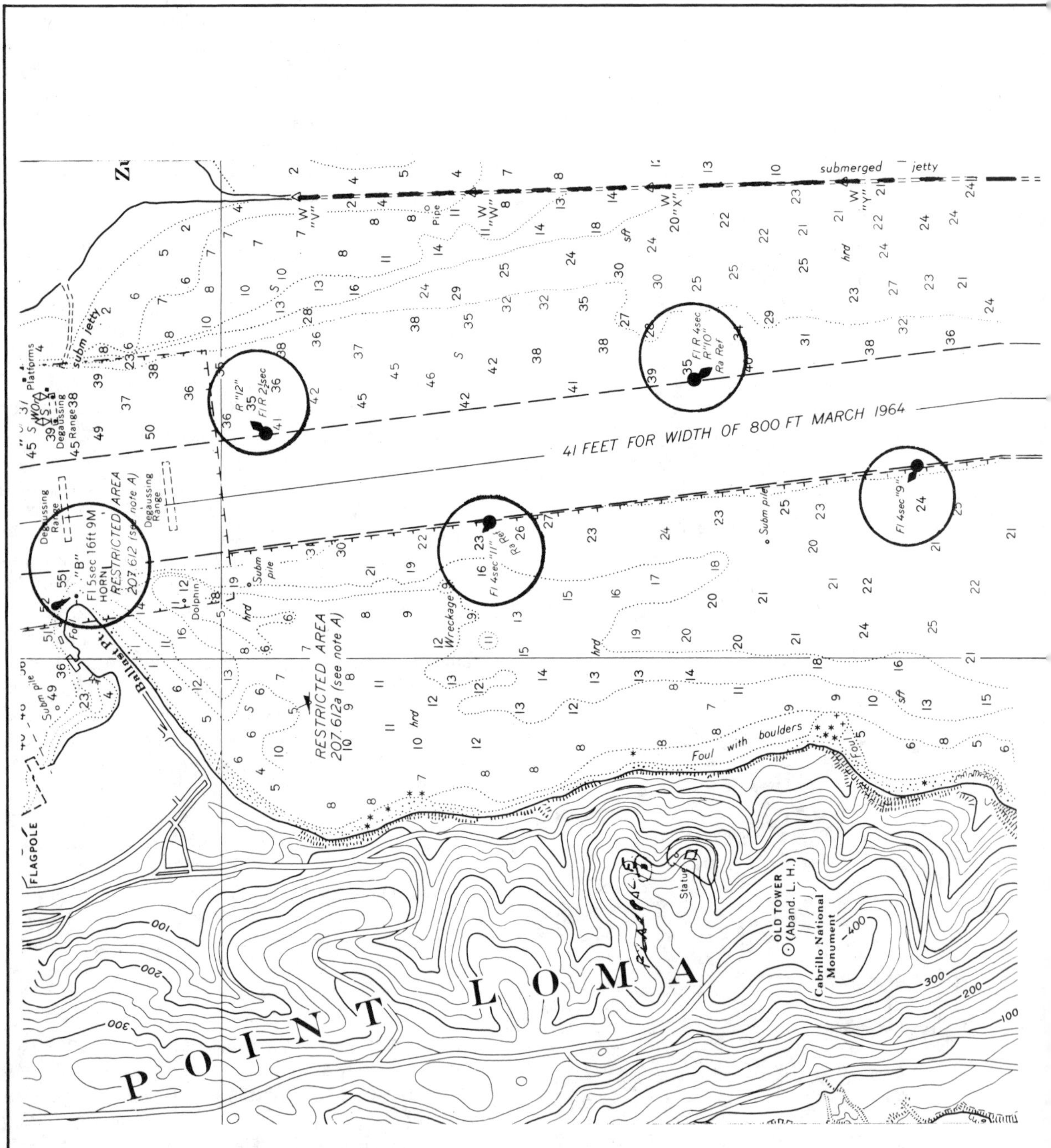
41 FEET FOR WIDTH OF 800 FT MARCH 1964
POINT LOMA
RESTRICTED AREA 207.612 (see note A)
RESTRICTED AREA 207.612a (see note A)
"B" Fl 5sec 16ft 9M HORN
R "12" Fl R 2½sec
Fl R 4sec R "10" Ra Ref
Fl 4sec "11"
Fl 4sec "9"
Degaussing Range
Dolphin
Subm pile
Wreckage
Foul with boulders
submerged jetty
subm jetty
Platforms
Pipe
Ballast Pt.
FLAGPOLE
Statue
OLD TOWER (Aband. L. H.)
Cabrillo National Monument

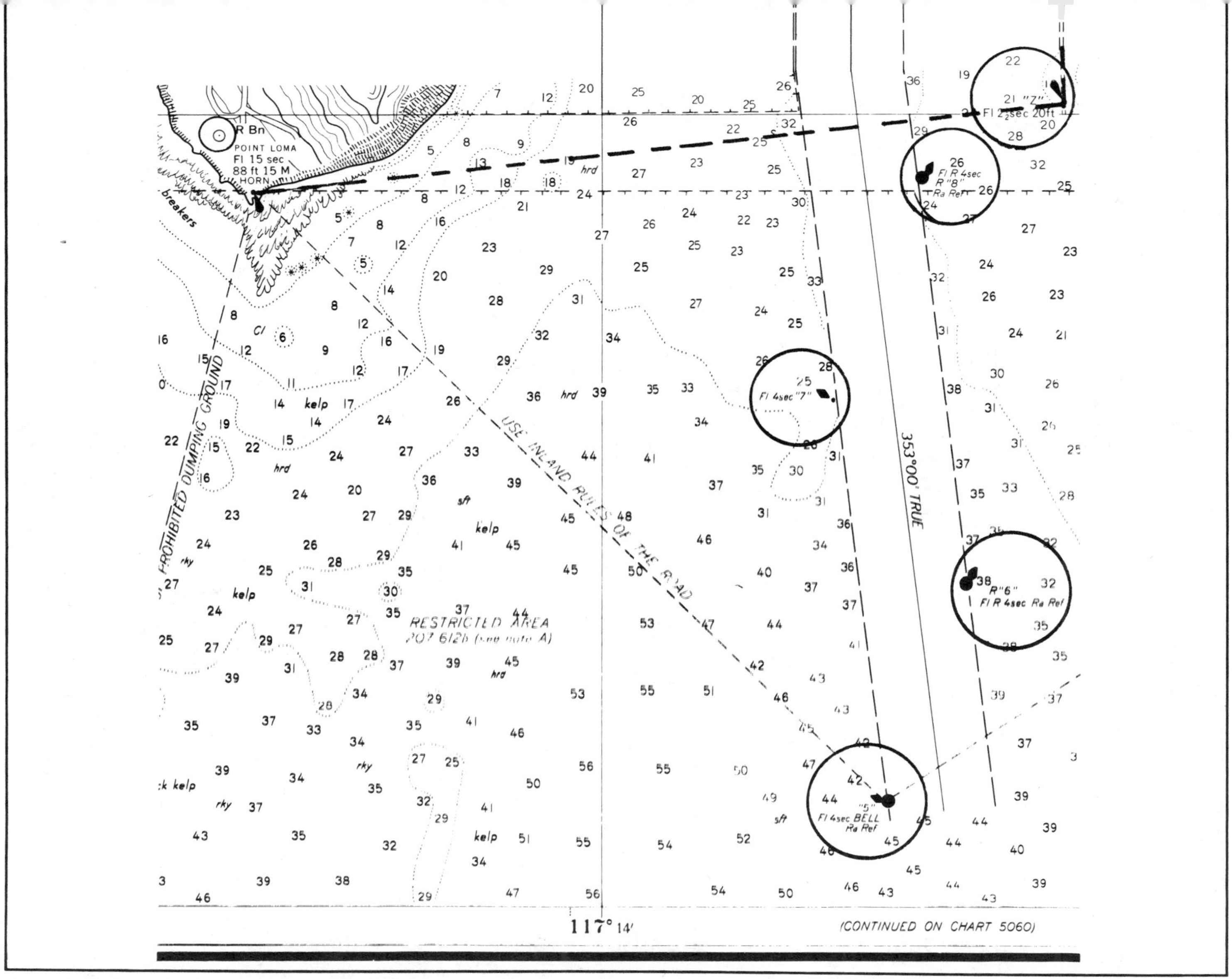
R Bn
POINT LOMA
Fl 15 sec
88 ft 15 M
HORN
breakers
PROHIBITED DUMPING GROUND
USE INLAND RULES OF THE ROAD
RESTRICTED AREA
353°00' TRUE
"Z"
Fl R 4sec
R "8"
Ra Ref
Fl 4sec "7"
R "6"
Fl R 4sec Ra Ref
"5"
Fl 4sec BELL
Ra Ref
117° 14'
(CONTINUED ON CHART 5060)

Fig. 3-18. Chart section showing channel marked by different buoys.

Coast, Gulf Coast, or Pacific Coast, a vessel is neither coming from or going to seaward. In order to maintain consistency in the coloring and numbering of offshore buoys, an arbitrary system was adopted. Proceeding south along the Atlantic Coast, north and then west along the Gulf coast, and north along the Pacific Coast are considered as coming from seaward. Coming from seaward is to proceed clockwise around the United States coasts. On the western rivers, moving upstream is uniformly coming from seaward regardless of compass directions. On the Great Lakes, the outlet of each lake is its seaward end, and so offshore buoys will go up in number to the west and north except on Lake Michigan. Lake harbors are marked as though coming in from the lake were coming in from seaward in a saltwater coastal port.

In summary, returning-from-seaward red buoys of whatever size or type will have even numbers and indicate the right side of the navigable channel, Blacks, no matter what size or type, are odd-numbered and mark the left side of the channel. Red and black *both* in horizontal stripes on whatever type buoy will appear on a buoy with *no number.* It will be lettered. It can be passed on either side, but the top stripe indicates which is the better side.

The black and white vertically striped mid-channel buoy, although technically part of the lateral system, really has little lateral significance because it indicates only that there is safe water on both sides of it. When buoys of any color other than those already mentioned are sighted, look them up on the chart. They are *not* channel markers; they mark something else entirely.

INTRACOASTAL WATERWAY AIDS

Because some readers are sure to be located and operating along the immense lengths of the Intracoastal Waterways (ICW), some further explanation of the aids used on that waterway is required. Note initially that the returning-from-seaward-direction throughout the ICW is the same as that used for offshore buoys—southward along the Atlantic portion, then north, and west along the Gulf section. Red buoys and fixed aids are on the right (mainland) side when proceeding all the way from New Jersey to Florida, and then to Texas regardless of the varying compass headings encountered on the way.

Both buoys and fixed aids are of exactly the same types as those used on other federally marked waters. Unlighted buoys are the normal cans and nuns. Lighted buoys, sound, and combination buoys are also the same types as used elsewhere. Both light and sound characteristics are also the same as those used elsewhere for either buoys or fixed aids.

The one distinctive difference separating ICW aids from all others is that all ICW aids carry somewhere on them a prominent yellow mark in the form of a stripe, a square, or a triangle (Fig. 3-9). All buoys carry a prominent yellow stripe. Daybeacons are in the normal square (left side of channel), and triangular (right side of channel) shapes. Both also have a prominent yellow stripe.

In its long course, the ICW crosses many other waterways: harbor entrances, river estuaries, bays, and sounds. As it crosses these waterways, it also crosses their associated buoyage systems. In some cases, both waterways follow a common channel for some distance before branching out in different directions. When the ICW crosses—and certainly when it joins another channel—there are buoys, beacons, or other aids that are dual-purpose devices, serving as aids for both channels at the same time. When this happens the ICW mark on these aids is again yellow, but it becomes either a yellow square or a yellow triangle.

Any aid bearing a yellow square is a left-side marker for the Intracoastal Waterway whatever its overall shape or color might be. It could be a red nun, a black whistle, or a red light flashing four seconds marking some harbor entrance channel. If it has a yellow square, it is also a ICW left-side channel marker. Similarly, the yellow triangle is the right side *ICW* marker regardless of its significance on the other channel.

UNIFORM STATE WATERWAY MARKING SYSTEM

The individual states each have both the authority and the responsibility to regulate and control navigation on waters lying entirely within their own boundaries. This includes establishing and maintaining aids to navigation. Because each state is legally free to use whatever system it wants for this purpose, the initial consequence was a considerable variety in the systems used by different states. The popularity of trailering boats from place to place included much crossing of state lines which, in turn, produced a lot of confusion among skippers as they tried to unravel the meaning of various objects that had originally been intended to guide not to puzzle him.

In consequence, although the states technically retain their independence, they have recently agreed to adopt a single, consistent marking system called the Uniform State Waterway Marking System. Under this system, channel markers conform to the federal lateral system of buoyage (Fig. 3-11). Black buoys mark the left side and red buoys mark the right side of the channel when proceeding toward the head of navigation. On a river, this would mean running upstream. On a lake, it means proceeding from the outlet end toward the inlet end.

If there is no well-defined channel, or hazards are scattered irregularly and can be approached from various directions—as on a lake—a *cardinal buoyage system* is used. Under this system, a white buoy with a black top means safe water is to the north or east of the buoy. If it is white with a red top, stay south or west of it. If it is vertically striped, alternately red and white, do not pass between it and the shore because foul ground lies between. The cardinal system is used in the United States only on state waters—never on federal waters. Although many foreign countries use cardinal buoyage systems on their national waters, the United States does not.

In addition to channel and hazard markers, the USWMS (Fig. 3-11) includes precautionary, regulatory, and informative markers as well. An open diamond in orange on a white background, whether on a buoy or a daybeacon, means danger (Fig. 3-11). An orange diamond with a cross inside it indicates "keep out!" An orange circle with a message inside it is a mandatory regulation. It gives a speed limit or limits or prohibits some other activity such as anchoring or waterskiing. Simple rectangular signs may give distances, point to locations, or give other useful information.

Chapter 4

The Compass

THE FACT THAT A PIECE OF IRON CAN BE MAGnetized, causing it to attract another piece of iron, has been known for thousands of years. The reason for this remained obscure until recent discoveries relating to atomic structure indicated that magnetism is a form of electrical phenomenon. The interrelationship between electricity and magnetism becomes clearly apparent when the magnetic field that exists around a current carrying wire is observed. Such fields in the vicinity of electric wiring can cause considerable difficulty by deflecting the compass when they happen to be located too close to it.

All magnets have two poles of opposite nature where the maximum force of the fields surrounding them is concentrated (Fig. 4-1). These are termed north and south poles. The force field around a bar magnet is conventionally shown as a series of curved arrows radiating out from the north pole and converging at the south pole. These arrows indicate the direction of the lines of force as well as the shape of the field surrounding the magnet.

When one magnet is brought within the field of influence of another, a curious reaction takes place. Like poles repel each other; unlike poles are attracted. North repels another north, but attracts a South. It is because of this simple law of magnetism—opposites attract and likes repel—that the magnetic compass functions as it does.

MAGNETIC FIELD OF THE EARTH

Although the origin of its magnetism is not fully understood, for many centuries it has been known that the earth is a gigantic magnet. The magnetic field of the earth (Fig. 4-2) has a pattern roughly similar to what one would expect if a short, very powerful bar magnet had been placed near its center. As Fig. 4-2 clearly shows, the geographic poles and the magnetic poles of the earth do not by any means coincide. In addition, the magnetic poles are not 180° apart. In spite of these discrepancies, the planet has a very clearly definable magnetic field. Within that field, any freely suspended bar magnet—even a very small one—will align itself with the planetary field so that its north *seeking* (unlike) pole will point to the north magnetic pole of the planet.

CONSTRUCTION OF THE MAGNETIC COMPASS

Because the north-seeking pole of a simple bar magnet will point toward the north magnetic pole of the planet, if free to do so; theoretically the construction of a magnetic compass is a very simple

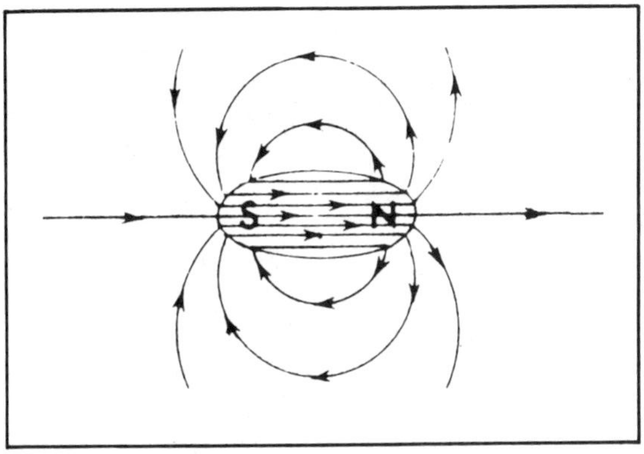
S
N

Fig. 4-1. Magnetic field of a bar magnet.

matter indeed. Merely suspend a bar magnet, leaving it free to move in a horizontal plane, and it will align itself with the magnetic field of the earth so that one end will point to magnetic north. In a stable, stationary location this presents no complicated technical difficulties.

Your boat at sea is by no means a stable, stationary platform. It rolls, it pitches, it twists, it squirms, and it vibrates; and on occasion, all at the same time. Yet with all this activity going on, the compass must unwaveringly continue to point in the same direction. In addition to various types of movement, the compass is also exposed to wide fluctuations in temperature. These requirements make the design and construction of an accurate, dependable, and sufficiently rugged instrument rather complicated.

A typical small boat marine compass is shown in cross section in Fig. 4-3. Normally more than one bar magnet is used to provide alignment with the magnetic field of the earth. In the compass illustrated, four long, thin ones are used. Each compass is held in one of four tubular holders mounted parallel to each other on a nonmagnetic frame. On top of this frame is mounted the compass card, which is a light, thin disc marked around its circumference in order that directions can be read as it turns.

Under the center of the magnet supporting

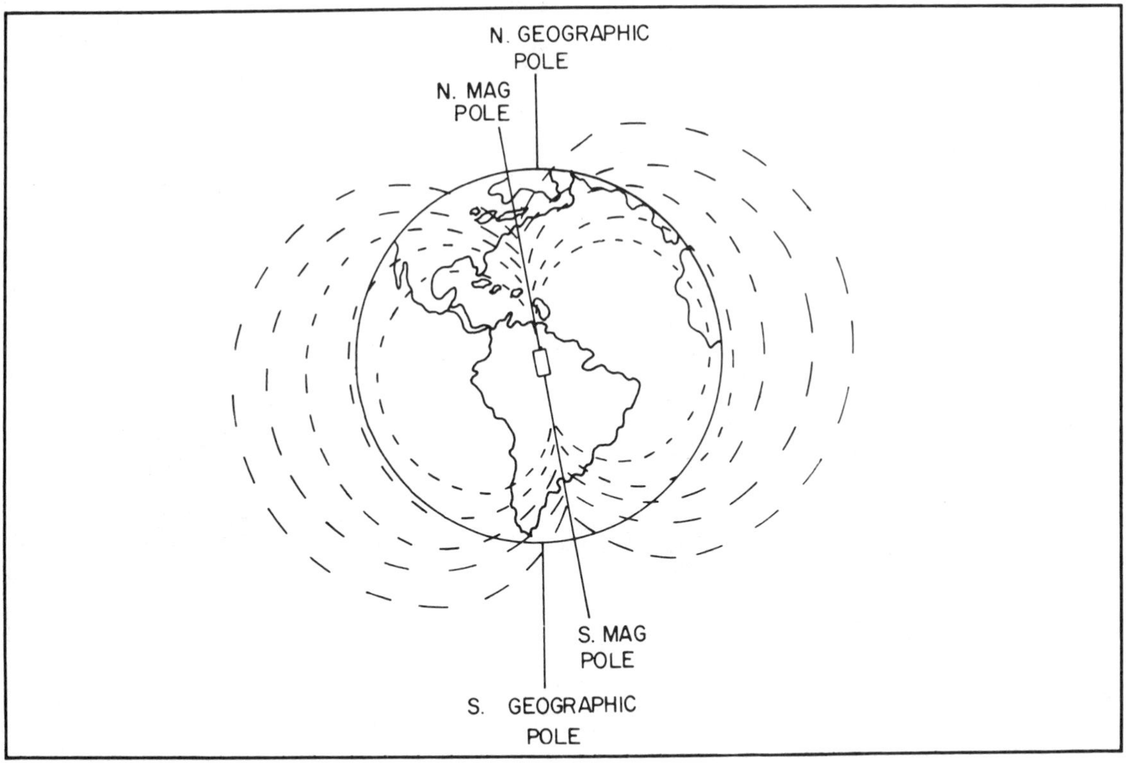
N. GEOGRAPHIC
POLE
N. MAG
POLE
S. MAG
POLE
S. GEOGRAPHIC
POLE

Fig. 4-2. Magnetic field of the earth.

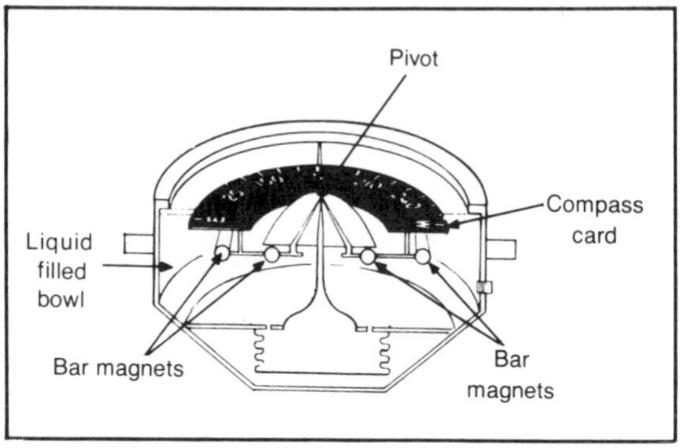
Pivot
Compass card
Liquid filled bowl
Bar magnets
Bar magnets

Fig. 4-3. Diagram of compass in cross section.

frame is a bearing that rests on top of the pivot. The pivot is a sharp point, often jeweled, that forms the top of a support rod. The support rod projects up from the bottom of the bowl, which constitutes the outer case of the complete compass. Above the card, a transparent cover is sealed to the top of the bowl. The cover might be flat or it might be hemispherical. In order to both reduce friction and damp vibration and oscillation, the bowl is filled with a nonfreezing liquid.

Either inside or outside the case, *gimbals* are provided so that the compass card may remain approximately level at all times regardless of the rolling or pitching motion of the vessel. Gimbals are a pair of rings, one inside the other, set up so that one pivots on a fore and aft axis while the other pivots on a thwartship axis. The combination of the two permits the compass to remain level.

Many compasses (Fig. 4-4) are furnished with a U-shaped mounting bracket that permits them to be mounted either on a horizontal, a vertical, or a slanted surface. Others (Fig. 4-5) are made only for flush or binnacle mounting in a horizontal surface. Still others (Fig. 4-6) are made to be inset into a vertical or a slanted bulkhead. The flush mount is most commonly used on power boats and the bulkhead mount is most often found on sailboats. The U bracket is a universal mount found on either sail or power vessels. Obviously it is going to be wise to choose your compass after a decision has been made as to where it will be mounted so that the compass chosen has a mount suitable to the location.

Compasses are often equipped with a light for night use. This light will be red and rather dim so as not to disturb the night vision of the person at the helm. When night vision is disturbed, it becomes somewhere between difficult and impossible for the helmsman to make out lights on buoys or on other vessels. Note, however, that it is a poor idea indeed to run at night using a compass that is not equipped with a light. From time to time, someone will light it up with a flashlight—which is much too bright and will interfere with the helmsman's night vision— or there will be a tendency to steer by hunch rather than by instrument and that is a direct route to catastrophe.

In addition to the pivot mounted magnets used to align the compass card with the magnetic field of the earth, the compass also contains four other magnets. These are called *compensating magnets* and they are used to reduce deviation of the compass. They are discussed further in connection with the explanation of deviation that comes later.

READING THE COMPASS

Above the pivot suspended magnets (Fig. 4-3), the compass card is mounted. Modern small-boat compass cards are marked in degrees (Fig. 4-7) from 0° up to 360°. On some cards, 0° is marked "N," 90° is "E," 180° is "S," and 270° is "W" for identifying the cardinal points or primary directions. On others,

Fig. 4-4. Compass in U-bracket mount.

Fig. 4-5. Compass in flush mount.

the cardinal points are both numbered and lettered. On larger compasses, not only the cardinal points—north, east, south, and west—are identified, but also the *intercardinals*—northeast (NE), southeast (SE), southwest (SW), and northwest (NW).

On many small-boat compasses, numbers appear only every 30°. For example, 30°, 60°, and 90° will be numbered, but 20°, or 40°, or 50° are usually not numbered. Every 5° will be marked with a short line and every 10° by a longer one. On anything other than a large ship's compass, the markings on a card graduated in single degrees will be too fine to be easily legible. In addition, as you'll soon discover, if you haven't already, a range of about 5° is the best that can be steered on a small boat in a seaway.

Markings on a compass card must first and foremost be large and clear if they are to be of any value. The constant movement of the boat in the

Fig. 4-6. Compass in bulkhead mount.

Fig. 4-7. Typical compass card.

seas, the constant small changes in direction as those seas strike her, plus the fact that the helmsman must watch the sea and other vessels in the vicinity as well as his proper course, all mean that he simply has not the time to decipher the meaning of fine markings. Rather, he needs large, bold markings that he can interpret correctly at a hasty glance.

Correct reading of the compass is going to depend on whether the one being used is a *top-reading compass* (Fig. 4-8) or a *front-reading compass* (Fig. 4-9). Every compass has a reference line called the *lubber line* fixed inside it, either in front of or behind the card. If the lubber line is in front of the card, it is a front-reading compass. If it is behind the card, it is a top-reading type.

Looking down on the card of a top-reading compass, the numbers indicating directions increase, moving clockwise around the card, this is a true representation of geographic directions relative to the boat. If you face due north, to your right (clockwise in the plane on which you are standing) will be east. Behind you will be south, and to your left is west. Looking down on a top-reading compass, this is precisely what you will see.

To a sailor accustomed to a top-reading compass, the front-reading model can be confusing because both numbers and directions seem to be reversed (Fig. 4-10). The lubber line marks the direction *toward* which the vessel is heading. This seeming reversal results from the fact that the location of the lubber line on the card has been reversed. This places geographic directions 180° away from their correct positions relative to the boat in order to align them with the lubber line.

Let us assume the vessel is moving toward the

240
W
300
210
S
CORSAIR
E
Fig. 4-8. Top-reading compass.

east. On a front-reading compass, the lubber line will quite correctly be on 90° (Fig. 4-9). Geographically, south is now to the right relative to the boat and north to the left. When you look at the compass, the numbers decrease from 60° through 30° toward north on the right side and increase on the left.

CHOOSING A COMPASS

For the coastal sailor, the single most important navigational tool aboard is the compass. Consequently, it should be chosen and installed with the greatest of care to ensure that it will operate reliably under adverse conditions. On a clear day, with visibility of 10 or 15 miles even with a compass that is absolute junk, you won't necessarily get into trouble. At night or in a fog or both, your compass is the device that tells you which way to head the boat. When you cannot see where you are going, the compass had better be right. An inexpensive compass hastily bought and carelessly installed can become the most expensive purchase you ever made.

A decent compass may be tilted at least 45° in any direction without the card sticking. It's ap-

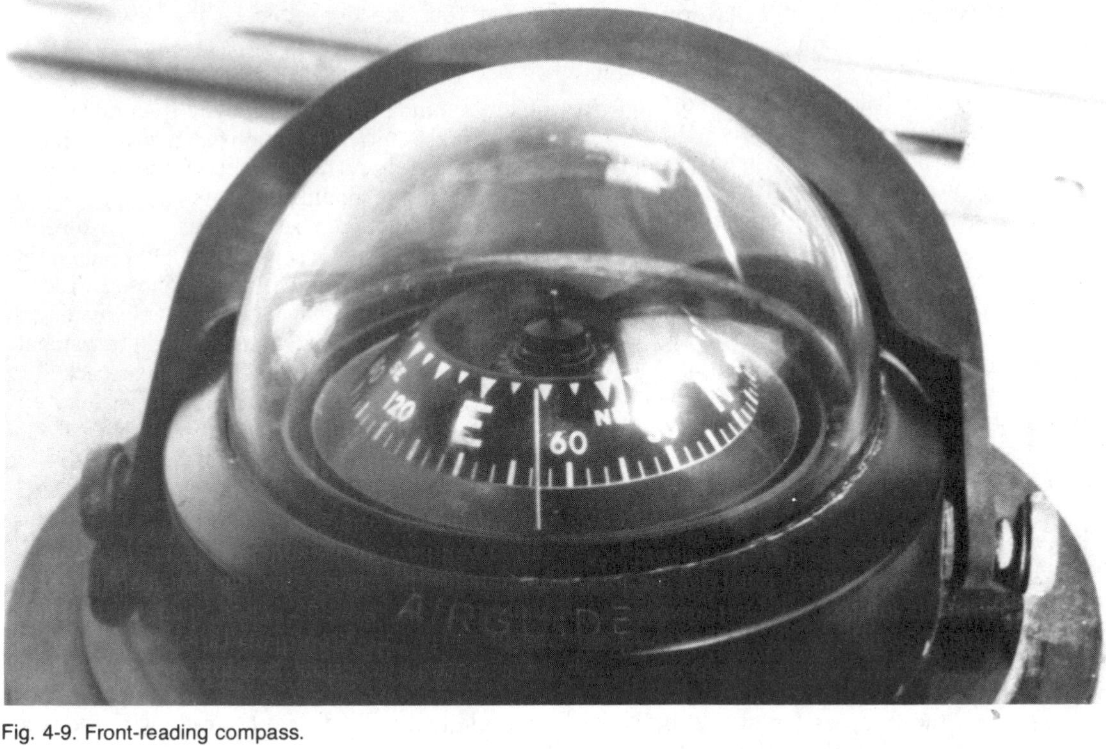
120
E
60
Fig. 4-9. Front-reading compass.

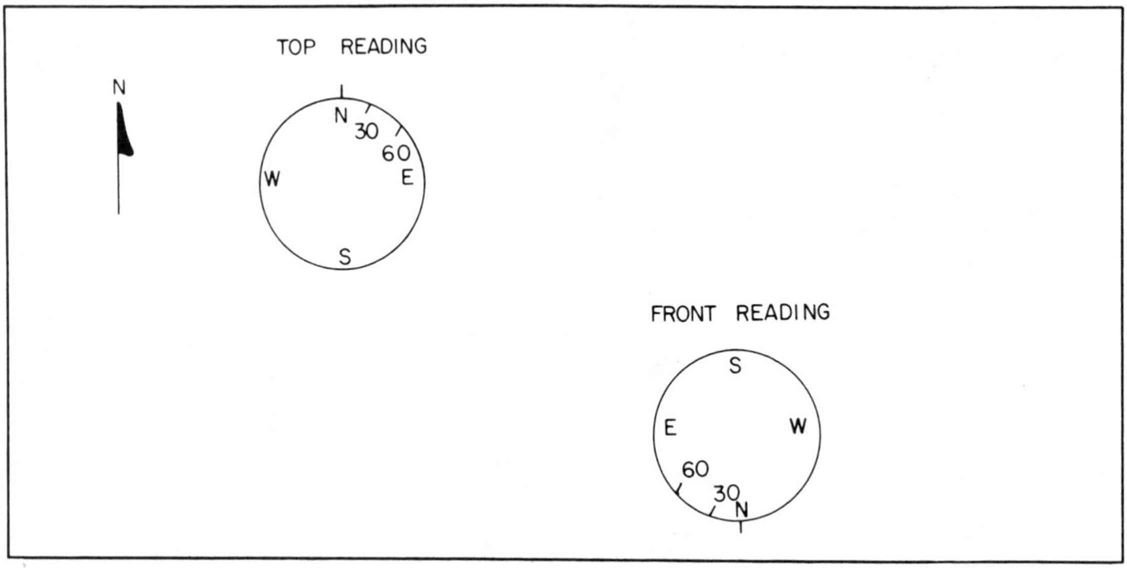
TOP READING
N
N
30
60
W
E
S
FRONT READING
S
E
W
60
30
N

Fig. 4-10. Diagram of difference; front- and top-reading compasses.

parent motion when turned in different directions is smooth and easy (not stiff and jerky). It will have to be mounted some several feet from the helmsman's eye. At that distance, the direction letters, degree numbers, and degree markings must be clearly legible at a hasty glance. It cannot be over emphasized that this instrument will be most important when conditions are at their worst!

If the boating budget calls for some economies, the compass is no place to skimp. Do not fall into the simple and obvious fallacy that a small boat manifestly calls for a small compass. The smaller the boat the more lively will be its motion in a seaway. As the movement of the boat becomes more lively, the importance of smoothness and stability in the compass increases. If the boat is bouncing about the compass card is bouncing about as well, there will be no possibility of maintaining a steady course in any direction. In general, the larger the compass the more stable it will be, and the smaller the boat the more important compass stability becomes. Get as large a compass as the mounting location will allow and of as high a quality as your bank account will allow.

Your compass should have built-in compensating magnets and it should have a built-in or clip-on, low-intensity light for night running. For small-boat use, the compass top should be hemispherical or domed rather than flat. This magnifies both numbers and markings and makes the compass vastly easier to read than flat-topped type. Consider the purchase of a compass as carefully as though your life depended on it—BECAUSE IT DOES!

COMPASS INSTALLATION

Before a compass can be installed, the first thing to do is to find a suitable location for it. That's simple; it should go directly in front of the helmsman. Right? Ideally it should, but that is not always possible. There might not be a suitable surface directly in front of the helm. If there is, it might result in the compass being mounted either too close or too far away from the helmsman for comfortable reading. If it is too far away, he must lean forward to watch it; and if it is too close, he might have to lean back. The surface might be fine at a suitable distance for eye comfort, but that location could be subject to unfavorable magnetic influences that cause excessive *deviation* of the compass readings.

Deviation can be caused by electrical devices. Therefore, engine instruments, radios, or other electrical equipment must be at least a couple of feet away from the compass location. Far better, they should be a good 6 feet away. That is easily said, but on a small boat that is not often possible. It might be hard enough to get two feet of clearance. The acid test will have to be made with the compass.

After a location has been selected, based on convenience of visibility and surface-mounting suitability, it will have to be tested with the compass for magnetic influences. In order to test a prospective location for magnetic influences with the compass itself, that compass first must be *zeroed in*. A new compass of decent quality should have been zeroed-in by the manufacturer before shipment, but it is advisable to check to make certain this has been properly done before using it to test a mounting location.

ZEROING IN

As mentioned above, the compass is built with internal compensating magnets (the purpose of which is to counteract, or at least minimize, local magnetic effects on the boat). Zeroing in is the process of adjusting those magnets initially so that they will have no effect at all on the compass. Later, after installation, we shall use them to deal with the deviation caused by the magnetic fields that exist on all boats. At the beginning we want them neutralized.

Zeroing the compass must be done ashore off the boat. Find a place free of any magnetic influences. There can be no cast-iron piping or galvanized piping nearby. Keep well away from radios, TVs or other electronic equipment. Do not do this on a table fastened together with steel nails or screws or containing any steel hardware. Keep off of a concrete slab containing steel reinforcing mesh or bars. Put aside the steel pocket knife, or any other steel objects in pockets or clothing, and remove all steel tools or other articles from the working area.

Ahead of time, a pair of wood blocks will have been prepared about a foot long by 6 inches or 8 inches wide and 3/4 of an inch thick. Trim them so the 1-foot-long edges of each block are both straight and exactly parallel. Now mount the compass on one block using brass or other nonmagnetic screws, with the lubber line aligned with the parallel edges. Precise alignment is not crucial. Block and compass (Fig. 4-11) are now placed on a flat and level surface clear of magnetic influences, as mentioned above, and turned until the compass reads exactly north. The second block is now placed snugly alongside the first one on which the compass stands. While holding the second block steady as a reference, the first one (with the compass on it) is now reversed end for end and replaced alongside the second. With uncommonly good luck, the compass will now read exactly south.

With more average luck, it will not read exactly south. The compass instructions will show which screw head is the N-S compensator. With a nonmagnetic screwdriver (file down a thin brass rod, a brass woodscrew, or a brass machine screw to make one), adjust the N-S compensator gently until half the difference between the reading and south has been removed. Now swivel the compass, block and all, until the compass reads exactly south. Using the second block as the reference, reverse the first block—returning the compass back to north. If it now reads exactly north all is well. If not, remove half the difference, realign the compass exactly on north, and repeat the entire process until the compass can be aligned exactly on north and reversed against the reference block to read exactly south. When this has been accomplished, the compass readings coincide with the local magnetic meridian.

With north-south out of the way, repeat the entire procedure with east-west. Align the compass reading on either east or west. Reverse the compass reading on either east or west. Halve the difference using the E-W compensator and repeat until the compass can be reversed between East and West and will read each one exactly. If after a

Fig. 4-11. Compass with blocks set up for zeroing.

reasonable number of tries the compass cannot be adjusted so that it will exactly reverse on both east-west and north-south, it is time to suspect that an unknown magnetic influence exists at the location chosen for zeroing in. Find another likely location and try again.

TESTING FOR MAGNETIC FIELDS

With the compass zeroed in, the prospective location for it on the boat can now be checked for magnetic influences in its immediate area. First, of course, careful visual inspection will have been made to ensure that all electronic equipment, electrical controls, wiring, and instruments are suitably spaced away from the spot chosen—away both horizontally and vertically. Everything on a horizontal plane with the chosen position might appear to be satisfactorily spaced, but diagonally about a foot and a half above it there might be an electric windshield wiper that could disrupt the compass at the worst possible time (when visibility is rotten and it is necessary to use that windshield wiper to see anything at all).

To test for magnetics, first place the compass in the position it will occupy when installed. Now slowly, gently, and very smoothly move it around that location without altering the alignment of the lubber line with the centerline of the boat. If the proposed mounting position is on a flat plane, the two blocks used for zeroing in might be helpful for maintaining that alignment while moving the compass back and forth. Watch to see if the compass card swings at all. If it does not, place it back on location and move all metal objects that are moved in normal operation of the boat (such as steering wheel, throttle, and gear shift to see if any of them affect the compass when operated).

If results are still happily negative, try out all electrical equipment. Turn lights, radio, depth sounder, bilge pump, and anything else electrical on and off to see if any of them have any effect. If results are still negative the location is fine.

If the compass card moves when the compass is moved about the desired location, only a magnetic field can cause this. Start looking for some iron or steel or some magnetized object in the vicinity that up to now has been missed. It could be something as simple as a steel screw that could be easily replaced with brass.

If the operation of any of the electrical equipment caused a reaction, possibly the device or its wiring can be relocated. If operation of the throttle, gearshift, or steering wheel caused compass movement, the chances are another installation location will have to be sought because those items are not readily relocated.

COMPASS MOUNTING

After the projected compass location has been checked out for unwanted magnetic influences with a properly zeroed-in compass—and found suitable—the compass can safely be fastened in place. Ideally, that location will be on the center line of the hull, and the compass will be physically oriented so that a line from the center of the card through the lubber line is exactly in line with the center line of the boat. Alas, all too seldom do we encounter the ideal. The chosen location is probably off center.

Actually, there is no particular need for the compass to be on the center line of the boat, except that it is a good deal easier to align it properly from there. What is crucial is that the line from the compass card center through the lubber line be accurately *parallel* to the centerline of the boat. Depending on the type of hull and superstructure, that centerline will have to be established by whatever means is feasible and then very carefully transferred to the compass mounting location.

On a small sailboat, it is safe to assume that the mast is stepped on the centerline. A piece of light twine or fishing line stretch tightly between the mast and the bow or the mast and the center of the transom will establish the centerline of the boat. On a small powerboat, the same light line stretched between the center of the windshield and bow or transom center will equally well establish the boat centerline. Normally, if the compass mounting location is to be on a main transverse bulkhead (Fig. 4-6), that bulkhead will already be constructed accurately at right angles to the centerline of the boat. Thus mounting the compass at right angles again to the bulkhead will align it accurately with the centerline of the boat.

When properly aligned, the compass must be very firmly attached to a very firm and solid mounting, preferably an integral part of the hull. The mounting bracket should be leveled, using shims if necessary, so that when the boat is standing level at the dock the compass will rest level in its gimbals.

EXISTING COMPASSES

If you have acquired a boat with a compass already installed, it could be a serious mistake to assume that the installation was done properly. First check the lubber line alignment with the boat centerline. Also, did the old skipper leave a deviation card?

If the lubber line alignment is no good, suspect the entire installation and redo it from the start. Take the compass ashore, zero it in, and test for magnetic effects at the mounting location. If it tests acceptable, realign and put it back. If magnetic problems are found, deal with them if possible or move the compass to a more suitable spot. If a deviation card was left, check it out using methods discussed later in this chapter.

COMPASS ERRORS

The standardized use of the term *compass errors* in nautical circles tends to give the newcomer an unfortunate impression. In everyday conversation, the word error is apt to imply a mistake, a blunder, or something that is just plain wrong. In navigation, as in various engineering fields, the meaning is quite different. *Instrument error* in navigation and other technical fields refers to a known and understood inaccuracy that is inherent in the nature of the instrument. Compass errors are well understood and easily dealt with by applying the proper correction factors. The point to remember is that a properly installed, good-quality compass is a reliable, trustworthy instrument. Its "errors" are readily corrected by simple addition or subtraction (making it an accurate instrument on which the mariner can and should depend). The mariner might make mistakes or blunders. The compass cannot.

The compass is designed to respond to, and align itself with, the magnetic field of the planet—and thus point north. As noted previously, geographic north and magnetic north are in two different places. When the magnetic compass accurately points to magnetic north, from most places on the planet, it is in error because it is not pointing to geographic north. Compass error caused by the magnetic field of the planet is termed *variation*. Variation affects equally all compasses in the same geographic vicinity.

As mentioned in connection with compass installation, the compass can also be very considerably influenced by magnetic forces in its immediate

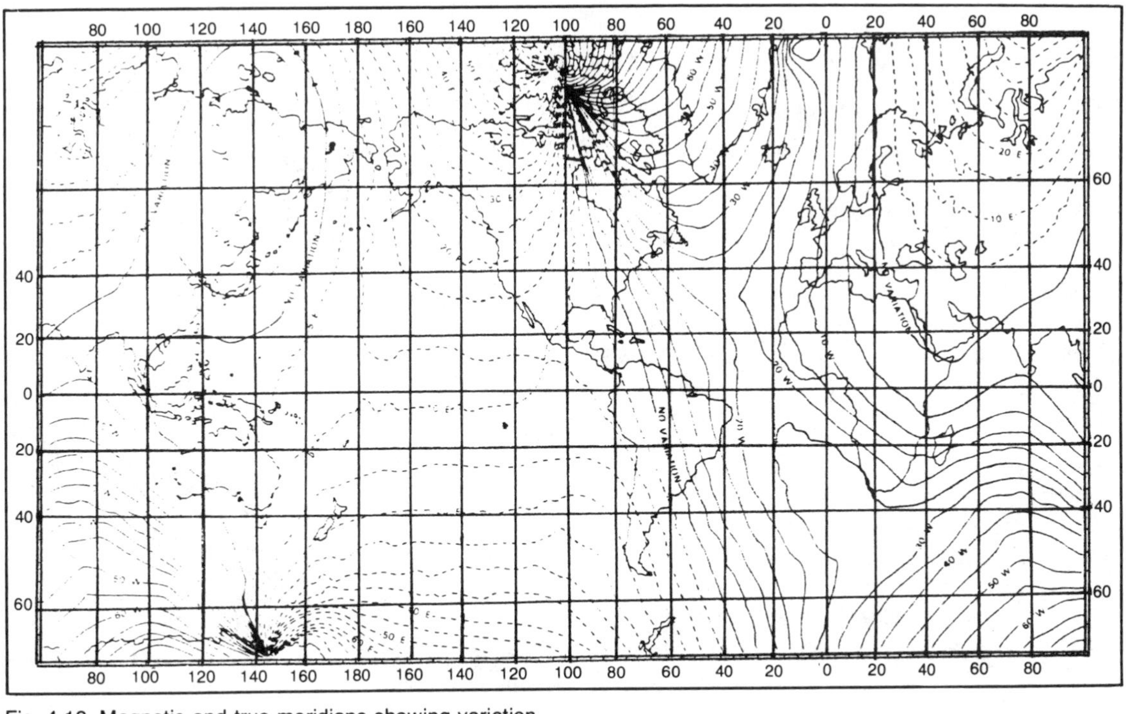
80 100 120 140 160 180 160 140 120 100 80 60 40 20 0 20 40 60 80
60
40
20
0
20
40
60
NO VARIATION
VARIATION
20 W
10 W
40 W
50 W
60 W

Fig. 4-12. Magnetic and true meridians showing variation.

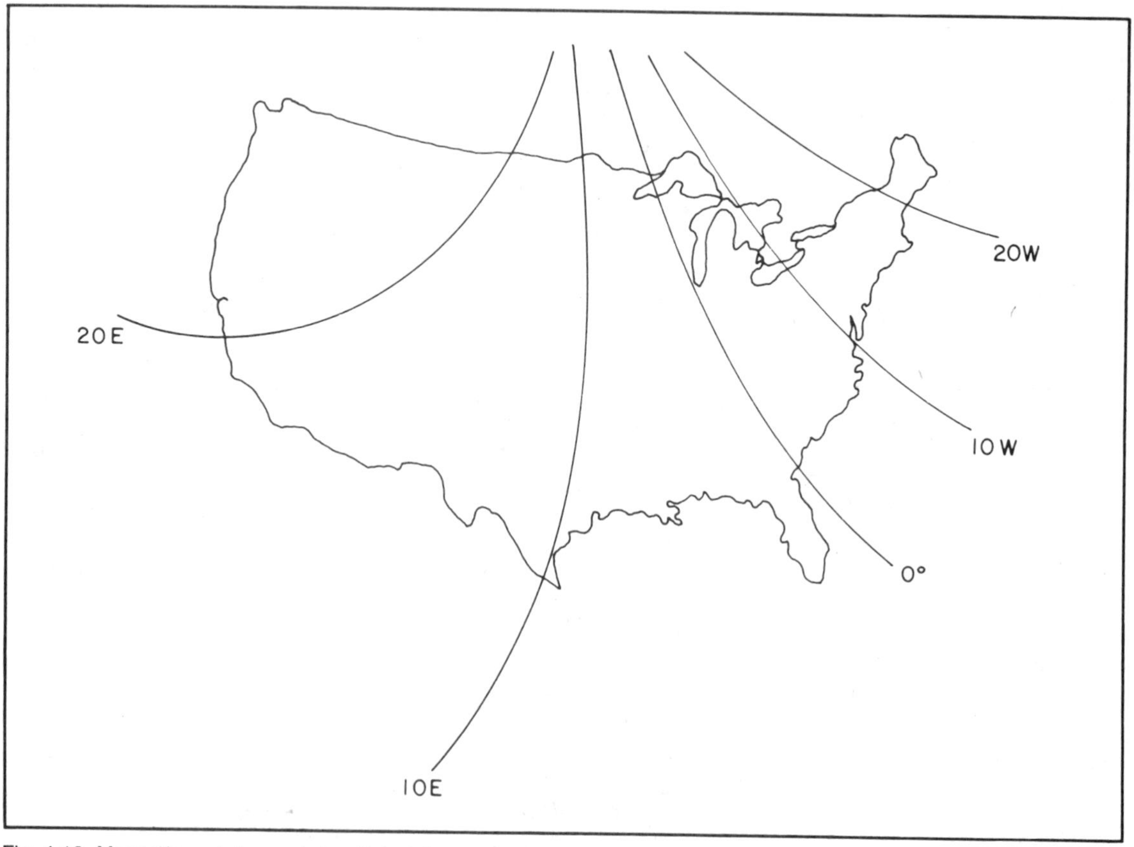
20E
20W
10W
0°
10E

Fig. 4-13. Magnetic variation over the United States.

vicinity on the boat. These influences will differ from boat to boat, and from place to place, on the same boat. These magnetic influences result in another type of compass error termed *deviation*. Deviation has different effects on each specific compass at each specific location on each particular boat. Variation is caused by the earth and affects all compasses in the area. Deviation is caused on the boat and effects only the compass on that boat.

VARIATION

The difference between true north and the magnetic meridian at any particular location is the *variation* for that place. This will be the difference between true north and the direction toward which a compass completely free of any local magnetic influcences will point. Such a compass would have to be mounted on a boat made entirely of nonmagnetic materials with no equipment containing magnetic materials aboard as well.

In such an ideal, if unlikely, situation the compass will point either east or west of true north depending on (Fig. 4-12) whether the magnetic meridian is pointed east or west of true north at that location. Therefore, variation must be designated either east or west. On the East Coast of the United States, it is generally west. On the west coast it is generally east. Figure 4-13 gives a general idea of the trends and extents of variation over the continental United States and its coasts.

Because the earth is by no means a homogeneous mass, its magnetic field is by no means uniform either. Consequently, the magnetic meridians are by no means nice, straight, regularly spaced lines as are meridians of longitude. They are actually extremely irregular. As a result, on a moderately long coastal passage, variation will change considerably. On the sort of passages usually made over a weekend, however, the change will not be great.

In any event, as long as the charts for the area

being sailed are aboard and the position of the boat is reasonably well known (which it will be if you follow the methods shown here), the variation for the location of the boat will also be known. Variation is given on all nautical charts in the form of one or more compass roses (Fig. 2-13) scattered about the chart. Use the one nearest to the position of the boat.

A compass rose consists of two concentric circles marked at every second degree for 360°. Each mark thus represents 2°. Numbers appear every 30°; 30°, 60°, 90°, 120°, and so on are numbered. The star at 0° on the outer circle represents true geographic north. The 0° mark on the inner circle will be out of alignment with the 0° mark on the outer one. The difference represents the variation for that locality. When the inner 0° mark is to the left of the outer one, the variation is to the west. When it is to the right, variation is to the east. Inside of the second circle, and in alignment with it, is a third circle marked off according to the old 32 compass point system. Because it is largely obsolete, it will not be discussed here. Inside of all three and printed around the center of the third circle is the variation for the area given in degrees (°) and minutes of angle ('). The year for which the variation given is accurate, is noted, and so is the annual local rate of increase or decrease of variation.

As we have seen, the magnetic field of the earth is highly irregular. In addition, for reasons that are not at all well understood, the field is constantly changing. The result is that variation at any specific location will either increase or decrease at a reasonably steady rate for a number of years. Then it becomes substantially static for a time; after which, it reverses its direction of change. Although the reason for these changes are not understood, the rates of change can be predicted with a high degree of accuracy for several years at a time, and do not exceed a few minutes (') of angle per year. A typical compass rose might read: Var. 13°25'E (1980) Annual Increase 4'. By 1982, in that area the variation has become 13°33'E which you will round off at 14°. The best of helmsmen on a small boat are going to wobble constantly by a few degrees left and right of the desired course. Hence, there is obviously no point in being concerned about 27' of angle which is less than ½ of one degree. Make it a standard procedure for steering corrections to round off parts of a degree. If the fraction is less than ½°, round off at the next lower degree. If more than ½°, round up to the next higher (as we have just done).

What that 14° E variation means to you is that your compass is reading 14° too low. When your boat is heading straight at geographic north (Fig. 4-14), which is 0°, the compass will read only 346°. Looking at it the other way—if your objective is geographically due north of your present position—you must aim at 346° magnetic to actually be pointing at it.

Variation, as we can now plainly see, is a

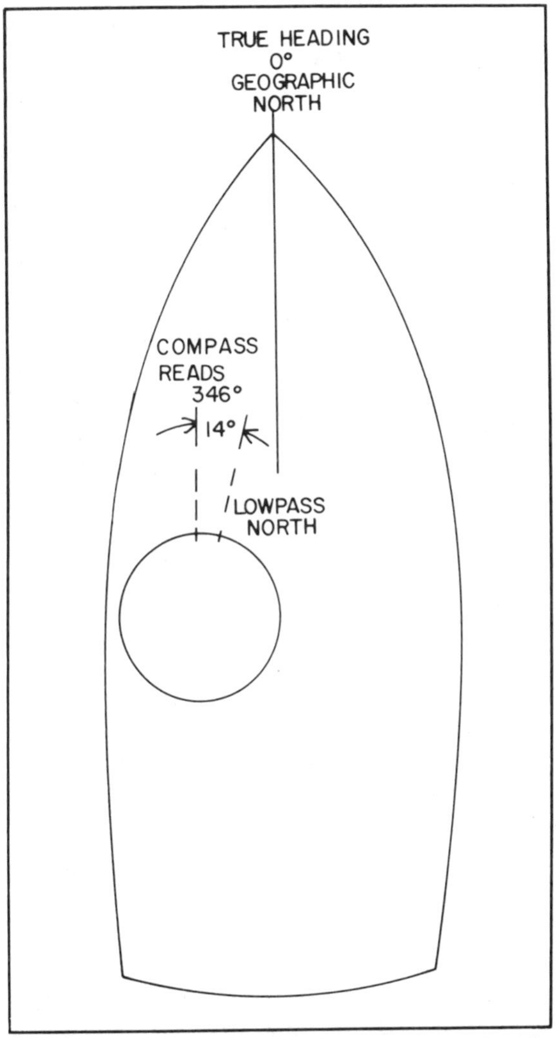
TRUE HEADING
0°
GEOGRAPHIC
NORTH
COMPASS
READS
346°
14°
LOWPASS
NORTH

Fig. 4-14. Boat heading geographic north (0 degrees T) while compass reads 346 degrees.

compass instrument error that is inherent in the irregularities of the magnetic field of the earth. There is absolutely nothing we can do about *that*. Although these irregularities differ in both direction and magnitude from place to place (and differ over time as well), we are saved by the fact that we are dealing with known quantities. Anyone who deals with measuring instruments of any type on a day-to-day basis is aware it makes no difference how great an instrument error could be as long as it is known. As long as we know that a clock is running 7 minutes fast, we also know that when it reads 1:27 it is actually 1:20. In the same way, if variation in an area is charted at 14° E, all compasses in that area will read 14° too low. By adding that 14° to the readings of any of them, that instrument error will be removed. Or in nautical terminology it will be "corrected."

DEVIATION

Deviation is another type of compass error that is also inherent in the nature of the instrument. Deviation differs significantly from variation. Variation is the same for all vessels in an area. Also it is the same regardless of the direction in which the boat is heading because it is caused by forces totally independent of the boat.

Deviation, by contrast, is caused by forces on or in each individual boat. Consequently, deviation is not the same for any two boats and it remains the same as the boat changes from one heading to another. If this sounds as though it can be a whole lot more confusing than variation, that is absolutely correct. Nevertheless, the direction and magnitude of deviation on different headings of the boat *can* be accurately determined. When that has been done, it makes no difference how great an instrument error is as long as its magnitude and direction are known.

Deviation changes with the heading of the boat, but on a specific heading it will always be the same. It does not change with geographic location or with time. It only changes when major changes are made in the location or amount of ferrous metal aboard or when major electrical changes are made.

Causes of Deviation

The compass points to magnetic north because it is responding to and aligning itself with the magnetic field of the earth. Because even the most expensive of compasses is of limited intelligence—it only knows how to respond to a magnetic field—it is totally unable to distinguish one field from another. Consequently, any magnetic materials or fields on the boat confuse it, causing it to deviate from magnetic north.

The direction and magnitude of the deviation will depend on how strong the local magnetic force is and where it lies relative to magnetic north on a particular heading of the boat (Fig. 4-15). When the local force on the boat lies to the right of magnetic north, the deviation will be to the right. While to the boat and those on it this is to starboard, the limited intelligence of the compass interprets this as east. It is an easterly deviation. When the local force lies to the left or port, of the compass, the deviation becomes westerly.

A variety of local influences on the boat can cause deviation. Any large concentration of ferrous material is a likely culprit (that very often is an engine). Other causes might be any of the various electrical devices aboard or the wiring leading to them. An electrical current passing through a wire creates a magnetic field (as do many of the devices themselves). One major difficulty with the effect of electrical fields on compasses is that they are usually intermittent. When an electrical device is in operation, its field can affect the compass, but its influence stops when it is turned off. This is why, before choosing a compass mounting location, you must test a prospective location by temporarily placing the compass there, and then operating *all* electrical equipment to determine if any of it affects the compass.

In connection with local influences on a compass, remember that when you are under way *never* leave a wrench, a screwdriver, a pair of pliers, a can opener, or a ferrous-metal beverage can on the dash near the compass. Any such hardware nearby will throw the compass way off.

On one occasion, while sailing as navigator, I gave the helmsman a course of about 170° during a run from the Isles des Saintes to the island of Dominica in the Caribbean. An hour or so later, he had Dominica dead ahead but on a course by compass of about 210°. That should have put him out of sight of the island by many miles to the west. It was a good thing he was sailing by the sun, because the entire time he had kept a steel beverage can within a foot of the compass and it threw the compass off by close to 40°.

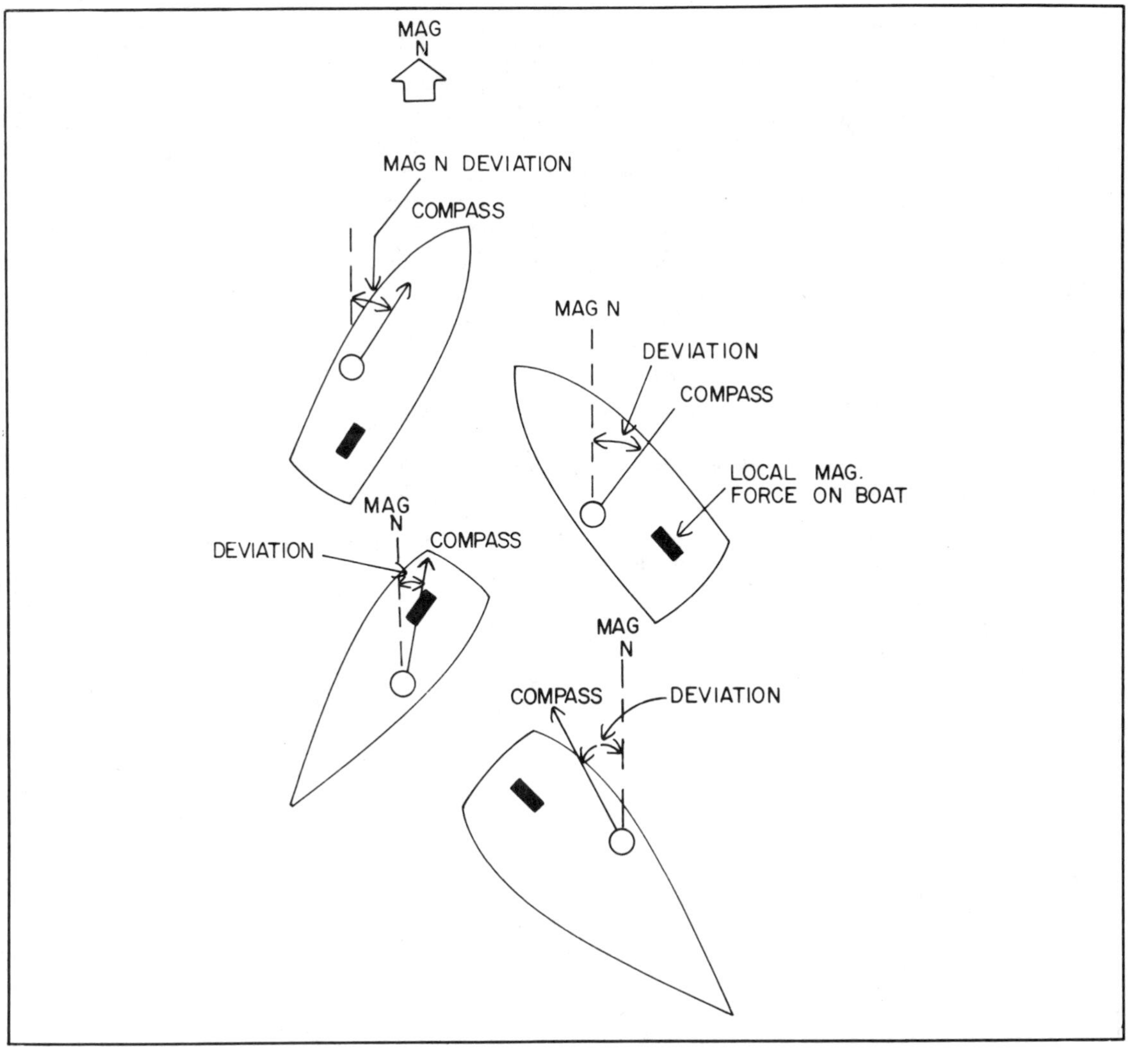
MAG
N
MAG N DEVIATION
COMPASS
MAG N
DEVIATION
COMPASS
LOCAL MAG.
FORCE ON BOAT
MAG
N
DEVIATION
COMPASS
MAG
N
COMPASS
DEVIATION

Fig. 4-15. Deviation caused by magnetism on boat.

Another friend wasn't so lucky. As a result of the same kind of foolishness, he completely missed the island of Antigua and didn't figure out what was wrong until a couple of hours after he should have been there. He ended up very late for dinner!

Tabulating Deviation

Deviation is the difference between the compass direction and the magnetic direction. That difference varies with the heading of the boat. What we need to determine is the magnitude and direction of that difference on a variety of headings. When this is known for a good many headings, ideally about every 15°, a *deviation card* is then compiled for converting back and forth between compass and magnetic courses.

When the compass is located on the boat in a position such that bearings can be taken directly over it, a deviation card for every 15° can be made quite simply by "swinging ship." First find two charted objects (Fig. 4-16) for which the magnetic bearing can be found from a nearby compass rose on the chart. On a calm day two people take the boat out. One will operate the boat while the other reads bearings.

First cross the range with the ships compass reading 0° and read and record the bearing of the range. Then recross with the compass reading 180° (the reciprocal of 000°) and read and record the range bearing again. Next, cross the range on a compass course of 15° and recross on its reciprocal 195° reading the bearing of the range on each crossing. Continue crossing and recrossing the range until the list of bearings is complete for every 15° from 0° compass up to 345° compass.

The deviation for each compass heading is the difference between the magnetic bearing of the range as taken from the chart and the bearing as actually read from the compass while the boat was on that heading. Table 4-1 is an imaginary set of bearings that might have resulted from an expedition such as that just described.

The size of the deviations in Table 4-1 are larger than would be considered acceptable for navigational use. Remember, however, that this table was taken with a compass that had been zeroed in prior to installation. Its compensating magnets have been carefully neutralized. By the time the compass has been compensated, most of this deviation will have been removed.

When a compass is located in a position where bearings cannot be taken over it, as on the bulkhead dividing the cockpit and the cabin on a sailboat, another method of assembling a deviation card will have to be used. Without being able to sight over the compass, a deviation card with neatly spaced intervals of 15° is not going to be possible. Nevertheless, enough deviations, even though taken at somewhat irregular intervals, will do the

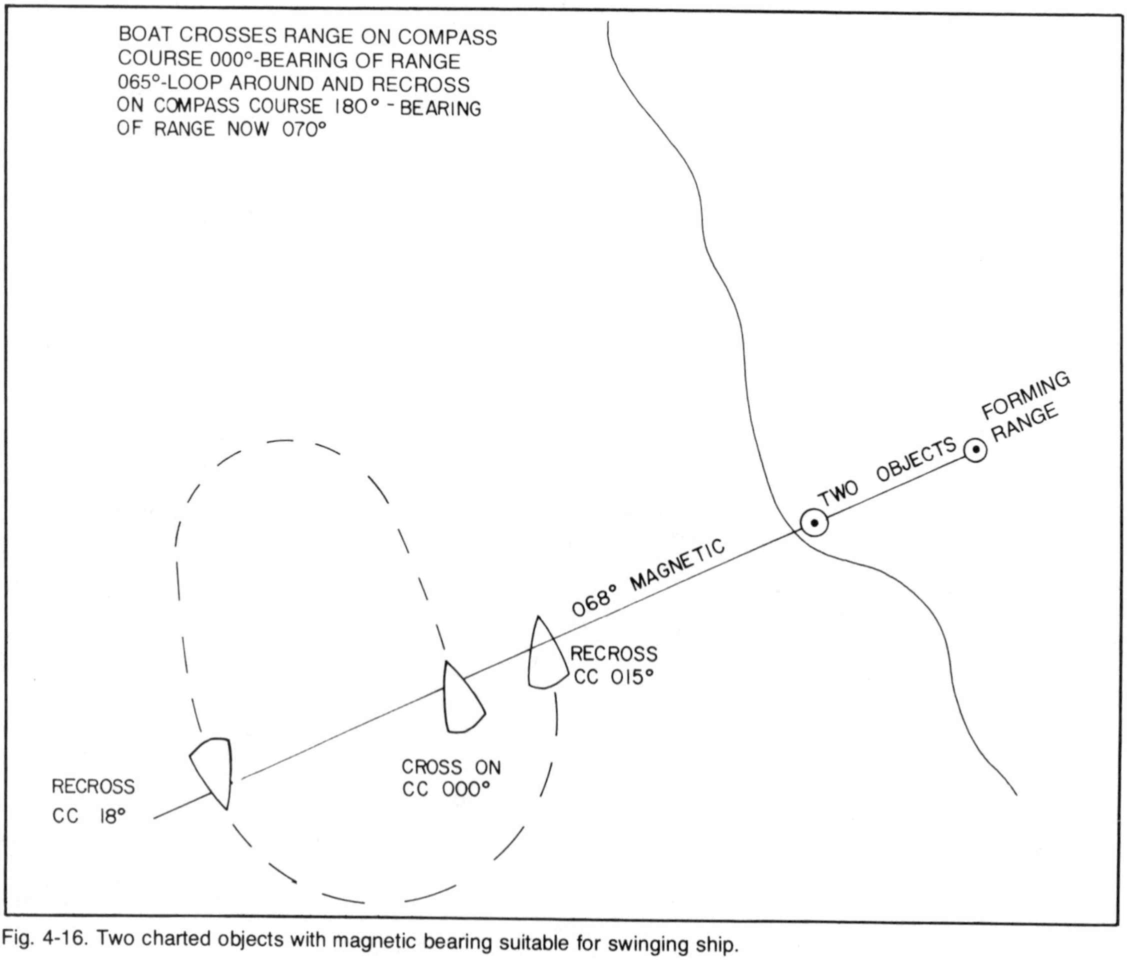
BOAT CROSSES RANGE ON COMPASS
COURSE 000°-BEARING OF RANGE
065°-LOOP AROUND AND RECROSS
ON COMPASS COURSE 180° - BEARING
OF RANGE NOW 070°
TWO OBJECTS FORMING RANGE
068° MAGNETIC
RECROSS
CC 015°
CROSS ON
CC 000°
RECROSS
CC 18°

Fig. 4-16. Two charted objects with magnetic bearing suitable for swinging ship.

Table 4-1. An Imaginary Set of Bearings.

MAGNETIC BEARING OF RANGE: 068°

SHIPS HEAD PER COMPASS	RANGE BEARING PER COMPASS	DEVIATION
000°	065°	3 E
015°	063°	5 E
030°	062°	6 E
045°	061°	7 E
060°	060°	8 E
075°	159°	9 E
090°	161°	7 E
105°	062°	6 E
120°	065°	3 E
135°	066°	2 E
150°	068°	0
165°	069°	1 W
180°	071°	3 W
195°	072°	4 W
210°	073°	5 W
225°	075°	7 W
240°	076°	8 W
255°	077°	9 W
270°	076°	8 W
285°	074°	6 W
300°	071°	3 W
315°	069°	1 W
330°	068°	0
345°	067°	1 E

job adequately. A harbor chart (Fig. 4-17) containing many charted landmarks and aids to navigation can provide numerous ranges for which magnetic bearings can be plotted using a convenient compass rose to find the bearings.

By taking the boat out and aligning with each of these ranges head on, the compass heading found on each range can be recorded and then compared with the charted magnetic bearing for each as taken from the chart. The difference, in each case, between the compass reading and the charted bearing is the deviation for that heading. When the compass reading is a smaller number than the charted bearing, the deviation is east. When the compass reading is larger, the deviation is west. As an example, when the magnetic bearing of a range is 167° a compass reading 162° (when heading down that range) has a deviation of 5° E. A compass with the same 5° of deviation, but this time to the west, would read 172°.

A deviation card derived from a group of range bearings in a local harbor might look like Table 4-2. This card also shows deviations in excess of those you will have to deal with in the practice of coastal navigation (again assuming an uncompensated compass). These deviations might also be a good deal larger than the ones you will find after mounting a properly zeroed-in compass on your own boat. Even if the deviations you find in your compass are much less than those shown here, it is a poor idea to assume that because the errors are small you can forget them.

Remember, your compass is going to be most important when you have a night run to make, a run in poor visibility, or both. Even with the best of steering on a small boat, there is every likelihood of being off by a couple of degrees one way or the other. If in addition to an unavoidable steering error, the course being steered was wrong by another 5° or 6° of deviation, the cumulative error becomes quite significant after a surprisingly short run. If the cumulative error altogether is a mere 5° after a run of only a little over 5 1/2 miles, the boat will be about 1/2 mile off course.

If the cumulative error reaches 10° after running the same distance, the boat is a whole mile off course. Obviously, inaccuracies of this magnitude in coastal operation are totally unacceptable. Therefore, the compass should be carefully compensated in order to reduce deviation error as close to zero as possible on as many headings as possible. Then the residual deviation should be checked and accurately recorded using either of the methods just described so that proper allowance can be made for it when sailing any heading on which it appears.

COMPASS COMPENSATION

Prior to installation, the compass was carefully zeroed in to totally neutralize the effect of its internal compensating magnets. This leaves it free to align itself with the magnetic field of the earth. Now that it is installed on the boat it is subject to magnetic influences that did not exist when it was zeroed in. These influences causing it to deviate from its alignment with the magnetic field of the earth can in large measure be counteracted by adjustment of those same compensating magnets. This is a simple job. A mighty mind is not required nor is either mighty strength or surpassing dexterity. Plodding patience and careful attention to detail are required.

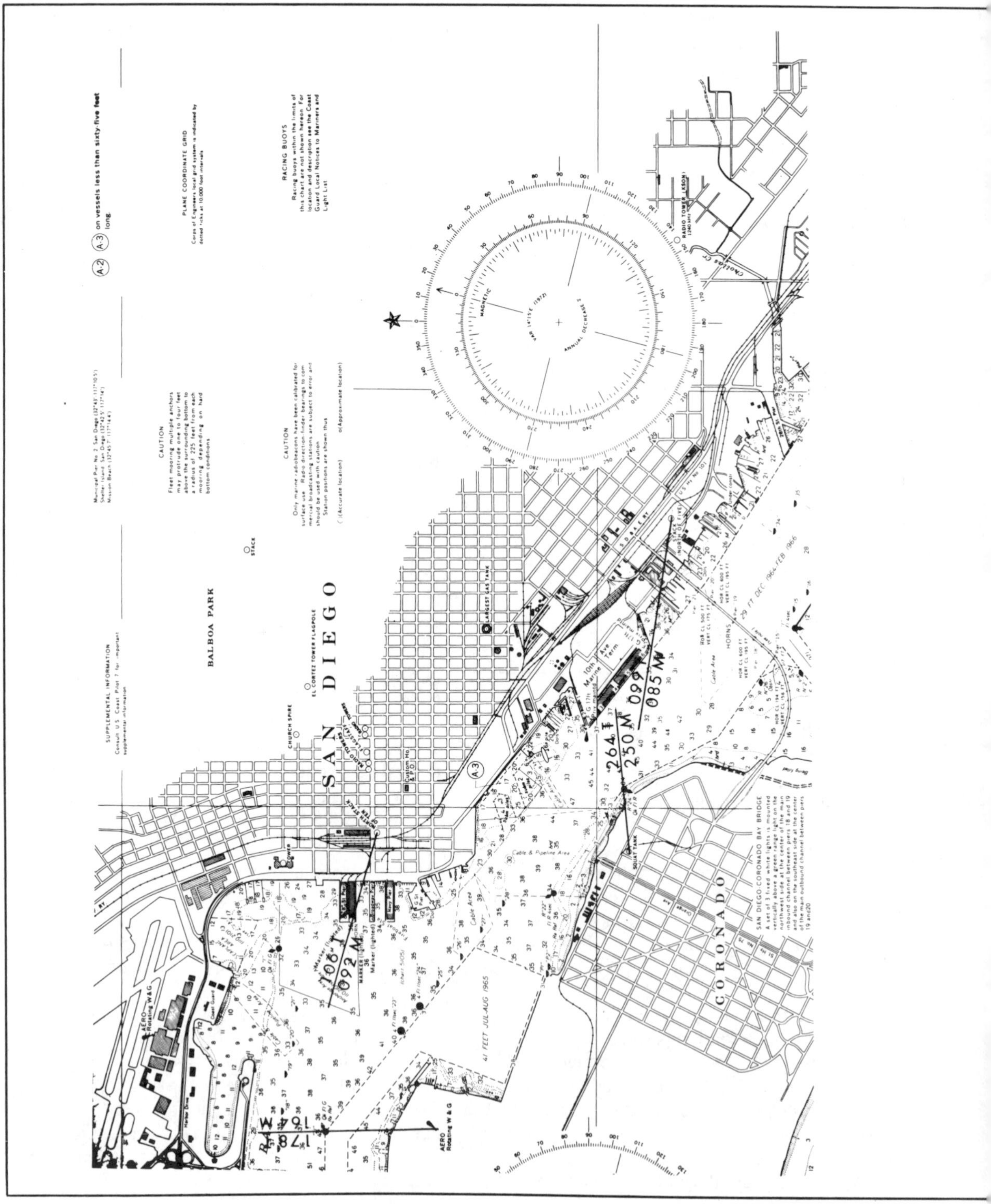

SUPPLEMENTAL INFORMATION
Consult U.S. Coast Pilot 7 for important supplemental information
BALBOA PARK
CAUTION
Fleet mooring multiple anchors may protrude one to four feet above the surrounding bottom to a radius of 225 feet from each mooring depending on hard bottom conditions
CAUTION
Only marine radiobeacons have been calibrated for surface use. Radio direction-finder bearings to commercial broadcasting stations are subject to error and should be used with caution
Station positions are shown thus
(Accurate location)
(Approximate location)
PLANE COORDINATE GRID
Corps of Engineers local grid system is indicated by dotted ticks at 10,000 feet intervals
RACING BUOYS
Racing buoys within the limits of this chart are not shown hereon. For location and description see the Coast Guard Local Notices to Mariners and Light List
A-2 A-3 on vessels less than sixty-five feet long.
SAN DIEGO
CORONADO
EL CORTEZ TOWER FLAGPOLE
CHURCH SPIRE
STACK
LARGEST GAS TANK
RADIO TOWER (KSON)
MAGNETIC
ANNUAL DECREASE
10th Ave Marine Term
SAN DIEGO-CORONADO BAY BRIDGE
A set of 3 fixed white lights is mounted vertically above a green range light on the northwest side at the center of the main inbound channel between piers 18 and 19 and also on the southeast side at the center of the main outbound channel between piers 19 and 20
41 FEET JUL-AUG 1965
AERO Rotating W & G
264 T
250 M
099 T
085 M

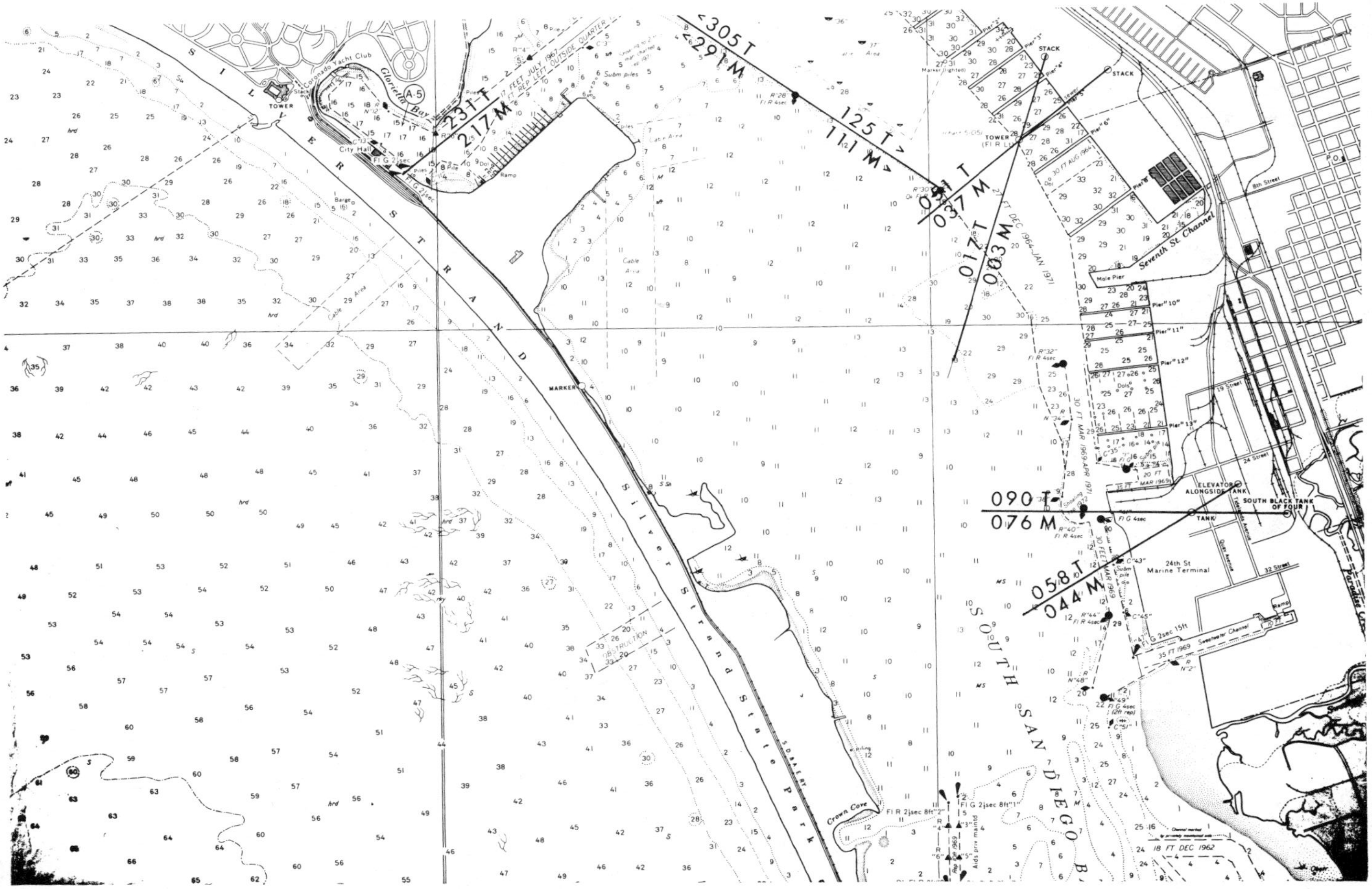

305 T
291 M
125 T
111 M
051 T
037 M
017 T
003 M
231 T
217 M
090 T
076 M
058 T
044 M
SILVER STRAND
Silver Strand State Park
SOUTH SAN DIEGO BAY
Glorietta Bay
Coronado Yacht Club
City Hall
TOWER
STACK
MARKER
Crown Cove
Seventh St. Channel
Mole Pier
Pier "10"
Pier "11"
Pier "12"
Pier "13"
ELEVATOR TANK ALONGSIDE
SOUTH BLACK TANK OF FOUR
TANK
24th St Marine Terminal
Sweetwater Channel
8th Street
24 Street
32 Street
Cable Area
Ramp
30 FT MAR 1969-APR 1971
27 FT DEC 1964-JAN 1971
18 FT DEC 1962
35 FT 1969

Fig. 4-17. Harbor chart with various ranges for deviation checks.

Table 4-2. Range Bearings.

RANGE BEARING	COMPASS READING	DEVIATION
008°	017°	9° W
014°	021°	7 W
058°	056°	2 W
066°	063°	3 E
093°	086°	7 E
132°	122°	10 E
178°	165°	13 E
191°	177°	14 E
208°	196°	12 E
236°	228°	8 E
248°	245°	3 E
262°	269°	7 W
288°	305°	17 W
296°	315°	19 W
318°	336°	18 W
324°	357°	15 W
355°	006°	11 W

The same two small screws on the compass case marked N-S and E-W that were used to zero the compass will now be used again to compensate for deviation. The nonmagnetic screwdriver will also be needed again to adjust those same screws. Before proceeding, every magnetic and electrical article or device on the boat must be stowed in its normal place. Every such article not normally aboard must be removed. Oh, and the crescent wrench and the beer can opener that you left by the compass—put them where they belong. Perhaps now you are ready to start.

The compass is to be adjusted by running reciprocal courses: north—south, then east—west. The actual adjustments will be made in exactly the same way as was done when the compass was zeroed. The zeroing was very simple; all you had to do was align the compass on a board, reverse it, align again, and repeat until the readings were exact. Now you have to align the whole boat, reverse it, and align again. This sounds more complicated than it really is.

A number of disposable markers will be needed. These can easily be made from empty milk cartons or plastic bottles. Add a handful of sand in the bottom of each to hold it upright when it is thrown over the side. Now with the markers at hand, everything aboard properly stowed, and the nonmagnetic screwdriver ready, it is time to begin.

Pick a buoy or daybeacon from which it is possible to run at least 1/2 to 3/4 of a mile due north *by ship's compass*. Holding a steady course of 0° per compass, make such a run from the buoy or beacon. When somewhere between 1/2 and 3/4 of a mile from the starting point, drop a milk carton or plastic bottle to form a range with the original buoy and then turn sharply to port and execute a full turn (Fig. 4-18).

Come back on course so that the centerline of the boat, the milk carton, and the original buoy are all in line. The boat is now facing exactly 180° from its original course. The compass should now read 180°, but what does it actually read? As when you zeroed it, for it to read 180° is too much to expect. Let us suppose it reads 190°. Holding course visually now on the original buoy, use the nonmagnetic screwdriver on the N-S screw to remove 1/2 of the difference between 180° and what the compass reads. This means setting it at 185°.

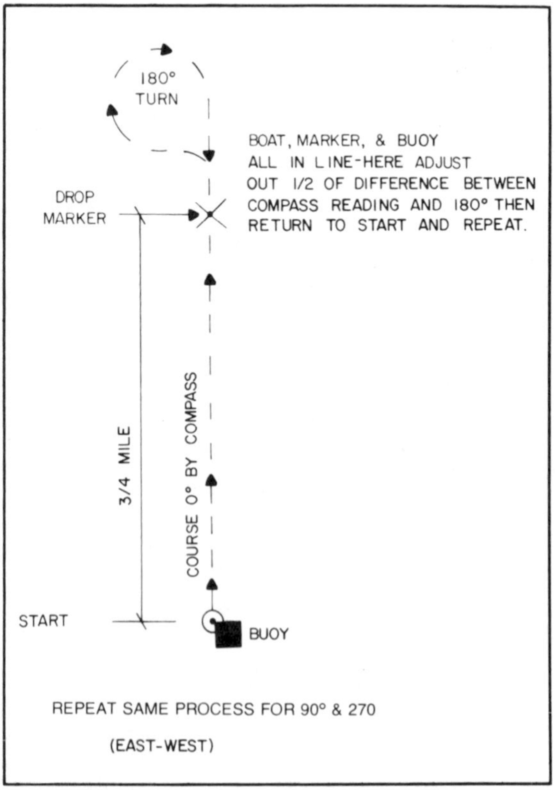
180° TURN
BOAT, MARKER, & BUOY ALL IN LINE-HERE ADJUST OUT 1/2 OF DIFFERENCE BETWEEN COMPASS READING AND 180° THEN RETURN TO START AND REPEAT.
DROP MARKER
3/4 MILE
COURSE 0° BY COMPASS
START
BUOY
REPEAT SAME PROCESS FOR 90° & 270
(EAST-WEST)

Fig. 4-18. Dropping marker and making 180-degree turn to compensate compass.

Now go back to the starting point and repeat the entire process until a 180° turn results in a 180° difference in the compass reading—no more and no less. With N-S adjusted turn next to E-W. Put the boat on a compass course of 090°, run 1/2 to 3/4 of a mile drop a marker, and repeat the entire process until a 180° turn on the east-west axis results in a 180° difference in the compass reading.

Unfortunately, perfect compensation is often impossible to achieve. The residual deviation that remains need not be a problem as long as it is known. This calls for the preparation of a final deviation table based on the compensated compass. This one will be made in exactly the same way as the first one. The obvious difference will be that the deviations found now will be vastly smaller. The final deviation table can be kept in list form or it can be transferred to a graphic deviation card form similar to Fig. 4-19. In any case, it should be available for ready reference at any time.

HEELING ERROR

Those with powerboats can forget this one, but it can be significant in some cases on sailboats. Heel-

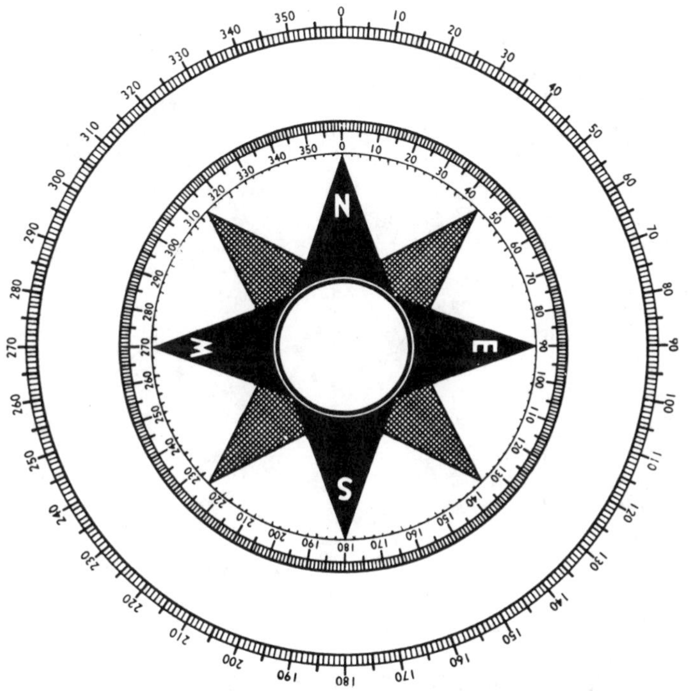
N
E
S
W

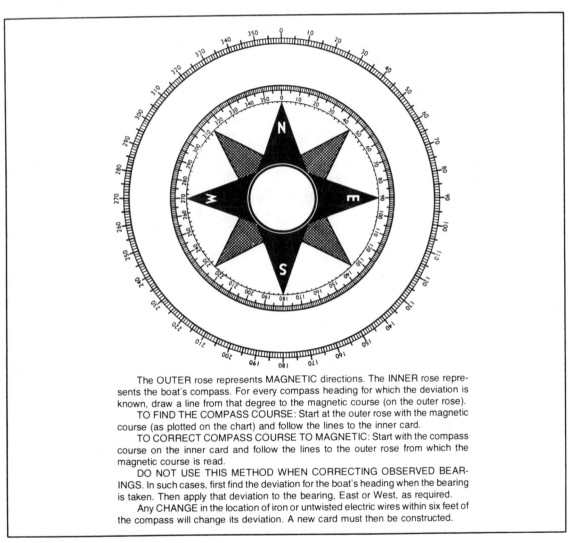

The OUTER rose represents MAGNETIC directions. The INNER rose represents the boat's compass. For every compass heading for which the deviation is known, draw a line from that degree to the magnetic course (on the outer rose).

TO FIND THE COMPASS COURSE: Start at the outer rose with the magnetic course (as plotted on the chart) and follow the lines to the inner card.

TO CORRECT COMPASS COURSE TO MAGNETIC: Start with the compass course on the inner card and follow the lines to the outer rose from which the magnetic course is read.

DO NOT USE THIS METHOD WHEN CORRECTING OBSERVED BEARINGS. In such cases, first find the deviation for the boat's heading when the bearing is taken. Then apply that deviation to the bearing, East or West, as required.

Any CHANGE in the location of iron or untwisted electric wires within six feet of the compass will change its deviation. A new card must then be constructed.

Fig. 4-19. Blank deviation card.

ing error results from the fact that the relationship of magnetic forces on a boat can be rather different when she is heeled over at say 10° or 20° than when she is upright. This, in turn, can cause deviation to change. Should you find that course calculations are not working out properly on some headings with the vessel running heeled, the cause could be heeling error. If so, this is a job for a professional compass adjuster—not an amateur.

COMPASS CORRECTION CALCULATIONS

All courses steered must be steered by compass. All bearings taken on aids to navigation or landmarks are taken by compass as well. The true direction in which the boat must proceed to get from point A to point B will be found on the chart as will the true locations of any aids to navigation or landmarks on which bearings are taken.

The navigator must, therefore, be able quickly to convert a true course from the chart to a compass course for steering or a compass bearing to a true bearing for plotting a line of position. Rapid and accurate conversions back and forth between true and compass courses and bearings should become simple and effortless for the competent navigator. All that is required is a little practice.

Converting from a compass course using deviation to get to magnetic and then variation to arrive at true is termed *correcting*. Working the other way, from true through magnetic to a compass direction, is termed *uncorrecting*. All that is involved is elementary addition or subtraction. The only possible difficulty is the question of whether to add or subtract in a particular case.

To clarify the correcting and uncorrecting of directions, a few examples will be helpful. In Fig. 4-20, two boats are both on a true course of 048°. Boat A is in an area having a local variation of 11°E and boat B (many hundreds of miles away) is in a locality with a variation of 11°W. Where A is sailing, the 0° mark on his compass is already pointing at 11° True. In order to aim at 048° True, he subtracts that 11° from 048° and turns to 037° by his compass.

The situation at boat B is very different. The 0° mark on his compass is pointing at 349° true, which is 11° to the west of true north. To put it another way, true north is already 011° by his compass; to take a heading of 048° true he has to *add* that 48° to the 11° of the variation giving him a

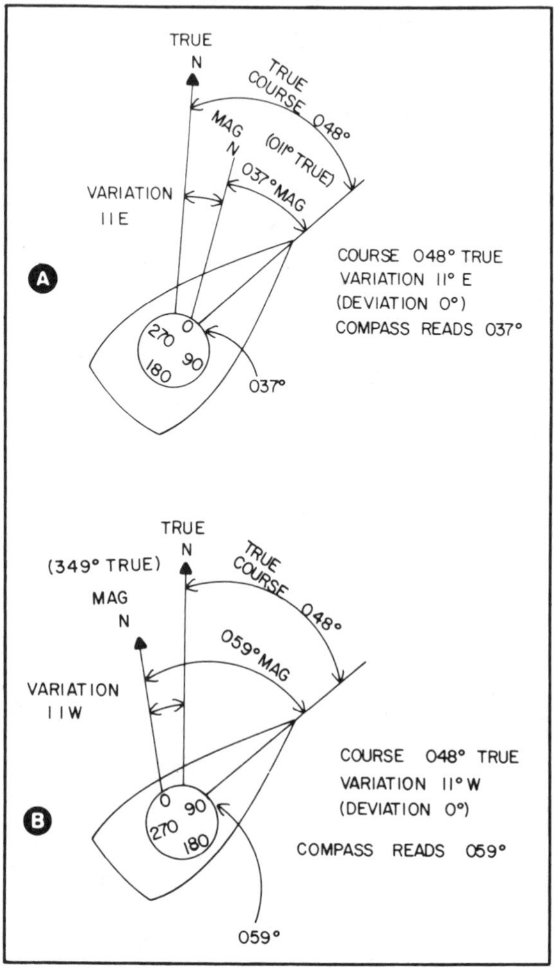

TRUE
N
TRUE COURSE 048°
MAG N
(011° TRUE)
037° MAG
VARIATION
11E
A
COURSE 048° TRUE
VARIATION 11° E
(DEVIATION 0°)
COMPASS READS 037°
0
270
90
180
037°
TRUE
N
(349° TRUE)
MAG
N
TRUE COURSE 048°
059° MAG
VARIATION
11W
B
COURSE 048° TRUE
VARIATION 11° W
(DEVIATION 0°)
COMPASS READS 059°
0
90
270
180
059°

Fig. 4-20. Two boats on 048-degrees True: a variation = 11 degrees E; B variation = 11 degrees W.

compass heading of 059°. Variation, remember, is the same for all boats in an area—large or small, sail or power—because variation is an irregularity in the magnetic field of the earth.

Two more examples of variation are given in Fig. 4-21. Boat A is sailing a course of 141° magnetic. Because the variation in this area is 9°W, his compass reads 9° more than the true direction of his heading, which is 132°. Boat B making good a course of 241° true. With a 12° easterly variation in his area, his compass will read less than his true course by that 12° (or 229°).

The math required for deviation corrections or uncorrections is exactly the same as for variation.

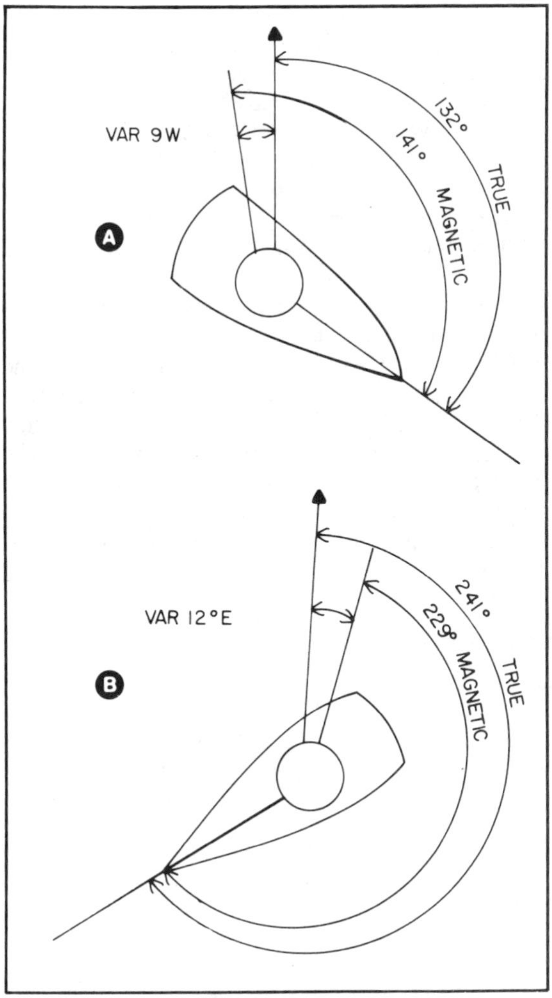
VAR 9W
132°
141°
TRUE
MAGNETIC
A
VAR 12°E
241°
229°
MAGNETIC
TRUE
B

Fig. 4-21. Further examples of E and W variation.

Easterly deviation gives a compass reading lower (smaller number) than true. Westerly produces a larger number on the compass. While the math is the same, do not forget the big difference. Deviation is different on *every* boat, and it is not constant. It changes with each heading of that boat. To figure deviation accurately, the deviation card for the boat is needed.

When both variation and deviation are involved, correction from compass to true or uncorrection from true to compass might require two additions or two subtractions or one of each. There are four possible combinations of variation:

- ☐ Variation E - Deviation E.
- ☐ Variation W - Deviation W.
- ☐ Variation E - Deviation W.
- ☐ Variation W - Deviation E.

Figure 4-22 shows four different boats in four very different areas, but all on a true course of 091°.

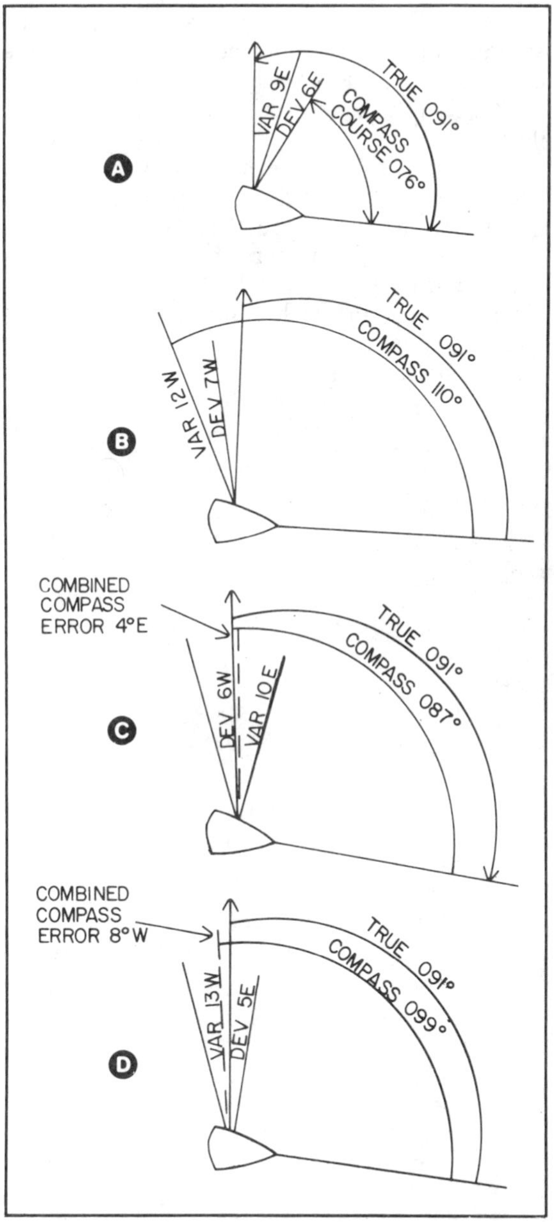
A
VAR 9E
DEV 6E
TRUE 091°
COMPASS COURSE 076°
B
VAR 12W
DEV 7W
TRUE 091°
COMPASS 110°
COMBINED COMPASS ERROR 4°E
C
DEV 6W
VAR 10E
TRUE 091°
COMPASS 087°
COMBINED COMPASS ERROR 8°W
D
VAR 13W
DEV 5E
TRUE 091°
COMPASS 099°

Fig. 4-22. Four types of combined compass errors: deviation and variation.

Vessel A has both variation and deviation east. Consequently, his compass course reflects a number smaller than the true direction by the amounts of both. To correct the compass course, add the easterly errors to reach true. To uncorrect the true to compass subtract them.

Vessel B has both variation and deviation westerly. Therefore, the compass course to be steered is the sum of the true direction, plus the deviation, plus the variation—making a total of 110° as the compass course required to head toward 091° true.

Vessel C has a little of everything. He has a variation of 10°E but a deviation of 6°W. Because he has errors in both directions he subtracts the lesser one from the greater. The result is the combined compass error. It is 4°E, which is treated as a single easterly error. It would be added to the compass course to give true or subtracted from true for the compass heading.

The last example, vessel D, also has errors in both directions. This time variation is west and deviation east. Again subtracting the lesser, 5°E, from the larger, 13°W, leaves a residual compass error of 8°W, which is now dealt with as a single westerly error.

One very basic procedure is the use of bearings on aids to navigation and charted landmarks to produce lines of position. These bearings require the use of the compass and the conversion of compass bearings to true for plotting on the chart. A common mistake that occurs in making these conversions is that people will inadvertently use the deviation off the boat's card for the bearing rather than the deviation for the heading when converting the bearing to true. *Never* use the deviation of the bearing for anything at all! Use only the deviation for the *heading*. This means when a bearing is recorded the heading the boat was on at the time must also be recorded with it.

Chapter 5

QUASAR

Dead Reckoning and Piloting

SAFELY DIRECTING A VESSEL FROM ONE PLACE to another is the definition of navigation. Dead reckoning and piloting are the two major divisions of navigation with which we are primarily concerned in coastal operation. These two divisions are so closely interrelated in coastal running that I shall discuss them as parts of the same chapter.

INSTRUMENTS

Because many of the instruments used in dead reckoning are also used in piloting, and vice versa, we'll get acquainted with the whole kit at once. Don't panic. There are only a few instruments you will need to know how to use, and they are very simple ones.

Charting Instruments

We use the chart to draw course lines and bearings so as to find the present position of the boat as well as to project future positions. This requires a few instruments similar to those used in mechanical drafting. One of these is called dividers (Fig. 5-1).

Dividers consist of two short metal bars connected by a pivot pin. The other end of each bar terminates in a sharp point. Be careful of those points. You do not want to dull or break them off. Get dividers made specifically for use aboard a boat. A pair that would be excellent for use in a drafting room on land will not do. Marine dividers are made of metal that will not corrode in the marine environment.

Dividers are used to measure distances on the chart and to exactly measure latitudes and longitudes. It is these latitude and longitude measurements that give us the precise position of the boat relative to various charted objects. The dividers are also used to answer time, speed, and distance questions with the help of the logarithmic speed scale (Fig. 2-17) printed on the chart.

The method to use for measuring distance with dividers depends on whether the distance to be measured is a short one, meaning within the span of the dividers, or a longer one, meaning several times that span. To measure short distances, place one point of the dividers on each end of the lines to be measured. Now maintaining the divider opening, move to the distance scale on the chart (Fig. 2-17) and read off the distance between the points. The distance scale is the best gauge to use on charts of the *Harbor Series* (Fig. 5-1). On the *Coast Series*, the latitude scales at the left- and right-hand sides of the chart are more accurate. As you should remember, one minute (1′) of latitude equals one nautical mile, and the latitude scale at the sides of

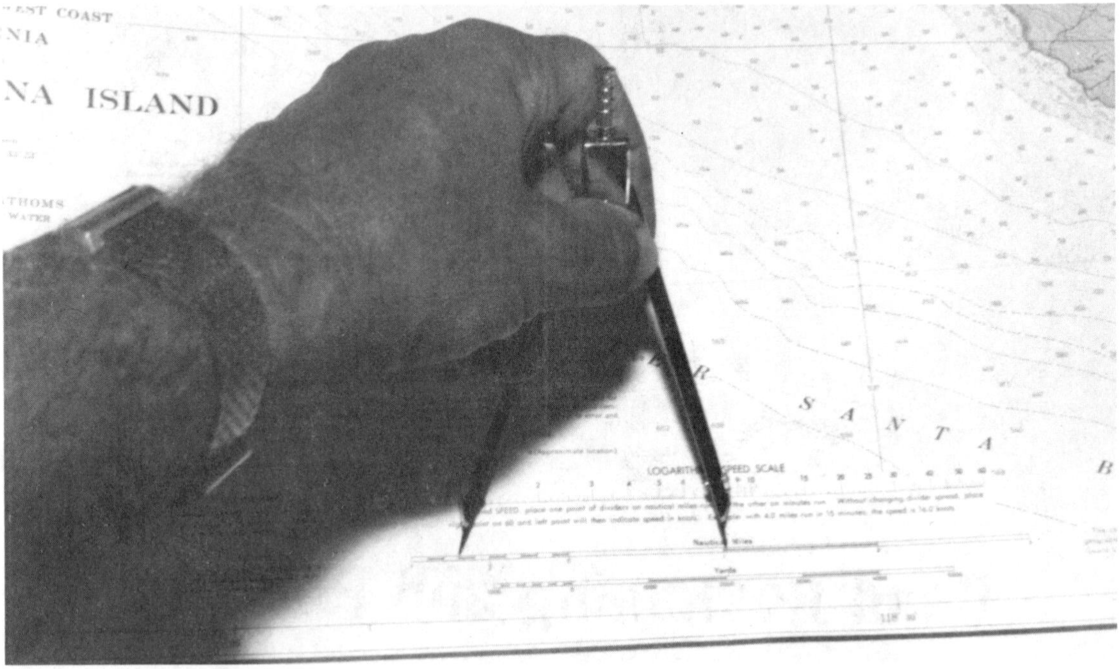
ISLAND

Fig. 5-1A. Measuring distance within one span of dividers on a distance scale.

the chart are marked (Fig. 2-15) in minutes and tenths. By counting the number of minutes and tenths across the divider opening (Fig. 2-16), you will have the number of nautical miles and tenths at the same time. *Be sure* to make distance measurements against the *latitude* scales at the *sides* of the chart. Never use the longitude scales at the top and bottom for this purpose.

To measure the distance represented by a line longer than the span of the dividers, go first to the latitude scale on the side of the chart. Set the dividers on an arbitrary distance (Fig. 5-2) shows dividers set at 1 mile). Next, flop the dividers along the line maintaining the preset span exactly. In this instance, the dividers were set for 1 mile and the length of the line allowed the dividers to flop five times before reaching a remainder that fell within that span. The five flops of the dividers equals 5 miles. Now adjust the divider to span only the remainder, take that to the latitude scale (in this case it measures 0.3 miles), and add the measurement found to the 5 miles found earlier. The complete length is 5.3 miles.

The determination of precise latitude and longitude of a given point on the chart is discussed and

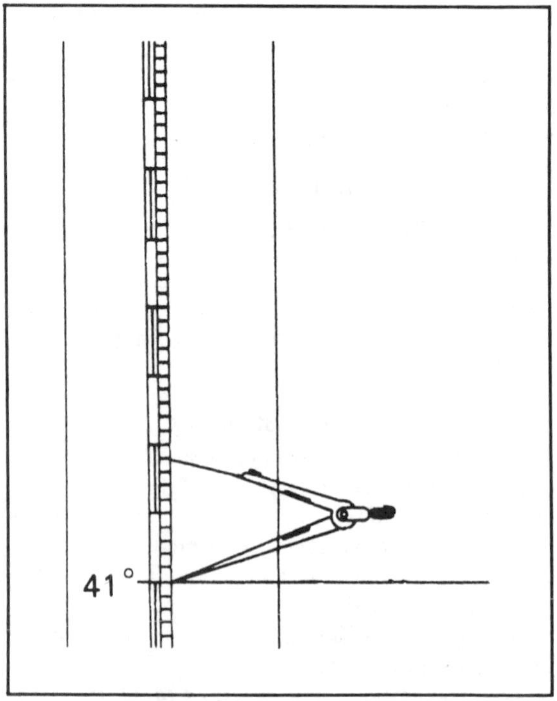
41°

Fig. 5-1B. Showing 1.8 miles on a latitude scale.

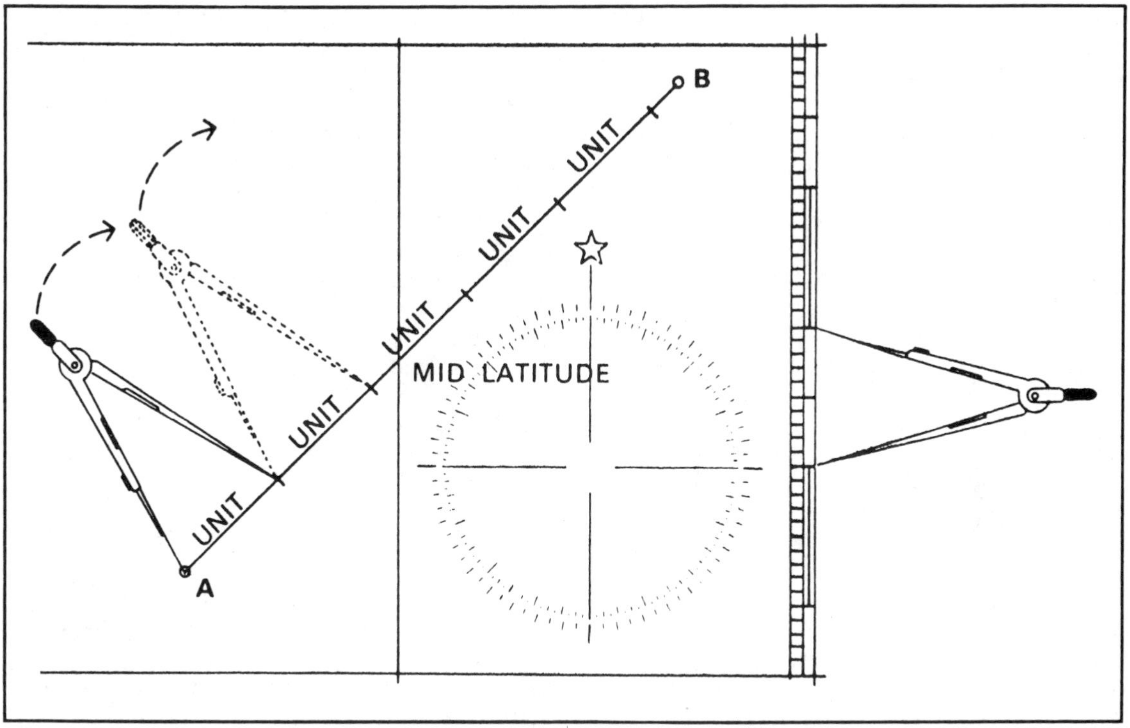
B
UNIT
UNIT
UNIT
UNIT
UNIT
MID LATITUDE
A
Fig. 5-2. Measuring distance greater than one span of dividers.

illustrated in Chapter 2. Always remember when making these measurements that in the Northern Hemisphere (where we are) latitude always increases as you work *up* from the bottom toward the top of the chart. Similarly, in the United States longitude will always increase from right to left.

To mark course lines, bearings, speeds, times, and other information on charts, use a pencil. *Never* use a pen. Only marks relating to the trip currently in progress should be on the chart. All others should be erased. Pen marks do not erase well!

For chart work, your pencil must be very sharp at all times. For this reason, use of an ordinary wood pencil is not advised. It cannot conveniently be kept really sharp. For several years, I have used a special mechanical drafting pencil of the type shown in Fig. 5-3. These pencils carry a supply of very thin leads internally. The leads are .5 millimeters thick and thus need no sharpening. Lead is manually fed from the internal supply.

Because these pencils are primarily for drafting work, leads are available ranging from very soft to very hard. For chart work, a lead that is too soft will smudge; one that is too hard will engrave the paper of the chart and not erase well. While many authorities recommend a 2H lead, I prefer an H. In any event, you surely should not use anything harder than a 2H or softer than an F. The amount of pressure that is comfortable when drawing a line on the chart differs for different people. Consequently, it would be a good idea for you to try F, H, and 2H to see which works best for you.

Because you are drawing with pencil, you will want a soft pencil eraser as well. Charts are printed on very heavy paper and are intended to resist considerable drawing and erasing. The more lightly you can manage to both draw and erase, however, the more service you will get from your charts.

Several devices are available to help you draw your course and bearing lines on the chart to the angles you need. These are parallel rules, course plotter, course protractor, and drafting triangles. There is no need to be horrified. You will not need them all! Most navigators get accustomed to one of the four and stay with it. A few use more than one. Each has certain advantages.

Parallel Rules. Parallel rules consist of two strips of transparent plastic (Fig. 5-4). They are connected by two short, pivoted metal or plastic strips that permit the rulers to be moved apart or back together, remaining always exactly parallel to each other. Parallel rules can be set on a bearing line. By alternately holding one side and moving the other, they can be "walked" to the nearest compass rose. There the bearing direction can be read. The course direction between two points is found in the same way by walking the rules from the course line to a compass rose. The reverse can also be done. To set a course of 035°, for example, from point A simply set the parallel rules on 035° at a nearby compass rose and walk them to point A. There draw the line and you have the course you want.

Because the parallel rules have no calibration marks on them, they are as accurate at angular measurement as the compass rose on the chart—which is very accurate indeed. But because this is a mechanical device with four pivot points, there is always a possibility of wear or looseness at one of those pivot points introducing error when the rules are walked.

As a consequence, they should periodically be checked for accuracy by walking them back and forth between printed horizontals or verticals on the chart. When walking parallel rules from one area to another on the chart, the stationary side must be held absolutely tight in place while the other side is moved. If there is the slightest slippage, the readings obtained will not be accurate.

Course Plotter. The course plotter is also transparent plastic. It is wider and thinner than either of the pieces used to make parallel rules (Fig. 5-5). A number of different models vary in the supplementary scales provided. Nevertheless, they are all similar in being marked with a series of parallel lines running lengthwise. In the middle of the plotter is a semicircle marked in degrees. Outside it is marked starting at 0° on the right going to 180° at the left. Inside it goes from 180° to 360°.

Inside the semicircle is a second arc also marked in degrees. This one starts at 120° outside on the right and ends at 240°. Inside it starts at 300° to the right going up to 360°/0° at the center. There it starts over at 0° and goes up to 60° at the left. The semicircle and the arc inside it are centered on a star or other identifying point.

The angles of courses or bearings are measured with the plotter directly by sliding it along the line until its star is centered on one of the charted vertical lines, indicating longitude, or on one of the horizontals marking latitude. As shown in Fig. 5-5, the plotter is on a vertical. If the course or bearing line is running from left to right, its angle is read where the longitude line passes through the scale on the *outside* of the semicircle as 70°. If it is

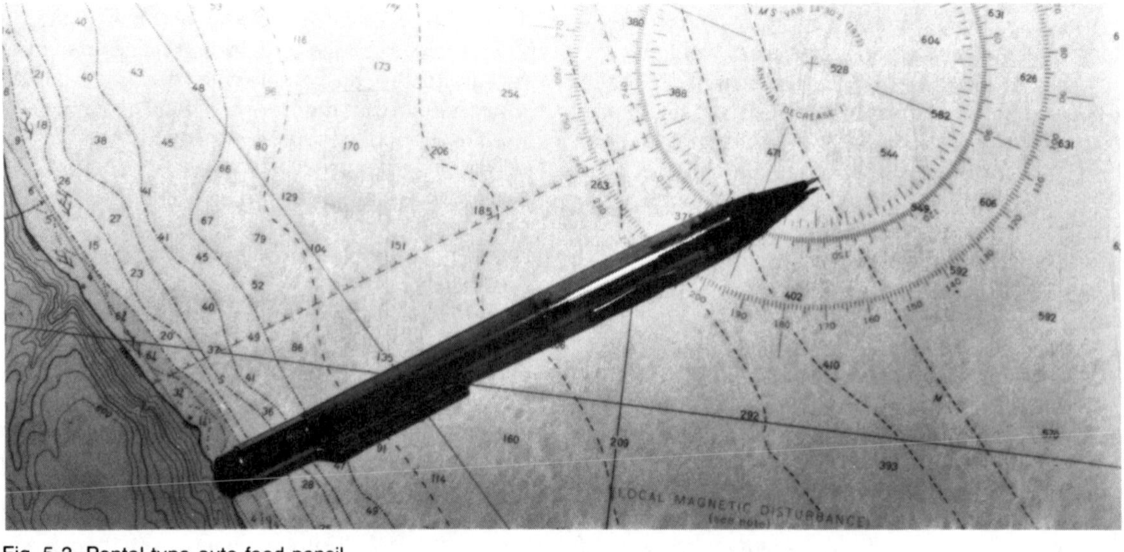
LOCAL MAGNETIC DISTURBANCE

Fig. 5-3. Pentel type auto-feed pencil.

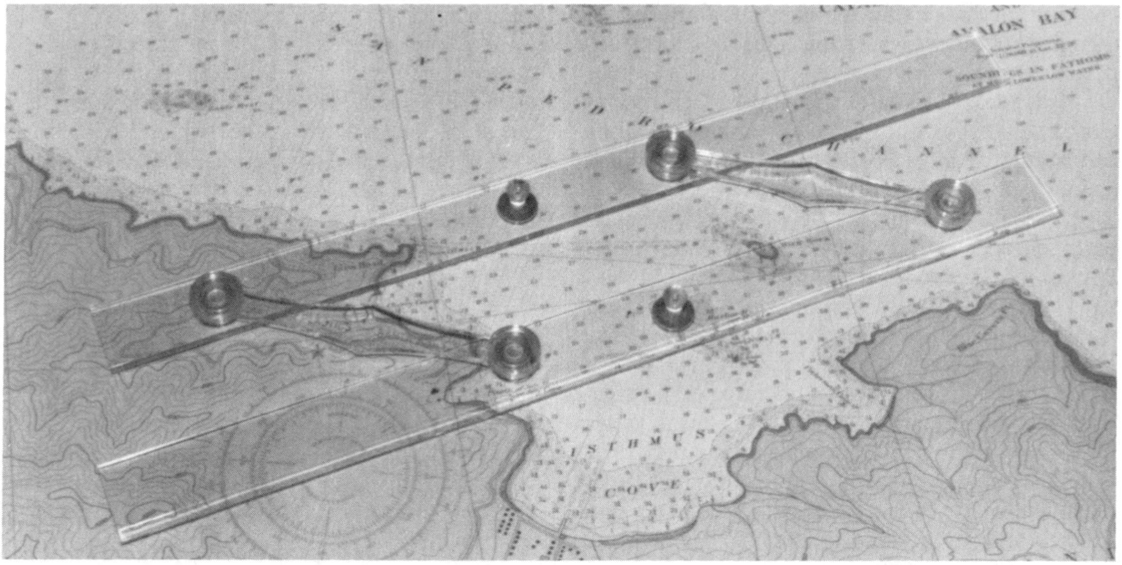
AVALON BAY

Fig. 5-4. Parallel rules.

running the other way—from right to left—it is read on the *inside* of the semicircle as 250°.

Another way to remember when to read outside and when to read inside of the semicircle is when the line is going anywhere east (right) of the vertical you read outside. When it is pointing *west* (left) of vertical read inside.

The inner arc is for reading angles using a horizontal or latitude line as the reference. When the star is on a horizontal line, move the plotter (Fig. 5-5) down the page a little. Lines heading north or above horizontal are read inside. Lines

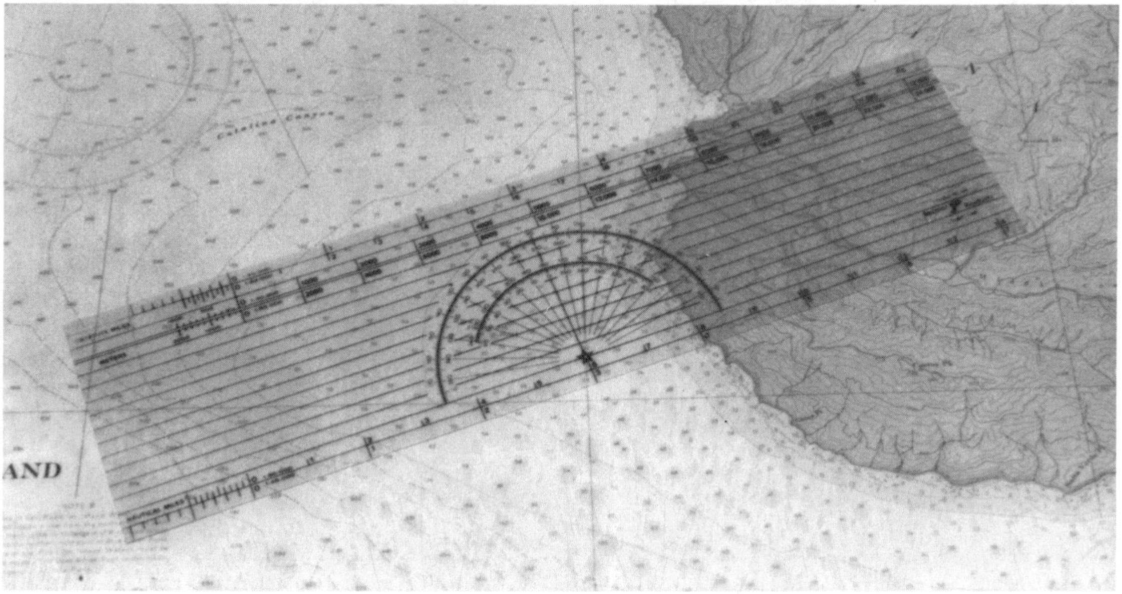
AND

Fig. 5-5. Course plotter.

pointing south or below the horizontal are read on the inside of the arc where the horizontal intersects it.

All course or bearing readings on the course plotter are *true*. If magnetic or compass readings are needed, variation and deviation must be accounted for (as shown in Chapter 4).

Because the course plotter has no mechanical parts, there is no way it can have any mechanical difficulties. Its accuracy, however, is only as good as the accuracy and legibility of the markings printed on it. Price differences generally show up as differences in printing accuracy and legibility.

Course Protractor. The course protractor consists of a compass rose printed on a transparent plastic square (Fig. 5-6). Attached to its center by a brass grommet is a swiveling arm. Alignment of the plastic square with any charted horizontal or vertical line aligns the compass rose with true north. Subsequent alignment of the swivel arm with a course or bearing line permits its direction to be read from the protractor compass rose.

Like the course plotter, the course protractor is only as accurate as the printing job on its compass rose. I have never been able to make friends with any of the course protractors I have tried. I have found it a rather clumsy instrument to use. Don't let my experience deter you from trying one; you might be comfortable with it. After all, the reason there are several plotting instruments available is that some navigators like one while others prefer another. Try them all. Then choose the one you will use purely on the basis of what you like. Properly handled they are all accurate.

Drafting Triangles. For a good many years, and for no particularly good reason, I have used a simple pair of drafting triangles (Fig. 5-7) for plotting. I use a 12-inch 30° × 60° and either an 8-inch or a 10-inch 45° × 45°. I do not claim for an instant that these are inherently better in any way than any of the instruments previously mentioned. I use them solely because I became accustomed to them. The way they are handled is simple. They are "walked" from a course or bearing line to a nearby compass rose by holding one in place while sliding the other along one of its edges. Clearly the stationary one must be held very firmly to yield accurate readings.

Directions and Bearings

Hand-Bearing Compass. The direction of travel

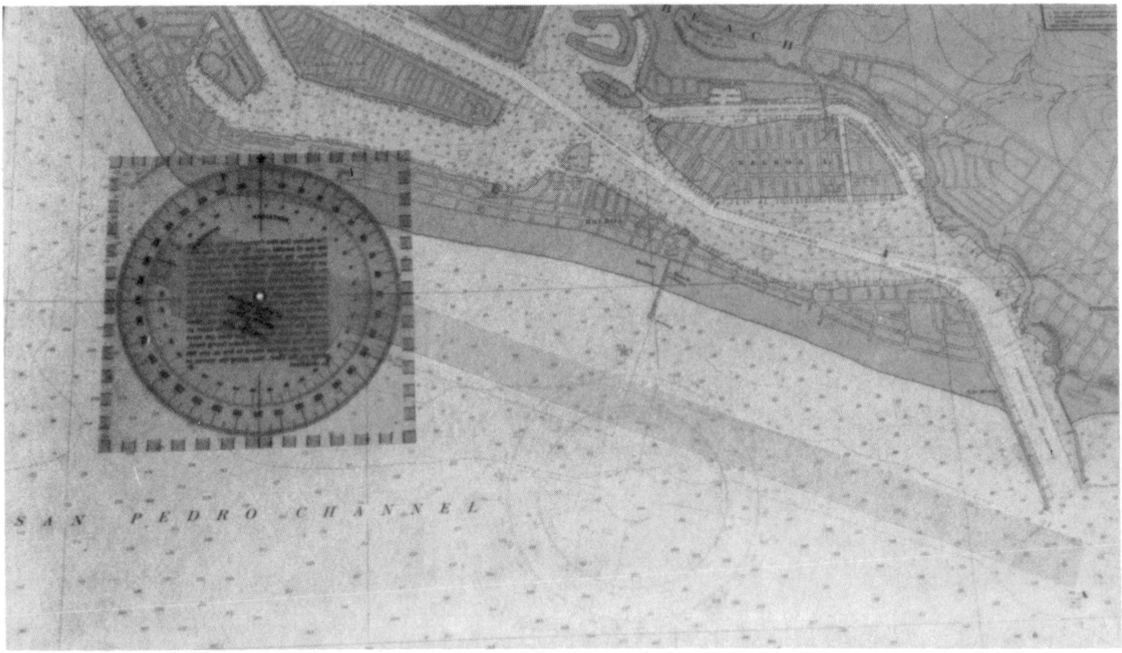
S A N P E D R O C H A N N E L

Fig. 5-6. Course protractor.

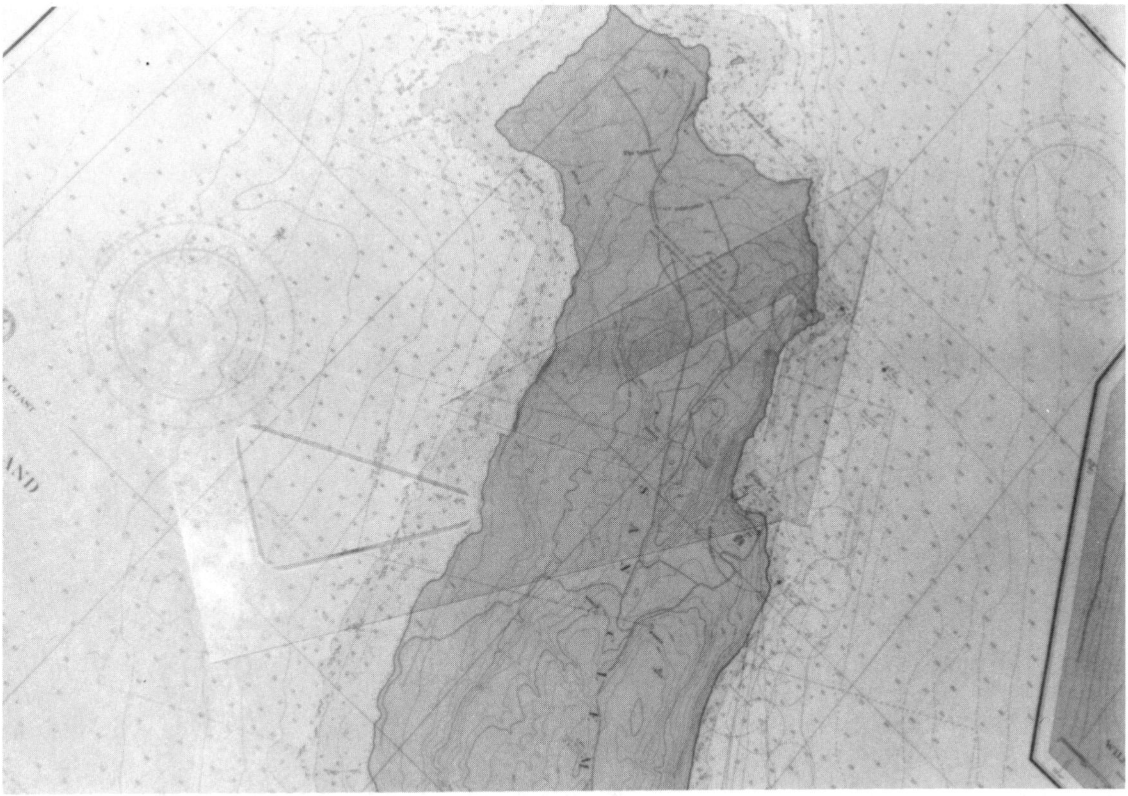

Fig. 5-7. Drafting triangles.

of the boat is found by reading the ship's compass. You have installed and checked it for deviation as described in Chapter 4, right? Nevertheless, the directions of significant objects in the area as seen from the boat are usually found with other instruments.

A most useful instrument for taking directional bearings that will produce lines of position is a hand-bearing compass (Fig. 5-8). A considerable variety of these are available (including some extremely compact models). By looking around, one can be found to fit in the most absurdly small storage space. As with your main compass, get one as large as storage space will allow. The larger it is the easier it will be to read, and the steadier the card will be. The movements of the boat will make this compass more difficult to read than the ship's compass. It will certainly be smaller.

A good many of these units, particularly the less expensive ones, are calibrated at 5° intervals. With these, it is necessary to interpolate by eye to get intermediate degrees. The more expensive models are calibrated in individual degrees.

I have one calibrated to single degrees, but I have often used 5° models. On a large boat that provides a fairly steady platform from which to take bearings, the added accuracy of the 1° card has value. On small, bouncy, unsteady boats, I am not convinced that the 1° card has any advantages at all.

Most hand-bearing compasses are equipped with battery-powered lights for night use. Check to ensure that the one you are getting is so equipped. Unless you do a lot of night running, it is a good idea to remove the batteries after each use. Most of us do little night running. If you leave the batteries in the compass, there is a lively possibility that they will go dead by the time you need them again. In accordance with Murphy's law, it is certain you will have no spares aboard that night. If you know you have to put batteries in the hand-bearing compass to use it on the odd-night run, then the batteries are more likely to be fresh. In addition, old dry cells

SE
150
120
E
NE
60
30
Fig. 5-8. Hand-bearing compass.

have been known to burst and corrode the container case quite badly.

The Pelorus. The instrument for taking bearings on objects relative to your boat is called a pelorus (Fig. 5-9). For years I wondered about the origin of that word because it seemed to have no relation to piloting, navigation, or directions. It appears that a chap named Pelorus guided Hannibal safely out of Italy; so there is a connection after all. The pelorus is also called a *dumb compass*. It is actually a dummy or false compass. It has a compass card calibrated at 360° that can be both swiveled about and clamped in place manually. Above that is a sight vane that also swivels above the compass card.

The pelorus can be used in either of two ways. When the pelorus card is set with its zero in alignment with the bow of the boat, all bearings taken will be *relative bearings*. A bearing was defined in Chapter 1 as the direction toward an object or place from another object or place expressed in degrees from 000° to 360°. When the bow of the boat is the reference point, relative bearings on objects around that boat are measured clockwise around the boat from the bow in degrees of angle (Fig. 5-10). The cupola (a slender tower on top of a building) bears 073° relative only to the boat. To find its true bearing, you need to know the direction toward which the boat is heading.

This brings us to a second way in which the pelorus is used. Because the pelorus card can be moved, it can readily be set to match the compass heading. When this is done, a pelorus bearing becomes at the same time a compass bearing. By accounting for deviation and variation, as described in Chapter 4, the compass bearing becomes a true bearing. As we shall presently see, that true bearing is drawn on the chart as a "line of position." At the time the bearing was taken, the boat was somewhere on the line.

The difficulty involved in this type of bearing is the matter of synchronizing the setting of the pelorus with the compass. As you will soon discover, if you have not already, it is very hard to maintain an exact compass heading for any length of time on a small boat under way. If the pelorus is set to a compass heading, but then the boat's bow wanders somewhat before the bearing is taken, that bearing is useless.

A better way to do it is to leave the pelorus set for relative bearings so it reads 000° parallel to the centerline of the boat. Now, place one person at the pelorus and a second person at the helm watching the compass. When the person at the pelorus has

Fig. 5-9. Pelorus.

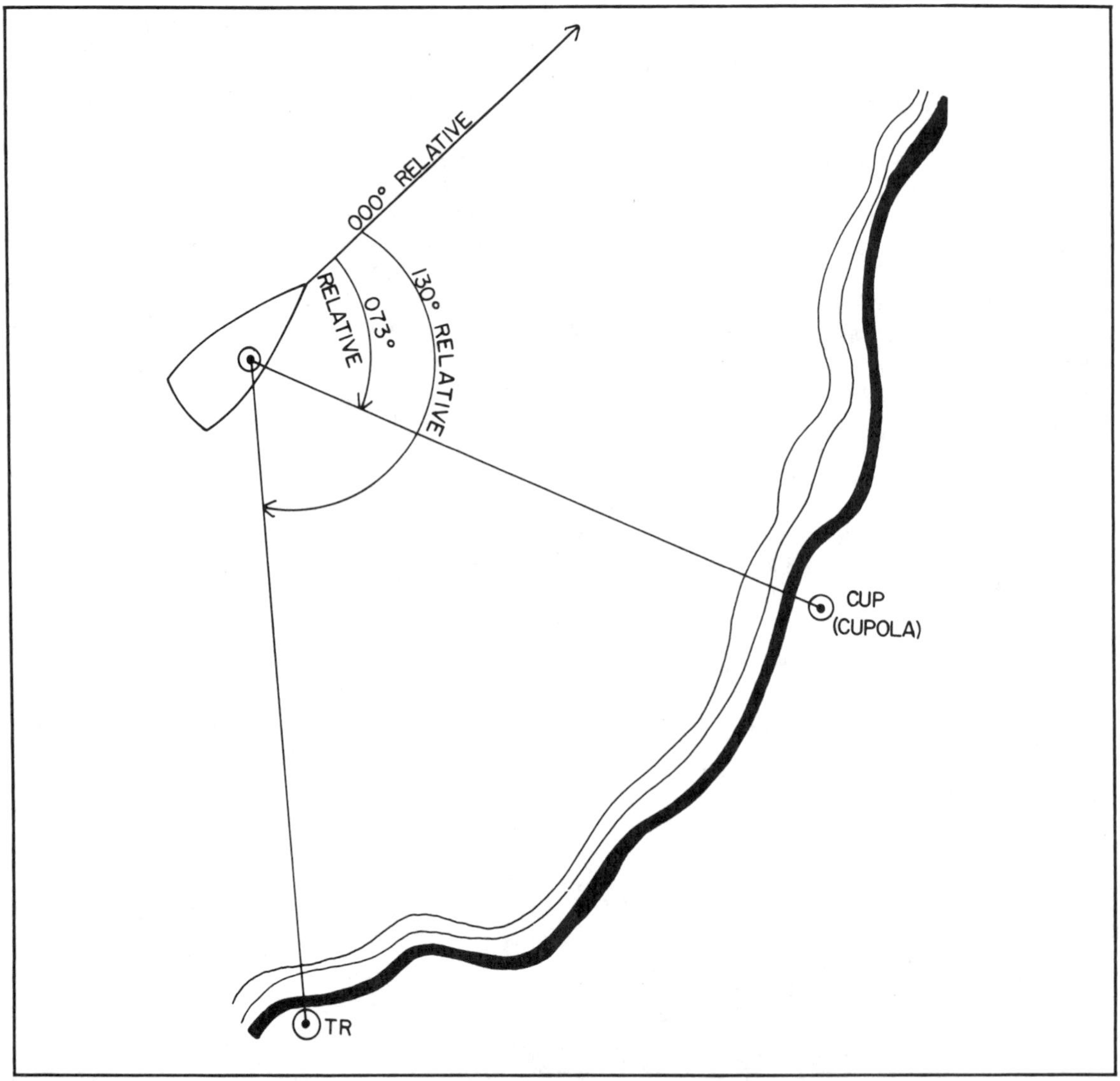
000° RELATIVE
073° RELATIVE
130° RELATIVE
CUP
(CUPOLA)
TR

Fig. 5-10. Relative bearings.

the desired object aligned in his sights, he is to call loud and clear to the helmsman "mark."

The helmsman notes the exact reading of the compass at that instant and calls it back to the person on the pelorus—who immediately writes down the compass reading, his pelorus reading, and the exact time. By adding the pelorus reading to the compass reading, a compass bearing has been obtained (Fig. 5-11). As shown in Fig. 5-11, note that the compass heading (315°) plus the relative bearing (125°) exceeds 360°. The final compass bearing is then found by subtracting 360° from the total.

The compass *bearing* in this case was 080° while the compass *heading* was 315°. When correcting that bearing in order to plot a line of position, remember that deviation depends on the *heading* of the boat. Therefore, be sure to use the deviation for the heading (315°), *not* the deviation for the bearing of 080°. The deviation for 315° is to be added to or subtracted from the 080° bearing to arrive at the correct magnetic bearing. Adding or subtracting the variation for the area will now produce the true bearing which, when plotted on the chart, becomes a true line of position.

Radio Direction Finder. Many readers may think of the radio direction finder (RDF) as a large, complicated, and very expensive instrument suitable only for very large vessels. Not so. Many small, comparatively inexpensive models are available that can be operated using a selfcontained battery bank. Or they can also be powered by the 12-volt battery of the boat. Because they normally cover the AM frequency band as well as the marine radio beacon band, they can be used to provide news, music, and weather reports when not in use for direction finding.

A more elaborate RDF includes reception on FM, citizen's band (CB), and the VHF/FM marine communications bands, as well as the marine beacon and AM bands. The five-band models do get more expensive, but they are still small, light (8 to 12 pounds), and either self-powered or they also can be connected to the boat battery.

With small, portable AM radios, you might have noticed that the volume on a given station can be changed considerably by facing the set in different directions. This is because the internal loop antenna picks up the signal better when it is at right angles to the direction of the transmitter. It fades when the loop is in line with that same direction. This simple fact is the basis for the operation of an RDF.

An RDF (Fig. 5-12) as used on small boats is simply a good-quality portable radio receiver that has a compass rose and a swiveling directional antenna on top. It also has, in addition to the normal tuning dial on its front, a ***null meter***. The null meter indicates the changes in the strength of the signal being picked up by the directional antenna as it is rotated in different directions.

The RDF can be installed anywhere that happens to be convenient. Just be certain it is at least 3 feet away from the compass. The RDF speaker contains a magnet that will completely upset the compass if it gets too close. It makes no difference which way the RDF is faced because the directional

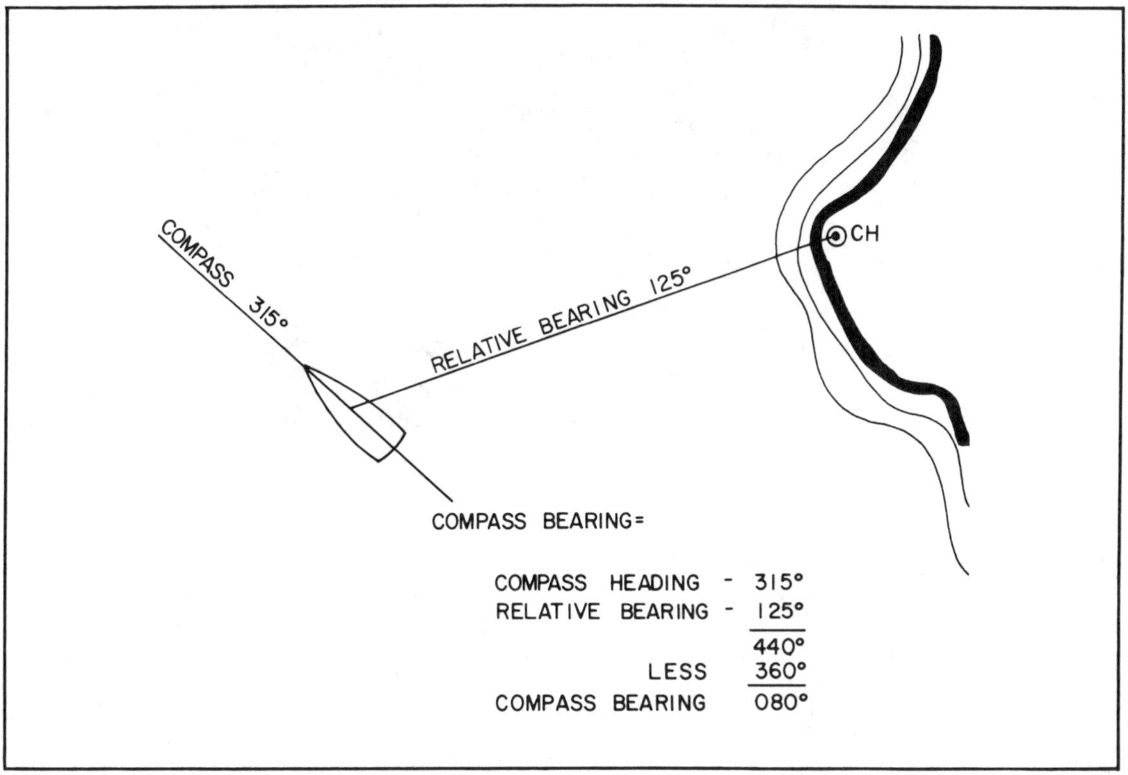
COMPASS 315°
RELATIVE BEARING 125°
CH
COMPASS BEARING=
COMPASS HEADING - 315°
RELATIVE BEARING - 125°
440°
LESS 360°
COMPASS BEARING 080°

Fig. 5-11. Relative bearing with compass heading becomes compass bearing.

RAY JEFF
660/ADF
SENSE VERIFY DIAL
MAN ADF LIGHT
EAR
MODE
BECN
AM
CB
VHF
FM
VOLUME
LOG

Fig. 5-12. Radio direction finder.

antenna on its top will rotate through 360° and the compass rose under the antenna can be rotated as well.

With the RDF located in the boat, its compass rose must be set so that the 000° mark is aligned with the bow of the boat. To take a radio bearing, a procedure similar to that used when taking a pelorus bearing is followed. One person is on the RDF and another is at the helm.

Tune the RDF to a beacon or broadcast station whose transmitter antenna location is known. Rotate the RDF antenna until the null meter shows minimum signal strength. Read the instructions that come with the instrument. On some models, minimum reading is at the top of the scale and on others it is at the bottom.

When the person at the RDF has found the minimum reading he calls "mark" to the helmsman, who calls back the compass reading at that moment. The RDF directional antenna is now showing two readings on its compass rose, 180° apart. Based on the compass course of the boat, its roughly estimated position, and the known location of the transmitter, one of these is generally logical as the direction of the station. The other is normally absurd. If you have been plowing about in a fog and are completely lost so that neither direction showing on the RDF is necessarily absurd, the instrument has a sensing antenna and circuit to discriminate between the two.

The marine radio beacon system, as discussed in Chapter 3, is operated by the Coast Guard. All beacons are noted in the *Light Lists* that give the exact transmitter locations. They also contain Radiobeacon Charts giving station frequencies, identification signals, and schedules of operation.

Some radiobeacons operate continuously and others are *sequenced.* A sequenced beacon operates on the same frequency with up to five other beacons. Each one broadcasts for one minute at a time and then goes off while the others take their turns. The order of these sequences can be found in the *Light List* and on the charts. When a Roman numeral follows the number indicating the beacon's broadcast frequency, that numeral shows its place in sequence. Sequenced beacons are grouped together for convenient identification on the radiobeacon charts.

In addition to the specially maintained radiobeacons, the RDF can be used to take bearings on any station in the standard broadcast band for which the transmitting antenna location is known. Occasionally the antenna is at the same location as the studios, but quite often it is several miles away. In some cases, where an antenna structure is visible from sea, it is charted and its station call letters and broadcast frequency given. For a station not so charted but whose signal is particularly strong where you are sailing, you can chart it yourself. Call or visit the station and ask for the exact geographic location of their antenna as given on the station license in latitude and longitude. Mark that spot accurately on your chart and you will have an excellent object to use for lines of position.

The RDF is subject to deviation errors that result from reflection of radio signals by rigging wires or other metal objects on the boat. A deviation card for the RDF can be readily prepared by taking simultaneous relative bearings on the RDF and the pelorus using a visible beacon as the objective. As with the compass, if you get deviation readings about every 15°, you will be in good shape. RDF deviation varies with the bearing and not with the heading of the boat, as is the case with a compass.

Other Useful Instruments

In addition to knowing which way the boat is going and what the directions of various objects are from the boat, some other types of information are also useful to the person trying to keep track of where the boat is. Knowledge of the speed of the boat through the water coupled with the time it has been running lets you calculate roughly how far you have moved. That calculation will not be entirely accurate because the effects of wind, current, and steering errors will throw it off. An approximation is better than nothing, however, so an instrument to measure speed is going to be helpful.

When you are working in close to shore or in narrow channels—even when you have a very accurate plot of your position and the chart indicates enough water under you—you are much safer if you can take a direct sounding of the depth of that water. An electronic depth sounder, or at least a lead line, will help here.

Speedometers. Two basic types of speedometers are used on small boats. One type consists of a through-hull sensor connected by a cable to the dial on the instrument panel. On most newer units, the sensor is activated by a small rotor or paddlewheel. Many older units used a Pitot tube. In either case, if you are trailering the boat, it must be loaded and unloaded very carefully in order to avoid damage to the sensor. Most paddlewheel sensors can be removed for servicing even while the boat is in the water. This is an important feature. With the sensor protruding outside the hull, it can easily be damaged or jammed by floating debris.

Speedometers are also available with a cumulative log that keeps a record of the distance run. These logs can be zeroed and reset for each trip. Always remember that the distance shown on a cumulative log is distance through the water. As we shall see, this is not the same as distance over the ground. If we are to move 10 miles over the ground in an hour against a 2-knot current we shall have to move 12 miles through the water. By the same token if that same 2-knot current is behind us—in order to move 10 miles over the ground in an hour—we'll only have to move 8 miles through the water. The movement of the water supplies the other 2 miles.

The other type of speedometer is the hand-held unit (Fig. 1-1). These are really not as accurate as the through-hull type; they are more difficult to read and are often rather a nuisance to use. Nevertheless, they are vastly less expensive. They are not subject to the sensor damage of the through-hull unit, and for short trips a high degree of accuracy is not required.

Depth Sounders. The depth sounder emits sound from a part called the transducer mounted in the hull. The time required for that sound to reach the bottom and bounce back to the transducer is converted by the instrument into a reading of the water depth at that spot. Always remember that the instrument reading is the water depth from the transducer location to the bottom, not the surface, and not the bottom of your keel either unless that is where the transducer is mounted which is unlikely. If the transducer is mounted 1½ feet below the surface—and the bottom of your keel is 2′ below that—when the depth sounder reads 6 feet you have only 4 feet of water under the keel.

Some sounders give their readings as a flashing spot on a circular dial; others have a digital readout. The flasher type is more difficult to read accurately, but an experienced operator can get much more information from it. The character of the flash indicates the nature of the bottom. Certain kinds of multiple flashes indicate, for fishermen, the presence of fish and their depth. Some models are equipped with a depth alarm that will alert the helmsman when the water becomes dangerously shallow.

If there simply is not space for a depth sounder or the bank account will not cover fixing the kids' teeth and a sounder as well, then either get or make a lead line. This consists simply of a length of light line with a weight at the end and plastic tags marking various distances along that line. Drop the weight in the water, and when it hits bottom the plastic tags tell you how much line is out. The major disadvantage with a lead line is that the boat must be either stopped or moving very slowly in order to get an accurate sounding.

Remember also that it has a couple of very big advantages: it is not affected by a power failure, and it is not subject to mechanical or electronic breakdown. Even if you have an electronic depth sounder, it is not a bad idea to keep a lead line handy just in case of breakdown. Again in accordance with Murphy's law, failure will only occur when you are feeling your way across shoal water at dusk in a pea soup fog, and you really *need* that depth sounder.

Timepiece

A quality timepiece is an essential tool in both dead reckoning and piloting. Our concern with time has to do mainly with elapsed time. Again and again we need to know how long we have been running on a particular course or exactly when a particular bearing was taken. Consequently, we need either a digital watch or a standard watch with large numbers and a sweep second hand, making it easy to read it at a glance.

Presently, very good digital watches are available at reasonable cost, and most are equipped with internal lights for convenient reading at night.

Binoculars. A good pair of binoculars is a must for successful piloting. The correct power for the purpose is 7 × 35 or 7 × 50. The seven here refers to the magnification. On a small boat, avoid magnifications higher than that because the combination of movement and vibration on the boat will make them difficult to use.

The second number is the diameter of the front lens (in millimeters). The larger lens becomes important if you expect to operate a lot at night. The larger lens is also more expensive. If you do not expect to do much night operating, save a few dollars and use the 7 × 35.

DEAD RECKONING

In Chapter 1, the scope of dead reckoning is briefly outlined. Using dead reckoning, you will project the position of your boat in time and space without regard for the deflecting effects of wind, current, steering errors, or anything else. Because wind, current, and steering errors do alter both the course and speed of the boat, you are probably wondering why you should bother to work out DR positions at all if you know ahead of time that they will be inaccurate. Perhaps so, but not as inaccurate as you might think.

You might be astonished to learn that Christopher Columbus (*Ital.* Cristoforo Colomob / *Span.* Cristobal Colon), one of the great navigators of all time, navigated four times back and forth across the Atlantic Ocean, as well as in and around the West Indies again and again, *solely by dead reckoning*. He had an astrolabe, an early sighting instrument, but he did not know how to use it! He also had a quadrant (another early sighting device). On one occasion, using a quadrant, he took a sight for latitude from an island that was actually at 21° N. By mistaking another star (Alfirk) for Polaris, he came up with a latitude of 42° N which is south of Boston near Plymouth, Massachusetts)! Nevertheless, he was a superlative DR navigator.

Yes, the inherent errors in DR navigation are such that you can be absolutely certain at the end of one or two hours running time that the one place on the entire chart where you are *not* is the DR position you have computed for that time. But you can be equally sure that, when you are able to fix your position exactly, your fix will be *near* that DR. The value of the DR is that, in the absence of additional information, it provides a helpful approximation of the position of the boat.

When running in conditions of poor visibility—or in a fog with no visibility at all—accurate recording of time, speed, and course, together with careful plotting and good steering, can get you to safety by dead reckoning alone. If only for this purpose, competence at dead reckoning is worth acquiring.

The Fix

All DR computations start from a position that is accurately known. This position is called a *fix*. The easy way to get an accurate fix from which to start is to come alongside a charted buoy and record the time (Fig. 5-13). As shown in Fig. 5-16, we have come alongside lighted buoy #22 to use it as our known point of departure. On the chart, draw a small circle on whatever side of the buoy you happen to be, put a dot in the center, and record the time: 0930 hrs.

The circle with the dot in its center is the standard symbol used in chart work to indicate a fix. No further explanation is needed. The time and the dot give the necessary starting information from which subsequent positions of the boat can be calculated.

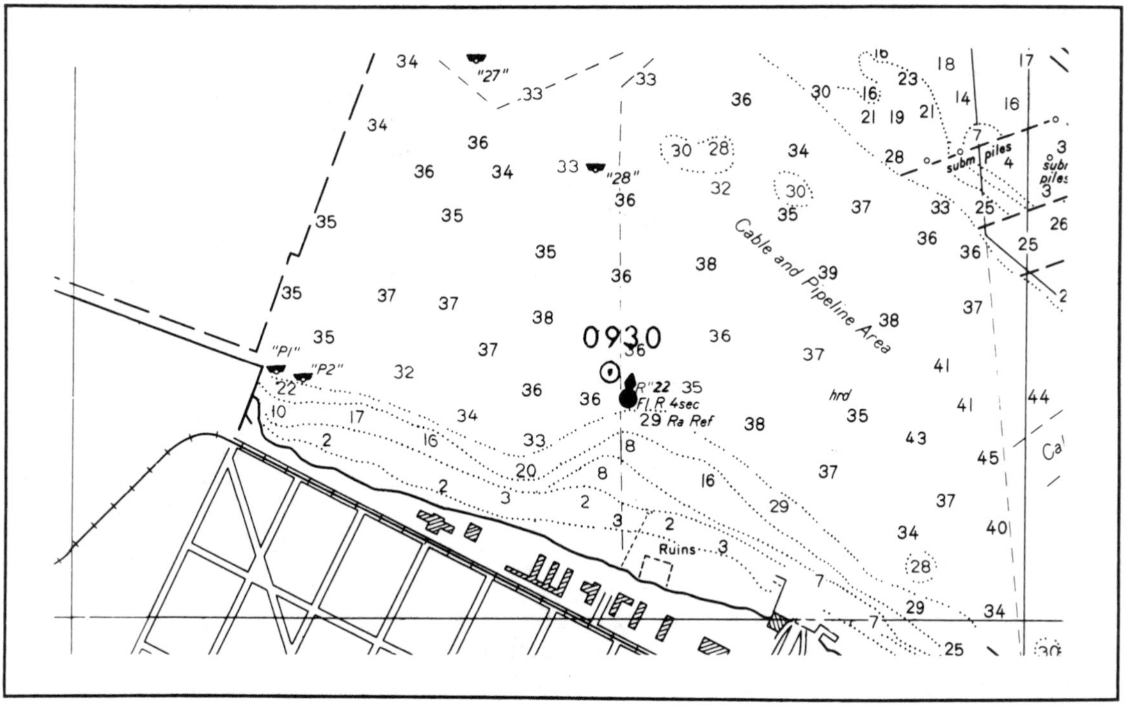

"27"
"28"
"P1"
"P2"
"22"
0930
R "22"
Fl. R. 4sec
Ra Ref
Cable and Pipeline Area
hrd
Ruins
subm piles

Fig. 5-13. Fix at buoy for start of DR plot.

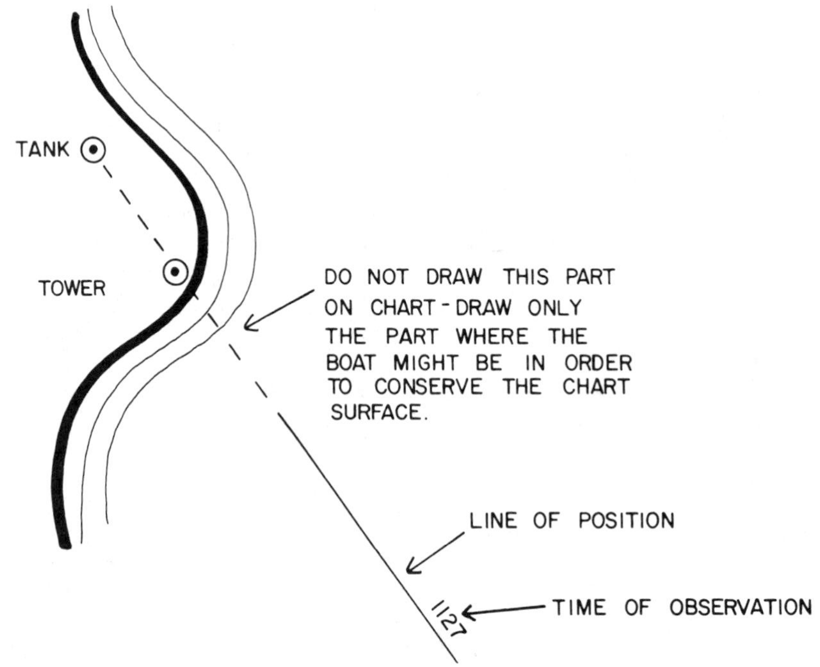
TANK
TOWER
DO NOT DRAW THIS PART ON CHART - DRAW ONLY THE PART WHERE THE BOAT MIGHT BE IN ORDER TO CONSERVE THE CHART SURFACE.
LINE OF POSITION
1127
TIME OF OBSERVATION

Fig. 5-14. LOP from range using charted objects.

This is fine if there happens to be a buoy or some other object handy where you want to start the DR plot. If not, some other way will have to be found to determine accurately the starting point. An excellent way is to cross two *lines of position* (LOPs). Correctly done, this fixes the boat at the intersection of the two lines.

A line of position is a line from some object that includes the position occupied by the boat. Our boat must be somewhere along that line, but we do not yet know where. A *range* constitutes a particularly good line of position. A range consists of any two charted objects aligned with each other (Fig. 5-14). Always note the time on an LOP.

Another reliable line of position is obtained from a bearing on a charted object (Fig. 5-15)—in this case a chimney. Such a bearing can be taken using a hand-bearing compass, or a pelorus, or can be taken over the permanently installed boat compass if its location permits. When using the hand-bearing compass, stand well clear of the engine or other large metal objects and take its reading as a magnetic bearing. As such, it can be plotted on the chart directly using the magnetic compass rose as the source of direction for the line. When this is done, the LOP is marked with the time above, in four digits, and the bearing direction in three digits below followed by the letter M to indicate that the direction noted is magnetic. When the bearing is corrected to true before plotting, that direction is noted below the LOP in three digits followed by the letter "T" to show it was corrected and plotted true as in Fig. 5-15.

When the pelorus is used to take the bearing, use the method described previously in this chapter. One person takes a relative bearing while a second person notes the compass heading at the time. The compass *heading* is then corrected for deviation before adding the relative bearing to that heading to obtain the magnetic bearing. Compass correction is discussed in Chapter 4. The magnetic bearing can be corrected for variation and plotted true or it can be taken as it is and plotted as magnetic. Just be sure an M or a T is there to show what was done.

When the bearing is taken over the ship's compass, the most common blunder people make is to correct for deviation using the bearing numbers instead of the *heading*. Sorry, this won't work!

After you have one line of position based either on a range or a single charted object, you need a second LOP to cross it and produce a fix. The second LOP (in this case a water tank) is taken in the same way as the first using some other object. Your first choice of objects to use for bearings should be fixed objects ashore. Floating aids to navigation should be your second choice because they move around their charted locations. Remember, the charted location of a buoy is the place where its mooring is dropped. The buoy is attached to that mooring by a chain that necessarily allows it some range of movement around the mooring location. Also, while it is not an everyday occurrence, storms, currents, or other forces occasionally move floating aids out of position. With two LOPs crossing each other, we now have (Fig. 5-16) a fix to use as the starting point for a DR plot.

Note: the fix in Fig. 5-13 was a circle with a dot in the center. This one is a circle around the crossing point of the two bearings. Either one indicates a fix and should be labeled with the time only.

The Dead Reckoning Plot

A DR plot that shows projected positions of the boat

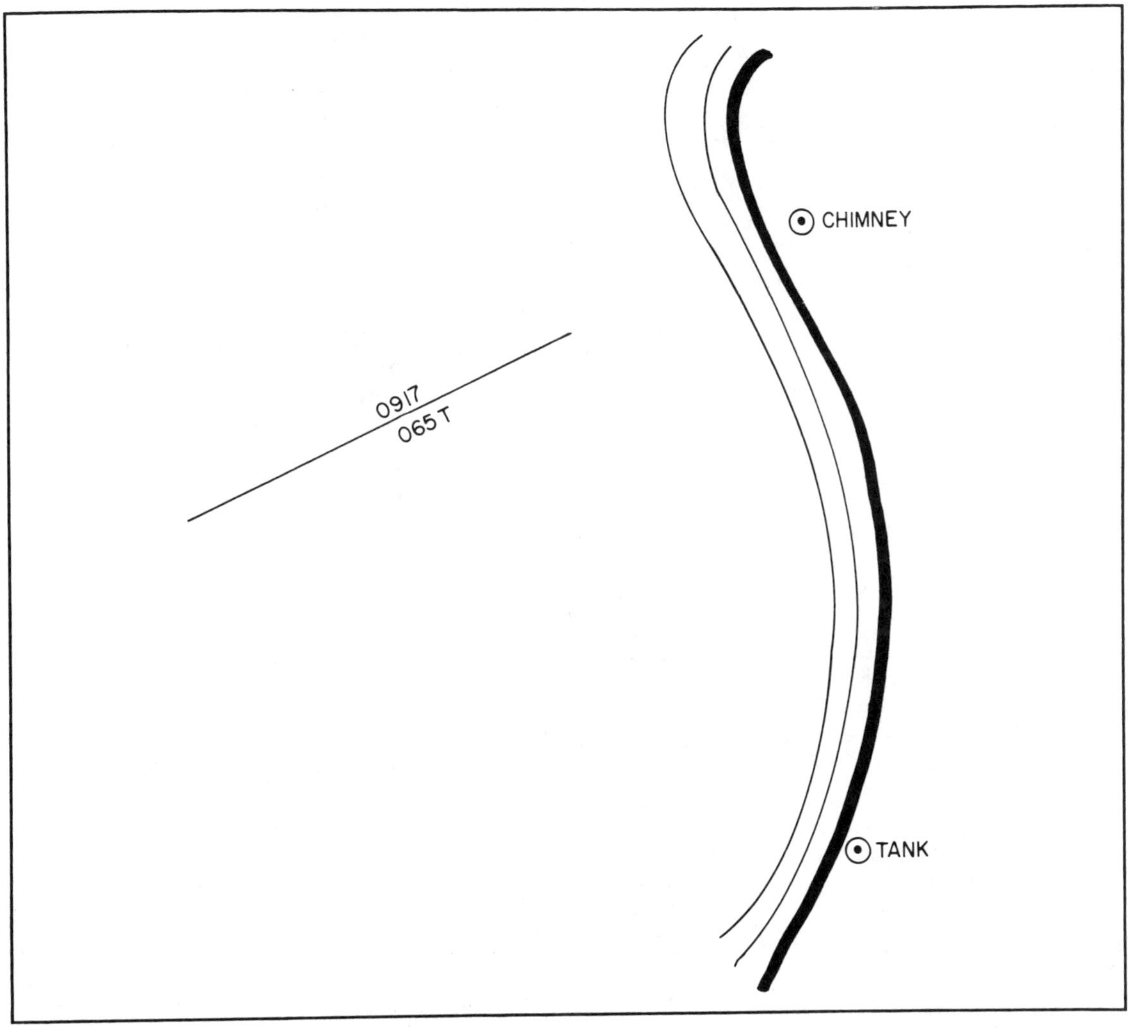
CHIMNEY
0917
065 T
TANK

Fig. 5-15. LOP from bearing.

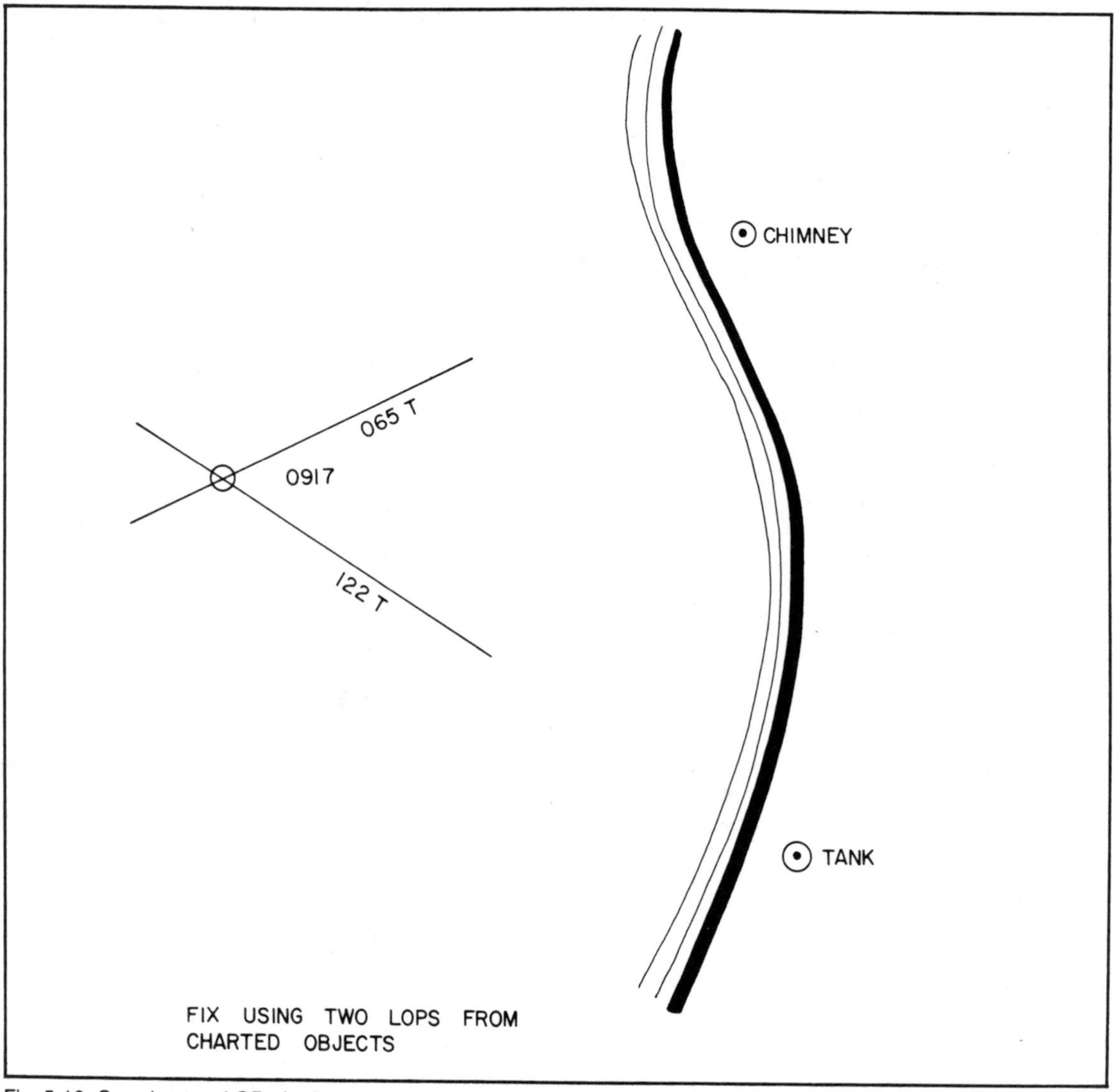
CHIMNEY
065 T
0917
122 T
TANK
FIX USING TWO LOPS FROM
CHARTED OBJECTS

Fig. 5-16. Crossing two LOPs for fix.

is often drawn on the chart in advance of starting a trip. This is done to give courses by which to steer and approximations of required running time.

Figure 5-17 shows an example of a simple plot of this type. Starting point "A" will be an easy one to fix visually when you get there, because it lies between two lighted markers at the ends of a pair of jetties. This point is termed the *departure*. Place a dot there and put a circle around it. From here we wish to proceed to point "E" on the east side of Point Loma.

Obviously, we cannot go directly there because land lies in the way. In addition, the chart—as well as local knowledge—tells us that all the way down along the coast there are kelp beds. This is West Coast Giant Kelp, big, thick, tough plants that will offer considerable interference to our boat. Therefore, we want to go outside the kelp beds. The plants grow as long as 100 feet or more so we want the water under us to be that deep or deeper in order to stay outside them. This being a Coastal Series Chart the soundings are in fathoms. A fathom is 6 feet. If we plan to stay outside the 10 fathom curve on the chart (60 feet), we will be clear of most of the kelp. It is easy to keep track of this line because the area inside the 10 fathom curve is tinted light blue on the chart. Outside it is white.

Taking our departure from point A, the first thing to do is to get plenty of sea room so as to stay outside the kelp. To accomplish this, we plan a run of 1½ miles straight out to sea in line with the channel we are leaving. This brings us to point B. By walking that course line with parallel rules up to the compass rose in the upper left-hand corner of the chart, we find we are on 249° magnetic (or 263° true). We've got to steer by compass so let's stay with the magnetic number. Because the compass is probably marked in 5° increments, it will not have a mark at 249°; but it will have one at 250°, making that an easy course to steer. For the moment we are ignoring deviation, OK?

If instead of the parallel rules you used a course plotter to find that course direction, the plotter shows 263° *true*. From that, subtract the 14° easterly variation shown in the center of the compass rose, in the upper left corner, which results in the same 249° magnetic found with the parallel rules. Again, 249° cannot be steered, but 250° can.

The course protractor will produce the same true reading as the plotter; therefore, it will be used in the same way. Many course protractors have an adjustable inner rose that can be set to the angle of the local variation. With these instruments, magnetic directions can be read directly. The drafting triangles will walk up to the compass rose in a similar manner to the parallel rules. Therefore, the triangle readings will be used in the same way as those from the parallel rules.

Having laid out a course to point B, we shall want to proceed from there in a southerly direction parallel to the coast and outside the kelp in order to reach our ultimate objective—point E. Starting this time at the compass rose, we find that due south true (180°) leaves us trying to steer 166° magnetic. Again move over 1° to 165° to get a more convenient course to steer. Transfer this direction to point B and draw a second course line toward what will be point C.

Around the intersection of the two course lines, draw a half circle. The half circle indicates a DR position at which, in this instance, a course change will be made. Because a change is to be made at that point, from one course to another, it is obviously necessary to note what those two courses will be. Therefore, the line coming from the departure point A is marked 250° *above* the line followed by the letter M to show that 250° magnetic is indicated. The line going south from point B is labeled 165° M.

Following the course of 165° M southward, we see that a short distance beyond Point Loma the 10 fathom curves begins to slant diagonally off toward the east. This being the case, at any convenient point in that area a course change may be made. The new one will slant down to the main ship channel running back up on the east side of the Point to position E (the desired objective).

When we come to actually run these courses, it will be much easier if the distances to be run are simple numbers. From point B, a distance of an even 6 miles will put us at point C. This looks like a good place for a course change. From there an easy diagonal will keep us outside the 10 fathom curve until we are in the main ship channel just beyond a line between buoys #1 and #3. After walking back and forth to the compass rose a couple times, we settle on a course of 110° M from point C; 110° M is divisible by 5° and hence will be found on the steering compass.

At point C, a half circle at the intersection of the course lines again defines the point as a DR position. Also, the third course line must be labeled as 110° M.

From point C, a distance of 3 miles (exactly) places us just barely beyond the channel limit marked by the odd-numbered buoys. Therefore, we plan to run another ½ mile, making point D a distance of 3.5 miles from point C. From D to E, we set a distance of 2.5 miles and a course angle of 345° M (another number that will be marked on the steering compass). At D, we again place a semicircle on the course intersection and label the final course 345° M. The final semicircle at position E completes the DR plot for this trip.

Speed, Time, and Distance

Chapter 1 points out that dead-reckoning navigation enables us to project positions of a boat ahead in time and space. This can be done using a very simple math. If fifth-grade multiplication or division causes difficulties, take along a pocket calculator. Joking aside, a pocket calculator is very useful on

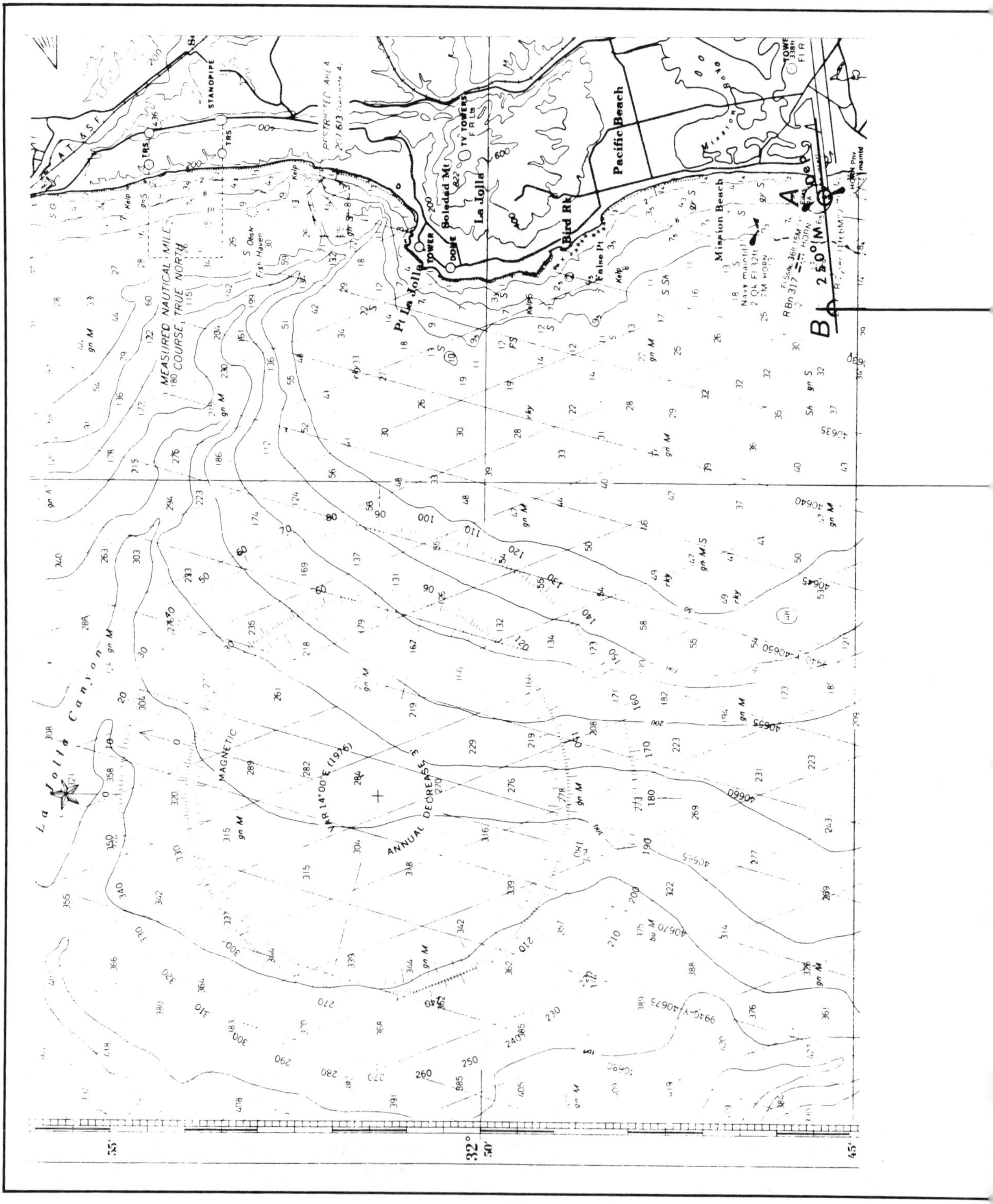

La Jolla Canyon
MEASURED NAUTICAL MILE
COURSE, TRUE NORTH
Pt La Jolla
Soledad Mt
La Jolla
Bird Rk
False Pt
Pacific Beach
Mission Beach
MAGNETIC
VAR 14°00'E (1976)
ANNUAL DECREASE 3'
STANDPIPE
TV TOWERS

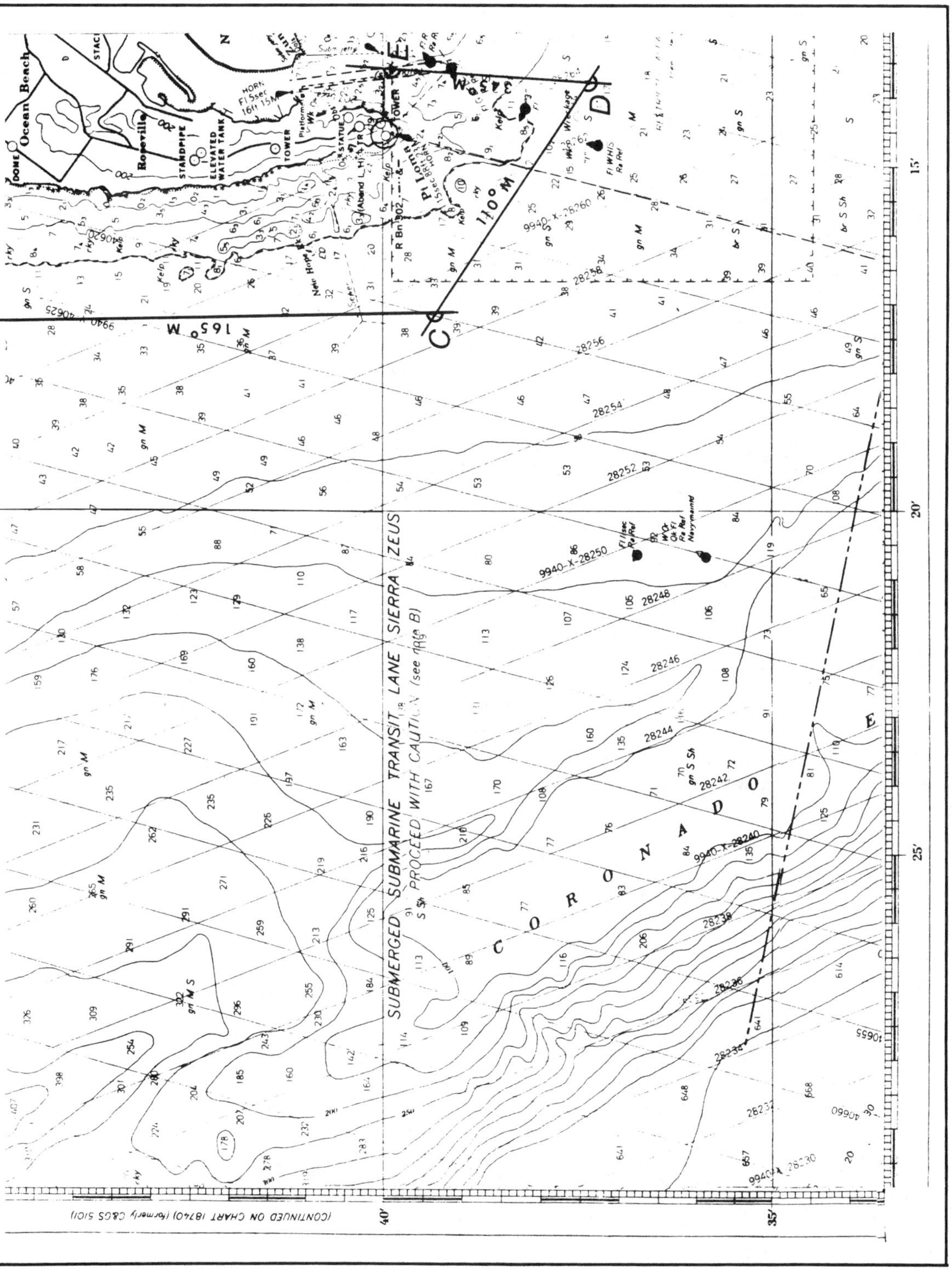
Ocean Beach
Roseville
STANDPIPE
ELEVATED WATER TANK
TOWER
Pt Loma
110° M
165° M
SUBMERGED SUBMARINE TRANSIT LANE SIERRA ZEUS
PROCEED WITH CAUTION (see note B)
C O R O N A D O
(CONTINUED ON CHART 18740) (formerly C&GS 5101)

Fig. 5-17. DR plot on chart (Mission Bay to Point Loma).

the boat. It is fast, it takes up no space, and it ensures against simple, careless, or hasty mathematical errors. Speed, time, and distance are related to each other by a simple formula:

$$60 \times D = S \times T$$

$$60 \times \text{Distance} = \text{Speed} \times \text{Time}$$

Some people find it easy to remember if they think of it as an address:

Sixty D Street (60 D = S T)

With this formula, when any two quantities are known the third can be found by simple multiplication and/or division. For example, if a boat runs at 14 knots for 20 minutes how far will it travel? Speed at 14 knots times a time of 20 minutes equals 280 divided by 60 equals a distance of 4.66667 or 4⅔ miles.

$$S \times T = 60 \times D$$

$$14 \times 20 = 280 = 60 \times D$$

$$D = \frac{280}{60} = 4.6667$$

If a boat travels 7.3 miles in 28 minutes what is its speed?

$$60\ D = S\ T$$

$$60 \times 7.3 = 438 = S \times 28 = \frac{438}{28} = 15.6 \text{ knots}$$

A person is planning to make a trip of 14.6 miles at a speed of 12 knots. How long will this trip take?

$$60 \times D = S \times T$$

$$60 \times 14.6 = 876 = 12 \times T$$

$$= \frac{876}{12} = 73 \text{ minutes} = 1 \text{ hour and } 13 \text{ minutes}$$

Because the math involved here is not very difficult, let us now see if this formula can be of use to us when it comes time to actually make the trip for which we laid out course directions in Fig. 5-17. For one thing, once we arbitrarily decide on a speed we can add the distances of the various courses we laid out and easily find out how long the trip will take.

The formula can be even more helpful in another way. Suppose we separately take the distance of each course, shown in Fig. 5-17, and set a speed at which the boat will run. Then using the formula, figure the running time for each course individually. The course distances were:

A to B	1.5 Miles
B to C	6.0 Miles
C to D	3.5 Miles
D to E	2.5 Miles

Arbitrarily setting a speed of 12 knots, the running times will be:

$\underline{60 \times D = S \times T}$

$60 \times 1.5 = S \times T = 90$ from A to B. $\quad T = \frac{90}{12} = 7.5$ minutes

$60 \times 6.0 = S \times T = 360$ from B to C $\quad T = \frac{360}{12} = 30$ minutes

$60 \times 6.0 = S \times T = 210$ from C to D $\quad T = \frac{210}{12} = 17.5$ minutes

$60 \times 2.5 = S \times T = 150$ from D to E $\quad T = \frac{150}{12} = 12.5$ minutes

Now take the boat to point A, make sure it is in the right place halfway between the ends of the two jetties, set the bow on 250° magnetic, and the throttle at 12 knots. Hold that course for exactly 7 minutes and 30 seconds by the watch. The boat is now at B so turn directly to 165° magnetic and go for 30 minutes precisely to get to C. There turn to 110° magnetic and hold for 17 minutes 30 seconds to get to D. Turn now to 345° magnetic for 12½ minutes to reach E.

Sailing by dead reckoning—as just described in 1 hour 7 minutes and 30 seconds—the boat should be at point E. Realistically, it is not going to be exactly at point E. The effects of wind, currents, and steering inaccuracies will place it off somewhat. Nevertheless, if the course directions, running times, and speed are maintained substantially accurately, the boat will be very *close* to point E.

The various factors just mentioned will force a boat away from its intended course and schedule while under way. Therefore there are several methods of fixing position en route. Course corrections are then made based on actual positions of the boat. These procedures are discussed later in connection with piloting.

First, let us look at another DR plot. This is a

little longer trip, and the conditions are a bit different. We are to meet a friend in his boat at a point a little north of La Jolla (Fig. 5-18). There is nothing to mark the spot he has in mind, so he has given the coordinates of 32° 51.2′ N latitude and 117° 16.1′ W longitude as the meeting place. We are to meet at 11:30 AM Saturday morning.

Our departure will be from the F1 G Bell southeast of Point Loma. We locate the destination by means of the latitude and longitude scales. Latitude is increasing upward on the scale at the left of the chart: 32° 50′ is clearly marked; 1.2′ above this mark will be 32° 51.2′ N latitude.

With dividers or parallel rules, transfer this level to La Jolla and draw a short, light line for the latitude of the destination. At the bottom of the chart, 117° 15′ and 117° 20′ are marked with line at 117° 20′. Measure back from that reference line to 117° 16.1′ with the dividers. Now transfer that distance up to La Jolla to the latitude line just drawn. Put a dot there and circle it to identify the destination.

The chart now shows where the trip will start and where it will end. We need next to determine the route to be followed to get from one to the other. Fuel is expensive and we do not want to make the course unnecessarily long and round about. Nevertheless, let us make it long enough to stand well clear of all known obstructions. Let us also lay out course legs of lengths and directions that will be easy to work with when we compute speed and time, and that will be easy to steer when making the trip.

Starting from F1 G Bell, it would not be wise, as we already know, to try to go immediately westward. We would very quickly be in thick kelp. Therefore, let us stand southward until a westerly leg will be well clear of it. A course of 180° M stays in the buoyed approach channel and is clear of the kelp.

At a distance of 1.5 miles, a 90° change to a course of 270° M gives a second leg that will be clear of obstruction. After 2 miles on that course (1′ of latitude = 1 nautical mile), it is time to start northward. Obviously to go due north (True) will not work out. Such a course is too close to the shore and passes through miles of kelp. From position C, a course of 340° M is satisfactory for much of the northerly leg, but gets in a bit close off La Jolla; 335° M goes perhaps a little further out than is absolutely necessary, but not by much. There will be a mark on the compass to use to steer 335°, and at exactly 12.5 miles on that course there is a good turning point at D.

From there, 040° M is a convenient steering number, and 2 miles even is a simple distance with which to work. At E turn to course 100° M. After proceeding for 1 mile, we should meet our friend.

The chart now shows a departure point, a destination, and the courses and distances to be traveled in order to go from one to the other. In order to be at the destination at 1130, a running speed must be selected. Then the running times for the various legs of the trip computed individually. They are next added together.

The total subtracted from 1130 will determine when the boat must leave point "A" if it is to be at point "F" by 1130.

If the Pacific Ocean is being pacific on Saturday morning, a small boat could run comfortably at 15 knots on this trip. Using a speed of 15 knots, what will be the times for the individual legs of the trip? What will the total running time be? When should we depart F1 G Bell?

A to B = 1.5 mi. Speed 15 knots

$\underline{60 \times D = S \times T}$

$60 \times 1.5 = S \times T = 90 \quad T = \frac{90}{15} = 6$ min. from A to B

B to C = 2.0 mi. Speed 15 knots

$\underline{60 \times D = S \times T}$

$60 \times 2.0 = S \times T = 120 \quad T = \frac{120}{15} = 8$ min. from B to C

C to D = 12.5 mi. Speed 15 knots

$\underline{60 \times D = S \times T}$

$60 \times 12.5 = S \times T = 750 \quad T = \frac{750}{15} = 50$ min. from C to D

D to E = 2.0 mi. Speed 15 knots

$\underline{60 \times D = S \times T}$

$60 \times 2.0 = S \times T = 120 \quad T = \frac{120}{12} = 8$ min. from D to E

E to F = 1 mi. Speed 15 knots

$\underline{60 \times D = S \times T}$

$60 \times 1.0 = S \times T = 60 \quad T = \frac{60}{15} = 4$ min. from E to F

Total distance = 19 mi. Total running time at 15 knots: 76 min. = 1 hr. 16 min.

To be at rendezvous at 1130 after a run of 1 hr. 16 min.

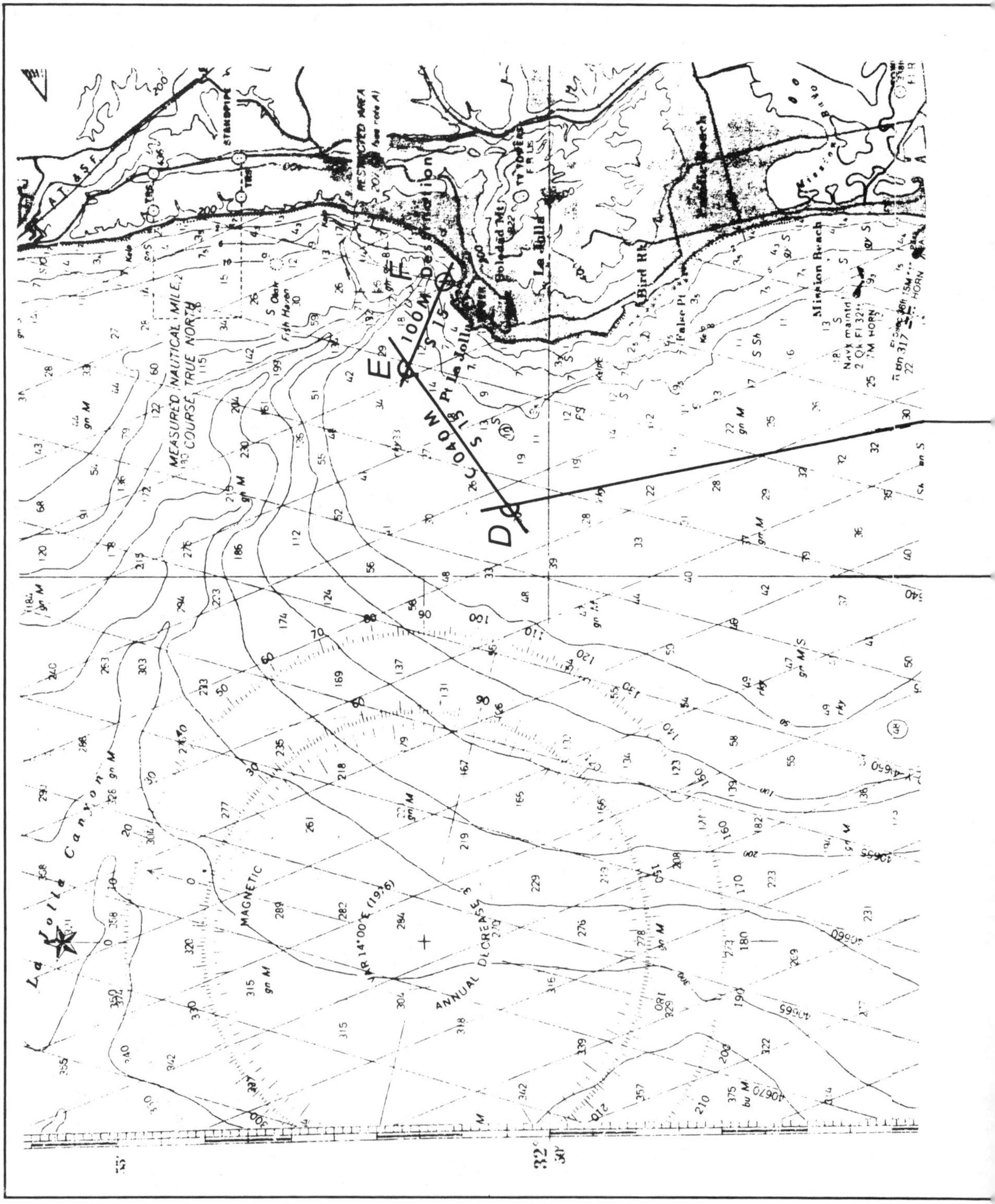

MEASURED NAUTICAL MILE
COURSE TRUE NORTH
RESTRICTED AREA
La Jolla
Pt La Jolla
Bird Rk
False Pt
Mission Beach
Fish Haven
La Jolla Canyon
MAGNETIC
ANNUAL DECREASE
D
E
F
C 040 M 15 S
100 M 15 S

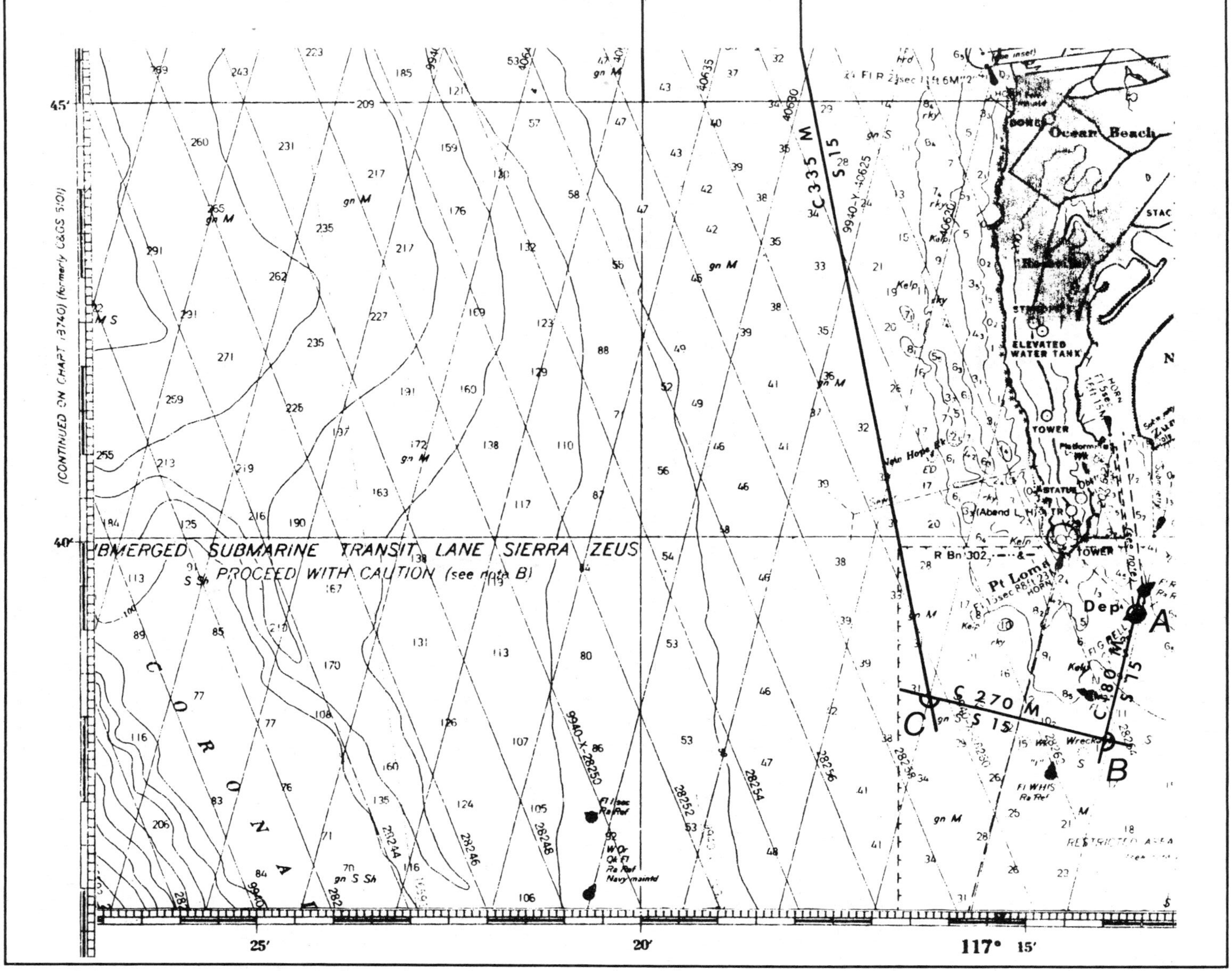

Ocean Beach
ELEVATED WATER TANK
TOWER
Pt Loma
Dep
A
B
C
C 335 M
S 15
C 270 M
S 15
C 180 M
S 15
9940-X-28250
SUBMERGED SUBMARINE TRANSIT LANE SIERRA ZEUS
PROCEED WITH CAUTION (see note B)
CORONA
(CONTINUED ON CHART 18740) (formerly C&GS 5101)
45'
40'
25'
20'
117° 15'

Fig. 5-18. DR plot on chart (Point Loma to La Jolla Shores).

```
  11 30
–  1 16
  10 14
```

Depart Fl G Bell buoy at 1014.

Time

Use of the time, speed, and distance formula should make clear the importance of time as an aid to keeping track of the position of a boat under way. At sea, time is recorded somewhat differently from what we are accustomed to ashore. While we all know a day consists of 24 hours, we are used to splitting them into 12 hours AM (ante meridian passage) and PM (post meridian after meridian passage. With this system, each hour number (1, 2, 3, 4, 5, 6, etc.) appears twice each day and must be followed by a postscript of either AM or PM to determine which of the two is meant.

Long ago people in the nautical and astronomical fields found this system cumbersome and changed to use of the 24-hour clock. The military has adopted the 24-hour system as well. Now all references to time in relation to nautical matters appear using 24-hour notation. This system is used, as described in Chapter 6 and Chapter 7, in compiling both tide tables and current tables. If for no other reason than to be able to read and use those tables, it is necessary to understand 24-hour timekeeping. Once you get accustomed to it, you will find the method very simple.

The 24-hour method expresses time in four digits. The first two digits are hours and the second two are minutes. The 24-hour day starts at midnight, which is written down as 0000 hours; no hours and no minutes of the new day have passed. At 17 minutes past midnight, the time is written 0017; no complete hours, but 17 minutes of the new day have passed.

The time you probably are used to writing down as 2:25 AM appears in the other notation as 0225. In addition, 10:25 AM is simply 1025; 11:25 AM is merely 1125, but 12:25 PM shows up as 1225. It cannot be confused with 12:25 AM because that was written 0025.

Now 1:25 8PM becomes 1325 (1200 + 125 = 1325); 2:25 PM is 1425 and so on through the second 12 hours until midnight is reached, which is 2400 hours (2400 hours is also 0000 hours, and marks the start of another day.).

In addition to preventing any possibility of confusion between AM and PM hours, the 24-hour notation system has another advantage. Because all time notations must be made in 4 digits, many inadvertent omissions are also prevented; 1030 cannot be miswritten 103 (the last zero dropped off) without raising questions as to whether the writer meant 0103, or 1003, or 1030.

Another very important point to remember regarding time is that, when adding and subtracting times, you are not dealing with the customary number system based on 10. Time is based on 60 seconds to the minute, 60 minutes to the hour, and 24 hours to the day. For example:

☐ You are to start on a run at 1039. That run will take 2 hr. 27 min. When will you arrive?

```
1039
 227
1266 ? ? ?
```

Because we have no 66 minute hours your arrival time will be *1306* hrs. (1:06 PM).

☐ You are out fishing. Friends are due at the dock to take you out to supper at 6:60 PM . It will take you 3 hours and 45 minutes to get back. What is the latest time you can start back?

```
6:30 PM = 1830 hr.
       1830 becomes
less    345

       1790
less    345
       1445 (2:45 PM)
```

You cannot subtract 45 from 30! You must borrow 1 hour from the 18. That gives you 60 minutes to add to the 30 already there: 1830 = 1790.

☐ It is now 2310 hrs. High tide is due at 0206. How long do we have to wait?

```
0206   becomes        2606
2310                  2310

       which becomes  2566
                      2310
                       256
```

We wait 2 hours 56 minutes.

In spite of the many rumors to the contrary, sailors are really very staid, conservative, and conventional people. Time is conventionally noted in four digits, and it is also placed in conventional locations on the charts. The time at which a bearing is taken is always written *above* the bearing line (as in Figs. 5-14 and 5-15). The number *below* the bearing line is always a three-digit number, and is the *direction* of the bearing. We shall come back to this number again.

The time of a fix is written *off* of the lines of position (LOPs) that meet to form that fix (as in Fig. 5-16). When two bearings meet to constitute a fix, there is no need to label them individually with the time. Bearings taken within a few moments of each other can be considered as being taken substantially, simultaneously, and time noted accordingly.

PILOTING

The dead reckoning (DR) plot is the projection of route and schedule we would *like* to follow. The techniques of piloting enable us to utilize charted information to determine exactly where we *actually* are at various times. With this information, course corrections and revised time estimates are made as needed. This is accomplished by developing LOPs at opportune times, crossing LOPs to exactly fix our position whenever possible, and then comparing the actual location of the boat at a specific time with the intended DR position at that time.

Lines of Position (LOPs)

The line of position is the real core of piloting. It tells you not where you planned, or wished, or hoped, or guessed, or yearned, or calculated you are. On the contrary, it tells you where you actually are. You have made the acquaintance of the LOP as used to fix the start of a DR plot. This is done with bearings on charted objects.

The value of a bearing used as an LOP depends, of course, on its accuracy. This, in turn, depends on the accuracy of the instrument used to take the bearing as well as the skill of the person using it. This is a skill none of us was born with. It has to be acquired by practice. Sitting in the cockpit at the dock, and sighting over a hand-bearing compass or a pelorous at a flagpole across the bay does not seem difficult at all—probably because it's *not* difficult. But from a small boat bobbing about in the middle of that bay it is a different story.

A boat does not normally bob and leap about in open water in a random or erratic manner; it moves rather in response to wave patterns. The waves are created by wind, and are quite regular and rhythmic in nature. When taking sights, it is necessary to adjust oneself to that rhythm. On a given day, the waves are passing at 8, 5, or 12 or whatever second intervals. The boat will go through a series of movements repeated at the same intervals. A point in that cycle when the boat is most nearly level is the time to take the sight. Take it half a dozen times at least at the same point in the cycle. When you are adjusted to the rhythm of the sea and are getting essentially the same reading repeatedly, you probably have a good *cut* (a nautical term for a satisfactory sight).

The most reliable LOP is from a bearing taken on a range. Next in order of reliability is LOP from a bearing on a fixed object ashore, and third is a floating aid to navigation such as a buoy. For our purposes, because we are not going to try to locate the pair of pliers we lost overboard last week, buoys are plenty accurate enough.

When taking bearings with the pelorus, no matter how we do it, we will be involved with the ship's compass. This means the deviation for the heading of the boat at the time of the bearing must be applied. When using the hand-bearing compass, stand well clear of ferrous metal and electrical devices and take its reading as a magnetic bearing ignoring deviation.

When drawing bearings on the chart, they can appear as either true or magnetic. The Navy likes everything to be charted true, but we sloppy civilian boatmen can do what we like as long as we know what we are doing and are consistent about it. Whether you draw true or magnetic depends partly on the charting instruments you have chosen to do the drawing. If, for example, you have come to like the course plotter and are most comfortable with it, you will plot everything true. This is because the course plotter is used by aligning it with a vertical longtitude line or a horizontal latitude line printed on the chart, and these lines are true north-south, and east-west lines.

Both parallel rules and drafting triangles must be walked to or from a compass rose for directional alignment. Once at the compass rose, both true and magnetic directions are available graphically. No computation is needed.

The course protractor has an outer rose that is aligned with the charted verticals or horizontals the same as the plotter. Nevertheless, it also has an inner rose that rotates independently, and can be set to match the variation of the area. In this way, it can be used to provide either true or magnetic directions without having to walk it about as must be done with parallel rules or triangles. As you can see, the various charting instruments handle differently enough to account for considerable diversity in personal taste.

In any event, in order to avoid confusing yourself, it is wise to pick either true or magnetic and chart everything the same way. In order to avoid confusing others who sail with you, be sure to identify all bearings and courses as you chart them (Fig. 5-15) with either an M or a T to show which you have used.

Thus far, all LOPs have been straight lines to something from our boat. We can also use a curved LOP called a *circle of position*. This line is found by first determining how far the observer is away from some charted object. Then draw a circle (Fig. 5-19), or in practice only a part of that circle, using that object as its center—and a radius equal to the observer's distance off. As an example, when the observer can be determined to be 2.5 miles away from a charted tower—then if a circle with a radius equal to 2.5 miles is drawn with the tower as its center—the observer must be somewhere on that circle.

One way of finding distance off from an object is by the use of what are called bow and beam bearings (Fig. 5-20). A bearing is taken when the object lies 45° off either port or starboard bow relative to the boat, and time is recorded as usual. The boat proceeds on a steady course and at a steady speed until the same object lies at 90° relative to the boat. A second bearing is now taken and time again is noted. Using the speed, time, and distance formula, the time between bearings and the speed at which the boat has been running are used to determine the distance run during that interval. By the simplest of trigonometry, the distance run has to be equal to the distance off. A 45° – 45° – 90° triangle is what is called isosceles (meaning that it has two equal sides). Finding the length of one gives you the other one as well.

This is the principle behind a second method of finding distance off. This method is very similar to the first in that it involves two bearings. Actually,

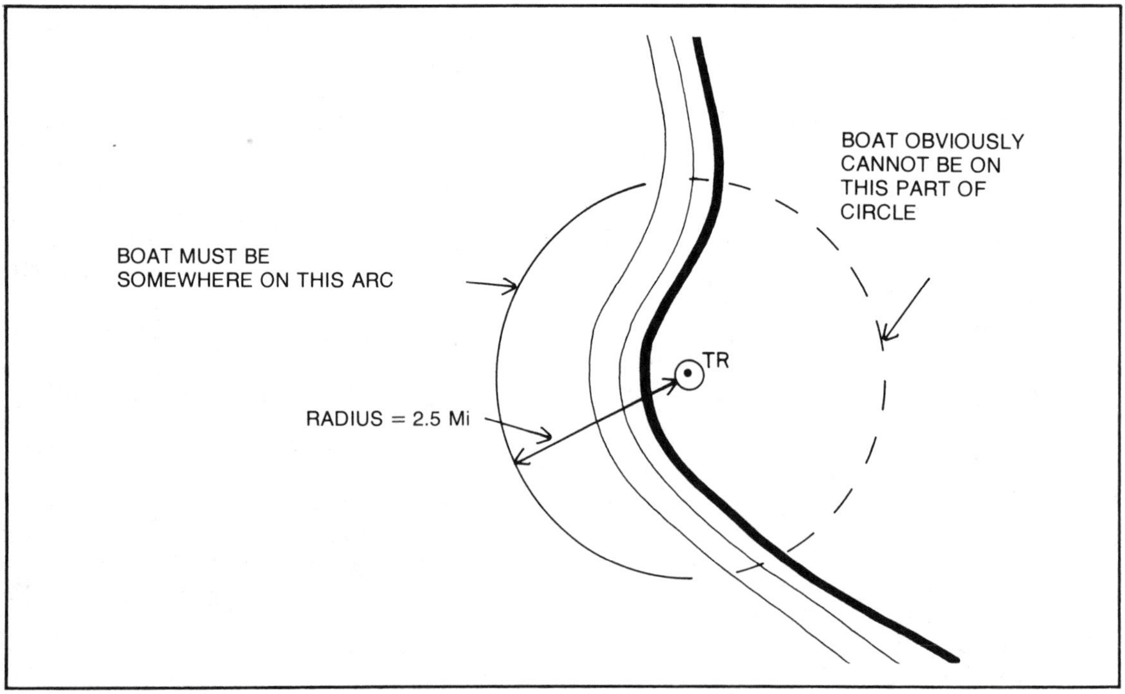
BOAT OBVIOUSLY CANNOT BE ON THIS PART OF CIRCLE
BOAT MUST BE SOMEWHERE ON THIS ARC
TR
RADIUS = 2.5 Mi

Fig. 5-19. Circle of position.

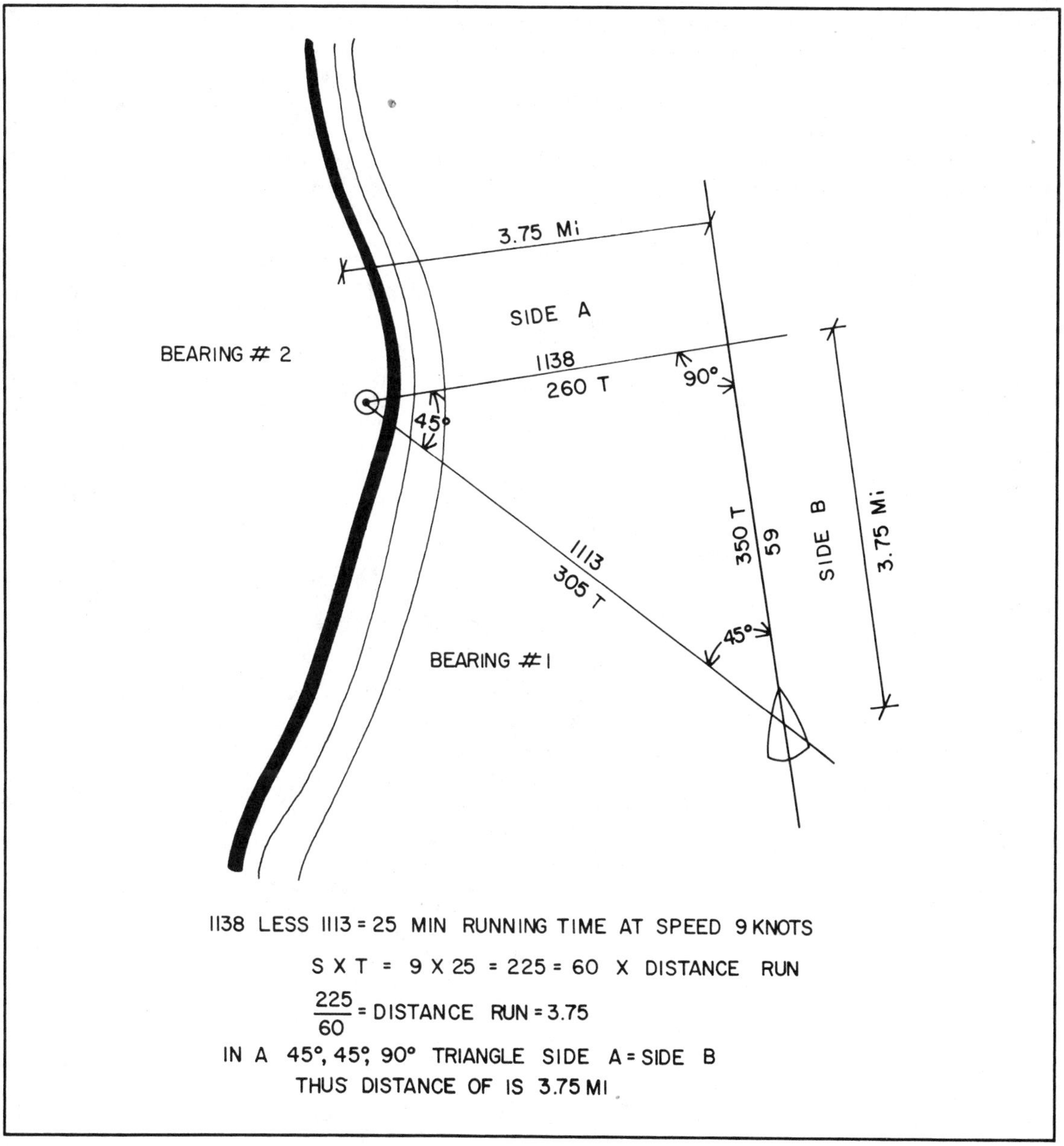
3.75 Mi
SIDE A
BEARING # 2
1138
260 T
90°
45°
1113
305 T
350 T
59
SIDE B
3.75 Mi
45°
BEARING # 1
1138 LESS 1113 = 25 MIN RUNNING TIME AT SPEED 9 KNOTS
S X T = 9 X 25 = 225 = 60 X DISTANCE RUN
225/60 = DISTANCE RUN = 3.75
IN A 45°, 45°, 90° TRIANGLE SIDE A = SIDE B
THUS DISTANCE OF IS 3.75 MI

Fig. 5-20. Bow and beam bearings for distance off.

the bow and beam bearing is a special case of this method termed *doubling the angle on the bow.* To play double the angle on the bow, take a bearing on an object at any convenient time and note its angle relative to either port or starboard bow. Proceed on a steady course at a constant speed until the bearing of the object (Fig. 5-24) is exactly double what it originally was. Now take a second bearing and note the time.

Using the speed that has been maintained—and the time interval between bearings as S and T in the time, speed, distance formula—work out how far the boat has traveled in the interim. Doubling the angle on the bow has set up another isosceles triangle in which the distance the boat has traveled is also its distance away from the object at the time of the second bearing. As can be seen in Fig. 5-21, any triangle that contains two equal angles also must have two equal sides.

In order to use either bow and beam bearings or doubling the angle on the bow as methods for determining distance away from an object, a pelorus and two people are necessary. Also, the accuracy of the result will depend on how closely the speed used in the computation agrees with actual speed *over the ground.* When a boat is moving at 10 knots through the water, but it is running against a 2 knot current, its actual forward movement—or as it is properly termed Speed of Advance (SOA)—is only 8 knots. This consideration is further discussed in Chapter 7 on Currents.

Distance off can be determined by taking two bearings other than ones that double the angle on the bow. This requires the use of Table 7 from *Bowditch,* which is not likely to be aboard small boats. *Bowditch* is a very big book (in two volumes).

Distance off can also be found by taking vertical sextant angles on an object of known height such as a lighthouse. Lighthouse heights are given on the charts. But to do this, both a sextant and Table 9 out of *Bowditch* are required. Neither is likely to be aboard our small craft.

A pocket range finder (Fig. 5-22) can easily be carried aboard a small boat, and it is a very handy

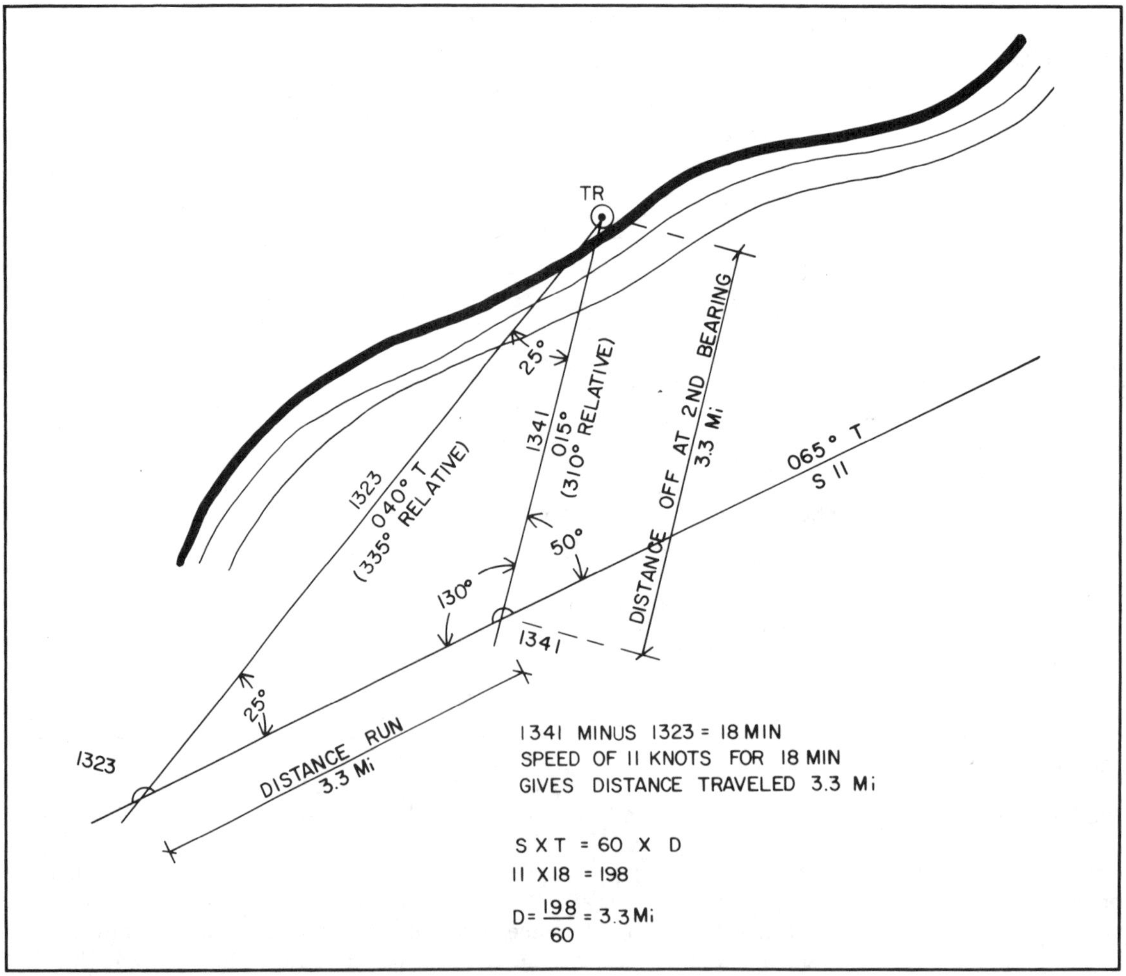

TR
25°
1341
015°
(310° RELATIVE)
DISTANCE OFF AT 2ND BEARING
3.3 Mi
1323
040° T
(335° RELATIVE)
50°
130°
065° T
S 11
1341
25°
1323
DISTANCE RUN
3.3 Mi
1341 MINUS 1323 = 18 MIN
SPEED OF 11 KNOTS FOR 18 MIN
GIVES DISTANCE TRAVELED 3.3 Mi
S X T = 60 X D
11 X 18 = 198
D = 198/60 = 3.3 Mi

Fig. 5-21. Distance off by doubling the angle on the bow.

Fig. 5-22. Pocket range finder. (Instrument courtesy Davis Instruments Corporation).

and inexpensive instrument to use for finding distance off (which will then yield a circular LOP).

The final instrument from which an LOP can be derived is the radio direction finder (Fig. 5-12). The correcting procedure that must precede plotting an RDF bearing requires dealing with two kinds of deviation (Fig. 5-23). The compass heading must, as always, be corrected for deviation to find the magnetic course. Then the RDF bearing must also be corrected for deviation (if it has any on that bearing). Remember: compass deviation varies with the boat *heading*; RDF deviation varies with

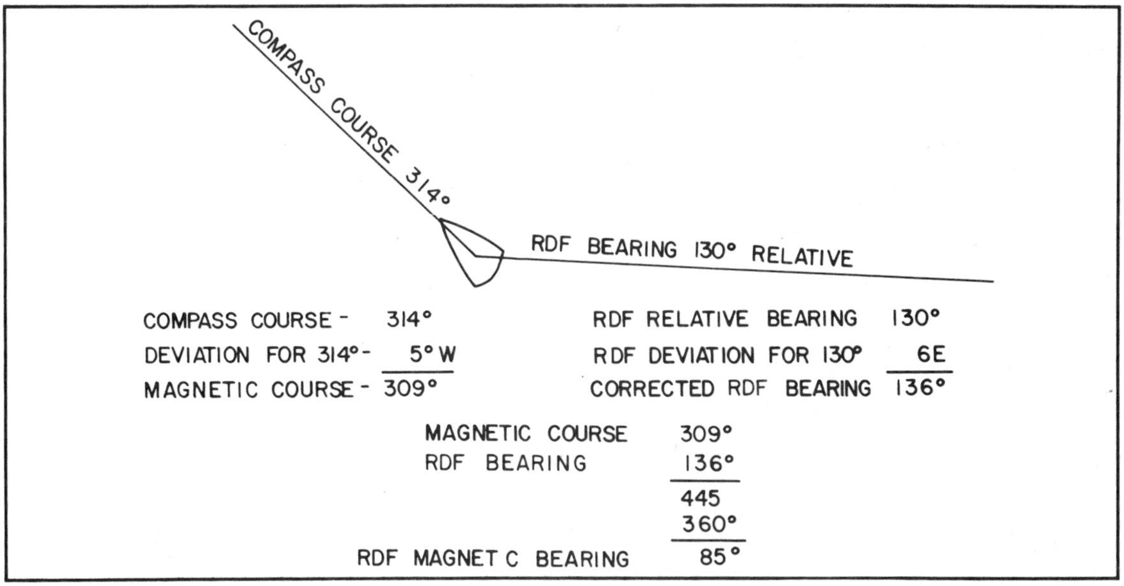
COMPASS COURSE 314°
RDF BEARING 130° RELATIVE
COMPASS COURSE - 314°
DEVIATION FOR 314°- 5° W
MAGNETIC COURSE - 309°
RDF RELATIVE BEARING 130°
RDF DEVIATION FOR 130° 6E
CORRECTED RDF BEARING 136°
MAGNETIC COURSE 309°
RDF BEARING 136°
445
360°
RDF MAGNET C BEARING 85°

Fig. 5-23. Correction of RDF bearing.

the *bearing*. Do not confuse the two!

With both compass heading and RDF bearing individually corrected for deviation, they are added together in the usual manner to produce a magnetic bearing that can be plotted as such or corrected to true before plotting. The great advantage of the RDF is that it will give an LOP when absolutely no visual references are available. As you will see, it

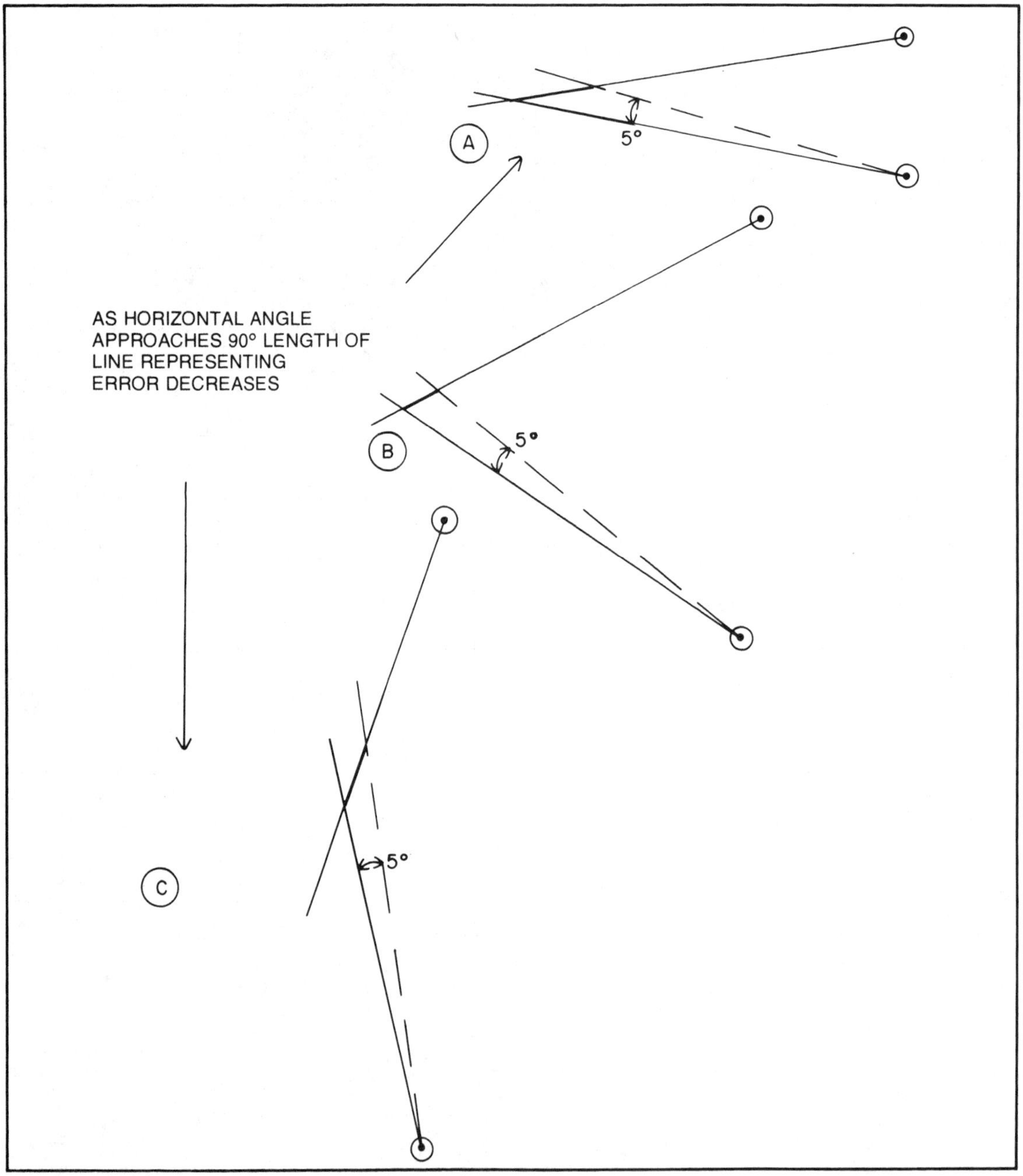

A
5°
AS HORIZONTAL ANGLE
APPROACHES 90° LENGTH OF
LINE REPRESENTING
ERROR DECREASES
B
5°
C
5°

Fig. 5-24. Effect on position of 5-degrees error in one sight.

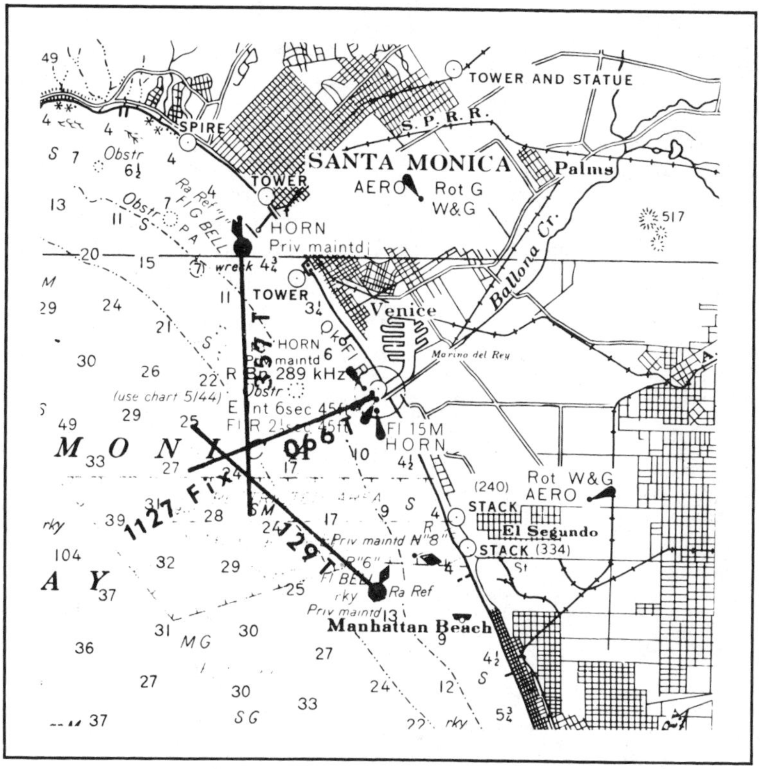

TOWER AND STATUE
S. P. R. R.
SPIRE
SANTA MONICA
Palms
TOWER
AERO
Rot G
W&G
HORN
Priv maintd
TOWER
Venice
Ballona Cr.
HORN
289 kHz
357° T
066° T
1127 Fix
129° T
FI 15M
HORN
Rot W&G
AERO
STACK
El Segundo
STACK (334)
Ra Ref
Manhattan Beach
M O N
A Y

Fig. 5-25. Three-point fix; three LOPs form a small triangle.

also makes possible a fix (not a running fix) when only one visible reference is available.

Fixing Position

A line of position (LOP) is found, as we have seen by determining with one of several instruments the direction from the boat to some reference object. Such a line transferred to the chart must pass through the position occupied by the boat at the time that direction was determined. The line also passes through a vast number of other positions as well. Only when at least two LOPs are crossed, as shown in Fig. 5-16, does the navigator know where his boat lies on each line.

When taking sights and plotting LOPs to fix the position of a boat, there is always a possibility of a mistake occurring. The sighting instrument can be used incorrectly or it can be read incorrectly. An error could occur when writing down the instrument reading. Also, the reading might be inaccurately plotted.

The effect on the location of the fix that will result from a mistake in one of two sights (Fig. 5-24) varies quite considerably depending on the horizontal angle between the two objects being sighted. As that angle increases, the error in the plotted location of the fix decreases, assuming the magnitude of the mistake remains constant. The error in the fix decreases with increase of the horizontal angle up to 90°. Above 90° it begins to increase again. Therefore, avoid fixes based on sights using two objects either very close together or spaced very widely apart.

Three-Sight Fix

Because of the extent to which a fairly small mistake in one sight can misplace a two-sight fix, it is considered a better practice, whenever possible, to base the fix on three sights (Fig. 5-25). A three-point fix, when plotted, most often results in defining a small triangle rather than a single point. In such cases, the position of the boat is considered as being most probably at the center of that triangle.

In the event that the triangle formed by three LOPs is disproportionately large or misshapen, this is a signal that one or more of the sights was poor or some other mistake has been made. If this should happen, do not waste time or effort trying to figure out where the mistake was made. Take another round of sights and plot them. Only if the second plot gives another large or odd-shaped triangle do you make a serious effort to find the trouble.

The most common difficulty, particularly among the inexperienced, is sloppy plotting. Good plotting is a precision operation. The pencil must be sharp. When walking parallel rules or a triangle, there must be absolutely *no* slippage. When using a course plotter or course protractor, alignment with printed chart horizontals or verticals must be *exact*. Acquiring adequate skill in the use of these instruments is purely a matter of practice, and more practice, and a little more after that. The same is true of taking sights. The more you practice, the better will be the cut you get. The more both sighting instruments and plotting instruments are used the more accurate both sights and plots become. Speed is also improved as well as confidence in the results.

Fix by Circle and Bearing

A circular LOP shown in Fig. 5-19 can be combined with a straight LOP to produce an excellent fix. The circle of position derived through use of a range-finder is likely to be more reliable than one based on either bow and beam bearings or doubling the angle on the bow. The accuracy of either of the latter two methods is only as good as the accuracy of the computation of travel over the ground—not through the water—during the time interval between the first and second bearings.

The examples shown in Figs. 5-20 and 5-21 are pure dead reckoning. No correction has been for any wandering from the course caused by windage, current, or steering lapses; although all three of

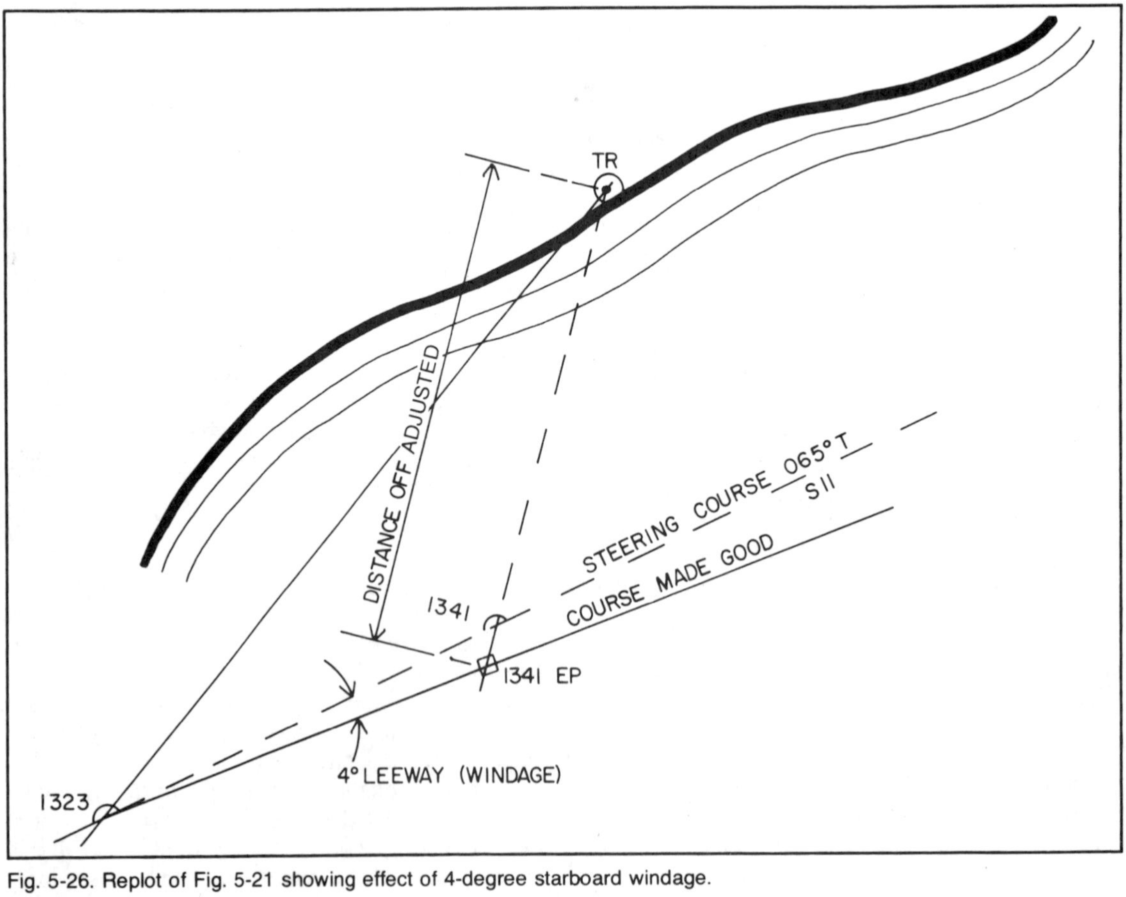
TR
DISTANCE OFF ADJUSTED
STEERING COURSE 065° T
S 11
COURSE MADE GOOD
1341
1341 EP
4° LEEWAY (WINDAGE)
1323

Fig. 5-26. Replot of Fig. 5-21 showing effect of 4-degree starboard windage.

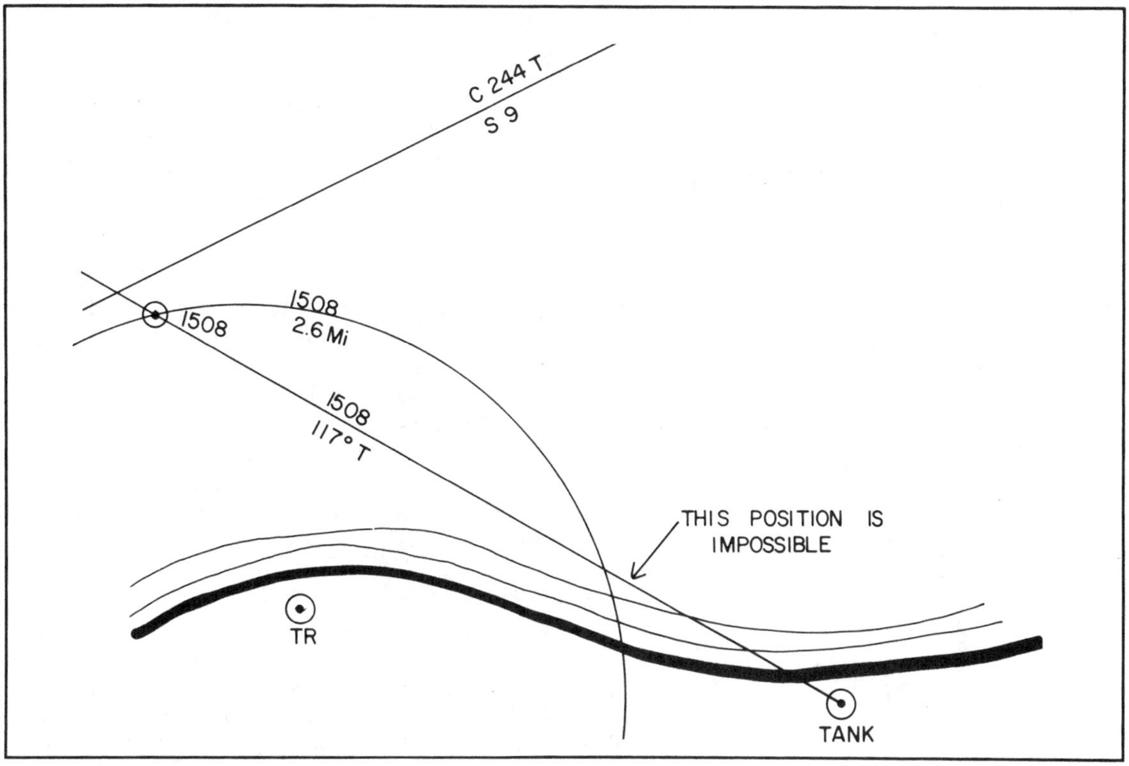
C 244 T
S 9
1508
1508
2.6 Mi
1508
117° T
THIS POSITION IS IMPOSSIBLE
TR
TANK

Fig. 5-27. Circle of position and bearing for fix.

these influences are likely to affect the boat. Currents and how to deal with them is discussed in Chapter 7. Sometimes the effect of windage can be seen when the wake of the boat is not running out straight behind the stern, but is at a slight angle. When such an effect can be seen, it should be worked into the plot (Fig. 5-26). If there is a fresh breeze from the port side and the wake consistently trails off 3° or 4° to port of dead astern, the boat is making leeway to starboard due to the wind by about the amount of that angle.

To show the effect of that leeway (Fig. 5-26) let us take the plot shown in Fig. 5-21 and see what happens when we work in an estimated leeway of 4° to starboard. Start with the same DR position at 1323 (the time of the first bearing). The steering course is the same 065° T, but by the time the angle on the bow has been doubled the boat has been moved by the wind off to the right of that course line to the position shown as 1341 EP (EP stands for *estimated position*).

An EP is the position of the boat after one or more factors not accounted for in the DR have been figured in. The accuracy of an EP is better than a DR position, but not nearly as reliable as a fix. A square around the line intersection is the symbol for an EP.

Once the distance off from an object has been determined, by whatever means, a bearing is taken on another object. A circle of position is drawn using the first object as its center (Fig. 5-27), and then the bearing is plotted as a second LOP. If the bearing crosses the circle at two points, one of them will be absurd as the position of the boat. The bearing of the tank, in this case, would be right but the position of the tower, the shore, and other charted objects would be totally wrong. Consequently, the intersection of the two LOPs in the vicinity of the DR course line is the fix.

When the distance off a charted object has been determined, it is possible to use the same object for a directional LOP by taking a sight on it. In this way, it is possible to get a positional fix from only one charted object by crossing the directional LOP and the circle of position. When running down an undistinguished coastline with very few charted landmarks, this is a good trick to be able to use.

Fix Using Two Circles

Next is a technique you will not use very often. Postulate the possibility that the pelorus could be damaged or the hand-bearing compass dropped, making it impossible to take directional bearings.

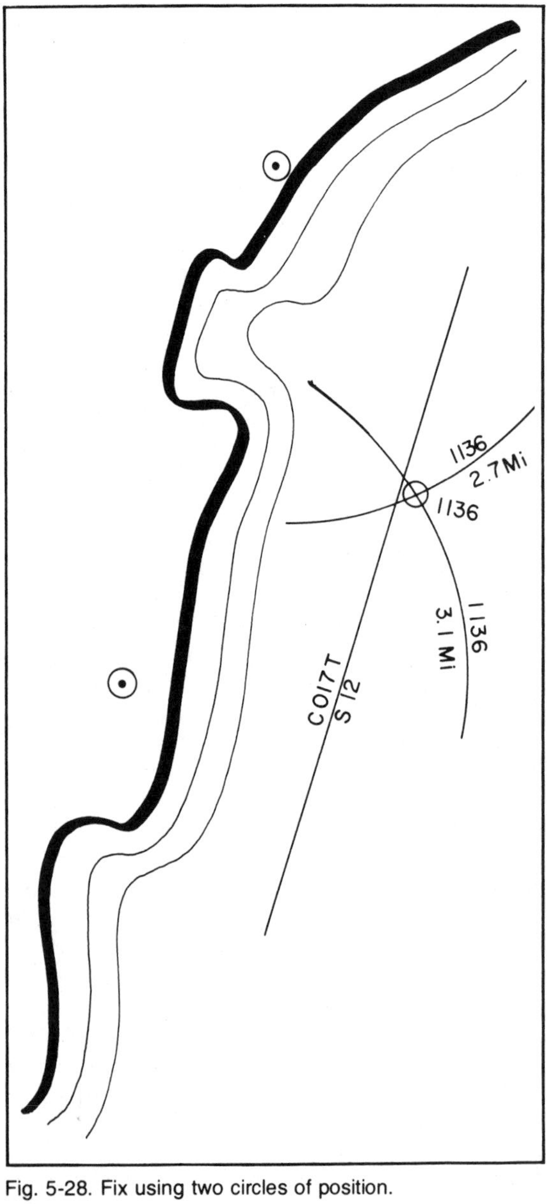
1136
2.7Mi
1136
1136
3.1 Mi
C017T
S12

Fig. 5-28. Fix using two circles of position.

The steering compass is undamaged. Therefore, a course can be properly steered, but its location makes the taking of bearings impossible. The rangefinder is available. In this case instead of bearings, get distances off from two charted objects (Fig. 5-28), draw two circles of position and find the fix where they intersect.

Fix Using Radio Directional LOPs

Another technique can be used in a situation where a fix is wanted, but only one visual landmark is available at the time. A visual bearing can be taken and crossed with an RDF bearing on a known transmitter location. RDF bearings are not nearly as accurate as visuals. At best they will be off by two or three degrees. For this reason it is a good idea (Fig. 5-29) to mark the bearing line "RDF" and sketch lines 3° either side of the RDF bearing to show on the visual LOP the area that lies within the normal range of error of the RDF. Set a new course from the fix in the normal manner, but remember that as a starting fix it is not of the same order of reliability as one based purely on visual LOPs.

In conditions of poor visibility—rain, haze, fog, darkness, or any combination of these—there might be no visual landmarks available at all. In these conditions, RDF lines—while not as accurate as visuals—certainly beat having nothing at all.

Take two or three RDF bearings and plot them in the normal manner. Then at 3° on either side of each bearing line sketch two lines where the bearings meet (Fig. 5-30). The boat is probably somewhere in the diamond-shaped area defined by the 3° lines either side of the bearing lines. Set the new course from the intersection of the bearing lines, but remain particularly alert for further information (primarily visual) that will enable you to fix your position more accurately.

Running Fix

When cruising along a coast, particularly in conditions of poor visibility, the navigator is often able to get an LOP from only one object at a time. If he has no RDF to fall back on, it is now impossible to get a normal fix on his position. In such circumstances, he could take a bearing on one object (Fig. 5-31) and then run until he gets an LOP on a second object. He then advances the first LOP for the distance and in the direction the boat has traveled in the interim. The point at which the second LOP is crossed by the first one is a running fix.

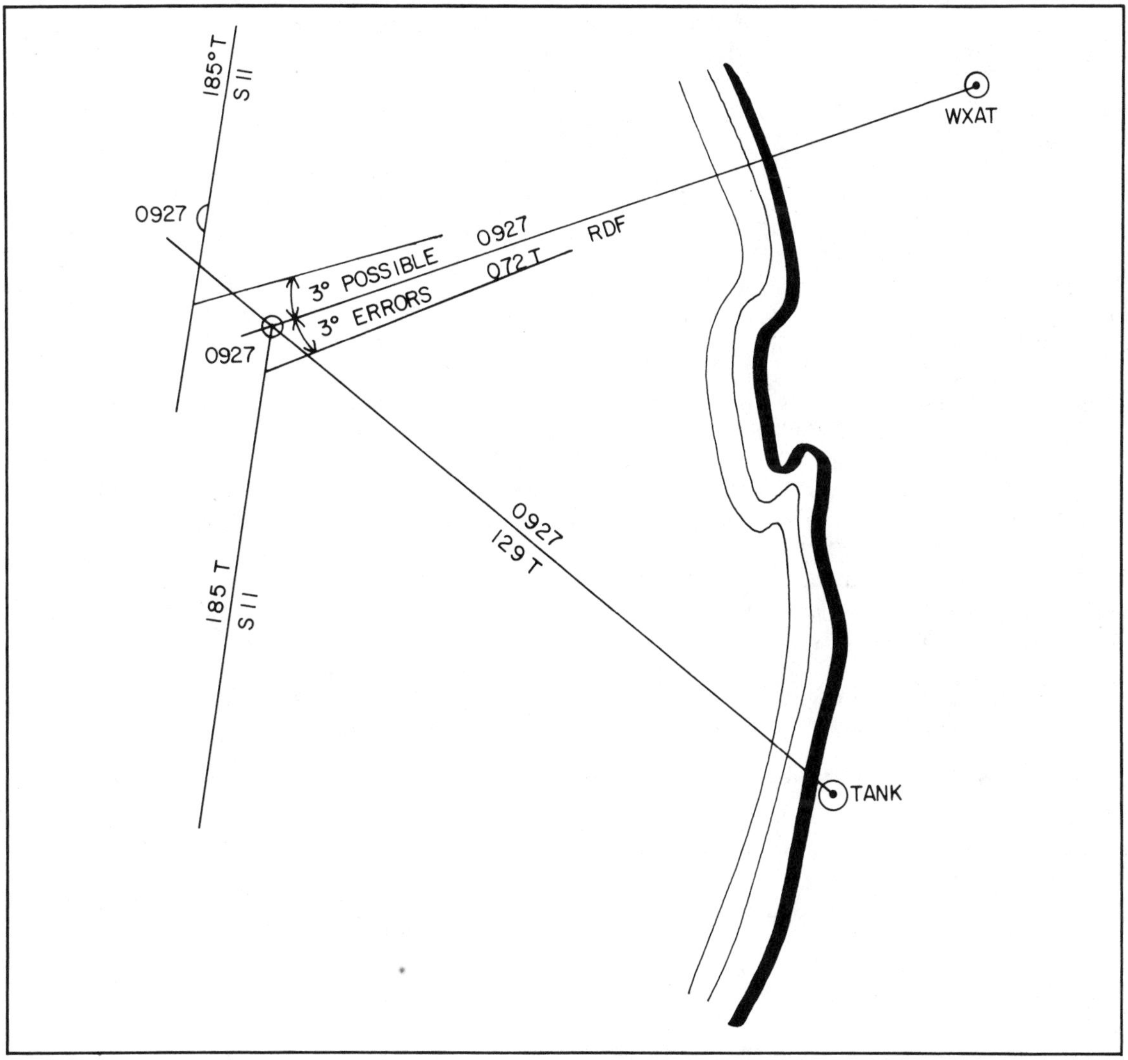
185° T
S 11
WXAT
0927
0927
RDF
3° POSSIBLE
072 T
3° ERRORS
0927
0927
129 T
185 T
S 11
TANK

Fig. 5-29. Fix using visual and RDF bearings.

A running fix is not as accurate as a fix obtained by taking two bearings on two different objects simultaneously. This is because its accuracy depends on how closely the estimated speed and direction of travel in the interval between sights corresponds to what actually happened. As we know, speed through the water and speed over the earth are not necessarily the same. Also, direction steered and direction actually traveled are not always the same either. Nevertheless, a running fix gives us a good deal better approximation of the position of the boat than pure dead reckoning.

A running fix can also be obtained (Fig. 5-32) by taking two bearings on the same object. To do this, advance the first bearing for time and distance to cross the second. Notice the labeling on the advanced LOP. It shows the times of both the first and the second LOP. Again, when the running fix was found, the original DR track was abandoned and a new one started. Notice also that the symbol for a running fix is the same circle around the intersection of LOPs that is used for a fix. The labeling is different. A fix shows time only. A running fix is labeled "R Fix" along with the time. This is to emphasize that it is a fix of lesser reliability than one derived from two simultaneous bearings.

Use of a Lone LOP

A single LOP cannot show you where you are at a given time. Nevertheless, it does provide some useful guidance as to where you are *not* at that time. Also combined with the DR plot, it furnishes at least a partial check on how closely that plot is being followed. Crossing the DR plot with one bearing (Fig. 5-33) produces another estimated position (EP). At 1000 hr., the boat might very well not be exactly at the position shown as the EP because of wind or current leeway that was not considered or because of faulty steering. It is clear, however, that the boat appears to be running behind schedule. A fix or a running fix further on will corroborate this.

Piloting a Planned Trip

You should now know a number of ways to find the actual position of the boat while under way. This will enable you to alter course, or speed, or both in order to compensate for whatever forces might cause the boat to deviate from the intended track and schedule. The sea might not allow the boat safely to maintain the desired speed, but you will surely be able to find the intended destination. Also—and most important—if trouble should develop and it is necessary to call for help, you can tell them where to find you.

Let's look back now to the short trip for which a DR track was drawn in Fig. 5-17. The chart shows various objects that can be used to provide LOPs for fixes or running fixes under way. With these, the progress of the boat can be monitored as the trip is being made. Here is one way it might be done.

We planned to take departure from a point midway between the ends of the breakwaters shielding the channel leading from Mission Bay ("A" on Fig. 5-17) and did so (Fig. 5-34). The DR plot gives an initial course of 250° M. A speed of 12 knots was projected for a distance of 1.5 miles, which would take 7½ minutes. With speed and steering correct, the light tower on the north breakwater should bear 070° M, and the Navy Oceanographic tower - "T" - 031° M (070° M is the reciprocal or opposite of the initial course of 250° M).

Departure is taken at 1000 hrs. exactly. At 1007 30 (7½ minutes later), sights are taken on the two objects. Readings are 068° on the breakwater

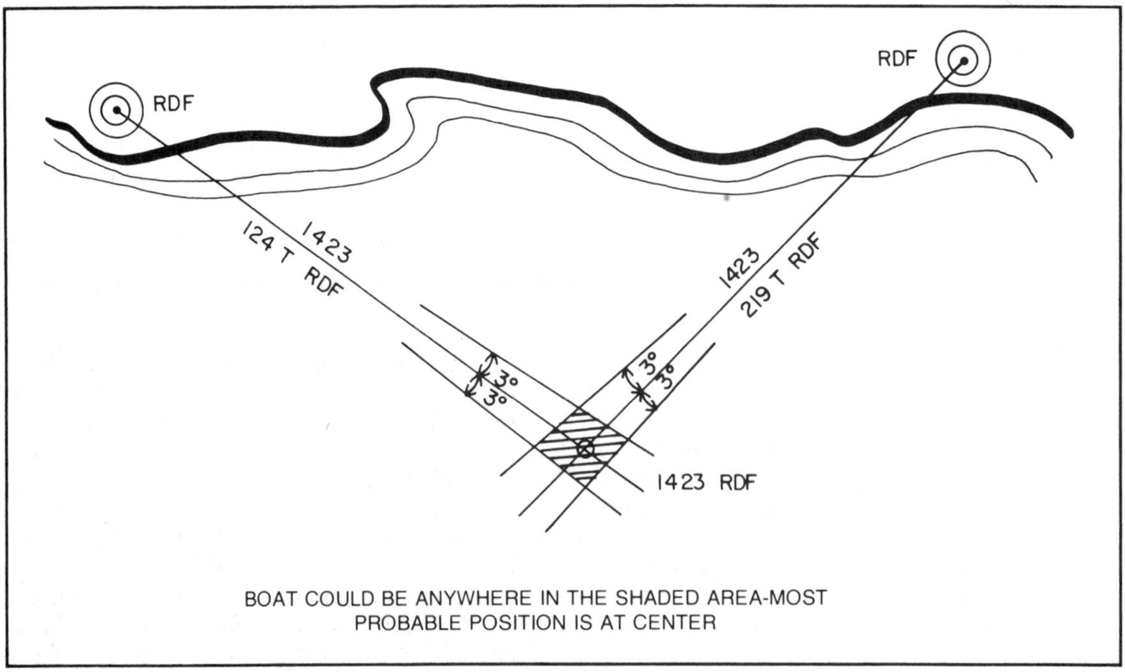
RDF
RDF
1423
124 T RDF
1423
219 T RDF
3°
3°
3°
3°
1423 RDF
BOAT COULD BE ANYWHERE IN THE SHADED AREA-MOST
PROBABLE POSITION IS AT CENTER

Fig. 5-30. RDF fix.

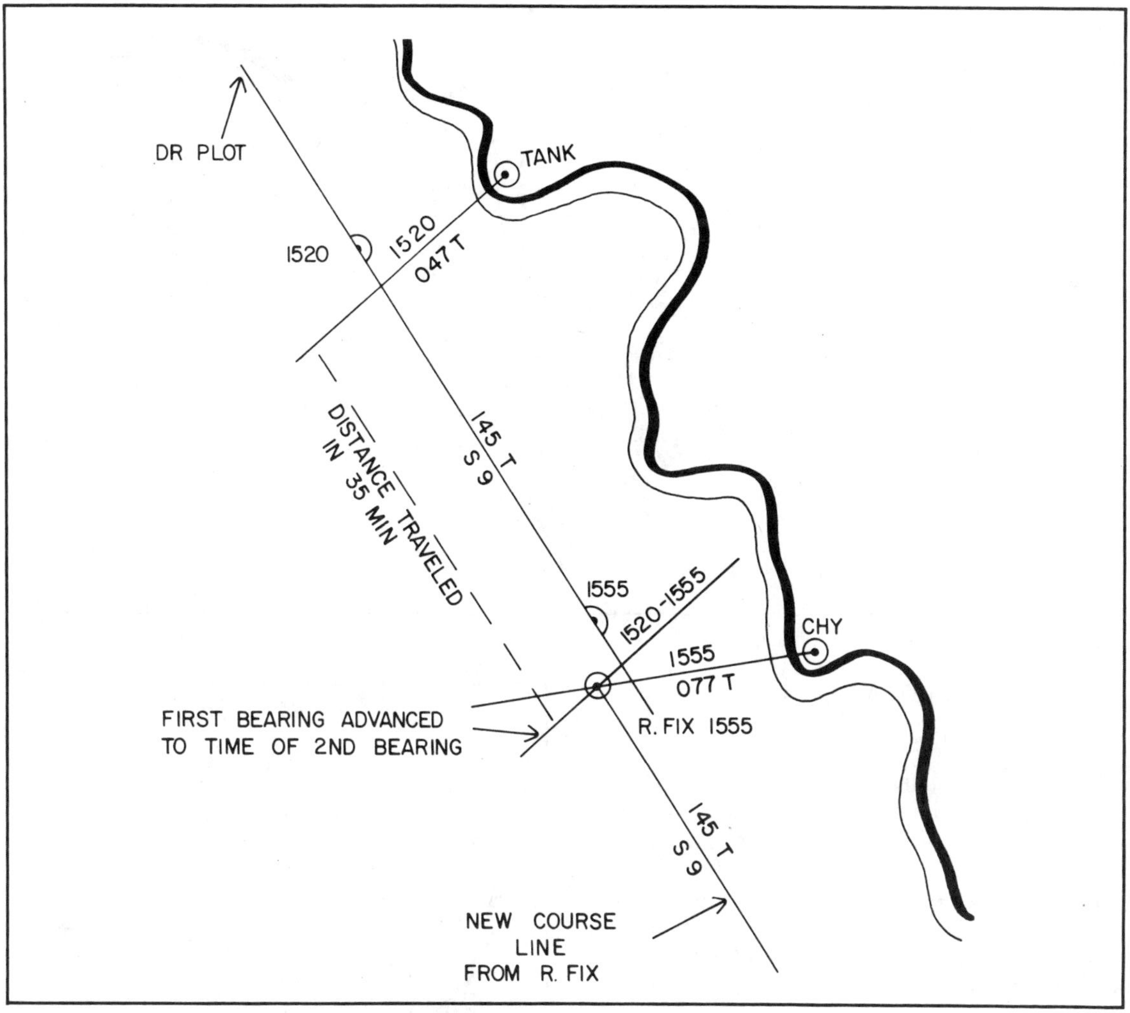

DR PLOT
TANK
1520
1520
047 T
DISTANCE TRAVELED
IN 35 MIN
145 T
S 9
1555
1520-1555
CHY
1555
077 T
FIRST BEARING ADVANCED
TO TIME OF 2ND BEARING
R. FIX 1555
145 T
S 9
NEW COURSE
LINE
FROM R. FIX

Fig. 5-31. Running fix; LOP on one object advanced to time of LOP on second object.

and 032° on the tower. That is close enough. DR position "B" is circled as a fix and labeled 1008. Course is changed to 165° M and a speed of 12 knots is maintained.

The second leg calls for a run of 30 minutes at 12 knots to go 6 miles. The decision is made to verify position in 15 minutes; at that time sights are taken on the elevated water tank ("U") and Point Loma Light. At 1023, the tank bears 066° M and Point Loma bears 123° M. When these bearings are plotted, the 1023 fix shows the boat to be about .4 mi. southeast of the 1023 DR position. Also, instead of moving 3 miles in 15 minutes, the boat has made good a distance over the ground of 3.2 miles.

$$60 \times D = S \times T \quad 60 \times 3.2 = 192$$

$$\frac{192}{15} = \text{Speed} = 12.8 \text{ knots}$$

The boat is traveling faster than expected. By finding the direction of the line from "B" to 1023 fix, the boat is found to be making 5° leeway. By leaving speed and steering direction as they are, the track of the boat over the ground for the next 15 minutes is represented by the line from 1023 fix to the square representing the 1038 EP. Assuming that leeway and actual speed over the ground remain constant, so that the boat reaches the EP shown at 1038 Point Loma Light, it will then bear 041° M from the boat at that time. While the heading being

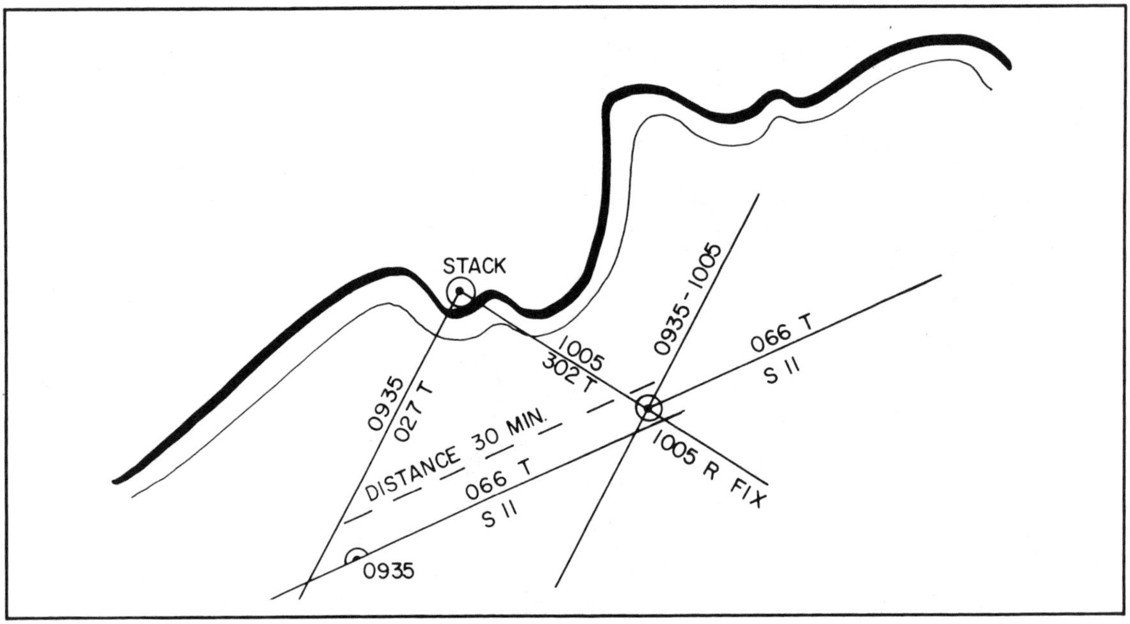

STACK
0935
027 T
1005
302 T
0935 - 1005
066 T
S 11
DISTANCE 30 MIN.
066 T
S 11
1005 R FIX
0935

Fig. 5-32. Running fix; two LOPs on same object.

steered remains 165° M, the direction of the expected track has become 160° M (which allows for the leeway).

At 1038 the light bears 044° M. This is quite close; it puts the boat within about .1 mi. of the EP along the track. Leaving the speed setting the same, the course is now changed to 110° M. The original DR called for a run of 3.5 miles on this course. Due to the actual position of the boat at the time of switching course, a run of 3.0 miles will be adequate to place the boat at a suitable location in the channel.

By looking back to the run from "B" to the 1023 fix, the difference between the 1023 DR location and the 1023 fix is a distance of .4 mi. in a direction of 104° M.

$$60 \times D = S \times T \quad 60 \times .4 = \frac{24}{T}$$

$$\frac{24}{15} = \text{Speed of set} = 1.6 \text{ knots}$$

When steering is changed from 165° M to 110° M, the effect of the forces causing the leeway will change as well. On a course of 110° M, the 104° M set will be almost directly behind the boat. If the speed setting on the boat is kept at 12 knots, its speed over the ground will be increased on the 110° M heading by very nearly 1.6 knots of 13.6. The run

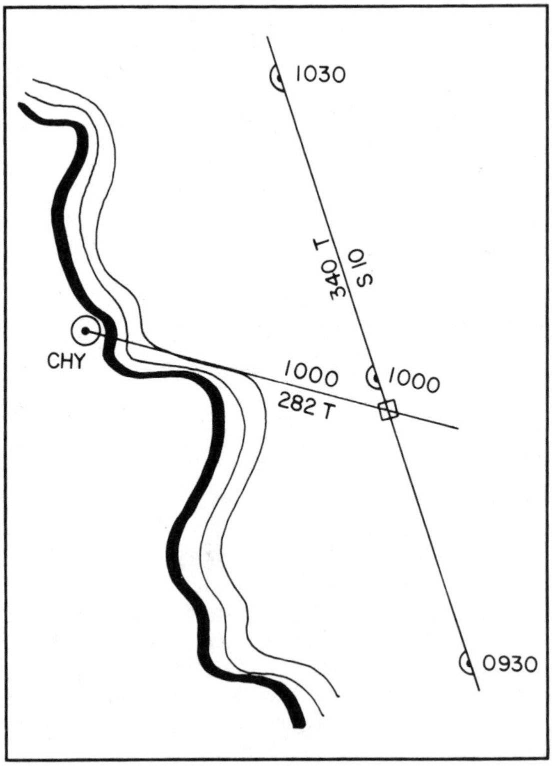

1030
340 T
S 10
CHY
1000
282 T
1000
0930

Fig. 5-33. LOP crossing DR for EP.

of 3.0 miles to the next turning point in the channel at that speed will take only a bit over 13 minutes. This is considerably faster than originally expected.

$$60 \times D = S \times T \quad 60 \times 3.0 = 180$$

$$\frac{180}{13.6} = \text{Time} = 13.4 \text{ minutes}$$

At the end of 13 minutes, Point Loma Light should bear 326° M if the boat has made good 3.0 miles over the ground in the direction of 110° M. Sight is taken at 1051, showing the light bearing 330° M. When this bearing is plotted, the boat is not at the 1051 DR position. Advancing the 1038 bearing for 3 miles along the 110° M course line until it crosses the 1051 bearing, a running fix results placing the boat south and west of the DR position. How the boat got west of the DR position when all the sets up to now have been south and east is hard to tell. Perhaps it is due to poor steering or an undetected current change.

In any event, from the running fix a final course of 345° M is taken, and engine speed is kept at 12 knots to bring the boat to its destination at "E." From there, the pilot will change to the harbor chart and make his way visually to his dock in the inner harbor. Distance of the final leg is approximately 3.0 miles. At 12 knots, this will take another 15 minutes. Total running time for the trip has been 65.5 minutes. Looking back to the time estimate based on the original DR plot it was 67.5 minutes. A difference of only 2 minutes is not bad at all!

Obviously, this procedure enables a boatman to plan a trip ahead of time and then make the trip in very nearly the planned time. This was accomplished even though, once under way, the boat deviated from both planned courses and speed requiring various corrections to be made en route. The key lies in early detection and prompt corrections for variations from the plan.

Now, let's work through a somewhat longer trip (Fig. 5-35). This time departure will be taken from Bell Buoy 5, southeast of Point Loma with Oceanside as the destination. The first step is to lay out the DR track. Next, the speed will be set in order to project the running time for the trip as a whole as well as the parts of the trip. Also, the chart will be carefully examined for landmarks and aids to navigation that may be used to check position along the way.

The DR plot for this trip is found in Fig. 5-35. Departure will be taken from the Bell Buoy on a course of 185° M for a short leg of only 1½ miles to a point about halfway between Buoys 3 and 1. There course will be changed to 265° M for a run of 2 miles. From here a track at 335° M goes straight in to Oceanside. Once at Oceanside, the inset chartlet is used to enter harbor.

Ocean swells in this area come normally from the northwest. This means that if there is a sea running when we make the trip, it will probably be diagonally on the port bow. It will be a considerably more comfortable trip and much easier on the boat if it is done at a moderate speed so the projected speed will be 10 knots.

The first leg of 1½ miles on course 185° M at 10 knots will take 9 minutes:

$$(60 \times 1.5 = 10 \times \text{Time} = \frac{90}{10} = 9 \text{ minutes})$$

The second leg of 2 miles on course 265° M will take 12 minutes at 10 knots:

$$(60 \times 2 = 10 \times \text{Time} = \frac{120}{10} = 12 \text{ minutes})$$

The third leg—the long straight shot up to Oceanside on course 335° M—measures off at 35.3 miles. At 10 knots this will take 3 hours 32 minutes:

$$(60 \times 35.3 = 10 \times \text{Time}$$

$$T = \frac{2118}{10} = 211.8 \text{ minutes}$$

212 minutes = 3 hr. 32 min.

Total travel time for the trip will thus be:

9 min.
12 min.
3 hr 32 min.
3 hr. 53 minutes

Ideally, if departure is at 1000 hr. from Bell Buoy 5, arrival at Oceanside harbor entrance will be at 1353 hrs. (1:53 PM). This assumes, of course, that a speed of exactly 10 knots over the ground is maintained for the entire time and that no steering errors are made.

Because—to put it mildly—this sort of ideal run is unlikely, a study of the chart shows both landmarks and aids to navigation that can be used to fix the position of the boat along the way. For example, at the end of the first 1½ mile leg on

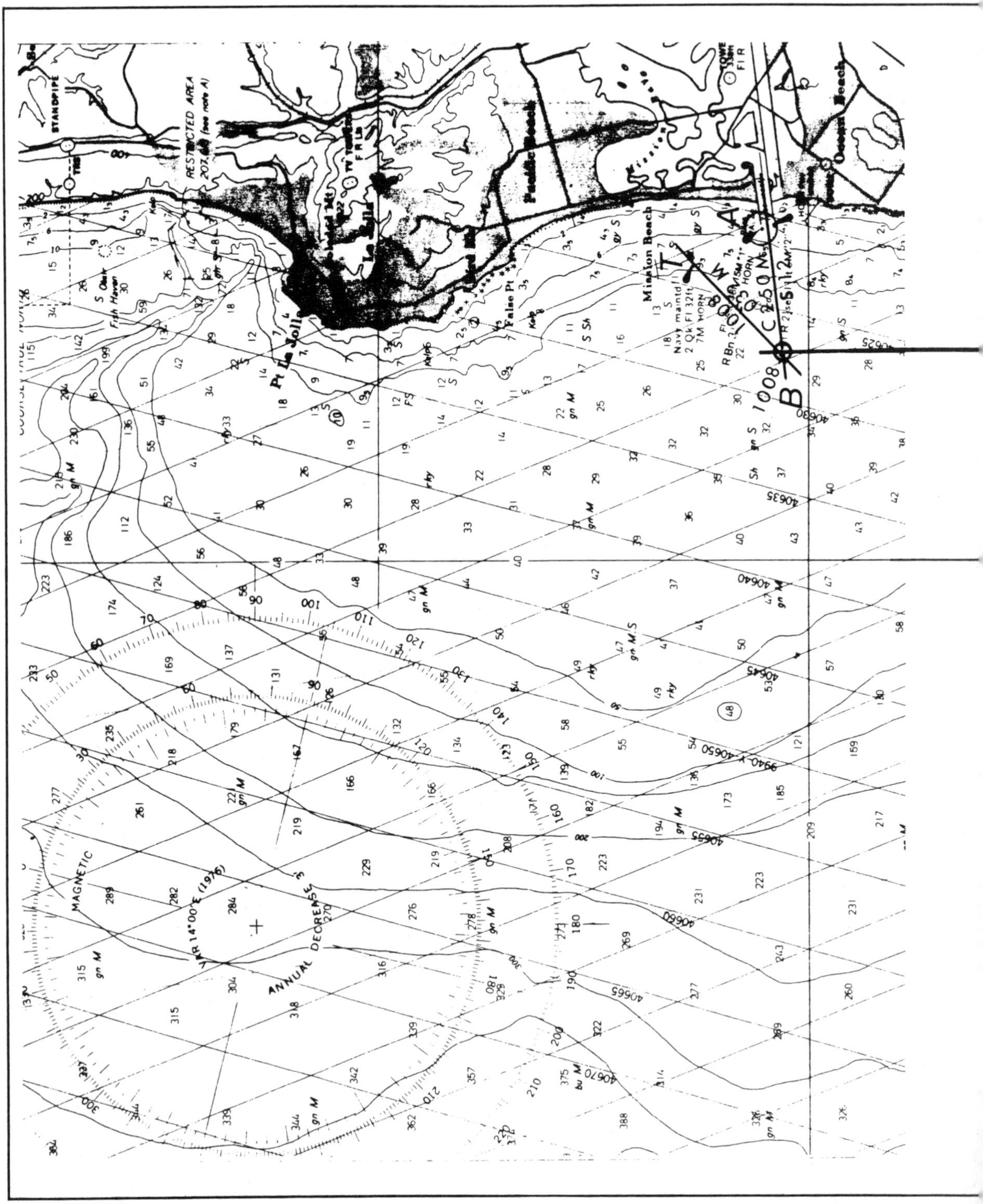
STANDPIPE
RESTRICTED AREA
Pt La Jolla
False Pt
Pacific Beach
Mission Beach
Ocean Beach
MAGNETIC
ANNUAL DECREASE

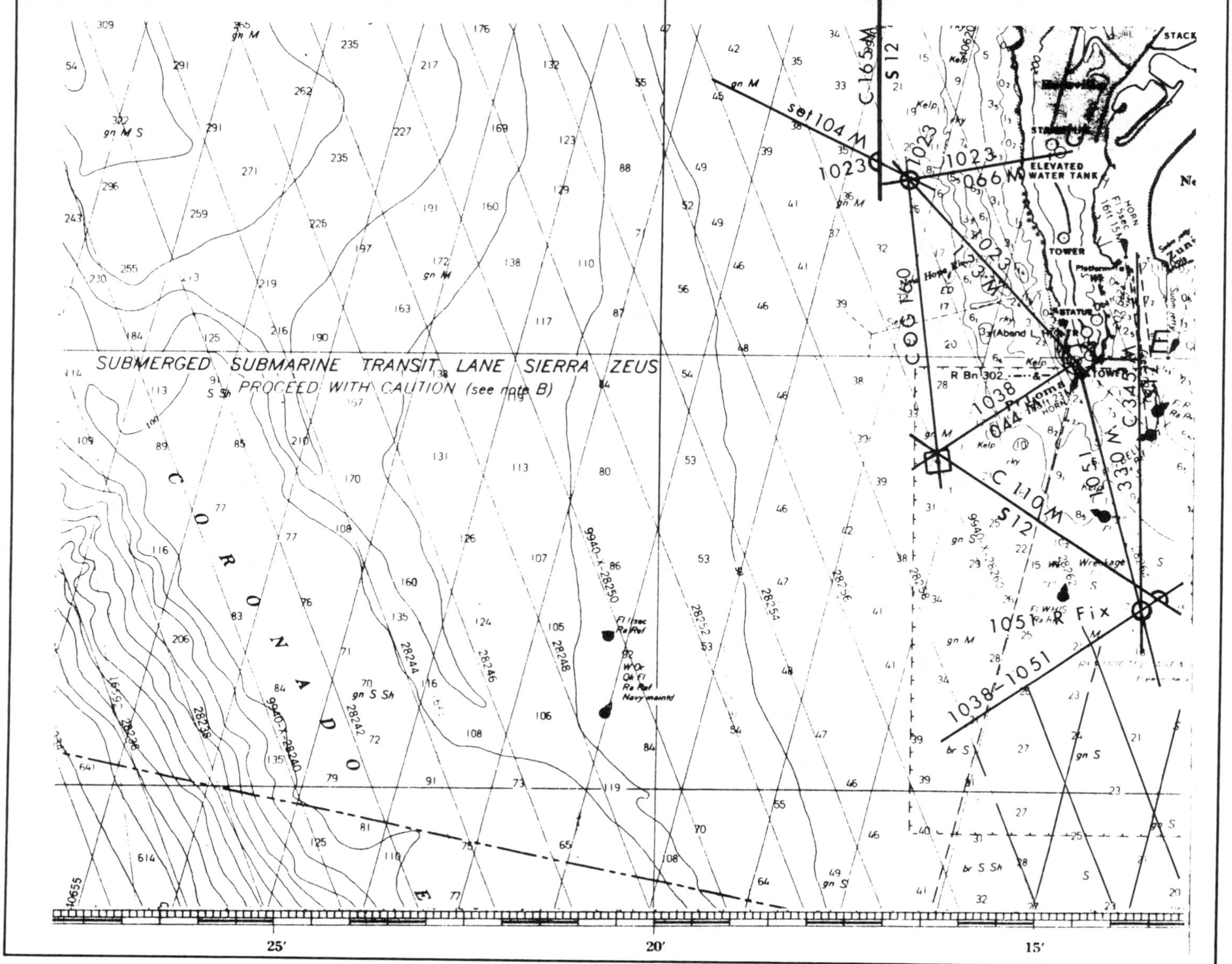

SUBMERGED SUBMARINE TRANSIT LANE SIERRA ZEUS
PROCEED WITH CAUTION (see note B)
C O R O N A D O
ELEVATED WATER TANK
TOWER
STATUE
HORN
set 104 M
C 165 M
S 12
1023
COG 140
C 110 M
S12
1038
044
105 R Fix
1038–1051
330 W
1051
25′
20′
15′

Fig. 5-34. Plot of actual trip (Mission Bay to Point Loma).

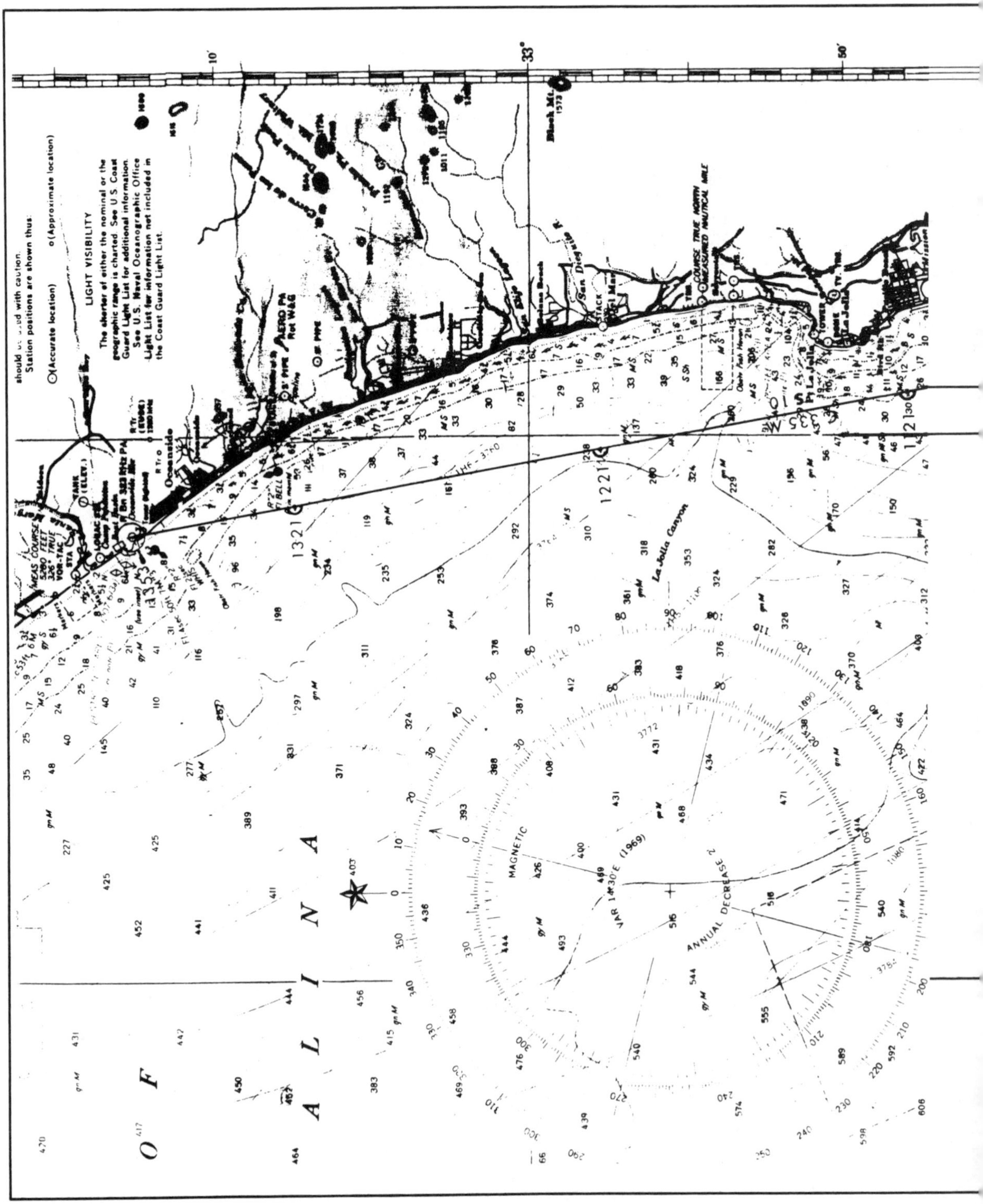

should be used with caution.
Station positions are shown thus:
⊙(Accurate location) o(Approximate location)
LIGHT VISIBILITY
The shorter of either the nominal or the geographic range is charted. See U.S. Coast Guard Light List for additional information. See U.S. Naval Oceanographic Office Light List for information not included in the Coast Guard Light List.
COURSE TRUE NORTH
MEASURED NAUTICAL MILE
La Jolla Canyon
MAGNETIC
ANNUAL DECREASE 2'

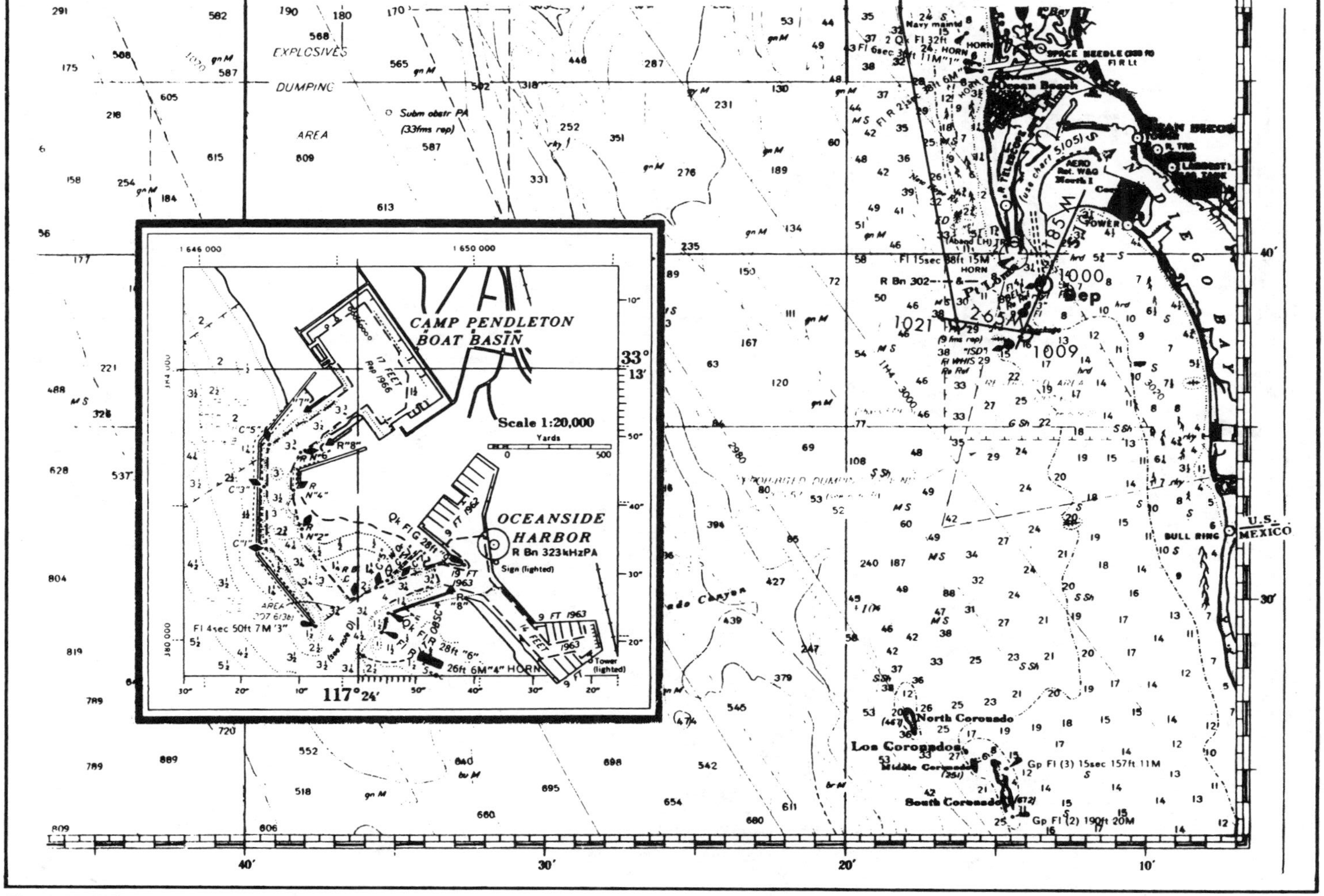
CAMP PENDLETON BOAT BASIN
OCEANSIDE HARBOR
Scale 1:20,000
EXPLOSIVES DUMPING AREA
Los Coronados
North Coronado
South Coronado
U.S. MEXICO

Fig. 5-35. DR plot for trip from Point Loma to Oceanside.

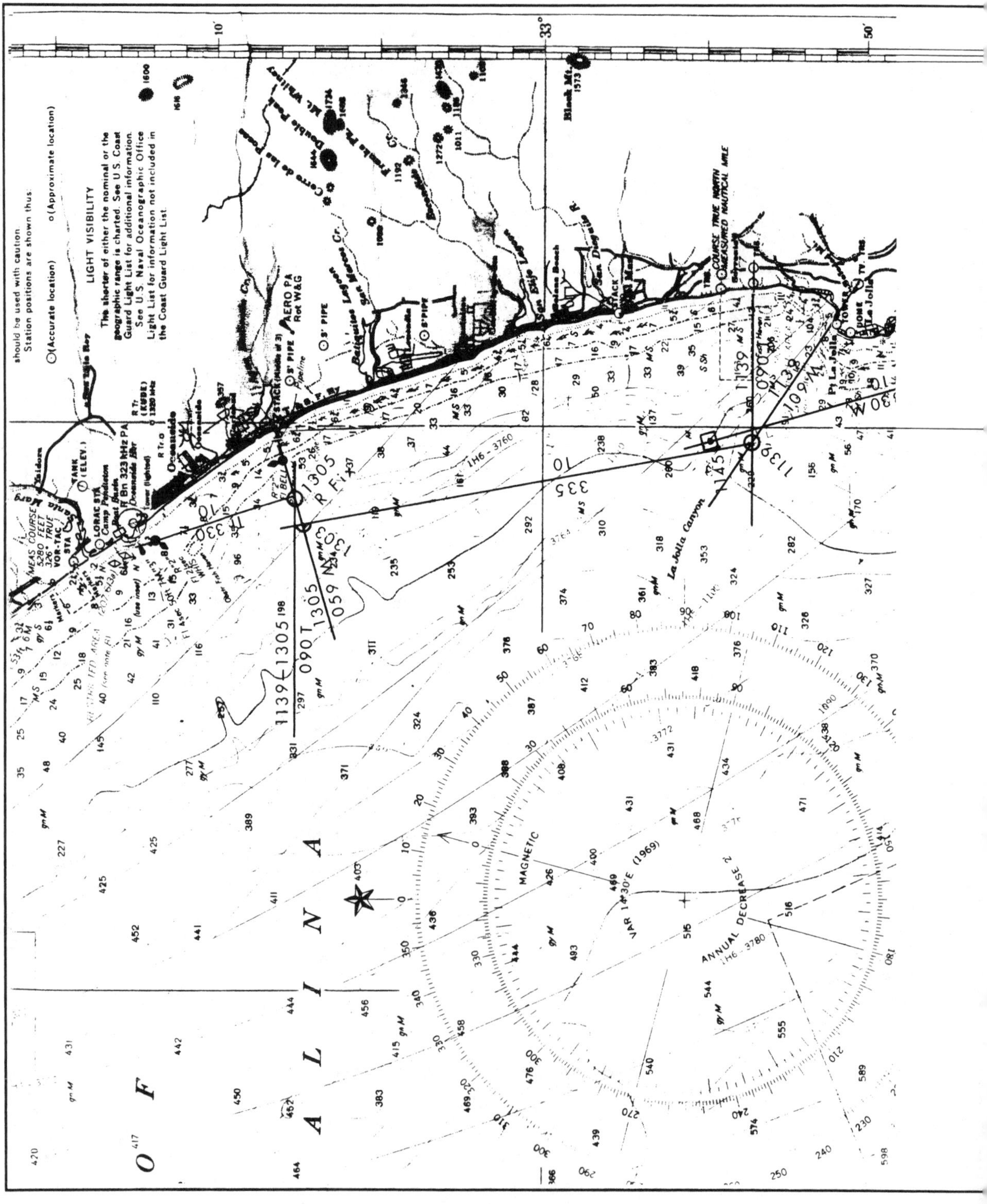
should be used with caution.
Station positions are shown thus:
⊙(Accurate location) o(Approximate location)
LIGHT VISIBILITY
The shorter of either the nominal or the geographic range is charted. See U.S. Coast Guard Light List for additional information. See U.S. Naval Oceanographic Office Light List for information not included in the Coast Guard Light List.
MEAS COURSE 5280 FEET 326° TRUE
LORAC STA Camp Pendleton
Oceanside
AERO PA Rot W&G
STACK
COURSE TRUE NORTH MEASURED NAUTICAL MILE
Black Mt. 1573
La Jolla Canyon
Pt La Jolla
O F
A L I N A
MAGNETIC
VAR 14°30'E (1969)
ANNUAL DECREASE 2'

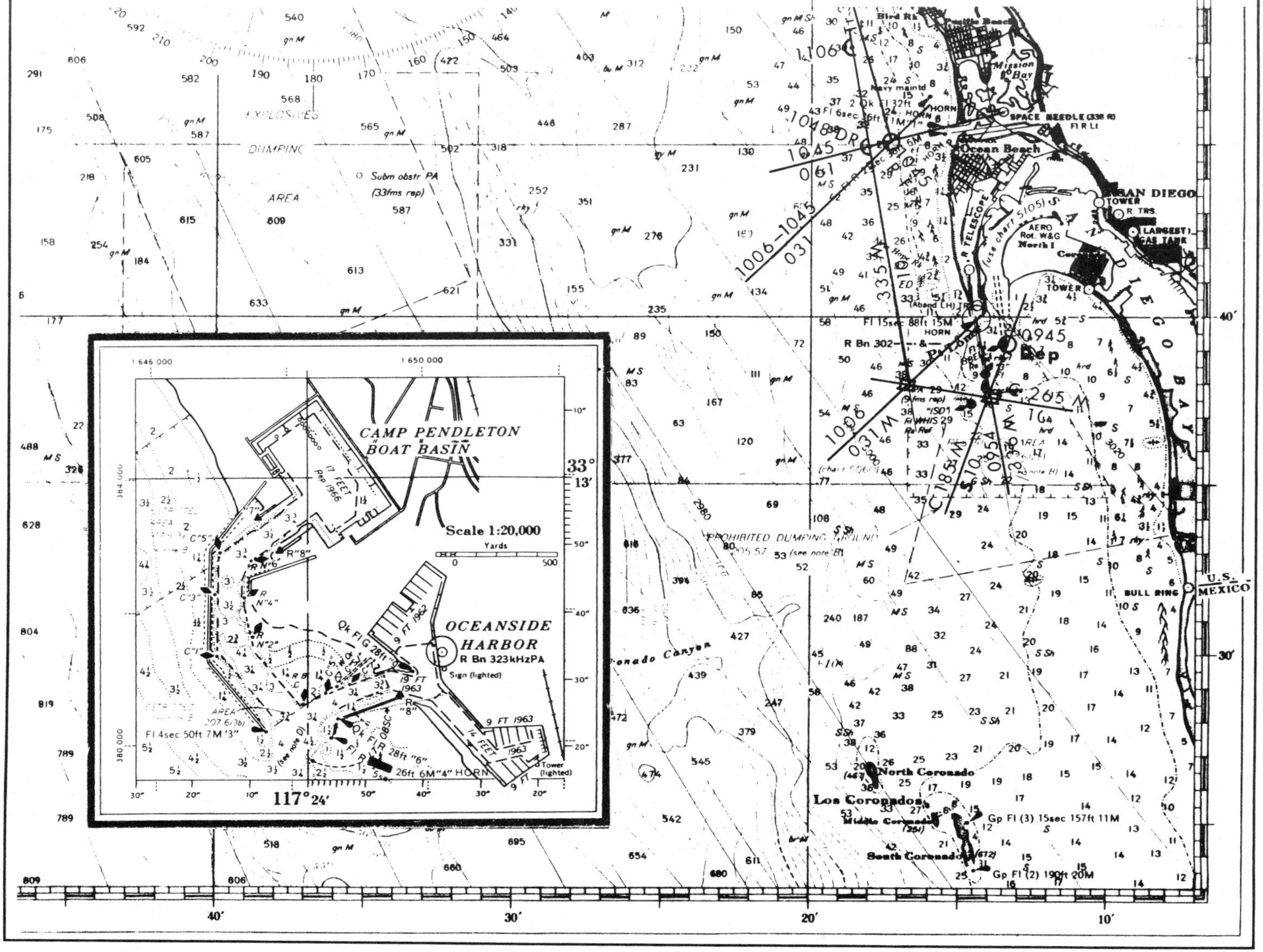

SAN DIEGO
Ocean Beach
Mission Bay
SPACE NEEDLE
DIEGO BAY
U.S. MEXICO
BULL RING
North Coronado
Middle Coronado
South Coronado
Los Coronados
PROHIBITED DUMPING GROUND
EXPLOSIVES DUMPING AREA
Subm obstr PA (33fms rep)
CAMP PENDLETON BOAT BASIN
OCEANSIDE HARBOR
R Bn 323kHzPA
Scale 1:20,000
117°24′
33° 13′

Fig. 5-36. Plot of trip from Point Loma to Oceanside.

course 185° M Buoys 2 and 3 should both be visible about equally distant from the boat and Point Loma Light should bear 334° M. After sailing from there on course 265° M, a distance of 2 miles, Point Loma should bear 028° M, at which time the course is changed to 335° for the long run to the destination at Oceanside Harbor entrance.

Looking north from Point Loma, the Space Needle 338 feet high should be an object on which bearings can be taken for a while. Perhaps we can get it lined up as a range with one of the lights at the end of the breakwaters just north of Ocean Beach. There is also some kind of a light 32 feet high marked "Navy maintd" north of those two that might be lined up with the Space Needle to make a range.

The TV towers on Soledad Mountain and the tower and dome in La Jolla are the next things to look for. Following those are two ranges marking a measured mile. We could even plan to change to a true north course while passing from one to the other. This would allow us to use them to see if there is any significant difference between our speed over the ground, and what we believe is our speed through the water as read on the speedometer.

From the measured mile north, there is only a stack in Del Mar, and a standpipe in Leucadia until we get to the Bell Buoy south of Carlsbad. Well, OK, there are three standpipes along the way. Not having had the best of luck finding standpipes in the past, I would not depend on them. Spotting the Bell Buoy in daylight from a mile away on a small boat will depend somewhat on sea conditions, but the stacks on shore beyond it certainly should be easy to find. From there, it is a short distance in to the destination.

With the DR laid out and various objects noted with which to check position and progress along the way, we are ready to make the trip. On the appointed day, we make our way to Bell Buoy 5 to depart (Fig. 5-36) for Oceanside. Because we are 15 minutes early, we mark Departure at 0945. Following the DR timing and course plan, the boat runs for 9 minutes at 10 knots on course 185° M. At that time (0954), a sight is taken on Point Loma Light with the hand-bearing compass. The reading is 336° M and a turn is made to course 265° M.

The intersection of the bearing with the course line is marked with a square indicating EP (estimated position) because it is based on the line of position from a single bearing. At 1106 after 12 minutes on course 265° M at 10 knots, a second bearing is taken again on Point Loma. This time it reads 031° M.

Because a bearing of 028° M had been expected, the boat is apparently slightly further offshore than the DR position. Again this position is marked with the EP square, and the course is changed to 335° M. Speed is maintained at 10 knots. At 1045 after 39 minutes, the north Mission Bay breakwater light is on range with the Space Needle bearing 061° M. According to the DR line, that range should not have been reached until 1048. The boat is off its DR course. Advancing the 1006 bearing on Point Loma to 1045, a running fix is found east of the DR line on the 1045 LOP (the range from the Breakwater Light to the Space Needle).

Some combination of forces—wind, seas, steering error, or currents—are setting the boat east (to starboard) of its intended course. Comparing the direction of the DR line with the line from the 1006 EP to the 1045 R fix, the difference is about 5°. Because the cause is unknown, it must be assumed that the same set will continue until or unless information to the contrary is found. Therefore, the course being steered must now be changed. In order to progress in the direction of 335° M, a course of 330° M will have to be steered in order to make up for the 52 set we have just discovered.

But we are already off course. If we progress in the direction 335° M, we'll no longer get to our destination. To make up what has been lost, the course change will have to be more than 5°. Actually about 8° would do it, but with a compass calibrated in 5° increments there is no way we can steer an 8° change. The change will be 10° to the west; instead of steering 335° the course to be *steered* becomes 325° M.

The original DR line is now abandoned and a new intended track starts from the running fix. The boat will be steered on a course of 325° M. Taking into account the expected 5° set to starboard, the course actually traveled is expected to be 330° M. A track line of 330° is now drawn and projected for 10 miles, which is one hour in running time. This gives an 1145 EP (estimated position). This is an EP not a DR because it allows for expected leeway.

At 1139, the south range of the measure nautical mile shown on the chart is in line, and from the chart it is aligned with 090° T. A bearing is taken at the same time on the TV towers on top of Soledad Mountain. They bear 109° M. These two bearings produce an 1139 fix that is now west of the expected track. Whatever force was setting the boat off to starboard has apparently moderated. The next projected track now starts at the 1139 fix. From here we can return to the original steering course of 335° M producing a track that ends a little west of Oceanside. This is good in case some set to starboard continues.

Proceeding on, it develops that, as was feared, the stack at Del Mar and the standpipes further along cannot be found. The next LOP will have to be taken on the stack close to Bell Buoy R 2 south of Carlsbad. When those two objects are in range the bearing will be 059° M. From the last fix, the distance along the intended track will be 14 miles. Continuing to run at 10 knots, the running time should be 1 hour 24 minutes.

$$(60 \times 14 = 10 \times \text{Time} = \frac{840}{10}$$

$$84 \text{ minutes} = 1 \text{ hr. } 24 \text{ min.})$$

The Bell Buoy and the stack should be in line at 1303. They are not aligned until 1305. Advancing the 1139 LOP of 090° T to cross the 1305 LOP on the buoy and stack, a running fix is found. It indicates that again there has been a starboard (or easterly) set.

The track is now picked up at the 1305 running fix and the final steering course is set at 325° M in order to make good a track of 330° M for the final 5 miles. It will require 30 minutes running time to arrive at the harbor entrance.

The preceding examples illustrate how the navigator prepares a DR plot and schedule in advance of starting a trip. The DR plan is then used to set courses and speeds when the trip is begun. Once under way, various piloting procedures are employed to determine where the boat has actually gone. Based on the information developed by these piloting procedures, the mariner can intelligently and accurately make such changes in courses and speeds as are required to get him where he intends to go.

Chapter 6

QUASAR

Tides and Tide Tables

WHEN MAKING PASSAGES CLOSE TO THE COAST and certainly when moving about in bays and harbors, a primary concern of any sensible sailor is the question of how much water he will have under his keel when he reaches his destination. He had best keep track of what he will have under him while underway as well!

In all saltwater areas and for varying distances up all rivers emptying into them, the depth of water changes at different times of the day, and also from one day to the next due to tides. Knowledge of tidal action and how the height of the tide affects water depths alerts the prudent boatman as to when he can safely cross a shoal or bar or pass under a bridge.

Inadequate knowledge of tidal depth has stranded many an unwary mariner and wrecked many more. Those lucky enough to ground in sand or mud may suffer no more than minor inconvenience. However, those who ground on rocks or coral, with a bit of a sea running, are lucky indeed if all they lose is the boat.

The ability to determine the height of the tide at a particular time plus knowledge as to how much higher it will rise as well as how much lower it will fall in a few hours, or over night, are absolutely necessary for safe anchoring and for tying up to fixed docks or bulkheads. While a detailed discussion of anchoring and mooring is well beyond the scope of this book, it is certainly pertinent to note that it is somewhere between foolish and dangerous to anchor or tie up to a dock of fixed height in ignorance of the state of the tide at that time.

As an example (Fig. 6-1), suppose it is about sundown and you have decided to anchor at a place you like. You find the water depth is about 10 feet. Because there are other boats nearby, you do not want to take up too much swinging room. Therefore, you decide to go with a scope of 5 to 1. You let out 50 feet of anchor line and happily go below. You "splice the main brace," eat, and go to sleep. No one notices that you anchored about 2½ hours after low water. The tide in this locality is due to rise another 4 feet. The boat will then be in 14 feet of water. The anchor scope will now be reduced from 5 to 1 down to a not-as-safe 3.6 to 1.

While boat people are a generally happy-go-lucky, cheerful lot, to a man they will be irritated if awakened by someone else's boat banging against theirs because it dragged anchor. When anchoring, try to allow a scope that will be at least 5 to 1 *at high tide*. This means it is necessary to know when high tide is due and how high it will be at that time.

While the height of the tide varies from one hour to the next on any given day—and also varies

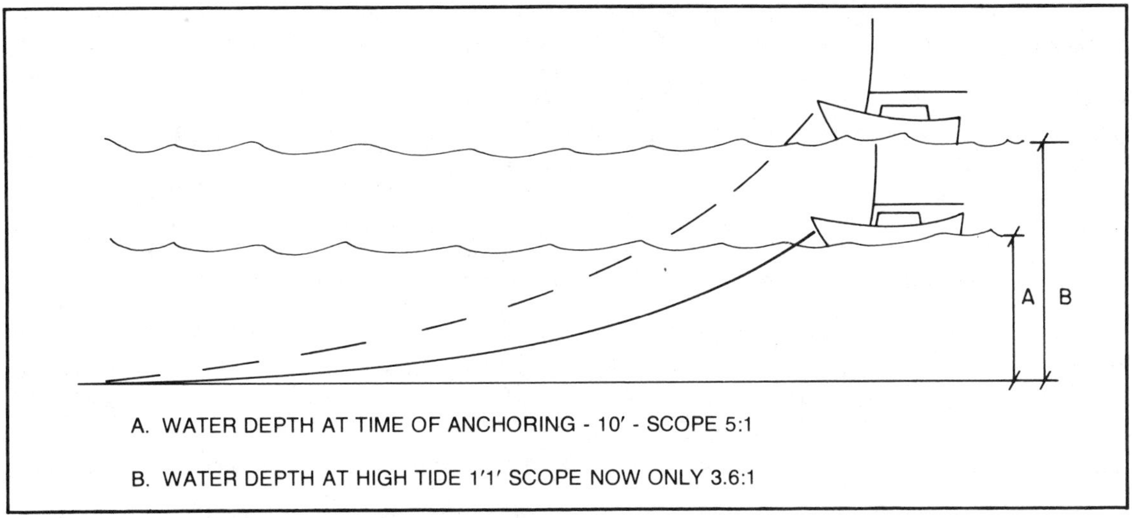
A
B
A. WATER DEPTH AT TIME OF ANCHORING - 10′ - SCOPE 5:1
B. WATER DEPTH AT HIGH TIDE 1′1′ SCOPE NOW ONLY 3.6:1

Fig. 6-1. Change in water depth; anchoring time to high tide.

from one day to the next—reasonably accurate predictions of tidal highs and lows can be made far in advance for a vast number of places. This is because the primary forces causing tides are related to the predictable movements of astronomical bodies.

TIDE GENERATING FORCES

Those who have sailed in tidal waters will have noticed not only that the time of high and low tides changes from day to day, but also that the maximum height of the high water as well as the depth remaining at low water changes daily. Understanding the forces that cause the tides makes clear the reasons behind this seemingly erratic phenomenon.

Earth and Moon Effect

The strongest tide generating effect on the oceans is that of the gravitational attraction between the earth and the moon, coupled with the centrifugal forces resulting from the revolution of both bodies around a common center. No, that little old lady didn't lie to you back in grade school. The moon does revolve around the earth, but at the same time the earth also revolves (Fig. 6-2) around the common center of mass of the two bodies. That common center lies *inside* the earth—about 810 miles inside.

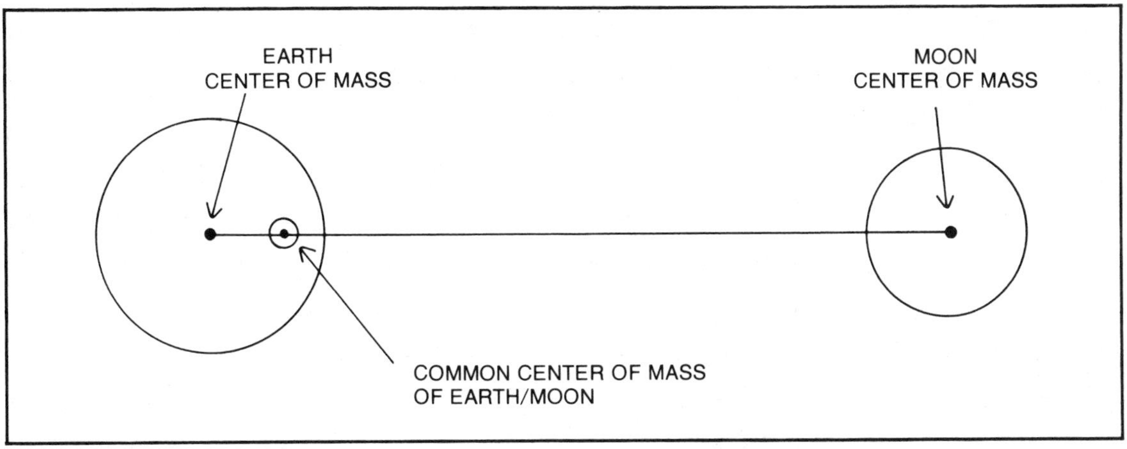
EARTH
CENTER OF MASS
MOON
CENTER OF MASS
COMMON CENTER OF MASS
OF EARTH/MOON

Fig. 6-2. Earth and moon; common center of mass.

The gravitational forces of the two bodies tend to draw them together while the centrifugal forces tend to drive them apart. Because these two forces overall are in balance the earth and moon, neither collide nor fly away from each other, but continue happily to rotate.

While the earth together with the moon comprises a rotating system that is in overall equilibrium, the individual particles of matter making up the earth are subjected to forces that are not by any means similarly balanced. As the system rotates, the centrifugal forces are the same all over the earth (Fig. 6-3) and always parallel to the line connecting the center of mass of the two planets. Gravitational forces, by contrast, are not everywhere the same (Fig. 6-4) because, as distance from the moon increases across the earth, the gravitational force of the moon decreases. The effective direction of that force changes as well.

The gravitational force of the moon is exerted not on a line parallel to the centers of mass, but from any point on earth directly toward the center of the moon. The combination of centrifugal and gravitational forces acting in opposing directions produces resulting forces on the surface of the earth (as diagrammed in Fig. 6-5). These combined forces are strongest on the area of the earth's surface directly facing the moon, and are of nearly as great intensity in the area directly opposite because there centrifugal forces most heavily overbalance the

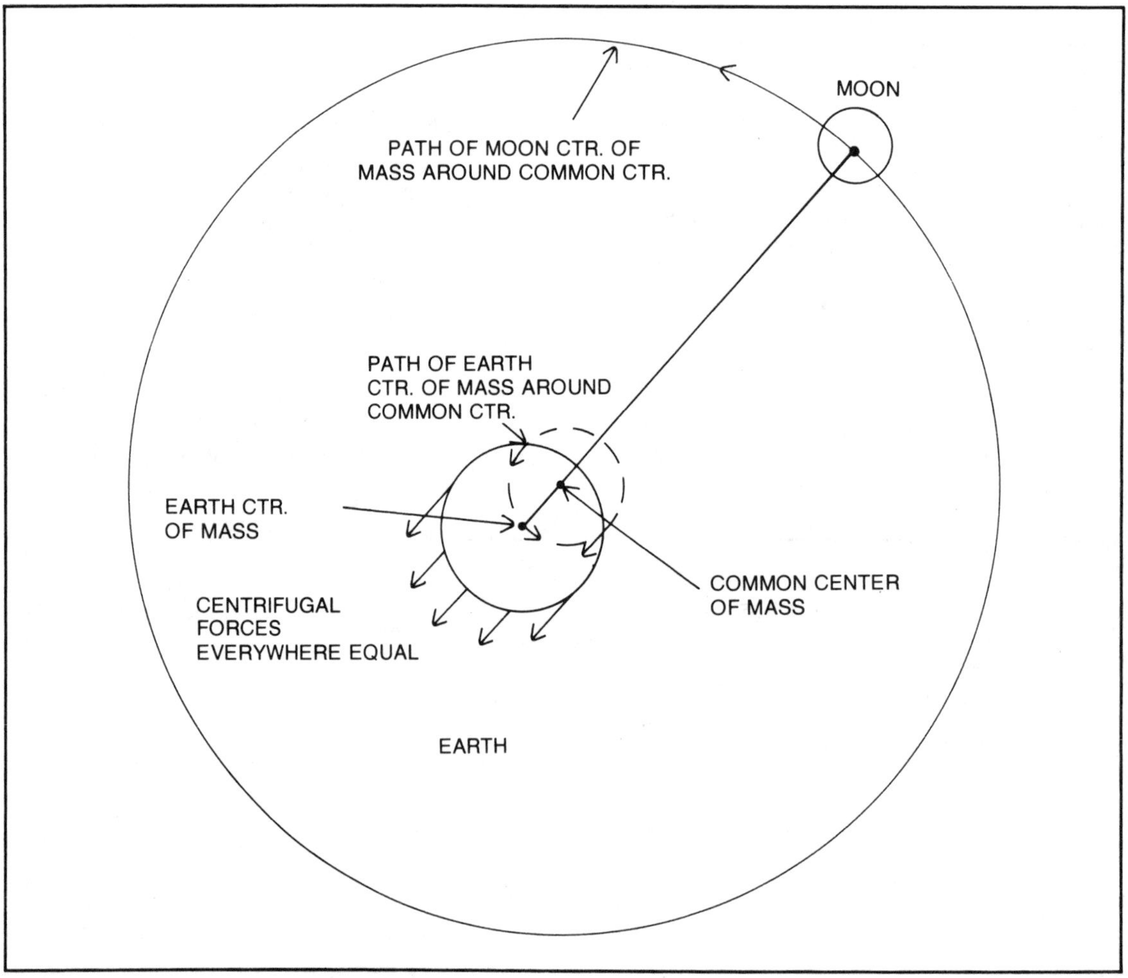

MOON
PATH OF MOON CTR. OF
MASS AROUND COMMON CTR.
PATH OF EARTH
CTR. OF MASS AROUND
COMMON CTR.
EARTH CTR.
OF MASS
COMMON CENTER
OF MASS
CENTRIFUGAL
FORCES
EVERYWHERE EQUAL
EARTH

Fig. 6-3. Earth and moon; centrifugal forces.

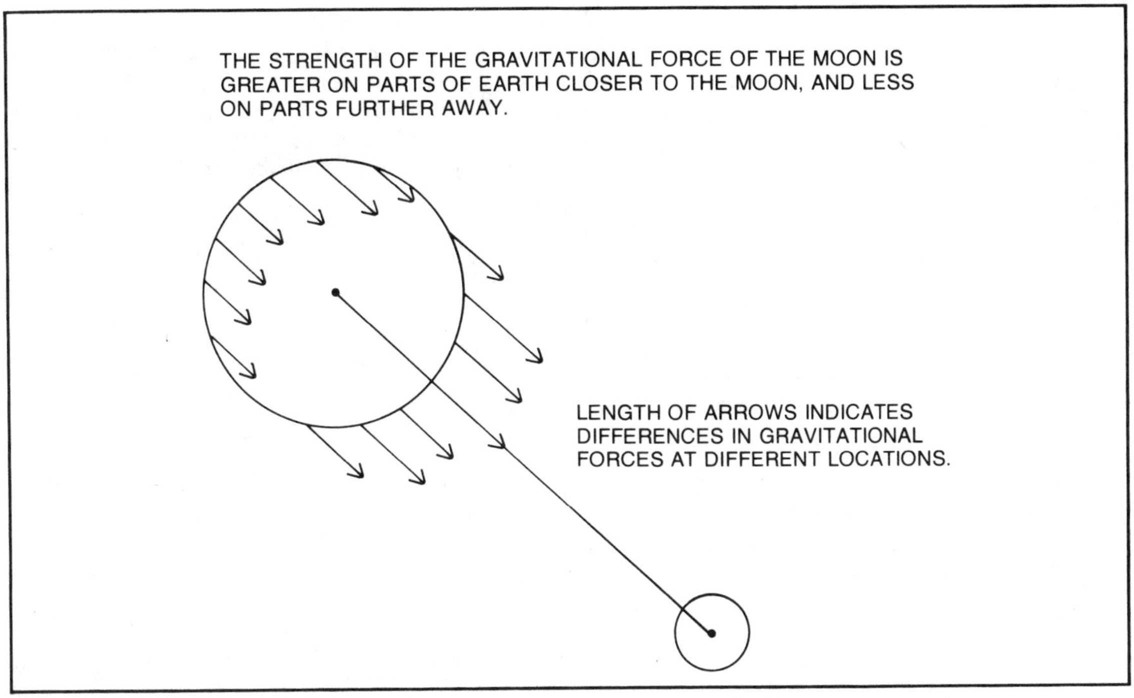
THE STRENGTH OF THE GRAVITATIONAL FORCE OF THE MOON IS GREATER ON PARTS OF EARTH CLOSER TO THE MOON, AND LESS ON PARTS FURTHER AWAY.
LENGTH OF ARROWS INDICATES DIFFERENCES IN GRAVITATIONAL FORCES AT DIFFERENT LOCATIONS.

Fig. 6-4. Earth and moon; gravitational force of moon.

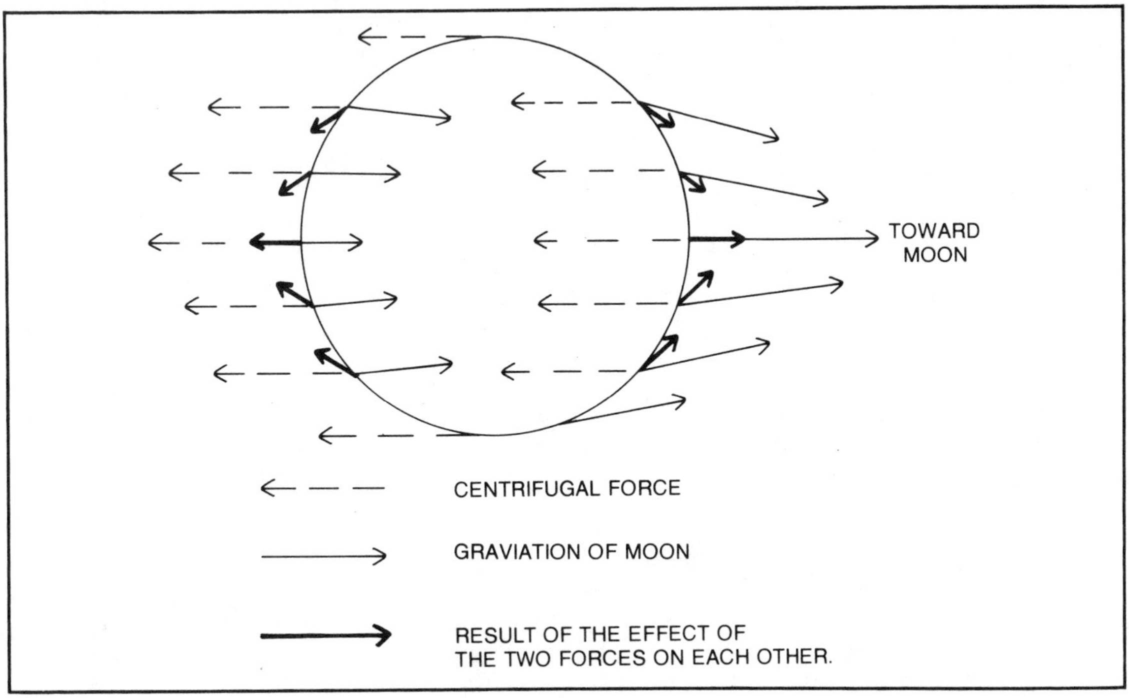
TOWARD MOON
CENTRIFUGAL FORCE
GRAVIATION OF MOON
RESULT OF THE EFFECT OF THE TWO FORCES ON EACH OTHER.

Fig. 6-5. Combined effect of centrifugal and gravitational forces.

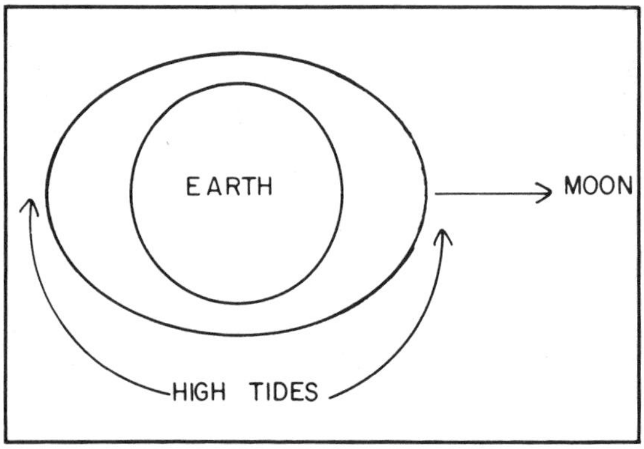
EARTH
MOON
HIGH TIDES

Fig. 6-6. Earth with tidal bulges due to moon.

gravitational pull on the moon.

This combination of centrifugal and gravitational forces are exerted over the entire surface of the earth. While the land masses do not move in response to them, the oceans do. This results in a tidal bulge on the side facing the moon and another on the side opposite (Fig. 6-6).

While the earth rotates around its axis every 24 hours by the time it has completed one full rotation the moon will have moved in its orbit around the earth. The result is that one full "tidal day" is 24 hours and 50 minutes. This is the time required for two successive passes of the moon over a specific point on the earth.

Earth and Sun Effect

The moon is the major influence in the generating of the tides, but not the only one. The sun, while having only 47 percent as powerful an effect as the moon, is still a major factor. The patterns of both gravitational and centrifugal forces caused by the sun are exactly the same as those of the moon except that they are not as powerful. This is because—while the sun is a vastly larger object than the moon—it is also vastly further away, and these forces are weakened by distance. The oceans respond to the sun just as they do to the moon, but in a less pronounced manner. Thus the oceans are moving in response to both sun and moon at any given time.

As the moon revolves around the earth during its monthly cycle, the alignment of the earth, moon, and sun relative to each other changes from day to day. At the time of new moon, the three are in an alignment such that the tidal forces of both sun and moon reinforce each other (Fig. 6-7). This occurs again at full moon. The highest high and the lowest low tides of the month occur at these times. At the times of first and last quarter sun and moon are at a 90° angle to earth and their tidal forces are at cross purposes to each other, making for the smallest tide ranges of the month. The high is not very high and the low is not very low. As the moon moves from new to first quarter, the tides decrease in height each day. From first quarter to full they increase daily. From full moon, tides decrease daily until third quarter. Then they increase daily until new moon when the entire cycle starts again.

Declination Effect

Certainly you have noticed the apparent movement of the sun, with the seasons north in the summer and south in the winter. The angle of the position of the sun with the equator of the earth any particular time is its *declination*. The moon is also constantly changing in declination. This causes a difference in the heights of two consecutive high tides. As shown in Fig. 6-8, the high tide at point A will be higher than it will be 12 hours and 25 minutes later when that point reaches point B. Because of this declination effect, the two high tides and the two low tides each day are seldom equal. Other factors contribute to inequality between two daily tides, but declination is a major factor.

Other Factors Affecting Tides

As the tidal bulges in the oceans caused by the combined solar and lunar gravitational and centrifugal forces moves around the earth, their movements would be reasonably simple and predictable if the earth were a plain sphere uniformly covered with water. In spite of the monthly declination cycle of the moon (from 28.5° north to 28.5° south) and the annual declination cycle of the sun (from 23.5° north to 23.5° south), if these were the only complicating factors, the computations would be quite easy.

The oceans vary tremendously in depth and bottom configurations. As the tidal waters move over and around these varying shapes, they are in turn considerably affected by them. In some cases, the combination of land and ocean basin shapes minimize tidal effects, as in the Gulf of Mexico. In other instances they magnify them, as in the Gulf of

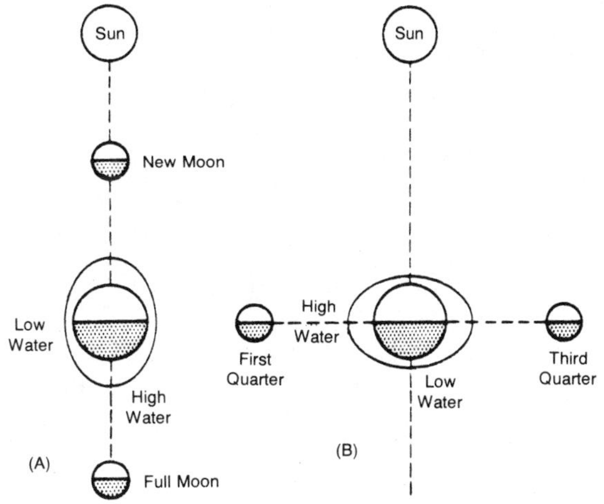
Sun
New Moon
Low Water
High Water
(A)
Full Moon
Sun
High Water
First Quarter
Low Water
Third Quarter
(B)

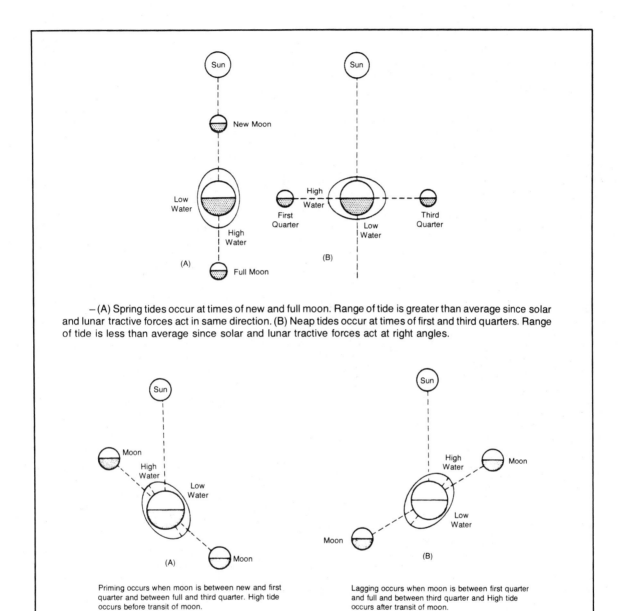

–(A) Spring tides occur at times of new and full moon. Range of tide is greater than average since solar and lunar tractive forces act in same direction. (B) Neap tides occur at times of first and third quarters. Range of tide is less than average since solar and lunar tractive forces act at right angles.

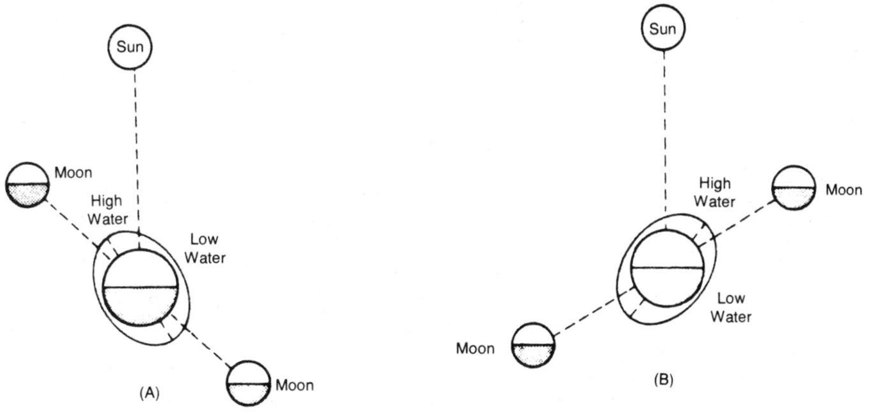
Sun
Moon
High Water
Low Water
(A)
Moon
Sun
High Water
Moon
Low Water
Moon
(B)

Priming occurs when moon is between new and first quarter and between full and third quarter. High tide occurs before transit of moon.

Lagging occurs when moon is between first quarter and full and between third quarter and High tide occurs after transit of moon.

Fig. 6-7. Earth/moon/sun. Angular relationships at: new moon, full moon, first and last quarter.

California. Because local conditions have such a large effect on tides, daily tidal predictions are made by National Ocean Survey for about 6000 places. These are based on a combination of local observations over many years, combined with astronomical predictions of the movements of earth, moon, and sun.

TYPES OF TIDES

As the great waves of the two tides roll continually over the oceans, seas, bays, and gulfs of the earth, yet another factor affects them. Every body of water has a natural period of oscillation. That period depends on the dimensions of the body. The oceans, due to their great sizes and irregular

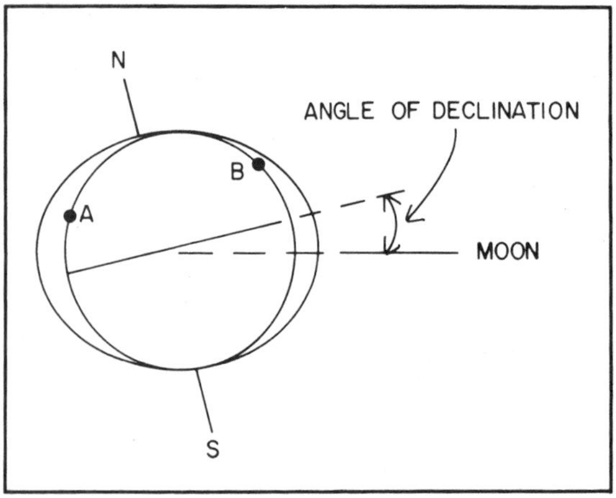
N
ANGLE OF DECLINATION
B
A
MOON
S

Fig. 6-8. Declination effect.

shapes, do not act as simple oscillating bodies. Instead they subdivide into a number of oscillating basins. As these basins are acted upon by the tide producing gravitational and centrifugal forces, some respond readily to the two tidal cycles each day. Others respond to one tidal cycle per day. And yet others respond by producing two daily cycles, but very unequal ones.

Semidiurnal is the term for a type of tide pattern characterized by two high and two low waters each day, such that the inequality between the two highs and the two lows is comparatively small. The tidal patterns on the East Coast of the United States are of this type (Fig. 6-9).

Diurnal is a tide pattern consisting of only one high and one low water per tidal day. In the United States, this type of tide is found along the coast of the Gulf of Mexico from Florida to Louisiana (Fig. 6-10).

Mixed tides combine the characteristics of both semidiurnal and diurnal. There are definitely two high and two low waters each tidal day. This is basically semidiurnal, but either the two highs, or the two lows, or both are extremely unequal (Fig. 6-11). In Seattle, the greater inequality is usually in the low waters. In Los Angeles, both are typically quite unequal. They also are in Honolulu but with a very different pattern. In the United States, mixed tides are found along the Pacific Coast and in some areas of the Gulf of Mexico.

As shown in Fig. 6-12, the type of tide in some places changes from semidiurnal, to mixed, to diurnal, and back again during the course of the month. This cycle can be seen in the charts for both Los Angeles and Honolulu. In Seattle, a few days of semidiurnal tides are scattered into a general pattern of mixed tides. By contrast New York is consistently semidiurnal.

TIDE RANGES AND REFERENCE LEVELS

Looking again at Fig. 6-12, it is apparent that at each of the ports illustrated the tidal variations in water level are in constant change—from hour to hour to hour, from day to day—throughout the month and throughout the year. These changes are

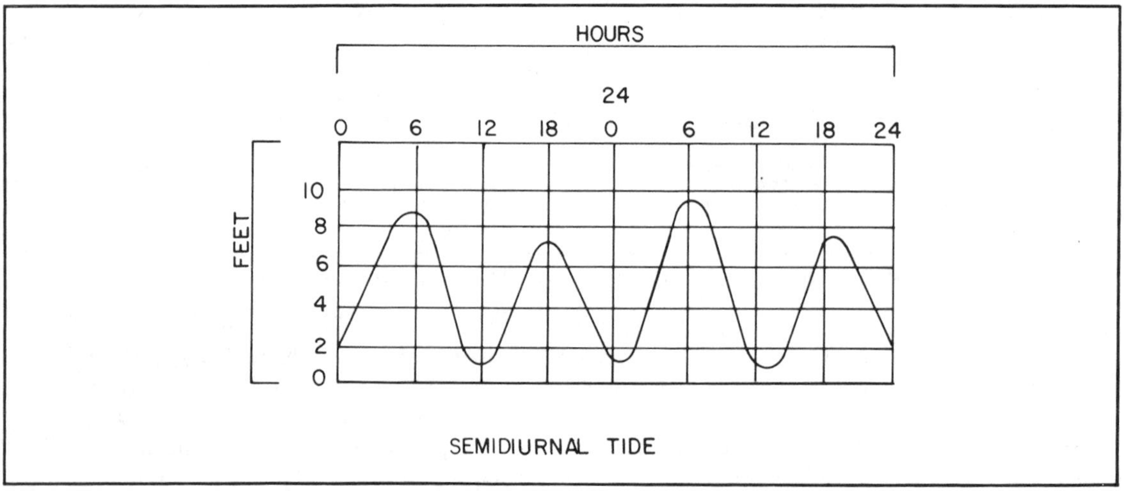
HOURS
24
0 6 12 18 0 6 12 18 24
FEET
10
8
6
4
2
0
SEMIDIURNAL TIDE

Fig. 6-9. Semidiurnal tide.

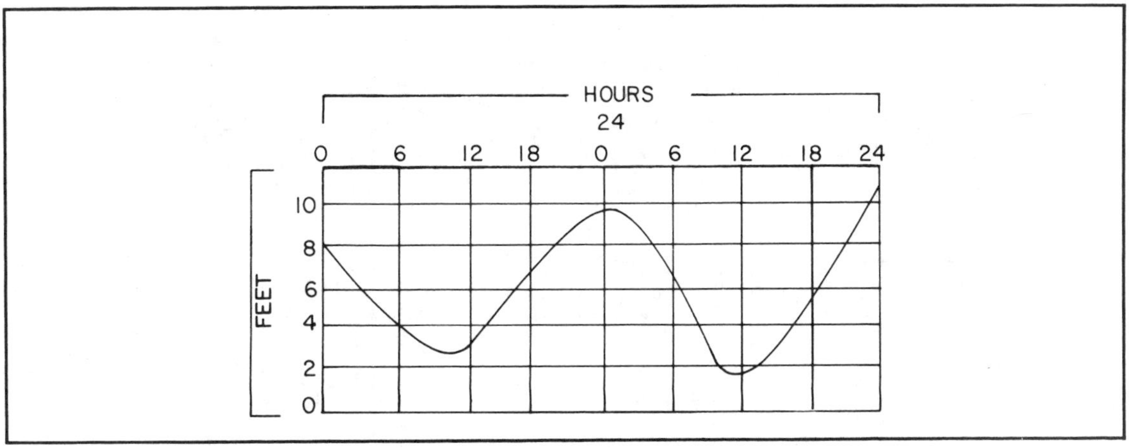
HOURS
24
0
6
12
18
0
6
12
18
24
FEET
10
8
6
4
2
0

Fig. 6-10. Diurnal tide.

given in feet, generally above and occasionally below, a zero reference line. These reference lines are called *tidal datums.*

Because of the different types of tides as well as the very great differences in tidal ranges at varying locations, a number of different datum levels are used. These datum levels are mentioned in Chapter 2 under the discussion of nautical charts.

In any locality, the datum level used as the basis for charted depth soundings must be the same as that used for figuring tidal depth changes. The purpose of coordinating the two is that the mariner should be able to depend on having under his vessel at least the charted depth of water regardless of the state of the tide. This is generally true. Nevertheless, for a few hours on a few days during some months "minus" tides occur in many places. Instances of such tides can be seen in Fig. 6-12 at New York, Seattle, and Los Angeles, where occasionally the tide graph dips below the "0" reference line.

The datum levels on which tidal predictions are based differ in different areas. Further explanation of at least a couple of them should be helpful.

Mean Low Water

Mean low water is the datum level used on NOS

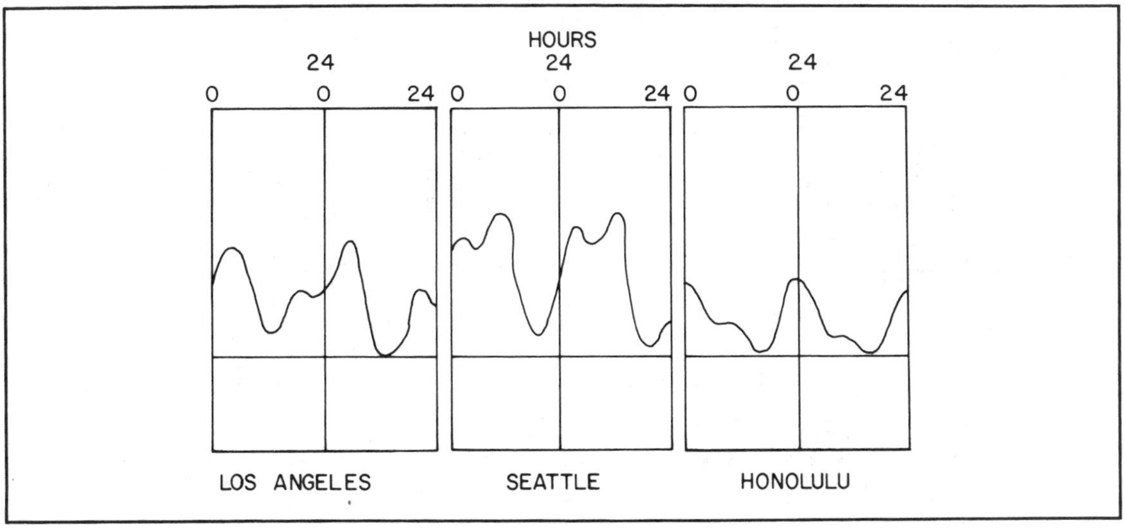
HOURS
24
0
0
24
24
0
0
24
24
0
0
24
LOS ANGELES
SEATTLE
HONOLULU

Fig. 6-11. Mixed tides.

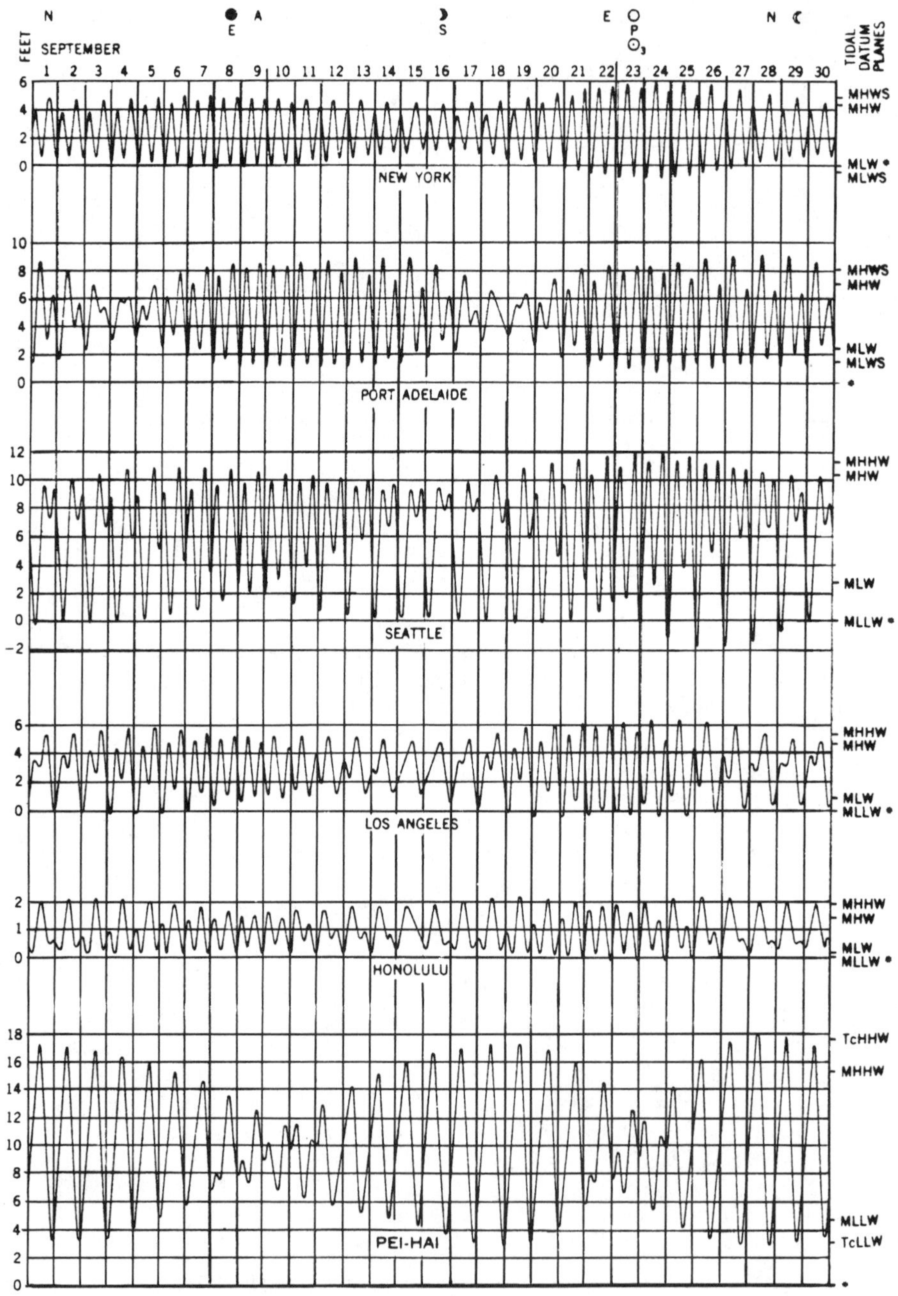
FEET
SEPTEMBER
TIDAL DATUM PLANES
N
A
E
S
P
$\odot_3$
NEW YORK
MHWS
MHW
MLW •
MLWS
PORT ADELAIDE
MHWS
MHW
MLW
MLWS
SEATTLE
MHHW
MHW
MLW
MLLW •
LOS ANGELES
MHHW
MHW
MLW
MLLW •
HONOLULU
MHHW
MHW
MLW
MLLW •
PEI-HAI
TcHHW
MHHW
MLLW
TcLLW

●, new moon; ☽, first quarter; ○, full moon; ☾, last quarter; E, moon on the Equator; N, S, moon farthest north or south of the Equator; A, P, moon in apogee or perigee; $\odot_3$, sun at autumnal equinox.
• chart datum.

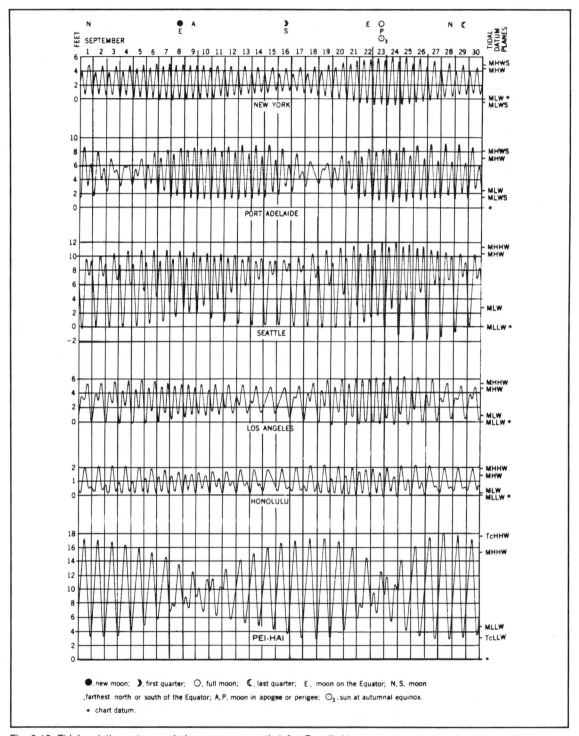

Fig. 6-12. Tidal variations at several places over a month (after Bowditch).

charts of the Atlantic Coast as well as Puerto Rico and the Virgin Islands. Tides in most of this area are semidiurnal, making the two lows of each tidal day very similar. The level used at New York (Fig. 6-12) is the average of all low tides.

When the datum level is the average of all low tides, this means that a good many low tides will be below the reference level. This is precisely what happens at New York. When the predictions of such tides are given in the Tide Tables, they are noted as minus numbers. For example, the low tide on September 24 might appear as −1.2 feet. Gulf Coast low water datum is essentially the same thing as mean low water. This term can be found on Gulf Coast charts.

Mean Lower Low Water

The types of tides on the Pacific Coast, Alaska, and Hawaii are generally mixed. This means that the two low tides in a tidal day are liable to be very different, with one much higher than the other. In this situation, an average of the lower of the two daily lows is more useful in ensuring adequate water depth than mean low water would be. As the graph of Los Angeles tides (Fig. 6-12) clearly shows, even using this as the datum level there will be occasional minus tides. This is the datum level used on the NOS charts of the Pacific Coast, Alaska, and Hawaii.

Tide Range Variations

The range of a tide is the difference in depth between high water and low water at a particular place (Fig. 6-13). The range changes from day to day in response to the daily changes in alignment of the earth, sun, and moon. Variation in the alignment of these bodies alters the intensity of the tide producing gravitational forces.

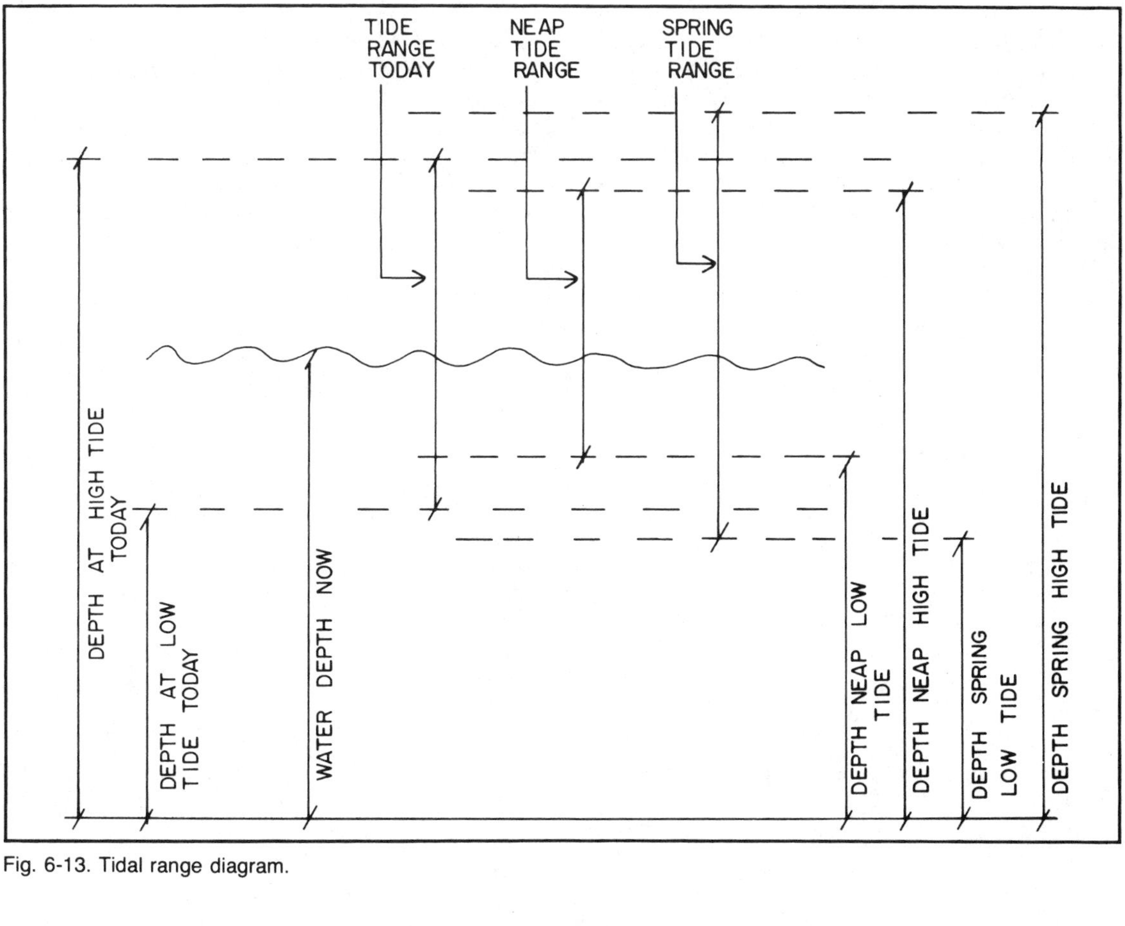
TIDE RANGE TODAY
NEAP TIDE RANGE
SPRING TIDE RANGE
DEPTH AT HIGH TIDE TODAY
DEPTH AT LOW TIDE TODAY
WATER DEPTH NOW
DEPTH NEAP LOW TIDE
DEPTH NEAP HIGH TIDE
DEPTH SPRING LOW TIDE
DEPTH SPRING HIGH TIDE
Fig. 6-13. Tidal range diagram.

Tidal ranges also vary tremendously from one locality to another. An average tide range in the Bay of Fundy is about 45 feet. In San Juan it is about 1 foot. In Boston it is about 8 feet, in San Diego around 5 feet, and in Honolulu it is down to perhaps 2 feet. The reasons for these geographical variations in tidal ranges are rather complex. While it might be interesting to explore them, what is important to the coastal navigator is not why the tide range varies in different places, but simply to be aware that this does happen. The navigator is hereby put on notice that the tidal range in his home port, and in other ports and anchorages—even some quite close by—might be quite different. Before going into an unfamiliar area, look it up so you will know what conditions to expect.

SOURCES OF TIDAL INFORMATION

Daily Newspapers. Usually the same page with the daily weather reports, local daily newspapers will give the predicted times of high and low tides together with the heights of these tides above, or below, the datum level used on the NOS charts of the immediate area. Both times and heights are generally given for a specific location that is named. In some cases, it is a place at the mouth of the harbor; in others it might be a point well inside. The location for which the prediction is given could be quite far away from where you will be in a large harbor. This could make an appreciable difference in times, height, or both.

Radio and TV Broadcasts. Tide predictions are often given several times a day on commercial radio and TV stations as part of the local news broadcasts. I have seldom heard broadcasters state the specific location for which the prediction is made. For the reason noted above, this omission might or might not be significant.

Tables from Marine Suppliers. As a convenience for their customers marine suppliers in many places offer, either gratis or for a nominal price, abbreviated Tide Tables covering only a limited nearby area. Such tables are normally based on the appropriate NOS tables and therefore are very accurate. The sample shown in Fig. 6-14 is from a convenient pocket size table (4¼ × 2¾ inches), giving each month on a separate page. For the period during which daylight-saving time is in effect locally, the local tide table gives its predictions in daylight time.

Cover Jackets of Small Craft Charts. As noted in Chapter 2, the SC chart series come in cover jackets that contain a wealth of useful information in capsule form. In many cases, this includes daily predictions for high and low tides in the area covered by the chart for the year of publication. If you are using an SC chart you bought last year, the tide tables are absolutely useless this year. Only tide tables for the current year are valid.

The daily predictions on SC charts are for a specific point in the area. These charts also have a schedule giving the facilities and services available at different marinas noted by number. The same schedule gives approximate time differences from the daily predictions for the tides at those marinas.

Tide Tables of the National Ocean Survey. The basic authority for all of the above sources of tidal information is the set of Tide Tables published annually by National Ocean Survey (NOS). These tables are published in four volumes that between them cover the entire planet. Any individual will have use for no more than one of these. If you are located on either the East Coast or the Gulf Coast, you will use *Volume #2,* which covers the east coasts of both North and South America. If you are located on the West Coast, use *Volume #3,* which covers the west coasts of both continents. Alaska and Hawaii are included in *Volume #3.*

Each book contains seven different tables accompanied by explanatory texts describing their use. Table 1 gives detailed tidal predictions for every day of the year for a limited number of places that are termed *reference stations.* Table 2 lists a large number of places termed *subordinate stations.* It also gives expected time and tidal height differences for each subordinate station based on one of the reference stations.

With Tables 1 and 2, the times and expected heights of high and low tides at a great many places can be found. By using Table 3, the height of the tide at any time in between predicted highs and lows can be found for those places. Tables 4, 5, 6, and 7 contain additional interesting information, but are not used directly in predicting tidal times and levels.

Using Table 1. A sample page from Table 1 for the West Coast appears in Fig. 6-15. This page covers the months of July, August, and September for the reference station of San Francisco. Daily predictions for the remaining months of the year are

429	MARCH 1982							
	LOW TIDE				HIGH TIDE			
	AM	Ht.	PM	Ht.	AM	Ht.	PM	Ht.
	Sunrise 6:27		-PST-		Sunset 5:58			
1 M	7:38	0.8	6:55	1.8	12:42	5.2	1:41	3.3
2 Tu	9:17	0.6	8:11	2.3	1:42	5.2	3:50	3.1
3 W	10:50	0.1	9:54	2.5	3:04	5.3	5:43	3.4
4 Th	11:59	—0.5	11:27	2.2	4:27	5.5	6:42	3.8
5 F	——	——	12:51	—1.0	5:37	5.9	7:26	4.3
	Sunrise 6:21		-PST-		Sunset 6:02			
6 Sa	12:28	1.8	1:36	—1.3	6:35	6.3	8:03	4.7
7 Su	1:19	1.3	2:15	—1.5	7:24	6.6	8:37	5.0
8 M	2:03	0.9	2:50	—1.4	8:09	6.6	9:09	5.2
9 Tu	2:45	0.6	3:22	—1.1	8:48	6.4	9:38	5.4
10 W	3:26	0.4	3:52	—0.7	9:27	6.1	10:07	5.4
	Sunrise 6:14		-PST-		Sunset 6:06			
11 Th	4:04	0.4	4:44	—0.1	10:05	5.5	10:35	5.3
12 F	4:41	0.5	4:49	0.5	10:44	4.9	11:04	5.2
13 Sa	5:23	0.6	5:14	1.1	11:22	4.2	11:34	5.0
14 Su	6:11	0.9	5:36	1.6	——	——	12:11	3.6
15 M	7:11	1.1	5:54	2.2	12:08	4.8	1:18	3.0
	Sunrise 6:08		-PST-		Sunset 6:09			
16 Tu	8:40	1.2	6:26	2.6	12:48	4.5	3:46	2.7
17 W	10:28	1.0	8:47	2.9	1:57	4.3	6:30	3.0
18 Th	11:40	0.6	11:00	2.8	3:36	4.3	6:52	3.4
19 F	——	——	12:23	0.2	4:57	4.5	7:14	3.7
20 Sa	12:01	2.5	12:59	—0.1	5:54	4.9	7:34	4.0
	Sunrise 6:02		-PST-		Sunset 6:13			
21 Su	12:41	2.0	1:30	—0.4	6:36	5.3	7:54	4.4
22 M	1:15	1.5	1:58	—0.6	7:15	5.6	8:16	4.7
23 Tu	1:50	1.0	2:24	—0.7	7:52	5.8	8:40	5.0
24 W	2:25	0.6	2:53	—0.6	8:29	5.9	9:06	5.3
25 Th	3:01	0.2	3:21	—0.4	9:06	5.8	9:33	5.6
	Sunrise 5:55		-PST-		Sunset 6:16			
26 F	3:40	—0.1	3:50	0.0	9:47	5.4	10:03	5.8
27 Sa	4:25	—0.3	4:24	0.5	10:33	5.0	10:38	5.9
28 Su	5:14	—0.3	4:57	1.1	11:24	4.3	11:18	5.8
29 M	6:13	—0.2	5:36	1.7	——	——	12:31	3.7
30 Tu	7:29	0.0	6:32	2.3	12:08	5.6	2:07	3.3
31 W	9:02	0.0	8:09	2.7	1:12	5.3	4:11	3.3

(2   9   ) 17   ● 25

429	APRIL 1982							
	LOW TIDE				HIGH TIDE			
	AM	Ht.	PM	Ht.	AM	Ht.	PM	Ht.
	Sunrise 5:49		-PST-		Sunset 6:20			
1 Th	10:28	—0.2	10:10	2.6	2:39	5.1	5:37	3.7
2 F	11:35	—0.6	11:35	2.1	4:13	5.2	6:29	4.2
3 Sa	——	——	12:28	—0.8	5:27	5.4	7:02	4.7
4 Su	12:33	1.5	1:10	—0.9	6:27	5.6	7:37	5.1
5 M	1:19	0.9	1:47	—0.8	7:15	5.7	8:05	5.4
	Sunrise 5:43		-PST-		Sunset 6:23			
6 Tu	2:00	0.4	2:19	—0.6	8:00	5.7	8:34	5.6
7 W	2:36	0.1	2:48	—0.3	8:39	5.5	8:59	5.7
8 Th	3:13	—0.1	3:13	0.2	9:16	5.2	9:25	5.8
9 F	3:47	—0.2	3:39	0.6	9:53	4.8	9:50	5.7
10 Sa	4:25	—0.2	4:03	1.1	10:29	4.3	10:15	5.5
	Sunrise 5:36		-PST-		Sunset 6:26			
11 Su	5:01	0.0	4:25	1.6	11:10	3.8	10:41	5.3
12 M	5:42	0.2	4:45	2.0	11:59	3.4	11:07	5.0
13 Tu	6:34	0.5	4:58	2.5	(1:11	3.0)	11:39	4.7
14 W	7:41	0.7	——	——	——	——	——	——
15 Th	9:12	0.8	——	——	12:40	4.4	——	——
	Sunrise 5:30		-PST-		Sunset 6:30			
16 F	10:34	0.6	10:27	3.0	2:13	4.1	6:09	3.5
17 Sa	11:27	0.3	11:32	2.5	3:57	4.2	6:27	3.9
18 Su	——	——	12:06	0.1	5:08	4.4	6:46	4.3
19 M	12:18	1.9	12:38	—0.1	6:01	4.8	7:08	4.7
20 Tu	12:53	1.2	1:10	—0.2	6:46	5.0	7:32	5.2
	Sunrise 5:25		-PST-		Sunset 6:33			
21 W	1:32	0.5	1:40	—0.2	7:31	5.2	7:58	5.7
22 Th	2:08	—0.1	2:13	0.0	8:14	5.3	8:27	6.1
23 F	2:49	—0.7	2:44	0.3	8:59	5.2	8:57	6.4
24 Sa	3:31	—1.0	3:19	0.6	9:44	4.9	9:32	6.5
Pacific Daylight Time Starts Sunday, April 25 - 2:00 a.m.								
25 Su	5:19	—1.2	4:55	1.1	11:38	4.5	11:10	6.5
	Sunrise 6:19		-PDT-		Sunset 7:37			
26 M	6:12	—1.2	5:33	1.6	(12:36	4.1)	11:54	6.3
27 Tu	7:11	—1.0	6:22	2.2	——	——	1:50	3.7
28 W	8:22	—0.7	7:36	2.6	12:47	5.9	3:23	3.5
29 Th	9:40	—0.5	9:24	2.8	1:54	5.4	4:56	3.8
30 F	10:55	—0.4	11:15	2.5	3:23	5.0	6:05	4.2

(1   8   ) 16   ● 23

Fig. 6-14. Sample pages from local tide table for San Diego.

found on two pages preceding, and the page following the one shown. The days of each month are listed in two vertical columns. Times of high and low waters are given in accordance with the 24-hour clock (explained in Chapter 5). Heights are shown in both feet and meters above, and occasionally below, charted depths. On most days, four times are given and followed by numbers in feet and meters indicating heights.

On July 9, the first time given (Fig. 6-15) is 0022 (12:22 midnight). At that time, the height of tide is predicted to be 5.5 feet above charted depth at Golden Gate. At 0708 on the same day, the height of the tide will be −0.5 feet. On July 15, the first time noted is 0023; at that time the depth will be 1.1 feet above charted soundings. At 0645 that day, depths will be 3.7 above chart datum. On the 9th, the first tide of the day is a high tide. On the 15th the first one is a low. Thus on any particular day to determine whether a tabulated time indicates a high or a low tide, it is necessary to look to the height column.

Looking again at these same two dates on the 9th, the first high tide is 5.5 feet followed by a low of −0.5 for a range of 6 feet. The second varies only from 4.6 down to 3.1 feet for a range of only 1.5 feet. This is a very pronounced inequality. On the 15th, the first low-to-high-tide range is 2.6 feet while the second range is 4.2 feet. Again, here is a decided inequality with extremes at very different times of day. Clearly the state of the tide at the end of the afternoon a few days ago has little bearing on today!

At the bottom of Fig. 6-15, note two significant bits of information that will be found on all pages of Table 1. First the time meridian (120°W) is the one for Pacific Standard Time. This is local time at this reference station, and is the basis for the times on this page. In addition, all heights of tides are given with reference to the same datum level used for the nautical charts of the area. In this instance, it happens to be mean lower low water.

Using Table 2. Compiling and publishing of complete daily predictions, as in Table 1, is limited to a relatively small number of major ports. Tide

SAN FRANCISCO (Golden Gate), CALIFORNIA, 1982

Times and Heights of High and Low Waters

JULY								AUGUST								SEPTEMBER							
Day	Time h m	Height ft	Height m	Day	Time h m	Height ft	Height m	Day	Time h m	Height ft	Height m	Day	Time h m	Height ft	Height m	Day	Time h m	Height ft	Height m	Day	Time h m	Height ft	Height m
1	0221	0.4	0.1	16	0122	0.3	0.1	1	0319	0.0	0.0	16	0250	-0.8	-0.2	1	0359	-0.1	0.0	16	0405	-0.6	-0.2
Th	0903	3.9	1.2	F	0815	3.9	1.2	Su	1040	4.5	1.4	M	1011	4.9	1.5	W	1108	4.8	1.5	Th	1103	5.5	1.7
	1339	2.1	0.6		1247	2.2	0.7		1458	3.0	0.9		1439	2.7	0.8		1559	2.4	0.7		1617	1.3	0.4
	2015	5.9	1.8		1927	6.4	2.0		2100	6.0	1.8		2055	6.8	2.1		2159	5.8	1.8		2237	6.2	1.9
2	0303	0.0	0.0	17	0216	-0.4	-0.1	2	0354	-0.2	-0.1	17	0340	-1.1	-0.3	2	0431	-0.2	-0.1	17	0446	-0.4	-0.1
F	1007	4.1	1.2	Sa	0928	4.2	1.3	M	1119	4.6	1.4	Tu	1057	5.1	1.6	Th	1133	4.9	1.5	F	1138	5.6	1.7
	1428	2.5	0.8		1343	2.5	0.8		1540	3.0	0.9		1532	2.4	0.7		1633	2.1	0.6		1703	0.9	0.3
	2049	5.9	1.8		2015	6.7	2.0		2139	6.0	1.8		2148	6.9	2.1		2238	5.7	1.7		2327	5.9	1.8
3	0342	-0.3	-0.1	18	0307	-1.0	-0.3	3	0430	-0.4	-0.1	18	0427	-1.3	-0.4	3	0501	-0.2	-0.1	18	0525	0.0	0.0
Sa	1057	4.3	1.3	Su	1028	4.6	1.4	Tu	1151	4.7	1.4	W	1139	5.3	1.6	F	1202	5.0	1.5	Sa	1213	5.6	1.7
	1514	2.7	0.8		1442	2.6	0.8		1618	2.9	0.9		1626	2.1	0.6		[illegible]38	1.9	0.6		1748	0.7	0.2
	2125	5.9	1.8		2105	6.9	2.1		2215	6.0	1.8		2240	6.8	2.1		2320	5.6	1.7				
4	0418	-0.5	-0.2	19	0357	-1.5	-0.5	4	0504	-0.5	-0.2	19	0512	-1.2	-0.4	4	0533	0.0	0.0	19	0017	5.5	1.7
Su	1144	4.4	1.3	M	1119	4.9	1.5	W	1223	4.7	1.4	Th	1217	5.4	1.6	Sa	1227	5.1	1.6	Su	0604	0.5	0.2
	1556	2.9	0.9		1537	2.6	0.8		1653	2.8	0.9		1715	1.8	0.5		1745	1.6	0.5		1247	5.6	1.7
	2201	5.9	1.8		2156	7.1	2.2		2253	5.9	1.8		2332	6.5	2.0						1834	0.6	0.2
5	0453	-0.6	-0.2	20	0444	-1.7	-0.5	5	0535	-0.5	-0.2	20	0554	-0.9	-0.3	5	0002	5.4	1.6	20	0108	5.1	1.6
M	1222	4.5	1.4	Tu	1207	5.1	1.6	Th	1251	4.7	1.4	F	1256	5.4	1.6	Su	0604	0.3	0.1	M	0642	1.1	0.3
	1634	3.0	0.9		1633	2.6	0.8		1729	2.7	0.8		1806	1.6	0.5		1259	5.2	1.6		1320	5.5	1.7
	2236	5.9	1.8		2248	7.0	2.1		2328	5.8	1.8						1826	1.3	0.4		1921	0.6	0.2
6	0525	-0.6	-0.2	21	0532	-1.7	-0.5	6	0607	-0.4	-0.1	21	0024	6.0	1.8	6	0047	5.1	1.6	21	0201	4.7	1.4
Tu	1301	4.5	1.4	W	1253	5.2	1.6	F	1321	4.8	1.5	Sa	0636	-0.4	-0.1	M	0639	0.7	0.2	Tu	0724	1.8	0.5
	1713	3.1	0.9		1727	2.4	0.7		1807	2.5	0.8		1334	5.5	1.7		1329	5.4	1.6		1352	5.4	1.6
	2309	5.8	1.8		2340	6.8	2.1						1859	1.4	0.4		1909	1.1	0.3		2008	0.7	0.2
7	0559	-0.7	-0.2	22	0618	-1.5	-0.5	7	0007	5.6	1.7	22	0113	5.5	1.7	7	0136	4.8	1.5	22	0304	4.3	1.3
W	1334	4.6	1.4	Th	1335	5.3	1.6	Sa	0639	-0.2	-0.1	Su	0718	0.2	0.1	Tu	0715	1.2	0.4	W	0806	2.4	0.7
	1749	3.1	0.9		1822	2.3	0.7		1351	4.9	1.5		1414	5.5	1.7		1403	5.5	1.7		1430	5.3	1.6
	2344	5.7	1.7						1849	2.4	0.7		1951	1.4	0.4		2001	0.9	0.3		2103	0.8	0.2
8	0635	-0.6	-0.2	23	0031	6.4	2.0	8	0049	5.2	1.6	23	0209	4.9	1.5	8	0239	4.5	1.4	23	0419	4.1	1.2
Th	1409	4.6	1.4	F	0705	-1.1	-0.3	Su	0711	0.0	0.0	M	0800	0.9	0.3	W	0758	1.8	0.5	Th	0902	2.9	0.9
	1831	3.1	0.9		1420	5.3	1.6		1423	5.0	1.5		1452	5.5	1.7		1443	5.7	1.7		1510	5.2	1.6
					1921	2.2	0.7		1935	2.2	0.7		2051	1.3	0.4		2102	0.8	0.2		2203	0.9	0.3

9	0022	5.5	1.7	24	0125	5.8	1.8	9	0134	4.9	1.5	24	0311	4.4	1.3	9	0352	4.2	1.3	24	0549	4.1	1.2
F	0708	-0.5	-0.2	Sa	0750	-0.6	-0.2	M	0747	0.5	0.2	Tu	0843	1.6	0.5	Th	0848	2.4	0.7	F	1015	3.3	1.0
	1441	4.6	1.4		1503	5.4	1.6		1455	5.2	1.6		1533	5.4	1.6		1531	5.8	1.8		1603	5.1	1.6
	1916	3.1	0.9		2022	2.1	0.6		2033	1.9	0.6		2153	1.3	0.4		2209	0.6	0.2		2310	1.0	0.3
10	0101	5.2	1.6	25	0221	5.2	1.6	10	0231	4.5	1.4	25	0429	4.0	1.2	10	0523	4.1	1.2	25	0711	4.3	1.3
Sa	0745	-0.3	-0.1	Su	0836	0.0	0.0	Tu	0829	1.0	0.3	W	0938	2.2	0.7	F	0955	2.9	0.9	Sa	1137	3.4	1.0
	1516	4.7	1.4		1548	5.5	1.7		1534	5.4	1.6		1615	5.4	1.6		1628	5.9	1.8		1705	5.0	1.5
	2007	2.9	0.9		2130	1.9	0.6		2133	1.6	0.5		2302	1.2	0.4		2322	0.3	0.1				
11	0146	4.9	1.5	26	0323	4.5	1.4	11	0339	4.1	1.2	26	0603	3.9	1.2	11	0655	4.3	1.3	26	0016	0.9	0.3
Su	0822	0.0	0.0	M	0926	0.7	0.2	W	0915	1.6	0.5	Th	1043	2.7	0.8	Sa	1117	3.1	0.9	Su	0808	4.5	1.4
	1551	4.9	1.5		1632	5.5	1.7		1618	5.6	1.7		1705	5.4	1.6		1736	6.0	1.8		1246	3.3	1.0
	2106	2.7	0.8		2242	1.6	0.5		2242	1.2	0.4										1811	5.0	1.5
12	0239	4.5	1.4	27	0440	4.0	1.2	12	0511	3.8	1.2	27	0008	1.0	0.3	12	0033	0.0	0.0	27	0111	0.7	0.2
M	0904	0.4	0.1	Tu	1017	1.4	0.4	Th	1013	2.1	0.6	F	0734	4.0	1.2	Su	0808	4.6	1.4	M	0849	4.6	1.4
	1630	5.1	1.6		1718	5.6	1.7		1706	5.9	1.8		1153	3.0	0.9		1234	3.0	0.9		1339	3.0	0.9
	2212	2.3	0.7		2354	1.3	0.4		2351	0.7	0.2		1758	5.4	1.6		1843	6.1	1.9		1911	5.1	1.6
13	0345	4.1	1.2	28	0613	3.7	1.1	13	0654	3.9	1.2	28	0107	0.8	0.2	13	0135	-0.3	-0.1	28	0200	0.5	0.2
Tu	0953	0.8	0.2	W	1112	2.0	0.6	F	1119	2.6	0.8	Sa	0844	4.3	1.3	M	0901	4.9	1.5	Tu	0921	4.8	1.5
	1709	5.4	1.6		1803	5.6	1.7		1800	6.1	1.9		1258	3.1	0.9		1341	2.7	0.8		1423	2.6	0.8
	2321	1.8	0.5										1854	5.5	1.7		1949	6.2	1.9		2006	5.2	1.6
14	0509	3.8	1.2	29	0056	1.0	0.3	14	0057	0.2	0.1	29	0159	0.6	0.2	14	0231	-0.6	-0.2	29	0242	0.3	0.1
W	1045	1.3	0.4	Th	0743	3.8	1.2	Sa	0818	4.2	1.3	Su	0929	4.5	1.4	Tu	0945	5.2	1.6	W	0950	4.9	1.5
	1752	5.7	1.7		1215	2.5	0.8		1231	2.8	0.9		1356	3.1	0.9		1438	2.3	0.7		1501	2.2	0.7
					1850	5.7	1.7		1900	6.4	2.0		1946	5.6	1.7		2050	6.3	1.9		2055	5.3	1.6
15	0023	1.1	0.3	30	0149	0.6	0.2	15	0156	-0.4	-0.1	30	0244	0.3	0.1	15	0319	-0.7	-0.2	30	0317	0.2	0.1
Th	0645	3.7	1.1	F	0859	4.0	1.2	Su	0919	4.5	1.4	M	1007	4.6	1.4	W	1027	5.3	1.6	Th	1015	5.0	1.5
	1144	1.8	0.5		1314	2.8	0.9		1338	2.8	0.9		1441	2.9	0.9		1530	1.8	0.5		1536	1.7	0.5
	1838	6.0	1.8		1936	5.8	1.8		1959	6.6	2.0		2035	5.7	1.7		2145	6.3	1.9		2140	5.4	1.6
				31	0237	0.3	0.1					31	0324	0.1	0.0								
				Sa	0955	4.3	1.3					Tu	1039	4.7	1.4								
					1409	2.9	0.9						1522	2.7	0.8								
					2018	5.9	1.8						2117	5.8	1.8								

Time meridian 120° W. 0000 is midnight. 1200 is noon.
Heights are referred to mean lower low water which is the chart datum of soundings.

Fig. 6-15. Tide Tables West Coast 1982; sample page from Table 1.

NO.	PLACE	POSITION Lat.	POSITION Long.	DIFFERENCES Time High water	DIFFERENCES Time Low water	DIFFERENCES Height High water	DIFFERENCES Height Low water	RANGES Mean	RANGES Diurnal	Mean Tide Level
		° ' S	° ' W	h. m.	h. m.	ft	ft	ft	ft	ft
	CALIFORNIA San Pedro Channel Time meridian, 120°W			on LOS ANGELES, p.68						
459	Santa Monica..........................	34 00	118 30	+0 01	+0 05	-0.1	0.0	3.7	5.4	2.8
	Santa Barbara Channel									
461	Mugu Lagoon (ocean pier)...............	34 06	119 06	+0 02	+0 09	*0.98	*0.98	3.7	5.3	2.7
463	Port Hueneme...........................	34 09	119 12	+0 09	+0 11	0.0	0.0	3.7	5.4	2.8
465	Ventura................................	34 16	119 17	+0 08	+0 14	0.0	0.0	3.7	5.4	2.8
467	Santa Barbara..........................	34 25	119 41	+0 23	+0 21	*0.98	*0.98	3.6	5.3	2.8
469	Gaviota................................	34 28	120 13	+0 38	+0 35	*0.98	*0.98	3.6	5.3	2.8
	Santa Barbara Islands									
471	Wilson Cove, San Clemente Island........	33 00	118 33	-0 04	-0 05	*0.96	*0.96	3.6	5.2	2.7
473	Catalina Harbor, Santa Catalina Island..	33 26	118 30	+0 10	+0 15	*0.96	*0.96	3.6	5.2	2.7
475	Avalon, Santa Catalina Island...........	33 21	118 19	+0 05	+0 07	*0.98	*0.98	3.7	5.3	2.7
477	Santa Barbara Island....................	33 29	119 02	-0 03	+0 02	*0.94	*0.94	3.5	5.1	2.6
479	San Nicolas Island......................	33 16	119 30	+0 09	+0 19	*0.91	*0.91	3.3	4.9	2.5
481	Prisoners Harbor, Santa Cruz Island.....	34 01	119 41	+0 24	+0 24	*0.93	*0.93	3.4	5.0	2.6
483	Bechers Bay, Santa Rosa Island..........	34 00	120 03	+0 36	+0 33	*0.98	*0.98	3.6	5.3	2.8
485	Cuyler Harbor, San Miguel Island........	34 03	120 21	+0 32	+0 32	*0.96	*0.96	3.5	5.2	2.7
	Outer Coast									
487	Point Arguello.........................	34 35	120 39	+0 44	+0 41	*0.96	*0.96	3.5	5.2	2.7
489	Avila Beach, San Luis Obispo Bay........	35 10	120 44	+0 47	+0 52	*0.98	*0.98	3.6	5.3	2.8
491	Morro Beach, Estero Bay................	35 24	120 52	+0 55	+0 54	*0.96	*0.96	3.5	5.2	2.8
493	San Simeon.............................	35 38	121 11	+0 59	+0 56	*0.96	*0.96	3.5	5.2	2.7
495	Carmel Cove, Carmel Bay................	36 31	121 56	+1 11	+1 11	*0.96	*0.96	3.5	5.2	2.8
				on SAN FRANCISCO, p.72						
497	Monterey, Monterey Bay..................	36 36	121 54	-1 16	-0 58	-0.5	0.0	3.5	5.3	2.8
499	Santa Cruz, Monterey Bay...............	36 58	122 01	-1 19	-1 04	-0.5	0.0	3.5	5.3	2.8

501	Ano Nuevo Island.......................	37 06	122 20	-1 28	-1 10	-0.6	-0.1	3.5	5.2	2.7
503	Princeton, Halfmoon Bay................	37 30	122 29	-1 10	-0 56	-0.2	0.0	3.8	5.5	3.0
505	Southeast Farallon Island..............	37 42	123 00	-0 43	-0 25	-0.2	0.0	3.8	5.6	3.0
507	San Francisco Bar......................	37 46	122 38	-0 39	-0 37	-0.1	0.0	3.9	5.6	3.0
509	Ocean Beach, outer coast...............	37 46	122 31	-0 53	-0 41	+0.2	0.0	4.2	6.0	3.2
	San Francisco Bay									
511	Bonita Cove, Golden Gate...............	37 49	122 32	-0 24	-0 06	+0.1	0.0	4.1	5.8	3.1
513	SAN FRANCISCO (Golden Gate)............	37 48	122 28		Daily predictions			4.1	5.8	3.2
515	Alcatraz Island........................	37 50	122 25	+0 10	+0 12	+0.1	0.0	4.1	5.8	3.1
517	San Francisco, North Point, Pier 41.....	37 49	122 25	+0 13	+0 11	+0.1	0.0	4.2	5.9	3.2
519	Rincon Point, Pier 22 1/2..............	37 47	122 23	+0 23	+0 25	+0.3	0.0	4.4	6.1	3.3
521	Yerba Buena Island.....................	37 49	122 22	+0 23	+0 32	+0.3	0.0	4.3	6.0	3.2
523	Oakland Pier...........................	37 48	122 20	+0 29	+0 42	+0.3	0.0	4.3	6.0	3.2
525	Alameda................................	37 46	122 18	+0 35	+0 42	+0.7	0.0	4.7	6.4	3.5
527	Oakland Harbor, Grove Street...........	37 48	122 17	+0 29	+0 36	+0.5	0.0	4.5	6.2	3.3
529	Oakland Harbor, Park Street Bridge......	37 46	122 14	+0 40	+0 44	+0.6	0.0	4.6	6.3	3.4
531	Bay Farm Island Bridge.................	37 45	122 14	+0 41	+0 52	+0.8	0.0	4.8	6.5	3.5
533	Oakland Airport........................	37 44	122 12	+0 40	+0 40	+0.8	0.0	4.8	6.5	3.5
535	Potrero Point..........................	37 46	122 23	+0 29	+0 40	+0.6	0.0	4.6	6.3	3.4
537	Hunters Point..........................	37 44	122 21	+0 32	+0 46	+0.8	0.0	4.9	6.6	3.6
538	Roberts Landing, 1.3 miles west of......	37 40	122 12	+0 48	+1 22	+1.5	+0.1	5.4	7.2	3.9
539	South San Francisco....................	37 40	122 23	+0 45	+1 02	+1.1	0.0	5.2	6.9	3.7
540	Oyster Point Marina....................	37 40	122 23	+0 48	+1 07	+1.1	0.0	5.2	6.9	3.7
541	Point San Bruno........................	37 39	122 23	+0 34	+1 04	+1.2	+0.1	5.1	6.9	3.7
542	Seaplane Harbor........................	37 38	122 23	+0 51	+1 11	+1.3	0.0	5.4	7.1	3.8
543	Coyote Point...........................	37 36	122 19	+0 49	+1 14	+1.5	+0.1	5.5	7.3	4.0
545	San Mateo Bridge.......................	37 35	122 15	+0 52	+1 20	+1.8	+0.1	5.8	7.6	4.1
547	Coyote Hill Slough entrance............	37 34	122 08	+0 54	+1 26	+2.1	+0.1	6.0	7.8	4.2
548	Bay Slough, west end...................	37 33	122 15	+0 55	+1 35	+1.8	0.0	5.9	7.6	4.0
549	Bay Slough, east end...................	37 33	122 13	+0 56	+1 59	+1.4	-0.2	5.7	7.2	3.8
550	Redwood Creek Marker #8................	37 32	122 12	+1 00	+1 35	+2.1	+0.1	6.1	7.9	4.2
551	Redwood Creek entrance (inside).........	37 31	122 12	+1 02	+1 32	+2.2	+0.1	6.1	7.9	4.2
552	Corkscrew Slough.......................	37 30	122 13	+1 03	+1 42	+2.2	+0.1	6.2	8.0	4.3
553	Redwood City, Wharf 5..................	37 30	122 13	+0 58	+1 32	+2.2	+0.1	6.2	8.0	4.3
554	West Point Slough......................	37 30	122 12	+1 03	+1 36	+2.2	+0.1	6.2	8.0	4.3
555	Smith Slough...........................	37 30	122 14	+1 11	+1 52	+2.2	0.0	6.2	7.9	4.2
556	Newark Slough..........................	37 31	122 05	+1 11	+1 58	+2.6	+0.1	6.6	8.4	4.2
557	Dumbarton Highway Bridge...............	37 30	122 07	+1 07	+1 44	+2.5	+0.1	6.5	8.3	4.4
558	Ravenswood Slough <17>.................	37 30	122 10	+1 05	- - -	- -	- -	- -	- -	- -
559	Granite Rock...........................	37 30	122 13	+1 03	+1 38	+2.2	+0.1	6.2	8.0	4.3
560	Palo Alto Yacht Harbor.................	37 27	122 06	+0 52	+1 48	+2.9	+0.1	6.8	8.6	4.6
561	Calaveras Point, west of...............	37 28	122 04	+1 01	+1 43	+2.9	+0.1	6.8	8.5	4.6
562	Mud Slough railroad bridge.............	37 28	121 58	+1 04	+2 06	+3.5	+0.1	7.4	9.1	4.9
563	Alviso (bridge), Alviso Slough.........	37 26	121 59	+1 20	+2 18	+3.3	+0.1	7.2	9.0	4.8

Endnotes can be found at the end of table 2.

Fig. 6-16. Tide Tables West Coast 1982; sample page from Table 2.

predictions for a large number of additional stations can be made by applying differences known to exist between each of these subordinate stations and an applicable reference station. Table 2 is the listing of the subordinate stations with the names of the reference stations with which they are associated. It also gives the differences that are to be applied to the data from the reference station to arrive at proper times and heights of tides at the subordinate station. Figure 6-16 is a sample page from Table 2.

Starting with Monterey, Monterey Bay, about halfway down the page, Fig. 6-16 lists a number of places for which predictions can be made using San Francisco as the reference station by applying the time and height differences listed for each one. In addition to time and height differences for each subordinate station, Table 2 gives the latitude and longitude where these differences apply as well as data regarding tidal ranges and mean tide level. While the coastal navigator will be interested in the positioning information, the range and tide level data are important. The sequential number found in the left-hand column is for use as an aid in locating any particular subordinate station from the alphabetical index in the back of the book.

Time differences are given separately for high and low waters because they are not very often the same. A plus (+) means hours or minutes to be added to the time of the tide at the reference station. A minus (−) means time to be subtracted. Height corrections are made in the same way. Where an asterisk (*) appears before a height correction, this indicates a ratio to be applied to the height given at the reference station. For example, the high water difference given for San Simeon (#493) of *0.96 means take the high water for Los Angeles for the day and multiply by .96 to find the high at San Simeon.

Although time intervals and height changes are not constant at the reference stations, constant differences for both times and heights are given for subordinate stations. For this reason, predictions for subordinate stations based on these constants will not be as accurate as those at the reference stations. This means that although predictions for subordinate stations will be reasonably accurate, when using such predictions leave some leeway. Do not try to cut it close on either time or height. Leave yourself at least an hour's time or a foot of water to spare.

Using Table 3. Table 1 consists of a great many pages, and Table 2 takes up quite a few as well. By contrast, Table 3 consists of one page only (Fig. 6-17). With Tables 1 and 2, it is possible to find the times of high and low waters for any day of the year at a great many places. Generally, one of those places will be close enough to where you are to give you a workable approximation of the high- and low-water times at your location. Tables 1 and 2 also provide information on the daily tide ranges and the heights of high and low water, relative to charted depths.

This is fine except that most of the specific times for which a sailor needs to know the state of the tide do not coincide with tabulated highs or lows. This is where Table 3 comes in. By using this table, the state of the tide at any time between tabulated highs and lows can easily be determined. This table is divided into two parts. The upper section deals with time. The lower section deals with height of water above charted datum.

Having determined a time for which the state of the tide is required, the first step is to find from Tables 1 and 2 the nearest times both before and after it that either a high or a low occur (one will be a high and one a low). Having found those, the interval between them is the duration of rise or fall.

The upper section of Table 3 is entered with that interval in the left-hand column. Using the interval as a starting point, move to the right along its line to a time equal to the interval between the desired time and the *nearest* high or low water. The vertical column in which the final answer will be found has now been located.

Go back now to Tables 1 and 2 to find the range of the tide for the day and place in question, and locate that range in the left-hand column of the bottom section of Table 3. Follow that range line to the right until it intersects the vertical column just found. The number at that intersection is the correction to be applied to the tide that was the nearest high or low water from which the time interval was taken.

Examples. The explanations of the use of Tide Tables 1, 2, and 3 will be clearer to you in light of how they are employed to answer some specific questions. First let us find the state of the tide on a particular day at a reference station, and at a time that is *not* close to either high or low water. We want to know the height of the tide at San Francisco at the Golden Gate at 5:15 PM Pacific daylight time on Sunday August 22, 1982. To use the tables, this becomes 4:15 Pacific Standard time because in August San Francisco is on daylight time.

Looking to Fig. 6-18, we have the page from Table 1 covering San Francisco for the months of July, August, and September of 1982. Looking down the fourth column from the left, which starts with August 16th, find Sunday the 22nd. The tide times and heights on that date are:

Time	Height	
0113	5.5 ft.	High
0718	0.2 ft.	Low
1414	5.5 ft.	High
1951	1.4 ft.	Low

Our desired time of 4:15 PM translates on the 24-hour clock to 1615.

1200 Noon
+ 415
1615 = 16 hours since midnight + 15 minutes

The nearest tide to 1615 is the one at 1414 at which time the height will be 5.5 ft. The next one after that is at 1951 with a height of 1.4 ft.

5.5 ft.
−1.4 ft.
4.1 ft. is the *range* of this tide

The duration of this tide is the time interval from 1414 (high tide) to 1951 (low tide).

1951 Low tide
−1414 High tide
537 or 5 hrs. 37 min. (5 37) = duration

The time interval from the nearest high or low tide to our desired time is the interval between 1414 and 1615:

1615 Desired Time
−1414 High Tide
201 or 2 hrs. 1 min. (2 01) = Interval

Now we have the information necessary to enter Table 3 (Fig. 6-19). The left-hand column of the upper section of Table 3 is marked "Duration of rise or fall." The duration of the tide was found to be 5 37, which is close enough to 5 40. Going across the 5 40 line we come to 2 05, which is very close to the 2 01 that we just found will be the interval from the nearest high water to the desired time. This is the correct vertical column. The answer will be in this column, but in the lower part of the table.

The range of the tide being worked on is 4.1 feet. Looking down the "Range of tide" column on the left side of the lower section, the number 4.0 is found. Again, this number is close enough for our purposes. By following across the line to the vertical column in which 2 05 was found, the number 1.2 ft. appears at the intersection.

Because 1414 was high tide, and 1615 is later, the tide has been going down for the last 2 hours. This means that the answer of 1.2 ft. must be *subtracted* from the height of the tide at 1414, which was 5.5 ft:

5.5 ft.
−1.2 ft.
4.3 ft.

At 1615, or 4:15 PM on Sunday, August 22, the height at Golden Gate is going to be 4.3 ft. above charted depths.

The next example requires the determination of the times and heights of high and low tides at a subordinate station on a given date using San Francisco as the reference station. This time the date is Friday, September 10, at Redwood City, Wharf 5.

Looking at Fig. 6-20, and this time at the month of September, on the 10th the tides at San Francisco will be:

0523	4.1 ft.
0955	2.9 ft.
1628	5.9 ft.
2322	0.3 ft.

Redwood City, Wharf 5 (Fig. 6-21) differs from San Francisco as follows:

Times-		h m
	High water	+0 58
	Low water	+1 32
Height-		ft
	High water	+2.2
	Low water	+0.1

Duration of rise or fall, see footnote	Time from the nearest high water or low water														
h. m.	h. m.	h. m.	h. m.	h. m.	h. m.	h. m.	h. m.	h. m.	h. m.	h. m.	h. m.	h. m.	h. m.	h. m.	h. m.
4 00	0 08	0 16	0 24	0 32	0 40	0 48	0 56	1 04	1 12	1 20	1 28	1 36	1 44	1 52	2 00
4 20	0 09	0 17	0 26	0 35	0 43	0 52	1 01	1 09	1 18	1 27	1 35	1 44	1 53	2 01	2 10
4 40	0 09	0 19	0 28	0 37	0 47	0 56	1 05	1 15	1 24	1 33	1 43	1 52	2 01	2 11	2 20
5 00	0 10	0 20	0 30	0 40	0 50	1 00	1 10	1 20	1 30	1 40	1 50	2 00	2 10	2 20	2 30
5 20	0 11	0 21	0 32	0 43	0 53	1 04	1 15	1 25	1 36	1 47	1 57	2 08	2 19	2 29	2 40
5 40	0 11	0 23	0 34	0 45	0 57	1 08	1 19	1 31	1 42	1 53	2 05	2 16	2 27	2 39	2 50
6 00	0 12	0 24	0 36	0 48	1 00	1 12	1 24	1 36	1 48	2 00	2 12	2 24	2 36	2 48	3 00
6 20	0 13	0 25	0 38	0 51	1 03	1 16	1 29	1 41	1 54	2 07	2 19	2 32	2-45	2 57	3 10
6 40	0 13	0 27	0 40	0 53	1 07	1 20	1 33	1 47	2 00	2 13	2 27	2 40	2 53	3 07	3 20
7 00	0 14	0 28	0 42	0 56	1 10	1 24	1 38	1 52	2 06	2 20	2 34	2 48	3 02	3 16	3 30
7 20	0 15	0 29	0 44	0 59	1 13	1 28	1 43	1 57	2 12	2 27	2 41	2 56	3 11	3 25	3 40
7 40	0 15	0 31	0 46	1 01	1 17	1 32	1 47	2 03	2 18	2 33	2 49	3 04	3 19	3 35	3 50
8 00	0 16	0 32	0 48	1 04	1 20	1 36	1 52	2 08	2 24	2 40	2 56	3 12	3 28	3 44	4 00
8 20	0 17	0 33	0 50	1 07	1 23	1 40	1 57	2 13	2 30	2 47	3 03	3 20	3 37	3 53	4 10
8 40	0 17	0 35	0 52	1 09	1 27	1 44	2 01	2 19	2 36	2 53	3 11	3 28	3 45	4 03	4 20
9 00	0 18	0 36	0 54	1 12	1 30	1 48	2 06	2 24	2 42	3 00	3 18	3 36	3 54	4 12	4 30
9 20	0 19	0 37	0 56	1 15	1 33	1 52	2 11	2 29	2 48	3 07	3 25	3 44	4 03	4 21	4 40
9 40	0 19	0 39	0 58	1 17	1 37	1 56	2 15	2 35	2 54	3 13	3 33	3 52	4 11	4 31	4 50
10 00	0 20	0 40	1 00	1 20	1 40	2 00	2 20	2 40	3 00	3 20	3 40	4 00	4 20	4 40	5 00
10 20	0 21	0 41	1 02	1 23	1 43	2 04	2 25	2 45	3 06	3 27	3 47	4 08	4 29	4 49	5 10
10 40	0 21	0 43	1 04	1 25	1 47	2 08	2 29	2 51	3 12	3 33	3 55	4 16	4 37	4 59	5 20

	Correction to height														
Ft.	*Ft.*	*Ft.*	*Ft.*	*Ft.*	*Ft.*	*Ft.*	*Ft.*	*Ft.*	*Ft.*	*Ft.*	*Ft.*	*Ft.*	*Ft.*	*Ft.*	*Ft.*
0.5	0.0	0.0	0.0	0.0	0.0	0.0	0.1	0.1	0.1	0.1	0.1	0.2	0.2	0.2	0.2
1.0	0.0	0.0	0.0	0.0	0.1	0.1	0.1	0.2	0.2	0.2	0.3	0.3	0.4	0.4	0.5
1.5	0.0	0.0	0.0	0.1	0.1	0.1	0.2	0.2	0.3	0.4	0.4	0.5	0.6	0.7	0.8
2.0	0.0	0.0	0.0	0.1	0.1	0.2	0.3	0.3	0.4	0.5	0.6	0.7	0.8	0.9	1.0
2.5	0.0	0.0	0.1	0.1	0.2	0.2	0.3	0.4	0.5	0.6	0.7	0.9	1.0	1.1	1.2
3.0	0.0	0.0	0.1	0.1	0.2	0.3	0.4	0.5	0.6	0.8	0.9	1.0	1.2	1.3	1.5
3.5	0.0	0.0	0.1	0.2	0.2	0.3	0.4	0.6	0.7	0.9	1.0	1.2	1.4	1.6	1.8
4.0	0.0	0.0	0.1	0.2	0.3	0.4	0.5	0.7	0.8	1.0	1.2	1.4	1.6	1.8	2.0
4.5	0.0	0.0	0.1	0.2	0.3	0.4	0.6	0.7	0.9	1.1	1.3	1.6	1.8	2.0	2.2
5.0	0.0	0.1	0.1	0.2	0.3	0.5	0.6	0.8	1.0	1.2	1.5	1.7	2.0	2.2	2.5
5.5	0.0	0.1	0.1	0.2	0.4	0.5	0.7	0.9	1.1	1.4	1.6	1.9	2.2	2.5	2.8
6.0	0.0	0.1	0.1	0.3	0.4	0.6	0.8	1.0	1.2	1.5	1.8	2.1	2.4	2.7	3.0

Range of tide, see footnote															
6.5	0.0	0.1	0.2	0.3	0.4	0.6	0.8	1.1	1.3	1.6	1.9	2.2	2.6	2.9	3.2
7.0	0.0	0.1	0.2	0.3	0.5	0.7	0.9	1.2	1.4	1.8	2.1	2.4	2.8	3.1	3.5
7.5	0.0	0.1	0.2	0.3	0.5	0.7	1.0	1.2	1.5	1.9	2.2	2.6	3.0	3.4	3.8
8.0	0.0	0.1	0.2	0.3	0.5	0.8	1.0	1.3	1.6	2.0	2.4	2.8	3.2	3.6	4.0
8.5	0.0	0.1	0.2	0.4	0.6	0.8	1.1	1.4	1.8	2.1	2.6	2.9	3.4	3.8	4.2
9.0	0.0	0.1	0.2	0.4	0.6	0.9	1.2	1.5	1.9	2.2	2.7	3.1	3.6	4.0	4.5
9.5	0.0	0.1	0.2	0.4	0.6	0.9	1.2	1.6	2.0	2.4	2.8	3.3	3.8	4.3	4.8
10.0	0.0	0.1	0.2	0.4	0.7	1.0	1.3	1.7	2.1	2.5	3.0	3.5	4.0	4.5	5.0
10.5	0.0	0.1	0.3	0.5	0.7	1.0	1.3	1.7	2.2	2.6	3.1	3.6	4.2	4.7	5.2
11.0	0.0	0.1	0.3	0.5	0.7	1.1	1.4	1.8	2.3	2.8	3.3	3.8	4.4	4.9	5.5
11.5	0.0	0.1	0.3	0.5	0.8	1.1	1.5	1.9	2.4	2.9	3.4	4.0	4.6	5.1	5.8
12.0	0.0	0.1	0.3	0.5	0.8	1.1	1.5	2.0	2.5	3.0	3.6	4.1	4.8	5.4	6.0
12.5	0.0	0.1	0.3	0.5	0.8	1.2	1.6	2.1	2.6	3.1	3.7	4.3	5.0	5.6	6.2
13.0	0.0	0.1	0.3	0.6	0.9	1.2	1.7	2.2	2.7	3.2	3.9	4.5	5.1	5.8	6.5
13.5	0.0	0.1	0.3	0.6	0.9	1.3	1.7	2.2	2.8	3.4	4.0	4.7	5.3	6.0	6.8
14.0	0.0	0.2	0.3	0.6	0.9	1.3	1.8	2.3	2.9	3.5	4.2	4.8	5.5	6.3	7.0
14.5	0.0	0.2	0.4	0.6	1.0	1.4	1.9	2.4	3.0	3.6	4.3	5.0	5.7	6.5	7.2
15.0	0.0	0.2	0.4	0.6	1.0	1.4	1.9	2.5	3.1	3.8	4.4	5.2	5.9	6.7	7.5
15.5	0.0	0.2	0.4	0.7	1.0	1.5	2.0	2.6	3.2	3.9	4.6	5.4	6.1	6.9	7.8
16.0	0.0	0.2	0.4	0.7	1.1	1.5	2.1	2.6	3.3	4.0	4.7	5.5	6.3	7.2	8.0
16.5	0.0	0.2	0.4	0.7	1.1	1.6	2.1	2.7	3.4	4.1	4.9	5.7	6.5	7.4	8.2
17.0	0.0	0.2	0.4	0.7	1.1	1.6	2.2	2.8	3.5	4.2	5.0	5.9	6.7	7.6	8.5
17.5	0.0	0.2	0.4	0.8	1.2	1.7	2.2	2.9	3.6	4.4	5.2	6.0	6.9	7.8	8.8
18.0	0.0	0.2	0.4	0.8	1.2	1.7	2.3	3.0	3.7	4.5	5.3	6.2	7.1	8.1	9.0
18.5	0.1	0.2	0.5	0.8	1.2	1.8	2.4	3.1	3.8	4.6	5.5	6.4	7.3	8.3	9.2
19.0	0.1	0.2	0.5	0.8	1.3	1.8	2.4	3.1	3.9	4.8	5.6	6.6	7.5	8.5	9.5
19.5	0.1	0.2	0.5	0.8	1.3	1.9	2.5	3.2	4.0	4.9	5.8	6.7	7.7	8.7	9.8
20.0	0.1	0.2	0.5	0.9	1.3	1.9	2.6	3.3	4.1	5.0	5.9	6.9	7.9	9.0	10.0

Obtain from the predictions the high water and low water, one of which is before and the other after the time for which the height is required. The difference between the times of occurrence of these tides is the duration of rise or fall, and the difference between their heights is the range of tide for the above table. Find the difference between the nearest high or low water and the time for which the height is required.

Enter the table with the duration of rise or fall, printed in heavy-faced type, which most nearly agrees with the actual value, and on that horizontal line find the time from the nearest high or low water which agrees most nearly with the corresponding actual difference. The correction sought is in the column directly below, on the line with the range of tide.

When the nearest tide is high water, subtract the correction.

When the nearest tide is low water, add the correction.

Fig. 6-17. Tide Tables; Table 3.

SAN FRANCISCO (Golden Gate), CALIFORNIA, 1982

Times and Heights of High and Low Waters

JULY

Day	Time h m	Height ft	Height m	Day	Time h m	Height ft	Height m
1	0221	0.4	0.1	16	0122	0.3	0.1
Th	0903	3.9	1.2	F	0815	3.9	1.2
	1339	2.1	0.6		1247	2.2	0.7
	2015	5.9	1.8		1927	6.4	2.0
2	0303	0.0	0.0	17	0216	-0.4	-0.1
F	1007	4.1	1.2	Sa	0928	4.2	1.3
	1428	2.5	0.8		1343	2.5	0.8
	2049	5.9	1.8		2015	6.7	2.0
3	0342	-0.3	-0.1	18	0307	-1.0	-0.3
Sa	1057	4.3	1.3	Su	1028	4.6	1.4
	1514	2.7	0.8		1442	2.6	0.8
	2125	5.9	1.8		2105	6.9	2.1
4	0418	-0.5	-0.2	19	0357	-1.5	-0.5
Su	1144	4.4	1.3	M	1119	4.9	1.5
	1556	2.9	0.9		1537	2.6	0.8
	2201	5.9	1.8		2156	7.1	2.2
5	0453	-0.6	-0.2	20	0444	-1.7	-0.5
M	1222	4.5	1.4	Tu	1207	5.1	1.6
	1634	3.0	0.9		1633	2.6	0.8
	2236	5.9	1.8		2248	7.0	2.1
6	0525	-0.6	-0.2	21	0532	-1.7	-0.5
Tu	1301	4.5	1.4	W	1253	5.2	1.6
	1713	3.1	0.9		1727	2.4	0.7
	2309	5.8	1.8		2340	6.8	2.1
7	0559	-0.7	-0.2	22	0618	-1.5	-0.5
W	1334	4.6	1.4	Th	1335	5.3	1.6
	1749	3.1	0.9		1822	2.3	0.7
	2344	5.7	1.7				
8	0635	-0.6	-0.2	23	0031	6.4	2.0
Th	1409	4.6	1.4	F	0705	-1.1	-0.3
	1831	3.1	0.9		1420	5.3	1.6
					1921	2.2	0.7

AUGUST

Day	Time h m	Height ft	Height m	Day	Time h m	Height ft	Height m
1	0319	0.0	0.0	16	0250	-0.8	-0.2
Su	1040	4.5	1.4	M	1011	4.9	1.5
	1458	3.0	0.9		1439	2.7	0.8
	2100	6.0	1.8		2055	6.8	2.1
2	0354	-0.2	-0.1	17	0340	-1.1	-0.3
M	1119	4.6	1.4	Tu	1057	5.1	1.6
	1540	3.0	0.9		1532	2.4	0.7
	2139	6.0	1.8		2148	6.9	2.1
3	0430	-0.4	-0.1	18	0427	-1.3	-0.4
Tu	1151	4.7	1.4	W	1139	5.3	1.6
	1618	2.9	0.9		1626	2.1	0.6
	2215	6.0	1.8		2240	6.8	2.1
4	0504	-0.5	-0.2	19	0512	-1.2	-0.4
W	1223	4.7	1.4	Th	1217	5.4	1.6
	1653	2.8	0.9		1715	1.8	0.5
	2253	5.9	1.8		2332	6.5	2.0
5	0535	-0.5	-0.2	20	0554	-0.9	-0.3
Th	1251	4.7	1.4	F	1256	5.4	1.6
	1729	2.7	0.8		1806	1.6	0.5
	2328	5.8	1.8				
6	0607	-0.4	-0.1	21	0024	6.0	1.8
F	1321	4.8	1.5	Sa	0636	-0.4	-0.1
	1807	2.5	0.8		1334	5.5	1.7
					1859	1.4	0.4
7	0007	5.6	1.7	22	0113	5.8	1.7
Sa	0639	-0.2	-0.1	Su	0718	0.2	0.1
	1351	4.9	1.5		1414	5.5	1.7
	1849	2.4	0.7		1951	1.4	0.4
8	0049	5.2	1.6	23	0209	4.9	1.5
Su	0711	0.0	0.0	M	0800	0.9	0.3
	1423	5.0	1.5		1452	5.5	1.7
	1935	2.2	0.7		2051	1.3	0.4

SEPTEMBER

Day	Time h m	Height ft	Height m	Day	Time h m	Height ft	Height m
1	0359	-0.1	0.0	16	0405	-0.6	-0.2
W	1108	4.8	1.5	Th	1103	5.5	1.7
	1559	2.4	0.7		1617	1.3	0.4
	2159	5.8	1.8		2237	6.2	1.9
2	0431	-0.2	-0.1	17	0446	-0.4	-0.1
Th	1133	4.9	1.5	F	1138	5.6	1.7
	1633	2.1	0.6		1703	0.9	0.3
	2238	5.7	1.7		2327	5.9	1.8
3	0501	-0.2	-0.1	18	0525	0.0	0.0
F	1202	5.0	1.5	Sa	1213	5.6	1.7
	[illegible]08	1.9	0.6		1748	0.7	0.2
	2320	5.6	1.7				
4	0533	0.0	0.0	19	0017	5.5	1.7
Sa	1227	5.1	1.6	Su	0604	0.5	0.2
	1745	1.6	0.5		1247	5.6	1.7
					1834	0.6	0.2
5	0002	5.4	1.6	20	0108	5.1	1.6
Su	0604	0.3	0.1	M	0642	1.1	0.3
	1259	5.2	1.6		1320	5.5	1.7
	1826	1.3	0.4		1921	0.6	0.2
6	0047	5.1	1.6	21	0201	4.7	1.4
M	0639	0.7	0.2	Tu	0724	1.8	0.5
	1329	5.4	1.6		1352	5.4	1.6
	1909	1.1	0.3		2008	0.7	0.2
7	0136	4.8	1.5	22	0304	4.3	1.3
Tu	0715	1.2	0.4	W	0806	2.4	0.7
	1403	5.5	1.7		1430	5.3	1.6
	2001	0.9	0.3		2103	0.8	0.2
8	0239	4.5	1.4	23	0419	4.1	1.2
W	0758	1.8	0.5	Th	0902	2.9	0.9
	1443	5.7	1.7		1510	5.2	1.6
	2102	0.8	0.2		2203	0.9	0.3

9	0022	5.5	1.7	24	0125	5.8	1.8
F	0708	-0.5	-0.2	Sa	0750	-0.6	-0.2
	1441	4.6	1.4		1503	5.4	1.6
	1916	3.1	0.9		2022	2.1	0.6
10	0101	5.2	1.6	25	0221	5.2	1.6
Sa	0745	-0.3	-0.1	Su	0836	0.0	0.0
	1516	4.7	1.4		1548	5.5	1.7
	2007	2.9	0.9		2130	1.9	0.6
11	0146	4.9	1.5	26	0323	4.5	1.4
Su	0822	0.0	0.0	M	0926	0.7	0.2
	1551	4.9	1.5		1632	5.5	1.7
	2106	2.7	0.8		2242	1.6	0.5
12	0239	4.5	1.4	27	0440	4.0	1.2
M	0904	0.4	0.1	Tu	1017	1.4	0.4
	1630	5.1	1.6		1718	5.6	1.7
	2212	2.3	0.7		2354	1.3	0.4
13	0345	4.1	1.2	28	0613	3.7	1.1
Tu	0953	0.8	0.2	W	1112	2.0	0.6
	1709	5.4	1.6		1803	5.6	1.7
	2321	1.8	0.5				
14	0509	3.8	1.2	29	0056	1.0	0.3
W	1045	1.3	0.4	Th	0743	3.8	1.2
	1752	5.7	1.7		1215	2.5	0.8
					1850	5.7	1.7
15	0023	1.1	0.3	30	0149	0.6	0.2
Th	0645	3.7	1.1	F	0859	4.0	1.2
	1144	1.8	0.5		1314	2.8	0.9
	1838	6.0	1.8		1936	5.8	1.8
				31	0237	-0.3	0.1
				Sa	0955	4.3	1.3
					1409	2.9	0.9
					2018	5.9	1.8

9	0134	4.9	1.5	24	0311	4.4	1.3
M	0747	0.5	0.2	Tu	0843	1.6	0.5
	1455	5.2	1.6		1533	5.4	1.6
	2033	1.9	0.6		2153	1.3	0.4
10	0231	4.5	1.4	25	0429	4.0	1.2
Tu	0829	1.0	0.3	W	0938	2.2	0.7
	1534	5.4	1.6		1615	5.4	1.6
	2133	1.6	0.5		2302	1.2	0.4
11	0339	4.1	1.2	26	0603	3.9	1.2
W	0915	1.6	0.5	Th	1043	2.7	0.8
	1618	5.6	1.7		1705	5.4	1.6
	2242	1.2	0.4				
12	0511	3.8	1.2	27	0008	1.0	0.3
Th	1013	2.1	0.6	F	0734	4.0	1.2
	1706	5.9	1.8		1153	3.0	0.9
	2351	0.7	0.2		1758	5.4	1.6
13	0654	3.9	1.2	28	0107	0.8	0.2
F	1119	2.6	0.8	Sa	0844	4.3	1.3
	1800	6.1	1.9		1258	3.1	0.9
					1854	5.5	1.7
14	0057	0.2	0.1	29	0159	0.6	0.2
Sa	0818	4.2	1.3	Su	0929	4.5	1.4
	1231	2.8	0.9		1356	3.1	0.9
	1900	6.4	2.0		1946	5.6	1.7
15	0156	-0.4	-0.1	30	0244	0.3	0.1
Su	0919	4.5	1.4	M	1007	4.6	1.4
	1338	2.8	0.9		1441	2.9	0.9
	1959	6.6	2.0		2035	5.7	1.7
				31	0324	0.1	0.0
				Tu	1039	4.7	1.4
					1522	2.7	0.8
					2117	5.8	1.8

9	0352	4.2	1.3	24	0549	4.1	1.2
Th	0848	2.4	0.7	F	1015	3.3	1.0
	1531	5.8	1.8		1603	5.1	1.6
	2209	0.6	0.2		2310	1.0	0.3
10	0523	4.1	1.2	25	0711	4.3	1.3
F	0955	2.9	0.9	Sa	1137	3.4	1.0
	1628	5.9	1.8		1705	5.0	1.5
	2322	0.3	0.1				
11	0655	4.3	1.3	26	0016	0.9	0.3
Sa	1117	3.1	0.9	Su	0808	4.5	1.4
	1736	6.0	1.8		1246	3.3	1.0
					1811	5.0	1.5
12	0033	0.0	0.0	27	0111	0.7	0.2
Su	0808	4.6	1.4	M	0849	4.6	1.4
	1234	3.0	0.9		1339	3.0	0.9
	1843	6.1	1.9		1911	5.1	1.6
13	0135	-0.3	-0.1	28	0200	0.5	0.2
M	0901	4.9	1.5	Tu	0921	4.8	1.5
	1341	2.7	0.8		1423	2.6	0.8
	1949	6.2	1.9		2006	5.2	1.6
14	0231	-0.6	-0.2	29	0242	0.3	0.1
Tu	0945	5.2	1.6	W	0950	4.9	1.5
	1438	2.3	0.7		1501	2.2	0.7
	2050	6.3	1.9		2055	5.3	1.6
15	0319	-0.7	-0.2	30	0317	0.2	0.1
W	1027	5.3	1.6	Th	1015	5.0	1.5
	1530	1.8	0.5		1536	1.7	0.5
	2145	6.3	1.9		2140	5.4	1.6

Time meridian 120° W. 0000 is midnight. 1200 is noon.
Heights are referred to mean lower low water which is the chart datum of soundings.

Fig. 6-18. Sample page Table 1 showing Aug. 22.

Duration of rise or fall, see footnote	Time from the nearest high water or low water														
h. m.	h. m.	h. m.	h. m.	h. m.	h. m.	h. m.	h. m.	h. m.	h. m.	h. m.	h. m.	h. m.	h. m.	h. m.	h. m.
4 00	0 08	0 16	0 24	0 32	0 40	0 48	0 56	1 04	1 12	1 20	1 28	1 36	1 44	1 52	2 00
4 20	0 09	0 17	0 26	0 35	0 43	0 52	1 01	1 09	1 18	1 27	1 35	1 44	1 53	2 01	2 10
4 40	0 09	0 19	0 28	0 37	0 47	0 56	1 05	1 15	1 24	1 33	1 43	1 52	2 01	2 11	2 20
5 00	0 10	0 20	0 30	0 40	0 50	1 00	1 10	1 20	1 30	1 40	1 50	2 00	2 10	2 20	2 30
5 20	0 11	0 21	0 32	0 43	0 53	1 04	1 15	1 25	1 36	1 47	1 57	2 08	2 19	2 29	2 40
5 40	0 11	0 23	0 34	0 45	0 57	1 08	1 19	1 31	1 42	1 53	2 05	2 16	2 27	2 39	2 50
6 00	0 12	0 24	0 36	0 48	1 00	1 12	1 24	1 36	1 48	2 00	2 12	2 24	2 36	2 48	3 00
6 20	0 13	0 25	0 38	0 51	1 03	1 16	1 29	1 41	1 54	2 07	2 19	2 32	2 45	2 57	3 10
6 40	0 13	0 27	0 40	0 53	1 07	1 20	1 33	1 47	2 00	2 13	2 27	2 40	2 53	3 07	3 20
7 00	0 14	0 28	0 42	0 56	1 10	1 24	1 38	1 52	2 06	2 20	2 34	2 48	3 02	3 16	3 30
7 20	0 15	0 29	0 44	0 59	1 13	1 28	1 43	1 57	2 12	2 27	2 41	2 56	3 11	3 25	3 40
7 40	0 15	0 31	0 46	1 01	1 17	1 32	1 47	2 03	2 18	2 33	2 49	3 04	3 19	3 35	3 50
8 00	0 16	0 32	0 48	1 04	1 20	1 36	1 52	2 08	2 24	2 40	2 56	3 12	3 28	3 44	4 00
8 20	0 17	0 33	0 50	1 07	1 23	1 40	1 57	2 13	2 30	2 47	3 03	3 20	3 37	3 53	4 10
8 40	0 17	0 35	0 52	1 09	1 27	1 44	2 01	2 19	2 36	2 53	3 11	3 28	3 45	4 03	4 20
9 00	0 18	0 36	0 54	1 12	1 30	1 48	2 06	2 24	2 42	3 00	3 18	3 36	3 54	4 12	4 30
9 20	0 19	0 37	0 56	1 15	1 33	1 52	2 11	2 29	2 48	3 07	3 25	3 44	4 03	4 21	4 40
9 40	0 19	0 39	0 58	1 17	1 37	1 56	2 15	2 35	2 54	3 13	3 33	3 52	4 11	4 31	4 50
10 00	0 20	0 40	1 00	1 20	1 40	2 00	2 20	2 40	3 00	3 20	3 40	4 00	4 20	4 40	5 00
10 20	0 21	0 41	1 02	1 23	1 43	2 04	2 25	2 45	3 06	3 27	3 47	4 08	4 29	4 49	5 10
10 40	0 21	0 43	1 04	1 25	1 47	2 08	2 29	2 51	3 12	3 33	3 55	4 16	4 37	4 59	5 20

	Correction to height														
Ft.	Ft.	Ft.	Ft.	Ft.	Ft.	Ft.	Ft.	Ft.	Ft.	Ft.	Ft.	Ft.	Ft.	Ft.	Ft.
0.5	0.0	0.0	0.0	0.0	0.0	0.0	0.1	0.1	0.1	0.1	0.1	0.2	0.2	0.2	0.2
1.0	0.0	0.0	0.0	0.0	0.1	0.1	0.1	0.2	0.2	0.2	0.3	0.3	0.4	0.4	0.5
1.5	0.0	0.0	0.0	0.1	0.1	0.1	0.2	0.2	0.3	0.4	0.4	0.5	0.6	0.7	0.8
2.0	0.0	0.0	0.0	0.1	0.1	0.2	0.3	0.3	0.4	0.5	0.6	0.7	0.8	0.9	1.0
2.5	0.0	0.0	0.1	0.1	0.2	0.2	0.3	0.4	0.5	0.6	0.7	0.9	1.0	1.1	1.2
3.0	0.0	0.0	0.1	0.1	0.2	0.3	0.4	0.5	0.6	0.8	0.9	1.0	1.2	1.3	1.5
3.5	0.0	0.0	0.1	0.2	0.2	0.3	0.4	0.6	0.7	0.9	1.0	1.2	1.4	1.6	1.8
4.0	0.0	0.0	0.1	0.2	0.2	0.4	0.5	0.7	0.8	1.0	1.2	1.4	1.6	1.8	2.0
4.5	0.0	0.0	0.1	0.2	0.3	0.4	0.6	0.7	0.9	1.1	1.3	1.6	1.8	2.0	2.2
5.0	0.0	0.1	0.1	0.2	0.3	0.5	0.6	0.8	1.0	1.2	1.5	1.7	2.0	2.2	2.5
5.5	0.0	0.1	0.1	0.2	0.4	0.5	0.7	0.9	1.1	1.4	1.6	1.9	2.2	2.5	2.8
6.0	0.0	0.1	0.1	0.3	0.4	0.6	0.8	1.0	1.2	1.5	1.8	2.1	2.4	2.7	3.0

Range of tide, see footnote															
6.5	0.0	0.1	0.2	0.3	0.4	0.6	0.8	1.1	1.3	1.6	1.9	2.2	2.6	2.9	3.2
7.0	0.0	0.1	0.2	0.3	0.5	0.7	0.9	1.2	1.4	1.8	2.1	2.4	2.8	3.1	3.5
7.5	0.0	0.1	0.2	0.3	0.5	0.7	1.0	1.2	1.5	1.9	2.2	2.6	3.0	3.4	3.8
8.0	0.0	0.1	0.2	0.3	0.5	0.8	1.0	1.3	1.6	2.0	2.4	2.8	3.2	3.6	4.0
8.5	0.0	0.1	0.2	0.4	0.6	0.8	1.1	1.4	1.8	2.1	2.6	2.9	3.4	3.8	4.2
9.0	0.0	0.1	0.2	0.4	0.6	0.9	1.2	1.5	1.9	2.2	2.7	3.1	3.6	4.0	4.5
9.5	0.0	0.1	0.2	0.4	0.6	0.9	1.2	1.6	2.0	2.4	2.8	3.3	3.8	4.3	4.8
10.0	0.0	0.1	0.2	0.4	0.7	1.0	1.3	1.7	2.1	2.5	3.0	3.5	4.0	4.5	5.0
10.5	0.0	0.1	0.3	0.5	0.7	1.0	1.3	1.7	2.2	2.6	3.1	3.6	4.2	4.7	5.2
11.0	0.0	0.1	0.3	0.5	0.7	1.1	1.4	1.8	2.3	2.8	3.3	3.8	4.4	4.9	5.5
11.5	0.0	0.1	0.3	0.5	0.8	1.1	1.5	1.9	2.4	2.9	3.4	4.0	4.6	5.1	5.8
12.0	0.0	0.1	0.3	0.5	0.8	1.1	1.5	2.0	2.5	3.0	3.6	4.1	4.8	5.4	6.0
12.5	0.0	0.1	0.3	0.5	0.8	1.2	1.6	2.1	2.6	3.1	3.7	4.3	5.0	5.6	6.2
13.0	0.0	0.1	0.3	0.6	0.9	1.2	1.7	2.2	2.7	3.2	3.9	4.5	5.1	5.8	6.5
13.5	0.0	0.1	0.3	0.6	0.9	1.3	1.7	2.2	2.8	3.4	4.0	4.7	5.3	6.0	6.8
14.0	0.0	0.2	0.3	0.6	0.9	1.3	1.8	2.3	2.9	3.5	4.2	4.8	5.5	6.3	7.0
14.5	0.0	0.2	0.4	0.6	1.0	1.4	1.9	2.4	3.0	3.6	4.3	5.0	5.7	6.5	7.2
15.0	0.0	0.2	0.4	0.6	1.0	1.4	1.9	2.5	3.1	3.8	4.4	5.2	5.9	6.7	7.5
15.5	0.0	0.2	0.4	0.7	1.0	1.5	2.0	2.6	3.2	3.9	4.6	5.4	6.1	6.9	7.8
16.0	0.0	0.2	0.4	0.7	1.1	1.5	2.1	2.6	3.3	4.0	4.7	5.5	6.3	7.2	8.0
16.5	0.0	0.2	0.4	0.7	1.1	1.6	2.1	2.7	3.4	4.1	4.9	5.7	6.5	7.4	8.2
17.0	0.0	0.2	0.4	0.7	1.1	1.6	2.2	2.8	3.5	4.2	5.0	5.9	6.7	7.6	8.5
17.5	0.0	0.2	0.4	0.8	1.2	1.7	2.2	2.9	3.6	4.4	5.2	6.0	6.9	7.8	8.8
18.0	0.0	0.2	0.4	0.8	1.2	1.7	2.3	3.0	3.7	4.5	5.3	6.2	7.1	8.1	9.0
18.5	0.1	0.2	0.5	0.8	1.2	1.8	2.4	3.1	3.8	4.6	5.5	6.4	7.3	8.3	9.2
19.0	0.1	0.2	0.5	0.8	1.3	1.8	2.4	3.1	3.9	4.8	5.6	6.6	7.5	8.5	9.5
19.5	0.1	0.2	0.5	0.8	1.3	1.9	2.5	3.2	4.0	4.9	5.8	6.7	7.7	8.7	9.8
20.0	0.1	0.2	0.5	0.9	1.3	1.9	2.6	3.3	4.1	5.0	5.9	6.9	7.9	9.0	10.0

Obtain from the predictions the high water and low water, one of which is before and the other after the time for which the height is required. The difference between the times of occurence of these tides is the duration of rise or fall, and the difference between their heights is the range of tide for the above table. Find the difference between the nearest high or low water and the time for which the height is required.

Enter the table with the duration of rise or fall, printed in heavy-faced type, which most nearly agrees with the actual value, and on that horizontal line find the time from the nearest high or low water which agrees most nearly with the corresponding actual difference. The correction sought is in the column directly below, on the line with the range of tide.

When the nearest tide is high water, subtract the correction.

When the nearest tide is low water, add the correction.

Fig. 6-19. Table 3 showing correction for 1615 on Aug. 22 at San Francisco.

SAN FRANCISCO (Golden Gate), CALIFORNIA, 1982

Times and Heights of High and Low Waters

JULY

Day	Time h m	Height ft	Height m	Day	Time h m	Height ft	Height m
1	0221	0.4	0.1	16	0122	0.3	0.1
Th	0903	3.9	1.2	F	0815	3.9	1.2
	1339	2.1	0.6		1247	2.2	0.7
	2015	5.9	1.8		1927	6.4	2.0
2	0303	0.0	0.0	17	0216	-0.4	-0.1
F	1007	4.1	1.2	Sa	0928	4.2	1.3
	1428	2.5	0.8		1343	2.5	0.8
	2049	5.9	1.8		2015	6.7	2.0
3	0342	-0.3	-0.1	18	0307	-1.0	-0.3
Sa	1057	4.3	1.3	Su	1028	4.6	1.4
	1514	2.7	0.8		1442	2.6	0.8
	2125	5.9	1.8		2105	6.9	2.1
4	0418	-0.5	-0.2	19	0357	-1.5	-0.5
Su	1144	4.4	1.3	M	1119	4.9	1.5
	1556	2.9	0.9		1537	2.6	0.8
	2201	5.9	1.8		2156	7.1	2.2
5	0453	-0.6	-0.2	20	0444	-1.7	-0.5
M	1222	4.5	1.4	Tu	1207	5.1	1.6
	1634	3.0	0.9		1633	2.6	0.8
	2236	5.9	1.8		2248	7.0	2.1
6	0525	-0.6	-0.2	21	0532	-1.7	-0.5
Tu	1301	4.5	1.4	W	1253	5.2	1.6
	1713	3.1	0.9		1727	2.4	0.7
	2309	5.8	1.8		2340	6.8	2.1
7	0559	-0.7	-0.2	22	0618	-1.5	-0.5
W	1334	4.6	1.4	Th	1335	5.3	1.6
	1749	3.1	0.9		1822	2.3	0.7
	2344	5.7	1.7				
8	0635	-0.6	-0.2	23	0031	6.4	2.0
Th	1409	4.6	1.4	F	0705	-1.1	-0.3
	1831	3.1	0.9		1420	5.3	1.6
					1921	2.2	0.7

AUGUST

Day	Time h m	Height ft	Height m	Day	Time h m	Height ft	Height m
1	0319	0.0	0.0	16	0250	-0.8	-0.2
Su	1040	4.5	1.4	M	1011	4.9	1.5
	1458	3.0	0.9		1439	2.7	0.8
	2100	6.0	1.8		2055	6.8	2.1
2	0354	-0.2	-0.1	17	0340	-1.1	-0.3
M	1119	4.6	1.4	Tu	1057	5.1	1.6
	1540	3.0	0.9		1532	2.4	0.7
	2139	6.0	1.8		2148	6.9	2.1
3	0430	-0.4	-0.1	18	0427	-1.3	-0.4
Tu	1151	4.7	1.4	W	1139	5.3	1.6
	1618	2.9	0.9		1626	2.1	0.6
	2215	6.0	1.8		2240	6.8	2.1
4	0504	-0.5	-0.2	19	0512	-1.2	-0.4
W	1223	4.7	1.4	Th	1217	5.4	1.6
	1653	2.8	0.9		1715	1.8	0.5
	2253	5.9	1.8		2332	6.5	2.0
5	0535	-0.5	-0.2	20	0554	-0.9	-0.3
Th	1251	4.7	1.4	F	1256	5.4	1.6
	1729	2.7	0.8		1806	1.6	0.5
	2328	5.8	1.8				
6	0607	-0.4	-0.1	21	0024	6.0	1.8
F	1321	4.8	1.5	Sa	0636	-0.4	-0.1
	1807	2.5	0.8		1334	5.5	1.7
					1859	1.4	0.4
7	0007	5.6	1.7	22	0113	5.5	1.7
Sa	0639	-0.2	-0.1	Su	0718	0.2	0.1
	1351	4.9	1.5		1414	5.5	1.7
	1849	2.4	0.7		1951	1.4	0.4
8	0049	5.2	1.6	23	0209	4.9	1.5
Su	0711	0.0	0.0	M	0800	0.9	0.3
	1423	5.0	1.5		1452	5.5	1.7
	1935	2.2	0.7		2051	1.3	0.4

SEPTEMBER

Day	Time h m	Height ft	Height m	Day	Time h m	Height ft	Height m
1	0359	-0.1	0.0	16	0405	-0.6	-0.2
W	1108	4.8	1.5	Th	1103	5.5	1.7
	1559	2.4	0.7		1617	1.3	0.4
	2159	5.8	1.8		2237	6.2	1.9
2	0431	-0.2	-0.1	17	0446	-0.4	-0.1
Th	1133	4.9	1.5	F	1138	5.6	1.7
	1633	2.1	0.6		1703	0.9	0.3
	2238	5.7	1.7		2327	5.9	1.8
3	0501	-0.2	-0.1	18	0525	0.0	0.0
F	1202	5.0	1.5	Sa	1213	5.6	1.7
	[illegible]38	1.9	0.6		1748	0.7	0.2
	2320	5.6	1.7				
4	0533	0.0	0.0	19	0017	5.5	1.7
Sa	1227	5.1	1.6	Su	0604	0.5	0.2
	1745	1.6	0.5		1247	5.6	1.7
					1834	0.6	0.2
5	0002	5.4	1.6	20	0108	5.1	1.6
Su	0604	0.3	0.1	M	0642	1.1	0.3
	1259	5.2	1.6		1320	5.5	1.7
	1826	1.3	0.4		1921	0.6	0.2
6	0047	5.1	1.6	21	0201	4.7	1.4
M	0639	0.7	0.2	Tu	0724	1.8	0.5
	1329	5.4	1.6		1352	5.4	1.6
	1909	1.1	0.3		2008	0.7	0.2
7	0136	4.8	1.5	22	0304	4.3	1.3
Tu	0715	1.2	0.4	W	0806	2.4	0.7
	1403	5.5	1.7		1430	5.3	1.6
	2001	0.9	0.3		2103	0.8	0.2
8	0239	4.5	1.4	23	0419	4.1	1.2
W	0758	1.8	0.5	Th	0902	2.9	0.9
	1443	5.7	1.7		1510	5.2	1.6
	2102	0.8	0.2		2203	0.9	0.3

9	0022	5.5	1.7	24	0125	5.8	1.8	9	0134	4.9	1.5	24	0311	4.4	1.3	9	0352	4.2	1.3	24	0549	4.1	1.2
F	0708	-0.5	-0.2	Sa	0750	-0.6	-0.2	M	0747	0.5	0.2	Tu	0843	1.6	0.5	Th	0848	2.4	0.7	F	1015	3.3	1.0
	1441	4.6	1.4		1503	5.4	1.6		1455	5.2	1.6		1533	5.4	1.6		1531	5.8	1.8		1603	5.1	1.6
	1916	3.1	0.9		2022	2.1	0.6		2033	1.9	0.6		2153	1.3	0.4		2209	0.6	0.2		2310	1.0	0.3
10	0101	5.2	1.6	25	0221	5.2	1.6	10	0231	4.5	1.4	25	0429	4.0	1.2	10	0523	4.1	1.2	25	0711	4.3	1.3
Sa	0745	-0.3	-0.1	Su	0836	0.0	0.0	Tu	0829	1.0	0.3	W	0938	2.2	0.7	F	0955	2.9	0.9	Sa	1137	3.4	1.0
	1516	4.7	1.4		1548	5.5	1.7		1534	5.4	1.6		1615	5.4	1.6		1628	5.9	1.8		1705	5.0	1.5
	2007	2.9	0.9		2130	1.9	0.6		2133	1.6	0.5		2302	1.2	0.4		2322	0.3	0.1				
11	0146	4.9	1.5	26	0323	4.5	1.4	11	0339	4.1	1.2	26	0603	3.9	1.2	11	0655	4.3	1.3	26	0016	0.9	0.3
Su	0822	0.0	0.0	M	0926	0.7	0.2	W	0915	1.6	0.5	Th	1043	2.7	0.8	Sa	1117	3.1	0.9	Su	0808	4.5	1.4
	1551	4.9	1.5		1632	5.5	1.7		1618	5.6	1.7		1705	5.4	1.6		1736	6.0	1.8		1246	3.3	1.0
	2106	2.7	0.8		2242	1.6	0.5		2242	1.2	0.4										1811	5.0	1.5
12	0239	4.5	1.4	27	0440	4.0	1.2	12	0511	3.8	1.2	27	0008	1.0	0.3	12	0033	0.0	0.0	27	0111	0.7	0.2
M	0904	0.4	0.1	Tu	1017	1.4	0.4	Th	1013	2.1	0.6	F	0734	4.0	1.2	Su	0808	4.6	1.4	M	0849	4.6	1.4
	1630	5.1	1.6		1718	5.6	1.7		1706	5.9	1.8		1153	3.0	0.9		1234	3.0	0.9		1339	3.0	0.9
	2212	2.3	0.7		2354	1.3	0.4		2351	0.7	0.2		1758	5.4	1.6		1843	6.1	1.9		1911	5.1	1.6
13	0345	4.1	1.2	28	0613	3.7	1.1	13	0654	3.9	1.2	28	0107	0.8	0.2	13	0135	-0.3	-0.1	28	0200	0.5	0.2
Tu	0953	0.8	0.2	W	1112	2.0	0.6	F	1119	2.6	0.8	Sa	0844	4.3	1.3	M	0901	4.9	1.5	Tu	0921	4.8	1.5
	1709	5.4	1.6		1803	5.6	1.7		1800	6.1	1.9		1258	3.1	0.9		1341	2.7	0.8		1423	2.6	0.8
	2321	1.8	0.5										1854	5.5	1.7		1949	6.2	1.9		2006	5.2	1.6
14	0509	3.8	1.2	29	0056	1.0	0.3	14	0057	0.2	0.1	29	0159	0.6	0.2	14	0231	-0.6	-0.2	29	0242	0.3	0.1
W	1045	1.3	0.4	Th	0743	3.8	1.2	Sa	0818	4.2	1.3	Su	0929	4.5	1.4	Tu	0945	5.2	1.6	W	0950	4.9	1.5
	1752	5.7	1.7		1215	2.5	0.8		1231	2.8	0.9		1356	3.1	0.9		1438	2.3	0.7		1501	2.2	0.7
					1850	5.7	1.7		1900	6.4	2.0		1946	5.6	1.7		2050	6.3	1.9		2055	5.3	1.6
15	0023	1.1	0.3	30	0149	0.6	0.2	15	0156	-0.4	-0.1	30	0244	0.3	0.1	15	0319	-0.7	-0.2	30	0317	0.2	0.1
Th	0645	3.7	1.1	F	0859	4.0	1.2	Su	0919	4.5	1.4	M	1007	4.6	1.4	W	1027	5.3	1.6	Th	1015	5.0	1.5
	1144	1.8	0.5		1314	2.8	0.9		1338	2.8	0.9		1441	2.9	0.9		1530	1.8	0.5		1536	1.7	0.5
	1838	6.0	1.8		1936	5.8	1.8		1959	6.6	2.0		2035	5.7	1.7		2145	6.3	1.9		2140	5.4	1.6
				31	0237	-0.3	0.1					31	0324	0.1	0.0								
				Sa	0955	4.3	1.3					Tu	1039	4.7	1.4								
					1409	2.9	0.9						1522	2.7	0.8								
					2018	5.9	1.8						2117	5.8	1.8								

Time meridian 120° W. 0000 is midnight. 1200 is noon.
Heights are referred to mean lower low water which is the chart datum of soundings.

Fig. 6-20. Table 1 showing Sept. 10.

NO.	PLACE	POSITION Lat.	POSITION Long.	DIFFERENCES Time High water	DIFFERENCES Time Low water	DIFFERENCES Height High water	DIFFERENCES Height Low water	RANGES Mean	RANGES Diurnal	Mean Tide Level
		° ' S	° ' W	h. m.	h. m.	ft	ft	ft	ft	ft
	CALIFORNIA San Pedro Channel Time meridian, 120°W			on LOS ANGELES, p.68						
459	Santa Monica...........................	34 00	118 30	+0 01	+0 05	-0.1	0.0	3.7	5.4	2.8
	Santa Barbara Channel									
461	Mugu Lagoon (ocean pier)................	34 06	119 06	+0 02	+0 09	*0.98	*0.98	3.7	5.3	2.7
463	Port Hueneme............................	34 09	119 12	+0 09	+0 11	0.0	0.0	3.7	5.4	2.8
465	Ventura.................................	34 16	119 17	+0 08	+0 14	0.0	0.0	3.7	5.4	2.8
467	Santa Barbara...........................	34 25	119 41	+0 23	+0 21	*0.98	*0.98	3.6	5.3	2.8
469	Gaviota.................................	34 28	120 13	+0 38	+0 35	*0.98	*0.98	3.6	5.3	2.8
	Santa Barbara Islands									
471	Wilson Cove, San Clemente Island........	33 00	118 33	-0 04	-0 05	*0.96	*0.96	3.6	5.2	2.7
473	Catalina Harbor, Santa Catalina Island..	33 26	118 30	+0 10	+0 15	*0.96	*0.96	3.6	5.2	2.7
475	Avalon, Santa Catalina Island...........	33 21	118 19	+0 05	+0 07	*0.98	*0.98	3.7	5.3	2.7
477	Santa Barbara Island....................	33 29	119 02	-0 03	+0 02	*0.94	*0.94	3.5	5.1	2.6
479	San Nicolas Island......................	33 16	119 30	+0 09	+0 19	*0.91	*0.91	3.3	4.9	2.5
481	Prisoners Harbor, Santa Cruz Island.....	34 01	119 41	+0 24	+0 24	*0.93	*0.93	3.4	5.0	2.6
483	Bechers Bay, Santa Rosa Island..........	34 00	120 03	+0 36	+0 33	*0.98	*0.98	3.6	5.3	2.8
485	Cuyler Harbor, San Miguel Island........	34 03	120 21	+0 32	+0 32	*0.96	*0.96	3.5	5.2	2.7
	Outer Coast									
487	Point Arguello..........................	34 35	120 39	+0 44	+0 41	*0.96	*0.96	3.5	5.2	2.7
489	Avila Beach, San Luis Obispo Bay........	35 10	120 44	+0 47	+0 52	*0.98	*0.98	3.6	5.3	2.8
491	Morro Beach, Estero Bay.................	35 24	120 52	+0 55	+0 54	*0.96	*0.96	3.5	5.2	2.8
493	San Simeon..............................	35 38	121 11	+0 59	+0 56	*0.96	*0.96	3.5	5.2	2.7
495	Carmel Cove, Carmel Bay.................	36 31	121 56	+1 11	+1 11	*0.96	*0.96	3.5	5.2	2.8
				on SAN FRANCISCO, p.72						
497	Monterey, Monterey Bay..................	36 36	121 54	-1 16	-0 58	-0.5	0.0	3.5	5.3	2.8
499	Santa Cruz, Monterey Bay................	36 58	122 01	-1 19	-1 04	-0.5	0.0	3.5	5.3	2.8
501	Ano Nuevo Island........................	37 06	122 20	-1 28	-1 10	-0.6	-0.1	3.5	5.2	2.7
503	Princeton, Halfmoon Bay.................	37 30	122 29	-1 10	-0 56	-0.2	0.0	3.8	5.5	3.0

505	Southeast Farallon Island...............	37 42	123 00	-0 43	-0 25	-0.2	0.0	3.8	5.6	3.0
507	San Francisco Bar.......................	37 46	122 38	-0 39	-0 37	-0.1	0.0	3.9	5.6	3.0
509	Ocean Beach, outer coast................	37 46	122 31	-0 53	-0 41	+0.2	0.0	4.2	6.0	3.2
	San Francisco Bay									
511	Bonita Cove, Golden Gate................	37 49	122 32	-0 24	-0 06	+0.1	0.0	4.1	5.8	3.1
513	SAN FRANCISCO (Golden Gate).............	37 48	122 28	Daily predictions				4.1	5.8	3.2
515	Alcatraz Island.........................	37 50	122 25	+0 10	+0 12	+0.1	0.0	4.1	5.8	3.1
517	San Francisco, North Point, Pier 41.....	37 49	122 25	+0 13	+0 11	+0.1	0.0	4.2	5.9	3.2
519	Rincon Point, Pier 22 1/2...............	37 47	122 23	+0 23	+0 25	+0.3	0.0	4.4	6.1	3.3
521	Yerba Buena Island......................	37 49	122 22	+0 23	+0 32	+0.3	0.0	4.3	6.0	3.2
523	Oakland Pier............................	37 48	122 20	+0 29	+0 42	+0.3	0.0	4.3	6.0	3.2
525	Alameda.................................	37 46	122 18	+0 35	+0 42	+0.7	0.0	4.7	6.4	3.5
527	Oakland Harbor, Grove Street............	37 48	122 17	+0 29	+0 36	+0.5	0.0	4.5	6.2	3.3
529	Oakland Harbor, Park Street Bridge......	37 46	122 14	+0 40	+0 44	+0.6	0.0	4.6	6.3	3.4
531	Bay Farm Island Bridge..................	37 45	122 14	+0 41	+0 52	+0.8	0.0	4.8	6.5	3.5
533	Oakland Airport.........................	37 44	122 12	+0 40	+0 40	+0.8	0.0	4.8	6.5	3.5
535	Potrero Point...........................	37 46	122 23	+0 29	+0 40	+0.6	0.0	4.6	6.3	3.4
537	Hunters Point...........................	37 44	122 21	+0 32	+0 46	+0.8	0.0	4.9	6.6	3.6
538	Roberts Landing, 1.3 miles west of......	37 40	122 12	+0 48	+1 22	+1.5	+0.1	5.4	7.2	3.9
539	South San Francisco.....................	37 40	122 23	+0 45	+1 02	+1.1	0.0	5.2	6.9	3.7
540	Oyster Point Marina.....................	37 40	122 23	+0 48	+1 07	+1.1	0.0	5.2	6.9	3.7
541	Point San Bruno.........................	37 39	122 23	+0 34	+1 04	+1.2	+0.1	5.1	6.9	3.7
542	Seaplane Harbor.........................	37 38	122 23	+0 51	+1 11	+1.3	0.0	5.4	7.1	3.8
543	Coyote Point............................	37 36	122 19	+0 49	+1 14	+1.5	+0.1	5.5	7.3	4.0
545	San Mateo Bridge........................	37 35	122 15	+0 52	+1 20	+1.8	+0.1	5.8	7.6	4.1
547	Coyote Hill Slough entrance.............	37 34	122 08	+0 54	+1 26	+2.1	+0.1	6.0	7.8	4.2
548	Bay Slough, west end....................	37 33	122 15	+0 55	+1 35	+1.8	0.0	5.9	7.6	4.0
549	Bay Slough, east end....................	37 33	122 13	+0 56	+1 59	+1.4	-0.2	5.7	7.2	3.8
550	Redwood Creek Marker #8.................	37 32	122 12	+1 00	+1 35	+2.1	+0.1	6.1	7.9	4.2
551	Redwood Creek entrance (inside).........	37 31	122 12	+1 02	+1 32	+2.2	+0.1	6.1	7.9	4.2
552	Corkscrew Slough........................	37 30	122 13	+1 03	+1 42	+2.2	+0.1	6.2	8.0	4.3
553	Redwood City, Wharf 5...................	37 30	122 13	+0 58	+1 32	+2.2	+0.1	6.2	8.0	4.3
554	West Point Slough.......................	37 30	122 12	+1 03	+1 36	+2.2	+0.1	6.2	8.0	4.3
555	Smith Slough............................	37 30	122 14	+1 11	+1 52	+2.2	0.0	6.2	7.9	4.2
556	Newark Slough...........................	37 31	122 05	+1 11	+1 58	+2.6	+0.1	6.6	8.4	4.2
557	Dumbarton Highway Bridge................	37 30	122 07	+1 07	+1 44	+2.5	+0.1	6.5	8.3	4.4
558	Ravenswood Slough <17>................	37 30	122 10	+1 05	- - -	- -	- -	- -	- -	- -
559	Granite Rock............................	37 30	122 13	+1 03	+1 38	+2.2	+0.1	6.2	8.0	4.3
560	Palo Alto Yacht Harbor..................	37 27	122 06	+0 52	+1 48	+2.9	+0.1	6.8	8.6	4.6
561	Calaveras Point, west of................	37 28	122 04	+1 01	+1 43	+2.9	+0.1	6.8	8.5	4.6
562	Mud Slough railroad bridge..............	37 28	121 58	+1 04	+2 06	+3.5	+0.1	7.4	9.1	4.9
563	Alviso (bridge), Alviso Slough..........	37 26	121 59	+1 20	+2 18	+3.3	+0.1	7.2	9.0	4.8

Endnotes can be found at the end of table 2.

Fig. 6-21. Table 2 showing differences for Redwood City.

Duration of rise or fall, see footnote	Time from the nearest high water or low water														
h. m.	*h. m.*	*h. m.*	*h. m.*	*h. m.*	*h. m.*	*h. m.*	*h. m.*	*h. m.*	*h. m.*	*h. m.*	*h. m.*	*h. m.*	*h. m.*	*h. m.*	*h. m.*
4 00	0 08	0 16	0 24	0 32	0 40	0 48	0 56	1 04	1 12	1 20	1 28	1 36	1 44	1 52	2 00
4 20	0 09	0 17	0 26	0 35	0 43	0 52	1 01	1 09	1 18	1 27	1 35	1 44	1 53	2 01	2 10
4 40	0 09	0 19	0 28	0 37	0 47	0 56	1 05	1 15	1 24	1 33	1 43	1 52	2 01	2 11	2 20
5 00	0 10	0 20	0 30	0 40	0 50	1 00	1 10	1 20	1 30	1 40	1 50	2 00	2 10	2 20	2 30
5 20	0 11	0 21	0 32	0 43	0 53	1 04	1 15	1 25	1 36	1 47	1 57	2 08	2 19	2 29	2 40
5 40	0 11	0 23	0 34	0 45	0 57	1 08	1 19	1 31	1 42	1 53	2 05	2 16	2 27	2 39	2 50
6 00	**0 12**	**0 24**	**0 36**	**0 48**	**1 00**	**1 12**	**1 24**	**1 36**	**1 48**	**2 00**	2 12	2 24	2 36	2 48	3 00
6 20	0 13	0 25	0 38	0 51	1 03	1 16	1 29	1 41	1 54	2 07	2 19	2 32	2 45	2 57	3 10
6 40	0 13	0 27	0 40	0 53	1 07	1 20	1 33	1 47	2 00	2 13	2 27	2 40	2 53	3 07	3 20
7 00	0 14	0 28	0 42	0 56	1 10	1 24	1 38	1 52	2 06	2 20	2 34	2 48	3 02	3 16	3 30
7 20	0 15	0 29	0 44	0 59	1 13	1 28	1 43	1 57	2 12	2 27	2 41	2 56	3 11	3 25	3 40
7 40	0 15	0 31	0 46	1 01	1 17	1 32	1 47	2 03	2 18	2 33	2 49	3 04	3 19	3 35	3 50
8 00	0 16	0 32	0 48	1 04	1 20	1 36	1 52	2 08	2 24	2 40	2 56	3 12	3 28	3 44	4 00
8 20	0 17	0 33	0 50	1 07	1 23	1 40	1 57	2 13	2 30	2 47	3 03	3 20	3 37	3 53	4 10
8 40	0 17	0 35	0 52	1 09	1 27	1 44	2 01	2 19	2 36	2 53	3 11	3 28	3 45	4 03	4 20
9 00	0 18	0 36	0 54	1 12	1 30	1 48	2 06	2 24	2 42	3 00	3 18	3 36	3 54	4 12	4 30
9 20	0 19	0 37	0 56	1 15	1 33	1 52	2 11	2 29	2 48	3 07	3 25	3 44	4 03	4 21	4 40
9 40	0 19	0 39	0 58	1 17	1 37	1 56	2 15	2 35	2 54	3 13	3 33	3 52	4 11	4 31	4 50
10 00	0 20	0 40	1 00	1 20	1 40	2 00	2 20	2 40	3 00	3 20	3 40	4 00	4 20	4 40	5 00
10 20	0 21	0 41	1 02	1 23	1 43	2 04	2 25	2 45	3 06	3 27	3 47	4 08	4 29	4 49	5 10
10 40	0 21	0 43	1 04	1 25	1 47	2 08	2 29	2 51	3 12	3 33	3 55	4 16	4 37	4 59	5 20

	Correction to height														
Ft.	*Ft.*	*Ft.*	*Ft.*	*Ft.*	*Ft.*	*Ft.*	*Ft.*	*Ft.*	*Ft.*	*Ft.*	*Ft.*	*Ft.*	*Ft.*	*Ft.*	*Ft.*
0.5	0.0	0.0	0.0	0.0	0.0	0.0	0.1	0.1	0.1	0.1	0.1	0.2	0.2	0.2	0.2
1.0	0.0	0.0	0.0	0.0	0.1	0.1	0.1	0.2	0.2	0.2	0.3	0.3	0.4	0.4	0.5
1.5	0.0	0.0	0.0	0.1	0.1	0.1	0.2	0.2	0.3	0.4	0.4	0.5	0.6	0.7	0.8
2.0	0.0	0.0	0.0	0.1	0.1	0.2	0.3	0.3	0.4	0.5	0.6	0.7	0.8	0.9	1.0
2.5	0.0	0.0	0.1	0.1	0.2	0.2	0.3	0.4	0.5	0.6	0.7	0.9	1.0	1.1	1.2
3.0	0.0	0.0	0.1	0.1	0.2	0.3	0.4	0.5	0.6	0.8	0.9	1.0	1.2	1.3	1.5
3.5	0.0	0.0	0.1	0.2	0.2	0.3	0.4	0.6	0.7	0.9	1.0	1.2	1.4	1.6	1.8
4.0	0.0	0.0	0.1	0.2	0.3	0.4	0.5	0.7	0.8	1.0	1.2	1.4	1.6	1.8	2.0
4.5	0.0	0.0	0.1	0.2	0.3	0.4	0.6	0.7	0.9	1.1	1.3	1.6	1.8	2.0	2.2
5.0	**0.0**	**0.1**	**0.1**	**0.2**	**0.3**	**0.5**	**0.6**	**0.8**	**1.0**	**1.2**	1.5	1.7	2.0	2.2	2.5
5.5	0.0	0.1	0.1	0.2	0.4	0.5	0.7	0.9	1.1	1.4	1.6	1.9	2.2	2.5	2.8
6.0	0.0	0.1	0.1	0.3	0.4	0.6	0.8	1.0	1.2	1.5	1.8	2.1	2.4	2.7	3.0

Range of tide, see footnote															
6.5	0.0	0.1	0.2	0.3	0.4	0.6	0.8	1.1	1.3	1.6	1.9	2.2	2.6	2.9	3.2
7.0	0.0	0.1	0.2	0.3	0.5	0.7	0.9	1.2	1.4	1.8	2.1	2.4	2.8	3.1	3.5
7.5	0.0	0.1	0.2	0.3	0.5	0.7	1.0	1.2	1.5	1.9	2.2	2.6	3.0	3.4	3.8
8.0	0.0	0.1	0.2	0.3	0.5	0.8	1.0	1.3	1.6	2.0	2.4	2.8	3.2	3.6	4.0
8.5	0.0	0.1	0.2	0.4	0.6	0.8	1.1	1.4	1.8	2.1	2.6	2.9	3.4	3.8	4.2
9.0	0.0	0.1	0.2	0.4	0.6	0.9	1.2	1.5	1.9	2.2	2.7	3.1	3.6	4.0	4.5
9.5	0.0	0.1	0.2	0.4	0.6	0.9	1.2	1.6	2.0	2.4	2.8	3.3	3.8	4.3	4.8
10.0	0.0	0.1	0.2	0.4	0.7	1.0	1.3	1.7	2.1	2.5	3.0	3.5	4.0	4.5	5.0
10.5	0.0	0.1	0.3	0.5	0.7	1.0	1.3	1.7	2.2	2.6	3.1	3.6	4.2	4.7	5.2
11.0	0.0	0.1	0.3	0.5	0.7	1.1	1.4	1.8	2.3	2.8	3.3	3.8	4.4	4.9	5.5
11.5	0.0	0.1	0.3	0.5	0.8	1.1	1.5	1.9	2.4	2.9	3.4	4.0	4.6	5.1	5.8
12.0	0.0	0.1	0.3	0.5	0.8	1.1	1.5	2.0	2.5	3.0	3.6	4.1	4.8	5.4	6.0
12.5	0.0	0.1	0.3	0.5	0.8	1.2	1.6	2.1	2.6	3.1	3.7	4.3	5.0	5.6	6.2
13.0	0.0	0.1	0.3	0.6	0.9	1.2	1.7	2.2	2.7	3.2	3.9	4.5	5.1	5.8	6.5
13.5	0.0	0.1	0.3	0.6	0.9	1.3	1.7	2.2	2.8	3.4	4.0	4.7	5.3	6.0	6.8
14.0	0.0	0.2	0.3	0.6	0.9	1.3	1.8	2.3	2.9	3.5	4.2	4.8	5.5	6.3	7.0
14.5	0.0	0.2	0.4	0.6	1.0	1.4	1.9	2.4	3.0	3.6	4.3	5.0	5.7	6.5	7.2
15.0	0.0	0.2	0.4	0.6	1.0	1.4	1.9	2.5	3.1	3.8	4.4	5.2	5.9	6.7	7.5
15.5	0.0	0.2	0.4	0.7	1.0	1.5	2.0	2.6	3.2	3.9	4.6	5.4	6.1	6.9	7.8
16.0	0.0	0.2	0.4	0.7	1.1	1.5	2.1	2.6	3.3	4.0	4.7	5.5	6.3	7.2	8.0
16.5	0.0	0.2	0.4	0.7	1.1	1.6	2.1	2.7	3.4	4.1	4.9	5.7	6.5	7.4	8.2
17.0	0.0	0.2	0.4	0.7	1.1	1.6	2.2	2.8	3.5	4.2	5.0	5.9	6.7	7.6	8.5
17.5	0.0	0.2	0.4	0.8	1.2	1.7	2.2	2.9	3.6	4.4	5.2	6.0	6.9	7.8	8.8
18.0	0.0	0.2	0.4	0.8	1.2	1.7	2.3	3.0	3.7	4.5	5.3	6.2	7.1	8.1	9.0
18.5	0.1	0.2	0.5	0.8	1.2	1.8	2.4	3.1	3.8	4.6	5.5	6.4	7.3	8.3	9.2
19.0	0.1	0.2	0.5	0.8	1.3	1.8	2.4	3.1	3.9	4.8	5.6	6.6	7.5	8.5	9.5
19.5	0.1	0.2	0.5	0.8	1.3	1.9	2.5	3.2	4.0	4.9	5.8	6.7	7.7	8.7	9.8
20.0	0.1	0.2	0.5	0.9	1.3	1.9	2.6	3.3	4.1	5.0	5.9	6.9	7.9	9.0	10.0

Obtain from the predictions the high water and low water, one of which is before and the other after the time for which the height is required. The difference between the times of occurence of these tides is the duration of rise or fall, and the difference between their heights is the range of tide for the above table. Find the difference between the nearest high or low water and the time for which the height is required.

Enter the table with the duration of rise or fall, printed in heavy-faced type, which most nearly agrees with the actual value, and on that horizontal line find the time from the nearest high or low water which agrees most nearly with the corresponding actual difference. The correction sought is in the column directly below, on the line with the range of tide.

When the nearest tide is high water, subtract the correction.

When the nearest tide is low water, add the correction.

Fig. 6-22. Table 3 showing correction for 1530 on Sept. 10 at Redwood City.

Applying these differences to the times and heights given for San Francisco, the results for that day are:

Times

San Francisco	Diff.	Red City
0523	+0 58	0621
0955	+1 32	1127
1628	+0 59	1726
2322	+1 32	0054 (9/11)

Heights

San Francisco	Diff.	Red City
4.1	+2.2	6.3
2.9	+0.1	3.0
5.9	+0.1	0.4
0.3	+0.1	0.4

Note: the second low tide occurs at San Francisco on September 10, but by the time it reaches Redwood City the date has changed (it is after midnight) to Sept. 11. It is not uncommon for a change in date to occur between a reference station and a substation, as demonstrated in this example.

You now have the times and heights of high and low water at a listed substation based on tabulated difference between it and its reference station. It is now possible to predict the height of water at the substation at a chosen time between high and low tides. Using the data already worked out for Redwood City, what will the height of tide be at Wharf 5 at 3:30 PM on September 10?

First the desired time must be translated to the 24-hour clock:

$$\begin{array}{r} 1200 \\ +\ \underline{330} \\ 1530 \end{array}$$

At Redwood City, the two tides on either side of the 1530 hour will be 1127 and 1726. To use Table 3, the first requirement is the duration of the tide:

$$\begin{array}{r} 1726 \\ -\ \underline{1127} \end{array} \qquad \begin{array}{r} 1686 \\ -\underline{1127} \\ 559 \end{array} = 5\ 59 \text{ Duration of rise or fall}$$

The next thing needed is the interval between 1530 (the desired time) and the nearest or low water. 1530 is closer to 1726 than it is to 1127 so the interval needed is:

$$\begin{array}{r} 1726 \\ -1530 \end{array} = \begin{array}{r} 1686 \\ -\underline{1530} \\ 156 \end{array} = 1\ 56 \text{ Interval from nearest high or low water}$$

The last piece of information needed for Table 3 is the range of this tide:

$$\begin{array}{r} 8.1 \\ -\underline{3.0} \\ 5.1 \end{array} \text{ range}$$

Taking this data to Table 3 (Fig. 6-22), the duration of 5 59 is closest to the line for 6.00. Following that line to the right, 2 00 is the closest number to the 1 56 interval to nearest high water. 5.0 is nearest the 5.1 expected range. Going across from 5.0 and down from 2 00, they meet at 1.2. Because we are calculating ***back*** from the nearest high water (see notes at bottom of Table 3), this 1.2 ft. correction is to be subtracted from the expected high water height of 8.1:

$$\begin{array}{r} 8.1 \\ -\underline{1.2} \\ 6.9 \end{array} \text{ ft.}$$

At 1530 on September 10, the height of water to be expected at Redwood City, Wharf 5 is 6.9 ft. above charted datum.

The use of a standard form for calculating height of tide at a subordinate station at a specific time is helpful both to expedite the calculation and to minimize possible errors. Figure 6-23 shows a standard form used by the Navy for this purpose. It is filled out to illustrate the computations just discussed for Redwood City. This form is reproduced as a blank in the Appendix in order for you to have it reproduced.

Mistakes often made when working out height of water at a subordinate station are applying the high water difference to low water height at the reference stations, or vice versa, or using only one difference for both high and low water (they are seldom the same), or similarly confusing time differences. Also, when the nearest tide is high water be sure to *subtract* the Table 3 correction; when it is low water always *add*.

Other Tables. Tables 4, 5, and 6 are not needed by the coastal navigator. If you are interested in knowing the times of sunrise, sunset, moonrise, or moonset, the information is there. In light of the impending conversion of the United States to the metric system, Table 7 on converting feet to meters should prove useful.

Also included in each book is a glossary relating to tidal matters and an index of the stations for which data is provided.

Rule of 12ths. There are many instances when height of tide at a time between high and low is needed, but when a high degree of accuracy is not necessary. Many times an approximation will do perfectly well.

If you plan to cross a shoal charted at 6 feet with a boat drawing 5½ feet, accurate knowledge of water depth at the time will be important. The same will be true if you want to pass under a bridge charted at 34 feet with a 37-foot high mast. Suppose you want to anchor a boat that draws 3½ feet at a place where the fathometer shows 12 feet of water. At the moment you have plenty of water. But the tide range is 6 feet here. It would be helpful to know whether it is now high tide, low tide, or somewhere in between in order to gauge how much anchor line to let out. In this case, an approximation of the height of the tide at present will be entirely adequate.

A simple way to handle such a situation is to use the rule of 12ths. The duration of rise or fall of a semidiurnal or mixed tide is usually very close to 6 hours—plus or minus a bit. The change in height of tide over that 6-hour period generally follows a set pattern. During the first hour, the change will be 1/12th of the total expected range. During the second hour, the change increases to 2/12ths. For the third and fourth hours, the change increases to 3/12ths for both hours. The fifth hour the change drops back to 2/12ths. And the sixth hour accounts for the last 1/12th.

As an example look at Fig. 6-14. On April 23, there will be a low tide of +0.3 feet at 2:44 PM. At 8:57 PM the high tide will reach +6.4 feet. From 2:44 to 8:57 is a little over 6 hours. The range during that time from +0.3 feet to +6.4 feet is +6.1 feet. To make rough calculations, round things off and say that in 6 hours the tide will rise 6 feet.

In this instance, what will be the height of tide roughly at about 4:30 PM? From 2:44 to 4:30 is a little less than 2 hours. At rise of 1/12th for the first hour plus 2/12ths for the second hour gives a total of 3/12ths of that 6-foot range; 3/12ths of 6 feet equals 1½ feet. Adding the 1½-foot rise to the +0.3 feet that we had at 2:44 PM gives us an approximate height at 4:30 PM of +1.8 feet above charted datum.

When an approximation of tidal height will suffice, the rule of 12ths saves a lot of time. It is also very easy to use.

HT OF TIDE	
DATE	SEPT. 10, 1982
LOCATION	REDWD. CITY-WH5
TIME	1530
REF STA	SAN FRANCISCO
HW TIME DIFF	+ 0 58
LW TIME DIFF	+ 1 32
HW HT DIFF	+ 2.2 FT.
LW HT DIFF	+ 0.1 FT.
REF STA HW/LW TIME	0955/1628
HW/LW TIME DIFF	+ 132/+058
SUB STA HW/LW TIME	1127/1726
REF STA HW/LW HT	2.9/5.9
HW/LW HT DIFF	+0.1/+2.2
SUB STA HW/LW HT	3.0/8.1
DURATION RISE/FALL	5 59 RISING
TIME FM NEAR TIDE	1 56 FM HW
RANGE OF TIDE	5.1 FT.
HT OF NEAR TIDE	8.1 FT.
CORR TABLE 3	-1.2 FT.
HT OF TIDE	6.9 FT.
CHARTED DEPTH	
DEPTH OF WATER	
DRAFT	
CLEARANCE	

Fig. 6-23. Standard form for tide calculations filled in for Redwood City on Sept. 10 at 1530 hrs.

Chapter 7

QUASAR

Currents

CURRENTS ARE THE HORIZONTAL MOVEMENTS of water. There are two primary types of current with which the coastal navigator is concerned: tidal and ocean. Of the two, the coastal navigator will deal mostly with tidal currents. These currents are caused by and accompany the rise and fall of the tides.

TIDAL CURRENTS

The tidal current that accompanies a rising tide is termed the *flood current*. The one accompanying the falling tide is the *ebb current*. During each tidal cycle, there is a period called *slack water* during which there is no horizontal current movement. This is the period when the current changes from flood to ebb or ebb to flood.

The direction of flow, also called the *set*, of a flood current at a particular location might be exactly opposite to that of the ebb. In this case it is referred to as a *reversing current*. In many cases due to the irregularities in the shoreline or the bottom, the set of the two currents is different. Knowledge of this kind of situation is of importance when you must work out corrections for current.

Logic would seem to indicate that the times of minimum tidal current flow would coincide with the times of high and low water. Also the times of maximum current would be approximately in the middle of the tidal cycle. Curiously enough this is not usually the case. Most often the time of the change in direction of flow of the tidal current lags behind the turn of the tide by an interval that varies with local geographic characteristics. On a fairly smooth coastline with rather shallow indentations, the lag would tend to be small. In a large, deeply indented harbor, the lag between tide and current change can be considerable; it gets up to as much as three hours at times.

Tidal Current Tables

The navigator must be just as concerned with the direction of flow and velocity of tidal currents as he is with changes in water depth due to rise and fall of tides. Such currents can speed the progress of the boat, they can slow it down, or they can set it off course to one side or the other by enough to place it in danger if directions and velocities are not known. Fortunately, tidal currents can be predicted with reasonable accuracy for most of the affected areas in which you will be sailing.

Unlike heights of tides, current velocities and directions are not found in daily newspapers. Nor will your friendly marine supply store have a handy pocket guide for the local area, as he often does for times and heights of tides. The only authority to use for tidal currents is the Tidal Current Tables published in two volumes by the National Ocean Survey. They also publish the Tide Tables discussed in Chapter 6. The two volumes of Tidal Current Tables are titled *Atlantic Coast of North America*, and *Pacific Coast of North America and Asia*. You won't need both!

Like the Tide Tables, the Tidal Current Table books contain several different tables along with explanatory material covering their use. The format is very similar to that of the Tide Tables. Table 1 gives daily current predictions for every day of the year for a comparatively small number of reference stations. Table 2 gives time and velocity differences for a large number of subordinate stations. Table 3 enables the navigator to predict currents for any time of the day in between the maximum and minimum flow times found in Tables 1 and 2. Table 4 of the current tables has no equivalent in the Tide Tables. With it the period of slack water between tidal currents can be determined, based on the maximum velocity of the current preceding that slack.

In addition to the actual tables used by the navigator to predict tidal current for the locality through which he intends to pass, the Tidal Current Tables include additional explanatory material. This material relates to coastal tidal currents, wind-driven currents, and the effect produced by combined currents.

Using Table 1. Changes in water depth (tides) and variations in velocities of horizontal movement (currents) are aspects of the same phenomenon. Nevertheless, they are very different aspects. Consequently, the reference stations used for tidal prediction and those used for tidal current prediction are not necessarily the same (although in a few cases the same stations are used for both).

Repetition of the same name in both tables does not necessarily mean the same geographic location. For example, San Francisco and San Diego appear in both tables as reference stations for the West Coast of North America. Both Tide Tables and Tidal Current Tables at San Francisco give predictions for Golden Gate at the entrance to San Francisco Bay. At San Diego, the Tide Table gives predictions for Broadway, while the Tidal Current Table gives them for Ballast Point. These two places are approximately 4½ miles apart.

The format for Table 1 of the Tidal Current Tables is quite similar to that used in Table 1 of the Tide Tables. Figure 7-1 is a sample page from this table. It covers the months of July and August for the year 1982. The days of each month are listed in two vertical columns. The times of slack water, maximum current flow, velocity of that flow, and identification of the current as flood or ebb are given for each day. At the top of the page, the geographic directions in which both flood and ebb currents set are given.

Times of slack water and maximum currents are given in reference to the 24-hour clock; that is the same system used in the Tide Tables. At the bottom of each page is a note giving the time meridian (in this case 120° W) used for the times stated above in the tables. All times are local standard time based on that meridian.

Note in San Francisco, as well as most other parts of the United States, in July, Daylight-Saving Time will be in effect. To translate the times shown in the table to Daylight-Saving Time one hour will have to be added. Be careful to remember in the summer when using either Tide Tables or Tidal Current Tables that both are published using the standard time of the locality throughout.

Looking in Table 1 (Fig. 7-1) for the currents at Golden Gate, on July 9 there will be slack water at 0220 (2:20 AM) and again at 0938. In between there will be a current maximum of 4.5 knots at 0547. The 4.5 is followed by an E, meaning that current is an ebb current. Looking at the top of the page, the ebb at Golden Gate sets 245° True. The flood direction at the same place is given as 065° T. Subtracting 180° from 245° leaves 065°; thus Golden Gate has an exactly reversing tidal current. This is not necessarily true everywhere.

Following the 0938 slack water, the next maximum current is at 1239, with a flow of 3.4 knots. This one is a flood and thus is setting 065° T. After the next slack water is 1610, the following maximum current is a second ebb at 1823. The velocity this time is 2.3 knots, an entirely respectable velocity but a vast change from the earlier ebb maximum of 4.5 knots. On this date, no second flood maximum time or velocity is given because the next flood occurs at 0024 (or 24 minutes into the next day July 10). Notice that the velocities of the three maximums on this date vary quite considerably.

Look now at the bottom of the same column to

SAN FRANCISCO BAY ENTRANCE (Golden Gate), CALIF., 1982

F-Flood, Dir. 065° True   E-Ebb, Dir. 245° True

JULY

Day	Slack Water Time h.m.	Maximum Current Time h.m.	Maximum Current Vel. knots	Day	Slack Water Time h.m.	Maximum Current Time h.m.	Maximum Current Vel. knots
1 Th	0434 1031 1619 2202	0046 0741 1313 1920	3.6E 2.8F 1.9E 2.5F	16 F	0342 0951 1516 2115	0635 1206 1817	2.8F 2.2E 2.7F
2 F	0520 1128 1707 2243	0126 0832 1411 2003	3.9E 3.2F 1.8E 2.5F	17 Sa	0438 1058 1618 2206	0032 0739 1309 1916	4.6E 3.4F 2.2E 2.8F
3 Sa	0602 1217 1750 2322	0205 0913 1446 2039	4.2E 3.4F 1.9E 2.4F	18 Su	0531 1157 1714 2258	0129 0835 1408 2010	5.2E 4.0F 2.4E 3.1F
4 Su	0642 1301 1829 2359	0240 0954 1521 2114	4.4E 3.6F 1.9E 2.4F	19 M	0621 1250 1808 2350	0221 0926 1502 2102	5.7E 4.5F 2.6E 3.3F
5 M	0719 1341 1905	0315 1027 1552 2149	4.6E 3.6F 2.0E 2.5F	20 Tu	0710 1338 1859	0315 1015 1553 2153	6.0E 4.7F 2.8E 3.5F
6 Tu	0035 0755 1419 1939	0352 1100 1625 2224	4.7E 3.6F 2.1E 2.4F	21 W	0042 0758 1425 1951	0404 1101 1640 2242	6.1E 4.8F 3.0E 3.5F
7 W	0110 0830 1456 2012	0431 1131 1703 2300	4.7E 3.6F 2.1E 2.4F	22 Th	0134 0845 1509 2044	0452 1147 1729 2334	5.9E 4.7F 3.1E 3.4F
8 Th	0144 0904 1533 2049	0508 1203 1742 2341	4.7E 3.5F 2.2E 2.3F	23 F	0226 0931 1553 2140	0541 1233 1817	5.5E 4.4F 3.1E

AUGUST

Day	Slack Water Time h.m.	Maximum Current Time h.m.	Maximum Current Vel. knots	Day	Slack Water Time h.m.	Maximum Current Time h.m.	Maximum Current Vel. knots
1 Su	0540 1157 1729 2257	0138 0855 1427 2020	3.8E 3.2F 1.6E 2.2F	16 M	0515 1140 1705 2246	0110 0823 1355 1955	5.0E 3.9F 2.3E 3.0F
2 M	0621 1238 1809 2339	0218 0934 1502 2056	4.1E 3.4F 1.8E 2.4F	17 Tu	0606 1229 1759 2342	0208 0912 1450 2053	5.4E 4.3F 2.6E 3.3F
3 Tu	0659 1316 1846	0256 1005 1531 2131	4.4E 3.5F 2.0E 2.5F	18 W	0655 1313 1850	0302 1001 1538 2144	5.6E 4.5F 3.0E 3.6F
4 W	0019 0734 1351 1921	0334 1038 1605 2206	4.6E 3.6F 2.3E 2.7F	19 Th	0036 0740 1354 1940	0351 1041 1621 2233	5.6E 4.5F 3.4E 3.7F
5 Th	0057 0807 1424 1956	0411 1106 1641 2245	4.7E 3.6F 2.5E 2.7F	20 F	0128 0823 1434 2030	0435 1122 1707 2322	5.4E 4.4F 3.6E 3.7F
6 F	0134 0839 1457 2032	0446 1135 1717 2322	4.7E 3.6F 2.8E 2.7F	21 Sa	0219 0906 1513 2120	0520 1202 1751	4.9E 4.1F 3.7E
7 Sa	0212 0909 1529 2112	0525 1207 1757	4.6E 3.6F 3.0E	22 Su	0311 0947 1552 2213	0010 0604 1243 1832	3.4F 4.3E 3.7F 3.7E
8 Su	0253 0940 1601 2157	0003 0606 1245 1838	2.7F 4.3E 3.4F 3.2E	23 M	0405 1030 1631 2309	0101 0649 1321 1918	3.1F 3.6E 3.2F 3.6E

9 F	0220	0547	4.5E
	0938	1239	3.4F
	1610	1823	2.3E
	2130		
10 Sa		0024	2.1F
	0259	0629	4.3E
	1012	1316	3.3F
	1648	1906	2.4E
	2220		
11 Su		0109	2.0F
	0345	0714	3.9E
	1048	1359	3.1F
	1726	1955	2.6E
	2319		
12 M		0202	1.9F
	0440	0803	3.5E
	1128	1442	2.9F
	1807	2047	2.8E
13 Tu	0026	0303	1.8F
	0549	0858	3.0E
	1215	1531	2.8F
	1850	2140	3.1E
14 W	0135	0411	1.9F
	0711	0955	2.6E
	1309	1624	2.6F
	1936	2237	3.5E
15 Th	0241	0521	2.3F
	0835	1057	2.3E
	1411	1721	2.6F
	2024	2335	4.1E

24 Sa		0026	3.1F
	0320	0629	4.8E
	1017	1317	4.0F
	1637	1906	3.2E
	2239		
25 Su		0122	2.8F
	0418	0718	4.1E
	1104	1405	3.5F
	1721	1957	3.1E
	2344		
26 M		0225	2.4F
	0521	0807	3.3E
	1154	1454	3.0F
	1807	2050	3.1E
27 Tu	0052	0336	2.2F
	0631	0903	2.5E
	1248	1547	2.5F
	1854	2146	3.1E
28 W	0201	0456	2.1F
	0746	1007	1.9E
	1348	1645	2.2F
	1944	2247	3.1E
29 Th	0306	0615	2.3F
	0901	1115	1.5E
	1450	1750	2.0F
	2035	2352	3.3E
30 F	0404	0716	2.6F
	1010	1241	1.4E
	1550	1843	2.0F
	2125		
31 Sa		0050	3.6E
	0455	0811	2.9F
	1108	1352	1.5E
	1643	1935	2.1F
	2213		

9 M		0048	2.6F
	0339	0649	3.9E
	1013	1318	3.2F
	1635	1923	3.3E
	2248		
10 Tu		0140	2.4F
	0434	0738	3.4E
	1050	1402	3.0F
	1712	2012	3.5E
	2349		
11 W		0237	2.4F
	0541	0830	2.8E
	1135	1452	2.7F
	1755	2107	3.7E
12 Th	0057	0344	2.4F
	0700	0929	2.3E
	1230	1546	2.4F
	1845	2202	3.9E
13 F	0208	0500	2.5F
	0823	1036	1.9E
	1340	1647	2.3F
	1943	2304	4.2E
14 Sa	0316	0618	2.9F
	0939	1143	1.8E
	1455	1756	2.4F
	2045		
15 Su		0009	4.6E
	0418	0723	3.4F
	1045	1251	1.9E
	1604	1859	2.6F
	2147		

24 Tu		0155	2.8F
	0504	0738	2.9E
	1115	1407	2.6F
	1713	2007	3.4E
25 W	0010	0258	2.4F
	0608	0830	2.2E
	1207	1456	2.1F
	1759	2057	3.2E
26 Th	0115	0413	2.2F
	0719	0930	1.6E
	1308	1553	1.8F
	1851	2156	3.1E
27 F	0222	0536	2.2F
	0833	1036	1.3E
	1417	1701	1.6F
	1948	2259	3.1E
28 Sa	0325	0644	2.4F
	0940	1156	1.2E
	1522	1805	1.6F
	2047		
29 Su		0003	3.3E
	0421	0739	2.7F
	1037	1315	1.4E
	1618	1906	1.8F
	2142		
30 M		0103	3.5E
	0509	0824	3.0F
	1124	1401	1.6E
	1705	1955	2.1F
	2232		
31 Tu		0148	3.8E
	0551	0903	3.2F
	1203	1430	2.0E
	1746	2034	2.4F
	2318		

Time meridian 120° W. 0000 is midnight. 1200 is noon.

Fig. 7-1. Sample page from Table 1 of Tidal Current Tables.

July 15. Here the first slack water is at 0241. The first maximum current is at 0521, flooding at 2.3 knots. Compare this with July 9 when slack water was at 0220, 21 minutes earlier, and the first maximum current occurred at 0547, 26 minutes later than on the 15th. The period between slack and maximum current on the 9th is then a total of 3 h 27 m. On the 15th, a comparable interval is only 2 h 40 m (a difference of 47 m less).

Now scan down through the maximum currents predicted for July 15 and compare them to those expected on the 9th. On the 15th, maximums are expected of 2.3 k flood, 2.3 k ebb, 2.6 k flood, and 4.1 k ebb. On the 9th, the day starts with an ebb at 4.5 k, then a flood of 3.4 k, an ebb of 2.3 k, and a flood just after midnight at 2.1 k.

These very considerable variations in tidal current velocities, both for different tides on the same day and tides on different days, are typical not only of San Francisco, but all places having tides with marked diurnal inequality. On the East Coast of the United States where diurnal inequalities in tidal heights are normally far smaller, daily variations in tidal current velocity are vastly smaller. Nevertheless, considerable day to day variations do occur because of the differences that occur in tides from day to day during the monthly tide cycle.

Looking back again to Fig. 6-15 on July 9, a high tide of 5.5 feet is expected at 0022 at Golden Gate. But not until 0220 will there be slack water. Low tide will occur at 0708. In this case, the interval high and low tides is 6 h 46 m.

The point halfway between 0022 and 0708, or at about 0345, would be the time simple logic would lead one to expect to find maximum current flow. Figure 7-1 gives a time of 0547 instead. Times of slack water (no current) do not often coincide with the times of high and low water when the depth of water is not changing. Nor do the times of maximum current velocity often agree with a time in the midpoint of the cycle between high and low water (as one might expect).

This discrepancy in time makes absolutely no sense at all until one takes a second look at what is happening. Geographically, San Francisco Bay (Fig. 7-2) is a good-sized body of water connected to the ocean by a comparatively small opening, the Golden Gate. Through this small opening must flow all the water that raises and lowers the tidal levels throughout the rest of the bay. At the time when the

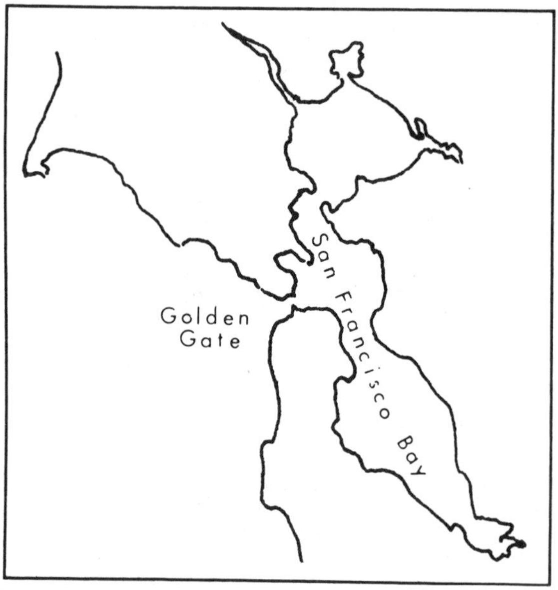
Golden Gate
San Francisco Bay
Fig. 7-2. Map sketch of San Francisco Bay.

great tidal wave circling the planet has reached its greatest height at Golden Gate, it has already passed through San Francisco Bay, which lies to the east. At the time when the tide is at its greatest height at Golden Gate, water must be flowing through that opening to allow the height of tide to drop east of Golden Gate. There high tide has already passed and the depth of the water is changing.

Similar situations occur in many bays and harbors on the East Coast as well. Chesapeake Bay, Delaware Bay, Long Island Sound, Pamilco Sound, and New York Harbor all show a variety of variations between times of stand of high or low tides and times of slack water with no tidal current flow.

Using Table 2. Because the Tidal Current Tables provide complete daily data on only a limited number of reference stations in Table 1, a second table is needed. Table 2 (Fig. 7-3) lists a large number of subordinate stations. For each one, it supplies correction factors for both time and velocity to be applied to the predictions at one of the reference stations. By taking the data at the reference station for a particular date and applying the correction factors given for the subordinate station times of slack water, maximum flood and maximum ebb can be found. Also, the current velocities at the times of those maximums can be calculated.

Table 2 also lists the latitude and longitude in

degrees and minutes of the subordinate station location as well as the directions toward which both flood and ebb currents will set. The number in the extreme left-hand column before each subordinate station name indicates the place of that subordinate station in sequence along the coast. On the East Coast, the sequence runs from north to south. On the West Coast, it runs south to north.

All of the subordinate stations listed on the sample page shown in Fig. 7-3 happen to refer to San Francisco, which is the reference station shown in Fig. 7-1. Time differences are in hours and minutes. A plus sign before the time difference (+) means that much time is to be added to the hour shown for the reference station to find the hours of slack water or maximum current at the subordinate station. A minus sign (−) means subtract that difference. Notice that the differences between the two stations for slack waters and for maximum current velocities are not necessarily the same. The time difference (Fig. 7-3) at #475, Sulsun Cutoff, for slack water is +3 35 (plus 3 hours 35 minutes) on San Francisco. Maximum current is to be found by adding 3 hours *55* minutes to the time predicted for maximums at San Francisco (a difference between differences of 20 minutes).

Current velocities at subordinate stations are consistently given as ratios. As an example, to find the velocity of the maximum flood current at Sulsun Cutoff on the afternoon of July 19, look first at the maximum current time difference at Sulsun—which is +3 55 (Fig. 7-3). Now go back to San Francisco Bay (Fig. 7-1) to July 19. The times and velocities of maximum currents there will be:

0221	5.7 Ebb
0926	4.5 Flood
1502	2.6 Ebb
2102	3.3 Flood

First, 3 hours 55 minutes must be added to the 0926 flood.

0926 + 3 55 = 1321 F

Because 1321 is the afternoon maximum flood, the other times are unnecessary. At that time, what will the velocity be at Sulsun because it will be 4.5 knots at San Francisco? At Sulsun (Fig. 7-3), it will be .6 × 4.5, which is 2.7 knots.

Note that, at this particular subordinate station, the velocity of the maximum flood currents is .6 as great as at San Francisco, but the maximum ebbs are only .5 as great. Looking up and down the two velocity ratio columns shown in Fig. 7-3, it is immediately apparent that while at some stations these ratios are the same for both floods and ebbs, there are many stations for which they differ. When calculating out the expected velocity at a subordinate station, be sure to use the correct ratio for the current being sought (be it flood or ebb).

Many bays and harbors contain the mouths of good-sized rivers. Examples of this are Mobile Bay, Delaware Bay, and New York Harbor. At such places, the tabulated predictions for current velocities are subject to variations resulting from storm or other conditions that temporarily can greatly swell the volume of water being discharged by the river. In any area fed by a river mouth, expect ebb velocities above and flood velocities below those predicted when the river is in flooding condition.

Using Table 3. Using Table 1 and Table 2, the hours of slack water, the hours of maximum current (both flooding and ebbing), the velocities of those currents, and the directions toward which they are set, can be determined for any day of the year and for a great many places.

All too often, however, the hour at which we want to pass through a channel does not coincide with any of the predicted slacks or maximum current flows. Perversely, it usually happens to fall somewhere in between. The Tidal Current Tables, like the Tide Tables, have a Table 3 with which the sailor can determine the approximate velocity of the tidal current at any time between a predicted slack and a predicted maximum current. Table 3 is shown in Fig. 7-4.

This Table is in two parts: a Table A and a Table B. The Table shown in Fig. 7-4 is from the Tidal Current book for the Pacific Coast. The book for the Atlantic Coast contains the same two part Table 3. Both are used in similar fashion. Table 3 A is used for most reference and subordinate stations in both books. Table 3 B is used only for reference stations Cape Cod, Hell Gate, and Chesapeake and Delaware Canal in the Atlantic book, and Deception Pass, Seymour Narrows, Sergius Narrows, and Isanotski Straight in the Pacific book. Table 3 B is also used for subordinate stations referring to all of the above reference stations in both books.

When a narrow passage connects two large bodies of water that periodically reach a consider-

TABLE 2.—CURRENT DIFFERENCES AND OTHER CONSTANTS

No.	PLACE	POSITION		TIME DIFFERENCES		VELOCITY RATIOS		MAXIMUM CURRENTS			
								Flood		Ebb	
		Lat.	Long.	Slack water	Maximum current	Maximum flood	Maximum ebb	Direction (true)	Average velocity	Direction (true)	Average velocity
		° ′	° ′	h. m.	h. m.			deg.	knots	deg.	knots
	SUISUN BAY	N.	W.								
			on SAN FRANCISCO BAY ENTRANCE, p.10								
	Time meridian, 120°W.										
450	Roe Island, south of	38 04	122 02	+2 40	+2 50	0.4	0.5	090	1.3	270	1.7
455	Chipps Island, south of	38 03	121 55	+3 40	+3 45	0.8	0.6	090	2.2	270	2.2
460	Suisun Slough entrance	38 07	122 04	+1 40	+1 25	0.4	0.4	290	1.2	110	1.3
465	Montezuma Slough, west entrance	38 08	122 03	+2 00	+1 25	0.5	0.4	355	1.4	175	1.4
470	Between Roe Island and Ryer Island	38 04	122 01	+3 05	+3 20	0.4	0.5	115	1.3	295	1.6
475	Suisun Cutoff	38 05	122 00	+3 35	+3 55	0.6	0.5	120	1.6	300	1.8
480	Spoonbill Creek, near bridge	38 04	121 54	+2 50	+2 55	0.5	0.4	105	1.5	285	1.3
485	Montezuma Slough, E. end, near bridge	38 05	121 53	+4 30	+4 50	0.3	0.4	135	1.0	315	1.2
490	New York Slough	38 02	121 52	+3 50	+4 00	0.4	0.4	110	1.2	295	1.3
	SACRAMENTO RIVER†										
495	Entrance, 0.7 mile SW. of Chain I	38 03	121 52	+3 40	+3 55	0.4	0.4	055	1.2	210	1.3
500	Point Sacramento, 0.3 mile NE. of	38 04	121 50	+3 30	+3 30	0.3	0.3	100	1.1	285	0.8
	SAN JOAQUIN RIVER†										
505	Point Beenar, 0.8 mile north of	38 03	121 50	+4 45	+4 55	0.4	0.4	155	1.0	355	1.4
510	Antioch Point, 0.3 mile east of	38 02	121 49	+4 20	+4 40	0.4	0.4	130	1.5	305	1.4
515	West Island Light, 0.5 mile SE. of	38 01	121 46	+4 20	+4 40	0.2	0.2	090	0.4	270	0.7
520	Vulcan Island, 0.5 mile east of	37 59	121 23	+5 45	+5 55	0.2	0.2	135	0.7	315	0.4
525	Brandt Bridge	37 52	121 19	+7 25	+7 50	0.3	0.3	135	0.7	315	1.0

	CALIFORNIA COAST—Continued										
530	Point Reyes‡	38 00	123 02	-1 10	-1 10	0.3	0.3	320	1.1	140	1.1
540	Salt Point‡	38 34	123 21	-1 20	-1 20	0.3	0.3	325	0.9	145	0.9
545	Point Arena‡	38 57	123 45	-1 30	-1 30	0.3	0.3	330	1.1	150	1.1
550	Point Cabrillo‡	39 21	123 50	-1 40	-1 40	0.3	0.3	345	1.0	165	1.0
555	Cape Vizcaino‡	39 44	123 50	-1 50	-1 50	0.3	0.3	325	0.9	145	0.9
560	Point Delgada‡	40 00	124 04	-1 35	-1 35	0.3	0.3	325	1.0	145	1.0
565	Punta Gorda‡	40 15	124 22	-1 35	-1 35	0.3	0.3	335	1.1	155	1.1
570	Cape Mendocino Lt., 4.6 miles W. of*	40 26	124 30	-----	-----	----	----	----	----	----	----
575	Table Bluff Light‡	40 42	124 17	-1 10	-1 10	0.3	0.3	010	0.8	190	0.8
	HUMBOLDT BAY										
580	Humboldt Bay entrance	40 46	124 14	-1 00	-0 46	0.6	0.6	125	1.6	310	2.0
585	Point Humboldt, channel west of	40 45	124 14	-1 10	-0 55	0.5	0.3	195	1.4	025	1.0
590	Eureka, channel west of	40 48	124 11	-1 05	-0 55	0.6	0.5	015	1.8	210	1.6
595	Eureka, channel north of	40 48	124 10	-1 15	-1 05	0.2	0.2	105	0.5	285	0.6
600	Samoa channel	40 49	124 11	-1 00	-1 10	0.4	0.3	045	1.2	205	1.1
	CALIFORNIA COAST—Continued										
605	Trinidad Head‡	41 03	124 10	-0 55	-0 55	0.3	0.3	005	1.0	185	1.0
610	Redding Rock Light‡	41 21	124 11	-0 50	-0 50	0.3	0.3	010	0.9	190	0.9
615	St. George Reef‡	41 49	124 20	-0 40	-0 40	0.3	0.3	005	1.0	185	1.0
	OREGON COAST										
620	Cape Sebastian‡	42 20	124 26	-0 25	-0 25	0.3	0.3	355	1.1	175	1.1
630	Cape Blanco‡	42 50	124 35	-0 10	-0 10	0.3	0.3	010	1.1	190	1.1

† Data do not apply during freshets.
‡ Data approximate.
* See "Coastal Tidal Currents," p. 235.

Fig. 7-3. Sample page from Table 2 of Tidal Current Tables.

Table A

Interval between slack and desired time	Interval between slack and maximum current													
	h. m. 1 20	*h. m.* 1 40	*h. m.* 2 00	*h. m.* 2 20	*h. m.* 2 40	*h. m.* 3 00	*h. m.* 3 20	*h. m.* 3 40	*h. m.* 4 00	*h. m.* 4 20	*h. m.* 4 40	*h. m.* 5 00	*h. m.* 5 20	*h. m.* 5 40
h. m.	*f.*	*f.*	*f.*	*f.*	*f.*	*f.*	*f.*	*f.*	*f.*	*f.*	*f.*	*f.*	*f.*	*f.*
0 20	0.4	0.3	0.3	0.2	0.2	0.2	0.2	0.1	0.1	0.1	0.1	0.1	0.1	0.1
0 40	0.7	0.6	0.5	0.4	0.4	0.3	0.3	0.3	0.3	0.2	0.2	0.2	0.2	0.2
1 00	0.9	0.8	0.7	0.6	0.6	0.5	0.5	0.4	0.4	0.4	0.3	0.3	0.3	0.3
1 20	1.0	1.0	0.9	0.8	0.7	0.6	0.6	0.5	0.5	0.5	0.4	0.4	0.4	0.4
1 40	......	1.0	1.0	0.9	0.8	0.8	0.7	0.7	0.6	0.6	0.5	0.5	0.5	0.4
2 00	......	......	1.0	1.0	0.9	0.9	0.8	0.8	0.7	0.7	0.6	0.6	0.6	0.5
2 20	......	......	......	1.0	1.0	0.9	0.9	0.8	0.8	0.7	0.7	0.7	0.6	0.6
2 40	......	......	......	......	1.0	1.0	1.0	0.9	0.9	0.8	0.8	0.7	0.7	0.7
3 00	......	......	......	......	......	1.0	1.0	1.0	0.9	0.9	0.8	0.8	0.8	0.7
3 20	......	......	......	......	......	......	1.0	1.0	1.0	0.9	0.9	0.9	0.8	0.8
3 40	......	......	......	......	......	......	......	1.0	1.0	1.0	0.9	0.9	0.9	0.9
4 00	......	......	......	......	......	......	......	......	1.0	1.0	1.0	1.0	0.9	0.9
4 20	......	......	......	......	......	......	......	......	......	1.0	1.0	1.0	1.0	0.9
4 40	......	......	......	......	......	......	......	......	......	......	1.0	1.0	1.0	1.0
5 00	......	......	......	......	......	......	......	......	......	......	......	1.0	1.0	1.0
5 20	......	......	......	......	......	......	......	......	......	......	......	......	1.0	1.0
5 40	......	......	......	......	......	......	......	......	......	......	......	......	......	1.0

TABLE B

Interval between slack and desired time (h. m.)	Interval between slack and maximum current: h. m. 1 20	h. m. 1 40	h. m. 2 00	h. m. 2 20	h. m. 2 40	h. m. 3 00	h. m. 3 20	h. m. 3 40	h. m. 4 00	h. m. 4 20	h. m. 4 40	h. m. 5 00	h. m. 5 20	h. m. 5 40
	f.	f.	f.	f.	f.	f.	f.	f.	f.	f.	f.	f.	f.	f.
0 20	0.5	0.4	0.4	0.3	0.3	0.3	0.3	0.3	0.2	0.2	0.2	0.2	0.2	0.2
0 40	0.8	0.7	0.6	0.5	0.5	0.5	0.4	0.4	0.4	0.4	0.3	0.3	0.3	0.3
1 00	0.9	0.8	0.8	0.7	0.7	0.6	0.6	0.5	0.5	0.5	0.4	0.4	0.4	0.4
1 20	1.0	1.0	0.9	0.8	0.8	0.7	0.7	0.6	0.6	0.6	0.5	0.5	0.5	0.5
1 40	......	1.0	1.0	0.9	0.9	0.8	0.8	0.7	0.7	0.7	0.6	0.6	0.6	0.6
2 00	......	......	1.0	1.0	0.9	0.9	0.9	0.8	0.8	0.7	0.7	0.7	0.7	0.6
2 20	......	......	......	1.0	1.0	1.0	0.9	0.9	0.8	0.8	0.8	0.7	0.7	0.7
2 40	......	......	......	......	1.0	1.0	1.0	0.9	0.9	0.9	0.8	0.8	0.8	0.7
3 00	......	......	......	......	......	1.0	1.0	1.0	0.9	0.9	0.9	0.9	0.8	0.8
3 20	......	......	......	......	......	......	1.0	1.0	1.0	1.0	0.9	0.9	0.9	0.8
3 40	......	......	......	......	......	......	......	1.0	1.0	1.0	1.0	0.9	0.9	0.9
4 00	......	......	......	......	......	......	......	......	1.0	1.0	1.0	1.0	0.9	0.9
4 20	......	......	......	......	......	......	......	......	......	1.0	1.0	1.0	1.0	0.9
4 40	......	......	......	......	......	......	......	......	......	......	1.0	1.0	1.0	1.0
5 00	......	......	......	......	......	......	......	......	......	......	......	1.0	1.0	1.0
5 20	......	......	......	......	......	......	......	......	......	......	......	......	1.0	1.0
5 40	......	......	......	......	......	......	......	......	......	......	......	......	......	1.0

Use table A for all places except those listed below for table B.
Use table B for Deception Pass, Seymour Narrows, Sergius Narrows, Isanotski Strait, and all stations in table 2 which are referred to these points.

1. From predictions find the time of slack water and the time and velocity of maximum current (flood or ebb), one of which is immediately before and the other after the time for which the velocity is desired.
2. Find the interval of time between the above slack and maximum current, and enter the top of table A or B with the interval which most nearly agrees with this value.
3. Find the interval of time between the above slack and the time desired, and enter the side of table A or B with the interval which most nearly agrees with this value.
4. Find, in the table, the factor corresponding to the above two intervals, and multiply the maximum velocity by this factor. The result will be the approximate velocity at the time desired.

Fig. 7-4. Table 3A from Tidal Current Tables with answer to first example.

SAN FRANCISCO BAY ENTRANCE (Golden Gate), CALIF., 1982

F-Flood, Dir. 065° True E-Ebb, Dir. 245° True

JULY

Day	Slack Water Time h.m.	Maximum Current Time h.m.	Maximum Current Vel. knots	Day	Slack Water Time h.m.	Maximum Current Time h.m.	Maximum Current Vel. knots
1		0046	3.6E	16	0342	0635	2.8F
Th	0434	0741	2.8F	F	0951	1206	2.2E
	1031	1313	1.9E		1516	1817	2.7F
	1619	1920	2.5F		2115		
	2202						
2		0126	3.9E	17		0032	4.6E
F	0520	0832	3.2F	Sa	0438	0739	3.4F
	1128	1411	1.8E		1058	1309	2.2E
	1707	2003	2.5F		1618	1916	2.8F
	2243				2206		
3		0205	4.2E	18		0129	5.2E
Sa	0602	0913	3.4F	Su	0531	0835	4.0F
	1217	1446	1.9E		1157	1408	2.4E
	1750	2039	2.4F		1714	2010	3.1F
	2322				2258		
4		0240	4.4E	19		0221	5.7E
Su	0642	0954	3.6F	M	0621	0926	4.5F
	1301	1521	1.9E		1250	1502	2.6E
	1829	2114	2.4F		1808	2102	3.3F
	2359				2350		
5		0315	4.6E	20		0315	6.0E
M	0719	1027	3.6F	Tu	0710	1015	4.7F
	1341	1552	2.0E		1338	1553	2.8E
	1905	2149	2.5F		1859	2153	3.5F
6	0035	0352	4.7E	21	0042	0404	6.1E
Tu	0755	1100	3.6F	W	0758	1101	4.8F
	1419	1625	2.1E		1425	1640	3.0E
	1939	2224	2.4F		1951	2242	3.5F
7	0110	0431	4.7E	22	0134	0452	5.9E
W	0830	1131	3.6F	Th	0845	1147	4.7F
	1456	1703	2.1E		1509	1729	3.1E
	2012	2300	2.4F		2044	2334	3.4F
8	0144	0508	4.7E	23	0226	0541	5.5E
Th	0904	1203	3.5F	F	0931	1233	4.4F
	1533	1742	2.2E		1553	1817	3.1E
	2049	2341	2.3F		2140		

AUGUST

Day	Slack Water Time h.m.	Maximum Current Time h.m.	Maximum Current Vel. knots	Day	Slack Water Time h.m.	Maximum Current Time h.m.	Maximum Current Vel. knots
1		0138	3.8E	16		0110	5.0E
Su	0540	0855	3.2F	M	0515	0823	3.9F
	1157	1427	1.6E		1140	1355	2.3E
	1729	2020	2.2F		1705	1955	3.0F
	2257				2246		
2		0218	4.1E	17		0208	5.4E
M	0621	0934	3.4F	Tu	0606	0912	4.3F
	1238	1502	1.8E		1229	1450	2.6E
	1809	2056	2.4F		1759	2053	3.3F
	2339				2342		
3		0256	4.4E	18		0302	5.6E
Tu	0659	1005	3.5F	W	0655	1001	4.5F
	1316	1531	2.0E		1313	1538	3.0E
	1846	2131	2.5F		1850	2144	3.6F
4	0019	0334	4.6E	19	0036	0351	5.6E
W	0734	1038	3.6F	Th	0740	1041	4.5F
	1351	1605	2.3E		1354	1621	3.4E
	1921	2206	2.7F		1940	2233	3.7F
5	0057	0411	4.7E	20	0128	0435	5.4E
Th	0807	1106	3.6F	F	0823	1122	4.4F
	1424	1641	2.5E		1434	1707	3.6E
	1956	2245	2.7F		2030	2322	3.7F
6	0134	0446	4.7E	21	0219	0520	4.9E
F	0839	1135	3.6F	Sa	0906	1202	4.1F
	1457	1717	2.8E		1513	1751	3.7E
	2032	2322	2.7F		2120		
7	0212	0525	4.6E	22		0010	3.4F
Sa	0909	1207	3.6F	Su	0311	0604	4.3E
	1529	1757	3.0E		0947	1243	3.7F
	2112				1552	1832	3.7E
					2213		
8		0003	2.7F	23		0101	3.1F
Su	0253	0606	4.3E	M	0405	0649	3.6E
	0940	1245	3.4F		1030	1321	3.2F
	1601	1838	3.2E		1631	1918	3.6E

9	0220	0547	4.5E
F	0938	1239	3.4F
	1610	1823	2.3E
	2130		
10		0024	2.1F
Sa	0259	0629	4.3E
	1012	1316	3.3F
	1648	1906	2.4E
	2220		
11		0109	2.0F
Su	0345	0714	3.9E
	1048	1359	3.1F
	1726	1955	2.6E
	2319		
12		0202	1.9F
M	0440	0803	3.5E
	1128	1442	2.9F
	1807	2047	2.8E
13	0026	0303	1.8F
Tu	0549	0858	3.0E
	1215	1531	2.8F
	1850	2140	3.1E
14	0135	0411	1.9F
W	0711	0955	2.6E
	1309	1624	2.6F
	1936	2237	3.5E
15	0241	0521	2.3F
Th	0835	1057	2.3E
	1411	1721	2.6F
	2024	2335	4.1E

24		0026	3.1F
Sa	0320	0628	4.8E
	1017	1317	4.0F
	1637	1906	3.2E
	2239		
25		0122	2.8F
Su	0418	0718	4.1E
	1104	1405	3.5F
	1721	1957	3.1E
	2344		
26		0225	2.4F
M	0521	0807	3.3E
	1154	1454	3.0F
	1807	2050	3.1E
27	0052	0336	2.2F
Tu	0631	0903	2.5E
	1248	1547	2.5F
	1854	2146	3.1E
28	0201	0456	2.1F
W	0746	1007	1.9E
	1348	1645	2.2F
	1944	2247	3.1E
29	0306	0615	2.3F
Th	0901	1115	1.5E
	1450	1750	2.0F
	2035	2352	3.3E
30	0404	0716	2.6F
F	1010	1241	1.4E
	1550	1843	2.0F
	2125		
31		0050	3.6E
Sa	0455	0811	2.9F
	1108	1352	1.5E
	1643	1935	2.1F
	2213		

	2157		
9		0048	2.6F
M	0339	0649	3.9E
	1013	1318	3.2F
	1635	1923	3.3E
	2248		
10		0140	2.4F
Tu	0434	0738	3.4E
	1050	1402	3.0F
	1712	2012	3.5E
	2349		
11		0237	2.4F
W	0541	0830	2.8E
	1135	1452	2.7F
	1755	2107	3.7E
12	0057	0344	2.4F
Th	0700	0929	2.3E
	1230	1546	2.4F
	1845	2202	3.9E
13	0208	0500	2.5F
F	0823	1036	1.9E
	1340	1647	2.3F
	1943	2304	4.2E
14	0316	0618	2.9F
Sa	0939	1143	1.8E
	1455	1756	2.4F
	2045		
15		0009	4.6E
Su	0418	0723	3.4F
	1045	1251	1.9E
	1604	1859	2.6F
	2147		

	2309		
24		0155	2.8F
Tu	0504	0738	2.9E
	1115	1407	2.6F
	1713	2007	3.4E
25	0010	0258	2.4F
W	0608	0830	2.2E
	1207	1456	2.1F
	1759	2057	3.2E
26	0115	0413	2.2F
Th	0719	0930	1.6E
	1308	1553	1.8F
	1851	2156	3.1E
27	0222	0536	2.2F
F	0833	1036	1.3E
	1417	1701	1.6F
	1948	2259	3.1E
28	0325	0644	2.4F
Sa	0940	1156	1.2E
	1522	1805	1.6F
	2047		
29		0003	3.3E
Su	0421	0739	2.7F
	1037	1315	1.4E
	1618	1906	1.8F
	2142		
30		0103	3.5E
M	0509	0824	3.0F
	1124	1401	1.6E
	1705	1955	2.1F
	2232		
31		0148	3.8E
Tu	0551	0903	3.2F
	1203	1430	2.0E
	1746	2034	2.4F
	2318		

Time meridian 120° W. 0000 is midnight. 1200 is noon.

Fig. 7-5. Tidal Current Table 1; July 24.

able difference in level due to tidal influences, a particularly swift current will occur. This is the situation at all of the reference stations just named. These currents are termed *hydraulic currents*. They pick up speed far more quickly than normal reversing tidal currents after a quite brief period of slack water. They also remain stronger for a longer period than the normal currents. Therefore they require a different table for prediction of any part of their cycles.

When current velocity is needed for a time other than the tabulated slacks and maximums, first go to Table 1, and then Table 2 as well if necessary, to find the nearest times before and after the desired hour at which a slack and a maximum current will occur. The interval between those two times is the interval between slack and maximum current. Find the column heading that most closely matches that interval in Table A (unless the station with which you are dealing is one of the exceptions that falls under Table B).

Now calculate the interval between the slack and the desired time. Slack might be before or it might be after the time for which velocity is needed. Suppose slack is at 1500 and the time for which velocity is required is 1700. The interval between slack and the desired hour is 2 h 00 m. If maximum flood is at 1500 and you still want current at 1700, the interval required to go into the table is the one to the *next slack,* which may occur until 2035. In this case, the interval needed in the left-hand column of Table 3 is 3 h 25 m. The closest interval in the table is 3 40.

Examples. The use of Tidal Current Tables 1, 2, and 3 will be much easier to understand after working through typical examples of their application in finding the velocity of current at specific locations, dates, and times of day. First, the question will be to find the current velocity at a reference station at a time between slack and maximum velocity. On the 24th of July, what will be the velocity of the current at Golden Gate at 0910 Pacific Daylight Time? The answer to this question will require the use of Tables 1 and 3. Table 2 is not needed here.

For starters, the Tables show only Standard Time. The time for which information is required was given as 0910 Pacific Daylight Time. This is the time in use in San Francisco on July 24. Changed back to Pacific Standard Time so the tables can be used, the target hour is 0810.

The Table 1 data for the date in question is found in the second column as shown in Fig. 7-5. Times of slack water, maximum currents, and maximum current velocities for that date are:

Slack Water	Max Current	Velocity
0320	0026	3.1 Flood
1017	0629	4.8 Ebb
1637	1317	4.0 Flood
2239	1906	3.2 Ebb

Maximum ebb current will be 4.8 knots at 0629 followed by slack water at 1017.

10 17	Flood
6 29	Ebb
3 48	Interval between maximum ebb and slack

The interval between maximum ebb and slack is 3 h 48 m. The interval between slack and desired time is 2 h 07 m.

10 17	Flood
08 10	Desired Time
2 07	Interval between slack and desired time

Moving now to Table 3 A (Fig. 7-4), the vertical column headed 3 h 40 m is the one closest to the 3 h 48 m interval between slack and maximum ebb current just found. The horizontal line starting with 2 h 00 m is the one closest to the 2 h 07 m interval between slack and desired time. The place where the two intersect contains the numbers 0.8. This is a ratio.

The maximum ebb current before the slack that follows the desired time was 4.8 knots. At the desired time of 0810 (2 h 07 m before slack), the current velocity will be 0.8 x 4.8 knots = 3.8 knots ebbing.

Determination of current velocity for a specific time at a subordinate station is really no more difficult than it is for a reference station. It is a slightly longer process because the reference station data must be transferred to the subordinate station first. This is how it should be done.

A boat is running north up the California coast and expects to put in for the night at Humbolt Bay at about 5:45 PM Pacific Daylight Time on the 19th of August. Will he have a favorable or an unfavorable current at the entrance at that time, and of what velocity?

Humbolt Bay entrance (Fig. 7-6) is found in Table 2 as a subordinate station to San Francisco

Bay entrance. Therefore it is necessary to start with the Table 1 data for 19 August at San Francisco (Fig. 7-7).

Slack Water	Max. Current	Velocity
0036	0351	5.6 Ebb
0740	1041	4.5 Flood
1354	1621	3.4 Ebb
1940	2233	3.7 Flood

Looking now at Humbolt Bay entrance (Fig. 7-6), slack waters are −1 00, or 1 hour earlier than at San Francisco. Maximum currents are −0 45 (or 45 minutes earlier). The time for which information is wanted is 5:45 PM (or 1745 *Daylight* Time). To make use of the tables, that must be changed back to 1645 Standard Time. Immediately, one sees an ebb maximum at 1621 (very close to 1645) in San Francisco. Subtracting 45 minutes to correct that time to Humbolt Bay gives 1536 (1621−45=1536) as the maximum ebb current.

The slack following the 1621 maximum ebb current is 1940 at San Francisco, which becomes 1840 at Humbolt Bay where slack waters are one hour earlier. To go into Table 3, the intervals between slack and maximum current and slack and desired time must be figured:

Slack	1840	
Max. Ebb	1536	
	304	Interval slack to Max. Current

Slack	1840	
Des. Time	1645	
	155	Interval Slack to Desired Time

In Table 3 (Fig. 7-8), the nearest slack to maximum current column to 3 04 is 3 00. The nearest line to 1 55 in the slack to desired time side is 2 00. Where these meet we find the ratio 0.9.

The ebb velocity at San Francisco was 3.4 at 1621. The ebb ration (Fig. 7-6) at Humbolt Bay is 0.6. The maximum velocity at San Francisco must first be changed to fit Humbolt Bay before the Table 3 ratio can be applied to adjust that velocity to the desired time.

$0.6 \times 3.4 = 2.0$ = maximum velocity of ebb at 1536 at Humbolt Bay
$0.9 \times 2.0 = 1.8$ = velocity of ebb at 1645 at Humbolt Bay

Yes, at Humbolt Bay Entrance at 1645 hr. on August 19, an adverse tidal current will be running at 1.8 knots. This adverse current can be avoided by delaying arrival by about 2 hours, at which time there will be slack water (at 1840).

Particularly at locations where there is a very strong tidal current and you have a very slow boat, it will be useful to know how long the slack water between strong currents will last. For this purpose Table 4 (Fig. 7-9) is included. Instructions for its use are to be found with the Table.

Similarly to Table 3, Table 4 is in two parts: A and B. Like Table 3, the A part is for normal use. Table 4 B applies to the same three East Coast and four West Coast reference stations and their subordinates that use Table 3 B. And for the same reason; areas with hydraulic currents reestablish strong current flow more rapidly than areas without them.

With a copy of the Tables available working out the predicted current velocity for any of the listed reference stations, or their subordinate stations, for any time on any day of the year is simple. All that is required is to find the right information in the Tables, and then perhaps do a bit of elementary adding, subtracting, or multiplying. People sometimes get in trouble and confusion from not working out the whole thing in an orderly fashion. Times, velocities, and ratios at reference stations and subordinate stations can get mixed up and strange results show up when the navigator fails to follow a standardized procedure.

The velocity for 1645 on August 19, 1982, at Humbolt Bay entrance is worked out on a current velocity form as shown in Fig. 7-10. This form arranges all the required information in an easily understood sequence. It provides a blank space for every bit of information that will be necessary. In this way, the form ensures that none of the steps needed to arrive at the correct answer are carelessly omitted. A blank copy of this form is included in the Appendix.

Tidal Current Charts

National Ocean Survey produces a series of tidal Current Charts covering a few areas where marine traffic is particularly heavy. There are only 11 such areas:

- ☐ Boston Harbor
- ☐ Naragansett Bay to Nantucket Sound

TABLE 2.—CURRENT DIFFERENCES AND OTHER CONSTANTS

No.	PLACE	POSITION		TIME DIFFERENCES		VELOCITY RATIOS		MAXIMUM CURRENTS			
								Flood		Ebb	
		Lat.	Long.	Slack water	Maximum current	Maximum flood	Maximum ebb	Direction (true)	Average velocity	Direction (true)	Average velocity
		° ′	° ′	h. m.	h. m.			deg.	knots	deg.	knots
	SUISUN BAY	N.	W.								
	Time meridian, 120°W.		on SAN FRANCISCO BAY ENTRANCE, p.10								
450	Roe Island, south of	38 04	122 02	+2 40	+2 50	0.4	0.5	090	1.3	270	1.7
455	Chipps Island, south of	38 03	121 55	+3 40	+3 45	0.8	0.6	090	2.2	270	2.2
460	Suisun Slough entrance	38 07	122 04	+1 40	+1 25	0.4	0.4	290	1.2	110	1.3
465	Montezuma Slough, west entrance	38 08	122 03	+2 00	+1 25	0.5	0.4	355	1.4	175	1.4
470	Between Roe Island and Ryer Island	38 04	122 01	+3 05	+3 20	0.4	0.5	115	1.3	295	1.6
475	Suisun Cutoff	38 05	122 00	+3 35	+3 55	0.6	0.5	120	1.6	300	1.8
480	Spoonbill Creek, near bridge	38 04	121 54	+2 50	+2 55	0.5	0.4	105	1.5	285	1.3
485	Montezuma Slough, E. end, near bridge	38 05	121 53	+4 30	+4 50	0.3	0.4	135	1.0	315	1.2
490	New York Slough	38 02	121 52	+3 50	+4 00	0.4	0.4	110	1.2	295	1.3
	SACRAMENTO RIVER†										
495	Entrance, 0.7 mile SW. of Chain I	38 03	121 52	+3 40	+3 55	0.4	0.4	055	1.2	210	1.3
500	Point Sacramento, 0.3 mile NE. of	38 04	121 50	+3 30	+3 30	0.3	0.3	100	1.1	285	0.8
	SAN JOAQUIN RIVER†										
505	Point Beenar, 0.8 mile north of	38 03	121 50	+4 45	+4 55	0.4	0.4	155	1.0	355	1.4
510	Antioch Point, 0.3 mile east of	38 02	121 49	+4 20	+4 40	0.4	0.4	130	1.5	305	1.4
515	West Island Light, 0.5 mile SE. of	38 01	121 46	+4 20	+4 40	0.2	0.2	090	0.4	270	0.7
520	Vulcan Island, 0.5 mile east of	37 59	121 23	+5 45	+5 55	0.2	0.2	135	0.7	315	0.4
525	Brandt Bridge	37 52	121 19	+7 25	+7 50	0.3	0.3	135	0.7	315	1.0

	CALIFORNIA COAST—Continued										
530	Point Reyes‡	38 00	123 02	-1 10	-1 10	0.3	0.3	320	1.1	140	1.1
540	Salt Point‡	38 34	123 21	-1 20	-1 20	0.3	0.3	325	0.9	145	0.9
545	Point Arena‡	38 57	123 45	-1 30	-1 30	0.3	0.3	330	1.1	150	1.1
550	Point Cabrillo‡	39 21	123 50	-1 40	-1 40	0.3	0.3	345	1.0	165	1.0
555	Cape Vizcaino‡	39 44	123 50	-1 50	-1 50	0.3	0.3	325	0.9	145	0.9
560	Point Delgada‡	40 00	124 04	-1 35	-1 35	0.3	0.3	325	1.0	145	1.0
565	Punta Gorda‡	40 15	124 22	-1 35	-1 35	0.3	0.3	335	1.1	155	1.1
570	Cape Mendocino Lt., 4.6 miles W. of*	40 26	124 30	-----	-----	----	----	----	----	----	----
575	Table Bluff Light‡	40 42	124 17	-1 10	-1 10	0.3	0.3	010	0.8	190	0.8
	HUMBOLDT BAY										
580	Humboldt Bay entrance	40 45	124 14	-1 00	-0 45	0.6	0.6	125	1.6	310	2.0
585	Point Humboldt, channel west of	40 45	124 14	-1 10	-0 55	0.5	0.3	195	1.4	025	1.0
590	Eureka, channel west of	40 48	124 11	-1 05	-0 55	0.6	0.5	015	1.8	210	1.6
595	Eureka, channel north of	40 48	124 10	-1 15	-1 05	0.2	0.2	105	0.5	285	0.6
600	Samoa channel	40 49	124 11	-1 00	-1 10	0.4	0.3	045	1.2	205	1.1
	CALIFORNIA COAST—Continued										
605	Trinidad Head‡	41 03	124 10	-0 55	-0 55	0.3	0.3	005	1.0	185	1.0
610	Redding Rock Light‡	41 21	124 11	-0 50	-0 50	0.3	0.3	010	0.9	190	0.9
615	St. George Reef‡	41 49	124 20	-0 40	-0 40	0.3	0.3	005	1.0	185	1.0
	OREGON COAST										
620	Cape Sebastian‡	42 20	124 26	-0 25	-0 25	0.3	0.3	355	1.1	175	1.1
630	Cape Blanco‡	42 50	124 35	-0 10	-0 10	0.3	0.3	010	1.1	190	1.1

† Data do not apply during freshets.
‡ Data approximate.
* See "Coastal Tidal Currents," p. 235.

Fig. 7-6. Tidal Current Table 2; Humbolt Bay Entrance.

SAN FRANCISCO BAY ENTRANCE (Golden Gate), CALIF., 1982 13

F-Flood, Dir. 065° True E-Ebb, Dir. 245° True

JULY

Day	Slack Water Time h.m.	Maximum Current Time h.m.	Maximum Current Vel. knots
1		0046	3.6E
Th	0434	0741	2.8F
	1031	1313	1.9E
	1619	1920	2.5F
	2202		
2		0126	3.9E
F	0520	0832	3.2F
	1128	1411	1.8E
	1707	2003	2.5F
	2243		
3		0205	4.2E
Sa	0602	0913	3.4F
	1217	1446	1.9E
	1750	2039	2.4F
	2322		
4		0240	4.4E
Su	0642	0954	3.6F
	1301	1521	1.9E
	1829	2114	2.4F
	2359		
5		0315	4.6E
M	0719	1027	3.6F
	1341	1552	2.0E
	1905	2149	2.5F
6	0035	0352	4.7E
Tu	0755	1100	3.6F
	1419	1625	2.1E
	1939	2224	2.4F
7	0110	0431	4.7E
W	0830	1131	3.6F
	1456	1703	2.1E
	2012	2300	2.4F
8	0144	0508	4.7E
Th	0904	1203	3.5F
	1533	1742	2.2E
	2049	2341	2.3F

Day	Slack Water Time h.m.	Maximum Current Time h.m.	Maximum Current Vel. knots
16	0342	0635	2.8F
F	0951	1206	2.2E
	1516	1817	2.7F
	2115		
17		0032	4.6E
Sa	0438	0739	3.4F
	1058	1309	2.2E
	1618	1916	2.8F
	2206		
18		0129	5.2E
Su	0531	0835	4.0F
	1157	1408	2.4E
	1714	2010	3.1F
	2258		
19		0221	5.7E
M	0621	0926	4.5F
	1250	1502	2.6E
	1808	2102	3.3F
	2350		
20		0315	6.0E
Tu	0710	1015	4.7F
	1338	1553	2.8E
	1859	2153	3.5F
21	0042	0404	6.1E
W	0758	1101	4.8F
	1425	1640	3.0E
	1951	2242	3.5F
22	0134	0452	5.9E
Th	0845	1147	4.7F
	1509	1729	3.1E
	2044	2334	3.4F
23	0226	0541	5.5E
F	0931	1233	4.4F
	1553	1817	3.1E
	2140		

AUGUST

Day	Slack Water Time h.m.	Maximum Current Time h.m.	Maximum Current Vel. knots
1		0138	3.8E
Su	0540	0855	3.2F
	1157	1427	1.6E
	1729	2020	2.2F
	2257		
2		0218	4.1E
M	0621	0934	3.4F
	1238	1502	1.8E
	1809	2056	2.4F
	2339		
3		0256	4.4E
Tu	0659	1005	3.5F
	1316	1531	2.0E
	1846	2131	2.5F
4	0019	0334	4.6E
W	0734	1038	3.6F
	1351	1605	2.3E
	1921	2206	2.7F
5	0057	0411	4.7E
Th	0807	1106	3.6F
	1424	1641	2.5E
	1956	2245	2.7F
6	0134	0446	4.7E
F	0839	1135	3.6F
	1457	1717	2.8E
	2032	2322	2.7F
7	0212	0525	4.6E
Sa	0909	1207	3.6F
	1529	1757	3.0E
	2112		
8		0003	2.7F
Su	0253	0606	4.3E
	0940	1245	3.4F
	1601	1838	3.2E

Day	Slack Water Time h.m.	Maximum Current Time h.m.	Maximum Current Vel. knots
16		0110	5.0E
M	0515	0823	3.9F
	1140	1355	2.3E
	1705	1955	3.0F
	2246		
17		0208	5.4E
Tu	0606	0912	4.3F
	1229	1450	2.6E
	1759	2053	3.3F
	2342		
18		0302	5.6E
W	0655	1001	4.5F
	1313	1538	3.0E
	1850	2144	3.6F
19	0036	0351	5.6E
Th	0740	1041	4.5F
	1354	1621	3.4E
	1940	2233	3.7F
20	0128	0435	5.4E
F	0823	1122	4.4F
	1434	1707	3.6E
	2030	2322	3.7F
21	0219	0520	4.9E
Sa	0906	1202	4.1F
	1513	1751	3.7E
	2120		
22		0010	3.4F
Su	0311	0604	4.3E
	0947	1243	3.7F
	1552	1832	3.7E
	2213		
23		0101	3.1F
M	0405	0649	3.6E
	1030	1321	3.2F
	1631	1918	3.6E

9	0220	0547	4.5E
F	0938	1239	3.4F
	1610	1823	2.3E
	2130		
10		0024	2.1F
Sa	0259	0629	4.3E
	1012	1316	3.3F
	1648	1906	2.4E
	2220		
11		0109	2.0F
Su	0345	0714	3.9E
	1048	1359	3.1F
	1726	1955	2.6E
	2319		
12		0202	1.9F
M	0440	0803	3.5E
	1128	1442	2.9F
	1807	2047	2.8E
13	0026	0303	1.8F
Tu	0549	0858	3.0E
	1215	1531	2.8F
	1850	2140	3.1E
14	0135	0411	1.9F
W	0711	0955	2.6E
	1309	1624	2.6F
	1936	2237	3.5E
15	0241	0521	2.3F
Th	0835	1057	2.3E
	1411	1721	2.6F
	2024	2335	4.1E

24		0026	3.1F
Sa	0320	0629	4.8E
	1017	1317	4.0F
	1637	1906	3.2E
	2239		
25		0122	2.8F
Su	0418	0718	4.1E
	1104	1405	3.5F
	1721	1957	3.1E
	2344		
26		0225	2.4F
M	0521	0807	3.3E
	1154	1454	3.0F
	1807	2050	3.1E
27	0052	0336	2.2F
Tu	0631	0903	2.5E
	1248	1547	2.5F
	1854	2146	3.1E
28	0201	0456	2.1F
W	0746	1007	1.9E
	1348	1645	2.2F
	1944	2247	3.1E
29	0306	0615	2.3F
Th	0901	1115	1.5E
	1450	1750	2.0F
	2035	2352	3.3E
30	0404	0716	2.6F
F	1010	1241	1.4E
	1550	1843	2.0F
	2125		
31		0050	3.6E
Sa	0455	0811	2.9F
	1108	1352	1.5E
	1643	1935	2.1F
	2213		

	2157		
9		0048	2.6F
M	0339	0649	3.9E
	1013	1318	3.2F
	1635	1923	3.3E
	2248		
10		0140	2.4F
Tu	0434	0738	3.4E
	1050	1402	3.0F
	1712	2012	3.5E
	2349		
11		0237	2.4F
W	0541	0830	2.8E
	1135	1452	2.7F
	1755	2107	3.7E
12	0057	0344	2.4F
Th	0700	0929	2.3E
	1230	1546	2.4F
	1845	2202	3.9E
13	0208	0500	2.5F
F	0823	1036	1.9E
	1340	1647	2.3F
	1943	2304	4.2E
14	0316	0618	2.9F
Sa	0939	1143	1.8E
	1455	1756	2.4F
	2045		
15		0009	4.6E
Su	0418	0723	3.4F
	1045	1251	1.9E
	1604	1859	2.6F
	2147		

	2309		
24		0155	2.8F
Tu	0504	0738	2.9E
	1115	1407	2.6F
	1713	2007	3.4E
25	0010	0258	2.4F
W	0608	0830	2.2E
	1207	1456	2.1F
	1759	2057	3.2E
26	0115	0413	2.2F
Th	0719	0930	1.6E
	1308	1553	1.8F
	1851	2156	3.1E
27	0222	0536	2.2F
F	0833	1036	1.3E
	1417	1701	1.6F
	1948	2259	3.1E
28	0325	0644	2.4F
Sa	0940	1156	1.2E
	1522	1805	1.6F
	2047		
29		0003	3.3E
Su	0421	0739	2.7F
	1037	1315	1.4E
	1618	1906	1.8F
	2142		
30		0103	3.5E
M	0509	0824	3.0F
	1124	1401	1.6E
	1705	1955	2.1F
	2232		
31		0148	3.8E
Tu	0551	0903	3.2F
	1203	1430	2.0E
	1746	2034	2.4F
	2318		

Time meridian 120° W. 0000 is midnight. 1200 is noon.

Fig. 7-7. Tidal Current Table 1; San Francisco, Aug. 19.

Table A

Interval between slack and desired time	Interval between slack and maximum current													
h. m.	*h. m.* 1 20	*h. m.* 1 40	*h. m.* 2 00	*h. m.* 2 20	*h. m.* 2 40	*h. m.* 3 00	*h. m.* 3 20	*h. m.* 3 40	*h. m.* 4 00	*h. m.* 4 20	*h. m.* 4 40	*h. m.* 5 00	*h. m.* 5 20	*h. m.* 5 40
	f.	*f.*	*f.*	*f.*	*f.*	*f.*	*f.*	*f.*	*f.*	*f.*	*f.*	*f.*	*f.*	*f.*
0 20	0.4	0.3	0.3	0.2	0.2	0.2	0.2	0.1	0.1	0.1	0.1	0.1	0.1	0.1
0 40	0.7	0.6	0.5	0.4	0.4	0.3	0.3	0.3	0.3	0.2	0.2	0.2	0.2	0.2
1 00	0.9	0.8	0.7	0.6	0.6	0.5	0.5	0.4	0.4	0.4	0.3	0.3	0.3	0.3
1 20	1.0	1.0	0.9	0.8	0.7	0.6	0.6	0.5	0.5	0.5	0.4	0.4	0.4	0.4
1 40		1.0	1.0	0.9	0.8	0.8	0.7	0.7	0.6	0.6	0.5	0.5	0.5	0.4
2 00			1.0	1.0	0.9	0.9	0.8	0.8	0.7	0.7	0.6	0.6	0.6	0.5
2 20				1.0	1.0	0.9	0.9	0.8	0.8	0.7	0.7	0.7	0.6	0.6
2 40					1.0	1.0	1.0	0.9	0.9	0.8	0.8	0.7	0.7	0.7
3 00						1.0	1.0	1.0	0.9	0.9	0.8	0.8	0.8	0.7
3 20							1.0	1.0	1.0	0.9	0.9	0.9	0.8	0.8
3 40								1.0	1.0	1.0	0.9	0.9	0.9	0.9
4 00									1.0	1.0	1.0	1.0	0.9	0.9
4 20										1.0	1.0	1.0	1.0	0.9
4 40											1.0	1.0	1.0	1.0
5 00												1.0	4.0	1.0
5 20													1.0	1.0
5 40														1.0

Table B

Interval between slack and desired time	Interval between slack and maximum current													
h. m.	*h. m.* 1 20	*h. m.* 1 40	*h. m.* 2 00	*h. m.* 2 20	*h. m.* 2 40	*h. m.* 3 00	*h. m.* 3 20	*h. m.* 3 40	*h. m.* 4 00	*h. m.* 4 20	*h. m.* 4 40	*h. m.* 5 00	*h. m.* 5 20	*h. m.* 5 40
	f.	*f.*	*f.*	*f.*	*f.*	*f.*	*f.*	*f.*	*f.*	*f.*	*f.*	*f.*	*f.*	*f.*
0 20	0.5	0.4	0.4	0.3	0.3	0.3	0.3	0.3	0.2	0.2	0.2	0.2	0.2	0.2
0 40	0.8	0.7	0.6	0.5	0.5	0.5	0.4	0.4	0.4	0.4	0.3	0.3	0.3	0.3
1 00	0.9	0.8	0.8	0.7	0.7	0.6	0.6	0.5	0.5	0.5	0.4	0.4	0.4	0.4
1 20	1.0	1.0	0.9	0.8	0.8	0.7	0.7	0.6	0.6	0.6	0.5	0.5	0.5	0.5
1 40	....	1.0	1.0	0.9	0.9	0.8	0.8	0.7	0.7	0.7	0.6	0.6	0.6	0.6
2 00	....	....	1.0	1.0	0.9	0.9	0.9	0.8	0.8	0.7	0.7	0.7	0.7	0.6
2 20	....	....	....	1.0	1.0	1.0	0.9	0.9	0.8	0.8	0.8	0.7	0.7	0.7
2 40	....	....	....	....	1.0	1.0	1.0	0.9	0.9	0.9	0.8	0.8	0.8	0.7
3 00	....	....	....	....	....	1.0	1.0	1.0	0.9	0.9	0.9	0.9	0.8	0.8
3 20	....	....	....	....	....	....	1.0	1.0	1.0	1.0	0.9	0.9	0.9	0.8
3 40	....	....	....	....	....	....	....	1.0	1.0	1.0	1.0	0.9	0.9	0.9
4 00	....	....	....	....	....	....	....	....	1.0	1.0	1.0	1.0	0.9	0.9
4 20	....	....	....	....	....	....	....	....	....	1.0	1.0	1.0	1.0	0.9
4 40	....	....	....	....	....	....	....	....	....	....	1.0	1.0	1.0	1.0
5 00	....	....	....	....	....	....	....	....	....	....	....	1.0	1.0	1.0
5 20	....	....	....	....	....	....	....	....	....	....	....	....	1.0	1.0
5 40	....	....	....	....	....	....	....	....	....	....	....	....	....	1.0

Use table A for all places except those listed below for table B.
Use table B for Deception Pass, Seymour Narrows, Sergius Narrows, Isanotski Strait, and all stations in table 2 which are referred to these points.

1. From predictions find the time of slack water and the time and velocity of maximum current (flood or ebb), one of which is immediately before and the other after the time for which the velocity is desired.
2. Find the interval of time between the above slack and maximum current, and enter the top of table A or B with the interval which most nearly agrees with this value.
3. Find the interval of time between the above slack and the time desired, and enter the side of table A or B with the interval which most nearly agrees with this value.
4. Find, in the table, the factor corresponding to the above two intervals, and multiply the maximum velocity by this factor. The result will be the approximate velocity at the time desired.

Fig. 7-8. Tidal Current Table 3A; answer to Humbolt Bay example.

The predicted times of slack water given in this publication indicate the instant of zero velocity, which is only momentary. There is a period each side of slack water, however, during which the current is so weak that for practical purposes it may be considered as negligible.

The following tables give, for various maximum currents, the approximate period of time during which weak currents not exceeding 0.1 to 0.5 knot will be encountered. This duration includes the last of the flood or ebb and the beginning of the following ebb or flood, that is, half of the duration will be before and half after the time of slack water.

Table A should be used for all places *except* those listed below for table B.

Table B should be used for **Decepton Pass, Seymour Narrows, Sergius Narrows, Isanotski Strait,** and all stations in table 2 which are referred to them.

Duration of weak current near time of slack water

TABLE A

Maximum current	Period with a velocity not more than—				
	0.1 knot	0.2 knot	0.3 knot	0.4 knot	0.5 knot
Knots	*Minutes*	*Minutes*	*Minutes*	*Minutes*	*Minutes*
1.0	23	46	70	94	120
1.5	15	31	46	62	78
2.0	11	23	35	46	58
3.0	8	15	23	31	38
4.0	6	11	17	23	29
5.0	5	9	14	18	23
6.0	4	8	11	15	19
7.0	3	7	10	13	16
8.0	3	6	9	11	14
9.0	3	5	8	10	13
10.0	2	5	7	9	11
11.0	2	4	6	8	10
12.0	2	4	6	8	10

TABLE B

Maximum current	Period with a velocity not more than—				
	0.1 knot	0.2 knot	0.3 knot	0.4 knot	0.5 knot
Knots	*Minutes*	*Minutes*	*Minutes*	*Minutes*	*Minutes*
1.0	13	28	46	66	89
1.5	8	18	28	39	52
2.0	6	13	20	28	36
3.0	4	8	13	18	22
4.0	3	6	9	13	17
5.0	3	5	8	10	13
6.0	2	4	6	8	11
7.0	2	4	5	7	9
8.0	2	3	5	6	8

When there is a difference between the velocities of the maximum flood and ebb preceding and following the slack for which the duration is desired, it will be sufficiently accurate for practical purposes to find a separate duration for each maximum velocity and take the average of the two as the duration of the weak current.

Fig. 7-9. Tidal Current Table 4; A and B.

VEL OF CURRENT	
DATE	AUG. 19, 1982
LOCATION	HUMBOLT BAY-ENT.
TIME	1645 P.S.T.
REF STA	SAN FRANCISCO
TIME DIFF SLACK WATER	- 1 00
TIME DIFF MAX CURRENT	-0 45
VEL RATIO MAX FLOOD	0.6
VEL RATIO MAX EBB	0.6
FLOOD DIR	125°
EBB DIR	310°
REF STA SLACK WATER TIME	1940
TIME DIFF	- 100
LOCAL STA SLACK WATER TIME	1840
REF STA MAX CURRENT TIME	1621
TIME DIFF	-045
LOCAL STA MAX CURRENT TIME	1536
REF STA MAX CURRENT VEL	3.4 K
VEL RATIO	0.6
LOCAL STA MAX CURRENT VEL	2.0 K
INT BETWEEN STACK AND DESIRED TIME	1 55
INT BETWEEN STACK AND MAX CURRENT	304
MAX CURRENT	2.0 K
FACTOR TABLE 3	0.9
VELOCITY	1 .8
DIRECTION	310°

Fig. 7-10. Humbolt Bay at 1645, Aug. 19 (worked out on form).

- ☐ Naragansett Bay.
- ☐ Long Island & Block Island Sounds.
- ☐ New York Harbor.
- ☐ Delaware Bay & River.
- ☐ Upper Chesapeake Bay.
- ☐ Charleston Harbor (S.C.).
- ☐ San Francisco Bay.
- ☐ Puget Sound, Southern Part.
- ☐ Puget Sound, Northern Part.

Each set consists of 12 charts. One chart is for each hour of the tidal cycle marked in terms of time before or after either slacks or current maximums. Figure 7-11 shows one plate from the Puget Sound, Southern Part set. The velocities shown on the tidal current charts are to be used in conjunction with the velocities found in the daily Tidal Current Tables. To find the expected current at a point covered in Fig. 7-11, it is necessary to know that predicted velocity from the Tidal Current Table for maximum flood at The Narrows, Puget Sound on the day in question.

The average weekend sailor is unlikely to carry a set of Tidal Current Charts on the boat. If he is operating in an area where fairly strong currents occur, and a set exists for his area, he may want to have a set at home. Use of these charts can help you to time passages so as to take advantage of favorable tidal currents and, perhaps more important, avoid battling with unfavorable ones.

Rotary Tidal Currents

Offshore and away from the constricting effects of the coast, tidal current becomes rotary. It flows continuously without slacks and also continuously changes direction through all points of the compass during a complete tidal cycle. With passage of time, the change in direction in the Northern Hemisphere is clockwise (north, to east, to south, to west, and back to north). Velocity will generally vary throughout the cycle along with the directional changes.

OTHER CURRENTS

While the coastal navigator's primary concern with currents will generally relate to tidal currents, he might from time to time encounter other types of currents. Probably the best known of all the ocean currents is the Gulf Stream, flowing northward from Florida along the eastern coast of the United States. The southern portion of this current is par-

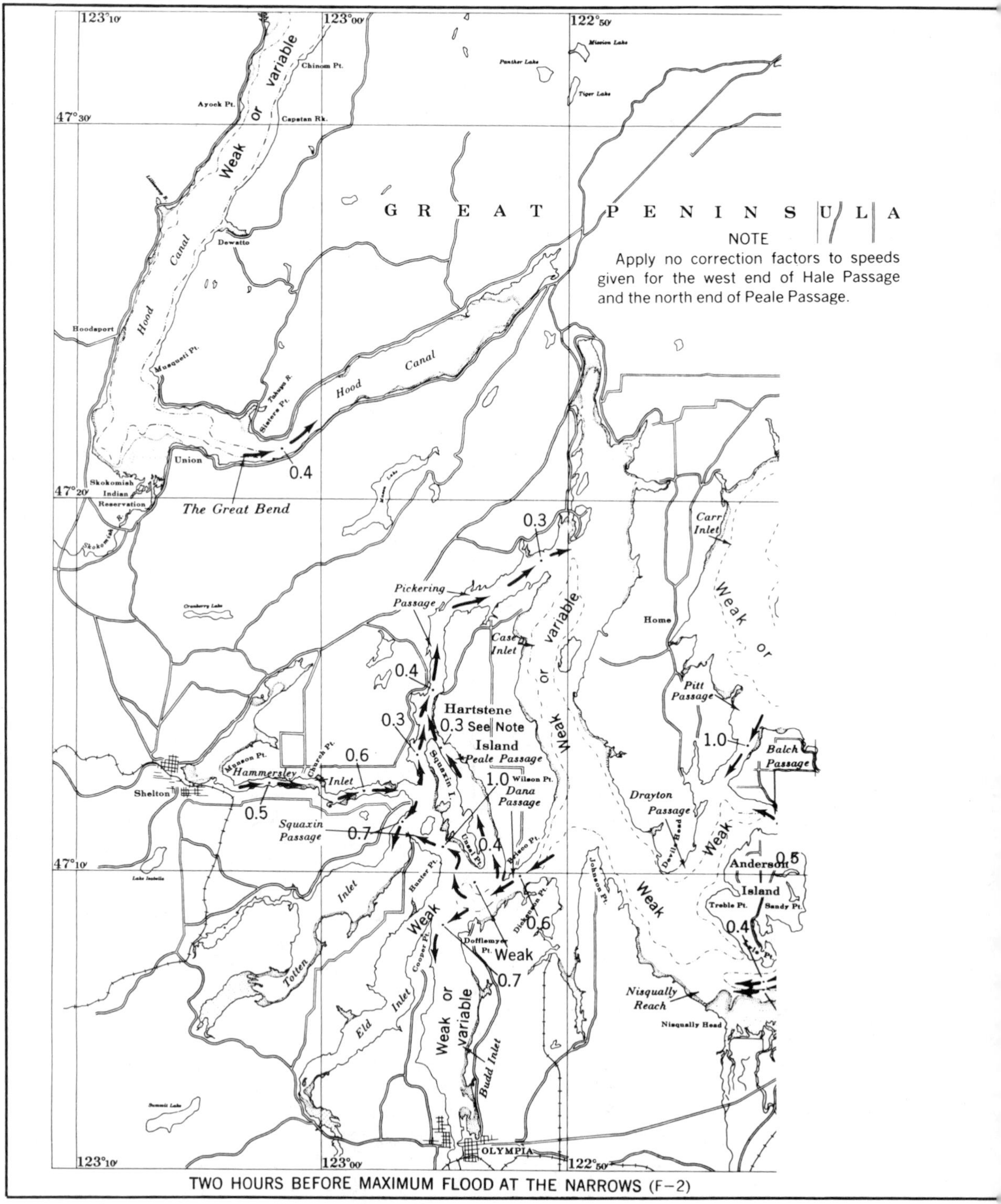

123°10′
123°00′
122°50′
47°30′
47°20′
47°10′
Ayock Pt.
Chinom Pt.
Capstan Rk.
Weak or variable
Mission Lake
Panther Lake
Tiger Lake
G R E A T P E N I N S U L A
NOTE
Apply no correction factors to speeds given for the west end of Hale Passage and the north end of Peale Passage.
Dewatto
Hood Canal
Hoodsport
Musqueti Pt.
Tahuya R.
Sisters Pt.
Hood Canal
Union
0.4
Skokomish Indian Reservation
The Great Bend
0.3
Carr Inlet
Pickering Passage
Weak or variable
Case Inlet
Home
Weak or
0.4
Hartstene
0.3
0.3 See Note
Island
Peale Passage
Pitt Passage
1.0
Balch Passage
Munson Pt.
Hammersley
Church Pt.
Inlet
0.6
Shelton
0.5
Squaxin I.
1.0 Wilson Pt.
Dana Passage
Drayton Passage
Squaxin Passage
0.7
Unsal Pt.
0.4
Brisco Pt.
Devils Head
Weak
0.5
Anderson
Island
Treble Pt.
Sandy Pt.
Johnson Pt.
Weak
Hunter Pt.
Inlet
0.6
0.4
Weak
Dickerson Pt.
Dofflemyer Pt.
Weak
0.7
Cooper Pt.
Totten
Nisqually Reach
Nisqually Head
Eld Inlet
Weak or variable
Budd Inlet
OLYMPIA
123°10′
123°00′
122°50′
TWO HOURS BEFORE MAXIMUM FLOOD AT THE NARROWS (F–2)

Fig. 7-11. Tidal Current Chart; sample sheet from Puget Sound.

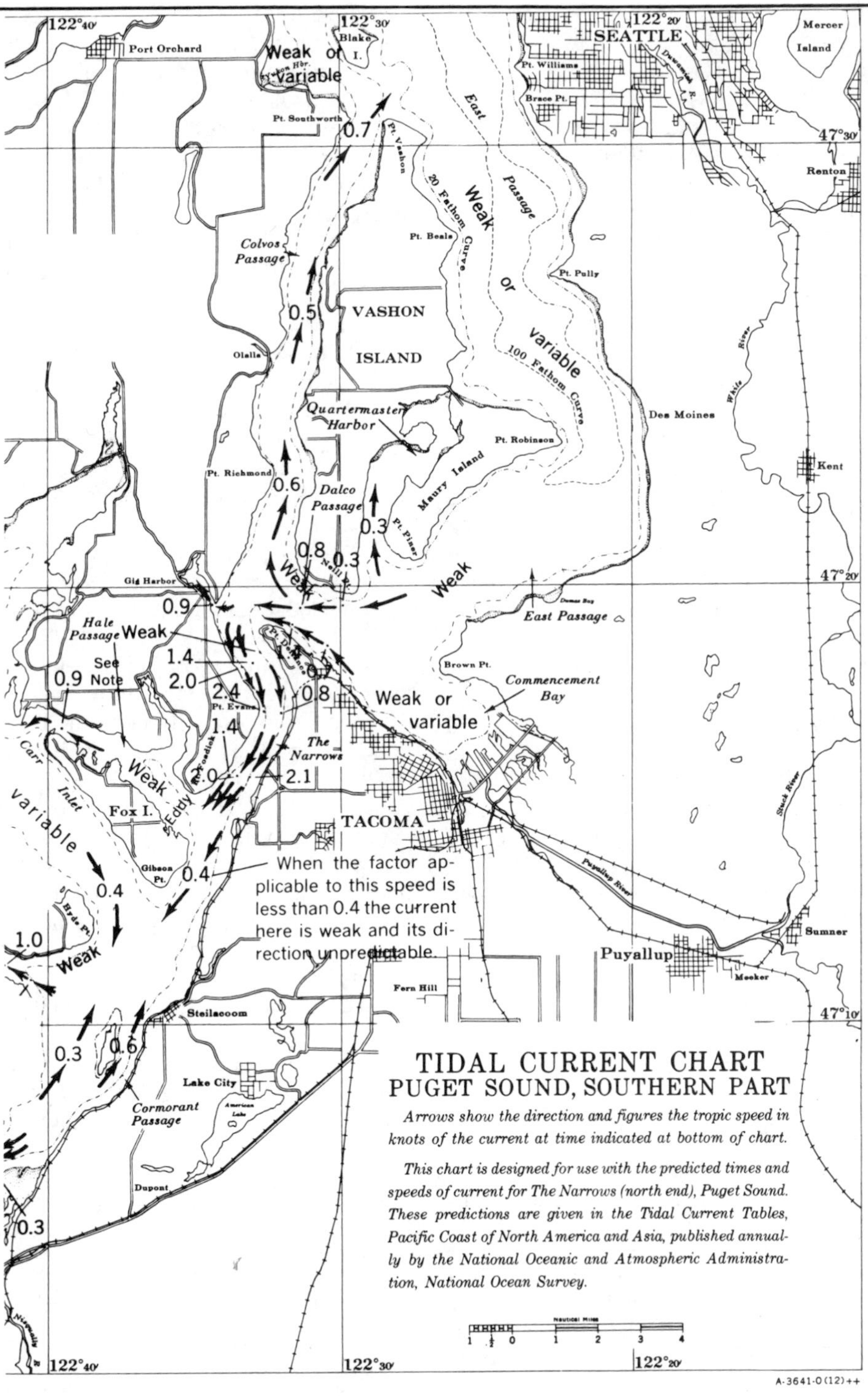

TIDAL CURRENT CHART
PUGET SOUND, SOUTHERN PART
Arrows show the direction and figures the tropic speed in knots of the current at time indicated at bottom of chart.
This chart is designed for use with the predicted times and speeds of current for The Narrows (north end), Puget Sound. These predictions are given in the Tidal Current Tables, Pacific Coast of North America and Asia, published annually by the National Oceanic and Atmospheric Administration, National Ocean Survey.
When the factor applicable to this speed is less than 0.4 the current here is weak and its direction unpredictable.
122°40′
122°30′
122°20′
47°30′
47°20′
47°10′
Port Orchard
SEATTLE
Mercer Island
Blake I.
Pt. Williams
Brace Pt.
Duwamish R.
Renton
Pt. Southworth
Pt. Vashon
Weak or variable
East Passage
20 Fathom Curve
100 Fathom Curve
Colvos Passage
Pt. Beals
Pt. Pully
VASHON ISLAND
Olalla
Quartermaster Harbor
Maury Island
Pt. Robinson
Des Moines
White River
Kent
Pt. Richmond
Dalco Passage
Pt. Piner
Gig Harbor
Hale Passage
See Note
East Passage
Brown Pt.
Commencement Bay
Pt. Evans
The Narrows
TACOMA
Carr Inlet
Fox I.
Eddy
Gibson Pt.
Hyde Pt.
Puyallup River
Stuck River
Puyallup
Sumner
Meeker
Fern Hill
Steilacoom
Lake City
American Lake
Cormorant Passage
Dupont
Nisqually R.
Weak
0.7
0.5
0.6
0.3
0.8
0.9
1.4
2.0
2.4
2.1
0.4
1.0
0.6
Nautical Miles
1 ½ 0 1 2 3 4
A-3641-0(12)++

ticularly strong and close to the coast. Boaters from Florida quite often get into this current. On the western coast a much weaker southerly setting current, the California Current, is found. This one will seldom affect the coastal boatman.

A steady wind from a constant direction will produce a wind-driven current. The velocity of such a current will depend on a combination of the velocity of the wind and the length of time it blows. Generally, the boatman will be more strongly affected by the leeway produced from wind blowing on his boat than he will be by wind-driven currents.

River discharge currents, particularly in the wake of heavy rains inland, are another source of horizontal water movements that affect a small boat. These can catch you unaware when they are caused, as often happens, by rainstorms or heavy snow melts at the source of the river many miles away from its mouth. The volume of water being discharged by the river can temporarily increase to a level considerably above normal. This can cause abnormal currents in the ocean near the river mouth.

Current Sailing

Current sailing is a way of adjusting course and speed that makes allowance for the expected effects of current. When it is well done, the intended track of the boat and its actual track very nearly coincide. For purposes of current sailing, the meaning of the word current is broadened to include all of the influences that can cause a boat to deviate from its intended DR course and schedule. Among the elements included in this broadened meaning are:

- ☐ Tidal current.
- ☐ Ocean current.
- ☐ Other currents.
- ☐ Sea conditions.
- ☐ Wind leeway.
- ☐ Steering errors.
- ☐ Uncorrected compass error.
- ☐ Speedometer, or other, error in determining speed.

Some combination of these factors will affect every trip you make. It is the actual combination working at any given time that will be considered as "current" in current sailing. First a few terms must be defined:

Estimated current—An evaluation of all known factors that will contribute to producing a current effect at particular time and place.

Actual current—Determined by the direction and distance between the DR position and an accurate fix at a specific time.

Estimated position (EP)—Most likely position of the boat at a particular time—allowance having been made for all estimated current effects.

Current triangle—Vector diagram of current effect. One side is current set and drift, one is boat DR course and speed, one side is actual track taken by boat.

Drift—Velocity of current (or combination of factors setting boat off intended DR track).

There are two types of current triangles you will want to use for current sailing. The first (Fig. 7-12) is used to project in advance the combined effect that best information, experience, and shrewd guesswork lead the sailor to expect. This is done by laying out one line to represent the DR course for a period of time. Next, from the DR position at the end of that time draw a line representing the expected direction and distance that the combined factors making up current will offset the boat during that time. The third side of the triangle becomes the expected track of the boat leading to the EP (estimated position) of the boat at the end of the allotted period of time.

In Fig. 7-13, an example is shown of the use of a current triangle to determine ahead of time the course and speed corrections that will be required to make a trip from Corona del Mar to Avalon Bay, a distance of 26.6 mi. Current and windage effects are expected to produce a combined set of 137° T at a velocity of 2 k.

The actual track the boat should follow over the ground to get from Corona del Mar to Avalon Bay is 236° T. With a current setting, however, the boat off to port steering 236° T will not get it to Avalon. The question is what course will get it there?

The skipper would like to make this run at a speed of 12 knots. For a distance of 26.6 miles, the time, speed, distance formula works out thus:

$$60 \times D = S \times T$$

$$60 \times 26.6 = 12 \times T \quad = \frac{1596}{12}$$

$$T = 133 \text{ minutes} = 2 \text{ hr. } 13 \text{ min.}$$

This shows that while the boat advances along the intended track at 12 knots, the current effects

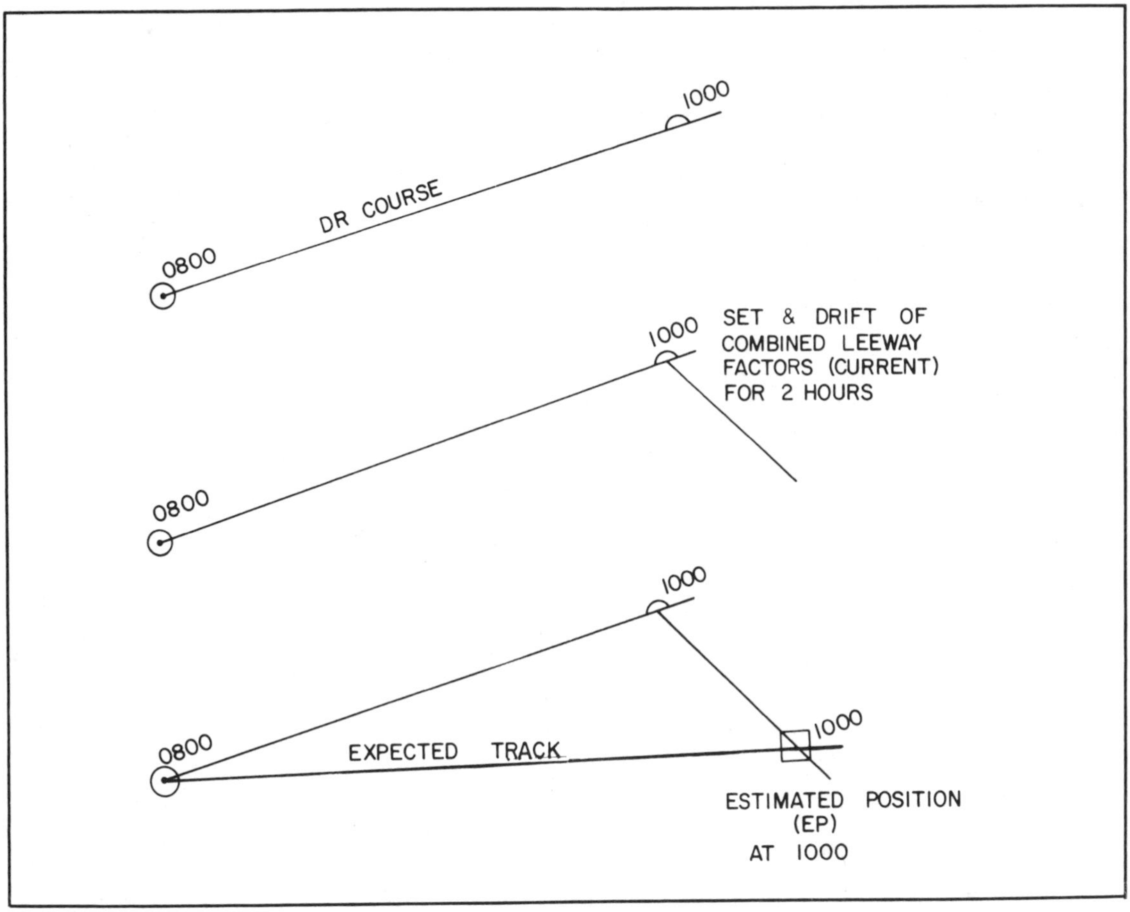
1000
DR COURSE
0800
1000
SET & DRIFT OF
COMBINED LEEWAY
FACTORS (CURRENT)
FOR 2 HOURS
0800
1000
1000
0800
EXPECTED TRACK
ESTIMATED POSITION
(EP)
AT 1000

Fig. 7-12. Current triangle; advance estimate

that are setting it off in the direction of 137° T at a velocity of 2 knots, will be influencing it for 133 minutes, or 2 hours 13 minutes. During that 133 minutes, exactly how far will the current move the boat in that 137° T direction. Again the time, speed, distance formula can tell us:

$$S \times T = 60 \times D$$

$$2 \times 133 = 60 \times D$$

$$D = \frac{266}{60} = 4.4 \text{ miles}$$

The boat must be steered in a direction and driven at a speed that will take it 26.6 miles in a direction of 236° T in 133 minutes, while at the same time counteracting a lateral set of 4.4 miles toward 137° T.

By drawing a line equal to 4.4 miles from Corona del Mar in the direction of 137° T the leeway for the entire trip is brought together in a single vector. A third line from that point (point X) to Avalon Bay now represents the direction (245° T) that must be steered, and the distance that will be traveled through the water to get there through the current that will be running. That distance turns out to be 27.7 miles.

The direct distance from Corona del Mar to Avalon Bay was 26.6 miles, but the boat will have to sail 27.7 miles through the water to get there. In that case, it will not arrive in 2 hr. 13 min. at a speed of 12 knots. Speed will have to be increased:

$$60 \times D = S \times T$$

$$60 \times 27.7 = S \times 133 = \frac{1662}{133}$$

$$S = 12.496 = 12.5 \text{ knots}$$

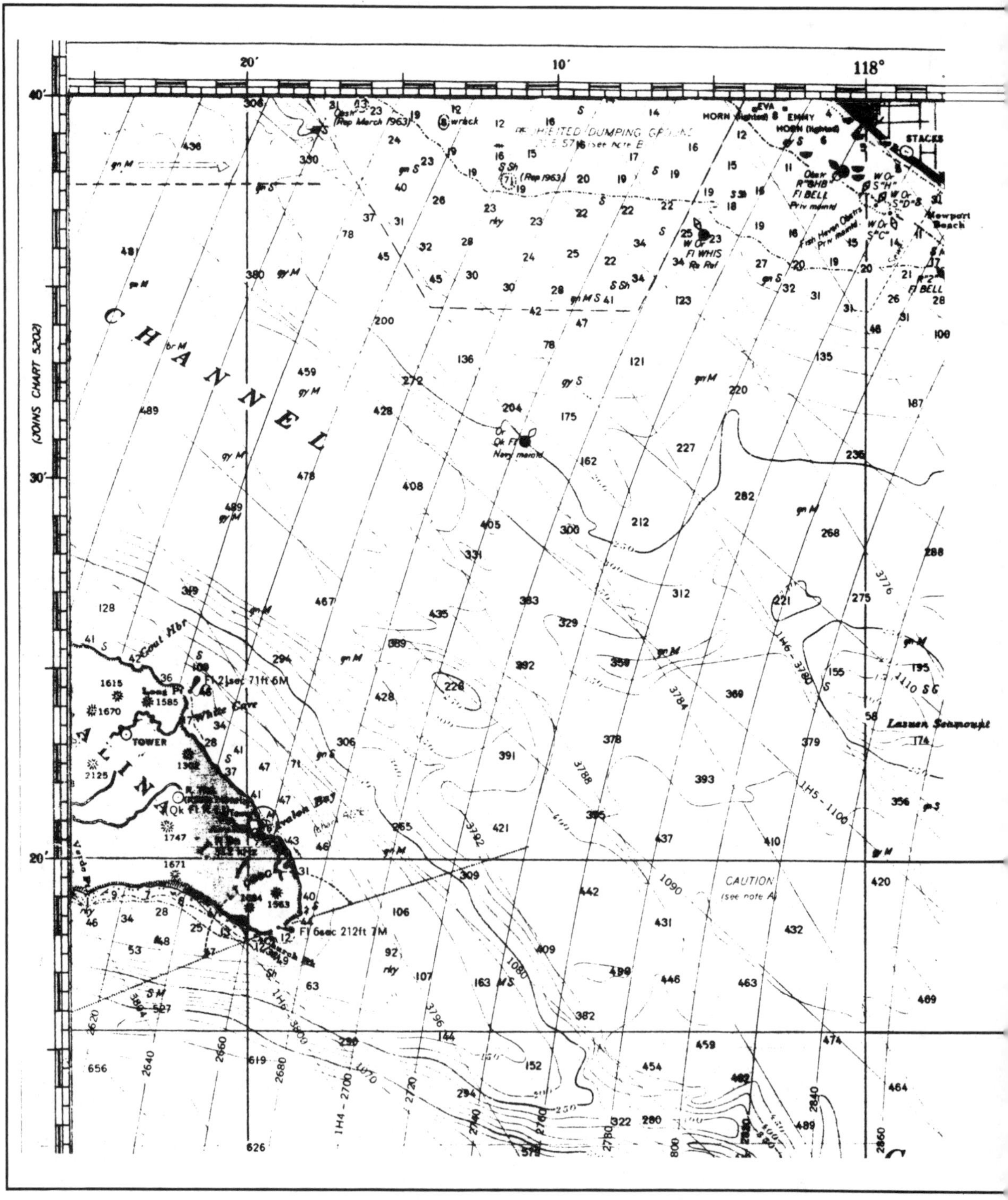
20′
10′
118°
40′
30′
20′
(JOINS CHART 5202)
CHANNEL
PROHIBITED DUMPING GROUND
HORN
EVA
EMMY
STACKS
Newport Beach
Fl BELL
Fl WHIS
Navy maintd
Goat Hbr
Long Pt
White Cove
TOWER
Avalon Bay
Fl 2 sec 71ft 6M
Fl 6sec 212ft 7M
CAUTION
(see note A)
Lasuen Seamount

Fig. 7-13. Chart showing advance plot for trip from Corona del Mar to Avalon.

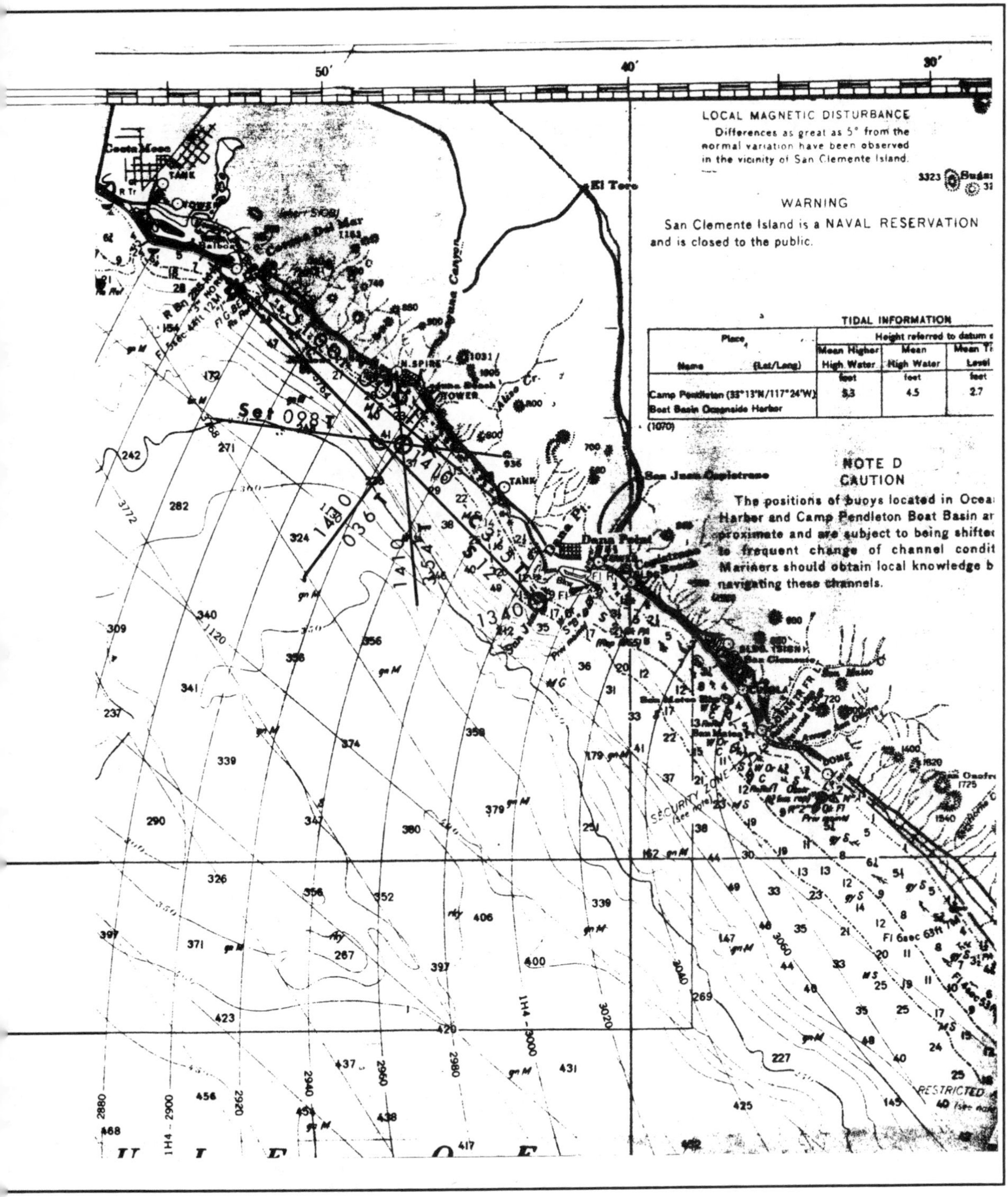
LOCAL MAGNETIC DISTURBANCE
Differences as great as 5° from the normal variation have been observed in the vicinity of San Clemente Island.
WARNING
San Clemente Island is a NAVAL RESERVATION and is closed to the public.
TIDAL INFORMATION
Place
Name
(Lat/Long)
Height referred to datum
Mean Higher High Water
Mean High Water
feet
Camp Pendleton (33°13'N/117°24'W)
Boat Basin Oceanside Harbor
5.3
4.5
2.7
(1070)
NOTE D
CAUTION
Mariners should obtain local knowledge
navigating these channels.
50'
40'
30'
Costa Mesa
El Toro
San Juan Capistrano
Dana Point
N. SPIRE
TOWER
TANK
DOME
SECURITY ZONE
RESTRICTED
Set 098 T
1410
036 T
1340

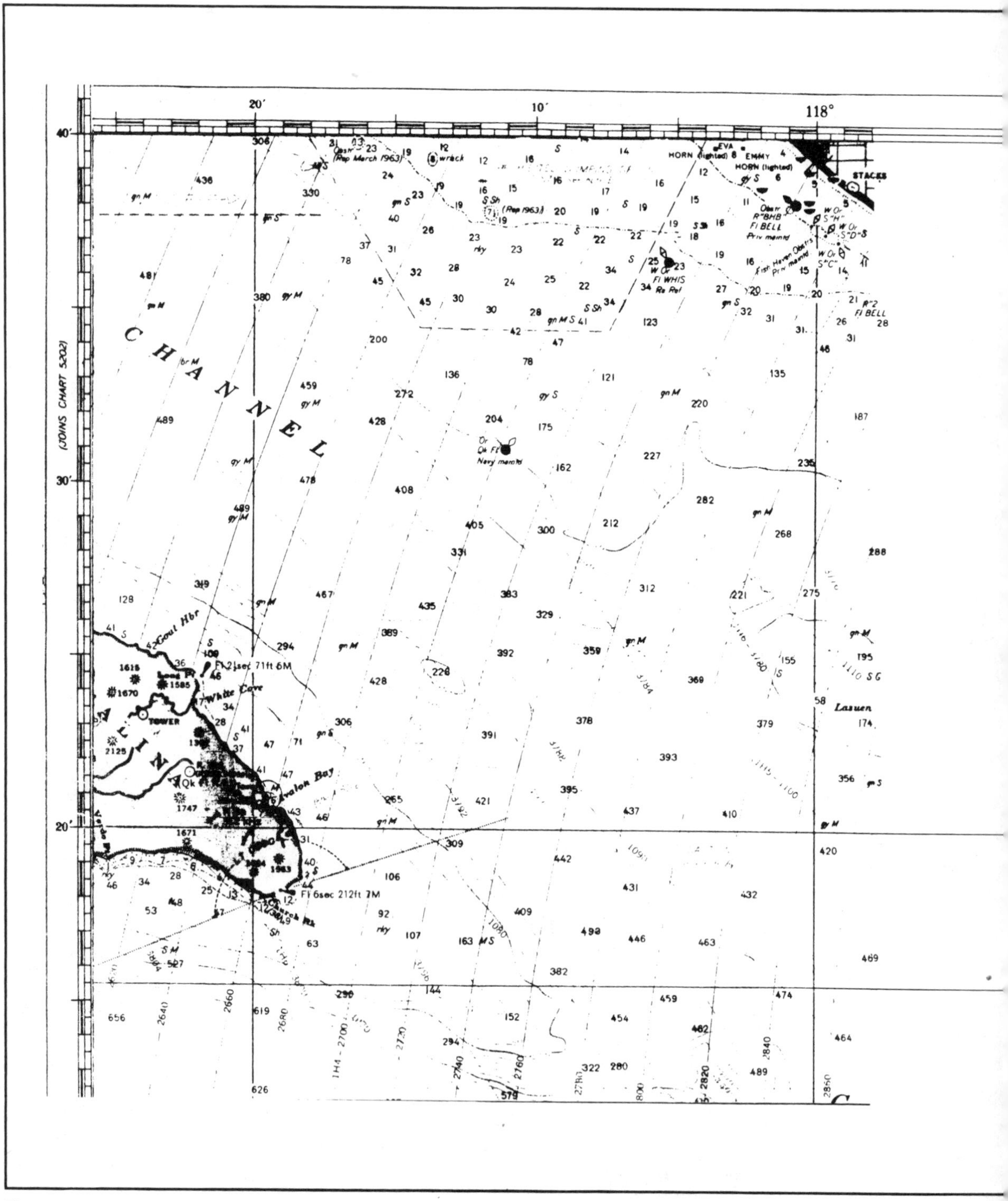

20′
10′
118°
40′
30′
20′
(JOINS CHART 5202)
CHANNEL
STACKS
HORN (lighted)
EVA
EMMY
HORN (lighted)
Fl WHIS
Navy maintd
Goat Hbr
White Cove
TOWER
Avalon Bay
Fl 2sec 71ft 6M
Fl 6sec 212ft 7M
Church Rk
Lasuen

Fig. 7-14. Chart showing course correction for current under way.

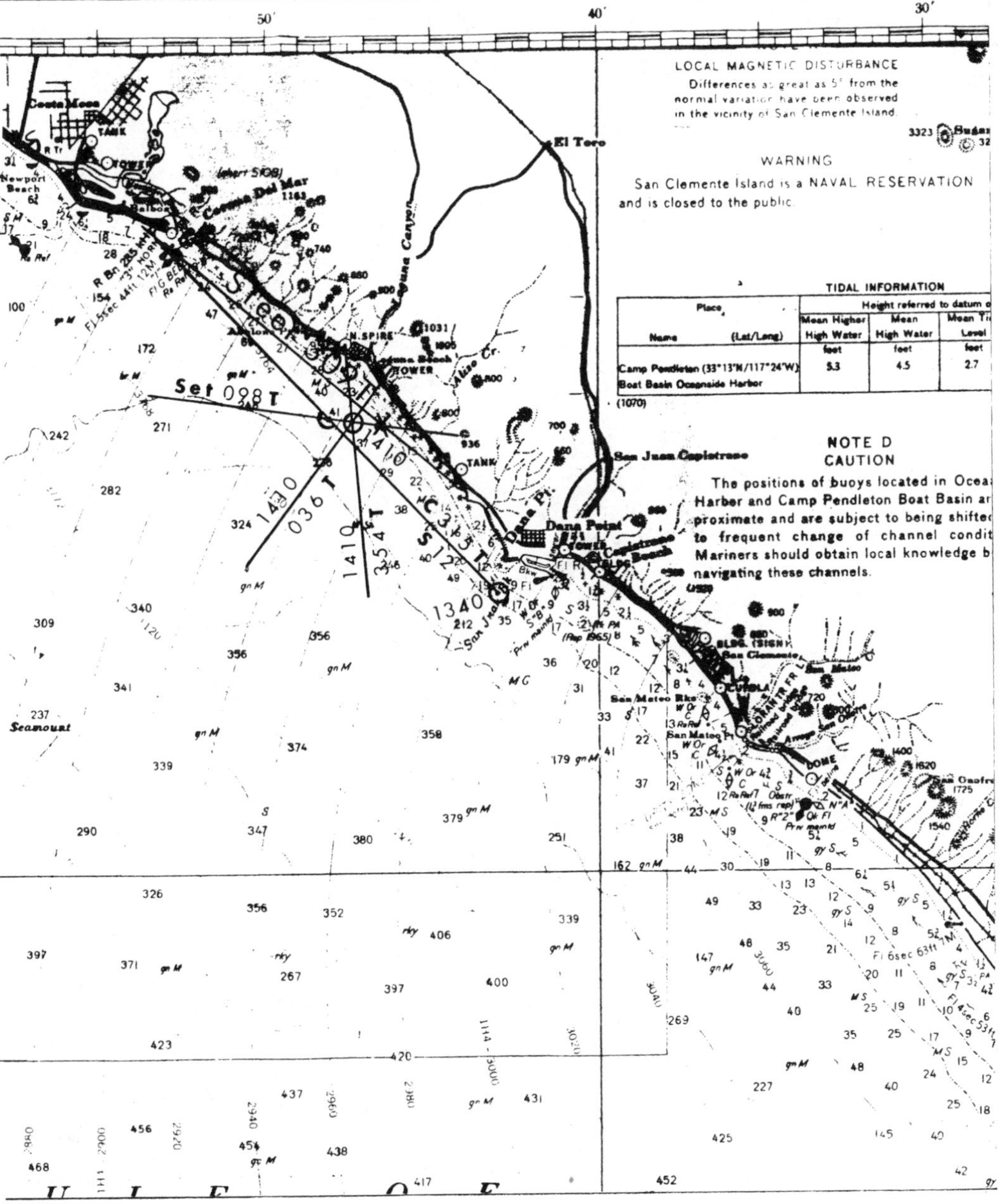

50′
40′
30′
LOCAL MAGNETIC DISTURBANCE
Differences as great as 5° from the normal variation have been observed in the vicinity of San Clemente Island.
WARNING
San Clemente Island is a NAVAL RESERVATION and is closed to the public.
TIDAL INFORMATION
Place
Name (Lat/Long)
Height referred to datum of
Mean Higher High Water
Mean High Water
Mean Tide Level
feet
Camp Pendleton (33°13′N/117°24′W) 5.3 4.5 2.7
Boat Basin Oceanside Harbor
(1070)
NOTE D
CAUTION
The positions of buoys located in Ocea Harbor and Camp Pendleton Boat Basin ar proximate and are subject to being shifted to frequent change of channel condit Mariners should obtain local knowledge b navigating these channels.
Costa Mesa
Newport Beach
Balboa
Corona Del Mar
El Toro
Laguna Canyon
Laguna Beach
Aliso Cr.
San Juan Capistrano
Dana Point
Dana Pt.
Capistrano Beach
San Clemente
San Mateo
San Mateo Pt.
San Onofre
Seamount
Set 098 T
036 T
354 T
1410
1340

At 12.5 knots and steering 245°T, the boat will make Avalon Bay in 2 hr. 13 min.

When planning a trip through an area where it is known that current effects will occur, the best available information should be used to determine, (as previously described) the course and speed corrections to use to compensate for the expected leeway. Once the trip is under way, the second type of current triangle comes into play. This time, instead of estimating set and drift to correct course, the actual set and drift are to be determined.

We had a fix (Fig. 7-14) at 1340 hrs. off Dana Point. We then set a course of 315°T toward Corona del Mar at a speed of 12 knots. The DR position in half an hour (at 1430 hrs.) should be off Laguna Beach. At 1410 hrs., bearings are taken on the Spire north of Laguna Beach and the Tower to the south. The 1410 fix is .7 mi. from the DR in the direction 098°T.

Because the boat is out of position by .7 mi., in half an hour the current drift is 1.4 knots and the set is 098°T. The distance over the ground from the 1340 fix to the 1410 fix is 4.5 mi., giving the boat a speed over the ground of 11 knots (4.5 mi. in ½ hr. equals a speed of 11 miles *per hour;* the definition of a knot is one nautical mile per hour).

Because the present steering course of 315°T is not going to get the boat to Corona del Mar, let's find one that will. From the 1410 position to Corona del Mar is a distance of 6.5 miles in the direction of 313°T. Because the boat is actually making good a speed of 11 knots over the ground, it will take it 35.5 minutes to get to Corona del Mar.

$$(60 \times 6.5 = \frac{390}{11} = 35.45)$$

During that 35.5 minutes, the same current set of 098°T will continue to act on the boat. Therefore a course must be found that will compensate for it. To do this, the total distance the boat will be set by current in 35.5 minutes is laid off on the line showing the 098°T set. This distance is .8 mi.

$$(1.4 \times 35.5 = \frac{49.7}{60} = .82)$$

As in the previous example, the line from the 1410 fix to point X is the total distance the current will displace the boat during the remaining time. The line from point X to Corona del Mar provides the steering course of 309°T.

Chapter 8

QUASAR

Weather

AN ELEMENTARY UNDERSTANDING OF WEATHer and weather systems is an absolute safety necessity for the small-boat coastal navigator. Most of us have seen those humorous little signs saying "O Lord, thy sea is so great, and my boat is so small." When the wind pipes up and the sea builds along with it, and if it is still a long way to port, that type of sign suddenly isn't so funny any more. To the practiced and attentive eye, there are many signals in the cloud formations, the wave trains, and the wind shifts that will alert the navigator to coming changes in the weather.

HEAT/WIND/PRESSURE

All weather effects and changes result ultimately from the heating and subsequent cooling of the atmosphere. Heating and cooling of air causes changes in humidity and pressure. Changes in pressure cause wind and wind moves masses of air about, altering the weather.

Heat is energy manifested by molecular motion, and it is transferred because of a temperature difference between things. This transfer can take place in any of three ways: conduction, convection, or radiation.

Conduction occurs when two different bodies at different temperatures are in direct contact. Some of the energy of molecular motion in the hotter one is transferred to molecules in the cooler one. The rate of heat flow from the hotter body to the cooler one will depend on two factors: the size of the temperature difference and the nature of the substances in contact. Air is a poor conductor while rocks or sand, as your bare feet probably have discovered, are pretty good conductors.

Convection occurs within a body of liquid or gas. When the air near the ground is heated on a sunny day (by conduction from the ground beneath), it expands, becomes lighter, and creates an upward-flowing, warm-air current (Fig. 8-1) that will be balanced by a down-flowing current of cooler air nearby.

Heat, in the form of electromagnetic radiation, can also flow between two bodies that are not in contact. This is precisely the way in which heat flows to the earth from the sun. The majority of the heat in the atmosphere gets there by conduction from the earth's surface. The surface absorbs solar radiation, becomes warmer than the air in contact with it, and then heats that air. Because air is a poor conductor, only a shallow layer is heated in that manner. The warming of air at higher altitudes occurs by convection.

Like all other substances air expands as it

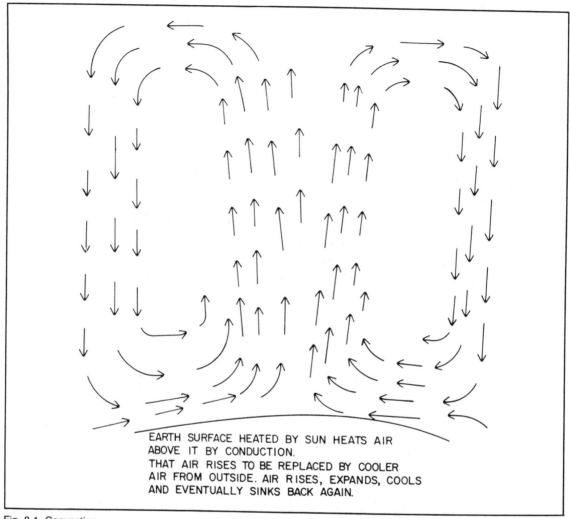

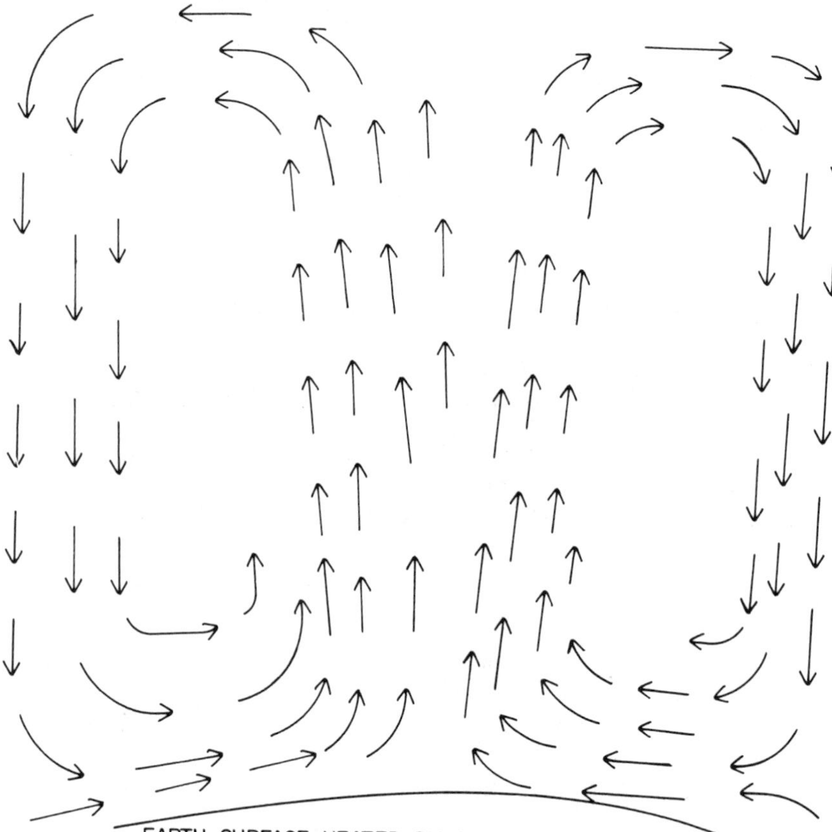
EARTH SURFACE HEATED BY SUN HEATS AIR
ABOVE IT BY CONDUCTION.
THAT AIR RISES TO BE REPLACED BY COOLER
AIR FROM OUTSIDE. AIR RISES, EXPANDS, COOLS
AND EVENTUALLY SINKS BACK AGAIN.

Fig. 8-1. Convection.

warms. This reduces the atmospheric pressure of the warmed air and brings cooler air at higher pressure in around it. This explains the generally consistent onshore airflow during the days, in June particularly, in Southern California. At that time of year, the deserts of eastern California and Arizona are intensely heated daily, causing the air to expand and rise resulting in a daily thermal low-pressure area inland. This causes a reasonably brisk daily afternoon breeze along the coast as cooler, higher-pressure marine air flows in from the Pacific Ocean to fill the "vacuum" of the low pressure area inland.

A similar temperature/pressure differential breeze over a far more limited geographical area often occurs, during summer months, over Great South Bay in New York. During the day, the sun heats the land on Long Island, creating a localized thermal low-pressure area. For a short distance out to sea, a breeze toward the land develops. Toward the end of the day the heating stops, and so does the breeze. During the evening, the land loses its heat and quite rapidly becomes cooler than the surrounding water. Now that the water is the warmer area, the air over it starts to warm, expand, and rise. This causes the breeze to reverse and blow now from the land toward the sea. This land breeze/sea breeze sequence is common in many other areas for the same reasons it occurs here.

The atmosphere draws most of its heat by conduction from the surface of the earth. That heating is necessarily very uneven due to the wide variations in the heat-absorbing and conducting characteristics of different areas of that surface. A sandy, rocky desert area will conduct heat to the air above it vastly better than a grassy prairie. The prairie will do a much better conducting job than a healthy stand of Douglas Fir trees. So although the amount of heat being radiated to the earth by the sun is uniform over sizeable areas, the amount being absorbed and conducted to the surrounding air varies considerably from place to place. This variation in conducted heat leads to accompanying variations in air pressure, as reflected in barometer readings. It is the variations in temperature and pressure, along with humidity, that result in day-to-day changes in weather.

AIR MASSES AND FRONTS

The air close to the surface of the earth is greatly affected by the characteristics of that surface. On a small scale, this becomes apparent in the localized sea breeze/land breeze phenomenon. In the same way that localized surface conditions cause localized effects in small areas, generally similar surface conditions over much larger areas cause much larger atmospheric effects. In winter in Canada, large areas covered by ice and snow—coupled with short days, meaning fewer hours of warming sun—result in thousands of square miles of very cold ground cooling the air above it. This cold air becomes comparatively dense, meaning high pressure, which causes it to move out toward areas of lower pressure. The result is north winds bringing freezing conditions over large areas of the United States.

Large-scale air formations of this type are termed *air masses*. The one just described, because it formed over a far northern land area, would be classified as a *polar continental* air mass. Other types of air masses are spawned where stable surface conditions spread over similarly large areas. Large tropical areas of uniformly warm water produce *tropical maritime* air masses. The cold northern oceans produce *polar maritime* air. Air masses are classified according to where they formed.

The movement of air masses once formed is influenced by several factors. One of these is the overall primary air circulation pattern of the planet (Fig. 8-2). From the equator to approximately Lat. 30°, both north and south, the predominant air movement is the easterly trade winds. From 30° to 60° north and south, the wind changes to the prevailing westerlies. Few readers of this book will venture in small boats further north than Lat. 60°. Air masses within these belts of predominantly easterly and westerly winds will tend to move in the same general direction as the rest of the air flow within those belts. How fast they move will depend on the temperature and pressure differentials between different air masses as well as the velocity at which other surrounding systems are moving.

When the air mass formed, it did so primarily in response to surface conditions over a large area. As it moves it will continue to be influenced by surface conditions below it. If it is colder than the surfaces it passes over, it will gradually warm. If it is warmer it will cool as it moves. As it moves away from its source region, its original characteristics change.

Where one air mass ends and another begins, a boundary line exists on either side of which the characteristics are decidedly different. It is these differences along the boundary lines, called *fronts*, between air masses that cause most of the bad weather we experience. Frontal bad weather follows certain predictable patterns, depending on the type of front moving through. The several types of frontal situations that can occur are variations of two basic conditions. In one case, a warm air mass is replacing a cooler one. In the other, a cool air mass is overtaking a warm one.

Warm Front Passage

The leading edge of a warm air mass replacing a colder one is defined as a warm front. On the weather map in the daily newspaper, a warm front (Fig. 8-3) is indicated by black semicircles drawn on the leading side of a line (indicating the location of that front). There is an extremely consistent weather sequence that accompanies the passage of a warm front (Fig. 8-4). Because warm air is lighter than cold, where they meet the warm air slides up over the top of the cold. Warm air absorbs and holds much more moisture than cold air. As it rises over the cooler air, however, it too cools as it rises. The cooler it gets the less moisture it can retain. So as it cools, some of its moisture condenses out in the form of clouds.

The first clouds to appear indicating the coming of a warm front (Fig. 8-5) will be high cirrus clouds; these are thin, wispy clouds at a very high altitude. As the front moves closer, these clouds thicken into cirro-stratus (Fig. 8-6) and are lower in altitude. As the front continues to move in, the clouds thicken, lower and become alto-stratus (Fig. 8-7), then low stratus (Fig. 8-8), and then merge finally into nimbo-stratus (Fig. 8-9) as the rain starts. This could be anywhere from 6 to 24 hours in advance of the final passage of the front at ground level.

The approximately 6-mile-high cirrus cloud advance guard will arrive anywhere from 600 to 900 miles ahead of the arrival of the front at ground level. The front will move at speeds between 20 and 30 miles per hour. It will cover anywhere from 450 miles to 700 miles per day. The first sighting of the high cirrus clouds is by no means the signal for panic. It means merely that bad weather is coming, and the prudent will prepare for it. How rapidly the bad weather will arrive can be gauged by how rapidly the cloud cover thickens and lowers. In spring and summer, the speed of frontal movements will be toward the slow end of the 20 to 30 mph range. In winter, it will be toward the faster end.

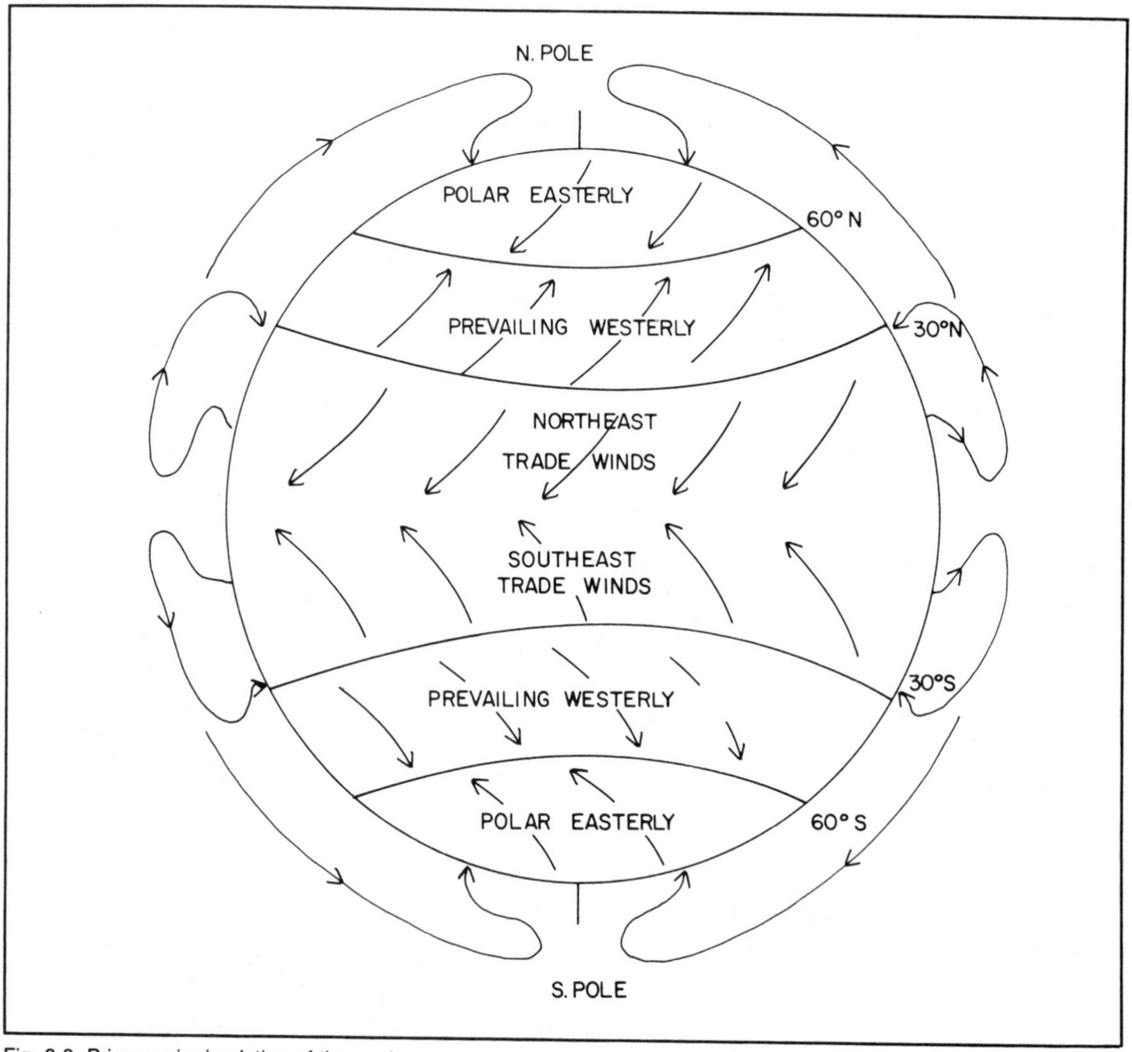
N. POLE
POLAR EASTERLY
60° N
PREVAILING WESTERLY
30°N
NORTHEAST
TRADE WINDS
SOUTHEAST
TRADE WINDS
PREVAILING WESTERLY
30°S
POLAR EASTERLY
60° S
S. POLE

Fig. 8-2. Primary air circulation of the earth.

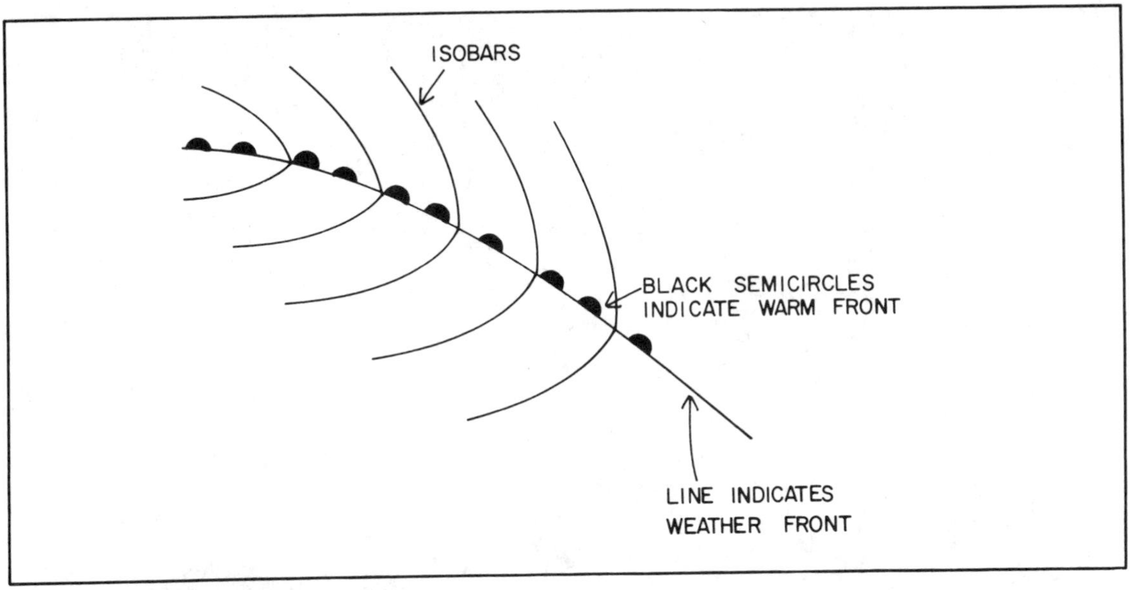
ISOBARS
BLACK SEMICIRCLES INDICATE WARM FRONT
LINE INDICATES WEATHER FRONT
Fig. 8-3. Warm front weather map symbol.

Winds in advance of a warm front will range from east to southeast and increase as the front approachs. If there is a barometer aboard, it will indicate steadily falling readings. Temperature will remain steady or rise, and visibility will remain good until shortly before the rains start.

As the warm front passes, the rains stop and the heavy clouds break up and start to clear. The wind will veer to the south and then to the southwest quite rapidly. The barometer readings will steady or they might continue to drop slowly. The temperature rises. Visibility improves from poor to fair. The sky remains mostly cloudy, some drizzle might continue, and then the weather will gradually clear.

Cold Front Passage

The weather sequence typical of the passage of a cold front differs considerably from the warm front passage just described. The cold front is shown on weather maps as a series of points or spikes along the line, indicating the location of the front. As with the semicircles of the warm front, the points of the cold front are on the side of the location line toward which the front is moving. (Fig. 8-10).

A cold front is the leading edge of a mass of air cooler than the air it is overtaking. Because cold air is heavier than warm air, it moves *under* rather than over the air in front of it (Fig. 8-11). Because the air close to the ground is slowed down by friction with

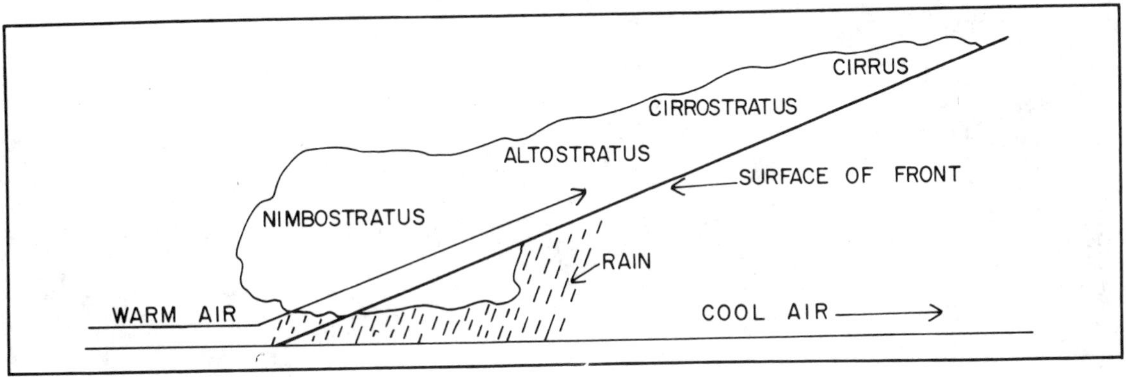
CIRRUS
CIRROSTRATUS
ALTOSTRATUS
SURFACE OF FRONT
NIMBOSTRATUS
RAIN
WARM AIR
COOL AIR
Fig. 8-4. Warm front in cross section.

Fig. 8-5. Cirrus clouds.

Fig. 8-6. Cirrostratus clouds.

Fig. 8-7. Altostratus clouds.

Fig. 8-8. Stratus clouds.

Fig. 8-9. Nimbostratus clouds.

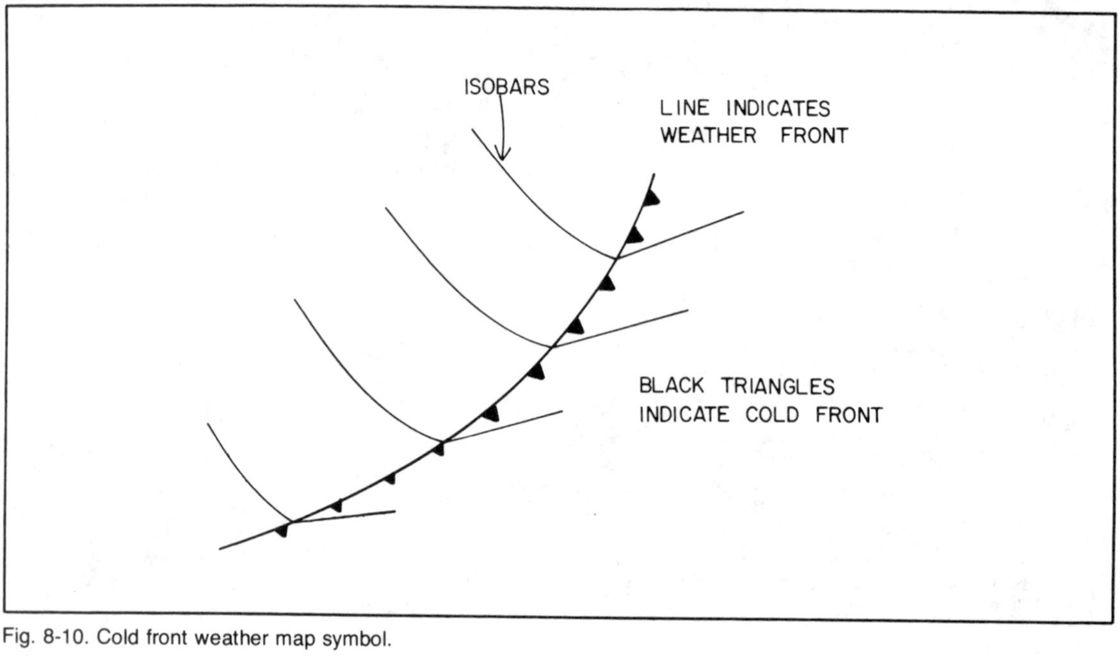

ISOBARS
LINE INDICATES
WEATHER FRONT
BLACK TRIANGLES
INDICATE COLD FRONT

Fig. 8-10. Cold front weather map symbol.

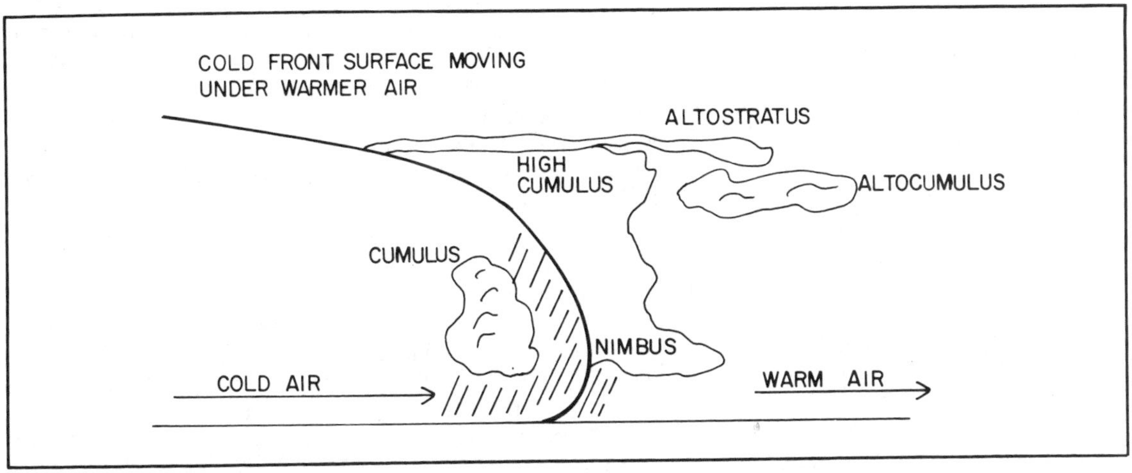
COLD FRONT SURFACE MOVING
UNDER WARMER AIR
ALTOSTRATUS
HIGH
CUMULUS
ALTOCUMULUS
CUMULUS
NIMBUS
COLD AIR
WARM AIR

Fig. 8-11. Cold front cross section.

the surface of the earth, the leading surface of a cold front becomes very steep. Normally, a cold front moves faster than the warmer air in front of it; this forces that warm air upward somewhat violently. This sudden uplifting of warm air causes rapid cooling which, in turn, produces cumulus and cumulonimbus type clouds (Fig. 8-12). These types of clouds give rise to frequent heavy showers.

Depending on the steepness of the front, the temperature differential between the air masses,

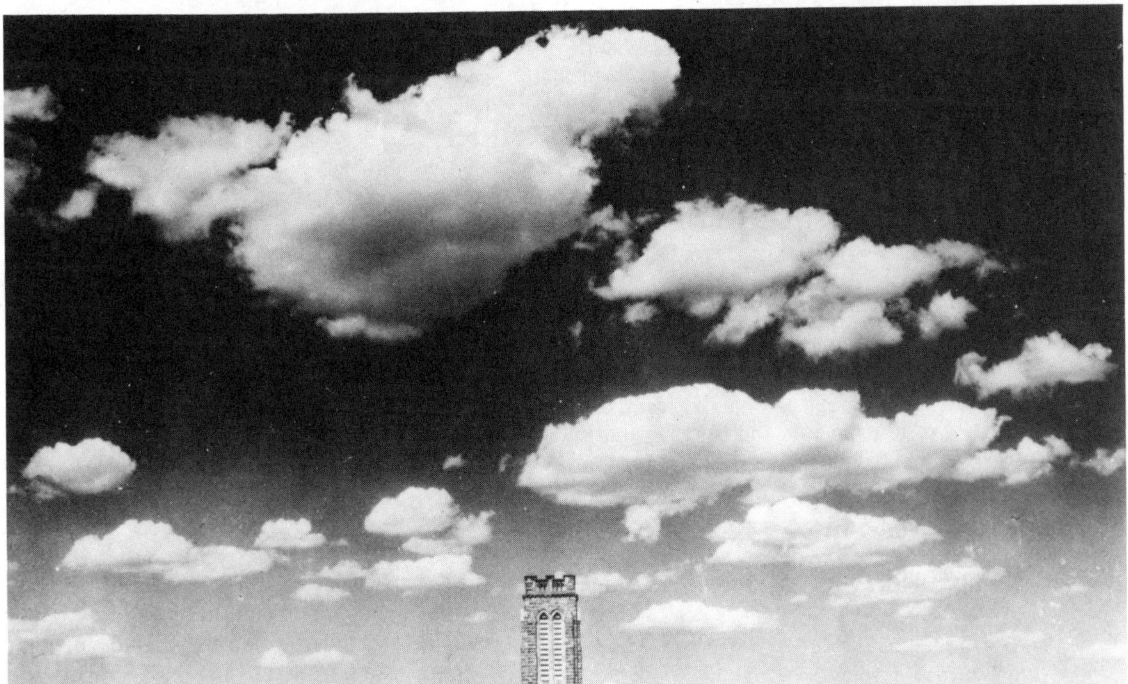

Fig. 8-12. Cumulus clouds.

and the temperature conditions within the warm mass, the resulting clouds and showers might develop as moderate to severe thunderstorms accompanied by extremely turbulent air conditions all along the front. Most of us have seen this cycle in the breakup of a summer heat wave by a series of thunderstorms followed by cooling weather.

For the sailor, the arrival of a cold front will be preceded by comparatively warm temperatures, high humidity, steady barometer readings, and scattered cumulus clouds. Winds will probably be south of west. As the front approaches, rising warm air will build up towering cumulus clouds that will become cumulonimbus as the front draws close. Heavy showers or thunderstorms follow and are accompanied by squally winds veering through west to northwest. The barometer will rise sharply with the arrival of cool, dense, high-pressure air. The temperature will drop abruptly, and visibility will greatly improve.

The cold front (after passing) will bring scattering cumulus clouds, strong northwest winds, a rising barometer, falling temperatures, and excellent visibility. All of the various changes in winds, temperatures, humidity, barometer readings, and visibility that occur with the passage of a cold front happen vastly more quickly than the changes that accompany the passage of a warm front. This is because the warm front passage is a gradual process occurring over a distance of 600 to 900 miles and a time span of one or two days; the cold front passage occurs in a matter of a few hours.

Stationary Front

In addition to the warm front passage and the cold front passage, other conditions and weather sequences can occur along meeting lines between air masses. Warm air replacing cold and cold replacing warm have both been discussed. In both instances the air masses were moving. Consider now the situation where two air masses—a warm and a cold—are in contact along a front but both are stationary. Conditions over a large geographical area are such that for a time both air masses are stopped. This is not an uncommon occurrence. It might continue for a matter of hours or for days.

From the point of view of the mariner, as long as the front remains stationary, the surface weather in its vicinity will resemble the weather pattern of the front described previously. When movement begins, often the cold air starts to move toward the warm. When this happens, the frontal surface slopes sharply downward in the direction of movement. The weather sequence takes on the characteristics of a common, garden variety cold front (which by now is exactly what it is).

Occluded Fronts

Another condition that can occur when air masses meet is termed an *occlusion*. When this happens, three air masses are involved: two cold and one warm. The two types of occlusions (Fig. 8-14) are a warm front occlusion and a cold front occlusion. When the coldest of the two cold masses is the last in line (Fig. 8-14A), it slides under both of the others. When the coldest is the first (Fig. 8-14B), both of the others ride up over it. In both types of occlusions as the front approaches, the cloud systems are approximately the same as those of the normal warm front because the long, tapering advance cloud wedge is the same. When the front passes, the clouds and precipitation take on the characteristics of a cold front passage.

To the small-boat sailor at sea, the warm front approach and the occluded front approach will be indistinguishable. The cloud sequences—steadily falling barometer, steady temperature, and east to southeast winds—are all the same. Radio weather reports might distinguish a warm front from an occlusion, but to that sailor at sea neither one is good news. In either case, rain, wind, and generally nasty conditions are coming. The best thing to do will be to get into a snug harbor as soon as possible.

TEMPERATE-ZONE CYCLONIC STORMS

As shown in Fig. 8-2, the primary air circulation system of the planet consists of easterly polar winds blowing from the poles down to latitudes of about 60° north and south. There the cold polar air meets warmer westerly winds from the temperate zone. At times, these winds flow smoothly by each other (Fig. 8-15A) and cause no disturbances. From time to time, however, polar air pushes south into the adjacent warm air. East of that intrusion of polar air, the warm temperate air bulges northward into the polar cold air (Fig. 8-15B).

The cold polar air continues to push southward, but develops a curve to the east (Fig. 8-15C).

Fig. 8-13. Cumulonimbus clouds.

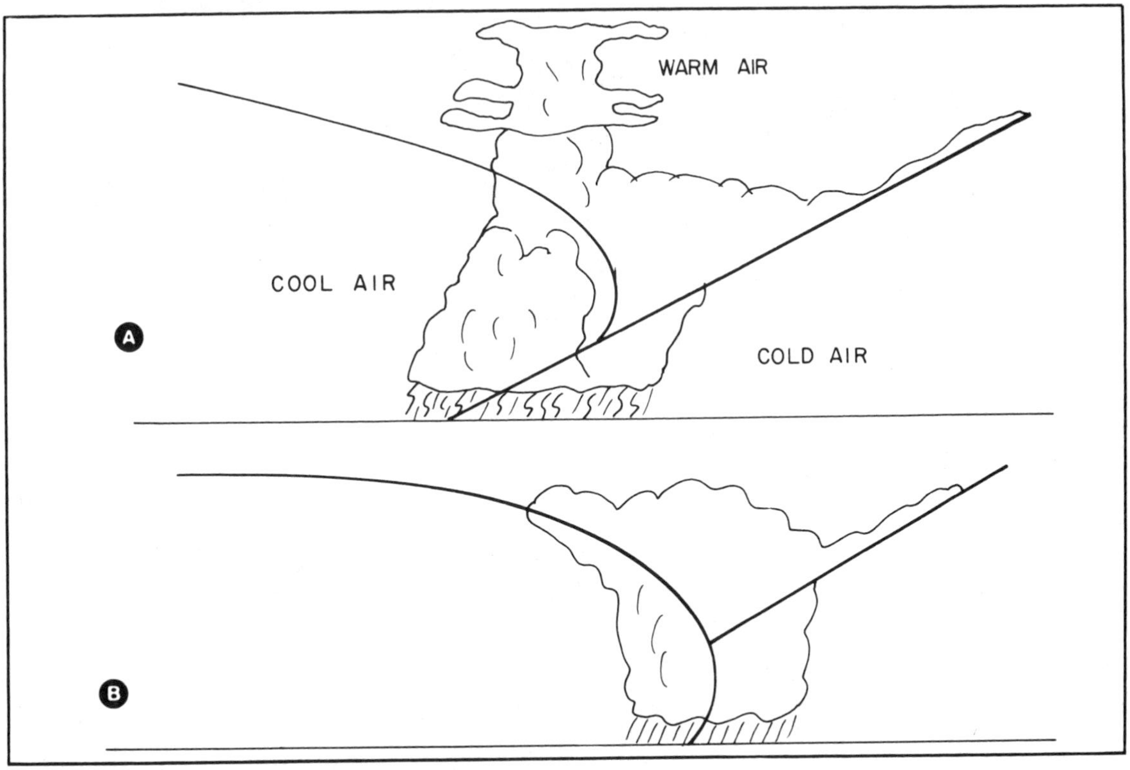
WARM AIR
COOL AIR
A
COLD AIR
B

Fig. 8-14. Occlusions (A) cold front (B) warm front.

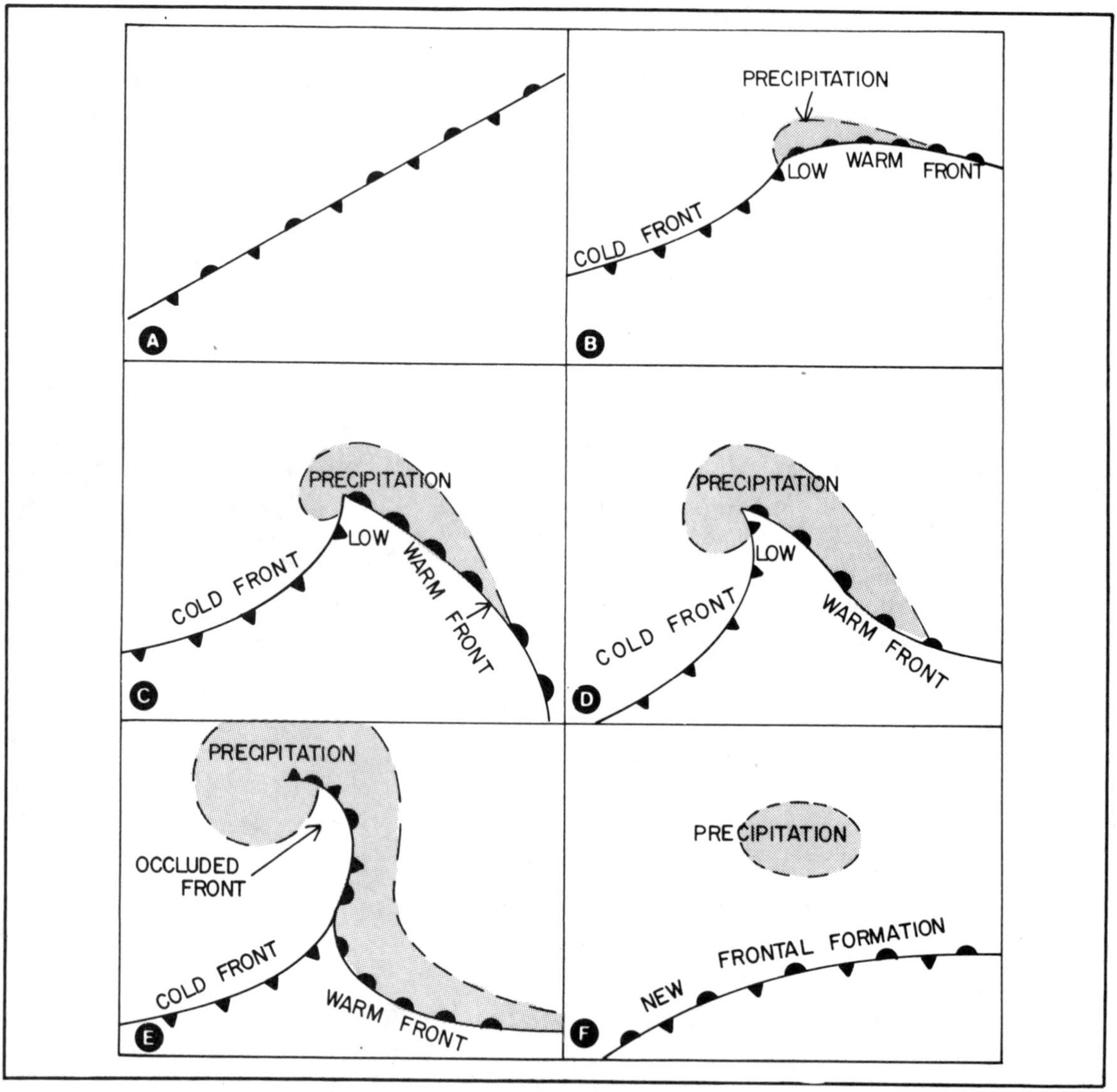
A
PRECIPITATION
LOW
WARM FRONT
COLD FRONT
B
PRECIPITATION
LOW
COLD FRONT
WARM FRONT
C
PRECIPITATION
LOW
COLD FRONT
WARM FRONT
D
PRECIPITATION
OCCLUDED FRONT
COLD FRONT
WARM FRONT
E
PRECIPITATION
NEW FRONTAL FORMATION
F

Fig. 8-15. Development of an extratropical cyclone (6 stages)

As the warm air bulge grows deeper it narrows. At the apex of the bulge, a distinct area of low-pressure air now exists. This is because the bulge consists of relatively warm air (the pressure of which is lower than the colder polar air around it).

A circular airflow swirls around the low-pressure center. This is followed by the development of two distinct fronts (Fig. 8-15D) curving south from the apex of the warm-air bulge. A warm front leads the movement of a warm-air mass, followed by a cold front in advance of the cold-air mass behind it. This is now a mature, fully developed cyclone.

For the observer located south of its center (Fig. 8-16), the first weather experienced will be the warm front passage as described previously. Cirrus clouds will be followed by cirrostratus, steadily lowering, thickening, and ending with nimbostratus and rain. Barometer readings will fall, temperature readings will rise, and the wind will be south of east. Passage of the front is marked by veering of the wind to southwest. The rain stops, the sky clears, the temperature rises, and everything seems fine. But that southwest wind, high humidity, and warm temperatures indicate that the cold front has yet to pass.

The fairly rapid appearance of large, cumulus clouds filling more and more of the sky signal the approach of the cold front. Gusty showers or thunderstorms indicate that it is here. Winds will veer through west to northwest and the barometer will rise as the temperature falls. With the return of clear skys and very good visibility, the cyclone has now passed and a period of good weather can be expected.

After reaching maturity, the cyclone itself is finally dissipated because the cold front moves faster than the warm one, and eventually overtakes it (Fig. 8-15E). This forms an occlusion that becomes longer and longer (Fig. 8-15F), cools the warm air by driving it higher and higher, and finally fills in the low-pressure center of warm air with high pressure cool air completing the dissipation of the storm.

Cyclonic storms do not necessarily occur singly. Particularly in winter (Fig. 8-17), but also at other times of the year, these storms occur in groups or families that result from a series of incursions of polar air into the temperate zone.

FOG

While more of a hazard in some areas than others, fog is present at times in all boating areas. In simple terms, fog is a cloud lying on the earth's surface instead of well above it. While in terms of its composition it is the same thing as a cloud, the two are formed quite differently. Clouds are formed primarily by rising air cooling down to its dew point; at that time a portion of its moisture content condenses out into very minute water droplets. Fog forms at the surface of the earth. Although fog and clouds are physically the same—being composed of a vast number of minute water droplets appearing to be suspended in the air—they differ in the processes by which they are formed.

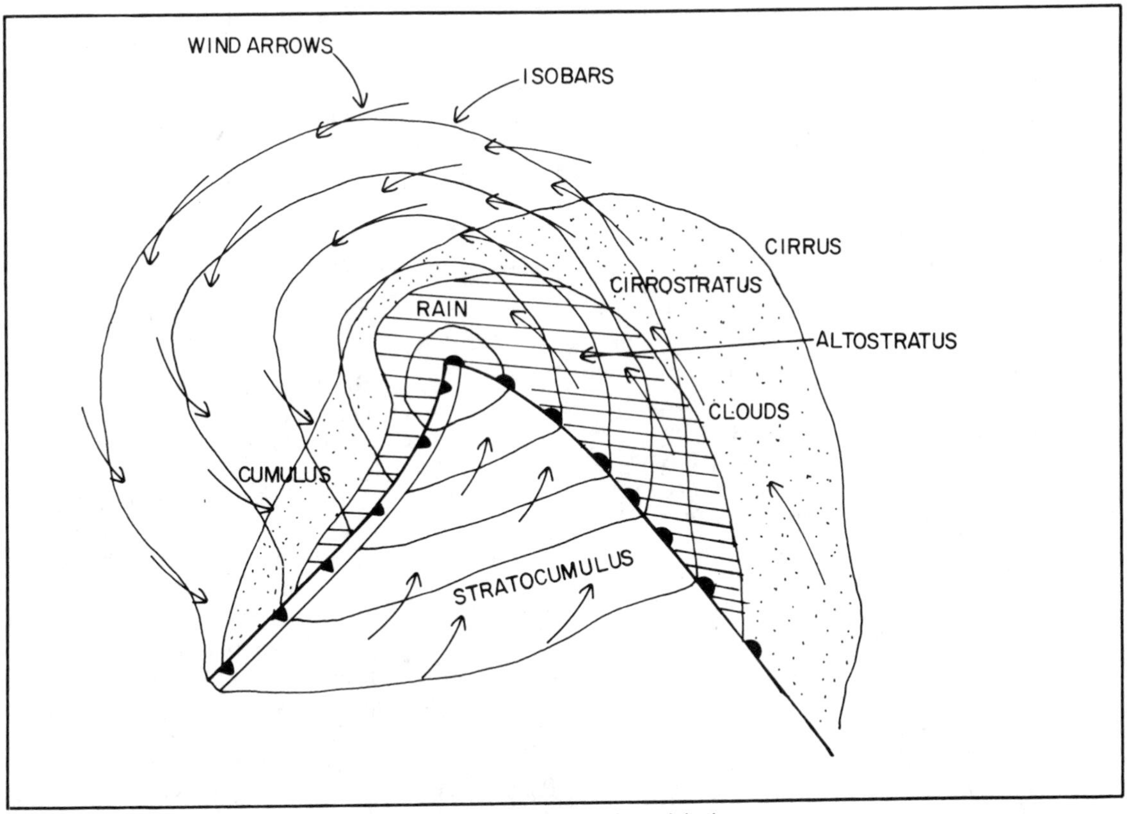
WIND ARROWS
ISOBARS
CIRRUS
CIRROSTRATUS
RAIN
ALTOSTRATUS
CLOUDS
CUMULUS
STRATOCUMULUS

Fig. 8-16. Fully mature cyclone; wind patterns, isobars, cloud and precipitation areas.

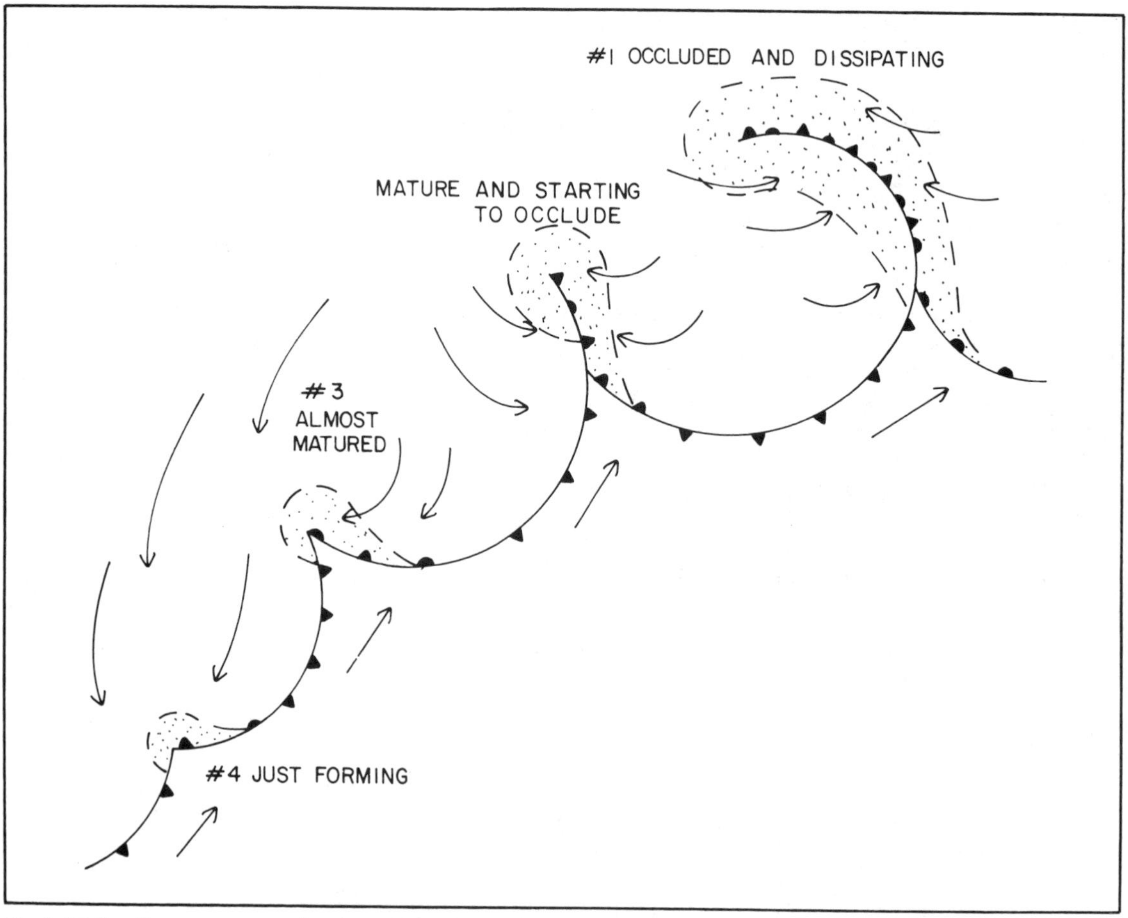
#1 OCCLUDED AND DISSIPATING
MATURE AND STARTING TO OCCLUDE
#3 ALMOST MATURED
#4 JUST FORMING

Fig. 8-17. Family or sequence of cyclones.

To the mariner, fog is a condition in which visibility is down to a point somewhere between terrible and nonexistent. The meteorologist, however, makes distinctions between the types of fog based on the ways in which they are formed. A modest knowledge of how fogs form is of considerable use to the sailor. Knowing how they form enables him often to predict such formation and take the precautions necessary to minimize danger and inconvenience. The various types of fog as classified by weathermen in order of their importance to the sailor are:

- ☐ Advection fog.
- ☐ Precipitation fog.
- ☐ Radiation fog.
- ☐ Sea smoke.
- ☐ Upslope fog.

Advection Fog

Advection is a technical term used to describe the horizontal movement of air. Advection fog results when warm, moist air blows over a water or land surface much colder than it. This kind of condition accounts for about four-fifths of all marine fogs. A wind somewhere between 4 and 15 knots must be blowing in order for advection fog to form. Once formed, the fog will continue as long as the wind direction and velocity remain constant. If the wind increases above about 15 knots, fog will usually lift and become low stratus clouds. As soon as the wind shifts so as to stop the flow of warm air over the cold surface, the fog will disappear.

Advection fog is particularly common on the Pacific Coast of the United States, where upwelling causes cold waters along the coast, and in the Great

Lakes in spring and early summer while the lake water is still cold from the previous winter.

Precipitation Fog

Another name for precipitation fog is *frontal fog* because it is associated with conditions in advance of the passage of a warm front overtaking a cold air mass. What happens is that warm air rises over a long wedge (Fig. 8-4) of retreating cold air. As it rises it cools. This causes its moisture to condense as clouds. The clouds thicken and finally this results in rain. As comparatively warm rain falls through the wedge of retreating cold air, it is partially evaporated as it falls. If the cold air becomes supersaturated with water vapor, which often happens, fog will result.

Any time a warm frontal system is predicted to pass through an area, a lively possibility exists that it will bring precipitation or frontal fog or both with it. This fog will change to rain as the front at ground level grows close. Precipitation will halt after the front has passed.

Radiation Fog

Radiation fog develops at night. It will happen on a clear night with very little breeze. On such a night, heat is radiated from the earth's surface into space, making that surface relatively cold. By conduction, the air next to the surface is cooled down to its dew point; this causes its moisture to condense into the minute water droplets of fog. A very light breeze, about 3 knots, is necessary to keep bringing warmer air in contact with the cold surface, thereby feeding the fog formation. This type of fog will form over land at night and often spreading out over adjacent waters. After sunrise, it dissipates as solar radiation rewarms the earth surface. The fog is evaporated from the bottom up in a process that reverses its formation. The same conditions favorable to the formation of radiation fog are also good indicators of fair weather for the following day.

Sea Smoke

Sea smoke occurs over tidal river estuaryles and bays, and open sea during very cold spells in winter. Occasionally it appears over lakes in the spring and fall. Sea smoke is not a serious problem for the average small-boat sailor because it occurs only when the air is very cold. Cold enough that most fellows will not want to be out on a bot! The process of its formation is almost a reversal of that for the formation of advection fog. In this case, very cold air passes over somewhat warmer water. By conduction, the surface air is warmed and moistened by contact with the water. As it mixes with the colder air above, the moisture picked up is condensed out as mist.

Upslope Fog

Upslope fog is strictly an inland phenomenon. It occurs when humid air flows over rising ground. The air cools as it rises, finally forcing the humidity to condense out as fog.

Boat Operation in Fog

The first point to be made about boat operation in a fog is simply do not operate unless it is absolutely necessary. When caught in a fog while under way, immediately drop anchor, if possible, and stay there until the fog lifts. Ring the bell, as required, to indicate to anyone silly enough to be moving about in the fog that a boat is there and anchored. Keep a sharp lookout.

Imagine a worst-case situation such that it is impossible to anchor—the water is too deep, or wind or tide conditions make anchorage impractical—and you are caught in fog underway at sea. There is no reason for panic. Because you are following the procedures discussed in Chapter 5, your vessel's present position is known with reasonable accuracy. From your present position, plot the course to the nearest buoy. Then work from buoy to buoy until a safe anchorage can be reached. It is better to make several short runs, even if this makes the total trip longer, than to make one straight, long run. By going from buoy to buoy, the progress of the vessel can be checked frequently. If one long run is made this cannot be done. A combination of steering errors and wind and current drift could place the vessel in danger.

Post lookouts both bow and stern. Sound proper fog signals. Proceed very slowly. If under engine, stop engines every so often to listen for nearby engine noises or other sounds. After reading Chapter 6, the compass was checked—now trust it! Sail by the compass; don't go by hunches and guesses. Steer all courses as carefully and accurately as possible. Let the helmsman concentrate on steer-

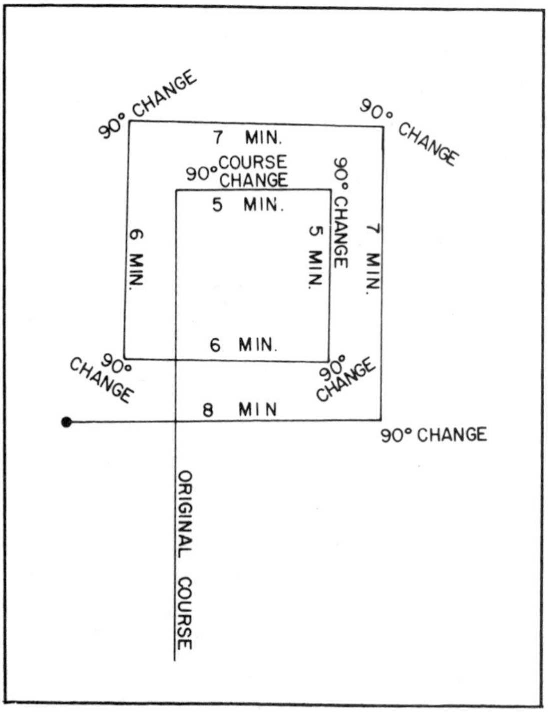
90° CHANGE
90° CHANGE
7 MIN.
90° COURSE CHANGE
90° CHANGE
5 MIN.
6 MIN.
5 MIN.
7 MIN.
6 MIN.
90° CHANGE
90° CHANGE
8 MIN
90° CHANGE
ORIGINAL COURSE

Fig. 8-18. Square search pattern.

ing while others handle the lookout chores. If there is a tachometer and a boat-speed curve, use time, speed, and distance computations along with the courses steered to project DR positions frequently. Above all proceed with calmness and deliberation.

As long as the buoy-to-buoy runs work out satisfactorily, continue them slowly and carefully. Should one of them not work out, so that at the expected time nothing can be found—*STOP*! Commence a square search pattern (Fig. 8-18) by turning 90° to starboard and running for 5 minutes at about 5 knots. Stop again. Listen for about 30 seconds. If nothing can be heard, turn 90° and run for another 5 minutes. Stop and listen. Turn 90° and run for another 6 minutes. Continue this pattern for between a ½ hour and an hour. Increase the running time by a minute after each two legs. If the search is still unsuccessful, stop it. Get out a sea anchor or drouge and wait until the fog lifts. Or if there is a radio telephone aboard, it is now time to call the Coast Guard and ask for an RDF fix on the boat's position. If they can give it, plot it on the chart and start over from there.

Remember that many situations can arise at sea in which the vessel and the people aboard her are most certainly in danger. Being merely lost in a fog is absolutely *not* one of them. It can cause definite inconvenience and possibly considerable discomfort as well, but a vessel lost in fog is not for that reason alone at any risk of sinking. Do not scream and whine to the Coast Guard the minute a buoy cannot be found and you have become confused about your location. Make every reasonable effort to solve the problem yourself. If all efforts fail, calling the Coast Guard for help in locating your position is justified. If they can help that's fine. If not simply wait it out. Shut down the engines to conserve fuel so when the fog lifts there will be enough left to make port. Shut off all lights except navigation lights to conserve batteries for engine starting when the fog lifts and for emergency radio transmission should a true emergency develop.

For reference regarding various common fog types, their origins, and their characteristics consult Fig. 8-19.

LOCALIZED HIGH-INTENSITY STORMS

The cold-core, temperate-zone cyclonic storm systems discussed previously are spread out over very large geographic areas—hundreds of square miles—but are of generally moderate intensity. Thunderstorms cover, by comparison very small geographic areas—a few square miles only—but are far more intense. Such storms can be extremely dangerous to small boats.

A thunderstorm begins as a cumulus cloud (Fig. 8-12). Such clouds are caused by the uplifting of warm air either by cold air moving under, as when a cold front arrives, or by convection resulting from air being heated by warm ground under it, making it expand and rise. In any case, it cools as it rises at a rate of about 5.5° per thousand feet until it reaches its dewpoint temperature. At that time moisture condenses and forms the cloud. When that happens, it usually slows down the current of rising air and brings the whole process to a gradual halt.

In cases when the air in the cloud continues to be warmer then the surrounding air, it continues to rise and develops quite a strong updraft (Fig. 8-20). By now the top of the cloud has reached heights where the temperature is well below freezing. Large amounts of raindrops and snowflakes have accumulated to the point where the updraft can no longer support them. Water begins to fall through

FACTOR	RADIATION FOG	ADVECTION TYPES: NORMAL	ADVECTION TYPES: LOCAL	ADVECTION TYPES: SEA BREEZE	ADVECTION TYPES: STEAM	PRECIPITATION
CAUSES	Nocturnal cooling of moist, stable air on clear nights with light winds	Moist, warm air blown by wind over cold surface	Moist, warm air blown by wind over cold surface	Moist, warm air blown by sea breeze over cold surface	Nearly saturated stable air blown by light wind over much warmer water surface	Warm rain falling through cold air near earth's surface
WHERE FORMED	Valleys, lowlands near lakes, rivers, swamps of middle latitudes	Sea coasts, blown inland, at sea	Lakes, coastal areas	Coastal areas	Rivers, small lakes, bays and harbors Extremely cold Arctic air over bays and tidal rivers	Any frontal area
CHARACTERISTICS	Local, forms at night, burns off after sun-rise, often patchy, can be dense	Extensive, drifts with wind, long lasting, often moderate, can be dense	Local, otherwise same as Normal	Local — moderate to thick	Local, often patchy, moderate to dense, forms in late evening or at night	Often extensive and long lasting if warm front type
EFFECT OF WINDS	Requires 3-5 mph. Stronger prevents formation	Carry fog, required for formation 4-10 mph.	REQUIRED FOR FORMATION			Strong winds will lift fog
CLOUDS	Night — hinder formation. Day hinder dissipation		HINDER FOG DISSIPATION			Provide rain for fog
SUNSHINE	Very little effect over water — causes fog to dissipate over land	None over water. Thins fog over land	SAME AS NORMAL		Clears fog in morning, warms air — reduces temperature contrast	Not available usually
LAND COOLING	Cause of fog	AIDS FORMATION OF FOG				
SEASON & TIME	Rare in summer, forms at night. More common in spring and fall when nights longer, days shorter	ANY — FORMS DAY OR NIGHT			Most frequent in fall — forms at night	Any — Forms day or night
DISSIPATION	Increase in wind. Warming of earth by sun	Increase in wind. Wind shift — Frontal passage	SAME AS NORMAL FOG			Passage of Front and wind shift.

Fig. 8-19. Fog table.

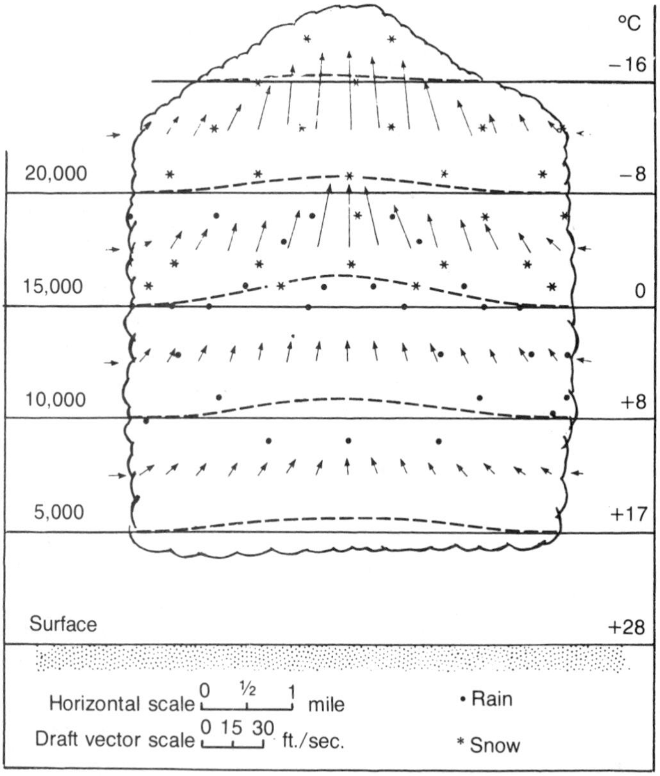
°C
−16
20,000
−8
15,000
0
10,000
+8
5,000
+17
Surface
+28
Horizontal scale 0 ½ 1 mile
Draft vector scale 0 15 30 ft./sec.
• Rain
* Snow

Schematic section through a cumulus cloud developing into a thunderstorm. The cloud is warmer than the surrounding air, and there is updraft more or less throughout the cloud. The diagram on the right shows typical temperature structure. *(After Byers and Braham.)*

Fig. 8-20. Development of a thunderstorm.

the cloud, turning part of the updraft into a downdraft.

At the ground level, a heavy downpour of rain begins; this marks the start of the mature stage (Fig. 8-21). At this point, updrafts and downdrafts are occurring side by side. The falling snow and rain cool the downdraft, which spreads out at ground level as a pool of wet, cool air (Fig. 8-22).

The start of the downdraft at ground level is marked by sudden strong gusts that are of brief duration, but which can reach velocities in excess of 70 mph. It is the gusty winds more than the rains of the mature thunderstorm that are a menace to the small boatman. As the mature stage progresses, the downdrafts overpower the updrafts, the cloud exhausts its water supply, the rain decreases, and finally the cloud disintegrates (Fig. 8-23).

The danger of being struck by lightning in a small boat is real. It does happen, but not very often. The truly serious danger presented by a thunderstorm to the operator of a small boat are those ferocious winds that occur with the onset of the downdraft as the storm matures.

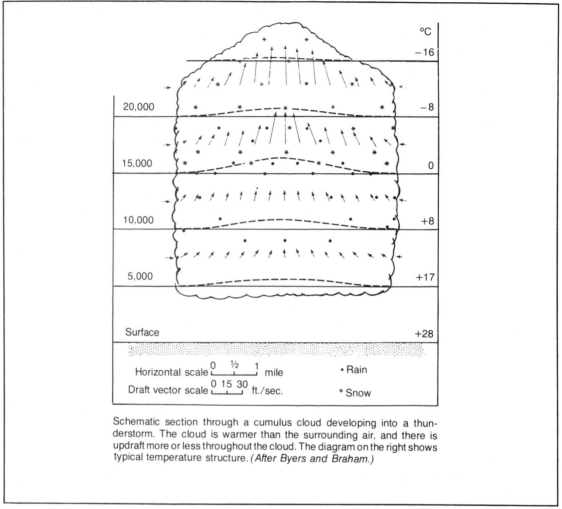

If you are in a small sailboat when a thunderstorm is seen approaching, play safe. Get the sails down. That downdraft gust can seemingly come out of nowhere and knock the boat down in a matter of seconds. If you are in a powerboat, secure anything that the wind might grab, head into the wind (face the coming storm), cut your speed to dead slow, and—when gusts hit—hold head to the wind until the blow passes.

Thunderstorms caused by the uplifting of warm air, which happens on the arrival of a cold front, can and do occur at any time of the day or night. Such storms result from a mass movement of air that is proceeding over a large geographical area independent of local conditions. The convection type of local origin develops within a more or less uniform air mass and is most likely to happen during hot summer afternoons.

When sailing, keep an eye on those fair weather puff ball clouds. If they begin to develop high, towering heads, watch for the typical anvil

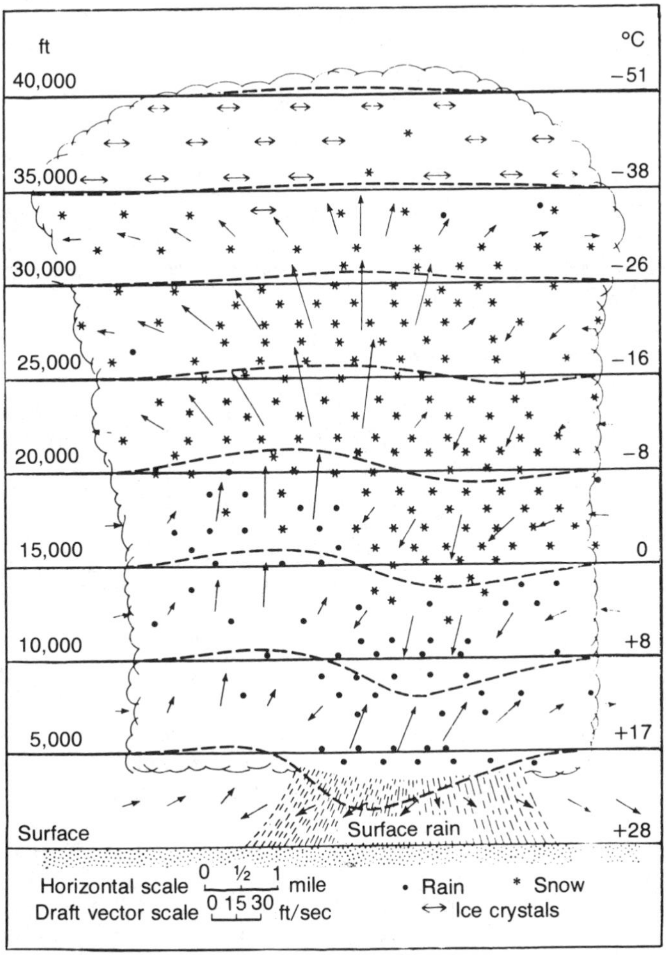

ft
°C
40,000
−51
35,000
−38
30,000
−26
25,000
−16
20,000
−8
15,000
0
10,000
+8
5,000
+17
Surface
Surface rain
+28
Horizontal scale 0 ½ 1 mile
Draft vector scale 0 15 30 ft/sec
• Rain
* Snow
↔ Ice crystals

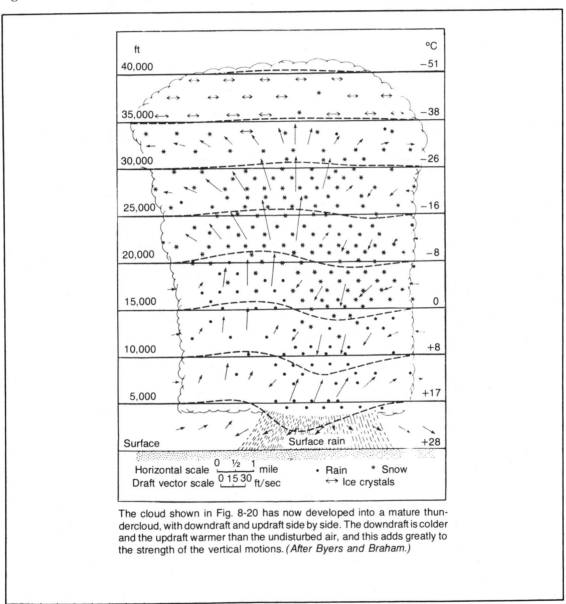

The cloud shown in Fig. 8-20 has now developed into a mature thundercloud, with downdraft and updraft side by side. The downdraft is colder and the updraft warmer than the undisturbed air, and this adds greatly to the strength of the vertical motions. *(After Byers and Braham.)*

Fig. 8-21. Mature thunderstorm.

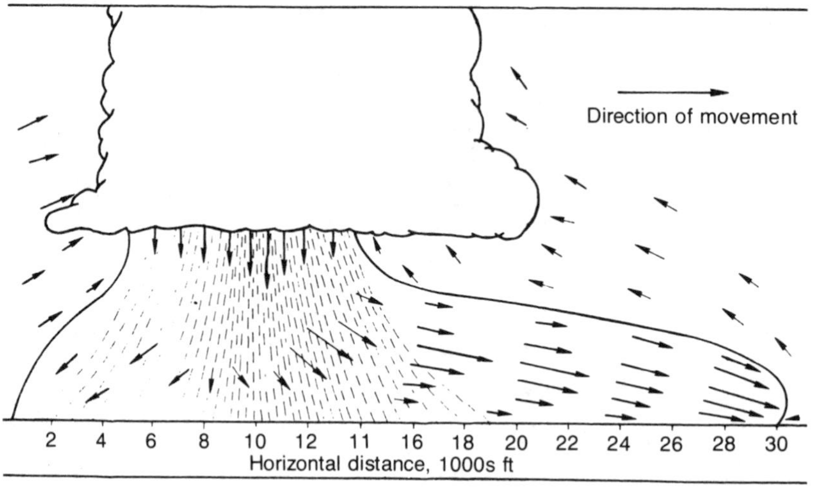

Direction of movement
2 4 6 8 10 12 11 16 18 20 22 24 26 28 30
Horizontal distance, 1000s ft

The downdraft spreads out like a wedge of cold air and arrives, with wind-gusts, ahead of the storm. *(After Byers and Braham.)*

Fig. 8-22. Ground section through mature thunderstorm.

shape indicative of a thunderhead (Fig. 8-24). Once that telltale, anvil-shaped head is spotted, track it to make certain it is not headed your way. Remember also that the head is not always visible. Any time the cumulus puff balls develop high tops and dark bottoms—watch out!

Tornadoes and Waterspouts

Tornadoes and waterspouts are closely related storm types. The tornado forms only over land. If its motion carries it out to sea, it becomes a waterspout. Although some waterspouts originate as tornadoes, others do not.

Fortunately, compared to other storm types, tornadoes cover very small areas; but where they hit they hit hard. The width of the storm varies from 20 or 30 yards across up to about a mile, and the length of the path along the ground averages between 3 and 6 miles. Wind speeds in the core have been impossible to measure as no gauge can stand up to them. Calculations based on the effects of those winds indicate velocities between 400 and 500 miles per hour must have occurred. Observed effects also indicate vertical air currents in the vicinity of 200 miles per hour in tornadoes.

In the Northern Hemisphere, tornadoes form most commonly in the spring and summer in the warm sector of a cyclone (Fig. 8-16). Once formed, they normally travel with the air mass toward the east to the northeast. They will commonly develop in the squall lines moving ahead of an advancing cold front. Thus they often occur in conjunction with thunderstorms. When conditions favorable to the formation of tornadoes occur, widespread warnings are issued immediately.

A sailor caught in a disturbance as violent as a tornado is not going to be able to do anything to protect himself. It is too late. A few hours earlier he could, and should, have protected himself by listening to the weather warnings on the radio. A day when thunderstorms and tornadoes are expected is just not a good day to go fishing.

Waterspouts are basically of two types. The tornado type forms over land and then moves out over the water. Consequently, it has all the same nasty characteristics as any other tornado. The true waterspout of marine origin is quite different. It is a convectional phenomenon normally associated with a heavy cumulus cloud. It can develop at any time in temperate or tropical latitudes in either generally fair weather or in foul.

Waterspouts often seem to start in two sections. First, the base of the cloud develops a small protuberance that grows into a funnel working its way slowly downward. Directly below this, the water surface becomes agitated, tossing spray, and the forming into a low mound of water that gradually grows upward into a funnel. It moves up toward the other funnel growing downward from the cloud. Finally they unite into a complete elongated whirling tube.

Once formed, the spout will last for perhaps half an hour, moving in the same direction as the parent cloud. It ends by either rolling up into the cloud or it thins in the center, dividing into two sections; then the upper part moves back up into the cloud while the lower part drops down into the water.

While occasionally a waterspout packs extremely violent winds, as often as not they are quite mild. That is they are mild compared to a tornado. While there are no recorded cases of modern ships being disasterously damaged by one, the vicinity of a waterspout is still no place for a small boat. Because they can be seen a long distance off and because they move fairly slowly, evasive action can be taken. I recall threading through three of them one day while making a passage of only about 40 miles from St. Thomas to Puerto Rico.

This discussion of violent storms would not be complete without mention of the hurricane, one of the most violent and awesome displays in nature. It

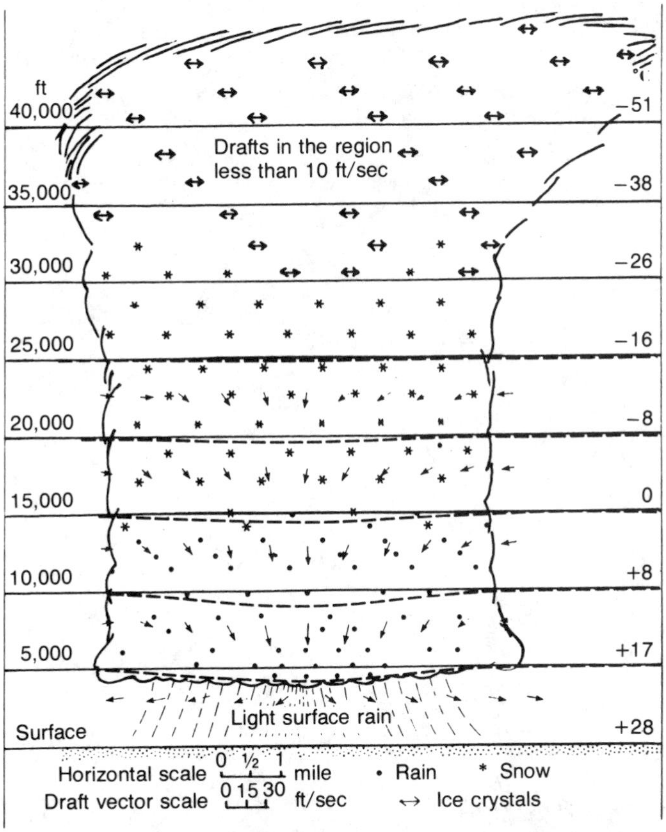

ft
40,000
35,000
30,000
25,000
20,000
15,000
10,000
5,000
Surface
−51
−38
−26
−16
−8
0
+8
+17
+28
Drafts in the region less than 10 ft/sec
Light surface rain
Horizontal scale 0 ½ 1 mile
Draft vector scale 0 15 30 ft/sec
• Rain
* Snow
↔ Ice crystals

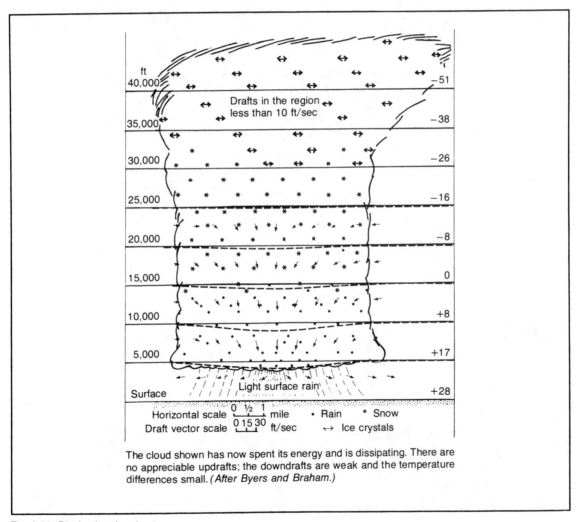

The cloud shown has now spent its energy and is dissipating. There are no appreciable updrafts; the downdrafts are weak and the temperature differences small. *(After Byers and Braham.)*

Fig. 8-23. Dissipating thunderstorm.

Fig. 8-24. Typical anvil-shaped cloud formation of a thunderhead.

is mentioned only for the purpose of pointing out why it will not be discussed in detail. Adequate information warning of the approach of a hurricane will enable the reader to be in port and safely secured well in advance of its arrival.

RADIO WEATHER BROADCASTS

An excellent series of Coastal Warning Facilities Charts updated annually are issued for the following areas:

- ☐ Eastport, ME to Montauk Point, NY.
- ☐ Montauk Pt., NY to Manasquan, NJ.
- ☐ Manasquan, NJ to Hatteras, NC.
- ☐ Hatteras, NC to Savannah, GA.
- ☐ Savannah, GA to Apalachicola, FL.
- ☐ Apalachicola, FL to Morgan City, LA.
- ☐ Morgan City, LA to Brownsville, TX.
- ☐ Point Conception, CA to the Mexican Border.
- ☐ Eurika, CA to Point Conception, CA.
- ☐ Canadian Border to Eurika, CA.
- ☐ Great Lakes: Michigan and Superior.
- ☐ Great Lakes: Erie, Huron and Ontario.
- ☐ Hawaiian Islands.
- ☐ Puerto Rico and Virgin Islands.
- ☐ Alaskan Waters.

These charts can be obtained from the Superintendent of Documents, U.S. Government Printing Office, Washington, D.C. 20402 if they are not available through local marine supply houses.

In addition to showing the locations of visual storm warnings, these charts list AM and FM commercial radio stations giving station call letters, broadcast frequency, times of weather broadcasts, and exact antenna locations so they can be used for positioning by radio direction finder.

In addition, the Weather Service operates a network of VHF stations broadcasting weather conditions in their local areas on a continuous basis. These stations report wind, weather, and sea conditions for a number of selected points nearby, summarize the major local weather influences, and provide short-term predictions (24 to 48 hours in advance).

The Coast Guard issues storm warnings along with other information relating to navigational hazards on VHF Channel 22A and AM. The average small boatman has a tendency to think that these weather reports are for commercial shipping. Not so! If anything, the small pleasure boatman needs them more than a commercial fisherman or a cargo carrier. The commercial vessel is far larger and can stand up to far worse weather conditions. The prudent small-boat captain will *always* check the current weather report before setting sail, and from time to time under way as well if conditions look at all questionable.

WEATHER OBSERVATION AND PREDICTION

Weather changes usually are not predictable for more than a few hours in advance when based on local observations only. But when such observations are combined with a study of the newspaper weather maps, the broadcast weather reports, and a lot of practice, it is possible to become very adept indeed at anticipating what is going to happen in an area with which the observer is familiar. Consider the kinds of things the sailor should watch as weather signals.

- ☐ Wind direction and velocity.
- ☐ Cloud types, amounts, speed, and direction of movement.
- ☐ Precipitation.
- ☐ Temperature and humidity.
- ☐ Pressure from a barometer if it is available.
- ☐ Sea conditions; wave height, direction, and type.
- ☐ Visibility; air clear or hazy.

Meaningful weather predictions cannot be made from one set of observations at one time. A series of observations over time are necessary to bring out trends and directions of movement and change. It becomes second nature for the experienced skipper to constantly watch, the wind, the clouds, the wave trains, and the changes that are gradually going on. Seldom will a sudden change in wind direction surprise him, and *never* will a rain or thunder squall find him unprepared in open waters. The darkening cumulonimbus cloud was visible many miles away a long time before it reached the position of the vessel.

Wind

Adequate estimates of wind velocity can be made without measuring instruments by observing its effect on the sea as well as on various objects on land such as trees, flags, or smoke from chimneys. The wind scale shown in Fig. 8-25 will be a helpful guide in learning to gauge wind velocities. Steady

BEAUFORT WIND SCALE

Wind Scale	Map Symbol	Seaman's Description of Wind	National Weather Service Terms	Knots	Estimating Velocities on Land
0		Calm	Calm	Less than 1	Smoke rises vertically.
1				1-2	
2		Light air	Light	3-7	Smoke drifts; wind vanes unmoved.
3		Light breeze		8-12	Wind felt on face; leaves rustle; ordinary vane moved by wind.
4		Gentle breeze	Gentle	13-17	Leaves and small twigs in constant motion; wind extends light flag.
5		Moderate breeze	Moderate	18-22	Raises dust and loose paper; small branches are moved.
6		Fresh breeze	Fresh	23-27	Small trees in leaf begin to sway; crested wavelets form on inland water.
7		Strong breeze	Strong	28-32	Large branches in motion; whistling heard in telegraph wires; umbrellas used with difficulty.
8		Moderate gale		33-37	Whole trees in motion; inconvenience felt in walking against the wind.
9		Fresh gale	Gale	38-42	Breaks twigs off trees; generally impedes progress.
10		Strong gale		43-47	Slight structural damage occurs.
11		Whole gale	Whole Gale	48-52	Trees uprooted; considerable structural damage occurs.
12					
13		Storm		53-57 58-62 63-67	Great structural damage.
14				68-72	
15		Hurricane	Hurricane	73-77	Greatest damage to waterfronts and buildings.

Fig. 8-25. Wind velocity scale.

Estimating Velocities on Sea	Sailing Conditions	Probable Mean Height of Waves in Feet	Description of Sea
Sea like a mirror.	Sailing vessels drift.	....	Calm (glassy)
Ripples form but without foam crests.	Sailing vessels have just enough wind to permit steerage way with wind free.	½	Rippled
Small wavelets. Crests have a glossy appearance and do not break.	Sailing vessels with topsails and light canvas are full-and-by and making about two knots.	1	Smooth
Large wavelets. Crests begin to break. Foam of glossy appearance. Perhaps scattered white caps.	Sailing vessels begin to heel over slightly under topsails and light canvas and make three knots full-and-by.	2½	
Small waves, becoming longer; fairly frequent white caps.	Sailing vessels heel over considerably on the wind under all sail. Motor boats may have some spray come over the bow.	5	Slight
Moderate waves, taking a more pronounced long form; many white caps are formed. Chance of some spray.	Sailing vessels begin to shorten sail. Motor boat skippers firmly hold the steering wheel and cushion the cruiser against wave shocks.	10	Moderate
Large waves begin to form. White foam crests are more extensive everywhere. Probably some spray.	Small craft warnings up and skippers of small vessels make for harbors.	15	Rough
Sea heaps up and white foam from breaking waves blown in streaks along direction of wind.	At sea, even larger sailing yachts and fishing smacks will heave to.	20	Very rough
Moderately high waves of greater length; edges of crests break into spindrift. Foam blown in well-marked streaks along direction of wind.	Storm warnings are hoisted. Large sailing yachts seek comfort lying to a sea anchor. Small cruisers certainly have no business out in such weather.	25	High
High waves. Dense streaks of foam along direction of wind. Sea begins to roll. Spray may affect visibility.	Steamships operate at reduced speed.	30	Higher
Very high waves with long, overhanging crests. Foam in great patches, blown in dense white streaks along direction of wind. Surface of sea takes a white appearance. The rolling of sea becomes heavy and shocklike. Visibility is affected.	Steamships operate at slowest speed.	35	Very high
Exceptionally high waves. (Small and medium-sized ships occasionally lost to view behind waves.) Sea completely covered with long white patches of foam lying along direction of wind. Edges of wave crests are blown into froth. Visibility affected.	Ships heave to or change course.	40	Exceptionally high
The air is filled with foam and spray. Sea completely white with driving spray. Visibility very seriously affected.	Ship's safety threatened.	45 or more	Phenomenal

practice both ashore and afloat for a couple months will help you develop an ability to judge wind velocity for the purpose of safely handling a small boat.

Anemometers (instruments for directly reading wind velocity) are often found on larger boats. They are fairly expensive gadgets and on a small boat a good many other instruments are likely to be higher on your priority list.

In Fig. 8-26, an excellent hand-held wind speed indicator is shown. This device is vastly less expensive than the larger anemometer and also has the additional advantage of requiring no installation. The handle folds to allow the unit to fit into a very compact storage case, and its accuracy is entirely adequate for your purposes.

Wind velocity and changes in it are very useful weather indicators. A steady wind indicates atmospheric stability and horizontal air movement with little vertical movement. Puffy, gusty winds are indicative of a considerable amount of vertical air movement. This type of movement accompanies the development of air-mass thunderheads. It also comes with the arrival of a cold front. This pushes warm air upward and produces squally weather such as occurs on the passage of the cold front of a cyclonic system.

A steady wind getting stronger from the northeast can mean the warm front of a cyclonic storm system is approaching. If the cloud cover is lowering and thickening at the same time, the warm front theory looks better yet. At this point, the warm front idea looks good if the wind *direction* fits.

The determination of wind direction on a moving boat is just a bit tricky. There is a big difference between *true wind* (the direction the wind is moving over the sea) and the *apparent wind*, which is the wind direction as perceived from the deck of a moving vessel (Fig. 8-27). The general rule of thumb is that the apparent wind (due to the movement of the vessel through the air) will always be stronger and further forward, relative to the ship's head, than the true wind. When in doubt as to true wind direction, the simple way to clear any question is to stop the boat. True wind and apparent wind will now be the same.

Figure 8-16 shows the wind patterns in the vicinity of a temperate zone cyclone, and clearly demonstrates the importance of wind *direction* as an

Wind Wizard
WIND SPEED INDICATOR

Fig. 8-26. Wind speed indicator.

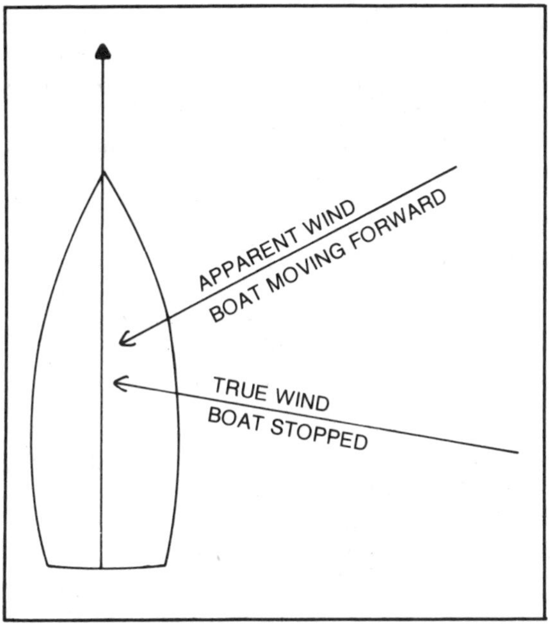
APPARENT WIND
BOAT MOVING FORWARD
TRUE WIND
BOAT STOPPED

Fig. 8-27. True and apparent wind.

indicator of coming weather. If the wind is from the east to southeast, bad weather is coming. If it is from the southwest, a period of fair weather will be followed by foul. When it moves to the northwest, fair weather should hold.

Clouds

The basic cloud types have been mentioned in connection with air masses and cyclonic systems. When high cirrus clouds are seen to gradually thicken and lower into heavier and heavier formations, the classic warm front approach seems to be in progress. Nevertheless, high cirrus "mare's tails" often appear, only to dissipate later in the day. Obviously they were not precursers of a warm front. Constant attention to the progression of cloud trains provides one of the best advance signals of coming weather changes and progressions.

The cloud formations observed while under way should be periodically compared with what would be expected in light of the weather reports prior to sailing. If those reports predicted a cloudy day, and it turned out clear—great! But, if they predicted a clear day, and it is not, keep track of what those clouds are saying. If they are layer type stratus clouds and they are getting constantly thicker, bad weather is coming; but it is coming slowly, and it is not likely to be particularly violent when it arrives.

If the forming clouds are cumulus types—and they are getting bigger and taller fairly rapidly—and it is still early in the day, thunderstorms are a lively possibility. If it is late in the day, the sun might drop low enough early enough to stop the vertical development of the clouds before the thunderstorm stage is reached. If an expected cold front moves in ahead of schedule, a squall line of tall, dark cumulus clouds is likely to define the edge of the advancing front, which is going to move rather rapidly. With it will come heavy rain and blustery winds, get into port ahead of it if at all possible!

Precipitation

Light rain or drizzle is likely to be persistent, particularly if accompanied by light to moderate winds. Those light winds indicate a slow-moving weather system. Heavy rain, particularly when accompanied by blustery winds, is likely to pass rapidly. Advection fog will persist until the wind either changes direction or velocity.

Temperature and Humidity

The normal daily fair-weather temperature cycle consists of gradually increasing temperature during the morning and early afternoon, decreasing again as the sun grows low in the afternoon sky. After sundown on land, there is rapid cooling of the ground and a consequent rapid cooling of the lower layers of air. Water, however, picks up heat slowly and loses it equally slowly. Thus the lower air layer over water does not cool nearly as sharply as over land after sundown.

Any variation in this normal daily temperature cycle indicates that a weather change is in progress. If it gets warm instead of cool at night, a warm air mass has moved in and rain or cloudy skies might come with it. If it cools instead of warming during the day, a cold mass might have moved in, bringing clear weather.

As temperature changes so will humidity. The humidity number that is given in weather reports is *relative humidity*. Warm air can hold more water vapor than cold air. The relative humidity percentage given in the weather summary is the percentage of water vapor in the air relative to the amount it could hold at its present temperature. As warm air cools, the absolute amount of water vapor in it has not changed, but its capacity to hold that vapor has. Consequently, dew, or fog at ground level, precipitates out of humid air. At varying altitudes, clouds form or rain falls. Dry air, that is air of low relative humidity, can cool considerably before dew or fog will form.

Pressure

The barometric pressure is another indicator of coming weather changes. A single barometer reading means nothing. A series of readings over time becomes meaningful by showing whether pressure is rising, dropping, or remaining constant. As a cyclonic system approaches, the barometer will steadily drop. With the passage of the warm front, it will stabilize. After the passage of a cold front, it rises sharply.

Whichever way the barometer is moving, both the direction of movement and the rate are significant. A barometer moving slowly upward indicates continued fair weather, with moderate winds and seas. Moving slowly downward will mean gradually worsening weather, but not violent storms. It is the rapid decline that accompanies the violent storm systems. The rapid rise, on the other hand, precedes rapid clearing with gusty winds and choppy seas.

Sea Condition

Only in very recent years have Westerners begun to realize how much we have to learn from the Polynesians and other Pacific Islanders about how to read the sea. Their navigators—with no clocks, sextants, compasses, charts, depth sounders, and or radio-direction finders—can locate an island invisible beyond the horizon by changes, impercepti ble to us, in the height, shape, and angle of wave trains.

We have a long way to go to reach that kind of capability, but the average sailor can still learn much from observation of the size, shape, and direction in which waves are moving. Very often wave trains moving in two or even three directions at the same time can be observed. On one occasion on the Ceiba Banks south of Ceiba Island in the Caribbean, I encountered wave trains coming from four directions at once!

The round-shaped rollers with long spaces between crests have come a long distance. Whatever wind or storm caused them is far away. It is the steeper waves, with sharper crests and shorter spaces between them, that originated close by. When the wind direction is the same as that of the seas, they will increase in size. Conditions will get worse.

If the seas are quite lumpy, but the wind direction differs from the seas, the wind will tend to knock the seas down and improve conditions. Any major storm system at sea will produce an advance guard of rising swells that will warn the observant sailor often before cloud changes or barometer readings have signaled coming trouble. The seasoned observer will combine the signals given by the sea condition with those given by cloud trains and wind directions to arrive at an estimate of what the weather is doing and what it is going to do.

A few years ago I was living in Puerto Rico, and I had occasion to review the Coast Guard records of serious boating accidents in the area over a period of a few years. These records covered noncommercial vessels (i.e., pleasure boats) and dealt only with serious injury, death to personnel, or extensive damage ranging to total loss of the vessels.

In an astonishing number of cases, the cause of the accidents was finally attributed to weather—adverse wind or sea conditions. In most cases, the skippers could and should have known that conditions were bad, and they should not have gone out. These people killed or injured themselves, their friends, and lost or damaged their vessels through ignorance or disregard of weather signals.

Chapter 9

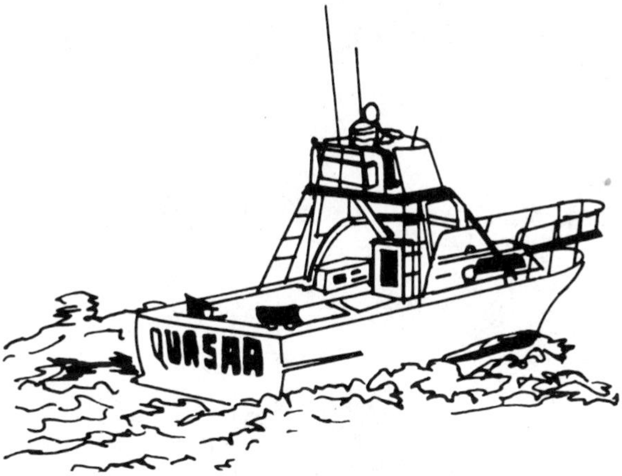
QUASAR

Safety

THE COAST GUARD KEEPS VERY EXTENSIVE records of pleasure-boat mishaps. A study of those records quickly reveals that most pleasure-boat mishaps, while charitably classified as accidents, are not accidents at all. An accident is defined as an unforseen or unexpected event proceeding from an unknown cause. Most boating "accidents" result from simple blunders on the part of the people involved.

Some were caused by mistakes in judgement resulting from inexperience, others resulted from inadequate care of hull, engine, or equipment, and still others resulted from navigational blunders. The essential point was that few indeed proceeded from an unknown cause.

A famous Admiral is reputed to have quipped, "An accident at sea can ruin your whole day." You do not need to have one to prove he was right! If you insist on having an "accident," the cause is likely to fall into one or more of these general categories:

☐ **The Boat:** poor maintenance—use of boat for wrong purpose—inoperative equipment—equipment missing.

☐ **Seamanship:** clumsy unskillful operation—ignorance of correct procedures or rules—sloppy housekeeping—tools or equipment aboard but inaccessible—reckless operation—disregard of weather warnings.

☐ **Navigation:** poor sights—sloppy plots—silly mathematical mistakes—outdated charts—wrong charts—no charts—no tidal information—no current information—unknown compass error—failure to keep track of position.

An extensive discussion of boat construction and maintenance or of seamanship is not a part of coastal navigation. Nevertheless, in any explanation of safety on the water all three become interlocked. Unhappy consequences often result not from a single cause, but rather from a combination of several factors joining to produce misfortune.

THE BOAT

Safely directing the movement of a boat from one place to another certainly requires that the navigator assure himself that the boat is of the type and in the proper condition to complete the intended trip. First comes the question of the type of boat.

A flat-bottom, shallow-draft, broad-beamed hull with a big deckhouse, large windows, and lots of living space is ideal for cruising rivers, harbors,

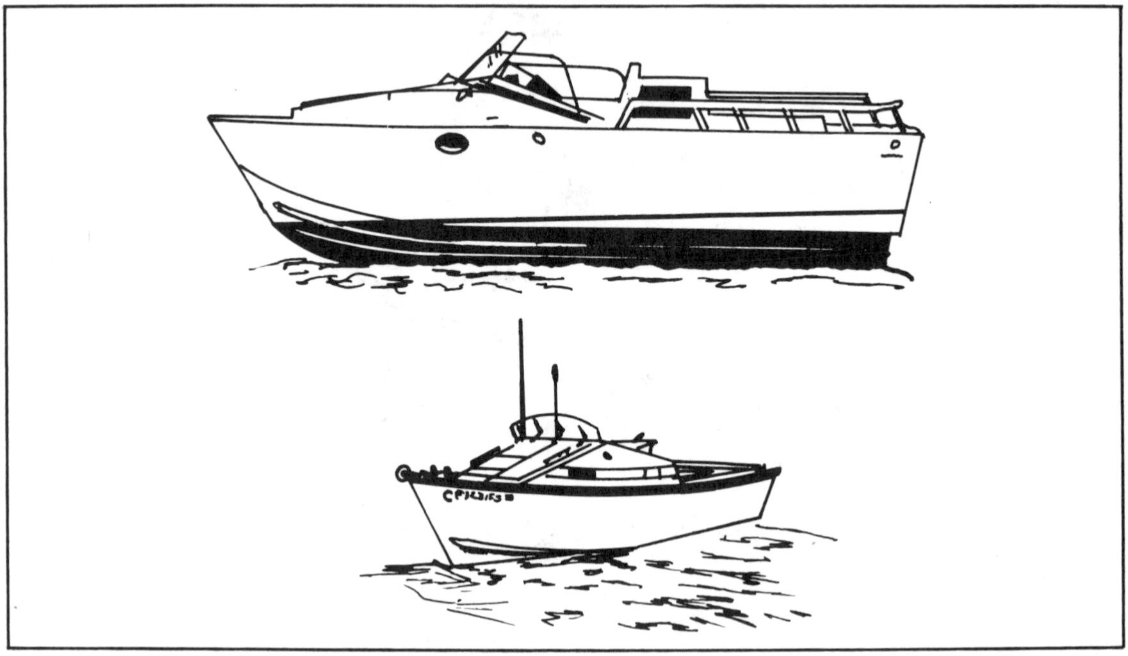

Fig. 9-1. Small V-bottom, open-sport fishing or ski boat.

and protected sounds where there might be numerous shoals. But such a boat will not be stable in heavy seas. To take this boat out in open ocean, except on a very, very calm day, is to invite disaster.

The high-speed, V-bottom, open-cockpit waterskiing and fishing boat (Fig. 9-1) takes its passengers quickly out to the fishing grounds and brings them back rapidly when the fishing is done. It can be operated safely in light to moderate seas. Living comfort (like the houseboat) it does not pretend to provide.

Lying somewhere between the previous two types, the small inboard/outboard cruiser (Fig. 9-2) is fairly fast, will stand up in a moderate sea, and provides much more protection and comfort than the open fishing boat.

For those who would rather sail than motor, the small cruising sailboat (Fig. 9-3) is an answer. Its a whole lot slower than a powerboat of the same size, but it rides vastly more comfortably in a seaway. It's quiet and wind power is much less expensive than gas or diesel fuel. The types with centerboards or retracting keels can come in from sea and operate in shoal water as well. The ones with fixed keels cannot go into the shoal areas, but they generally are roomier inside. The racing types have comparatively spartan accommodations, and are rigged and handled quite differently from the cruising sailboats.

Assuming the boat is of a type suitable for the intended trip and can comfortably accommodate the number of people it will carry, is it properly equipped and in satisfactory condition? The first indication is whether things simply look clean and orderly aboard. A boat that looks sloppy is very probably not well maintained.

Are the bilges clean and dry? Do the anchor and mooring lines look clean and sound or are they frayed and tired? Are engine and storage compartments neat and orderly or are they messy and confused?

Is the minimum required safety equipment aboard and accessible? This means lifejackets, fire extinguishers, a horn, a bell, running lights, and distress flares. In addition, is there a bilge pump, an anchor, spare lines, a first-aid kit, a tool kit, spare plugs for the engine, and tape to temporarily patch a torn sail on a sailboat? Safe operation cannot be expected unless all these items are aboard, and instantly available if needed.

The larger the boat, and the longer the trips

QUASAR

Fig. 9-2. Inboard/outboard cruisers (22 to 26 feet).

Fig. 9-3. Cruising sailboats (22 to 26 feet).

taken in her, the more extensive will be the measures necessary to provide for the comfort of the crew. These include food, drink (other than intoxicants), bedding and sleeping accommodations, warm clothing in case the weather turns cold, and foul weather gear in case it becomes stormy. If you were about to complain that while comfort is desirable it has nothing to do with safety—you are dead wrong! A cold, or wet, or hungry, or thirsty, or exhausted sailor is not by any means as alert as a comfortable, well-fed, well-rested one. The one who is not fully alert is the one who makes mistakes. Mistakes cause "accidents," remember?

All right, it appears that everything that should be on the boat is in fact here. Is everything also operating properly? Recently, an acquaintance went out for the day to a nearby offshore island. He started back late in the day; en route the engine died. There was no reason to be disturbed. After working over the engine for a while without success, he calmly picked up the radio-telephone and turned it on to call for assistance. Only then did he discover it was not working!

There might, after all, be some truth to the saying that God watches out for fools and drunks. This fool, who should have tested the radio before leaving the dock, was in luck. He and his passengers spent an uncomfortable, hungry, and thirsty night adrift before the wind finally came up the next day so he could sail back to port. While several families spent a worried night, things could have been a great deal worse.

When it is certain that the fuel tanks and the water tanks are filled, and the bilge pump, the running lights, and the radio are all operating, start the engine. After it has run a little while, is warmed up, is pumping a good stream of cooling water, and is firing smoothly, let go the mooring lines and get under way.

SEAMANSHIP

Successful boat handling involves partly the knowledge of various principles that apply to the operation of boats in general. It also involves practice in the application of those principles to the specific boat being used. Skill at boat handling comes only with practice. Just as dexterity at taking sights or plotting LOPs is only developed by working at it, smooth maneuvering of a boat is the result of suffering through a lot of not so smooth maneuvers.

The clumsiness of inexperience might cause damage no more serious than a scar on the bow of the boat or a splintered plank on the dock, but often the results are considerably worse. I watched a fellow in a small outboard ride the forward face rather than the back of a wave when entering a breaking inlet. As the crest of the wave broke, it hit his transom rather like a hammer hitting a nail. The boat and both occupants instantly disappeared in a welter of froth and foam. None survived.

About a year and a half ago, I made a run from San Diego to Oceanside (see Figs. 5-35 and 5-36). Some time before reaching Oceanside, we were caught in very dense fog. Immediately speed was cut to dead slow. When we heard what we thought might be the horn on the east jetty (for some reason there it is called the *south* jetty), we stopped to wait for the fog to lift. In an hour or so, it thinned considerably and gave us good visibility for entering the harbor. Immediately on entering, we went, as required, to the office of the harbor police to check in and get a dock assignment for the night. There we heard that about 20 minutes earlier someone following the sound of the horn to the harbor entrance had smashed on the rocks below it. He had come in at high speed, demolished the boat, and killed himself. Prudent seamanship would certainly not have allowed this unfortunate chap to run at high speed in thick fog.

Competent seamanship certainly includes knowledge as to how to handle the boat in adverse conditions of rough seas and high winds. It also includes the knowledge that the most masterful way of handling such conditions is to have noted the weather reports so that, instead of being out there getting pounded, you are here comfortably snugged down at the dock.

Dangerous departures from good seamanship usually result from either ignorance, lack of basic skills, or outright recklessness. For none of these is there a satisfactory excuse. Throughout the country, in nearly all communities where boating is popular, free classes in safe boating are offered by the U.S. Power Squadrons, the U.S. Coast Guard Auxiliary, or both. In addition, in many cities similar classes are offered as part of adult education programs or university extensions. The small-boat operator who is ignorant of nautical fundamentals would appear to remain so through sheer determination.

The lack of basic skills of the type that require practice—such as docking, leaving the dock, picking up a mooring, maneuvering in close quarters, or rescuing a person overboard under varying conditions of wind, sea, and current—can only be remedied by practice. This requires that you spend part of a morning or an afternoon on a number of different days practicing so as to get this experience under varying weather conditions. Go through each of these maneuvers over, and over, and over again. While you are doing this, you'll get a lot of kidding and hear a lot of lame attempts at humor from the dock. No matter!

Certainly, there is absolutely no question, it would be a lot more fun to be out fishing, waterskiing, snorkling, or doing just about anything other than backing and filling, and backing and filling again and again while being the butt of a lot of not-very-funny cracks from a seedy looking gang on the dock. Don't let it get to you. If those clowns had any wits at all, they too would be practicing things they need to learn and not wasting their time making fun of you!

Recklessness, machismo, or however you characterize the deliberate show-off, he is dangerous. That he is dangerous to himself is not what is important. He is a clear and very present menace to every person and every boat in his vicinity. A young chap was showing off to his girl friend, sitting next to him in a small outboard. He was going to give her a thrill by taking her through breaking surf. Whether she got the thrill or not we do not know. The way her legs were smashed she'll never dance again. Perhaps he is in luck. He won't have to live with what he did. His head was cracked open like an eggshell on the reef.

Not all of the reckless fools kill themselves. Another show-off trying to impress the girls at a hotel beach succeeded in very forcefully impressing an extremely beautiful one. He came roaring into the roped-off swimming area. Apparently he did not see the girl in the water. She dove to avoid being hit by the boat. She almost made it. The boat missed her but the propeller didn't. It got her once on the head and made six huge cuts across her back. She did recover, but she is not as beautiful now.

You were about to reassure yourself with the thought that these are not everyday accidents. Actually they are really fairly rare. Perhaps so, but that does not excuse them. They are not "accidents," they are the result of pure recklessness and complete disregard for the safety of others. Incidents of this type should not be rare; they should not happen at all!

Another factor that contributes to safe seamanship relates to equipment. The law requires that certain safety equipment be carried aboard boats; the requirements varying with the size of the boat. In addition to the legal requirements, there is a good deal of additional equipment that any prudent sailor will have aboard. Nevertheless, simply having all this stuff aboard accomplishes nothing unless you know how to use it and do use it at appropriate times. This naturally implies that when a piece of equipment is needed you can both find it and get it out so that it can be used.

When the boat is laboring in heavy seas, long *before* they might be needed, have the lifejackets broken out. Make certain the bilge pump is working before leaving the dock. Once the boat has started shipping water, it is time to use that pump—not test it. Should you need to fire a distress flare, you will not have a lot of time to remember in which locker the flares are stowed. There won't be much time to clear liquor bottles or cans of soda pop out of the way to get to them.

The competent seaman continually thinks ahead. He comes smoothly to dock in a brisk cross-wind because before he made his approach he planned his speed and angle to account for the wind. Once at the dock, the lines go out at once because they were in place and ready quite some time ago.

A skillful seaman is very seldom taken by surprise. Any time a fellow boatman attempts to entertain you with a hair-raising tale designed to demonstrate his intrepid courage and unparalleled skill in the face of the unexpected violence of wind or sea, he is making an admission of which he is unaware. What he is actually telling you is not how intrepid and skillful he is, but rather how careless he is. This is not to say he did not get into serious difficulties or that the efforts necessary to get out of them were less than heroic. The point is that, with very, very few exceptions, he should have seen what was coming and been prepared for it. Or better yet he should not have been at sea at all.

Just plain laziness is also the seaman's undoing from time to time. I suppose I am as guilty of this as the next fellow, but not just everybody has the distinction, as I do, of having very nearly lost a boat because of it. The boat was a 32-foot, ketch-rigged, wood-hull, Chesapeake Bay Bugeye. She had a great long centerboard that fitted into a great long centerboard trunk running down the middle of the cabin.

The centerboard drops from that trunk through the bottom of the hull into the water or is retracted into the trunk at will. In other words, a centerboard boat has a long narrow hole in its bottom. The only reason it doesn't sink is that the trunk, which is a housing for the board, goes well above the water line, *and* is very well sealed where it meets the hull.

With a wood boat, the way that joint is sealed is by caulking it. To do this the centerboard must be removed, an awkward operation, after which that narrow slot is still a very difficult place in which to work. So one spring, in Babylon, New York, while preparing the boat for its annual launching, I got a bit lazy. The previous summer that trunk had been tight enough not to cause any trouble. I decided to skip inspecting and working on it. Naturally, the perversity of inanimate objects being what it is, the wretched thing leaked from the time it was launched. The leak grew progressively worse until I finally had to enlist the help of a friend to take it back to the boatyard. All the way back, one of us sailed it while the other pumped to keep it afloat.

Laziness about keeping up the varnish will probably damage little more than appearances. Not so when it comes to the hull, through-hull fittings, routine engine maintenance, electrical system, or standing and running rigging on a sailboat.

NAVIGATION

From preceding chapters, you should be aware of some of the ways in which navigation, or more accurately navigational mistakes, can place a boat and its occupants in trouble or, worse yet, in danger. The distinction here is that trouble involves inconvenience, discomfort, expense, or any combination of the three. Danger means someone might be injured or killed. Careful, accurate navigation is vital to the safety of the boat and those who voyage in her.

The heart and core of navigation—whether along the coast or on the high seas—is knowing with reasonable accuracy where the boat is now, which way to go to get to its destination, and about how long it will take to get there. Everything I have discussed up to now is intended to contribute to answering these questions.

At this point, let's review some of these matters with particular reference to safety considerations. A logical place to start is with charts. With coastal navigation, there is no way that the importance of accurate charts and proper use of them can be exaggerated. The most common mistake people tend to make with regard to their charts (other than simply not having them aboard at all) is not keeping them up to date. There is a tendency sometimes to buy a chart along with the boat. Some 5 or 10 years later the same chart is still there.

One unfortunate factor contributing to this tendency is that new editions of charts are not issued on any sort of predictable schedule. Here's how it works. At intervals very widely spaced in time (often as long as 50 years!) A full-scale hydrographic survey is made of an area. After that a new edition of the chart is issued. The master drawings for that edition are kept at NOS.

From time to time, additional new information comes in to NOS regarding that area from various sources such as the Corps of Engineers report on the dredging of a channel, FCC reports on the approval of a broadcast antenna and its location or merchant ship captain reports an uncharted wreck. When enough additional information has been received and verified that NOS considers it warranted, a new edition is published.

How much is enough? This is a highly discretionary matter. A decision is based partly on the total number of changes that have piled up and partly on the importance of those changes to the safety of navigation. The result is that new editions of charts come out at totally irregular intervals. And when one does come out, your local newspapers, radio stations, and TV stations will mark this momentous occasion by taking no notice of it whatsoever. The only way you can find out about it is from a chart supplier or a fellow boatman who happened to hear about it. Well, yes, NOA puts out a monthly bulletin listing all the charts they publish with the dates of the latest editions, but we both know you are not going to bother to subscribe to it.

You are not going to bother to subscribe to the weekly *Notice to Mariners* either. You might see this posted at your yacht club or marina. It contains changes that have not yet appeared on the charts, and also changes of a temporary nature such as a beacon that is out while the light is being repaired.

In addition to keeping your charts up to date, be sure you have *all* available charts for the area in which you are sailing. It is very easy to skip paying $5 apiece for a couple harbor charts to places you don't go into very often anyway. It takes only one rotten night when you need one of those places as a harbor of refuge to more than justify the cost of the chart.

The most important precaution regarding the compass is to make that deviation table. Because you are sailing pleasure boats, you are normally out only in good weather with good visibility. Little discrepancies between the compass reading and the visible object don't seem very important. Check that compass against visible charted objects in daylight and clear weather. Then at night and in conditions of reduced visibility believe the instrument not your hunches!

In addition, be very careful not to leave anything near the compass that could disturb it. Remember my friend in the Caribbean who missed an entire island because a fellow came up to take over the wheel and dropped a pair of pliers too close to the compass.

The number of boats stranded or grounded due to inadequate or inaccurate tidal information is certainly enormous. If you are lucky and land on a sandbar, as I did once in Jones Inlet on Long Island, New York, you might escape with nothing more serious than acute embarrassment. If you land on rocks, you might be lucky to escape at all.

I have sailed on the northeast coast where 8-foot tides are not uncommon, the southwest coast where 4-foot to 6-foot tides are common, and in the Caribbean where the average tide is 1 foot and spring tides approach 2 feet. Sometimes the place with the very slight tide is the most dangerous. Where there is very little tide, the sailor has a tendency to forget it altogether. Most of the time this will not matter, but on the odd occasion when it does someone is in a world of trouble.

Strong tidal currents are found in areas that have considerable tidal rise and fall as well. The sailor operating in such places comes to expect them. What he must be careful about is the timing. High water and low water might also be very close to slack at one place while a couple miles away a very strong current is still running at the time of high and low waters. Depending on the speed of which a particular boat is capable, certain parts of a trip will have to be correctly timed or the boat will be incapable of getting through at all. On one occasion motoring a rather slow auxiliary sailboat down the East River in New York, I spent an hour between the Brooklyn and Manhattan Bridges fighting an adverse current. Finally, I tied up to wait for the current to change.

The sailor who fails to check the weather reports before setting out and who forgets to watch the weather changes while he is out is unwise indeed. In an inland lake surrounded by hills, there might be some excuse for being caught flatflooted by an adverse change in the weather. In open water, changes can be seen coming many miles and many hours away.

A few years ago on a regatta day in Long Island Sound, a sudden thunderstorm knocked down over 100 small sailboats in a matter of a few minutes. Among other things, this day is particularly remembered because of the very abnormality of it. Thunderstorms are among the most intense of weather disturbances. They can, however, be seen coming for quite a distance. There is no way that the people on over 100 boats failed to see that storm coming. Some underestimated its strength. Others were racing and, wanting to wait until the last minute to shorten sail, they ended by waiting too long.

When bad weather conditions are moving in, shorten sail and batten down too soon—not too late. Be prepared for the worst and smile brightly when it doesn't happen rather than the other way around.

Because positioning—knowing where the boat is—forms the most important part of navigation, the greatest care must be taken to avoid mistakes in this area. There are plenty of places where mistakes can and will creep in.

When taking bearings—whether with a hand-bearing compass or pelorus—it will not be possible to hold an object in the sights for any length of time when you are on a small boat. You've got to feel the rhythm of the boat's movement and catch the object in the sights several times at the same point in the cycle. Then average out the variations in the readings. Skill at taking bearings requires considerable work.

Plotting these bearings can open the door to lots of easy blunders. The most obvious, of course, is slippage of the plotting instrument. On a small boat, the area available for chart work will be small as well. Working in a cramped space on a boat that is squirming under you while you plot is not easy. You will have to plot several times before you become accurate at drawing course lines and bearings to find positions. This is another skill you were not born with!

After you've been bouncing around for a few hours, and your wits are a trifle addled anyway, it is not difficult to add 2 + 2 and get 5, 7 or even 9. Silly mathematical mistakes are quite common. Such mistakes usually show up in absurd totals, times, or locations.

While the list of things you can do wrong is almost endless—and to navigate properly places you on a very narrow path indeed—the first time you come in from sea and the place you were heading for is right dead ahead—you hit it exactly—there is a feeling of satisfaction that cannot be described. You have dealt with the elements: the wind, the sea, the boat, and the people on her. You have understood. You have tamed the forces around you, and in spite of them all you have placed that boat precisely where you wanted it to be.

Well done, captain!

Appendix

Distance of the horizon for heights of eye above sea level from 1′ to 920′ from The American Practical Navigator—DMAHC Pub. 9

TABLE 8

Distance of the Horizon

Height feet	Nautical miles	Statute miles	Height feet	Nautical miles	Statute miles	Height feet	Nautical miles	Statute miles
1	1.1	1.3	120	12.5	14.4	940	35.1	40.4
2	1.6	1.9	125	12.8	14.7	960	35.4	40.8
3	2.0	2.3	130	13.0	15.0	980	35.8	41.2
4	2.3	2.6	135	13.3	15.3	1,000	36.2	41.6
5	2.6	2.9	140	13.5	15.6	1,100	37.9	43.7
6	2.8	3.2	145	13.8	15.9	1,200	39.6	45.6
7	3.0	3.5	150	14.0	16.1	1,300	41.2	47.5
8	3.2	3.7	160	14.5	16.7	1,400	42.8	49.3
9	3.4	4.0	170	14.9	17.2	1,500	44.3	51.0
10	3.6	4.2	180	15.3	17.7	1,600	45.8	52.7
11	3.8	4.4	190	15.8	18.2	1,700	47.2	54.3
12	4.0	4.6	200	16.2	18.6	1,800	48.5	55.9
13	4.1	4.7	210	16.6	19.1	1,900	49.9	57.4
14	4.3	4.9	220	17.0	19.5	2,000	51.2	58.9
15	4.4	5.1	230	17.3	20.0	2,100	52.4	60.4
16	4.6	5.3	240	17.7	20.4	2,200	53.7	61.8
17	4.7	5.4	250	18.1	20.8	2,300	54.9	63.2
18	4.9	5.6	260	18.4	21.2	2,400	56.0	64.5
19	5.0	5.7	270	18.8	21.6	2,500	57.2	65.8
20	5.1	5.9	280	19.1	22.0	2,600	58.3	67.2
21	5.2	6.0	290	19.5	22.4	2,700	59.4	68.4
22	5.4	6.2	300	19.8	22.8	2,800	60.5	69.7
23	5.5	6.3	310	20.1	23.2	2,900	61.6	70.9
24	5.6	6.5	320	20.5	23.6	3,000	62.7	72.1
25	5.7	6.6	330	20.8	23.9	3,100	63.7	73.3
26	5.8	6.7	340	21.1	24.3	3,200	64.7	74.5
27	5.9	6.8	350	21.4	24.6	3,300	65.7	75.7
28	6.1	7.0	360	21.7	25.0	3,400	66.7	76.8
29	6.2	7.1	370	22.0	25.3	3,500	67.7	77.9
30	6.3	7.2	380	22.3	25.7	3,600	68.6	79.0
31	6.4	7.3	390	22.6	26.0	3,700	69.6	80.1
32	6.5	7.5	400	22.9	26.3	3,800	70.5	81.2
33	6.6	7.6	410	23.2	26.7	3,900	71.4	82.2
34	6.7	7.7	420	23.4	27.0	4,000	72.4	83.3
35	6.8	7.8	430	23.7	27.3	4,100	73.3	84.3
36	6.9	7.9	440	24.0	27.6	4,200	74.1	85.4
37	7.0	8.0	450	24.3	27.9	4,300	75.0	86.4
38	7.1	8.1	460	24.5	28.2	4,400	75.9	87.4
39	7.1	8.2	470	24.8	28.6	4,500	76.7	88.3
40	7.2	8.3	480	25.1	28.9	4,600	77.6	89.3
41	7.3	8.4	490	25.3	29.2	4,700	78.4	90.3
42	7.4	8.5	500	25.6	29.4	4,800	79.3	91.2
43	7.5	8.6	520	26.1	30.0	4,900	80.1	92.2
44	7.6	8.7	540	26.6	30.6	5,000	80.9	93.1
45	7.7	8.8	560	27.1	31.2	6,000	88.6	102.0
46	7.8	8.9	580	27.6	31.7	7,000	95.7	110.2
47	7.8	9.0	600	28.0	32.3	8,000	102.3	117.8
48	7.9	9.1	620	28.5	32.8	9,000	108.5	124.9
49	8.0	9.2	640	28.9	33.3	10,000	114.4	131.7
50	8.1	9.3	660	29.4	33.8	15,000	140.1	161.3
55	8.5	9.8	680	29.8	34.3	20,000	161.8	186.3
60	8.9	10.2	700	30.3	34.8	25,000	180.9	208.2
65	9.2	10.6	720	30.7	35.3	30,000	198.1	228.1
70	9.6	11.0	740	31.1	35.8	35,000	214.0	246.4
75	9.9	11.4	760	31.5	36.3	40,000	228.8	263.4
80	10.2	11.8	780	31.9	36.8	45,000	242.7	279.4
85	10.5	12.1	800	32.4	37.3	50,000	255.8	294.5
90	10.9	12.5	820	32.8	37.7	60,000	280.2	322.6
95	11.2	12.8	840	33.2	38.2	70,000	302.7	348.4
100	11.4	13.2	860	33.5	38.6	80,000	323.6	372.5
105	11.7	13.5	880	33.9	39.1	90,000	343.2	395.1
110	12.0	13.8	900	34.3	39.5	100,000	361.8	416.5
115	12.3	14.1	920	34.7	39.9	200,000	511.6	589.0

HT OF TIDE	
DATE	
LOCATION	
TIME	
REF STA	
HW TIME DIFF	
LW TIME DIFF	
HW HT DIFF	
LW HT DIFF	
REF STA HW/LW TIME	
HW/LW TIME DIFF	
SUB STA HW/LW TIME	
REF STA HW/LW HT	
HW/LW HT DIFF	
SUB STA HW/LW HT	
DURATION RISE FALL	
TIME FM NEAR TIDE	
RANGE OF TIDE	
HT OF NEAR TIDE	
CORR TABLE 3	
HT OF TIDE	
CHARTED DEPTH	
DEPTH OF WATER	
DRAFT	
CLEARANCE	

Blank Standard Form for Tide Calculation (after Dutton's).

VEL OF CURRENT	
DATE	
LOCATION	
TIME	
REF STA	
TIME DIFF SLACK WATER	
TIME DIFF MAX CURRENT	
VEL RATIO MAX FLOOD	
VEL RATIO MAX EBB	
FLOOD DIR	
EBB DIR	
REF STA SLACK WATER TIME	
TIME DIFF	
LOCAL STA SLACK WATER TIME	
REF STA MAX CURRENT TIME	
TIME DIFF	
LOCAL STA MAX CURRENT TIME	
REF STA MAX CURRENT VEL	
VEL RATIO	
LOCAL STA MAX CURRENT VEL	
INT BETWEEN SLACK AND DESIRED TIME	
INT BETWEEN SLACK AND MAX CURRENT	
MAX CURRENT	
FACTOR TABLE 3	
VELOCITY	
DIRECTION	

Form for Finding Velocity of Tidal Current at any time (after Dutton's).

WIND BAROMETER TABLE

WIND DIRECTION	BAROMETER REDUCED TO SEA LEVEL	CHARACTER OF WEATHER
SW to NW	30.10 to 30.20 and steady	Fair, with slight temperature changes for one or two days.
SW to NW	30.10 to 30.20 and rising rapidly	Fair followed within two days by rain.
SW to NW	30.20 and above and stationary	Continued fair with no decided temperature change.
SW to NW	30.20 and above and falling slowly	Slowly rising temperature and fair for two days.
S to SE	30.10 to 30.20 and falling slowly	Rain within twenty-four hours.
S to SE	30.10 to 30.20 and falling rapidly	Wind increasing in force, with rain within 12 to 24 hours.
SE to NE	30.10 to 30.20 and falling slowly	Rain in 12 to 18 hours.
SE to NE	30.10 to 30.20 and falling rapidly	Increasing wind and rain within 12 hours.
E to NE	30.10 and above and falling slowly	In summer with light winds rain may not fall for several days.
		In winter rain in 24 hours.
E to NE	30.10 and above and falling fast	In summer, rain probably in 12 hours.
		In winter, rain or snow, with increasing winds will often set in when the barometer begins to fall and the wind set in NE.
SE to NE	30.00 or below and falling slowly	Rain will continue 1 or 2 days.
SE to NE	30.00 or below and falling rapidly	Rain with high wind, followed within 36 hours by clearing and in winter colder.
S to SW	30.00 or below and rising slowly	Clearing in a few hours and fair for several days.
S to E	29.80 or below and falling rapidly	Severe storm imminent, followed in 24 hours by clearing and in winter colder.
E to N	29.80 or below and falling rapidly	Severe NE gale and heavy rain, winter heavy snow and cold wave.
Going to W	29.80 or below and rising rapidly	Clearing and colder.

Reproduced by Courtesy of National Weather Service.

Standard Chart Symbols from Chart No. 1.

A. The Coastline (Nature of the Coast) (see Introduction)

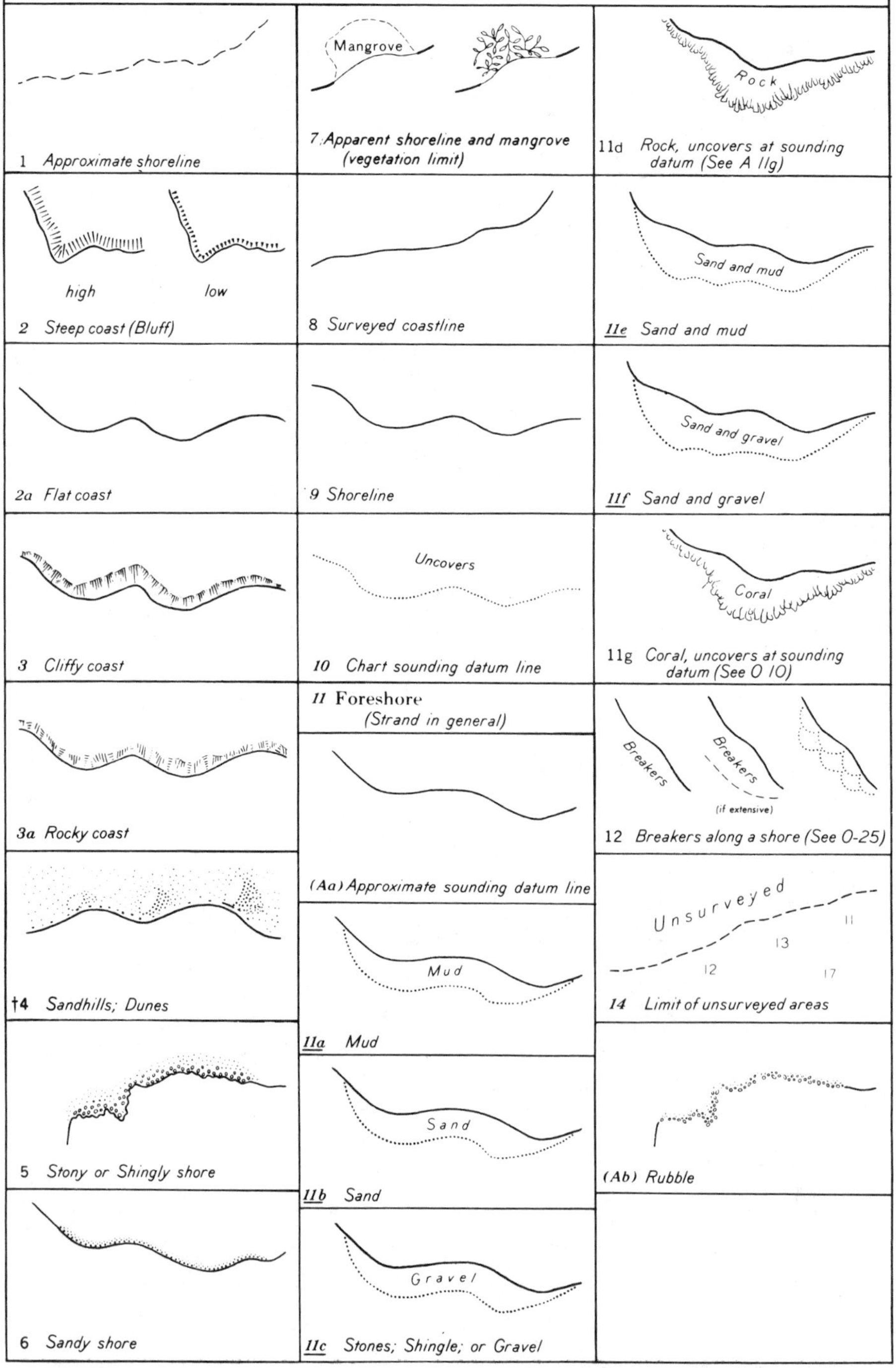
1 Approximate shoreline
Mangrove
7 Apparent shoreline and mangrove (vegetation limit)
Rock
11d Rock, uncovers at sounding datum (See A 11g)
high
low
2 Steep coast (Bluff)
8 Surveyed coastline
Sand and mud
11e Sand and mud
2a Flat coast
9 Shoreline
Sand and gravel
11f Sand and gravel
3 Cliffy coast
Uncovers
10 Chart sounding datum line
Coral
11g Coral, uncovers at sounding datum (See O 10)
3a Rocky coast
11 Foreshore (Strand in general)
Breakers
Breakers
(if extensive)
12 Breakers along a shore (See O-25)
†4 Sandhills; Dunes
(Aa) Approximate sounding datum line
Unsurveyed
13
11
12
17
14 Limit of unsurveyed areas
Mud
11a Mud
5 Stony or Shingly shore
Sand
11b Sand
(Ab) Rubble
6 Sandy shore
Gravel
11c Stones; Shingle; or Gravel

Symbols from Chart No. 1.

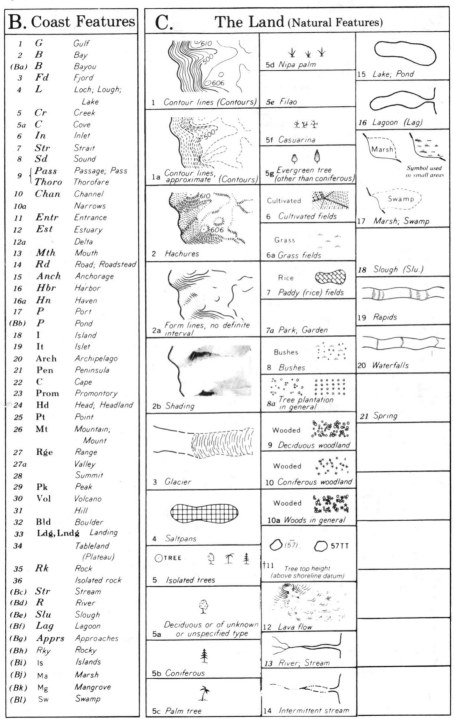

B. Coast Features

1	*G*	*Gulf*
2	*B*	*Bay*
(Ba)	*B*	*Bayou*
3	*Fd*	*Fjord*
4	*L*	*Loch; Lough; Lake*
5	*Cr*	*Creek*
5a	*C*	*Cove*
6	*In*	*Inlet*
7	*Str*	*Strait*
8	*Sd*	*Sound*
9	*Pass* / *Thoro*	*Passage; Pass* / *Thorofare*
10	*Chan*	*Channel*
10a		*Narrows*
11	*Entr*	*Entrance*
12	*Est*	*Estuary*
12a		*Delta*
13	*Mth*	*Mouth*
14	*Rd*	*Road; Roadstead*
15	*Anch*	*Anchorage*
16	*Hbr*	*Harbor*
16a	*Hn*	*Haven*
17	*P*	*Port*
(Bb)	*P*	*Pond*
18	I	*Island*
19	It	*Islet*
20	Arch	*Archipelago*
21	Pen	*Peninsula*
22	C	*Cape*
23	Prom	*Promontory*
24	Hd	*Head; Headland*
25	Pt	*Point*
26	Mt	*Mountain; Mount*
27	Rge	*Range*
27a		*Valley*
28		*Summit*
29	Pk	*Peak*
30	Vol	*Volcano*
31		*Hill*
32	Bld	*Boulder*
33	Ldg, Lndg	*Landing*
34		*Tableland (Plateau)*
35	*Rk*	*Rock*
36		*Isolated rock*
(Bc)	*Str*	*Stream*
(Bd)	*R*	*River*
(Be)	*Slu*	*Slough*
(Bf)	*Lag*	*Lagoon*
(Bg)	*Apprs*	*Approaches*
(Bh)	*Rky*	*Rocky*
(Bi)	Is	*Islands*
(Bj)	Ma	*Marsh*
(Bk)	Mg	*Mangrove*
(Bl)	Sw	*Swamp*

C. The Land (Natural Features)

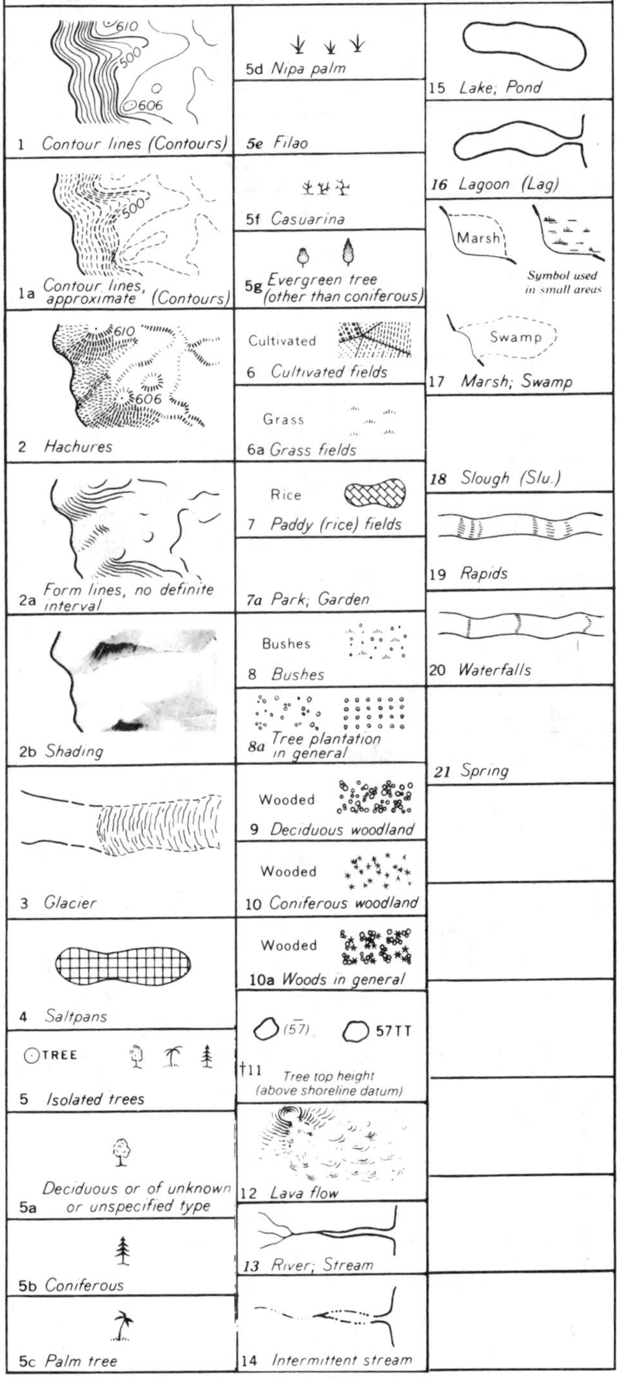
610
500
606
1 Contour lines (Contours)
500
1a Contour lines, approximate (Contours)
610
606
2 Hachures
2a Form lines, no definite interval
2b Shading
3 Glacier
4 Saltpans
TREE
5 Isolated trees
5a Deciduous or of unknown or unspecified type
5b Coniferous
5c Palm tree
5d Nipa palm
5e Filao
5f Casuarina
5g Evergreen tree (other than coniferous)
Cultivated
6 Cultivated fields
Grass
6a Grass fields
Rice
7 Paddy (rice) fields
7a Park; Garden
Bushes
8 Bushes
8a Tree plantation in general
Wooded
9 Deciduous woodland
Wooded
10 Coniferous woodland
Wooded
10a Woods in general
(57)
57TT
†11
Tree top height (above shoreline datum)
12 Lava flow
13 River; Stream
14 Intermittent stream
15 Lake; Pond
16 Lagoon (Lag)
Marsh
Symbol used in small areas
Swamp
17 Marsh; Swamp
18 Slough (Slu.)
19 Rapids
20 Waterfalls
21 Spring

Symbols from Chart No. 1.

D. Control Points

1	△		*Triangulation point (station)*
1a			*Astronomic station*
2	○	*(See In)*	*Fixed point (landmark, position accurate)*
(Da)	∘	*(See Io)*	*Fixed point (landmark, position approx.)*
3	· 256		*Summit of height (Peak) (when not a landmark)*
(Db)	 256		*Peak, accentuated by contours*
(Dc)	 256		*Peak, accentuated by hachures*
(Dd)			*Peak, elevation not determined*
(De)	⊙ 256		*Peak, when a landmark*
4	⊕	Obs Spot	*Observation spot*
**5*		BM	*Bench mark*
6	View X		*View point*
7			*Datum point for grid of a plan*
8			*Graphical triangulation point*
9		Astro	*Astronomical*
10		Tri	*Triangulation*
(Df)		C of E	*Corps of Engineers*
12			*Great trigonometrical survey station*
13			*Traverse station*
14		Bdy Mon	*Boundary monument*
(Dg)	◇		*International boundary monument*

E. Units

1	hr, h	*Hour*
2	m, min	*Minute (of time)*
3	sec, s	*Second (of time)*
4	m	*Meter*
4a	dm	*Decimeter*
4b	cm	*Centimeter*
4c	mm	*Millimeter*
4d	m^2	*Square meter*
4e	m^3	*Cubic meter*
5	km	*Kilometer(s)*
6	in, ins	*Inch(es)*
7	ft	*Foot, feet*
8	yd, yds	*Yard(s)*
9	fm, fms	*Fathom(s)*
10	cbl	*Cable length*
11	M, Mi, NMi, NM	*Nautical mile(s)*
12	kn	*Knot(s)*
12a	t	*Tonne (metric ton = 2,204.6 lbs.)*
12b	cd	*Candela (new candle)*
13	lat	*Latitude*
14	long	*Longitude*
14a		*Greenwich*
15	pub	*Publication*
16	Ed	*Edition*
17	corr	*Correction*
18	alt	*Altitude*
19	ht; elev	*Height; Elevation*
20	°	*Degree*
21	′	*Minute (of arc)*
22	″	*Second (of arc)*
23	No	*Number*
(Ea)	St M, St Mi	*Statute mile*
(Eb)	μsec, μs	*Microsecond*
(Ec)	Hz	*Hertz (cps)*
(Ed)	kHz	*Kilohertz (kc)*
(Ee)	MHz	*Megahertz (Mc)*
(Ef)	cps, c/s	*Cycles/second (Hz)*
(Eg)	kc	*Kilocycle (kHz)*
(Eh)	Mc	*Megacycle (MHz)*
(Ei)	T	*Ton (U.S. short ton = 2,000 lbs.)*

F. Adjectives, Adverbs, Nouns, and Other Words

1	gt	*Great*
2	lit	*Little*
3	Lrg	*Large*
4	sml	*Small*
5		*Outer*
6		*Inner*
7	mid	*Middle*
8		*Old*
9	anc	*Ancient*
10		*New*
11	St	*Saint*
12	CONSPIC	*Conspicuous*
13		*Remarkable*
14	D, Destr	*Destroyed*
15		*Projected*
16	dist	*Distant*
17	abt	*About*
18		*See chart*
18a		*See plan*
19		*Lighted; Luminous*
20	sub	*Submarine*
21		*Eventual*
22	AERO	*Aeronautical*
23		*Higher*
23a		*Lower*
24	exper	*Experimental*
25	discontd	*Discontinued*
26	prohib	*Prohibited*
27	explos	*Explosive*
28	estab	*Established*
29	elec	*Electric*
30	priv	*Private, Privately*
31	prom	*Prominent*
32	std	*Standard*
33	subm	*Submerged*
34	approx	*Approximate*
35		*Maritime*
36	maintd	*Maintained*
37	aband	*Abandoned*
38	temp	*Temporary*
39	occas	*Occasional*
40	extr	*Extreme*
41		*Navigable*
42	N M	*Notice to Mariners*
(Fa)	L N M	*Local Notice to Mariners*
43		*Sailing Directions*
44		*List of Lights*
(Fb)	unverd	*Unverified*
(Fc)	AUTH	*Authorized*
(Fd)	CL	*Clearance*
(Fe)	cor	*Corner*
(Ff)	concr	*Concrete*
(Fg)	fl	*Flood*
(Fh)	mod	*Moderate*
(Fi)	bet	*Between*
(Fj)	1st	*First*
(Fk)	2nd, 2d	*Second*
(Fl)	3rd, 3d	*Third*
(Fm)	4th	*Fourth*
(Fn)	DW	*Deep Water*
(Fo)	min	*Minimum*
(Fp)	max	*Maximum*
(Fq)	N'ly	*Northerly*
(Fr)	S'ly	*Southerly*
(Fs)	E'ly	*Easterly*
(Ft)	W'ly	*Westerly*
(Fu)	Sk	*Stroke*
(Fv)	Restr	*Restricted*
†*(Fw)*	Bl	*Blast*
†*(Fx)*	CFR	*Code of Federal Regulations*
†*(Fy)*	COLREGS	*International Regulations for Preventing Collisions at Sea, 1972*
†*(Fz)*	IWW	*Intracoastal Waterway*

Symbols from Chart No. 1.

G. Ports and Harbors

No.	Symbol	Abbreviation	Meaning
1	⚓	Anch	*Anchorage (large vessels)*
2	⚓ ⚓	Anch	*Anchorage (small vessels)*
3		Hbr	*Harbor*
4		Hn	*Haven*
5		P	*Port*
6		Bkw	*Breakwater*
6a			*Dike*
7			*Mole*
8			*Jetty (partly below MHW)*
8a			*Submerged jetty*
(Ga)			*Jetty (small scale)*
9		Pier	*Pier*
10			*Spit*
11			*Groin (partly below MHW)*
†12	ANCH PROHIBITED	ANCH PROHIB	*Anchorage prohibited (screen optional)(See P 25)*
12a			*Anchorage reserved*
12b	QUARANTINE ANCHORAGE	QUAR ANCH	*Quarantine anchorage*
13	Spoil Area		*Spoil ground (See P 11)-* *(Dump Site)*
(Gb)	Dumping Ground		*Dumping ground (depths may be less than indicated)* *(Dump Site)*
(Gc)	80 83 85 Disposal Area depths from survey of JUNE 1972 90 98		*Disposal area (Dump Site)*
(Gd)	Ⓟ		*Pump-out facilities*
14		Fsh stks	*Fisheries; Fishing stakes*
14a			*Fish trap; Fish weirs (actual shape charted)*
14b			*Duck blind*
15			*Tuna nets (See G 14a)*
15a	Oys	Oys	*Oyster bed*
16		Ldg, Lndg	*Landing place*
17			*Watering place*
18		Whf	*Wharf*
19			*Quay*

No.	Symbol	Abbreviation	Meaning
20			*Berth*
20a	(14)		*Anchoring berth*
20b	3		*Berth number*
21	∘	Dol	*Dolphin*
†22	∘		*Bollard*
23			*Mooring ring*
24			*Crane*
25			*Landing stage*
25a			*Landing stairs*
26		Quar	*Quarantine*
27			*Lazaret*
†28	Hbr Mr	Harbor Master	*Harbormaster's office*
29		Cus Ho	*Customhouse*
30			*Fishing harbor*
31			*Winter harbor*
32			*Refuge harbor*
33		B Hbr	*Boat harbor*
34			*Stranding harbor (uncovers at LW)*
35			*Dock*
36			*Drydock (actual shape on large-scale charts)*
37			*Floating dock (actual shape on large-scale charts)*
38			*Gridiron; Careening grid*
39			*Patent slip; Slipway; Marine railway*
39a		Ramp	*Ramp*
40	Lock		*Lock (point upstream) (See H 13)*
41			*Wetdock*
42			*Shipyard*
43			*Lumber yard*
44		Health Office	*Health officer's office*
45		Hk	*Hulk (actual shape on large-scale charts) (See O 11)*
46	PROHIBITED AREA	PROHIB AREA	*Prohibited area (screen optional)*
46a	(10)		*Calling-in point for vessel traffic control*
47			*Anchorage for seaplanes*
48			*Seaplane landing area*
49	Under construction		*Work in progress*
50			*Under construction*
51			*Work projected*
(Ge)	Subm ruins		*Submerged ruins*
†(Gf)	Dump Site		*Dump Site*

Symbols from Chart No. 1.

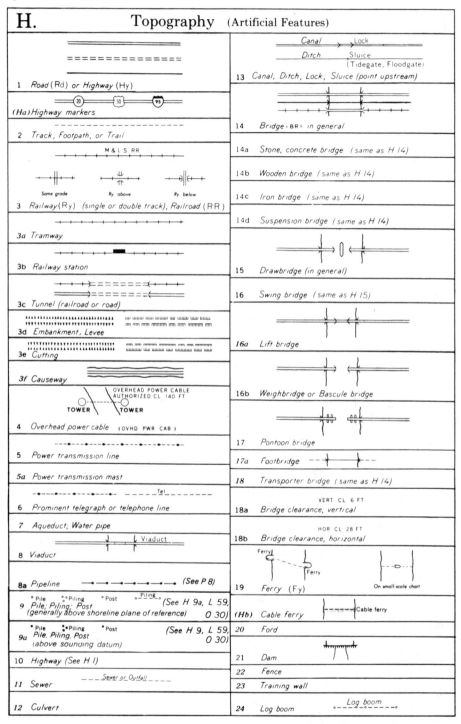

H. Topography (Artificial Features)

1 *Road* (Rd) *or Highway* (Hy)

(Ha) *Highway markers* (20, 50, 95)

2 *Track, Footpath, or Trail*

3 *Railway* (Ry) *(single or double track), Railroad* (RR) — M & L S RR; Same grade; Ry. above; Ry. below

3a *Tramway*

3b *Railway station*

3c *Tunnel (railroad or road)*

3d *Embankment, Levee*

3e *Cutting*

3f *Causeway*

4 *Overhead power cable* (OVHD PWR CAB) — TOWER; OVERHEAD POWER CABLE AUTHORIZED CL 140 FT; TOWER

5 *Power transmission line*

5a *Power transmission mast*

6 *Prominent telegraph or telephone line* — Tel

7 *Aqueduct; Water pipe*

8 *Viaduct* — Viaduct

8a *Pipeline* *(See P 8)*

9 *Pile; Piling; Post (generally above shoreline plane of reference)* — Pile, Piling, Post, Piling *(See H 9a, L 59, O 30)*

9a *Pile, Piling, Post (above sounding datum)* — Pile, Piling, Post *(See H 9, L 59, O 30)*

10 *Highway (See H 1)*

11 *Sewer* — Sewer or Outfall

12 *Culvert*

13 *Canal, Ditch, Lock, Sluice (point upstream)* — Canal, Lock; Ditch, Sluice (Tidegate, Floodgate)

14 *Bridge* (BR) *in general*

14a *Stone, concrete bridge (same as H 14)*

14b *Wooden bridge (same as H 14)*

14c *Iron bridge (same as H 14)*

14d *Suspension bridge (same as H 14)*

15 *Drawbridge (in general)*

16 *Swing bridge (same as H 15)*

16a *Lift bridge*

16b *Weighbridge or Bascule bridge*

17 *Pontoon bridge*

17a *Footbridge*

18 *Transporter bridge (same as H 14)*

18a *Bridge clearance, vertical* — VERT CL 6 FT

18b *Bridge clearance, horizontal* — HOR CL 28 FT

19 *Ferry* (Fy) — Ferry; Ferry; On small-scale chart

(Hb) *Cable ferry* — Cable ferry

20 *Ford*

21 *Dam*

22 *Fence*

23 *Training wall*

24 *Log boom* — Log boom

Symbols from Chart No. 1.

I. Buildings and Structures (see Introduction)

No.	Symbol	Abbreviation	Meaning
1			City or Town (large scale)
(Ia)			City or Town (small scale)
2			Suburb
3		Vil	Village
3a			Buildings in general
4		Cas	Castle
5			House
6			Villa
7			Farm
8			Church
8a		Cath	Cathedral
8b	○ SPIRE	Spire	Spire; Steeple
9			Roman Catholic Church
10			Temple
11			Chapel
12			Mosque
12a			Minaret
(Ib)			Moslem Shrine
13			Marabout
14		Pag	Pagoda
15			Buddhist Temple; Joss-House
15a			Shinto Shrine
16			Monastery; Convent
17			Calvary; Cross
17a	Cem		Cemetery, Non-Christian
18			Cemetery, Christian
18a			Tomb
19			Fort (actual shape charted)
20			Battery
21			Barracks
22			Powder magazine
23	Airport		Airplane landing field
24			Airport, large scale (See P-13)
(Ic)			Airport, military (small scale)
(Id)			Airport, civil (small scale)
25			Mooring mast
26	King St	St	Street
26a	Locust Ave	Ave	Avenue
26b	Grand Blvd	Blvd	Boulevard
27		Tel	Telegraph
28		Tel Off	Telegraph office
29		PO	Post office
30		Govt Ho	Government house
31			Town hall
32		Hosp	Hospital
33			Slaughterhouse
34		Magz	Magazine
34a			Warehouse; Storehouse
35	○MON	°Mon	Monument
36	○CUP	°Cup	Cupola
37	○ELEV	°Elev	Elevator
(Ie)		Elev	Elevation; Elevated
38			Shed
39			Zinc roof
40	Ruins	°Ru	Ruins
41	○TR	°Tr	Tower
(If)	○ ABAND LT HO		Abandoned lighthouse
42	○WINDMILL		Windmill
43			Watermill
43a	○WINDMOTOR		Windmotor
44	○CHY	°Chy	Chimney; Stack
45	○S'PIPE	°S'pipe	Water tower; Standpipe
46			Oil tank
47		Facty	Factory
48			Saw mill
49			Brick kiln
50			Mine; Quarry
51	°Well		Well
52			Cistern
53	○TANK	°Tk	Tank
54			Noria
55			Fountain

Symbols from Chart No. 1.

I. Buildings and Structures (continued)

No.	Symbol	Abbreviation	Meaning
61		Inst	*Institute*
62			*Establishment*
63			*Bathing establishment*
64		Ct Ho	*Courthouse*
65	▪	Sch	*School*
(Ig)	▪	HS	*High school*
(Ih)	▪	Univ	*University*
66	■ ▨ □	Bldg	*Building*
67		Pav	*Pavilion*
68			*Hut*
69			*Stadium*
70		T	*Telephone*
71	⊕ • ⊘		*Gas tank; Gasometer*
72	⊙ GAB	○ Gab	*Gable*
73			*Wall*
74			*Pyramid*
75			*Pillar*
†76	⊙		*Oil derrick*
(Ii)		Ltd	*Limited*
(Ij)		Apt	*Apartment*
(Ik)		Cap	*Capitol*
(Il)		Co	*Company*
(Im)		Corp	*Corporation*
(In)	⊙		*Landmark (position accurate)(See D 2)*
(Io)	○		*Landmark (position approximate)(See Da)*

J. Miscellaneous Stations

No.	Symbol	Abbreviation	Meaning
1		Sta	*Any kind of station*
2		Sta	*Station*
3	C G		*Coast Guard station (similar to Lifesaving Station, J 6)*
(Ja)	⊙ R TR C G WALLIS SANDS		*Coast Guard station (when landmark)*
4	⊙ LOOK TR		*Lookout station; Watch tower*
5			*Lifeboat station*
6	LS S		*Lifesaving station (See J 3)*
7		Rkt Sta	*Rocket station*
†8	Pilots ⊙ PIL STA		*Pilot station/Pilots*
9		Sig Sta	*Signal station*
10		Sem	*Semaphore*
11		S Sig Sta	*Storm signal station*
12			*Weather signal station*
(Jb)	⊙ NWS SIG STA		*Nat'l Weather Service signal sta*
13			*Tide signal station*
14			*Stream signal station*
15			*Ice signal station*
16			*Time signal station*
16a			*Manned oceanographic station*
16b			*Unmanned oceanographic station*
17			*Time ball*
18			*Signal mast*
18a	○ Mast		*Mast*
19	⊙ FS ○ FS ⊙ FP ○ FP		*Flagstaff; Flagpole*
19a	⊙ F TR	○ F Tr	*Flag tower*
20			*Signal*
21		Obsy	*Observatory*
22		Off	*Office*
(Jc)	○ BELL		*Bell (on land)*
(Jd)	○ HECP		*Harbor entrance control post*
(Je)	○ MARINE POLICE		*Marine police station*
(Jf)	○ FIREBOAT STATION		*Fireboat station*

Symbols from Chart No. 1.

K. Lights

1		*Position of light*
2	Lt	*Light*
(Ka)		*Riprap surrounding light*
3	Lt Ho	*Lighthouse*
4	AERO AERO	*Aeronautical light (See F-22)*
4a		*Marine and air navigation light*
5	Bn Bn	*Light beacon*
6		*Light vessel; Lightship*
8		*Lantern*
9		*Street lamp*
10	REF	*Reflector*
11		*Leading light*
12	RED RED	*Sector light*
13	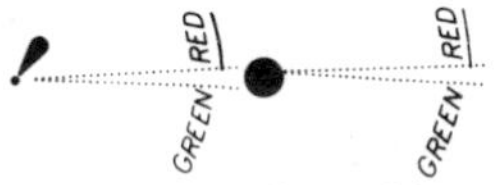RED RED GREEN GREEN	*Directional light*
14		*Harbor light*
15		*Fishing light*
16		*Tidal light*
17	Priv maintd	*Private light (maintained by private interests; to be used with caution)*
21	F	*Fixed (steady light)*
†22	Occ; Oc	*Occulting (total duration of light more than dark)*
23	Fl	*Single-Flashing (total duration of light less than dark)*
†(Kb)	L Fl	*Long-Flashing (2s or longer)*
	Fl (2+1)	*Composite group-flashing*
23a	Iso E Int	*Isophase (light and dark equal)*
†24	Qk Fl; Q	*Continuous Quick Flashing (50 to 79 per minute; 60 in U.S.)*
	Q (3)	*Group Quick*
25	Int Qk Fl; I Qk Fl; IQ	*Interrupted Quick Flashing*
†(Kc)	V Qk Fl; VQ	*Continuous Very Quick Flashing (80 to 159-usually either 100 or 120 per minute)*
	VQ (3)	*Group Very Quick*
	IVQ	*Interrupted Very Quick*
	UQ	*Continuous Ultra Quick (160 or more-usually 240 to 300 flashes per minute)*
	IUQ	*Interrupted Ultra Quick*
25a	S Fl	*Short Flashing*

†26	Alt; Al;	*Alternating*
†27	Gp Occ; Oc (2) Oc (2+3)	*Group-Occulting* *Composite group occulting*
†28	Gp Fl; Fl (3)	*Group Flashing*
28a	S-L Fl	*Short-Long Flashing*
28b		*Group-Short Flashing*
29	F Fl	*Fixed and Flashing*
30	F Gp Fl	*Fixed and Group Flashing*
30a	Mo (A)	*Morse Code light (with flashes grouped as in letter A)*
31	Rot	*Revolving or Rotating light*
41		*Period*
42		*Every*
43		*With*
44		*Visible (range)*
(Kd)	M; Mi; N Mi	*Nautical mile (See E-11)*
(Ke)	m min	*Minutes (See E-2)*
(Kf)	s; sec	*Seconds (See E-3)*
45	Fl	*Flash*
46	Occ	*Occultation*
46a		*Eclipse*
47	Gp	*Group*
48	Occ	*Intermittent light*
49	*SEC*	*Sector*
50		*Color of sector*
51	Aux	*Auxiliary light*
52		*Varied*
61	Vi	*Violet*
62		*Purple*
63	Bu	*Blue*
64	G	*Green*
65	Or; Y	*Orange*
66	R	*Red*
67	W	*White*
67a	Am	*Amber*
(Ko)	Y	*Yellow*
68	*OBSC*	*Obscured light*
68a	*Fog Det Lt*	*Fog detector light (See Nb)*

Figures in parentheses are examples

Symbols from Chart No. 1.

K. Lights (continued)

69		*Unwatched light*
70	Occas	*Occasional light*
71	Irreg	*Irregular light*
72	Prov	*Provisional light*
73	Temp	*Temporary light*
(Kg)	D. Destr	*Destroyed*
74	Exting	*Extinguished light*
75		*Faint light*
76		*Upper light*
77		*Lower light*
78		*Rear light*
79		*Front light*
80	Vert	*Vertical lights*
81	Hor	*Horizontal lights*
(Kh)	VB	*Vertical beam*
(Ki)	RGE	*Range*
(Kj)	Exper	*Experimental light*
(Kk)	TRLB	*Temporarily replaced by lighted buoy showing the same characteristics*
(Kl)	TRUB	*Temporarily replaced by unlighted buoy*
(Km)	TLB	*Temporary lighted buoy*
(Kn)	TUB	*Temporary unlighted buoy*

L. Buoys and Beacons (see Introduction)

1	o •	*Approximate position of buoy*
2		***Light buoy***
3	BELL BELL BELL	***Bell buoy***
3a	GONG GONG GONG	***Gong buoy***
4	WHIS WHIS	*Whistle buoy*
5	C C	*Can or Cylindrical buoy*
6	N N	*Nun or Conical buoy*
7	SP SP	*Spherical buoy*
8	S S	*Spar buoy*
†8a	P P	*Pillar or Spindle buoy*
9		*Buoy with topmark (ball) (see L-57)*
10		*Barrel or Ton buoy*
(La)		*Color unknown*
(Lb)	FLOAT FLOAT	*Float*
12	FLOAT FLOAT FLOAT	*Lightfloat*
13		*Outer or Landfall buoy*
14	BW BW	*Fairway buoy (BWVS)*
14a	BW BW	*Midchannel buoy (BWVS)*
15	R "2" R "2" R "2"	*Starboard-hand buoy (entering from seaward)*
16	"1" "1"	*Port-hand buoy (entering from seaward)*
†17	RB BR RB RB	*Bifurcation buoy*
†18	RB BR RB RB	*Junction buoy*
†19	RB BR RB RB	*Isolated danger buoy*
†20	RB BR RB G G G G G	*Wreck buoy*
†20a	RB BR RB G G	*Obstruction buoy*
21	Tel Tel	*Telegraph-cable buoy*
22		*Mooring buoy (colors of mooring buoys never carried)*
22a		*Mooring*
22b	Tel Tel	*Mooring buoy with telegraphic communications*
22c	T T	*Mooring buoy with telephonic communications*
23		*Warping buoy*
24	Y Y	*Quarantine buoy*
24a		*Practice area buoy*
25	Explos Anch Explos Anch	*Explosive anchorage buoy*
25a	AERO AERO	*Aeronautical anchorage buoy*
26	Deviation Deviation	*Compass adjustment buoy*
27	BW BW	*Fish trap (area) buoy (BWHB)*
27a		*Spoil ground buoy*
28	W W	*Anchorage buoy (marks limits)*
29	Priv maintd Priv maintd	*Private aid to navigation (buoy) (maintained by private interests, use with caution)*

L. Buoys and Beacons (continued)

No.	Symbol	Abbreviation	Description
30			*Temporary buoy (See Ki, j, k, l)*
30a			*Winter buoy*
31		HB	*Horizontal stripes or bands*
32		VS	*Vertical stripes*
33		Chec	*Checkered*
33a		Diag	*Diagonal bands*
41		W	*White*
42		B	*Black*
43		R	*Red*
44		Y	*Yellow*
45		G	*Green*
46		Br	*Brown*
47		Gy	*Gray*
48		Bu	*Blue*
48a		Am	*Amber*
48b		Or	*Orange*
51			*Floating beacon*
†52	△RW Bn △W Bn ▲R Bn ■G Bn △G Bn		*Fixed beacon (unlighted or daybeacon)*
	▲Bn		*Black beacon*
	△Bn		*Color unknown*
(Lc)	○MARKER ○Marker		*Private aid to navigation*
53		Bn	*Beacon, in general (See L 52)*
54			*Tower beacon*
55			*Cardinal marking system*

No.	Symbol	Abbreviation	Description
56	△ Deviation Bn		*Compass adjustment beacon*
†57	etc		*Topmarks (See L 9)*
58			*Telegraph-cable (landing) beacon*
59	Piles Piles		*Piles (See O 30; H 9, 9a)*
			Stakes
	Stumps		*Stumps (See O 30)*
			Perches
61	○ CAIRN ○Cairn		*Cairn*
62			*Painted patches*
63	○TR		*Landmark (position accurate) (See D 2)*
(Ld)	○ Tr		*Landmark (position approximate)*
64		REF	*Reflector*
65	○MARKER		*Range targets, markers*
(Le)	W Or W Or W Or W Or		*Special-purpose buoys*
66			*Oil installation buoy*
67			*Drilling platform (See Of, Og)*
70			*NOTE: Refer to new L-70, on page 11, for aid system used in certain foreign waters.*
(Lf)		Ra Ref	*Radar reflector (See M 13) (not charted on IALA Sys. "A" marks see L-70)*
			Superbuoys
†71			*LANBY (large auto. nav. buoy)*
†72			*TANKER terminal buoy (mooring)*
†73			*ODAS (Data buoy)*

Symbols from Chart No. 1.

M. Radio and Radar Stations

1	° R Sta	*Radio telegraph station*
2	° RT	*Radio telephone station*
3	◎ R Bn	*Radiobeacon*
4	◎ R Bn	*Circular radiobeacon*
† 5	◎ RD (RD 072°30')	*Directional radiobeacon; Radio range*
6		*Rotating loop radiobeacon*
7	◎ RDF	*Radio direction finding station*
(Ma)	⊙ ANTENNA (TELEM) / ⊙ TELEM ANT	*Telemetry antenna*
(Mb)	⊙ R RELAY MAST	*Radio relay mast*
(Mc)	⊙ MICRO TR	*Microwave tower*
9	⊙ R MAST	*Radio mast*
	⊙ R TR	*Radio tower*
9a	⊙ TV TR	*Television mast; Television tower*
10	⊙ R TR (WBAL) 1090 kHz	*Radio broadcasting station (commercial)*
10a	° R Sta	*QTG radio station*
11	◎ Ra	*Radar station*
12	◎ Racon	*Radar responder beacon*
13	⌣ Ra Ref	*Radar reflector (See L-Lf) (not charted on IALA Sys. "A" marks; see L-70)*
14	Ra (conspic)	*Radar conspicuous object*
14a		*Ramark*
15	D F S	*Distance finding station (synchronized signals)*
16	◎ AERO R Bn 302	*Aeronautical radiobeacon*
17	° Decca Sta	*Decca station*
18	° Loran Sta Venice	*Loran station (name)*
19	◎ CONSOL Bn 190 kHz MMF	*Consol (Consolan) station*
(Md)	◎ AERO R Rge 342	*Aeronautical radio range*
(Me)	◎ Ra Ref Calibration Bn	*Radar calibration beacon*
(Mf)	⊙ LORAN TR SPRING ISLAND	*Loran tower (name)*
(Mg)	⊙ R TR F R Lt	*Obstruction light*
(Mh)	⊙ RA DOME ⊙ DOME (RADAR) ° Ra Dome ° Dome (Radar)	*Radar dome*
(Mi)	uhf	*Ultrahigh frequency*
(Mj)	vhf	*Very high frequency*

N. Fog Signals

† 1	Fog Sig ⑊	*Fog-signal station*
2		*Radio fog-signal station*
3	*GUN*	*Explosive fog signal*
4		*Submarine fog signal*
5	*SUB-BELL*	*Submarine fog bell (action of waves)*
6	*SUB-BELL*	*Submarine fog bell (mechanical)*
7	*SUB-OSC*	*Submarine oscillator*
8	*NAUTO*	*Nautophone*
9	*DIA*	*Diaphone*
10	*GUN*	*Fog gun*
11	*SIREN*	*Fog siren*
12	*HORN*	*Fog trumpet*
13	*HORN*	*Air (foghorn)*
13a	*HORN*	*Electric (foghorn)*
14	*BELL*	*Fog bell*
15	*WHIS*	*Fog whistle*
16	*HORN*	*Reed horn*
17	*GONG*	*Fog gong*
18	◎	*Submarine sound signal not connected to the shore (See N 5,6,7)*
18a	◎∿∿	*Submarine sound signal connected to the shore (See N 5,6,7)*
(Na)	*HORN*	*Typhon*
(Nb)	*Fog Det Lt*	*Fog detector light (See K 68a)*
† (Nc)	Mo	*Morse Code fog signal*

O. Dangers

(25) (25)
†1 *Rock which does not cover (height above MHW)*

Uncov 2 ft *Uncov 2 ft*
(2) (2)
2 *Rock which covers and uncovers with height above chart sounding datum (see Introduction)*

3 *Rock awash at (near) level of chart sounding datum*
Dotted line emphasizes danger to navigation

(Oa) *Rock awash (height unknown)*
Dotted line emphasizes danger to navigation

4 *Submerged rock (depth unknown)*
Dotted line emphasizes danger to navigation

5 Rk
5 *Shoal sounding on isolated rock*

6 *Submerged rock not dangerous to surface navigation (See O 4)*

21 Rk 21 Obstr
6a *Sunken danger with depth cleared by wire drag*

Reef
7 *Reef of unknown extent*

Sub Vol
8 *Submarine volcano*

Discol Water
9 *Discolored water*

Coral Co Co Co
10 *Coral reef, detached (uncovers at sounding datum)*

Co 3 Reef line
Coral or Rocky reef, covered at sounding datum (See A-11d, 11g)

11 *Wreck showing any portion of hull or superstructure (above sounding datum)*

Masts
12 *Wreck with only masts visible (above sounding datum)*

13 *Old symbols for wrecks*

PA
13a *Wreck always partially submerged*

14 *Sunken wreck dangerous to surface navigation (less than 11 fathoms over wreck) (See O 6a)*

5½ Wk
15 *Wreck over which depth is known*

21 Wk
15a *Wreck with depth cleared by wire drag*

8 Wk
15b ***Unsurveyed wreck over which the exact depth is unknown, but is considered to have a safe clearance to the depth shown***

16 *Sunken wreck, not dangerous to surface navigation*

Foul
17 *Foul ground, Foul bottom (fb)*

Tide Rips (Symbol used only in small areas)
18 *Overfalls or Tide rips*

Eddies (Symbol used only in small areas)
19 *Eddies*

Kelp (Symbol used only in small areas)
20 *Kelp, Seaweed*

21	Bk	*Bank*
22	Shl	*Shoal*
23	Rf	*Reef (See A 11d, 11g, O 10)*
23a		*Ridge*
24	Le	*Ledge*

25 *Breakers (See A 12)*

26 *Submerged rock (See O 4),*

5½ Obstr
27 *Obstruction*

(Ob) *Obstr* *Well* *Subm well*
Obstr *Well* *Subm well (buoyed)*

Obstruction (fish haven)
(Oc) *Fish haven (artificial fishing reef)*

28 *Wreck (See O 11 to 16)*

Wreckage *Wks*
29 *Wreckage*

29a *Wreck remains (dangerous only for anchoring)*

Subm piles *Subm piling*
30 *Submerged piling (See H-9, 9a; L 59)*

Snags *Stumps*
30a *Snags; Submerged stumps (See L 59)*

31 *Lesser depth possible*

32	Uncov	*Dries (See A 10; O 2, 10)*
33	Cov	*Covers (See O 2, 10)*
34	Uncov	*Uncovers (See A 10; O 2, 10)*

3 *Rep (1958)*
Reported (with date)

Eagle Rk (rep 1958)
35 *Reported (with name and date)*

36 *Discol* *Discolored (See O 9)*
37 *Isolated danger*

38 *Limiting danger line*

rky
39 *Limit of rocky area*

41	PA	*Position approximate*
42	PD	*Position doubtful*
43	ED	*Existence doubtful*
44	P Pos	*Position*
45	D	*Doubtful*
46		*Unexamined*
(Od)	LD	*Least Depth*

Subm Crib Crib *(above water)*
(Oe) *Crib*

Platform (lighted)
HORN
(Of) *Offshore platform (unnamed)*

Hazel (lighted)
HORN
(Og) *Offshore platform (named)*

Index

Edited by Steven Bolt